The Romano-British Villa at Castle Copse, Great Bedwyn

The Romano-British Villa at Castle Copse, Great Bedwyn

ERIC HOSTETTER AND THOMAS NOBLE HOWE,
EDITORS

With contributions by
Enid Allison, Bradley Ault, Theodore V. Buttrey, Alan Clapham,
Bruce Eagles, Robert M. Ehrenreich, Laura Flusche, Fern Fryer,
Kathryn L. Gleason, David Frederick Grose, Margaret Guido, Eric Hostetter,
Thomas Noble Howe, Andrew K. G. Jones, David K. Keefer,
John F. Kenfield, Ruth Megaw, Vincent Megaw, Maryline Parca,
Rosemary Payne, Sebastian Payne, Valerie Hutchinson Pennanen,
Paul Robinson, Archer St. Clair, Anthony R. Wilmott

INDIANA
UNIVERSITY
PRESS
Bloomington and Indianapolis

MANUFACTURED IN THE UNITED STATES OF AMERICA

Library of Congress Cataloging-in-Publication Data

The Romano-British villa at Castle Copse, Great Bedwyn / Eric
Hostetter and Thomas Noble Howe, editors; with contribution by Enid
Allison . . . [et al.].
p.   cm.
Includes bibliographical references and index.
ISBN 0-253-32802-0 (cl)
1. Castle Copse Site (England) 2. Architecture, Domestic—
England—Great Bedwyn. 3. Great Bedwyn (England)—Antiquities,
Celtic. 4. Great Bedwyn (England)—Antiquities, Roman.
5. Architecture, Roman—England—Great Bedwyn. 6. Farm buildings—
England—Great Bedwyn. 7. Country homes—England—Great Bedwyn.
8. Britons—England—-Great Bedwyn. 9. Romans—England—Great
Bedwyn.   I. Hostetter, Eric.   II. Howe, Thomas Noble, date .
III. Allison, Enid.
DA147.C247R66 1997
936.2'317—dc20   94-47082

1 2 3 4 5 02 01 00 99 98 97

CONTENTS

Introduction

CHAPTER 1.
The Regional Setting: Environmental Geology and Geography

CHAPTER 2.
Chisbury Camp and Northeastern Wiltshire in the Iron Age

CHAPTER 3.
The Area around Cunetio in the Roman Period

CHAPTER 4.
The Romano-British Villa at Castle Copse, Great Bedwyn

CHAPTER 5.
The Area around Bedwyn in the Anglo-Saxon Period
BY BRUCE EAGLES / 378

ABBREVIATIONS

AE	copper alloy		m	meter(s)
alt	altitude		Max. Th.	maximum thickness
AS	Anglo-Saxon		Min. Th.	minimum thickness
A.Th.	average uniform thickness		ml	milliliter
A	Sector A		mm	millimeter
B	Sector B		O.D.	Ordnance Datum
C	Sector C		Th.	thickness
D	Sector D		W.	width
1–10	Evaluation Trench 1-10		I–XV	Phases
cm	centimeters		**1–489**	catalogue numbers, bold
D.	diameter			faced
Fe	iron			
ft	feet			Excavation units are recorded as follows:
g	gram(s)			A–D = excavation sector
GB	Great Bedwyn			arabic numeral = context
H.	height			roman numeral = phase
kg	kilogram(s)			Thus, A90:II, would be Sector A,
km	kilometer(s)			Context 90, Phase II.
L.	length			All measurements in the catalogue en-
l	liter			tries are expressed in meters.

LIST OF TABLES

LIST OF FIGURES

Photographs, unless otherwise credited, are by J. Crawford. Field maps, plan, and sections from the villa are by T. N. Howe with the assistance of C. Alexander, E. Brescia, N. Burch, L. Cockerham, M. Downs, B. Drone, S. Falatko, N. Griffiths, C. Horeische, L. Jaracz, D. Keefer, J. Klein, M. Lane, M. Lynch, J. Poor, T. Scott, L. Sisson, and O. Tolba. Objects from the villa are, unless otherwise credited, by K. L. Gleason, T. Scott, C. Alexander, B. Drone, and L. Cockerham. The environmental maps and flot/wet-sieving charts are by K. L. Gleason, E. Brescia, J. Poor, and O. Tolba. Figures for chapters 2 and 5 are by N. Griffiths. Catalogue numbers are in boldface type.

PREFACE

ERIC HOSTETTER

For nearly three decades, Alexander Abraham has been an active participant in the archaeological investigations conducted by a variety of American universities and research institutions. His involvement with archaeology began in 1964 when, invited to join the Fine Arts Visiting Committee of the Fogg Art Museum at Harvard University, he became deeply engaged in the joint Harvard-Cornell Expedition to the Lydian capital Sardis and in the American School of Oriental Research. In 1972 Mr. Abraham helped launch the exploration of the Etruscan town of Ghiaccio Forte in Tuscany. This project promptly yielded many insights into urban life in Etruria, and the handsome finds are now housed in the Archaeological Museum in Florence. From 1976 through 1983 Mr. Abraham served as a trustee of the Archaeological Institute of America and from 1980 to 1986 as a trustee of the American Schools of Oriental Research. In a different vein, Mr. Abraham also assisted in the restoration of the Tresantin Room in the Ashmolean Museum. Since 1983, Mr. Abraham has assisted several ongoing excavations throughout the Mediterranean and has helped initiate several field projects, including the collaborative exploration of the east slope of the Palatine Hill by the Soprintendenza Archeologica di Roma and the American Academy in Rome, and of the site which is the subject of this volume, the Romano-British villa at Castle Copse, Great Bedwyn.

Recounting Mr. Abraham's archaeological *cursus honorum* does not, however, fully convey the experience of working with him. Not content with being an interested observer, he, with his wife Helene, can be found every summer in the troweling line alongside the team. Through such engagement, Mr. Abraham has gained a deep understanding of the logistical problems associated with archaeology, an appreciation which makes his friendship and counsel invaluable both in the field and in the drive toward publication.

On the American side of the Atlantic, Mr. Abraham is an investment banker in New York, a profession that, as he has commented, tends to offer an overly abstract view of society. Mr. Abraham's other ventures run no risk of succumbing to such a danger. These include medical research and efforts to relieve the plight of the homeless. With their daughter Nancy, the Abrahams have started over ten shelters, some of which offer sanctuary exclusively to mothers and children.

Thus, the contributors in this volume wish both to extend their thanks to Mr. Abraham for his kind patronage of this project and to express their admiration for his estimable vision of revealing the past, ameliorating the present, and ensuring a future.

Alexander and Helene Abraham. (L. Robbennolt)

ACKNOWLEDGMENTS
ERIC HOSTETTER

The investigation of the Roman villa at Castle Copse by the Program in Classical Archaeology of Indiana University, Bloomington, in the years 1983–1986 was made possible thanks to the kindness and generosity of many on both sides of the Atlantic. Our thanks are owed first to Alexander Abraham, true *amicus artibus* for his support of the project throughout excavation, study, and publication.

Alistair and Ann Buchanan and Montgomery and Richard Charles, successive owners of Bedwyn Brail, the wooded ridge upon which the villa is situated, generously gave their consent to excavate, facilitated operations at every turn, and, at the end of the field work, generously consigned the material archive to The Museum in Devizes. Permission to place an evaluation trench near the church of St. Mary the Virgin on Manor Farm in Great Bedwyn was kindly given by Arnold and John Kerr, who also shared with us their intimate knowledge of regional geology, farming, and village history.

We are grateful to the English Heritage Commission and its predecessor, The Department of the Environment, for permission to excavate this scheduled site; in particular, we are indebted to Mr. David M. Evans and Dr. Geoffrey Wainwright for offering much sound counsel to a team whose field experience had, for the most part, concentrated south of the Alps.

From the start of the project until 1985, when Littlecote House changed owners, the Littlecote Roman Research Trust extended every kindness to the project. Seton Wills and Bryn Walters, founding trustee and director of the LRRT, respectively, are to be thanked especially, as are Peter Johnson, Luigi Thompson, and Bernard Phillips.

Kenneth Annable and Paul Robinson, successive curators of The Museum in Devizes, graciously accepted the material archive from Castle Copse. For conservation of some of these finds, we thank Michael Corfield and Margaret Robertson of the Salisbury County Conservation Laboratory, as well as Barry Cunliffe, Esther Cameron, and C. Mortimer of the Institute of Archaeology of Oxford University. Among the many others to whom we are indebted for advice and assistance in a variety of areas are: P. Austen, J. Bayley, A. Borthwick, H. Butzer, H. Cave-Penny, J. Chandler, J. A. Charles, A. J. Clark, R. Clarke, D. W. Cope, Jr., M. Corney, A. David, S. Davis, M. Downs, J. P. Gillam, J. Goodheart, G. Gould, N. A. Griffiths, D. R. Harris, J. Henderson, M. Henig, G. Hillman, S. Hirst, D. Hopkins, R. A. Housely, M. Hughes, E. Jarosewich, B. Levitan, A. MacGregor, D. F. MacKreth, C. McGill, G. Mees, N. F. Miller, S. Moorhouse, S. Murray, P. Northover, T. O'Connor, J. Olin, R. Perrin, S. Pressey, J. Price, P. Rahtz, R. Reece, V. Rigby, A. Robinson, S. Rushton, I. Stead, V. Swan, L. van Zelst, A. Vince, G. Webster, B. Wiggins, P. Wiggle, D. Yarçan, B. Yorke, and K. M. Zwilsky.

Publication of this volume by Indiana University Press was supported by a grant from the Edward Schrader Fund of the Program in Classical Archaeology, and the editors are grateful to John Gallman, director, and Robert J. Sloan, sponsoring editor, of Indiana University Press, for their patience and varied efforts in preparing the manuscript for publication. The critical time required for completion and editing of the manuscripts was made possible by a Research Board/Arnold A. Beckmann Award from the University of Illinois at Urbana-Champaign.

Finally, we thank the kind and gentle people of the villages of Great Bedwyn and Shalbourne for their warm hospitality, differences in dialects notwithstanding.

1994

INTRODUCTION
ERIC HOSTETTER

The Site

The ruins of the Roman villa at Castle Copse lie on the western brow of the three-kilo-meter-long wooded ridge known as Bedwyn Brail, immediately south of the village of Great Bedwyn, in southwest England (Figs. 1–4, 7–8).[1] These structures had long attracted the attention of both villagers in need of building material and early travellers. By the mid-nineteenth century the site also aroused the interest of antiquarian excavators and, by the 1930s, that of amateur archaeologists, whose combined activities revealed extensive constructions and several objects of notable quality.

The results of these early inquiries suggested that the site was worthy of further investigation. The scale of the villa alone, as indicated by the extent of the platform upon which it rests and the density of building debris, hinted at a structure of some promi-nence (Figs. 4, 7–9). Overlooking the Bedwyn Valley, the villa's position is strategically advantageous because of its situation at the head of two major valley systems—the Vale of Ham, leading to the Kennet and then to the Thames Valley to the northeast, and the Vale of Pewsey, leading to the southwest—both of which form natural passages (Figs. 11, 13–14). To the west ran the road connecting the Roman town of Cunetio (Black Field, Mildenhall), the regional administrative center, with Venta Belgarum (Winchester) (Figs. 1–2, 25).

Also of particular interest was the villa's evident longevity and proximity to major sites of preceding and succeeding periods. Crowning the hill across the Bedwyn Valley three kilometers to the north lies the Iron Age hillfort of Chisbury, probably abandoned by around B.C. 100, but with an extramural settlement immediately to the west, which was seemingly occupied until shortly after the Roman conquest (Figs. 2, 5). Sporadic finds within the fort suggest occupation, at some level, in the early Roman period. Whether there was significant occupation in the late or post-Roman periods is uncertain, but because the hillfort appears to be connected to the site of the villa by a cross-valley dyke of unknown date (Figs. 2, 161–62), the question is of some interest. Finally, mid-way between the villa and the hillfort, on the northern banks of the Bedwyn Stream, lies the village of Great Bedwyn (Fig. 6), known to have been a Saxon secondary market-town sufficiently important to have struck its own coinage. This cluster of three signifi-cant sites, morphologically and chronologically diverse, suggests that the area centering on the Bedwyn Valley might, over the course of successive periods, have retained a cer-tain regional prominence. The proximity of these sites suggested that an investigation of the villa might offer some insight into the question of regional continuity and change.

The project whose results are presented in this volume dealt mainly with the Roman villa proper and its immediate surroundings. A broader research strategy involving investigation of Chisbury hillfort and Saxon Great Bedwyn was not pursued, though limited efforts were made to understand the relationship between the sites within their geological and geographical setting. The intent of this volume is therefore solely to report on excavations at the villa at Castle Copse, although chapters on the region in the Iron Age and Roman and Saxon periods are included, in order to provide a broader context.

History of the Excavations

Perhaps the earliest mention of the villa at Castle Copse is by John Leland, commenting on his journey through Wiltshire of 1542: ". . . but whereas I harde ons that there was a castelle or forteres at *Greate Bedwine;* [the ruins and plot whereof is yet seene, VI.71.] I could there heere nothinge of it."[2] Certainly, one Roman villa in the vicinity was known at least as early as c. 1780, for in 1860 the Reverend John Ward, in his account of the village of Great Bedwyn, describes briefly a "Roman station" in Bedwyn Brail, discovered "about 80 years ago":[3]

> A small castramentation surrounding about two acres of land was the centre of the station. . . . It was situated about half a mile east of the Roman road . . . and between the station and the road were discovered . . . the remains of a villa, with valuable specimens of tesselated pavements, foundations of brick-work, and a massive lead cistern, which were all unfortunately destroyed.

The "station" in Bedwyn Brail may refer to the villa at Castle Copse, though the distance to the road, half a mile, would then be incorrect. Despite several attempts to locate the "villa" between the station and the road, its site remains unknown, even though several of the older inhabitants of Great Bedwyn confirmed the existence of a second "villa" somewhere along the western foot of Bedwyn Brail.

Ward further reports that in 1853 the Reverend W. C. Lukis, the avid explorer of prehistoric barrows in Wiltshire and elsewhere, discovered several mosaics near the same spot, at "The Old Castle," along with pottery, glass, coins and various metal objects, including a small gold ring engraved with a cross (Figs. 30, 112).[4] An account of a tour of the site given by Lukis appeared in 1860,[5] but, apart from the earlier report by Ward and the occasional mention of artifacts, Lukis's work was never published; a series of drawings and watercolors of the tesselated pavements are, however, preserved in The Museum at Devizes (Figs. 95, 96).[6] In this regard, Ward's comment that, following excavation, the pavements were "destroyed by idle boys" is suspect; the current excavations revealed not only the nails used by Lukis to execute his drawings, but also several neat cuts in the bedding of the mosaics, demonstrating that some sections were probably lifted.

Approximately eighty-two years later, in 1936 and 1937, E. R. Pole and the Paddington Great Western Railway Archaeological Society conducted limited trenching at the northwestern corner of the villa platform, work reported upon by F. C. Warren (Fig. 39).[7] According to one villager who participated in the excavations as a youth, these operations were conducted in a furtive manner for fear of being discovered by the landowner. Excavation took place primarily on weekends by members of the Society who "went down from London by car or train at irregular intervals and generally returned the same day." The report by Warren of 1938 included limited stratigraphic description, a schematic plan, and brief accounts of the pottery (by E. R. Pole and C. F. C. Hawkes) and animal bones (by D. M. A. Bate). In September of 1937, efforts were abandoned "in view of the difficulties of the site as compared with the resources of the Society."

In 1976, B. Walters included the villa in his Cardiff University undergraduate thesis on the villas of northeastern Wiltshire,[8] noting its hilltop setting, courtyard morphology, and the chronological range of surface pottery from shortly after the mid-first century to the later fourth century A.D.

The most recent excavations of the villa at Castle Copse are those reported upon here, the 1983–1986 summer campaigns conducted by Indiana University, Blooming-ton. At the start of this project, sporadic scatters of pottery, *tesserae,* and flints were visi-ble on the undulating surface of the forested site, while buttons, medicine bottles, and other artifacts suggested extensive disturbance during the last two centuries. Village elders recall material being carted away, presumably in the later nineteenth and earlier twentieth centuries, for road repair in and around Great Bedwyn.[9]

After clearing the villa platform of diseased elms, excavation was carried out in four sectors (A–D) (Figs. 8, 9) and in a series of small evaluation trenches.[10] This work estab-lished much of the villa's plan, function, and chronology. Slight remains of possible ear-lier (Iron Age?) structures were also revealed, as was part of a late structure postdating the Roman villa and extending into the courtyard.

Aerial photography, geophysical prospecting, and limited, noncollecting field sur-veys were undertaken both in and around the villa proper, but with mixed results. Aerial photography did not reveal any features not already discerned (Fig. 3, for earlier photo-graph). Field walking, except for one week in March 1985,[11] unfortunately had to take place during the summer months when dense vegetation camouflaged the terrain. And ten evaluation trenches, placed to test the results of both field walking and geophysical surveys (Figs. 87–88) showed that apparent patterns were not reliable (see Appen-dix 4).[12]

The term "villa" is used to refer to the Roman constructions at Castle Copse. The site displays numerous features of wealth and status: the building technology and archi-tectural vocabulary—mortared masonry, hypocausts, mosaics, frescoes, and the extensive courtyard plan—all reflect the desire on the part of the owner(s), whatever his or her birthright, to appear Romanized. Thus, despite recent calls to abandon the term "villa," it is here, as elsewhere in the empire, retained. As R. Hingley points out, for all its imper-fections, to abandon the term would be impractical.[13]

Notes

1. Bibliography on the villa and finds therefrom includes: Bruce 1854: 352; and 1855: 26; Jackson 1854: 177; Lukis 1854: 216; and 1857: 14; Ward 1860: 261–62; Anonymous 1860: 253; Goddard 1902: 188–89; 1908: 406; and 1913: 188–89; Cunnington and Goddard 1911: 51–52, nos. 400–416; Cunnington 1930: 174; Warren 1938: 318–20; Pole 1960; Walters 1976: 52–56; Hostetter 1985: 233–35; Frere 1985: 308, fig. 29; Hostetter and Howe 1986a: 97–102; Hostetter and Howe 1986b: 36–43; Hostetter, Howe, and Kenfield 1987: 52–56.

2. R. E. Jackson 1854: 177.

3. Ward 1860: 261.

4. To judge from a letter from Francis to his brother Jack (John Ward ?), dated March 6, 1852, which contained a sketch of an area (probably Sector A) of Lukis's excavations labelled "Old Castle," many of these discoveries may have occurred in the previous year. A photocopy of this letter was kindly given me by B. Walters.

5. Anonymous 1860: 253, wherein the date of the excavations is given as 1854: ". . . W. C. Lukis: who then conducted the party into the middle of a wood called Castle Copse where in 1854 he had discovered the site of a Roman villa . . ."

6. Other artifacts from the villa are believed to be in the museum on Guernsey, a letter of inquiry to which went unanswered. For a reproduction of one of Lukis's mosaic watercolors, see Hostetter and Howe 1986b: 41. On Lukis and this seminal period in British archaeology, see Marsden 1974: 54–57; and Levine 1987.

7. Warren 1938: 318–20. Even in the 1960s, Bedwyn Brail was still known as Castle Hill (Pole 1960).

8. Walters 1976.

9. Warren 1938: 318.

10. These efforts were directed by this writer, T. N. Howe, and J. F. Kenfield. Sector A was supervised by A. Wilmott throughout the four seasons of excavation. Sector B was directed by J. Howell in 1984 and 1985, then by B. Ault in 1986. Sector C was supervised by M. Burch in 1984 and by B. Ault in 1985, and Sector D by E. Hostetter. Evaluation trenches, both in and around the villa proper and in the village of Great Bedwyn, were supervised by J. Kenfield. Field drafting was done primarily by T. N. Howe, C. Alexander, M. Lynch, T. Scott, and M. Lane. Faunal and botanical retrieval was directed by K. Gleason, F. Fryer, and S. Payne, and find processing by M. Parca, A. St. Clair, E. Fry, and S. dell'Isola. Most photographs are by J. Crawford.

The excavation archive is stored at the School of Art and Design, Program in Art History, 408 East Peabody Drive, University of Illinois at Urbana-Champaign, Illinois 61820; and the finds, at The Museum, 41 Long St., Devizes, Wiltshire SN10 1NS.

11. By D. M. Evans, E. Hostetter, T. N. Howe, and K. Gleason.

12. Geophysical surveys were conducted by A. David, C. Gaffney, and C. Heron. Phosphate sampling was executed by G. Mees and K. L. Gleason.

13. Hingley 1989: 21. Far better, perhaps, to forsake the term "samian," virtually unused across the Channel.

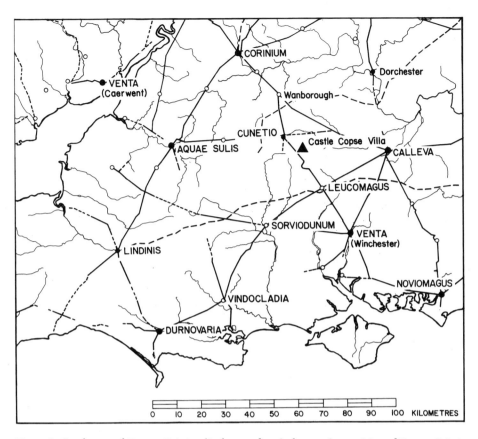

Figure 1. South-central Roman Britain. (Redrawn after Ordnance Survey Map of Roman Britain 1978.)

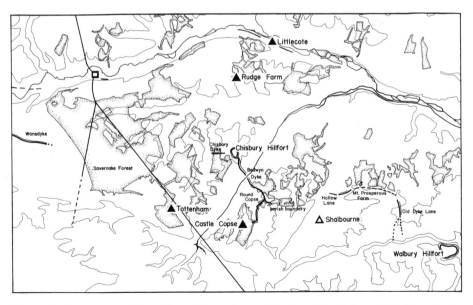

Figure 2. Area surrounding villa at Castle Copse, showing Wansdyke and Bedwyn Dyke. (T. N. Howe)

Figure 3. Aerial photograph of the southern area of Bedwyn Brail, showing relic field system. Villa remains are at northern edge of clearing in upper left (pale rectangle), off northern edge of squarish meadow. (Cambridge University. Photo courtesy of Wiltshire County Council.)

Figure 4. Castle Copse villa platform, toward west.

Figure 5. View north toward Chisbury hillfort, Bedwyn Dyke, and valley from northern edge of Bedwyn Brail.

Figure 6. View of Bedwyn Stream and Great Bedwyn (background, toward southwest).

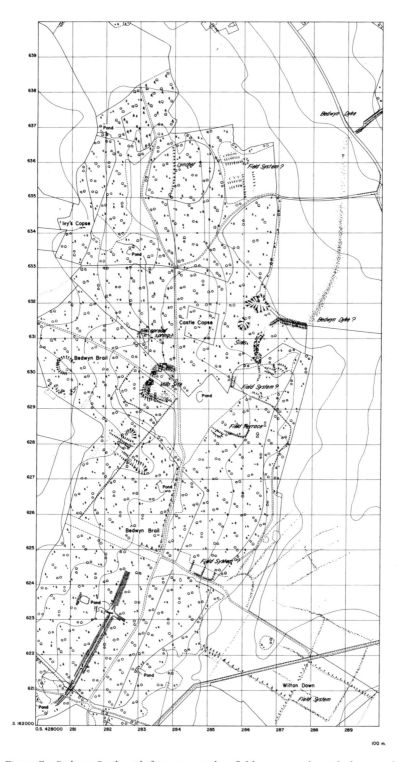

Figure 7a. Bedwyn Brail, with features noted in field survey and aerial photographs. (Redrawn after Ordnance Survey 1:2500 series, Sheet SU 2862 2962, contours after 1:10,000 series, Sheet SU 26 SE, with additional features.)

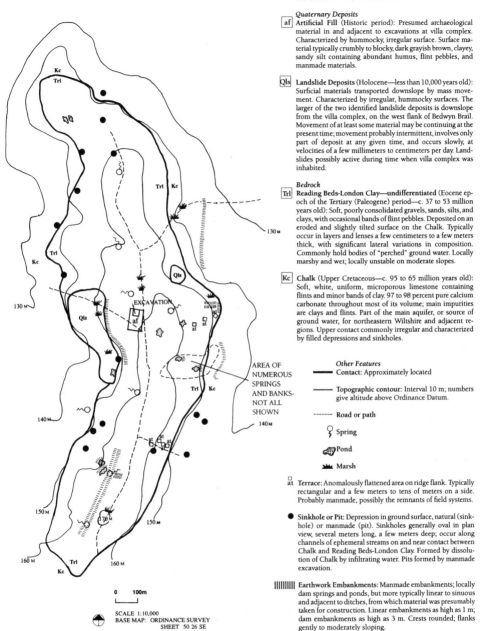

LEGEND TO FIGURE 7B

Quaternary Deposits

af **Artificial Fill** (Historic period): Presumed archaeological material in and adjacent to excavations at villa complex. Characterized by hummocky, irregular surface. Surface material typically crumbly to blocky, dark grayish brown, clayey, sandy silt containing abundant humus, flint pebbles, and manmade materials.

Qls **Landslide Deposits** (Holocene—less than 10,000 years old): Surficial materials transported downslope by mass movement. Characterized by irregular, hummocky surfaces. The larger of the two identified landslide deposits is downslope from the villa complex, on the west flank of Bedwyn Brail. Movement of at least some material may be continuing at the present time; movement probably intermittent, involves only part of deposit at any given time, and occurs slowly, at velocities of a few millimeters to centimeters per day. Landslides possibly active during time when villa complex was inhabited.

Bedrock

Trl **Reading Beds-London Clay—undifferentiated** (Eocene epoch of the Tertiary (Paleogene) period—c. 37 to 53 million years old): Soft, poorly consolidated gravels, sands, silts, and clays, with occasional bands of flint pebbles. Deposited on an eroded and slightly tilted surface on the Chalk. Typically occur in layers and lenses a few centimeters to a few meters thick, with significant lateral variations in composition. Commonly hold bodies of "perched" ground water. Locally marshy and wet; locally unstable on moderate slopes.

Kc **Chalk** (Upper Cretaceous—c. 95 to 65 million years old): Soft, white, uniform, microporous limestone containing flints and minor bands of clay. 97 to 98 percent pure calcium carbonate throughout most of its volume; main impurities are clays and flints. Part of the main aquifer, or source of ground water, for northeastern Wiltshire and adjacent regions. Upper contact commonly irregular and characterized by filled depressions and sinkholes.

Other Features
━━━ **Contact:** Approximately located

─── **Topographic contour:** Interval 10 m; numbers give altitude above Ordinance Datum.

------ **Road or path**

♀ **Spring**

Pond

Marsh

at **Terrace:** Anomalously flattened area on ridge flank. Typically rectangular and a few meters to tens of meters on a side. Probably manmade, possibly the remnants of field systems.

● **Sinkhole or Pit:** Depression in ground surface, natural (sinkhole) or manmade (pit). Sinkholes generally oval in plan view, several meters long, a few meters deep; occur along channels of ephemeral streams on and near contact between Chalk and Reading Beds-London Clay. Formed by dissolution of Chalk by infiltrating water. Pits formed by manmade excavation.

‖‖‖‖‖‖ **Earthwork Embankments:** Manmade embankments; locally dam springs and ponds, but more typically linear to sinuous and adjacent to ditches, from which material was presumably taken for construction. Linear embankments as high as 1 m; dam embankments as high as 3 m. Crests rounded; flanks gently to moderately sloping.

Figure 7b. Bedwyn Brail geologic map (after Ordnance Survey 1:10,000 series, Sheet SU 26 SE).

Figure 8. Contour plan of building platform and meadow to the south, with excavation sectors. (T. N. Howe)

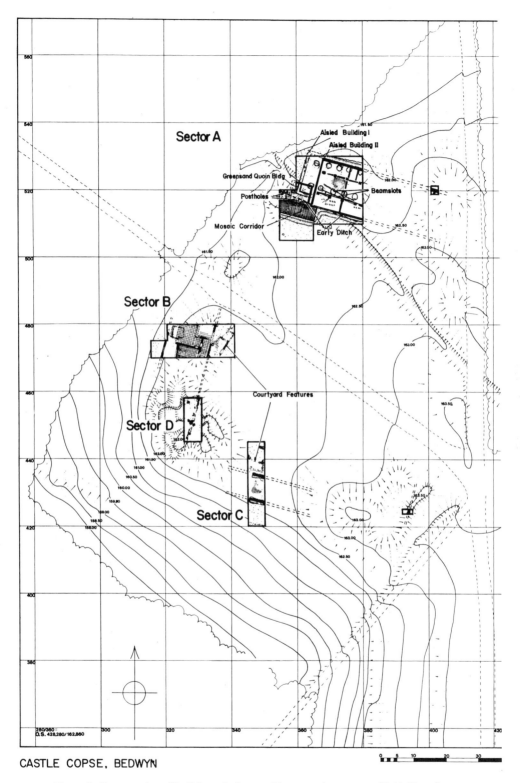

CASTLE COPSE, BEDWYN

Figure 9. Contour plan of building platform, with excavation sectors. (T. N. Howe)

The Romano-British Villa at Castle Copse, Great Bedwyn

CHAPTER 1

The Regional Setting:
Environmental Geology and Geography

DAVID K. KEEFER

Introduction

Chisbury hillfort, the Roman villa at Castle Copse, and the town of Great Bedwyn in northeastern Wiltshire are in a region that has a temperate marine climate, abundant rainfall of 700 to 1000 mm per year, fertile soils, and topography that includes both flat valley bottoms and rolling uplands. Altitudes in this region range from 55 m to 297 m above O.D.

Within 6 km of Chisbury, Castle Copse villa and Great Bedwyn are parts of four of southern England's major physiographic provinces: the valleys of the Thames River and its tributary, the Kennet; the Marlborough Downs (called the Berkshire Downs in adjoining Berkshire); the Vale of Pewsey and associated Vale of Shalbourne; and Salisbury Plain (Figs. 10-11). Also within 6 km are watershed boundaries dividing three major river basins: the Thames, the Salisbury Avon, and the Test. Chisbury hillfort, Castle Copse villa, and Great Bedwyn are thus in a region that contains several major valleys, uplands, and river systems. Because of this, the region also encompasses several physical environments and contains a variety of resources. The purposes of this chapter are to describe the geography, topography, geology, and hydrology of this region and to discuss the possible effects of these environmental conditions on the siting and developments of the hillfort, villa, and town.

Geography and Topography

Chisbury hillfort, Castle Copse villa, and Great Bedwyn are on a part of the Marlborough Downs that forms an upland between the valleys of the Kennet and Thames rivers to the north and east and the vales (valleys) of Pewsey and Shalbourne to the south (Fig. 11). The upland is about 40 km from east to west and 10 km from north to south. Its greatest width is in the Chisbury, Great Bedwyn, and Castle Copse area. Dissection of the upland by small valleys and combes (dry valleys) creates an irregular surface containing many isolated hills and ridges. The southern boundary of this part of the Marlborough Downs is a prominent escarpment (Fig. 13), locally as steep as 35% and as high as 158 m. The highest altitudes on the Marlborough Downs are at the top of this escarpment at Martinsell Hill (altitude 294 m O.D.; Fig. 11), Milk Hill (294 m O.D.), and Tan Hill (294 m O.D.), which are respectively 11, 19, and 20 km west of Castle Copse villa.

Chisbury, Great Bedwyn, and the villa are thus not built on the highest ground on the Marlborough Downs. Rather, they cluster in and around the valley of Bedwyn Brook, the only stream that has cut completely through the upland from the Vale of Pewsey to the Kennet Valley (Fig. 11). The valley of Bedwyn Brook has been an important transportation corridor in recent times, as both the Kennet-Avon Canal and the Great Western Railway pass through the upland there. The town of Great Bedwyn is in the valley of Bedwyn Brook itself (Figs. 6, 11) in an area where altitudes range from 118 to 143 m O.D. Chisbury hillfort and Castle Copse villa are on hilltops that are respectively 1.7 km north and 1.4 km south-southeast of the town's church.

Chisbury hillfort is on an irregular ridge, 4 km long, 2.5 km wide, and 57 m high (Figs. 5, 11). The highest part of the ridge, which is occupied by the hillfort, is triangular in plan. The maximum altitude on the ridge crest is 175 m O.D., and the minimum altitude of the hillfort embankments is 160 m O.D. The hillfort encloses about 11 hectares. The flanks of the ridge are gentle, with average slope inclinations of 2% to 8%; the gentlest flank is on the northeast, sloping down toward the Kennet Valley, whereas the steepest is on the south-southeast, sloping down toward Bedwyn Brook. Parts of the ridge, including the ditch and embankments of the hillfort, are wooded; other parts, including the central area of the hillfort, are open fields.

The Roman villa at Castle Copse is on Bedwyn Brail, an elongated, forested ridge 3 km long, 1 km wide, and 55 m high (Figs. 7, 11). The ridge has a broad, rounded crest and flanks with moderate slopes of about 5% to 20%. The maximum altitude is between 170 and 175 m O.D., at a point near the ridge's southern end. The villa is 1.5 km north-northeast of the highest point and is at an altitude of 162 m O.D. The southern flank of Bedwyn Brail is the northwest terminus of the Vale of Pewsey.

The Vale of Pewsey, one of southern England's largest valleys, stretches 45 km west from Bedwyn Brail to near Westbury (Figs. 10–11). The vale is 2–3 km wide near Bedwyn Brail and broadens to widths of 10–15 km near Westbury. The north wall of the vale is the south-facing escarpment of the Marlborough Downs (Figs. 11, 13), and the vale's south wall is a similar north-facing escarpment bounding Salisbury Plain (Figs. 11, 14). The floor of the vale contains a few low hills and a west-facing escarpment in the Devizes area, but otherwise is relatively flat (Figs. 11, 13). Altitudes of the vale floor decrease from about 140 m O.D. near Bedwyn Brail to about 40 m near Westbury.

East of Bedwyn Brail and separated from the Vale of Pewsey by a narrow, upland divide, 1.8 km wide (Fig. 11), is the Vale of Shalbourne, a valley 6 km in length, physiographically and geologically similar to the Vale of Pewsey (Figs. 10, 11, 14). At the eastern end of the Vale of Shalbourne another narrow, upland divide, only 0.7–1.0 km wide, separates the vale from the Thames Valley to the east (Fig. 11). These two divides at either end of the Vale of Shalbourne are the only upland bridges between the Marlborough and Berkshire Downs and Salisbury Plain (Figs. 10, 11).

Salisbury Plain stretches 30–40 km south from the two vales. This "plain" is a dissected upland, similar to the Marlborough Downs, consisting of numerous ridges and hills separated by small valleys and combes. The northern boundary of Salisbury Plain is a prominent north-facing escarpment; the highest point on the escarpment is 9 km east of Castle Copse villa at Walbury Hill, where the altitude is 297 m O.D. (Figs 11, 14). The regional slope of Salisbury Plain is southward, and the northern part nearest the Chisbury-Great Bedwyn-Castle Copse area contains the highest as well as some of the most rugged ground on the "plain."

The fourth major physiographic province near Chisbury, Great Bedwyn, and the villa consists of the valleys of the Thames and Kennet rivers (Figs. 10–11). The Kennet River has headwaters north of Avebury, 19 km west-northwest of Great Bedwyn, and flows east into the broader valley of the Thames 15 km north-northeast of Great Bedwyn, between Kintbury and Newbury (Fig. 11). North of Chisbury, the Kennet Valley consists of an alluvial plain about 500 m wide. Bedwyn Brook is one of the main tributaries to the Kennet and joins it at Hungerford, 8 km northeast of Great Bedwyn. From immediately east of the Vale of Shalbourne, the Thames Valley proper, southeastern England's broad and densely populated lowland, stretches east to London and the sea.

Geology

Bedrock in south-central England consists of sedimentary rocks of Triassic, Jurassic, Cretaceous, and Tertiary ages, which were deposited from c. 240 million years to c. 37 million years ago (Fig. 10).[1] These rocks have been uplifted, folded into a series of gentle anticlines (upwarps) and synclines (downwarps), locally faulted, and partly eroded to form the present topography. The rocks are covered nearly everywhere by modern soils and, in some areas, by other unconsolidated deposits of Quaternary age (c. 1.6 million years to the present) as well.

The oldest rocks in the region are in the west, and the youngest are in the east and south (Fig. 10). The oldest bedrock units are the Triassic, consisting of sandstones, conglomerates (cemented pebble beds), and marls (mixtures of clay and calcium carbonate) and the Lias, which consists primarily of clay, with some interbedded limestone. Overlying the Lias is a series of well-consolidated limestones with some interbedded clays (Inferior Oolite, Great Oolite, and Cornbrash). The limestones form a well-drained upland upon which the Roman Fosse Way was built. Stratigraphically above these limestones are the Oxford Clay, Corallian Beds (predominantly limestones), Kimmeridge Clay, Portland Group (primarily limestones and sandstones), Purbeck Group (limestones, marls, sandstones, and clays), Wealden (clays and marls), and Lower Greensand. In Wiltshire, these rocks are found primarily in lowland areas of the Clay Vale, the Vale of Wardour, and the western Vale of Pewsey (Fig. 10).

The younger Cretaceous and Tertiary rocks and Quaternary deposits that occur in and around northeastern Wiltshire are discussed below.[2]

BEDROCK AND ASSOCIATED SOILS

Distribution of the main bedrock units in the vicinity of Chisbury, Castle Copse villa, and Great Bedwyn is shown in Figs. 10, 12, and 15. Because the bedrock is covered virtually everywhere by modern soils or other Quaternary deposits, nearly all bedrock exposures are in man-made cuts or excavations. Bedrock units are described below in stratigraphic order from oldest to youngest.

Gault (Lower Cretaceous): The Gault consists of clay and marl, with a stratigraphic thickness of 30–70 m. Within the area of Fig. 12, the Gault is exposed at the surface only in the western part, more than 20 km from Great Bedwyn. However, the Gault is important to the hydrology of the Chisbury-Great Bedwyn-Castle Copse area, because it forms an impermeable barrier below the Upper Greensand (Fig. 15).

Upper Greensand (Lower Cretaceous): The Upper Greensand is 10 to 50 m of fine sands and sandstones that are locally silty, contain occasional nodules of chert, and are locally cemented into relatively hard layers known as "doggers." The green color in these materials results from the inclusion of grains of the green mineral, glauconite. The Upper Greensand underlies the floor of the Vale of Shalbourne and the floor of the Vale of Pewsey as far west as Devizes (Fig. 12).

Most soils developed on Upper Greensand are light, calcareous, sandy loams; in some places the soils also contain marl, clay, and/or gravel derived from Quaternary deposits or from colluvium washed from nearby slopes. Upper Greensand soils are generally fertile and are easily worked, supporting a wide variety of crops, orchards, and pastures.[3] The fertility of these soils is evidenced by population densities in the Vales of Pewsey and Shalbourne that are higher than those on the adjacent uplands.[4] The Upper Greensand is also important for water supply (see below).

Chalk (Upper Cretaceous): The Chalk is 175–320 m of soft, white, microporous limestone that, throughout much of its volume, is 97–98% pure calcium carbonate. The Chalk is divided stratigraphically into three units—Lower Chalk, Middle Chalk, and Upper Chalk (Figs. 12, 15). The Lower Chalk and Middle Chalk commonly form the lower parts of the escarpments bounding the Marlborough Downs and Salisbury Plain, whereas the Upper Chalk forms the upper parts of these escarpments and most of the rolling uplands themselves. Great Bedwyn is built on Upper Chalk (Figs. 12, 15).

The Chalk contains two main impurities: clay and flints. Lower Chalk contains the most clay and consists of a clay-calcium carbonate mixture called the Chalk Marl. Middle and Upper Chalk also contain minor bands of clay or marl. The clay content decreases upward in section so that the Upper Chalk is the purest. By contrast, flints are most common in the Upper Chalk and uppermost Middle Chalk, and the abundance of flints decreases gradually downward in the section. Flints occur along bedding planes, in veins, and as irregular nodules.

The calcium carbonate matrix of the Chalk is dissolved by rainwater and soil acids, and thus most soils on Chalk are composed largely of the small proportion of insoluble impurities in the Chalk mixed with unweathered Chalk rubble, material from overlying Tertiary and Quaternary deposits, and windblown silt and sand. Because of the greater clay content of the Lower Chalk, soils developed on this unit are relatively stiff and range in composition from marl to loam; these soils are fertile and particularly suitable for cereal grain and arable crop cultivation.[5] Middle Chalk soils are generally thin, well-drained loams containing numerous flints. These soils are used for pasture, but are of poor quality for cultivation.[6] Soils on the Upper Chalk are variable in thickness and composition. Where material from overlying Tertiary or Quaternary deposits is abundant, the soils are arable and suitable for cultivation (especially, in modern times, for cereal production) as well as grazing; where such materials are absent, the soils are thin, well-drained loams of poor quality, similar to the Middle Chalk soils.[7] Because of the hydrological properties of the Chalk (see below, Hydrology and Water Supply), the upland surfaces of the Marlborough Downs and Salisbury Plain are relatively dry and well-drained except where covered by clayey soils derived from Tertiary or Quaternary sediments.

Reading Beds, London Clay and Bagshot Beds (Tertiary): The Tertiary-age sediments in this region are a sequence of soft, poorly consolidated gravels, sands, silts and clays, with occasional bands of flint pebbles. These Tertiary sediments occur in isolated patches on the upland Chalk surface as far west as Savernake Forest (Fig. 12) and are also present throughout the Thames Valley (Fig. 10). Maximum stratigraphic thickness of these sediments in the vicinity of Chisbury, Castle Copse villa, and Great Bedwyn is probably less than 35 m.[8] The sediments vary significantly in composition both vertically and laterally. In most areas, the Reading Beds and Bagshot Beds are predominantly sand, whereas the London Clay is predominantly clay. The London Clay is also associated with numerous landslides and is commonly unstable on slopes as gentle as 14%.[9] In many places, the Bagshot Beds-London Clay contact is marked by a line of wet, marshy ground, as downward infiltration of water through the more permeable Bagshot Beds is retarded by the less permeable London Clay.

Two stratigraphic sections of Reading Beds were examined near Castle Copse villa. A 2.7 m thick section is exposed in a quarry approximately 1.2 km east-northeast of the villa (Fig. 16). There the sediments consist of layers, lenses, and channel deposits of fine, well-sorted, well-rounded sands, interbedded with moderately soft, fissured, plastic clays. The beds range 3–60 cm thick, and sands comprise an estimated 55–60% of the exposed stratigraphic section. Another stratigraphic section, 5.85 m thick, 300 m east-northeast of the villa on Bedwyn Brail itself, was exposed by digging a shallow trench. At this locality, the sediments consist of sandy clays, clayey sands, clays, and a single bed of moderately well sorted, fine-to-very-fine sand. Beds range in thickness from 20 to 85 cm (Fig. 17). Sediments in this section, however, are probably disturbed by soil- and slope-forming processes, slope wash, and soil creep, and thus are probably not as representative of the local stratigraphy as are the beds in the quarry section.

An 11 m–thick section of London Clay and Bagshot Beds at the Dods Down Brickworks on Wilton Brail, 1.2 km southwest of the villa, was described by H. J. O. White.[10] There, the London Clay contains 2.4 m of loam, 0.3 m of sandy clay, 3 m of clay, and 1.5 m of sand and loam containing flint pebbles (Fig. 18). The overlying Bagshot Beds contain 1.5 m of sand with clay seams, 1.2 m of alternating clay and sand, and 0.9 m of stiff clay with flint pebbles.

Castle Copse villa is built on Tertiary sediments (Figs. 12, 15), probably on London Clay just above its contact with the Reading Beds.[11] In northeastern Wiltshire, however, field identification of this contact is difficult because of the units' poor exposure and local similarity in composition, and thus the position of the contact on Bedwyn Brail is not precisely determined.

Chisbury hillfort is built partly on Bagshot Beds and partly on Quaternary Plateau Gravel (see below, Quaternary Deposits). Two stratigraphic sections of Bagshot Beds near Chisbury (on the roadcut on the south flank of the hill containing Chisbury and at Stock

Farm, 2 km to the southwest) were described as consisting primarily of sand with a little clay.[12] The London Clay may feather out below Chisbury, and thus under part of that hill the Bagshot Beds probably rest directly on the Reading Beds (Fig. 12).[13]

Soils developed on Tertiary sediments in the vicinity of Chisbury, Great Bedwyn, and Castle Copse villa typically contain more clay than do the chalk soils, but are variable in composition, reflecting both the variability of the bedrock and the extensive reworking of these sediments during the Quaternary. These soils are covered in many places by dense forest.

Geologic Structure: Rocks in the Chisbury, Great Bedwyn, and Castle Copse area have been uplifted and folded. The main folds are the Kingsclere-Pewsey Anticline, a moderate upwarp, and the London Basin, a broad syncline (downwarp). The axis of the anticline strikes east-southeast along the north side of the Vale of Pewsey and through the Vale of Shalbourne. Bedrock south of this axis dips to the south (Fig. 15). The axis of the London Basin, parallel to and north of the anticline, passes through Bedwyn Brail near the villa. This synclinal axis plunges down toward the east, and the villa is near the westernmost expression of the syncline, which is in Savernake Forest.[14] Rocks between the two fold axes dip toward the north, whereas rocks north of the synclinal axis dip toward the south (Fig. 15).

QUATERNARY DEPOSITS

Before the beginning of Quaternary glaciation, much of the Chalk was probably covered by Tertiary sediments.[15] However, late Tertiary uplift and erosion, and geomorphic processes operating in both near-glacial and interglacial conditions during Quaternary times removed these sediments from much of the Chalk, reworked them, and redeposited their material along with windblown silt and sand to form a complex and variable suite of Quaternary deposits in northeastern Wiltshire. The main Quaternary deposits in the Chisbury-Great Bedwyn-Castle Copse area are: Clay-with-flints, Coombe Rock, Brick Earths, Sarsens, Plateau Gravels, Valley Gravels, and Alluvium.

Clay-with-flints are deposits of clay and sand, derived from Tertiary sediments, and flints left as insoluble residues during erosion of parts of the Chalk. Clay-with-flints soils typically support dense forest growth. Such soils are present throughout much of Savernake Forest.

Coombe Rock consists of masses of chalk, flint, and clay, probably formed by frost-shattering of rocks and subsequent downslope movement under near-glacial conditions.

Brick Earths are loams used in making brick, tile, and pottery. They have a silt or fine-sand matrix and contain enough clay to remain coherent during firing. They were probably deposited partly by streams and partly by wind.[16]

Sarsens are very hard, irregularly shaped cobbles and boulders of quartzite (silica-cemented sandstone), silicified clay silt or silica-cemented conglomerate.[17] Sarsens occur on surfaces underlain by the Chalk; they are remnants of particularly hard layers in the Tertiary sediments that were lowered onto the Chalk surface when the rest of the Tertiary material was eroded. Some sarsen boulders are more than 7 m in diameter. The Marlborough Downs contain the greatest concentration of sarsens in southern England, and they are particularly abundant near Avebury.[18]

Plateau Gravels, Valley Gravels, and Alluvium are river and stream deposits. *Plateau*

Gravels were deposited by rivers flowing in valleys about 100 m higher in elevation than the present valley floors. The Plateau Gravels contain pebbles and subangular pieces of flint, sandstone, and quartzite, as well as small sarsens, and variable amounts of sand, silt and clay. The interior and some embankments of Chisbury hillfort are on Plateau Gravels (Figs. 12, 15), which there consist of subangular pieces of flint, rounded flint pebbles, and pieces of sarsen in a sandy matrix.[19] *Valley Gravels,* deposited about 20 m higher in elevation than present valley floors, are similar in composition to the Plateau Gravels, but also contain Chalk rubble, mammal fossils, and Paleolithic artifacts.[20] *Alluvium* denotes the deposits of modern rivers. These deposits are made up of clays, silts, sands, loams, and fresh-water marls.

BUILDING MATERIALS

Building stone in northeastern Wiltshire is not as good or as plentiful as in the limestone uplands to the west (Fig. 10); few layers in either the Chalk or Upper Greensand are durable enough to be quarried for building-stone blocks. The most durable local stone building materials are flints and sarsens, which have been used for construction in this area since the Neolithic. Sarsens can be split and shaped into blocks but have the disadvantage of condensing moisture on their surfaces under certain weather conditions.[21] Flints, found in the Chalk, Tertiary sediments, and Quaternary deposits, are also very hard and durable. Flints occur as pebbles, cobbles, or irregularly shaped nodules and are difficult to shape into blocks. Thus they are commonly mortared into walls in their original, irregular shapes or with only rough modification. The softer Chalk is used in a local variant of wattle-and-daub construction known as "cob" or "dob."[22] This unbaked mixture of chalk, straw, and clay has been used to build barns and cottages, which typically are thick-walled, rounded, and thatched. This material needs protection from rainfall and soil moisture; the cob is usually placed on a stone foundation, covered by whitewash or powdered chalk, and protected by a large overhang on the roof.[23] Chalk was also excavated and used directly in construction of the many barrows, earthwork embankments, and hillforts built on the Marlborough Downs and Salisbury Plain during the Neolithic, Bronze Age, and Iron Age.

A few of the harder layers in the Chalk and Upper Greensand, including one Chalk bed that occurs in the valley of Bedwyn Brook, have been quarried. Chalk blocks have been used for buildings, particularly for interior walls, and for paving roads.[24] Blocks of Upper Greensand absorb less water than brick and have been used for foundations and the lower parts of the walls in brick buildings.[25]

Local Brick Earths have been used for pottery-making since before the Roman arrival[26] and, more recently, for making brick. Brick, tile, and pottery have also been made from materials in the Clay-with-flints and Tertiary sediments. Brick, both local and imported, is probably the most popular modern construction material in the Chisbury-Great Bedwyn-Castle Copse area.

Beautiful and durable building stone has been quarried at distances of 23 to 50 km from Great Bedwyn from strata in the Corallian Beds, Great Oolite, Portland Group, and Purbeck Group (Fig. 10). The occurrence of such building stone closest to Great Bedwyn is 23 km to the north-northwest, where Purbeck and Portland limestone was quarried and used to build the old town of Swindon.[27] Since the Roman period, a golden-brown limestone, known as "Bath Stone," has been quarried from the Great Oolite near Bath and Box, 45–50 km west of Great Bedwyn. Bath Stone is also currently quarried near Corsham, 41 km west of Great Bedwyn.[28] A Corallian limestone, known as "Calne Freestone," is quarried near Calne, 29 km west-northwest of Great Bedwyn, and quarries in the Vale of Wardour, 45 km southwest of Great Bedwyn, have provided "Chilmark Stone," a cream to light gray, sandy limestone in the Portland Group.[29]

Hydrology and Water Supply

With 700–1000 mm average annual precipitation, northeastern Wiltshire has an abundant water supply. Water can be obtained from direct catchment of rainfall, from streams and rivers, and from subsurface (groundwater) sources tapped by wells or natural springs. The main rivers and streams in the Chisbury-Great Bedwyn-Castle Copse area are the Kennet and its tributaries, including Bedwyn Brook (Fig. 11). Numerous Roman villas and the Roman town of Cunetio are in the Kennet Valley near the river. However, groundwater is almost always less contaminated than surface water because of the natural filtering action of flow through rock and soil. Perhaps partly for this reason and perhaps partly for convenience or defense, wells were dug in Roman times even for settlements in the Kennet Valley; a well 20 m deep has been excavated at Cunetio, a well 8 m deep near Silbury Hill,[30] and a well more than 2 m deep at Littlecote villa. Great Bedwyn is today supplied by water from wells, despite the proximity of Bedwyn Brook and the Kennet-Avon Canal.[31] In the vicinity of Chisbury, Castle Copse villa, and Great Bedwyn, groundwater may be obtained from the large region-wide Chalk–Upper Greensand aquifer or, locally, from thin, permeable beds within the isolated occurrences of Tertiary and Quaternary deposits.

Groundwater in the Chalk flows primarily through fractures. Because of the solubility of calcium carbonate, the groundwater flow itself enlarges the fractures, producing a permeable aquifer. Water from precipitation infiltrates down from the ground surface to the water table (defined as the upper surface of the zone of saturation within the rock). Because of the resistance to water flow within the rock, the water table is not level, and in the area between Bedwyn Brail and Chisbury the slope of the water table is toward the northeast. As inferred from measurements in August 1976, the water table in the Chalk was at an approximate elevation of 122 m O.D. under the villa and 115 m O.D. under Great Bedwyn and Chisbury (Fig. 19).[32] Thus the August 1976 water table in the Chalk was only about 3 m below the ground surface under the lower part of Great Bedwyn, but 40 m below the surface at the villa and 45–60 m below the surface at Chisbury hillfort.

Fractures through the otherwise impermeable Lower Chalk extend into the permeable Upper Greensand and connect the Upper Greensand and the Chalk into a single aquifer. Thus, groundwater flow within the Upper Greensand is also controlled by the water table in the Chalk.[33] Where the water table intersects the ground surface, springs are formed, and because of the local geologic structure, numerous springs are present where the Upper Greensand crops out in the Vale of Pewsey (Figs. 12, 15). Because the water table does not fall below the base of the Chalk, these springs have year-round flow and have supplied water for many villages and other settlements. Many of these settlements date from Saxon times, and at least one—Bratton (38 km west-southwest of Castle

Copse villa)—from Roman times.[34] Four such year-round springs occur just southwest of Bedwyn Brail, 2–3.5 km from the villa.[35] These springs are the headwaters of Bedwyn Brook, and their flow has been dammed to form the present-day Wilton Water.

Castle Copse villa is built on Tertiary sediments; Chisbury hillfort, partly on Tertiary and partly on Quaternary deposits (Figs. 12, 15, 19). The Tertiary sediments consist of layers and lenses of permeable sands alternating with impermeable clays; at Chisbury the Tertiary sediments are capped by an additional, permeable layer of Plateau Gravel. Because the impermeable clays form barriers to downward infiltration, water flows laterally through the sandier strata, forming local bodies of groundwater "perched" above the regional groundwater body in the Chalk and Upper Greensand (Fig. 19). The presence of perched groundwater at Chisbury is suggested by a pond near the top of the hill, within the hillfort. The presence of perched groundwater on Bedwyn Brail is evidenced by many springs, ponds, marshes, and ephemeral streams. Within the north-dipping Tertiary sediments there, groundwater flows north from the highest parts of the ridge toward the villa. The quantity of water available from these Tertiary and Quaternary sediments is smaller and more seasonably variable than from the Chalk–Upper Greensand aquifer because of the small catchment areas, limited areal and vertical extent of the sediments, and the small proportion of permeable material.

Water-table elevations and quantities of groundwater available may vary over time because of seasonal or longer variations in climate, vegetation, or human water use. The most significant change in vegetation affecting groundwater conditions in northeastern Wiltshire was probably large-scale human clearing of the postglacial forests. Forest clearance tends to raise water tables by reducing evapo-transpiration and by allowing more precipitation to fall directly onto the ground surface. Clearance of the once extensive forests in southern England, however, began on a large scale in the Neolithic and was probably well advanced on the Chalk uplands before the beginning of the Iron Age.[36] Thus, its effect on groundwater conditions has probably been negligible since that time.

Climatic data from Iron Age Britain suggest that a particularly wet period began in south-central England as early as c. 500 B.C. and possibly as early as c. 800 B.C.[37] Limited data from Britain and elsewhere in northwestern Europe suggest that such wet conditions continued through c. A.D. 100 and that drier, though still moderately wet, conditions prevailed until at least c. A.D. 500. More complete data since A.D. 600 suggest additional wet periods c. A.D. 600 to 700, A.D. 800 to 950, and A.D. 1000 to 1100.[38] Archaeological evidence from Cranbourne Chase, 58 km southwest of Great Bedwyn, also suggests that the climate in south-central England was wetter in the Roman period than at present; this evidence consists of a Romano-British village with an extensive drainage network and a Roman period well with its bottom substantially above the probable elevation of the water table as measured in 1925.[39] These climatic and archaeological data thus suggest several periods of wet climate during the Iron Age, a climate slightly wetter than at present during the period of Romano-British occupation at Castle Copse villa, and alternating dry and wet conditions during Anglo-Saxon times.

A wetter climate would have increased the quantities of groundwater potentially available to the villa at Castle Copse and Chisbury hillfort from the Tertiary and Quaternary sediments. Because the present water table in the Chalk–Upper Greensand aquifer is almost at the surface under much of Bedwyn Valley (Fig. 19), however, this water table could not have risen more than a few meters even during exceptionally wet periods. Any wells at the hillfort or villa thus could not have tapped into the deeper and more plentiful groundwater in the Chalk at depths of less than about 35–40 m, and constructing wells of such depths would probably have been difficult.

Effects of Geographic, Geologic and Hydrologic Conditions

Chisbury hillfort, Castle Copse villa, and Great Bedwyn are near the center of southern England on a narrow upland between two major lowlands, the Thames Valley and the Vale of Pewsey. Within a few kilometers of the three sites are divides between three major river basins (the Thames, Test, and Salisbury Avon) and parts of four physiographic provinces (the Kennet-Thames Valley, Vale of Pewsey-Vale of Shalbourne, the Marlborough Downs, and Salisbury Plain). Thus, centrally located and in a major divide area, the sites are at a natural confluence of southern England's transportation routes, both lowland and upland.

The Valley of Bedwyn Brook, around which the three sites are arrayed, is the only tributary valley cut completely through the Marlborough Downs from the Vale of Pewsey to the Thames Valley. This tributary valley provides a natural lowland transportation route from the London area and Thames lowland, through the Vale of Pewsey, and to southwestern England. The Bedwyn Valley has been thus used in modern times for a major railroad and canal, and it could have been similarly used for lowland transportation during some earlier periods.

Castle Copse villa, Great Bedwyn, and Chisbury hillfort, as well as the two neighboring hillforts at Walbury and Fosbury (Fig. 11), are also located strategically with respect to upland transportation routes. Chalk uplands such as Salisbury Plain and the Marlborough Downs were the principal dry and open country in southern England in prehistoric times. These uplands were used extensively for transportation[40] and were probably particularly important during the wet period in the late Iron Age, when marshes were widespread in the lowland valleys.[41] Starting from the south, the Chalk uplands converge from the Dorset Downs, South Downs, North Downs, and Salisbury Plain onto the two narrow upland divides at either end of the Vale of Shalbourne (Figs. 10–12). From there the uplands broaden again to the north onto the Marlborough Downs, Berkshire Downs, and Chiltern Hills, on the northwest side of the Thames Valley. The three hillforts—Walbury, Fosbury, and Chisbury—and the villa are all on high points overlooking the two narrow upland divides that connect Salisbury Plain with the Marlborough Downs (Fig. 11). The hillforts (and the site of the villa) are thus situated to control the narrowest part of prehistoric southern England's upland transportation system: Walbury hillfort, on the highest point on the Salisbury Plain escarpment, dominates the divide east of the Vale of Shalbourne. Fosbury hillfort dominates the southern approach to the western divide while Bedwyn Brail and Chisbury hillfort dominate the northern approach (Fig. 11).

Additional strategic advantage for Chisbury, Great Bedwyn, and Castle Copse villa derives from their location on the east-west-trending upland between the Kennet River and the Vale of Pewsey, which is a natural defensive position between these two major valleys. The defensive position is enhanced by the broken, irregular nature of much of this ground and by the presence of dense woods, particularly on the Tertiary sediments and Clay-with-flints soils. Numerous hillforts and earthwork embankments, including the Wansdyke and Bedwyn Dyke, are located on this upland. It is conceivable that these form a chain-like series of earthworks from the upland's western terminus south of Calne, through Chisbury, to the north of Great Bedwyn and the villa; and it is possible that the trace continues through to the upland's eastern terminus and junction with Salisbury Plain at Walbury hillfort (see chapter 4.18) (Fig. 11). The clearest break in this series of dykes is in heavily wooded terrain in Savernake Forest. While many of the earthwork dykes are probably not contemporaneous in construction with the hillforts, the dykes and the hillforts could have been used simultaneously, at least in post-Roman times. Such a series of earthworks—if it continued as far as Walbury and if it is in all sections defensive in character—would have been positioned to defend the Vale of Pewsey from raiding from the north.

Chisbury hillfort, Castle Copse villa, and Great Bedwyn are thus at a convergence of four lines of transportation or defense: the valley of Bedwyn Brook, which connects the Vale of Pewsey with the Kennet-Thames Valley, the upland divide connecting the Marlborough Downs to Salisbury Plain, the Roman road between Cunetio and Winchester; and the (possible) east-west line of dykes and hillforts on the most defensible upland terrain between the lowlands of the Kennet and Thames and the Vale of Pewsey. In addition to this strategic location, Chisbury hillfort and Castle Copse villa are on hilltops with potential for water supply from Tertiary and or Quaternary sediments. This potential gives these sites a significant advantage over all but a few of the other hilltop sites in this area, as most hilltop sites are underlain by Chalk (Fig. 12).

Finally, in addition to these advantages, Castle Copse villa and its associated estate were well positioned to exploit a rich variety of agricultural soils and environments. Within three kilometers of the villa buildings are level, valley-bottom, Upper Greensand soils suitable for arable crops, orchards, and pastures; Lower Chalk soils for arable crops and cereals; Middle and Upper Chalk soils for grazing and cereal cultivation; dense woods on Tertiary sediments and Clay-with-flints soils; upland ground-water supply from the Tertiary sediments; and year-round springs fed by the Chalk–Upper Greensand aquifer. Sites farther north on the Marlborough Downs, or farther south, on Salisbury Plain, lack such access to the fertile Upper Greensand and Lower Chalk soils, to year-round springs and, in most places, to the Tertiary sediments, with their woodlands and potential for upland water supply.

NOTES

1. Welch and Crookall 1935; Melville and Freshney 1982.
2. Information on these materials is derived from field observations of the author; from Institute of Geological Sciences maps (IGS 1947, 1959, 1974, 1975; IGS and TWA 1978) and area reports (Jukes-Browne 1905 and 1908; H. White 1907 and 1925); and from the regional work of Sherlock (1960), Limbrey (1975), Barron (1976), and Melville and Freshney (1982).
3. Jukes-Browne 1905: 50; and 1908: 60.

4. Barron 1976: 94.

5. Jukes-Browne 1905: 50; H. White 1925: 94; and Barron 1976: 99.

6. Jukes-Browne 1905: 50; and H. White 1925: 94.

7. H. White 1925: 94; and Barron 1976: 116.

8. H. White 1907: 49, 65, 71.

9. Skempton and Hutchinson 1969.

10. H. White 1907: 68.

11. IGS 1947.

12. H. White 1907: 63.

13. H. White 1907: 68; and IGS 1947.

14. Sherlock 1960: 57.

15. Limbrey 1975: 176.

16. Limbrey 1975: 179–80.

17. Barron 1976: 85.

18. H. White 1925: 74; massive sarsens were used to construct the Neolithic stone circles at Avebury and Early Bronze Age circles at Stonehenge.

19. H. White 1907: 97.

20. H. White 1907: 97.

21. H. White 1907: 121.

22. Respectively, Barron 1976: 86; and H. White 1925: 96.

23. Barron 1976: 86, 124.

24. H. White 1907: 38; and Barron 1976: 86.

25. Barron 1976: 96–97.

26. H. White 1925: 96. Including at the southern end of Bedwyn Brail.

27. Barron 1976: 60–62.

28. Barron 1976: 42–43.

29. Barron 1976: 64, 137–39.

30. Whitaker and Edmunds 1925: 25–26.

31. IGS and TWA 1978.

32. IGS and TWA 1978; Thames Water Authority, oral communication, 1985.

33. Barron 1976: 77.

34. Barron 1976: 97–100.

35. IGS and TWA 1978.

36. Limbrey 1975: 184–88.

37. Lamb 1982: 144–46.

38. Lamb 1972–77: 2: 427; and 1982: 154.

39. Whitaker and Edmunds 1925: 15.

40. Barron 1976: 107.

41. Lamb 1982: 146.

Figure 10. Bedrock geology and physiographic provinces of south-central England. (Redrawn and modified from Melville and Freshney 1982: fig. 1.)

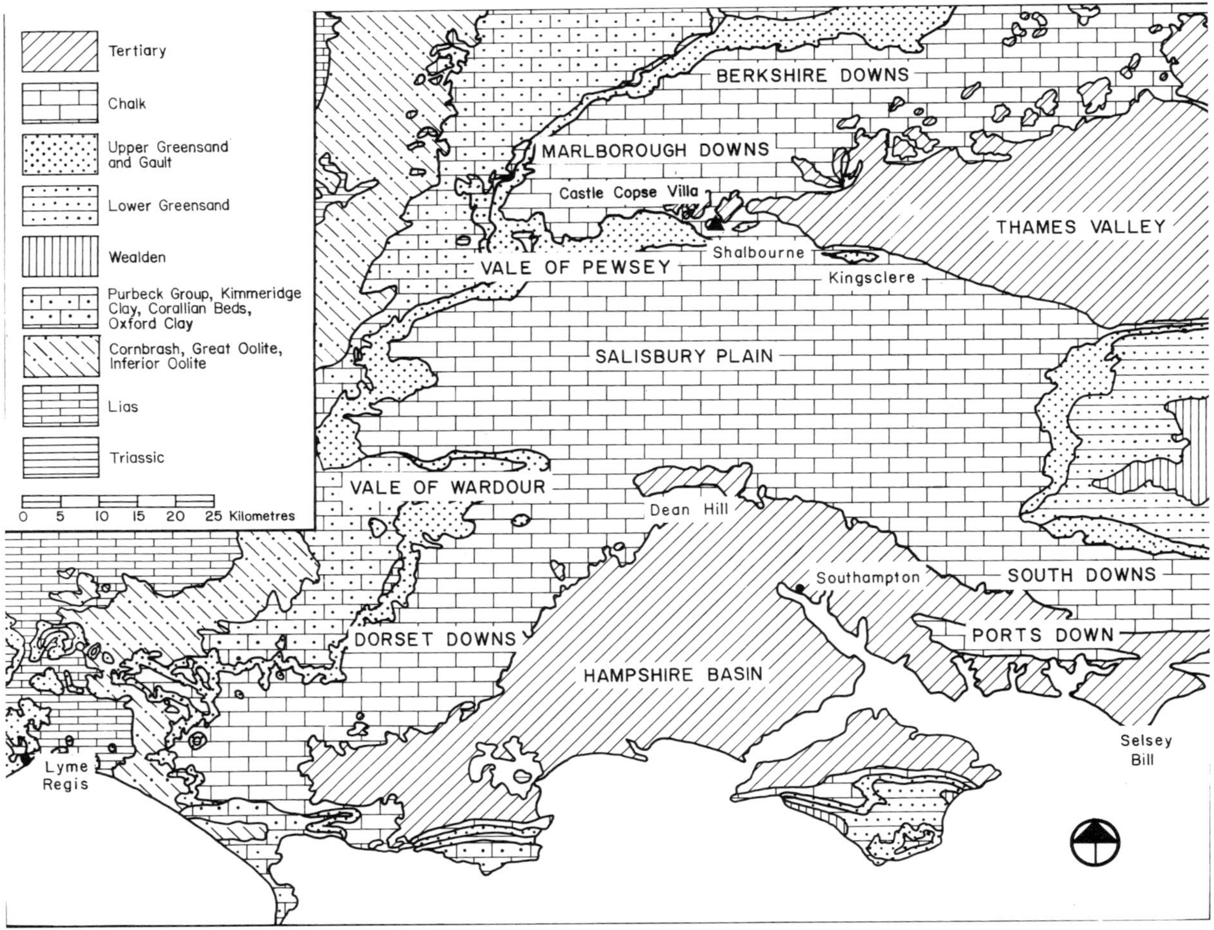

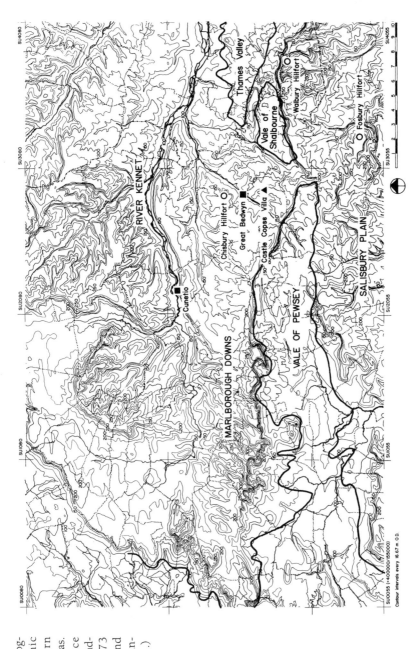

Figure 11. Geography, topography, and physiographic provinces of northeastern Wiltshire and adjacent areas. (Redrawn after Ordnance Survey 1:50,000 scale, Landranger Series Sheet 173 [Swindon and Devizes] and Sheet 174 [Newbury, Wantage and Surrounding Area].)

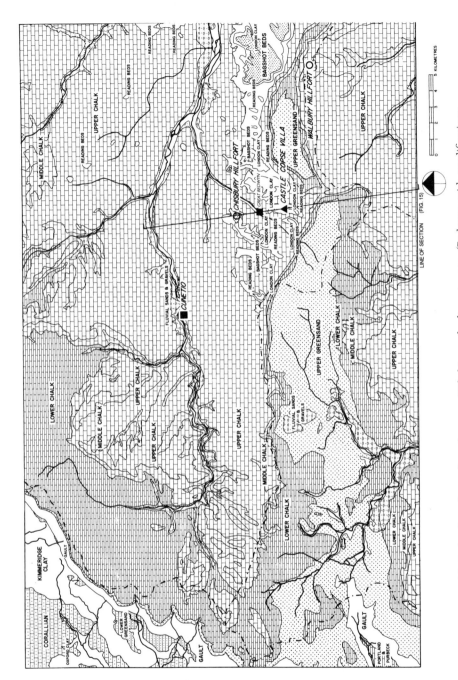

Figure 12. Bedrock geology of northeastern Wiltshire and adjacent areas. (Redrawn with modifications from Institute of Geological Sciences and Thames Water Authority [1978].)

Figure 13. Flat floor of Vale of Pewsey and steep escarpment that forms southern boundary of the Marlborough Downs and north wall of the vale. View east-northeast, with Martinsell Hill at top of scarp in background. (D. K. Keefer)

Figure 14. Prominent northfacing escarpment of Salisbury Plain and flat floor of Vale of Shalbourne. View west from Walbury Hill. (D. K. Keefer)

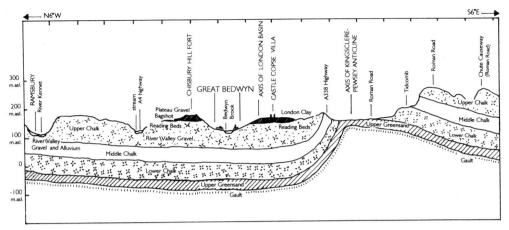

Figure 15. Geologic cross-section along line trending N6°W–S6°E from Ramsbury in the Kennet Valley; through Chisbury, Great Bedwyn, and villa at Castle Copse on the Marlborough Downs; through the western Vale of Pewsey; and onto the northern Salisbury Plain. (D. K. Keefer)

Key to Figures 16–18
Figure 16.
SECTION OF READING BEDS IN QUARRY, 1.2 KM EAST-NORTHEAST OF CASTLE COPSE VILLA
    I. Very fine, well sorted, well rounded sand with flint pebbles
    II. Light grey, moderately soft, plastic, fissured clay
    III. Very fine, well sorted sand—channel deposit
    IV. Clay, as above
    V. Fine, well sorted, well rounded sand, cream-colored with orange lenses
    VI. Clay, as above
    VII. Sand, as above except no orange lenses
  VIII. Light grey, moderately soft, plastic, fissured clay
    IX. Fine, well sorted, well rounded sand, cream-colored with orange lenses
    X. Clay, as above
    XI. Sand, as above
    XII. Clay, as above
  XIII. Sand, as above
  XIV. Clay, as above with some orange staining
   XV. Fine, well sorted, well rounded sand; cream-colored with orange at middle and bottom
  XVI. Light grey, moderately soft, fissured, plastic clay

Figure 17.
SECTION OF READING BEDS ON BEDWYN BRAIL, 0.3 KM EAST-NORTHEAST OF CASTLE COPSE VILLA
    I. Clay, dark greyish brown 2:16 (Munsell Color 10YR 4/2), slightly sandy, moderately soft, plastic—Topsoil
    II. Clay, plastic, fissured, moderately soft; mostly very pale brown (10YR 7/3) with mottlings of very dark grey (10YR 3/1); a few very pale brown sandstone pebbles, friable
    III. Sandy clay, moderately soft, plastic, brownish yellow (10YR 6/8) with mottlings of very pale brown (10YR 7/3); a few lenses of very fine grained sand
    IV. Clay, moderately soft, plastic, slightly sandy, very pale brown (10YR 8/3) with mottlings of dark greyish brown (10YR 4/2)
    V. Sand, fine to very fine, moderately well sorted, sub-rounded, slightly clayey, white (10YR 8/1)
    VI. Clay, moderately soft, plastic, sandy, very pale brown (10YR 7/3) with mottlings of greyish brown (10YR 5/2) and yellow (10YR 7/8)
    VII. Clay, moderately soft, fissured, dark brown (10YR 3/3); some lenses of silt and (or) sand
  VIII. Clay, moderately soft to soft, plastic, sandy, dark greyish brown (10YR 4/2)
    IX. Clayey sand or sandy clay; very fine grained, moderately soft, moderately plastic, dark brown (10YR 3/3)
    X. Clayey sand or sandy clay with sandy lens at top; mostly brown-dark brown (10YR 4/3); lens at top, very pale brown (10YR 7/4); sand very finely grained; clayeey sand/sandy clay soft and moderately plastic
    XI. Clayey sand or sandy clay, moderately plastic, moderately soft to soft, greyish brown (10YR 5/2) with mottlings of yellow (10YR 8/4)
    XII. Clayey sand, very fine grained, moderately soft, moderately plastic, brown (10YR 5/3) with mottlings of very pale brown (10YR 8/4)
  XIII. Clayey sand, very fine grained, moderately soft, moderately plastic, brown-dark brown (10YR 4/3); a few lumps of chalk
  XIV. Clayey sand, as above, with abundant lumps of chalk

Figure 18.
SECTION OF LONDON CLAY AND BAGSHOT BEDS AT DODS DOWN BRICKWORKS ON WILTON BRAIL, 1.2 KM SOUTHWEST OF CASTLE COPSE VILLA
    I. Stiff brown clay, full of black and white flint-pebbles up to 6 inches in diameter
    II. Alternate beds of light fawn and greyish-brown clay (impure pipe-clay) and buff sand
    III. Buff sand, with seams of light clay; layer of flint-pebbles at base
    IV. Grey, argillaceous sand with brown mottlings, passing down into red-brown ferruginous sand and loam; with seams of small and medium-sized flint-pebbles at base
    V. Dark, grey-brown, unctuous clay with regular joints
    VI. Dark grey sandy clay
  VII. Fine, green or grey-green loam; firm and strongly calcareous towards the top

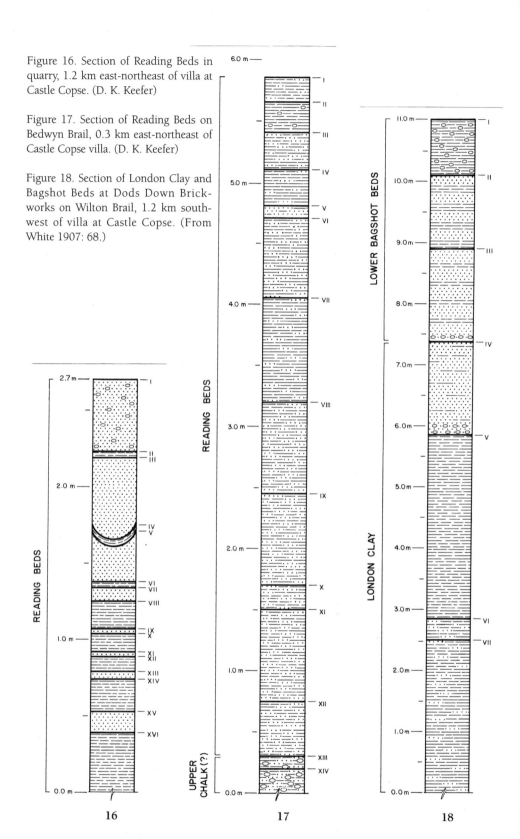

Figure 16. Section of Reading Beds in quarry, 1.2 km east-northeast of villa at Castle Copse. (D. K. Keefer)

Figure 17. Section of Reading Beds on Bedwyn Brail, 0.3 km east-northeast of Castle Copse villa. (D. K. Keefer)

Figure 18. Section of London Clay and Bagshot Beds at Dods Down Brickworks on Wilton Brail, 1.2 km southwest of villa at Castle Copse. (From White 1907: 68.)

16

17

18

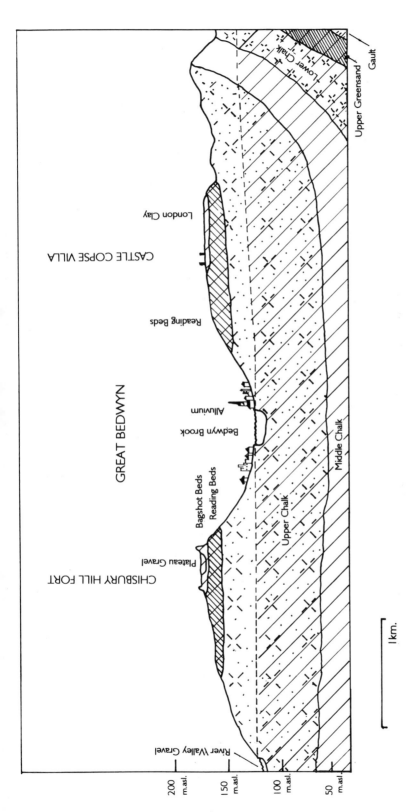

Figure 19. Hydrological cross-section of Chisbury-Great Bedwyn-Castle Copse area along part of same line of section shown in Fig. 15. Solid lines are contacts between geologic units. Dashed line is water table in Chalk as inferred from measurements in August 1976 (IGS and TWA 1978). Shaded areas show zones of saturation (groundwater), including bodies of perched groundwater under Chisbury and Bedwyn Brail, inferred from stratigraphy, geologic structure, and field observations. (D. K. Keefer)

CHAPTER 2

Chisbury Camp and Northeastern Wiltshire in the Iron Age

PAUL ROBINSON

Introduction

Within the last century, probably more excavations of sites of Iron Age date have been undertaken in Wiltshire than in most other counties of England. Nevertheless, in spite of the extensive and "classic" excavations at All Cannings Cross between 1911 and 1922[1] and at Little Woodbury in 1938 and 1939,[2] disappointingly few of these excavations have contributed as much to our understanding of this period in Wiltshire as we should initially have expected, in contrast to the situation elsewhere. While M. E. Cunnington (generally with her husband, B. H. Cunnington) undertook the excavation of a number of hillforts and other sites of Iron Age date, the limitations of their published excavation reports, as well as the complete absence of any excavation notes or other field records, mean that their work represents a sadly inadequate contribution to our knowledge of the period in Wiltshire. Rather than pave the way towards a major postwar excavation of a hillfort or other long-lived settlement site, as with Danebury in Hampshire[3] and South Cadbury in Somerset,[4] their work may possibly even have discouraged it.

This situation will, however, be remedied to a great extent in the near future with the publication in full of three important excavations of Iron Age sites in Wiltshire, carried out to more acceptable modern standards.

First, the excavation of the long-lasting farmstead on Cow Down in Longbridge Deverill, by S. Chadwick from 1956 to 1960,[5] which will provide much needed evidence for the history and development of a small settlement on the Wiltshire downland over a long period of time in the Early and Middle Iron Age. Second, the completion by B. W. Cunliffe of the excavations undertaken between 1959 and 1967 by D. Grant King at Bury Wood Camp hillfort in Colerne and their final publication will provide a long-awaited modern study of a major hillfort in Wiltshire.[6] In addition, Bury Wood Camp has produced a surprisingly large number of stratified finds, much more than any other site of this date in the county and will be indispensable for any survey of the material culture and economy of the Iron Age in Wiltshire. One regret, perhaps, is that Bury

Wood Camp lies at the western edge of the county, in the Cotswolds, and is very far from characteristic of hillforts in Wiltshire in general, in reality relating more to sites of this date in the Avon basin. Third, of indisputable importance will be the eventual publication of the partially investigated and very extensive settlement at Potterne, which was occupied from the middle of the second millennium B.C. until the Earliest Iron Age.[7] The site covered a considerable area of land and is at present unique in Britain as a possible urban settlement. Perhaps, above all, the fact of its recent discovery and recognition is a warning of the probable limitations of our present knowledge of the archaeology of southern England in the later prehistoric period. Finally, the Royal Commission on Historic Monuments (R.C.H.M.) has recently undertaken a comprehensive and detailed survey of prehistoric earthworks in Wiltshire, including a reexamination of their history and dating.[8] The publication of this project will certainly contribute a great deal to our knowledge of the hillforts and other visible major settlements of Iron Age date in the county.

B. W. Cunliffe's research into the archaeology of the Iron Age in southern England as a whole has involved the reevaluation of the excavations undertaken by the Cunningtons and others in Wiltshire earlier this century. His first synthesis of this, concentrating solely upon Wiltshire, was published in 1973 in the series *Victoria History of the Counties of England* and recently has been superseded by an overall survey of the Iron Age in Wessex as a whole.[9] It has, however, a particular emphasis on Wiltshire, although concentrating to a great extent on the central and southern areas of the county. Cunliffe identified nine consecutive ceramic phases within the Iron Age, which correspond to five chronological phases. These were based upon pottery sequences and overlaps at Iron Age sites in both Wiltshire (Potterne, All Cannings Cross) as well as outside the county, in particular at Danebury and Hengistbury Head in Hampshire and at various sites in Dorset. The five chronological phases, with their approximate dates, are according to this scheme:

Earliest Iron Age	B.C. 800–550
Early	B.C. 550–400
Middle	B.C. 400–100
Late	B.C. 100–10
Latest	B.C. 10–A.D. 50

This scheme with its divisions and dating will be followed below.[10]

Finally it should be remembered that our knowledge of the archaeology of Wiltshire in the Iron Age is unevenly spread, both geographically and chronologically. For example, in contrast to what we know of central and southern Wiltshire, we are comparatively ignorant of the archaeology of north Wiltshire, particularly the northeast area in the two early and the Middle Iron Age phases. While to some extent this may be fortuitous and due to the lack of any systematic investigation of many of the sites in this area, it may also be because the northeast of the county lay at the edge of, if not essentially outside, the main areas of settlement in both Wessex and the lower Thames Valley. In addition, present-day "Wiltshire" is a comparatively large geographical area, and we should not expect to find at this time a pattern and picture of comparative unity. Just (as we shall see) as in the Late and Latest Iron Age phases several different political and cultural groups of peoples can be identified in Wiltshire, so a similar diversity should be presumed to have also existed in earlier periods of the Iron Age in the county.

The Earliest and Early Iron Ages

The Earliest Iron Age (c. B.C. 800–550) was characterized by the use of large jars with S-shaped profiles; by jars with flaring rims that were often highly decorated with incised or stamped geometric motifs, which at times were infilled with chalk or a white paste; and by smaller, bipartite bowls that were sometimes given a hematite coating or decorated with furrowed grooves around the shoulder and neck. The last clearly copied bronze prototypes, such as the bowl found at Welby in Leicestershire. Iron appears to have been relatively scarce. Iron slag found at Boscombe Down East[11] and the unpublished iron fragments from Potterne confirm its early introduction into Wiltshire. The unstratified finds of socketed iron axes, reminiscent of late Bronze Age socketed bronze axes, at Cold Kitchen Hill in Brixton Deverill[12] and most recently at Bishopstone (North) in north Wiltshire,[13] should not be considered as necessarily dating from this early period. There is no evidence to suggest that local smiths were working in Wiltshire. There is also as yet no certain evidence that any of the sources of iron in Wiltshire (at Seend, Westbury,[14] Bromham, and Mere) were being worked at this date in the Iron Age, or indeed within the Iron Age at all. However, it should be noted that the settlement site at Potterne does lie fairly close to Seend and that an Earliest Iron Age site of uncertain type lies either on or very close to the nineteenth-century ironworks at Westbury.[15] Bronze continued to be widely used to make both working tools and weapons. Bone, and to a lesser extent, antler were also extensively used to make smaller tools as shown in particular at All Cannings Cross, but which are found at other sites, too.[16]

There was a wide range of settlement types. One of the more common forms was the farmstead or small hamlet consisting of a handful of dwellings and workplaces, which was sometimes but not always enclosed by a bank and ditch. The best known examples of these in Wiltshire are Little Woodbury, which is in fact of Early Iron Age date,[17] and Cow Down.[18] All Cannings Cross may also have been a farmstead or small hamlet of this same type, rather than a more substantial settlement, as the quantity and richness of the excavated finds might initially have suggested, since only a single hut circle appears in the plan of the site published by the excavators.[19] Many of the small farmsteads or hamlets continued in use for a considerable period of time. All Cannings Cross certainly lasted into at least the Middle Iron Age; Cow Down, until the second or first century B.C.; Little Woodbury, perhaps also for as long. Some were enclosed by substantial ditches of up to about 9.5 ft (2.9 m) in depth, which were clearly for the protection of the occupants, rather than merely serving to restrain the livestock.

Defended hilltop sites of the Earliest Iron Age include large enclosures defined by a comparatively slight rampart and ditch, with the interior occupied, but not densely, with well-built houses, as with Martinsell[20] and Walbury Camp. Other sites were more strongly fortified, their location clearly selected for strategic reasons and protected by more substantial defenses. Oliver's Camp occupied a spur of land projecting from the western edge of the downs and had a single approach only.[21] As with Lidbury, a rather enigmatic site of this period, the defenses are subrectangular.[22] At Liddington Castle, the hillfort defenses were recently sectioned by Rahtz and revealed three building phases in the Earliest Iron Age.[23] It is, however, uncertain whether or not these three phases succeeded each other fairly swiftly or were, in fact, phases within a single complex construction carried out at one time. Budbury Camp, which also was partially excavated more recently, again occupied an easily defended spur of land and was impressively protected by a double system of banks and ditches.[24]

The final hillfort or hilltop site to consider is Casterley Camp in Upavon.[25] Occupying an area of 62 acres, it is located at the northern end of the Dorset Ridgeway. An unpublished socketed bronze axe-head, found in the mid-nineteenth century in the makeup of the rampart, suggests that the hillfort was built at the close of the Bronze Age.[26] A bronze ribbed button or disk, of a type akin to that found at All Cannings Cross, supports this early dating and suggests that the site continued in use into the Earliest Iron Age. Its status as a site is uncertain, or rather, unexplained by the excavations that have taken place there as yet. Its location at the point where the Ridgeway meets the route north up the Avon from Hengistbury Head, as well as the number of particularly significant stray finds that have been found in the area, suggests that it may have owed its particular importance at this time to trade.

The comparative unity shown in the pottery of this period from different sites in Wessex illustrates that trading contacts were maintained within the region. Hengistbury Head, on the south coast, developed in this period,[27] and it was presumably through this and other harbors that trading contact was maintained with Brittany. The findspots of the characteristic "Breton" type of socketed bronze axe-head, which possibly served as a primitive currency, show a possibly significant concentration in central-eastern Wiltshire, where five examples have been found.[28] These are stray finds from East Kennet, Ogbourne St. Andrew, Chilton Foliat, and Shalbourne, as well as the excavated fragment from All Cannings Cross. The very rich "South Wiltshire hoard," found in about 1986 at Netherhampton, near Salisbury, included discarded scrap metal and casting waste, working tools and finished products[29] with a large number of Continental pieces and may represent the working stock of either a Breton merchant-trader of about this period or a local entrepreneur with trading links over the Channel. Items of shale were certainly also being traded from the Dorset coast to sites such as Potterne, where there is also evidence for the manufacture of bronze implements and other products.

In the Early Iron Age (c. B.C. 550–400), the characteristic pottery—hematite-coated bowls with horizontal cordons and scratched geometric decoration filled with white paste—is found at a number of sites in Wiltshire, predominantly in the central and southeastern areas of the county, and may indeed have been manufactured at a site located to the north of Salisbury. The farmsteads, All Cannings Cross, Little Woodbury, and Cow Down continued in use. The large hilltop enclosures ceased, as did some of the hillforts of the Earliest Iron Age, possibly including Liddington[30] and Oliver's Castle.[31] This latter site appears to have been succeeded by an open settlement near Mother Anthony's Well, close to the bottom of the spur on which the hillfort had been situated.[32] The size and, indeed, the exact nature of this settlement, which has not been closely investigated, but which appears to have lasted into at least the Middle Iron Age, is uncertain. Other hillforts, such as Lidbury[33] and Martinsell,[34] did continue in use. A number of small, more strongly defended hillforts which were broadly circular in form and had timber-revetted ramparts were built at this time, the best-known in Wiltshire being perhaps Yarnbury Castle.[35] Averaging 13 acres (5.261 hectares) in size, the interiors were quite densely settled.

Three separate stray finds of exotic, coral-studded jewelry of this date—two fibula brooches and an item which may be a plate brooch or a mount from a harness—which were found in the vicinity of Casterley Camp,[36] support the evidence of the site's pottery finds that the hillfort continued in use in this period and was of some particular importance, possibly primarily, because of its location close to the Avon and at the end of the Dorset Ridgeway. The characteristic hematite-coated pottery of this period tends to occur on sites close to the Salisbury Avon and its tributaries, suggesting that river routes were important both in its distribution and in trade in general.

The Middle Iron Age

The characteristic pottery of the Middle Iron Age (c. B.C. 400–100) in central and southern Wiltshire, as well as in Dorset, northeast of the river Stour were "saucepan pots" and round-shouldered jars decorated in the so-called Yarnbury-Highfield style.[37] The distribution of the pottery echoes that of the scratched-cordoned hematite-coated wares manufactured in the sixth century B.C. Approximately in the same area there occurs the distinctive La Tène I "Wessex" type of bronze fibula brooch, of which two examples were found at All Cannings Cross. These suggest the presence in this region of either a homogeneous ethnic community or a community with a tightly controlled economy. In northern Wiltshire above the Pewsey Vale there are fewer examples of both saucepan pots and round-shouldered jars, none of which are decorated in the distinctive Yarnbury-Highfield style, and this area must be regarded as essentially outside that region. Northern parts of Wiltshire and Berkshire share a separate "Thames Valley" style of saucepan pot, and presumably represent a different community of people in that area.[38]

The period saw, probably throughout Wessex as a whole, both a major increase in the size of the population and an improvement in the economy. These are reflected in the material culture as well as the settlement pattern. Iron was much more widely used for both tools and weapons; it is perhaps significant that weapons were more common than in earlier periods. Apart from the standard weapon, the iron spearhead, of which several examples were found in the ironwork hoard from Barbury Castle,[39] more prestigious weapons are now found. They include iron swords (fragments from Chisbury Camp and Broughton Gifford) (Fig. 21.4)[40] with their scabbards (several examples of scabbard shape from Cold Kitchen Hill),[41] shields (as from Wilsford N),[42] and chariots (fittings found include nave hoops from the Barbury Castle hoard and from Battlesbury,[43] as well as a linchpin from Barbury Castle).

Within this period, while a number of the earlier hillforts went out of use, there developed a smaller number of more heavily defended sites situated in more strategic, defendable positions on hilltops. These appear to have served several functions—as social, economic, and perhaps also religious centers of substantial individual territories, generally of about 35–45 miles² (c. 90.65–116.55 km²) in area. Some of these focal points were newly created hillforts, as was Chisbury Camp. Others were older hillforts that were either rebuilt or substantially enlarged, as with Yarnbury Castle itself, one of the two sites after which the characteristic pottery of the period is named,[44] and Oldbury Camp, which was refortified with more substantial ramparts and ditches.[45] These hill-forts were generally larger in area, the defenses enclosing 15–30 acres (c. 6.07–12.14 hectares). A number of burials found outside the northwest entrance of Battlesbury Camp have been interpreted as evidence for a massacre of its inhabitants.[46] Otherwise there is at present little actual evidence for warfare and the assaulting of hillforts in Wiltshire in the Middle Iron Age. How far, then, the growth in militarism in society, reflected both by the development of the hillforts and the increase in the number and type of weapons, is perhaps still open to question. The traditional Celtic love of mascu-line "show" could well be largely responsible for the latter.

The single farmsteads or small hamlets such as Little Woodbury and All Cannings Cross continued in use. All Cannings Cross would appear to have come to an end within this period. However, a first-century A.D. Roman site lies only a very short distance away, and it is possible that the site did continue, having merely moved a short distance from its earlier location. Larger unenclosed settlements also grew up, such as that near Battlesbury Camp, which may indeed be an extramural settlement of the hillfort.[47] An extensive unen-closed settlement at Boscombe Down West[48] is reminiscent of Potterne (the Middle Bronze to Earliest Iron Age settlement) in its near-urban size. Side by side with them, a new class of smaller enclosed settlement of the so-called banjo type also developed.

Evidence for trade and outside contact in the form of nonperishable luxury goods is difficult to identify, in contrast with both the earlier and the later periods in the Iron Age, and in spite of what would appear to have been an economically successful community.

The Latest Iron Age Period

The final phases of the Iron Age in Wiltshire, as well as in Wessex as a whole, saw a number of changes in material culture, settlement pattern, and burial custom. These were essentially due to an increase in contact with the Continent, both with the indepen-dent Gaulish kingdoms before their conquest by the Romans in the first century B.C., and subsequently with the now Roman Gaul for the purposes of trade. There is no evi-dence for migration on a large scale from Gaul into central and southwestern Britain. However, emigration on a smaller scale is historically illustrated when the Gaulish leader, Commius, went into exile in Britain following his defeat by Caesar, and was presumably accompanied by followers and retainers. He established a new dynasty over the Atrebates in the area of Hampshire and perhaps also eastern Wiltshire. Small-scale migration quite possibly had a ripple effect elsewhere in southern England. Commius need not have been the only Gaulish leader to have fled to Britain in the mid-first century B.C. The Marlborough Bucket, which is described below, may have been the treasured possession of another king or aristocratic leader who preferred living in an independent Celtic Britain to living under Roman rule in Gaul.

The first major change to consider is the general abandonment of the heavily defended hillforts of the middle period, shown in sites such as Chisbury Camp and Bury Wood Camp. In some there may have continued a localized settlement of a small area in the interior, as with Casterley Camp and possibly Ringsbury Camp in Purton, but it is evident that with few exceptions, such as Yarnbury Castle and other forts in Southern

Wiltshire, hillforts no longer exercised the same role that they had previously. At some there was perhaps a hasty revival at the very end of the Iron Age. Some hillforts in Wiltshire also show continued use, generally on a small scale, in the Roman period.

The political authority implied by the earlier heavily defended hillforts may in some instances have passed to strong double-ditched enclosure sites, such as that at Boscombe Down West on Salisbury Plain.[49] The dating of these sites, however, remains somewhat uncertain and they may date from a later period in the Iron Age. In eastern England, as well as in central southern England (e.g., Silchester and Winchester), the chief political authority was assumed by *oppida*—urban or near-urban settlements. It has been suggested that there may have been an *oppidum* in the vicinity of the parishes of Marlborough and Mildenhall, an area which clearly was of particular importance in the Late or Latest Iron Age.[50] This might have been focussed upon Black Field in Mildenhall, the site of the subsequent Roman town of Cunetio, or it may have lain a short distance to the south within the complex of earthworks and ploughed-out features at Forest Hill, which includes a large enclosure of about 27 acres (c. 10.93 hectares) as well as a further series of banks and ditches that remains difficult to interpret.[51] From Black Field itself, where only small-scale excavations have taken place to date, there are only four certain finds which are of Iron Age date. These are all coins—an Irregular Dobunnic coin of the "Upavon" type; the core of a plated quarter stater of an uncertain type; a bronze stater in the style of the Corieltauvi series of coin (all of which are in Devizes Museum); and a coin of an uncertain type listed by Haselgrove.[52] Other Iron Age coins have been found elsewhere in the parish of Mildenhall, while further coins are known to have been found in the parish, but it is uncertain whether or not they come from Black Field/Cunetio. An unusually high number of other coin finds, including a major hoard, have been recorded from just outside Mildenhall.[53] There are also important finds of decorative Late Iron Age metalwork from the area of Mildenhall.[54]

The main indication that the area of Marlborough-Mildenhall was of particular importance at the end of the Iron Age comes from the Marlborough Bucket.[55] Prior to the Late Iron Age, the chief burial rite practiced was excarnation, with the limited interment of parts of the corpse. Cremation was apparently introduced in this period, although there is no suggestion that it was adopted on a wide scale at all in the southwest. In particular, it occurs in the form of rich burials accompanied by large bronze-mounted buckets, which were objects of prestige and probably symbolic when placed in the grave, alluding to rebirth. The two important burials in Wessex of this type are at Hurstbourne Tarrant in Hampshire and St. Margaret's Mead in Marlborough, where in 1807 there was found beneath a now destroyed barrow, a cremation burial placed within a large bronze-mounted wooden bucket. The bucket is elaborately decorated with repoussé male and female heads, both facing and in profile, and with pairs of horses. It was probably made in north Gaul in the first century B.C. and was certainly a prestigious object in its own time and an indication of the wealth and status of its owner. Cremation, as stated above, was not widely adopted, it would appear. The rite of casual inhumation appears to have continued in Wessex, although relatively few burials dating from the end of the Iron Age have been identified in Wiltshire. The cemetery not far from Black Field, Mildenhall, which has sometimes been stated to be of this date, may instead date from the early Roman period, as the pottery associated with it is early Roman "Savernake Ware."[56]

In the Late and Latest Iron Age, between approximately B.C. 50 and the Roman Conquest, there is somewhat better evidence for the political division of Britain into separate kingdoms or tribes, the boundaries of which can sometimes be postulated.[57] The evidence for this comes primarily from the coins, struck in gold, silver, and copper or bronze, the use of which was first introduced into Britain at this phase. In Wiltshire, the main tribal coinages found are those attributed to the Durotriges, the Dobunni, and the Atrebates. A further local series issued by another tribe in central-eastern Wiltshire, probably independent of these, but whose name is not recorded, has also been identified.[58]

The coins of the Durotriges are chiefly found in Dorset, west Hampshire, and south Wiltshire. It has been suggested that the northern boundary of their territory in Wiltshire was either the river Wylye or the Nadder, but more recent finds of Durotrigian coins suggest that it ran to the north of this, perhaps along the northern edge of Salisbury Plain or within the Pewsey Vale. The Dobunni occupied primarily the territory of present-day Somerset and Gloucestershire. Their coins are also found in west Wiltshire, where they occur only rarely east of the Bristol Avon, as well as in the extreme northwest and north of Wiltshire. Coins of the Atrebates are rarer finds in Wiltshire than coins of the Durotriges and the Dobunni and are found in the east and northeast of the county. They include finds of coins of Tincommius and Verica from the area immediately to the west of Chisbury Camp. Because of their paucity it is questionable whether any parts of eastern Wiltshire actually fell within the Atrebatic kingdom. In the first century A.D., however, a client kingdom of the tribe of the Catuvellauni in eastern England was established in the northern parts of the Atrebatic kingdom, centered upon Silchester. Coins of its ruler, Epaticcus, are not uncommon in central-eastern Wiltshire, and it is possible that this part of the county may have been incorporated into this client kingdom by the close of the Iron Age, perhaps around A.D. 30–40.

P. Robinson[59] identified three main series of coins in gold, base-gold, and silver found almost exclusively in central-eastern Wiltshire and which appeared to be a local, independent tribal coinage. The silver coins have been described as "Irregular Dobunnic."[60] This is, however, a misnomer, as the two series of coins are, with one or two exceptions only, territorially exclusive.

The three series of coins are, first, a small number of gold and red-gold quarter staters of types Mack 68 and 74, that, from the proportion of gold within the alloy, probably date well within the first century B.C. The second series is of silver coins of type Mack 377 and 384a. The later may have been struck at an intended average weight of 1.1 g, which, if the weight standard relates to that of the coins of the neighboring tribe of the Dobunni, again suggests an early date as it corresponds to the weight of the first class of the Dobunnic series. (Too few examples of Mack 377 survive for the original weight to be determined.) A small group of these coins, probably a small hoard or purseful of coins, was found in Mildenhall in the mid-nineteenth century.[61] More recent finds of these coins confirm their association with central-eastern Wiltshire, although they are now known to occur just beyond the northeast boundary of the county (with findspots at Lechlade, Lambourn and Uffington). The third series comprises crudely designed, uniface staters struck in base-gold, of type Mack 62. Most of the surviving examples of this type come from the large hoard found in Savernake Forest in 1857,[62] where they were associated with silver coins of Epaticcus and Roman denarii. These indicate that the hoard was a late one, concealed certainly within the early Roman period. This and the light weight of the coins suggest that the base-gold staters date very late in the Iron Age and well into the first century A.D.

A fourth series has now been identified, comprising two further related types of silver coin. They are not in the standard works on Celtic coins and may be described as the "Upavon" type, after the principal find of the series made in that parish.[63] Their average weight of 0.85–0.95 g indicates that they are late, dating well after the second series above, possibly being either slightly older or contemporary with the third series of base gold staters.

The findspots of these four series of coins are centered upon the area of Marlborough and Mildenhall, the Pewsey Vale, and the northern edge of Salisbury Plain. The coins occur only very infrequently in north Wiltshire above the Marlborough Downs, and this area can reasonably be regarded as lying outside the circulation area. The people who issued the coins cannot then be identified as the Cornovii, after whom the Roman town Durocornovium at Wanborough was named, but probably represent another people whose name has been lost.

In the Late and Latest Iron Age, trade with the Continent probably increased with the demand from the Roman world for materials such as salt, hide, corn, and metals, as well as slaves. In return, luxury products such as wine were imported. Specific contact with the Continent is illustrated by finds of Continental coins—gold staters of the Namnetes of Brittany (from near Swindon) and the Aulerci Cenomani (from Amesbury); a bronze coin of the Aulerci Eburovices (from Mildenhall); and a potin coin of the Senones (from near Chisbury Camp).[64] A Celtiberian coin, an unstratified find from Westbury[65] suggests even more distant contact, but like the Celtiberian penannular "omega" brooch from near Martinsell hillfort,[66] might have been lost in the early Roman period by a Spanish auxiliary cavalryman. The coins should not be taken as specific evidence for trade, but could have reached Wiltshire as a result of other activities.

Overland contact with other areas of England is illustrated by finds of coins of tribes such as the Catuvellauni and the Corieltauvi, although some of these may have been lost early in the Roman period, rather than in the Iron Age. A bronze animal mask vessel mount in the Stourhead Collection at Devizes Museum,[67] unprovenanced but presumably from Wiltshire, finds a parallel in London and suggests that other decorative Late Iron Age metalwork may either have originated in eastern England or may have been traded to there.

Chisbury Camp

Although the evidence is far from satisfactory, Chisbury Camp appears to have been one of the strong centralized hillforts built in the Middle Iron Age. Enclosing an area of about 15 acres (c. 6.07 hectares), it is situated toward the eastern edge of Savernake Forest. It is bi-vallate in form, with an additional rampart on the southwest side. The evidence for its dating comes from the pottery recovered from a number of pits which were exposed when trenches were dug within the hillfort in 1932. Five of the pits were subsequently excavated by M. E. Cunnington, and a brief and extremely inadequate report of the work was published.[68] Strictly speaking, the association of the Iron Age sherds with the hillfort defenses is unproven. They could come from hypothetical settlement on the hilltop before the hillfort was built, while alternatively they need not necessarily be regarded as including the earliest finds from the site. All that may be said is that at present they provide the best evidence for the dating of the hillfort. Further excavations at Chisbury Camp in 1988 were on a small scale only and have not clarified the dating of the hillfort.

Altogether, about eighty potsherds, a stone spindle whorl, and a fragment of a possible crucible were recovered by M. E. Cunnington in her excavation of the pits exposed in the interior of Chisbury Camp (Figs. 20–21.3). The report illustrates five sherds or reconstructed vessels only, four of which are of Roman date. It does not indicate which sherds were associated together or from which pit they come. It gives neither the locations of the pits nor their relationship—if there was one. The sherds fall into two chronological groups. The earliest are of Middle Iron Age date and are from saucepan pots which are either straight-sided or have gently curved profiles, all without any decoration. The profiles that can be reconstructed are illustrated below (Fig. 20.1–4). The second group of sherds dates from shortly after the Roman Conquest and is described later in this section (Figs. 21.5, 22–23.1–3).

Recently, a number of casual finds have been recorded from outside the hillfort, chiefly on the west and southwest sides, presumably representing settlement immediately outside the hillfort defenses. They include two items which are certainly of Middle Iron Age date, but nothing which is chronologically earlier than this. The two items are a bronze strap union of a type with parallels at Old Sarum and Bury Wood Camp in Wiltshire (not illustrated), as well as from Danebury in Hampshire, and a fragment from the handle of a sword of anthropoid type (Fig 21.4).[69] These Middle Iron Age finds could antedate those from inside Chisbury Camp, they could be contemporary with them, or could be later in date, possibly indicating that habitation had ceased within the hillfort actually before the end of the Middle Iron Age.

There are no finds of any sort from the center of Chisbury Camp that date from either the Late or the Latest Iron Age, suggesting that, as with most other hillforts in Wiltshire, habitation had ceased within the camp by the end of the Middle Iron Age. A number of finds from these periods have, however, been found in the area immediately to the west of the hillfort, suggesting that the settlement continued in this area now. The finds, all Iron Age coins are as follows:

1. Gold quarter stater of type Mack 67 var.
2. Potin coin of the Gaulish tribe, the Senones.
3. Silver Atrebatic coin struck in the name of Verica, type Mack 129.
4–5. Two silver coins of Epaticcus, the Catuvellaunian client king over the northern Atrebates, type Mack 263.

These are all in private hands,[70] apart from no. 2, which is in Devizes Museum.[71] Two other coins said to have been found are:

6. Another gold quarter stater of an unrecorded type.
7. Coin described as an early Durotrigian quarter stater, and presumably to be identified as a quarter stater of the Gallo-Belgic D or the British O series, if not either an early white gold or silver quarter stater of the Durotriges.

Of these coins, nos. 1, 2, 6, and 7 should date from well into the first century B.C., although no. 2, at least, could possibly have been lost at a much later date. Nos. 3–5 date from the final years of the Iron Age and could indeed have been lost after the Roman Conquest. Finally, mention should be made of an iron crescent-headed linchpin from a chariot, said to have been found "at Chisbury Camp," but not certainly within the hill-fort. It dates either from the Late Iron Age or early Roman period.[72]

A number of finds of objects as well as coins confirm that the settlement to the west of Chisbury Camp continued after the Roman Conquest, but probably for not more than a decade or so. They include two Roman military pendants (Fig. 23.4–5) and three Claudian copper coins (a sestertius and two dupondii).[73] A group of five Roman denarii found close to the west entrance of the hillfort—three of them of Republican date, the two others of Augustus and Tiberius—are probably from a small dispersed hoard,[74] which is reminiscent of the recently found hoard from near Membury hillfort and which was deposited shortly after the conquest. No later finds are known from this area, suggesting that any settlement west of the fort probably ceased not long after about A.D. 60–80. Only a very few other later Roman finds have been made in other areas near the hillfort. Recently, an antoninianus of Salonina was found a short distance to the southeast of the site and a small hoard of late fourth century bronze coins to the east of it.[75] They suggest that there was only casual occupation on a very small scale subsequently in the Roman period. There is evidence for resumed habitation or use in some form of the hill-fort in approximately the same period, following the Roman conquest. The evidence for this comes primarily from the group of storage pits excavated in 1932. The pottery from these included sherds from bead rimmed jars in Savernake Ware, dated to c. the latter half of the first century A.D. (Figs. 21.5, 22.1–3); a fragment of an amphora of Haltern type 70, dated to B.C. 50–A.D. 50–70 (not illustrated); two sherds from a South Gaulish samian ware bowl, form Dragendorf 24/25, dated to the period c. A.D. 14–68 (Fig. 23.2); and a sherd from a reeded-rim carinated bowl, dated to c. the Flavian period (Fig. 23.1). An aureus of Augustus was found within the camp in 1959, but was probably lost after the Roman conquest rather than before it, and perhaps fairly shortly afterwards, rather than in the latter years of the first century.[76] The inference from the aureus and the amphora sherd is that a site of some status may have existed within the area of the hill-fort in the early Roman period, lasting perhaps into the latter half of the first century. There is no evidence to suggest that there was any substantial community living within the camp or that its defenses continued to be used. No finds of a later date within the Roman period are recorded from the hillfort. The casual record of a second century A.D. Roman brooch "from Chisbury" should be ignored, as it is unknown whether it was found within the camp as opposed to merely near it.

The use of hillforts in the Roman period took different forms. Certainly in some, substantial communities of the former Iron Age peoples continued to live. At Forest Hill, to the south of the Roman town of Cunetio, a prestigious building, possibly a villa or a religious site of some sort, was built within the area of the hillfort. In contrast, a much more mundane native farmstead was built within Casterley Camp. There is as yet no archaeological evidence for the hillfort's reuse at the end of the Roman period and in the post-Roman period, when there was revival of the use of hillforts as strategic and defensive sites. The late Roman coin hoard found near Chisbury Camp in 1981 suggests that people were living at least in the area at this time, but no conclusions beyond this can be drawn without more extensive excavation of the site, which would, of course, provide evidence for its history much more satisfactory than the brief and limited conclusions summarized above.

NOTES

1. M. E. Cunnington 1923.
2. Bersu 1940; and Brailsford 1948.
3. Cunliffe 1984a.
4. Alcock 1972; and 1980.
5. Grimes 1961.
6. P. Rahtz's excavation in 1976 at Liddington Castle, while of particular importance and interest in demonstrating the very early date of the hillfort and the method and history of the construction of its defenses, was on a small scale only: Hirst and Rahtz 1976.
7. Gingell and Lawson 1985.
8. Corney 1989.
9. Cunliffe 1984b.
10. Other chronological schemes have been proposed as alternatives, such as that advanced by S. M. Elsdon (1989):

Early Iron Age	B.C. 800–600 B.C.
Middle	B.C. 600–300 B.C.
Later	B.C. 300–100 B.C.
Late	B.C. 100–15/10 B.C.
Very Late	B.C. 15/10–A.D. 60

This particularly shortens the earlier period and extends the middle period. It is, however, beyond the scope of this brief survey to compare the two chronological schemes in any detail.
11. Richardson 1951.
12. Manning and Saunders 1972.
13. In Swindon Museum: WAR 1991:147, no. 20.
14. The site lies in the adjacent parish of Heywood, but is conventionally known as "Westbury Ironworks."
15. The "Westbury Ironworks" site essentially is unpublished. The finds recovered from it are all unstratified and not closely located. They are preserved in the Devizes Museum and include Iron Age pottery, loomweights, stone and bone tools, and an amber bead. The Iron Age site underlies a major Roman settlement.
16. M. J. Smith 1982.
17. Bersu 1940; and Brailsford 1948.
18. Grimes 1961.
19. M. E. Cunnington 1923.
20. Meyrick 1946; and G. Swanton 1987.
21. M. E. Cunnington 1908.
22. M. E. Cunnington 1917.
23. Hirst and Rahtz 1976.
24. Wainwright 1970.
25. Cunnington and Cunnington 1913.
26. Correspondence file in Devizes Museum.
27. Cunliffe 1978.
28. Dunning 1959.
29. This "hoard" is, at present, unpublished. One group of artifacts from it is preserved in Devizes Museum, while another group is in the British Museum.

30. Passmore 1914.
31. M. E. Cunnington 1908.
32. In 1951 M. H. Callender excavated a hearth of Iron Age date at Mother Anthony's Well in Bromham. This remains unpublished. The sherds found are in the Devizes Museum (accession no. 11.56.262). Other Iron Age sherds were found at the site during fieldwalking in 1975 (*WANHS Bulletin* 1976: 14 ff. and WAR 1980: 204, no. 65).
33. M. E. Cunnington 1917.
34. Meyrick 1946.
35. M. E. Cunnington 1933.
36. Hattat 1987: 1440–41; and WAR 1987: 141.
37. Cunliffe 1974.
38. Cunliffe 1984b.
39. MacGregor and Simpson 1963.
40. Both in the Devizes Museum.
41. In the Devizes Museum.
42. Cunnington and Goddard 1934.
43. M. E. Cunnington 1922.
44. M. E. Cunnington 1933.
45. H. Cunnington 1871.
46. M. E. Cunnington 1922.
47. Chadwick and Thompson 1956.
48. Richardson 1951.
49. Richardson 1951.
50. Robinson 1975; Cunliffe 1984b.
51. Corney 1989.
52. Haselgrove 1984: 154.
53. Robinson 1975.
54. From Ramsbury, a terminal in the form of a grotesque animal head (WAR 1991: 147, no. 22). From Bishopstone (North), a mount in the form of a grotesque mask (WAR 1988: 184, no. 19), while a small figurine in the form of a Barbury sheep, or perhaps a mouflon, may in fact be of earlier date (WAR 1990: 232, no. 35). From Poulton Hill, Mildenhall, comes a fragment of decorated sheet bronze which may be from a shield (unpublished, in Devizes Museum).
55. Fox 1958.
56. Devizes Museum, Meyrick collection.
57. D. F. Allen 1944; Sellwood 1984.
58. Robinson 1977a.
59. Robinson 1977a.
60. D. F. Allen 1961.
61. Robinson 1975.
62. Robinson 1975.
63. It is hoped that this dispersed hoard or assemblage will be published shortly. Other examples of the "Upavon" type have been found at the nearby parishes of Charlton, Chirton, Urchfont, and Potterne and at Cunetio (Robinson 1982). A further example in the National Museum of Wales was said to have been found at Easton Grey in northwest Wiltshire, but this is now doubted.
64. Robinson 1982.
65. Devizes Museum Day Book 408.
66. In Devizes Museum: WAR 1981: 206, no. 121.
67. Cunnington and Goddard 1934: no. 382.
68. M. E. Cunnington 1932.
69. The former is in private possession; the latter is in Devizes Museum: WAR 1983: 158, no. 28.
70. WAR 1983: 158, no. 28 and WAR 1986 242, no. 62, supplemented by information kindly given by B. Cavill.
71. Robinson 1982.

72. In Devizes Museum, but with no information on its provenance.
73. Griffiths 1983.
74. WAR 1983: 160, no. 50; see also WAR 1986: 242, no. 83.
75. Burnett 1983.
76. Robinson 1977b.

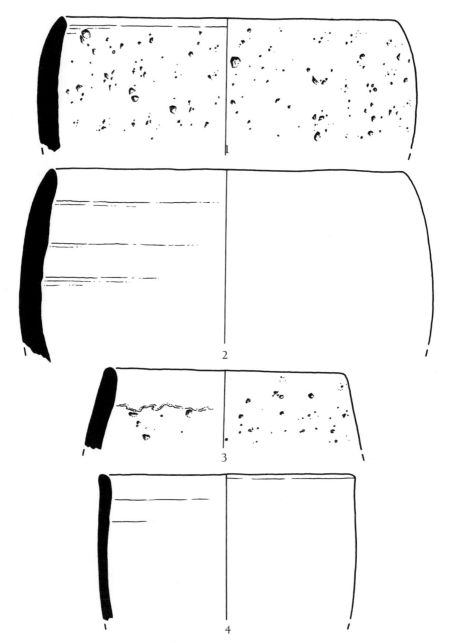

Figure 20. 1: Jar with inturned rim. Red fabric with chalk and flint infill that has largely leached out from both surfaces. Middle Iron Age. From pits in Chisbury Camp. 2: Jar with inturned rim. Dark buff to grey/black fabric with sand and chalk infill. Middle Iron Age. From pits in Chisbury Camp. 3: Jar with inturned rim. Grey/brown sandy texture. Middle Iron Age. From Chisbury Camp. 4: Straight-sided jar. Dark buff sandy fabric with wiped surfaces, now largely decayed. Middle Iron Age. From pits in Chisbury Camp. (1:2)

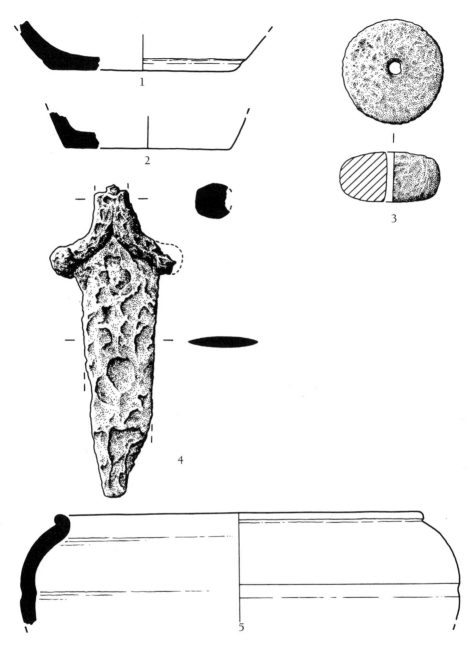

Figure 21. 1: Base of black pot of flint and grog-tempered fabric with the exterior surface burnished. Middle Iron Age (?). From pits at Chisbury Camp. 2: Base of dark grey pot in sandy fabric with some grass in the infill and with smoothed exterior surface. Middle Iron Age (?). From pits at Chisbury Camp. 3: Stone spindle whorl. Date uncertain but perhaps Middle Iron Age. From pits at Chisbury Camp. 4: Fragment of anthropoid sword. Middle Iron Age. Found to the west of Chisbury Camp. 5: Large bead rim jar in Savernake Ware, with pale orange exterior and grey interior. Early Roman period. From pits at Chisbury Camp. (1:2)

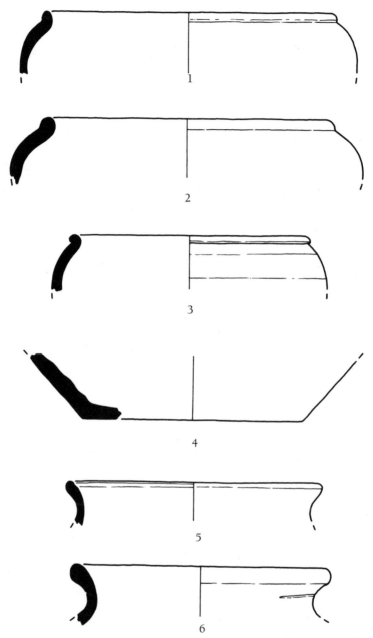

Figure 22. 1: Bead rim jar in Savernake Ware, with black exterior and buff interior. Early Roman period. From pits at Chisbury Camp. 2: Bead rim jar in Savernake Ware, in pale grey fabric. Early Roman period. From pits at Chisbury Camp. 3: Bead rim jar in Savernake Ware, in pale grey fabric. Early Roman period. From pits at Chisbury Camp. 4: Base of pot in Savernake Ware with grit and grog temper. Early Roman period. From pits at Chisbury Camp. 5: Rim sherd from a jar in black/dark grey burnished ware. Early Roman period? From pits at Chisbury Camp. 6: Rim sherd of jar in orange/buff fabric. Early Roman period? From pits at Chisbury Camp. (1:2)

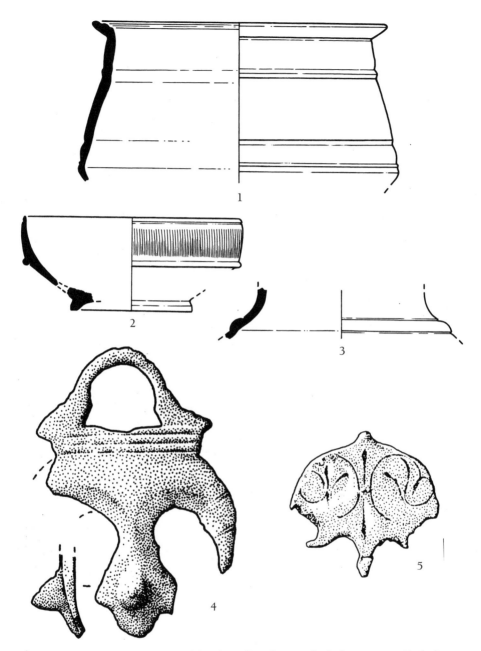

Figure 23. 1: Reeded-rim carinated bowl. Buff surfaces with dark grey core. Early Roman (Flavian period). From pits at Chisbury Camp. 2: Two sherds from a South Gaulish *terra sigillata* bowl, form Dragendorf 24/25. Early Roman (Tiberius to Nero). From pits at Chisbury Camp. 3: Sherd from the neck of a jar of "Atrebatic" style, in grey fabric with partially smoothed outside surface. Late Iron Age/Early Roman periods. From pits at Chisbury Camp. 4: Bronze military pendant of phallic type, found with Fig. 23.5. Early Roman (Claudian-Flavian). Found to the west of Chisbury Camp. 5: Bronze military pendant of trifoliate shape with traces of silvering and niello inlay, found with Fig. 21.5. Early Roman (Claudian-Flavian). Found to the west of Chisbury Camp. (1:1)

CHAPTER 3

The Area around Cunetio in the Roman Period

3.1 THE AREA AROUND CUNETIO

ERIC HOSTETTER

Introduction

This essay intends to survey selectively the region surrounding the small walled town of Cunetio (Black Field, Mildenhall), within whose territory the Roman villa at Castle Copse probably lay (Figs. 24–25).[1]

The relatively limited attention which this territory has received, when compared to other areas in the south, is perhaps owed to the lack therein of a *civitas* capital or other major town during the Roman period. While early travellers and antiquarians[2] commented upon and explored a number of sites and landscape features, as men of their epoch their attention was primarily attracted to the more spectacular Roman discoveries, among them Rudge villa (Froxfield), with its famous cup bearing images of western forts on Hadrian's wall, found in 1725, and Littlecote villa, with its "Orphic" mosaic unearthed four years later. Among the most active scholars earlier in this century were M. E. Cunnington, best known for her Iron Age excavations, and E. H. Goddard. Together they produced a fundamental catalogue (1911) on the holdings of The Museum in Devizes. Goddard also compiled a listing of the prehistoric, Roman, and Saxon material from Wiltshire by parishes (1913); and Cunnington, a lengthy summary of Romano-British remains in Wiltshire (1930). Other writers reporting on local discoveries include A. D. Passmore, author of a series of articles on Roman sites in northern Wiltshire, including the settlement of Durocornovium (Wanborough) (1921) and Rudge villa (1950). Since 1854, much of the archaeological scholarship appeared in the *Wiltshire Archaeological and Natural History Magazine,* and in 1957 the data was collected in L. V. Grinsell's grand *Victoria County History* 1:1 for Wiltshire.

In the last four decades, archeological interest in the area has intensified. In 1973 a survey of Roman Wiltshire by B. Cunliffe appeared in *Victoria County History* 1:2—a model contested by P. J. Fowler (1975b)—while J. Richards (1978) compiled a succinct survey of the archaeology of the Berkshire Downs in all periods, and C. J. Chandler (1989) produced a brief appraisal of the Thamesdown area in the Roman period.[3]

More specialized investigations on landscape archaeology, especially those on the Fyfield and Overton Downs, land allotment and linear features, and settlement patterns on the Marlborough Downs have also been carried out by, among others, P. J. Fowler and H. C. Bowen (e.g., Bowen 1978, 1990; Fowler 1967, 1975a; Bowen and Fowler 1962, 1966, 1978; and Bowen, Fowler, and Race 1978). D. J. Bonney studied the relationship between pagan Saxon burials and ancient and medieval boundaries and land allotments (1966, 1972, 1977, 1978) and Iron Age and Roman settlement in Wiltshire from a geological perspective (1968). B. Walters, B. Phillips, and other members of the Littlecote Roman Research Trust continue to record regional Roman sites and landscape features, but the major focus of their efforts has been the recently completed excavation (1978–91) of the villa at Littlecote Park.[4] J. Haslam, examining a medieval iron-smelting site at Ramsbury (1980), posited the existence of four Saxon *villae regales* whose boundaries may, in part, reflect Roman units of land tenure. Investigation of the territory's urban center, Cunetio, has lagged. Aerial photography, limited excavations by K. Annable (1955, 1958, 1959),[5] and the occasional fortuitous, if spectacular, find, such as the Cunetio hoard published by E. Besly and R. Bland (1983), have all contributed to an understanding of the town. The serious comparison of the evolution of town and country remains, however, problematic.

Somewhat farther north, but nevertheless important for the understanding of the area surrounding Cunetio, a variety of features of all periods in the path of the M4 motorway were recorded during 1969–71 by P. J. Fowler and B. Walters (1981). More recently, the survey of prehistoric and Roman landscapes surrounding Maddle Farm villa on the Berkshire Downs, coupled with limited trenching on the same, by V. Gaffney and M. Tingle (1989), has provided a more refined and invaluable understanding of land use and settlement in an area somewhat less wealthy than that surrounding Cunetio.[6]

The exemplary work conducted on several classes of locally manufactured pottery, particularly Oare and Savernake,[7] provides a basic picture of regional distribution and, for Savernake Ware, broader patterns of trade.

Least advanced, as ever, are faunal and botanical studies, a situation that obliges reliance upon the results obtained at the villa at Castle Copse and upon other better studied southern regions, especially the Upper Thames Valley.

Aerial photography,[8] field survey, and casual observation have steadily revealed an increasing density of sites around Cunetio. This expanding corpus of data has not, however, resulted in a clearer notion of settlement hierarchy, however defined, nor has it clarified the relationships between settlements or explicated the land units upon which they lay. Despite a lack of investigation and publication, it is plain that a broad range of "sites"—walled town, various types of villas, "larger" nucleated settlements or villages, hamlets, houses, cottages and farmsteads, and round and rectangular huts—is present and that, while distinctions between many of these are vague, the variety does reveal marked socioeconomic differences.[9] Additional factors hindering study are the undefined chronologies of the majority of these sites within the Roman period, particularly in the first and second centuries A.D., and the pace of site destruction from the plough, construction, and other forces.[10]

A.D. 43–Second Century

The relationship between the Roman military and native hillforts and *oppida* during and following the second stage of the Claudian invasion is little understood.[11] Secure archaeological evidence for local hostilities is lacking, but garrisons were probably strategically stationed to ensure peace with the natives (chap. 2). Several major Roman roads—e.g., the Fosse Way and Ermine Street—were probably constructed during the early period of military campaigning, as is suggested by the recovery of Roman pottery of A.D. 43–50 from the ditch of the Roman road at Dorcan Stream.[12] Whether, as has often been proposed, the Fosse Way ever formed a Claudian frontier has been questioned.[13]

Cunetio, which probably owes its name to the native appellation of the River Kennet, on whose southern bank it lay,[14] may owe its foundation to its strategic position at the foot of Forest Hill hillfort to the southwest and at the hub of no fewer than five major roads (Fig. 25).[15] These avenues ran: east along the Kennet Valley towards Spinis (Speen), beyond which it intersected the route between Calleva Atrebatum (Silchester) and Durocornovium (Wanborough); west to Verlucio (Sandy Lane) and Aquae Sulis (Bath); north to Durocornovium and Corinium (Cirencester); and south to a fork, with one branch leading to Sorviodunum (Old Sarum), the other to Venta Belgarum (Winchester).

Possible continuity of site occupation at Cunetio is hinted at by the recovery of Iron Age coins (see chap. 1), several early pieces of military metalwork, examples of which were also recovered from a Roman villa (?) within the hillfort of Forest Hill, *terra sigillata* pottery of c. A.D. 50–60, and several Republican and early imperial coins.[16] B. C. Burnham and J. Wacher suggest that much of this material might derive from the abandonment, in the early A.D. 60s, of a civilian settlement or fort.[17] The layout of early (pre-walled?) Cunetio appears to have been relatively regular with one north-south and two east-west streets, but, pending further excavation, questions of possible early fortifications and town planning will remain obscure.

Other traces of early military presence in the region may be attested at and near Chisbury hillfort. A trifoliate bronze pendant and a bronze phallic pendant, both popular among soldiers in the first century A.D., were recovered to the west of the hillfort in 1980 (Fig. 23.4–5),[18] and coinage of Augustus, Tiberius, and Claudius has been found within and to the west of the hillfort (see chap. 1).[19] At Littlecote, the excavators have interpreted a lengthy ditch and bank as a possible small military encampment enclosed by a timber palisade (c. A.D. 43–60), erected alongside a road of like date and possible military origin.[20]

In the second century, Cunetio must have prospered, becoming the regional market and distribution center within an increasingly currency-based imperial system of short- and long-range trade. The importance of the town is eventually made explicit by its inclusion in the Antonine Itinerary[21] and, perhaps, by the building of a double-ditched enclosure of c. 6 hectares with rounded corners, the date of which, however, has not been established.[22]

Neighboring roadside settlements, too, appear to have flourished at this time. Durocornovium, perhaps founded as a small fort at the junction of roads linking Corinium, Calleva, and Venta, hosted a civilian settlement by A.D. 75–80, which continued to develop in the early second century.[23] At an uncertain later date, the town received a probable *mansio*,[24] a feature that may underscore the settlement's intermediate position between the more prominent Cunetio and Corinium, both of which arrogated many of Durocornovium's potential functions.[25] In the later second or earlier third century, the center of the town may have been fortified.[26]

Stimulated by the demands of military supply and the Roman road system, the region around Cunetio undoubtedly began to develop, though at what pace is uncertain.[27] Roman and native landowners may have sought to increase production as surplus became readily salable in diverse and distant markets and, in turn, to acquire luxury goods from the Mediterranean and beyond.[28] However, if Roman control signified an expansion of land under the plough, Iron Age farmers may long have been accustomed to producing surplus for market, and in the early Roman period continuity rather than change in the countryside may have been the rule. The greater changes which were taking place, especially the clearing of woodlands, had begun in the Iron Age and before.[29]

The slopes overlooking the fertile Kennet Valley and the Vales of Pewsey and Ham proved attractive sites for Romanized farms and villas (see chap. 3.2).[30] At least twenty-four villas or possible villas displaying varying degrees of Romanized architectural pretension have been identified around Cunetio (Figs. 24–25, Appendix 1). These are for the most part located on chalk or clay-with-flints-on-chalk on valley slopes and are nearly always in relatively close proximity to the Roman road system running through the valleys, the avenues along which agricultural produce traveled to market. The lighter soils of the uplands, long inhabited, still offered good farming and grazing, and, at least at Fyfield Downs, some molluscan evidence suggests a shift from a shady to a more open landscape in the pre- and early Roman periods.[31]

In the absence of a sufficient number of investigated sites, the chronology of villa development around Cunetio remains problematic, and much depends upon the often vaguely defined moment at which a developing settlement or farmstead is reclassified as, or gains, a "villa." Several Romanized villas are preceded by native and Roman settlements of varying morphology, but the relationship between Celtic farmstead or settlement and Roman farmstead or Roman villa is ill-defined.[32] However attractive, the notion that such examples hint at Celtic villa-owners remains unsubstantiated—even if many natives undoubtedly owned Romanized villas.[33]

On the meager evidence of a few partially explored and essentially unpublished (but for one) sites, the development of Romanized villas around Cunetio may date from the later second and even third centuries—or when they assume their more familiar Roman architectural forms.[34] Here, as elsewhere,[35] many villas probably began as smaller "cottage" villas replacing native settlements.

The best explored, but as yet unpublished, villa is that at Littlecote Park, where, at the end of the first century A.D., circular native huts are replaced by two rectangular wooden buildings, one residential, the other a probable barn containing ovens, "corn-driers," wooden fermentation tanks and rotary grinding stones. These buildings probably represent a modest farmstead and are the precursors of the stone corridor villa and larger flint-walled barn erected around A.D. 170.[36]

In the west wing of the villa at Castle Copse, a stone building of the third century A.D. (B:III) succeeded earlier wooden constructions (B:I) of uncertain character, while in the north and south wings pottery deposits suggest occupation in the later first century A.D. (A965–971:I and C59:I). It is also possible that Romanized structures existed on-site in the second century: in the north wing, fragments of plain plaster were recovered in the sealed stylobate fills of the first aisled building (A960:VII) dating to after A.D. 198, and fragments of flue, pan, and cover tiles were recovered in the terrace gravel, the plat-form for the later villa,[37] laid down in the mid-to-late second century A.D.

The unexplored villa (?) built within the hillfort at Forest Hill offers one of the more striking examples of cultural superimposition, though not necessarily of continuity.[38] Southeast of Durocornovium, at Starveall, a halled-villa probably erected in the later third century, yielded Iron Age sherds, a first century A.D. sherd of *terra sigillata,* and a brooch of like date.[39] Similarly, at Maddle Farm villa, five kilometers to the west, con-struction of the stone villa buildings may date to the early third century, although earlier residual material associated with an earlier settlement also exists on the site.[40] At Badbury (Chiseldon), the masonry villa of the third–fourth century was preceded in the west range by timber structures and mid-first-century A.D. pottery; the construction of a barnlike structure in the east range may date to the second or third century A.D.[41]

Lastly, farther west, within the orbit of Aquae Sulis (Bath), recent excavations at Box villa suggest possible pre-Roman occupation west of the main villa site and occupation on the villa site and elsewhere by c. A.D. 150, before which date a stone building was constructed at the northeast corner of the villa.[42]

Larger nucleated settlements or villages are also present, especially from the second century A.D. on,[43] and not a few demonstrate likely continuity from the Iron Age.[44] In their 1966 survey of settlements in Dorset and Wiltshire, P. J. Fowler and H. C. Bowen called attention to the presence on the Marlborough Downs (West Overton and Fyfield Downs) of a series of contiguous and succeeding Iron Age and Roman settlements of wide variety and considerable extent and virtually all associated with "Celtic" fields.[45] Of particular importance was their observation that most settlements lay at about or above 274 meters O.D. (600 ft), those at lower elevations having been destroyed or obscured by later medieval occupation, ploughing, and other agencies. Such results demonstrated the potential limitations of field survey and aerial photography in determining ancient settlement patterns.

The best-explored of these chalkland settlements are those at West Overton and, far-ther to the north, Knighton Bushes, which is associated with the modest villa at Maddle Farm. The former is an enclosed pre-Roman Iron Age settlement with timber structures of around one hectare (two to three acres) and Celtic fields cultivated both before and dur-ing the early Romano-British period.[46] The earliest datable features at Knighton Bushes seem to be pre-Flavian, though Iron Age material is also present and appears to be associ-ated with a "Celtic" lynchet modified in the Roman period. An early second-century sub-rectangular enclosure of uncertain function is compared by the excavators with others found at more humble Roman sites such as Odstone Down, Botley Copse, and Ram's Hill;[47] the domestic area of the settlement appears to have lain beyond the enclosure. Another likely large settlement is what appears to be a village of c. 1.62 hectares (four acres) associated with a squarish earthwork and field systems south of Down Farm (Everleigh).[48] Situated upon the parish boundary and at some distance from the nearest known villa (Manningford Bruce),[49] it may suggest a community on the limit of a land unit. Still farther from Cunetio, the village of Chisenbury Warren (Enford) runs along more than 640 meters (700 yards) of a "street" on the northern slope of a valley, and covers over 5.50 hectares (c. 14.5 acres); possessing some eighty rectangular platforms, it is associated with both "Celtic" and more elongated fields.[50] Other unrecognized settlements are suggested by the occasional cluster of Roman period finds (Fig. 25).

Modest buildings, farmsteads, and small hamlets of varying shape on a smaller scale constituted the most common form of rural settlement in the Roman period, but, again, few in the vicinity of Cunetio have been investigated (Figs. 24–25, Appendix 1). At Littlecote Park, a farmstead with at least two rectangular Romanized buildings was built in the last decade of the first century A.D.[51] At Finches Farm (Baydon), work on the M4 Motorway revealed a possible modest Early Iron Age and Romano-British settlement, with circular structures, a series of postholes, and linear ditches, some of which formed rectangular enclosures and tiles.[52] Small-scale excavation on the shoulder of the motorway revealed a beamslot structure associated with pottery, whose date places the foundation date not later than A.D. 50–75. And near Badbury (Chiseldon), a short distance east of the road leading to Durocornovium, lies a small rectangular structure yielding material from the late first or second through the earlier fourth century A.D.[53]

Located Roman burials are few in the area around Cunetio.[54] Most graves document the continuation of the native ritual of inhumation (see Appendix 1),[55] but a few cremation burials are also present: the Roman (?) burial of Forest Hill (Folly) Farm (Mildenhall) in which an urn was placed beneath a brick arch;[56] the three tumulus burials surrounded by upright posts from Overton Hill (West Overton);[57] and the cemetery of cremation (?) burials north of Weir Farm (Broad Hinton).[58]

The rural economy was probably based on mixed farming,[59] at least to judge by the regional geology and geography, by the evidence of landscape features, limited published botanical and faunal data, and by the increasing numbers of farm-related constructions (barns, "corn-driers," tanks, ovens, stores) and artifacts (querns, iron and bronze implements, etc.).

While the conventional view—that farming intensified in the earlier Roman period—has been contested,[60] the agricultural expansion model is perhaps supported by F. J. Green's review of the range, complexity, and specialization in crop agriculture in Wessex[61] and by V. Gaffney and M. Tingle's survey of the Lambourn Downs. That survey shows that pottery dating between the late first and early second centuries and the fourth century, but with a concentration between c. A.D. 50 and 250, was scattered across nearly 2,000 hectares during manuring of fields; a series of fields "Celtic" in form appear in fact to be late first/early second century A.D.[62] Further, P. J. Fowler and H. C. Bowen also identified distinctively Roman fields amidst Celtic ones at Totterdown (Fyfield Down) that apparently date to the first/early second century A.D.,[63] demonstrating, as mentioned earlier, that "Celtic" fields visible on Marlborough

Downs represent only the upper limits of field systems that extended into the valleys below.[64] Many field systems appear to be associated with native settlements of the Roman period, some of which lie in close proximity to villas, e.g., the fields of elongated form on Totterdown, c. 3 km north of Fyfield villa, or Knighton Bushes, near Maddle Farm villa.

Judging by the evidence of the plant remains recovered at Maddle Farm villa and the associated settlement at Knighton Bushes, wheat, barley, and oats may have been among the principal crops, both being well suited to chalk soils,[65] and at Castle Copse villa, evidence for earlier production includes various cereals (see chap. 4.17).[66]

A. King and A. Grant suggest that in the Roman period cattle and pig increased in importance, while sheep decreased.[67] S. Payne notes that the animal bone from the villa at Castle Copse does not contradict this view (chap. 4.16).[68] Nor does the much smaller assemblage from Maddle Farm challenge it, since there cattle, caprovids and pig predominate. Horse and dog, domestic and wild birds, and red and road deer are also present.[69] The Lambourn Downs survey suggests that the fertility of the fields was maintained by the dispersal of settlement refuse and manure from herds, with a strong likelihood of dairy herds.[70] The raising of sheep for wool is also suggested by the common recovery of spindle whorls and loom weights, at Savernake Forest kilns, Tottenham House, and elsewhere.[71] Animal husbandry is further suggested by ditched enclosures and byres, such as the second-century enclosure tentatively interpreted as a corral at Knighton Bushes settlement and others.[72] Because some of these enclosures occasionally overlie "Celtic" fields, H. C. Bowen has suggested a possible shift to stock farming.[73]

Nonagricultural economic activities in the region include the manufacture of Savernake Ware, perhaps beginning on sites at Oare and, possibly, Broomsgrove Farm and west of Martinsell hillfort.[74] Numerous kilns have been excavated, especially in Savernake Forest (Tottenham House and Column Ride), as have clay pits (e.g., Bitham Pond).[75] The production of Savernake ware began soon after the invasion, and at Oare, where native forms were also produced, the introduction of Romanized forms may reflect the requirements of military supply.[76] Later, the industry was sustained by the growth of Cunetio, whose location facilitated its distribution. I. Hodder originally suggested a general market area for Savernake Ware of c. 16–24 km (c. 10–15 miles), with further distributions in the directions of the primary road systems; but subsequent reappraisal suggested a northwestern bias in the distribution, perhaps attributable to marketing of the wares in Dobunnic tribal territory.[77]

Other classes of locally produced pottery include molded imitation *terra sigillata* or "samian" ware of the late first century A.D.; North Wiltshire Color-coated Ware, possibly from the area of Wanborough, of the earlier second century A.D.; lead-glazed wares of the late first or early second century A.D., sherds of which have been found at kiln sites at Oare and in Savernake Forest; and a variety of coarse wares.[78]

Bricks and tiles, notably from Oare,[79] were also produced locally, probably at a variety of levels, as indeed they were until recently in the region (see chap. 1). As a rule, they are *sine textu,* though tiles stamped "IVC.DIGNI" have been recovered in third- and fourth-century contexts to the north of Cunetio at Burderop Down, Studley villa near Calne, Badbury villa, Wanborough, and Silchester.[80]

Of the local building stone (see chap. 1), flint nodules were the most commonly employed stone, chalk and greensands being less frequently used, owing to their soft-ness.[81] Sarsens, quarried on the Marlborough Downs since early prehistory,[82] were com-monly used for quoins and foundations, as well as for querns.[83]

Iron production has been posited south of Verlucio (Sandy Lane), and iron slag, perhaps originating as nodules and pans in Kimmeridge Clay, is common at Wanbor-ough.[84] Most iron-working was, however, probably associated with local smithing, rather than smelting operations; R. Ehrenreich suggests that at the villa at Castle Copse the iron may have been obtained from sources in the Weald, the Forest of Dean, and the Jurassic Ridge region (chap. 4.9).[85] Bronze-working is also attested indirectly by the clay triskelis mold from Castle Copse (?) (see chap. 10) and by furnaces in a barn at Littlecote.[86]

The Third and Fourth Centuries to c. A.D. 360

The third century, at least until its later decades, is often suspected to have been a period of decline or stagnation.[87] R. Reece's proposal[88] that the economic viability of Romano-British towns diminished dramatically in the third century has not been fully accepted in light of the continuing administrative, building construction, and commercial activities documented in third- and early fourth-century urban centers.[89] Still, a process of deterio-ration in the larger urban centers of the third century is often recognized and coincides with an increasingly decentralized economy and the period when many smaller towns appear to have peaked in size and economic vitality.[90]

Reece's corollary, that there was an apposite shift of prosperity to the countryside, has been better received. In his charting of villas, M. Gregson has shown that there was, over time, an increase in the number of villas and a decrease in their mean size, and that "the number and total area curves only begin to flatten off in the first half of the third century AD, perhaps implying the lateness of a relatively full 'saturation' of Britain by villas . . ."[91]

In the countryside around Cunetio, the later part of the third century appears to be a period of marked prosperity, at least for villa-owners. For those villas whose chronolo-gies are even minimally defined, there is expansion and a shift from wooden to masonry construction.[92] Extensive additions were undertaken between the years A.D. 200 and 270 at the winged corridor villa at Littlecote [93] while at Castle Copse a vast gravel plat-form, the foundation for the future stone villa, was laid down between the mid-/late sec-ond and the early third century A.D., a second phase of extensive posthole structures was erected after A.D. 198, and a large aisled building was constructed within the third century. To the north, the halled villa house at Starveall was probably constructed later in the third century.[94]

Cunetio and the surrounding countryside appear to have prospered in the later third century, a situation perhaps reflected in the greater distribution of regionally pro-duced pottery.[95] Disquiet, however, may or may not be suggested by several local hoards (see chap. 4.7). Two hoards of nearly sixty thousand coins were recovered south of Cunetio; one concealed in a Savernake Ware storage jar, was deposited around A.D. 270–71; the other, from a lead box, around A.D. 274–75.[96] A smaller hoard of the Gallic empire comes from Aldbourne,[97] and a fourth, of Diocletianic bronzes, from Upavon.[98]

When, in A.D. 314, Corinium became the capital of Britannia Prima, Cunetio may

have assumed added importance.[99] Economic strength may be indicated by the importation of significant volumes of diverse pottery—New Forest, Oxfordshire, Alice
Holt/Farnham, and other wares—from outside the region, and at the end of the third
and in the earlier fourth century, the numerous villas around Cunetio show evidence of
substantial capital investment.[100] Formerly modest villas are transformed by architectural
additions, the laying of extensive mosaics, and the decoration of walls with frescoes,
occasionally figural. Frequently advanced explanations for this prosperity include the
increasing irrelevance of towns, save for administrative functions, the wider appeal of the
"villa" as an economic asset and prestigious residence, restored confidence following earlier civil disturbances, and an often posited, but doubtful, influx of wealthy Roman
investors fleeing unrest in Gaul.[101]

    This rural prosperity coupled with the political and social changes occurring
empire-wide, could suggest a concomitant and continuing tendency toward the concentration of wealth in the hands of the owners of the larger Roman estates, with the expansion of larger villa estates at the expense of smaller holdings, and the abandonment of
less productive or marginal lands.[102] But this view is contested by P. J. Fowler[103] and
questioned by M. Millett, who views the increasing frequency of larger estates as the natural result of the elite's investment in the countryside.[104] M. Gregson's conclusions that,
contrary to expectations, there is, over time, a decrease in mean villa size with, in the
later period, fewer very large and very small villas and more of a medium size (i.e.,
500–1,000 m²)[105] may also argue against the domination of the few, though our general
bewilderment over land tenure hinders interpretation. Many small villas and their associated lands could easily represent single parcels in the collection of holdings of a few single wealthy "estates" or families. Gregson tentatively attributes the trend to more
Romanized, less socially constrained methods of property management in the decades
around A.D. 300, seemingly the period of greatest construction in the villas surrounding
Cunetio. If the lack of excavated sites around Cunetio disallows unambiguous state-
ments, it at least remains difficult to identify villas that were unquestionably abandoned
or in marked decline in the late third or earlier fourth century.[106]

    Also difficult to assess is the notion of a population decline in Wiltshire over the
course of the fourth century, a model at odds with the evident prosperity found in both
villas and, possibly, in the settlements around Cunetio, or the possibility that perceived
demographic change merely represents a shift of population from town to country.[107]

    The best-documented villa around Cunetio exemplifying rural prosperity in the late
third and earlier fourth centuries A.D. remains that at Littlecote. There, around A.D. 270,
the large industrial building to the north was narrowed, and subsequently a small bath
suite was built into the north corner along with further elaborations both within that
building and within and around the residential range to the west.[108] At Castle Copse
villa, the second aisled building was subdivided into luxury quarters after A.D. 331
(A:XI), on the evidence of a coin of the House of Constantine (**55**) recovered in a sealed
floor of the phase preceding those alterations. The small villa at Rudge Manor Farm, still
functioning in the fourth century, is well-known for the 1725 discovery of an enamelled
bronze cup depicting western forts along Hadrian's Wall; the site also produced a figural
mosaic and, in 1875, a small stone half-figure of Attis.[109] Although poorly documented,
other villas yielding fourth-century A.D. pottery include the winged villa at Brown's

Farm (Marlborough); a series of buildings, including Bath stone column fragments, found over an extensive area at South Farm (Chiseldon);[110] Aldbourne Gorse; and, possibly, the structures at Draycot Farm (Wilcot).[111]

Farther north, around Durocornovium, Badbury villa underwent significant rebuilding, with structure G, an aisled corridor building in the south range, being reworked in the third and early fourth centuries, and again in the fourth century.[112] At Starveall Farm, the foundation of the stone aisled hall villa appears to date to the later third century, and, on the evidence of a New Forest beaker sherd sealed in the column foundation, the building received many of its mosaics, wall painting, and a colonnade between A.D. 300 and 330.[113] The villa at Maddle Farm also underwent a secondary major phase of construction, which, though poorly dated, is likely to have occurred in the fourth century.[114] And to the west, the villa at Box was extensively increased in size in the late third and fourth centuries A.D.[115]

The degree to which the prosperity evident in the late villas extends downwards to more modest settlements is more difficult to assess.[116] At Overton Down, which earlier had an enclosed pre-Roman Iron Age settlement with timber structures of some two to three acres and "Celtic" fields cultivated before and during the early Roman-British period, there developed an entirely new settlement of up to perhaps one dozen structures lying among earlier "Celtic" fields. The two small rectangular stone-founded structures that P. J. Fowler excavated (site XII) are of probable fourth-century date,[117] and most of the material recovered from the settlement appears to be from the end of the third and fourth centuries A.D., including many coins of Constantine and ending with Arcadius. As Fowler suggests, at least modest or relative wealth may be implied by the nature of some finds, among which were various bronze artifacts, including jewelry and pottery, both from Savernake Forest kilns and from the New Forest and Oxford regions.

Mixed farming appears to have continued during this period and beyond. D. Miles posits an intensification of production in the late Roman period, linked to technological change, the introduction of coulters, asymetrical ploughshares, the threshing sledge and other implements, and the use of full crop rotation techniques.[118] However, V. Gaffney and M. Tingle recorded a marked (perhaps 70%) fall-off in the later Roman period in pottery deposited in the course of spreading manure in the fields around Maddle Farm. This suggests a decrease in the manuring of fields, which in turn hints at a possible decline in agricultural activity, perhaps due to overly ambitious marketing strategies in earlier periods or to soil exhaustion.[119] P. J. Fowler, too, has postulated a decline in cultivated land—given over to pasturage?—in the later Roman period in Fyfield and West Overton parishes on the Marlborough Downs.[120]

Clearly, the question is a vexed one, as the architectural evidence of many villas around Cunetio suggests prosperity in this period, and the facilities and implements of agriculture (increasing numbers of "corn-driers," ovens, tanks, cereal stores, and tools) and evidence of small-scale industry (crucibles, slag dumps, filings) are attested at many sites of varying status. Such technological innovation, with its implied investment in agriculture, must reflect the investment seen in the late villa buildings themselves.

Cattle and pigs continue to be economically important. A few faunal assemblages from villas in the south, e.g., Shakenoak, Bancroft, and Pitney, suggest industrial specialization in the processing of pig.[121] Around Cunetio few comparative faunal data are available apart from Castle Copse villa, whose bone assemblages, except for the odd late groups of pig bones discussed by S. Payne (chap. 4.16), generally fall within the expected ranges. Other local sites, such as Starveall Farm villa and, possibly, Aldbourne Gorse villa, which have probable stock enclosures but no obvious field systems, may have specialized in livestock.[122]

Even if the relative numbers of sheep bones on Romano-British sites appear to decline,[123] significant areas of the downlands may have been given over to sheep in this late period. Evidence for sheep rearing and wool production is present in the form of sheep shears found at Barton Court Farm;[124] two double-ended combs from Baydon;[125] another from a villa at Andover; a weaving card, two picks, and a shale spindle whorl from the villa at Castle Copse (**460, 478–480**); shale spindle whorls from Overton Down (XII) and Maddle Farm;[126] and in clay from various sites. W. H. Manning, followed by Wild, suggests that woolcombs of likely third- or fourth-century date may reflect flock distribution, with single-ended combs grouped near the chalklands of south Cambridgeshire and two-ended combs perhaps relating to downlands.[127] Whether or not there was a marked development of the sheep husbandry in the late Roman period,[128] the importance of sheep rearing and wool production in this period is seemingly supported by the listing of the British *byrrhus* and *tapete* in the *Edictum Diocletiani* (XIX, 48; XIX, 28, 29) and by the possible presence of an imperial weaving mill at Venta (Winchester?).

The Later Fourth Century and Beyond

The troubles of the mid- and later fourth century—the conspiracy of A.D. 367, loss of troops to imperial expeditions, disintegration of market systems and communications, a possible decline in population and various incursions—may, in part, be reflected in the archaeological record around Cunetio. Insecurity in the town may be indicated by the replacement of the earlier undated defenses with a stone wall, but on a slightly different trace, enclosing c. 7.5 hectares.[129] The walls, between 4.9 and 5.6 m wide, rested upon mortared flint rubble foundations, were faced with oolitic limestone, and were probably punctuated with external towers. A *terminus post quem* for their construction is offered by a coin of A.D. 354–358 recovered from the primary silt of a ditch sealed by the wall at the west gate, making this one of the latest sets of town walls in Roman Britain. Whether they are to be related to Theodosius's measures for the defense of the province cannot be known.

Within the walls, an apsidal structure and a suite of rooms with a facing corridor over forty meters in length of later fourth-century date have been excavated in the northwest corner, and aerial photography has revealed other buildings, including a possible courtyard complex.[130] Other clues to the late history of Cunetio have been sought in the recovery of a military buckle plate dating to c. 350–380 A.D.[131]

Though few offer secure examples of destruction in A.D. 367, a number of villas in the southwest appear to have suffered around the middle of the fourth century.[132] According to K. Branigan, several villas along the lower Bristol Avon River appear to have been damaged around this time, but the same pattern of events is seemingly not repeated by the contiguous inland group of villas.[133] Beyond Bath there may again be traces of raiding. At Box villa, several rooms were partially or entirely burned, perhaps after A.D.

364–378, and Atworth was also partially destroyed by fire between c. A.D. 340 and 375, though later reoccupied. At North Wraxall villa, three bodies were dumped into a well in the fourth century, but again the villa was reoccupied after c. A.D. 370. Indeed, the majority of the villas which might have suffered in A.D. 367 appear to have been reoccupied thereafter[134] and often received further and elaborate architectural additions.[135]

Around Cunetio, there are few or perhaps even no certain examples of villas destroyed or damaged in the A.D. 360s or thereabouts. On the contrary, the decade of the A.D. 360s at Littlecote villa was a period of expansion during which the triconch chamber paved with the well-known Orpheus mosaic was added, and for which a coin of Constantius II of A.D. 356–360 provides the *terminus post quem*.[136] When Littlecote does enter into decline, in the later fourth century, it appears to be a gradual process.[137] At the courtyard villa at Castle Copse, the mid-fourth century witnesses the subdivision of the second aisled building (A:XI, after A.D. 331), a change which had more to do with social exigencies than with decline, since the resulting chambers were handsomely appointed with frescoes and mosaics; even later, the assemblages of probable kitchen waste suggest continuing prosperity (see chaps. 4.16 and 4.17).

One possible candidate for assault is the villa at Rudge Manor Farm, although the date at which the four or five skeletons were dumped into a well has yet to be established.[138] At Starveall, well to the north, the excavator suggests destruction of indeterminate nature around A.D. 350–370 on the basis of sherds contained in the ash of a hypocaust overlain by destruction debris.[139] The picture presented by nearby Badbury villa is, on the other hand, one of staggered decline, with demolition, the propping of collapsing walls, a burial in the former bath, and continued occupation in a reduced building into the fifth century.[140] Such also appears to be the case at Maddle Farm villa.

Thus, the case for the broad destruction or damaging of villas in the A.D. 360s would appear tenuous. More compelling is the contrast between the prosperity of regional villas at the start of the fourth century and the material impoverishment of many of them by the end of the same century. The physical aspects of the process are familiar: grander rooms are subdivided, bath complexes cease to be used or are lived in, mosaics are crudely repaired with mismatching tesserae, industrial and farming activities— smithing, kilns for "corn-drying," dumps for food processing, stackyards—formerly restricted to peripheral rooms or outlying buildings, now occur in formerly elegant chambers. And, too, the pottery which reached these villas changes as some wares cease, other continuing wares reduce their repertoire of forms, and volumes decrease.[141] This deterioration has been variously interpreted. Some villa owners may have decamped, perhaps, in some cases, for the perceived safety of walled Cunetio or, in difficult times, labor and resources may have been invested solely in achieving estate self-sufficiency rather than in maintenance of villa buildings.

If the chronology for the abandonment of villas remains intractable as new coin issues cease and older issues slowly drop out of circulation, as Roman pottery production ends,[142] and as the economy shifts towards payment in kind, the chronology for the abandonment of more modest rural settlements is even more problematic. At Knighton Bushes, the settlement associated with Maddle Farm villa, activity continues after the demise of the villa proper,[143] and on Overton Down P. J. Fowler sees one excavated settlement continuing in the late fourth and into the fifth century, even while, over the course of the fourth century, significant tracts of arable land were going out of cultivation.[144] In the period after the native revolt of A.D. 409 and the abandonment of the province by Honorius a year later, the impressive walls of Cunetio may have extended the town's physical survival, however meaningless such urban environments may otherwise have become as both urban and rural populations fell, a deterioration in climate began, and even inland sites suffered sporadic raids from the Irish coast. At Durocornovium, pottery suggests limited occupation into the fifth century, though the Saxons ultimately chose to occupy a different site, a hill with Roman (villa?) constructions that later became Upper Wanborough.[145]

The desire to protect tracts of land and/or territory may be signaled by the Wansdyke, if a sub-Roman date is taken, and, possibly, by the undated Bedwyn Dyke, running at the very least from Chisbury hillfort to the villa site at Castle Copse (see chaps. 4.18 and 5). Like the second, post–A.D. 367 phase of the Bokerly Dyke,[146] such features may be among the few monumental landscape features of an obscure period, which could suggest organized response to external threats.

Sporadic evidence of casual Roman presence in and around several hillforts such as Chisbury (see chap. 2) is attested, but only Liddington hillfort, where a possible Saxon structure cut through a late Roman context, has yielded a potentially plausible example of regional refortification in this late period.[147] Perhaps significant is the late Roman hanging bowl escutcheon found nearby.[148] The hoard of ninety-nine bronze coins, the latest struck between A.D. 388 and 402, perhaps deposited around A.D. 400 and found c. 100 meters east of Chisbury hillfort in 1981, does not demonstrate reoccupation,[149] though it and other late hoards—e.g., that from Manton (Preshute), not far from the villa at Barton Down, containing pewter vessels, pottery, and coins, including twenty-six *siliquae* reaching as late as Honorius, deposited in the early fifth century,[150] or the small hoard from the West Kennet Long Barrow, reaching to the late fourth century[151]—may well attest to the unstable tenor of the times.[152]

The survival, in whatever form, of villas and villa estates into the fifth century is difficult to document.[153] K. Branigan suggests that in the southwest those villas or villa estates which endured longest may be those which were best defended, either because of their particular topographic situations, fortifications (as at Gatcombe), their proximity to the nearest secure town,[154] or the possible presence of military or mercenaries on or near the site.

At Castle Copse, the coin list reaches Arcadius (**85–86**).[155] Overwey Ware pottery of the end of the fourth century appears in the latest contexts, and at least one stratigraphically post-villa structure (B:IX) with humble but stone foundations was constructed in the courtyard, but on a different alignment from the villa (Figs. 34, 86). More promising is Upper Upham (Aldbourne). There, late Roman finds—including a late fourth-century military-type buckle, perhaps belonging to a mercenary, or merely the property of a villa-owner with civil or military responsibilities[156]—are associated with early Saxon material.[157] Also, as B. Eagles points out (chap. 5), the name Upper Upham belongs to that group of place-names ending in -*ham,* often with early Saxon settlement. Tottenham (Grafton), and Tockenham (north of), are also of this group and are known villa sites.[158] At Littlecote, evidence for post-Roman activity is suggested by a possible timber structure erected south of the west wing.[159] At North Farm villa in Aldbourne, the coins reach

Honorius,[160] while Stock Lane, Barton Down, and other villa sites also yielded coins of very late date.[161] Structure G of Badbury villa suggests continued, if impoverished, occupation into the fifth century, and there may be sixth-century occupation slightly farther afield from the villa.[162] Lastly, Maddle Farm villa appears to go out of use around the turn of the century; on the evidence of five sherds, four of which were unstratified, of organic-tempered pottery, it is posited that its associated settlement may have continued.[163]

Such handmade organic-tempered pottery has been taken as evidence for early Saxon occupation though it might also, in some instances, represent a response to the collapse of mass-produced pottery. Elsewhere in the region, this ware has been recovered at a variety of sites, including Littlecote, Round Hill Down (Ogbourne St. George), Southward Down (Aldbourne), Wellhead (Westbury), and Overton Hill (West Overton), where some sherds are associated with a Roman inhumation burial, outside of Liddington Castle (see chap. 5).[164]

D. J. Bonney estimated that one-eighth or 15% of the known Roman settlements in Wiltshire lie under later settlements.[165] Even cursory comparison of the distribution of Roman and Saxon sites and finds suggests considerable similarities in site selection both on the downlands and in the valleys,[166] the avenues along which the newcomers entered the region (see chap. 5). Examples are common. At Manor Farm (Ramsbury), medieval activity occurs near a late Roman villa or farmstead.[167] Garden construction in 1822 and in 1839 revealed a Saxon cemetery near the possible villa site at Basset Down (see chap. 5).[168] At Callas Hill (Wanborough), Roman material was recovered in the vicinity of a Saxon burial,[169] and at Cherhill a late Roman mosaic underlies a Saxon church.[170] Similar associations also appear at Manningford Bruce, where chalk walls and tesserae have been documented in the churchyard, and at Fyfield villa, where flue and stone tiles and evidence of mosaics were situated near the church.[171]

Existing land units and boundaries often appear to have been respected by the Saxons as well. D. J. Bonney estimated that over 40% of pagan Saxon burials in Wessex are found on or near existing settlements and parish or tithing boundaries, suggesting not only that such boundaries were in existence in the early Saxon period, but that many were probably present in the Roman period and before.[172] Around Cunetio, Saxon burials lying near or on such boundaries include: the "spoke" cemetery at Crofton (Great Bedwyn); the secondary burials at Thornhill Lane (Clyffe Pypard), Great Botley Copse (East Grafton) and within a barrow at West Overton; and the cemetery at Bassett Down (Lyliard Tregoze). J. Haslam has proposed the existence of four agglomerated Saxon *villae regales* focussing on Great Bedwyn, Ramsbury, Kintbury, and Lambourne, all of which utilize boundaries that probably reflect earlier Roman patterns of land tenure (see chapter 5)—though whether for the whole or parts is uncertain, as few large Roman estates were likely to have been single consolidated units.[173] Whatever the case, the significance of the relationship between Roman and Saxon settlements may rest more often with the advantages and resources of a site than with any social or economic continuity between the two cultures.[174] In the absence of knowledge regarding political control over the landscape of the fifth and sixth centuries A.D., archaeology will have difficulty resolving such questions.

NOTES

1. The great quantity and variety of Roman material present preclude any attempt at being comprehensive. I thank B. Eagles and M. Corney for their many valuable suggestions throughout this essay.

2. On early excavators, see Levine 1986 and Marsden 1974.

3. For an archaeological ranking of Wessex sites in need of investigation, see Ellison 1981. For surveys and appraisals of neighboring areas: Berkshire Downs: Richards 1978: 45–49; Upper Thames valley: Young 1986: 58–63; Dorset: Groube and Bowden 1982: 47–50.

4. Frere 1992: 301, fig. 23; 1990: 353–54, fig. 24 (architectural phase plan), with earlier bibliography in notes.

5. For a summary of Cunetio scholarship, Burnham and Wacher 1990: 148–52.

6. Gaffney and Tingle 1989: 90.

7. By F. K. Annable (1962a), I. Hodder (1974a, 1974c), V. Swan (1975, 1977, 1984), and A. S. Anderson (1978a–b, 1980a–b).

8. On the contribution of aerial photography in Romano-British archaeology, Miles 1989: 116–20.

9. On the problem of site definition and an attempt at clarification, see Hingley 1989, and 1991: 75–80; Miles 1989: 115–34; Esmonde Cleary 1989a: 242–43; and C. Taylor 1982: 1–15. On settlement hierarchy on the Berkshire Downs, Gaffney and Tingle 1989: 239, who list "substantial buildings" or villas, followed by "large settlements," and lastly "ephemeral scatters of pottey which form discrete foci while not being associated with any discernable settlement area."

10. For a bleak view, even in the 1960s, of the chances of attaining a reliable assessment of settlement patterns on the Marlborough Downs, see Bowen and Fowler 1966: 62.

11. See M. Todd 1985: 187–99; for cautionary views of invasion scholarship, Millett 1990: 40–64; and Maxfield 1989: 19–29.

12. Phillips and Walters 1977, with bibliography on earlier excavations in notes 5–6; Chandler 1989: 16.

13. For the case against, see Millett 1990: 55; and Maxfield 1989: 26–27, with earlier bibliography in notes; for arguments in favor, Cunliffe 1973: 440; and Webster 1970: 179–97.

14. On the name: Eagles, chapter 5; Rivet and Smith 1979: 328–29; K. Jackson 1970: 71–72; Gover, Mawer, and Stenton 1970: 8; Tomkins 1983: 62, 75; and Ekblom 1917: 107.

15. For a brief discussion of the roads and gates of Cunetio, see Burnham and Wacher 1990: 148, 150. See too, Margary 1973: 135; and Grundy 1918: 85–87. On the early development of towns in Britain, Millett 1990: 69–84.

16. Griffiths 1983: 53–55; Annable 1966: 9–24; 1976: 176–79; 1978b: 126–27; and Swan 1975: 43–44. The presence of a few fragments of military hardware could mean many things: the stationing of a small contingent of soldiers for surveying and town planning, the presence of a regular garrison defending a fort, the detritus of a passing unit, etc. On evidence for the Roman army at *oppida* in the southwest, Todd 1985: 195–97. On Late Iron Age settlement patterns and multiple ditch systems around Cunetio, see Corney 1989: 111–28.

17. Burnham and Wacher 1990: 148–51, figs. 42–43.

18. Griffiths 1983: 52; and WAR 1986: 242, no. 83.

19. Griffiths 1983: 52; and WAR 1983: 160, no. 50.

20. Phillips and Walters 1983: 5; 1985: 5, pl. 5; and Rankov 1982: 387.

21. Antonine Itinerary 486.5 (Iter XIV); Rivet 1970: 58–60.

22. Burnham and Wacher 1990: 150. On the walls of Cunetio, see Burnham and Wacher 1990: 150; R. J. Smith 1987: 358; and Crickmore 1984: 127–28.

23. On Wanborough: Burnham and Wacher 1990: 160-164, with earlier bibliography in notes; Chandler 1989: 18; R. J. Smith 1987: 5, 244–46; Anderson and Wacher 1980: 115–26; and Phillips and Walters 1977: 223–27.

24. Phillips and Walters 1977: 223–27.

25. Indeed, Chandler (1989: 20) suggests that Durocornovium may ultimately have proved

less successful than anticipated, noting that building in the town did not in all areas extend to the limits of the walls.

26. Burnham and Wacher 1990: 163.

27. On Roman army supply, Fulford 1989: 179–81, who suggests as provisioning possibilities the payment of taxes in kind (grain), or the selling of grain to a procurator who paid with tax revenues; Millett 1990: 56–57; Higham 1992: 18–24; and G. E. M. Jones 1991: 24–25.

28. Late Iron Age participation in long-range trade certainly existed, evidence for which, noted by Robinson (chap. 2), includes Later and Latest Iron Age finds of continental coins and other items at both Cunetio and from near Chisbury hillfort. The economic impact of pre-Roman exchange has been questioned (Haselgrove 1989: 14–16), primarily on the grounds of its small scale.

29. On changes in Roman landscape: G. E. M. Jones 1989: 127–34 and Miles 1989: 115–26.

30. The appearance of villas has been argued to represent consumption, rather than any increase in agricultural production: Millett 1990: 97.

31. Fowler and Evans 1965: 296.

32. On the process of change from Celtic farm to Roman villa, see Branigan 1982: 81–96.

33. On the social hierarchy, see Higham 1992: 24–28, who views villa-owners as those "with significant amounts of land or the surplus therefrom—that is, the indigenous landed gentry and aristocracy." However, contrary to some of the "nativist" arguments, the Romans were not inexperienced in appraising good land or unskilled at employing symbolism by appropriating prestigious native sites to make plain the new order. M. Todd (1978: 199) would have wealthy aristocracy and businessmen as villa-owners and, in decreasing numbers, peasant freeholders, craftsmen who had made money in towns to invest in the countryside, and soldiers as estate owners.

34. Branigan (1976: 122–26 and 1977a: 33, 35–36, 43) suggests that villa construction in the area of the Atrebates and eastern Belgae began in the early or mid-second century A.D. and in the eastern territory of the Dobunni from the late first and early second centuries A.D., but holds that second-century villas in the southwest are not common. This contrasts with villa development in the southeast, where E. W. Black (1987) documents the development of villas even in the later first century. In the Upper Thames Valley, Young (1986: 59) notes that the first Romanized rectangular buildings at North Leigh, Barton Court, and Shakenoak all date to before the end of the first century A.D.

35. E.g., Shakenoak, North Leigh, and Ditchley villas to the northeast, reviewed by Young 1986: 61.

36. Phillips and Walters 1983: 12; and 1985: 5–6, fig. 2; Frere 1985: 308; and 1992: 301, with earlier bibliography in note 215. Although unevenly received, Walthew (1975: 195–99) has made the suggestion that the winged corridor villa may have been an imported type beginning in the later first century A.D.; and Branigan (1977a: 51), that in the territory of the western Belgae and of the Dobunni, the winged corridor villa with intramural court may be a local specialty, with parallels in northern Gaul.

37. Terrace gravel, A:II, contexts 152, 422, 509, 523, 529, 534-535, 538, 541, 582, 629, 680, 878, 883, 927, 964.

38. Grinsell 1957: 88; M. E. Cunnington 1930: 197; and Annable 1955: 191–92. A military mount was recovered not far from the "villa": Annable 1978b: 126–27. A more probable example of continuity from hillfort to villa is Ditches (North Cerney): Trow and James 1989: 83–87.

39. Phillips 1981: 46.

40. Gaffney and Tingle 1989: 162–64 for a summary; on 240, the construction date of the villa building is given as c. A.D. 180–240.

41. Chandler 1989: 21; Fowler and Walters 1981: 99. Among the many other essentially unexplored villas yielding hints of earlier occupation are North Farm (Aldbourne), with coins as early as Tiberius, and the possible villa at Upper Uppham (Aldbourne), producing coins as early as Vespasian: Grinsell 1957: 22–23.

42. Hurst, Dartnall, and Fisher 1987: 21–22.

43. On rural development in Wiltshire, Cunliffe 1973: 442–45, who suggests that the growing number of sizeable nucleated settlements in Wiltshire at this time may in part have been owed to

the restrictions of Celtic land tenure in the face of the increased demands of Roman villa owners farming ever larger estates. On the recognition and scholarly rehabilitation of Romano-British villages: Millett 1990: 205–11; Miles 1989: 115–16; Hanley 1987; Leech 1976: 142–61; Bowen and Fowler 1966: 43–67; various authors in Thomas 1966 and Miles 1982; and Hallam 1964: 19–32.

44. Hanley (1987: 10) cites thirty-six of a total of c. one hundred forty Roman villages in the counties of Avon, Somerset, and Gloucestershire as having Iron Age antecedents; there are probably more. See, too, P. J. Fowler 1975a: 121–36.

45. Bowen and Fowler 1966: 57–63; P. J. Fowler 1975a: 121–23.

46. P. J. Fowler 1967: 16–33.

47. Gaffney and Tingle 1989: 142–43.

48. Grinsell 1957: 70.

49. Grinsell 1957: 84.

50. Fowler and Bowen 1966: 51–53, figs. 4–5. At Chalton in nearby Hampshire, B. Cunliffe has surveyed a large settlement of rectangular houses with Iron Age antecedents, surrounded by a complex field system, also of likely Iron Age date: Hanley 1987: 28 and Cunliffe 1977.

51. Phillips and Walters 1979, 1981, 1983 and 1985: passim.

52. Fowler and Walters 1981: 125–26.

53. Ravetz 1958: 24–29.

54. Robinson (chap. 2) suggests that a small cemetery near Cunetio, previously thought to be Iron Age, may be early Roman.

55. E.g., Annable 1962b, burials in Bath Stone and lead sarcophagi at Devizes. On three inhumation graves to the north at Upper Lambourn see Richards 1976: 21–28 and on one from Cunetio see Annable et al. 1980: 187–91; and Annable 1965.

56. Forest Hill (Folly) Farm: Grinsell 1957: 88; and Annable 1955: 191–92.

57. Smith and Simpson 1964.

58. Grinsell 1957: 50; and Passmore 1921: 390.

59. On the concept of "mixed" economies, see Branigan 1988: 42–44; and for a summary of recent scholarship of Romano-British agriculture, see Miles 1989: 121–24; and G. E. M. Jones 1989: 127–34. On Roman farming in general, see Miles 1982 and 1989; and G. E. M. Jones 1989; while on the continuation of Iron Age practices, see F. J. Green 1981: 129–53. For a brief appraisal of mixed farming in the Upper Thames Valley, see Young 1986: 61.

60. By M. Jones (1989: 129), who suggests that such a perception might be related more to different patterns of distribution than to increased production. See, too, Fulford 1989: 187. On the contrary, Jones (1982: 101–102; 1989: 131; and 1991: 21) suggests that, apart from hay and other specific crops, grain production may actually have stagnated from the early Roman period through the later third century A.D., and that new harvesting tools and crop strategies either precede the arrival of the Romans or, as with the introduction of new plough technology of the late third century, postdate it.

61. F. J. Green 1981: 129–58.

62. Gaffney and Tingle 1989: 93, 240. See, too, Ford et al. 1988: 401–404; and Fulford 1989: 187.

63. Fowler and Bowen 1966: 59, fig. 9; P. J. Fowler 1975a: 121–23. On other field systems: Rhodes 1950: 1–28; Bradley and Ellison 1975: 65–67, 69–71; Richards 1978; Miles 1989: 125; Ford et al. 1988: 401–404.

64. Work in the river valleys near Abingdon and Reading has shown that Roman field systems survive as earthworks sealed beneath Roman and medieval alluvial deposits (Miles 1989: 125), while Roman fields at Claydon Pike (Lechlade) are now known to have been used primarily for grazing (Miles 1982: 66; and 1984: 197–203).

65. Carruthers 1989: 179–82.

66. For a review of agriculture in Wessex as a whole, see F. J. Green 1981.

67. A. C. King 1978 and 1991; Grant 1989.

68. In the Upper Thames Valley, cattle seems to have been the most important animal type, followed by sheep: Young 1986: 61.

69. Brown 1989: 183–92.

70. Gaffney and Tingle 1985: 69–72; and 1989: 225–38.

71. Swan 1984: 114, 119; Gaffney and Tingle 1989: 165–66, figs. 12.4: 49–50, 54, 56.

72. On stock buildings and cattle stalls and byres, Morris 1979: 40–54.

73. Bowen 1978: 1; Bowen, Evans, and Race 1978: 149–53. On the "ranch boundaries" on the chalklands of Hampshire and Wiltshire, which run irregularly both between and across parcels and "Celtic" field systems, and often in relation to settlements and hillforts, see Bonney (1978: 50), who interprets them as both local and regional boundaries.

74. The North Wiltshire pottery industry is summed up by A. S. Anderson (1980a), with bibliography and location of kiln sites in figs. 1–2.

75. Annable 1962a: fig. 1; Swan 1975; and 1984: 43, 114, 116–17; and A. S. Anderson 1980a.

76. A. S. Anderson 1980a: 3; and Swan 1975.

77. Hodder 1974a–c; and 1979: 193–94; see, too, Fulford 1982: 411. On social considerations hindering interpretations of distribution patterns based solely on market-predictable patterns, Hingley 1982: 47–48.

78. Swan 1977; Anderson 1978a–b; and 1980a: 12–14.

79. Swan 1984: 119, map 18; and 1975: 38.

80. Grinsell 1957: 54, 56; M. E. Cunnington 1940: 117. Fowler and Walters (1981: 103) consider that these tiles may be residual and could therefore possibly date even to the second century; that the first three letters may be the tilemaker's name, the last five being for *Dignitas* or *Dignus*, "worthy of"; and that they may have been manufactured at a tile manufactory at Oaksey to the north.

81. On building materials in the southeast, see J. H. Williams 1971a, including Great Bedwyn and Cunetio (nos. 122–123), and 1971b.

82. On the sarsen industry, see N. E. King 1968, 83–93.

83. P. J. Fowler 1967: 28–29. Finer architectural details were more often of imported Bath Stone; other imported stones included pennant slate for roof tiles and Kimmeridge shale for jewelry.

84. Burnham and Wacher 1990: 164; Cunliffe 1973: 451.

85. On iron-working, see Fulford 1989: 189–90; and Cleere and Crossley 1985.

86. Phillips and Walters 1985: 9, Building 2, Room 13.

87. For a summary of arguments: Fulford 1989: 191–95; Wacher 1989: 94; C. E. King 1981.

88. Reece 1980.

89. For a review of the question, see Millett 1990: 142. Such, for example, appears not to have been the case at Calleva Atrebatum.

90. Hingley 1982: 39–41; Millett 1990: 143–51.

91. Gregson 1988: 27.

92. By comparison, Young (1986: 61) notes that, in the Upper Thames Valley, Ditchley and Shakenoak villas reach their greatest extent in the second century and may have declined c. A.D. 200, though North Leigh did not, demonstrating steady development into the fourth century.

93. Frere 1990: 353–54, fig. 24; Phillips and Walters 1985.

94. Phillips 1981: 46; Grinsell 1957: 42.

95. Fulford 1989: 196; Hingley 1982: 36–41.

96. Besly and Bland 1983; reviewed by Robinson 1984: 137–38. However, on the perils of associating coin hoards with political unrest, see Reece 1981: 84–87.

97. Besly 1983: 61–66; 1984: 63–68; and Moorhead 1990.

98. Burnett and Robinson 1984: 89–99.

99. In contrast, perhaps, with Wanborough, where it appears that although the earlier (?) *mansio* remains in use the third- and fourth-century A.D. buildings excavated to date appear to be modest, sarsen-founded, timber frame structures: Chandler 1989: 30; Burnham and Wacher 1990: 163–64; R. J. Smith 1987: 245–46; Anderson and Wacher 1980: 115–26.

100. Branigan 1976: 124–25 on the burst of villa foundations in the southwest in the last thirty years of the third century.

101. M. Todd (1989: 17) argues that a transfer of capital assets from Gaul to Britain would

have been "virtually impossible in the conditions of the third century," and J. T. Smith (1978a) refutes the theory of the "halled villa" as an architectural import to Britain resulting from Gallic immigration. For a short review of the question, Hingley 1989: 48–50.

102. As Cunliffe 1973: 460 and Todd 1978: 206.

103. Fowler 1975b.

104. Millett 1990: 186, 203. See, too, Arnold 1984: 58–59.

105. Gregson 1988: 27.

106. North of Cirencester, however, Ditches Villa was apparently abandoned and partially demolished before the end of the third century A.D. (Trow and James 1989: 84); and in the Upper Thames Valley, where there has been extensive survey and excavation, the villa at North Leigh may have expanded at the expense of Ditchley and Shakenoak: Young 1986: 61; Brodribb, Hands, and Walker 1978: 202–205. The difficulties and opportunities of interpreting settlements and their relationship to the landscape are particularly well illustrated by D. Miles (1988: 72), describing fieldwork at Claydon Pike.

107. Cunliffe 1973: 457; and P. J. Fowler 1975b: 301–303. Other population estimates postulate a rise through c. A.D. 400, followed by a precipitous decline: Hingley 1989: 3–4, fig. 1, after P. J. Fowler 1978: fig. 1. See, too, Arnold 1982: 456–57; 1984: 122–33; and M. E. Jones 1979.

108. Phillips and Walters 1979, 1981, 1983, and 1985; and Frere 1992, with earlier bibliography in note 215.

109. Grinsell 1957: 71–72; Wright 1952: 361–62; Anonymous 1932: 108–109; Passmore 1950: 332; Colt Hoare 1821: 123. On the unusual wealth of stone sculpture in southwestern villas, Branigan 1976: 129–30.

110. Grinsell 1957: 56.

111. Recorded in 1880 as having pillars and *tesserae,* more recent exploration failed to confirm such elegance: Grinsell 1957: 78; Thompson 1971: 71–75; Goddard 1928: 270.

112. Fowler and Walters 1981: 99.

113. Phillips 1981: 46–47.

114. Gaffney and Tingle 1989: 162–64, who note late pottery and an unstratified coin of Eugenius (A.D. 392–394).

115. Hurst, Dartnall, and Fisher 1987: 27–28.

116. At the settlement at Catsgore (Somerset), for example, there was significant construction in the late third and earlier fourth centuries: Leech 1976: 147, 159.

117. P. J. Fowler 1967: 26–33, Site XII on 26–30.

118. Miles 1982: 102; Rees 1979: 486; and M. Jones 1981: 113.

119. Gaffney and Tingle 1989: 241–43.

120. P. J. Fowler 1975a: 123.

121. Branigan 1988: 44.

122. Phillips 1981: 47, who notes the contrast with nearby Russley Park villa, which lies amidst field systems.

123. According to Wild (1982: 116), because of a shift away from a mutton diet, or because sheep are raised for wool rather than mutton and so find less representation among the bone assemblages. A. King (1991: 17–18) suggests that the wealthier inhabitants of villas may have been able to select their diet, thus creating assemblages that would not accurately reflect the economy of the area.

124. Haverfield 1900: 302

125. Cunnington and Goddard 1934: 194, no. 3.459, pl. 62.

126. P. J. Fowler 1967: 28; Gaffney and Tingle 1989: 165–66, figs. 12.4: 49–50, 54, 56.

127. Manning 1966a: 60–62; Wild 1982: 117–18.

128. Grant 1989: 143; *pace* C. C. Taylor 1967: 304–306, who dates many of the so-called late Roman enclosures to after the Roman period.

129. On other possible explanations, public works projects, walls as part of imperial policy directed from abroad, etc., see Arnold 1984: 34–36.

130. Burnham and Wacher 1990: 151–52.

131. Annable 1978a: 127–28, fig. 1, who also mentions a like buckle from North Wraxall

villa, recovered with skeletons interpreted as victims of a late fourth-century assault on the villa. See Poulett-Scope 1862: 59–75; and Böhme 1986: 481, 563, List 1, no. 50a.

132. Branigan 1976: 136–41; 1977a: 93–108; Arnold 1984: 49–50; and Webster 1969: 226–31, who suggests that a significant number of villas in the areas of Hampshire, Dorset, and Wiltshire may have ceased to be occupied before c. A.D. 360.

133. Branigan 1976: 136–41; and 1977a: 93–99.

134. A view supported by Branigan's analysis (1976: 139–40; 1977a: 98–99) of the coin lists from one hundred southwestern villas: only 40% of the villas had as their latest coins issues struck before A.D. 367, while 60% had later issues, with 17% minted between A.D. 395 and 408—and the latest coin present on site hardly equates with the end of occupation. Cp. too, the coin lists from the Shrine of Apollo at Nettleton, where there were 31 coins of Arcadius, 9 of Honorius and 116 of the House of Theodosius: Reece 1982: 112–118. See also Buttrey (chap. 4.7. Fig. 107).

135. E.g., Hucclecote and Ilchester Mead and possibly Whittington, Frocester Court, Chedworth, Barnsley Park, and Gatcombe.

136. The iconography of the mosaic, "Orpheus" with lyre surrounded by female seasons, has been used to attribute an "Orphic" religious function to the chamber: Walters 1983; and Toynbee 1981.

137. The excavators opine that much evidence may have been removed during the reoccupation of the site in the medieval period: Phillips and Walters 1985: 6.

138. Grinsell 1957: 71–72.

139. Phillips 1981: 47.

140. Fowler and Walters 1981.

141. Young 1977; and Fulford 1975b. See, for example, pottery from Maddle Farm and Knighton Bushes (Gaffney and Tingle 1989), or at Castle Copse, where Overwey Ware represents the latest ware (see chap. 4.11).

142. New Forest and Oxford kilns, still producing in the late fourth century, may have continued just into the fifth.

143. Gaffney and Tingle 1989: 111, 240.

144. P. J. Fowler 1975a: 123. Along the edge of the floodplain of the Lechlade area, D. Miles (1989: 126) has documented the disappearance of Romano-British settlements, roughly every kilometer, at a later date, by the middle of the fifth century; drainage systems were filled in, and some land was abandoned and some was converted to pasture.

145. Burnham and Walker 1990: 164; and Chandler 1989: 31.

146. Bowen 1990: 38–41.

147. Hirst and Rahtz 1976; Fowler and Walters 1981: 113. See, too: Fowler 1971: 204 on refortified hillforts in Wessex, where post-Roman refortification is not widespread; Ellison and Rahtz 1987: 72–75, on late/post-Roman occupation (Phases 4–7) at Whitsbury Castle Ditches hillfort in Hampshire, with possible refortifcation in Phase 6 of the sixth or seventh century A.D.; and Burrow 1979 and 1981, on the phenomenon, more common in Somerset and farther west.

148. On the escutcheon: Passmore 1914: 584; E. Fowler 1968: 300; and Fowler and Walters 1981: 113.

149. Burnett 1983: 144–45.

150. Grinsell 1957: 97; M. E. Cunnington 1930: 200, site 135; Colt Hoare 1821: 43.

151. Robertson 1970: 199–200.

152. On other coin hoards from the southwest, see Isaac 1976: 57–58 and Robertson 1970: 199.

153. For a summary of the problem, Millett 1990: 223–24 and Arnold 1984: 48–83.

154. Branigan (1977a: 104–105) cites four villas near Bath, one near Gloucester, and another near Ilchester.

155. Despite the fact that coins issued after A.D. 388 tend to be less common on rural sites: Ryan 1988.

156. Hawkes and Dunning 1961: 45, fig. 13g; Cunliffe 1973: 462. For an amphora-shaped military strap-end of probable late fourth-century date, recovered at Catsgore (Building 3.10), and a second outside the building, see Simpson 1976.

157. Haslam 1980: 60–61.

158. WAR 1978: 132 (Tockenham).

159. Walters and Phillips 1985: 6.

160. Grinsell 1957: 23.

161. E.g., coins of Arcadius and Theodosius II from the Roman well at Silbury: Brooke and Cunnington 1896–97: 167.

162. Fowler and Walters 1981: 91–110.

163. Gaffney and Tingle 1989: 111, 144, 240.

164. P. J. Fowler 1966: 31–37, with list of sites on 36; and 1967: 30; Fowler and Walters 1981: 113–15.

165. Bonney 1973: 483–84 and 1966: 29–30 n. 6. Hurst, Dartnall, and Fisher (1987: 32), considering the question of possible post-Roman continuity for the estate of Box villa, recall L. V. Grinsell's observation that 30% of the Domesday sites in Wiltshire have known Roman antecedents, and that 70% of the villas then known were the foci of Domesday manors.

166. About 17% (twelve) of the Romano-British sites listed in the Sites and Monuments Record (1986) for the concerned areas of Wiltshire, Berkshire, and Hampshire lie directly under, or in exceedingly close proximity to, a Saxon site, while about 33% (twenty-four) Romano-British sites lie less than one kilometer from a Saxon site.

167. Haslam 1980: 55.

168. Grinsell 1957: 83–84.

169. Passmore 1928: 244; and Grinsell 1957: 117–18.

170. Johnson and Walters 1988: 77–83, 89–91; and Blackford 1941.

171. Johnson and Walters 1988: 77, 84–91; M. E. Cunnington 1930: 189–90; and Colt Hoare 1821: 80.

172. Bonney 1966, 1972, and 1977. This notion is further supported by the manner in which the Bedwyn Dyke and the late or post-Roman Wansdyke disregards parish boundaries: Bonney 1972: 174–76.

173. Haslam 1980: 60–64. On the contrasting possibilities of division and agglomeration in the process of estate formation, see Bonney 1977: 50. Regarding the area around Cirencester, R. Reece (1976: 74–75) envisions the "break-up of single (Roman) estates into small units, perhaps interconnected, with appropriate fitting into the spaces left in the power structure as the owners of the farm-houses seem to have declined."

174. In Dorset, Groube and Bowden (1982: 53) put the question of associations between villa estates and early parishes well, suggesting that such "may not indicate an unbroken agricultural tradition but a common attraction to alluvial soil or clay-lands and a common avoidance of the exhausted chalklands. . . . The agricultural strategy initiated in the Roman period of exploiting the richer valley soils and expansion into wetter claylands was continued. . . . The survival of relatively intact early Iron Age field systems on so much of the chalklands is witness to their small arable role in post-Roman agriculture."

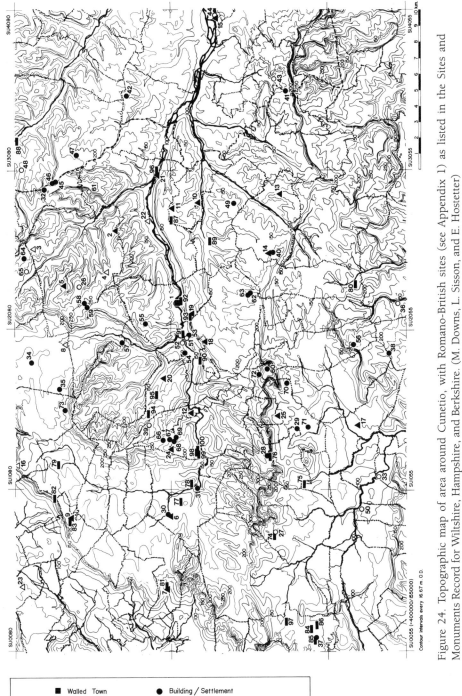

Figure 24. Topographic map of area around Cunetio, with Romano-British sites (see Appendix 1) as listed in the Sites and Monuments Record for Wiltshire, Hampshire, and Berkshire. (M. Downs, L. Sisson, and E. Hostetter)

■ Walled Town   ● Building / Settlement
▲ Villa   O Possible Building / Settlement
△ Possible Villa   ▬ Burial

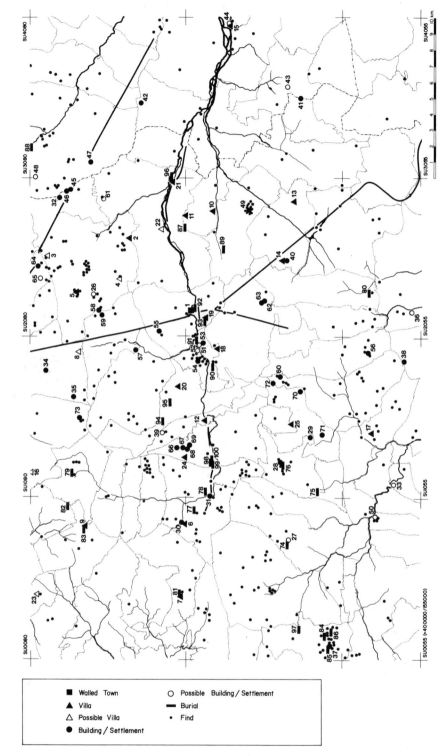

Figure 25. Map of area around Cunetio, with Romano-British sites and finds (see Appendix 1) as listed in the Sites and Monuments Record for Wiltshire, Hampshire, and Berkshire. (M. Downs, L. Sisson, and E. Hostetter)

■ Walled Town
▲ Villa
△ Possible Villa
● Building / Settlement
○ Possible Building / Settlement
▬ Burial
• Find

3.2 VILLA SITING

ERIC HOSTETTER AND LAURA FLUSCHE

The intent of this essay is to offer a brief characterization of the distribution of villa and settlement sites around Cunetio within the somewhat arbitrary thousand square mile area covered by the maps in Figures 24–25.[1] It is assumed that the listing of sites (Appendix 1) is partial, preservation biases favoring the identification of substantial villas as opposed to settlement or farmstead sites, and that masking and destructive factors such as dense vegetation, continuous settlement, soil movement, ploughing, and construction have disguised or altered the landscape. Nor do the maps pretend great accuracy with regard to site location[2] or site identification—such information often being vague—nor yet to completeness, although it is assumed that recently discovered sites will not, in most cases, significantly alter the overall picture. The purpose, however, is only general: to discern broad patterns of settlement and finds distribution. While later finds would certainly add to the lists, most would not significantly alter the patterns described.

Site classification in the Roman period is in many instances vague and based on scanty evidence, not the least so for distinctions between "villas" and "farmsteads."[3] Sites listed as "buildings/settlements" may in certain cases also have been villas, but appear to lack the more obvious signs of luxury. Buildings/settlements may include villages, farmhouses, cottages, huts, and kiln or other industrial sites. Multiple burials and clusters of finds may in some cases be suggestive of a nearby settlement. Further complicating the picture of the region is the fact that the maps represent palimpsests of all recorded (through 1986) Romano-British sites and finds over the entire Roman period, despite the fact that not all sites are contemporaneous and many will have changed morphology.

Number and Density of Sites

Seventy-two habitation sites are recorded for the Roman period: one town, twenty-four villas or possible villas, and forty-eight generally undifferentiated buildings and settlements.[4] Furthermore, twenty-seven Roman period burial sites are known, of which only seven contain a sufficient number of graves to be posited as possible settlements. Of these seven, all are located more than 500 m from an established settlement and therefore cannot be readily associated with known villas or settlements and may therefore reflect nearby unknown settlement.

Altogether, nine burial sites can be directly associated by reason of proximity with established villas or settlements. Expressed in percentages, the rural sites (i.e., excluding

Cunetio) would be: villas 24%; buildings/settlements 48%; and burials 27%. In the area surrounding Cunetio, the limits of which are both distorted and arbitrary,[5] the density of sites is:

Villas	1/41.67 km²
Settlements/Buildings	1/20.83 km²
Villas and Settlements/Buildings	1/13.89 km²

If multiple burials not associated with known settlements—i.e., which may reflect as yet unidentified settlements—are added to the latter figure, the density rises to 1/18.18 km².[6] Along the Kennet Valley, the mean distance between Roman villas is approximately every 5.42 km.[7]

All these figures, however, probably bear little relation to the likely pattern of Roman settlement, which was indubitably more dense, and systematic survey would radically change the picture. For the area southeast of Durocornovium, B. Phillips and B. Walters have proposed a pattern of villas spaced two to three kilometers apart, with homesteads in between.[8]

Drift Geology

Apart from a tendency to locate upon lighter chalk soils, no single geological factor appears to consistently determine the location of villas around Cunetio. Indeed, villa distributions may often be dependent primarily upon their poximity to roads and, as suggested by K. Branigan, upon the siting of urban centers, rather than upon the location of the most favorable soils.[9] Following D. J. Bonney's scheme,[10] the geological location of the villa and settlement sites can be categorized as follows:

CHALK		Villas	Buildings/Settlements
Light Soils	Chalk	9	24
	Valley Gravel on Chalk		
	Plateau Gravel on Chalk		
	Alluvium on Chalk	1	1
	Lower Chalk/Upper Greensand	1	
Heavy Soils	Clay-with-Flints on Chalk	6	11
NON-CHALK			
Light and	Upper Greensand		
Medium Soils	Corallian Limestone	1	
	Upper Greensand	2	3
	Alluvium	1	2
	Alluvium/River Terrace	1	1
	River Terrace	1	4
Heavy Soils	Reading Beds	1	
	London Clay		
	Reading Beds		
	Bagshot Beds		
	Gault		
	Kimmeridge Clay		1
	Bagshot Beds/Plateau Gravel		1

Of the twenty-four villas or possible villas around Cunetio, the majority, seventeen (70.8%), are situated on chalk and seven (29.2%), off chalk on a variety of generally low-lying formations with no single clear preference other than, perhaps, generally lower elevations.[11] Of the forty-eight settlements, thirty-six (75%) are again on chalk. Thus, of the seventy-two villas and buildings/settlements combined, fifty-three (73.6%) lie on clay-with-flints on chalk or on chalk, and eighteen (25%), of which seven are villas and twelve settlements, lie off chalk. Thus, in general, a slight preference for chalk—or perhaps merely a preference for being slightly off valley bottoms—may be present. This propensity concurs with J. C. Richards's appraisal of Roman settlement on the Berkshire Downs, where he suggests, with equal reservations, a slight preference for lighter soils.[12] The density of settlement on valley bottoms, however, may have been much greater than is now apparent.[13]

Elevation

Of the twenty-four villas or possible villas, twelve (50%) are located 150–199 m O.D. and nineteen (79%) 100–199 m O.D. Only one is located 50–99 m O.D. and one above 250 m O.D. The locations of the forty-eight Romano-British buildings and settlements are not markedly different, with 42% falling 150–199 m O.D. and thirty-two (67%) 100–199 m O.D. The breakdown of villa and building/settlement elevations are:

Elevation (m. O.D.)	Villas	Buildings/Settlements
250 +	1 (4%)	4 (8%)
200–249	3 (13%)	12 (25%)
150–199	12 (50%)	20 (42%)
100–149	7 (29%)	12 (25%)
50–99	1 (4%)	0 (0%)

Slight but significant differences exist: 33% of buildings and settlements, as compared with 17% of villas, are located at elevations greater than 200 m O.D., suggesting a slight preference, as has been noted elsewhere,[14] for higher elevations, though no account is taken here of the type of building/settlement occurring at different elevations. Presented otherwise, the elevations are:

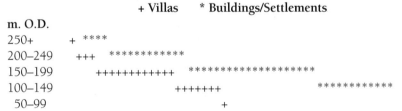

	+ Villas	* Buildings/Settlements
m. O.D.		
250+	+ ****	
200–249	+++ ***********	
150–199	+++++++++++ *******************	
100–149	+++++++ ***********	
50–99	+	

Topography

As the elevations of the villas or possible villas around Cunetio show, slope sites, often overlooking valleys, are preferred. Neither valley bottoms nor hilltops are avoided, though the latter are less common. Following K. Branigan's division,[15] their siting can be described:

Villa Siting	Villas	Percent
Hilltop	4	16.67%
Upper slope	7	29.17%
Lower slope	10	41.67%
Valley bottom	3	12.50%

Or, graphically:

Hilltop	++++
Upper slope	+++++++
Lower slope	+++++++++++
Valley bottom	+++

D. J. Bonney's examination of Roman sites in all of Wiltshire suggests that villas tend not to occupy hilltops, and more frequently to be found on valley slopes and bottoms, with a possible increase of "valley bottom, scarpfoot and lowland sites" in the later Roman period.[16] By contrast, in the Upper Thames Valley, D. Miles suggests that villas are infrequent on lower ground, where more humble farmsteads and settlements are more common.[17]

Proximity to Cunetio

Castle Copse and other regional villas probably functioned in relationship to the administrative and market center of Cunetio, where many of the wealthier individuals who owned villas resided. Several of the villas lying on the outermost edges of the area—e.g., St. James Church (Cherhill), Kennet and Avon Canal (Kintbury), and Tockenham (Tockenham)—may also have functioned in relation to neighboring centers such as Verlucio, Spinis, and Durocornovium.

As the crow flies, the mean distance from villas to Cunetio is 10.10 km, with some villas lying as far from the town as 20 km and others lying merely 1 km away.[18] The falloff for the 24 villas or possible from Cunetio is:

Distance from Cunetio (km)	Villas	Percent	
0–0.99	0	0%	2 villas
1.00–1.99	1	4%	between 0–4.99 km=8.3%
2.00–2.99	1	4%	
3.00–3.99	0	0%	
4.00–4.99	0	0%	
5.00–5.99	5	13%	15 villas
6.00–6.99	2	17%	between 5–9.99 km=62.5%
7.00–7.99	2	8%	
8.00–8.99	2	4%	
9.00–9.99	4	17%	
10.00–10.99	0	0%	3 villas
11.00–11.99	0	0%	between 10–14.99 km=12.5%
12.00–12.99	0	0%	
13.00–13.99	2	8%	
14.00–14.99	1	4%	

15.00–15.99	1	4%	3 villas
16.00–16.99	0	0%	between 15–19.99 km=12.5%
17.00–17.99	1	4%	
18.00–18.99	1	0%	
19.00–19.99	0	0%	
20.00–20.99	1	4%	1 villa
			over 20 km=4.16%

Or: **Villas less than 5 km from Cunetio =** 2 or   8.33%

10	17 or	70.83%
15	20 or	83.33%
20	23 or	95.83%
21	24 or	100%

Were the three outlying villas or possible villas which may fall all or in part within the orbit of Verlucio, Spinis, and Wanborough eliminated, the breakdown would be:

Villas less than 5 km from Cunetio = 2 or   9.52%

10	17 or	80.94%
15	20 or	95.22%
20	21 or	100%

Either way, the most favored range for villas lay between 5 and 10 km from the town (62.5% of the villas). Far fewer (8.33%) lay less than 5 km from town—where there is also less land—and there is a marked fall-off beyond 10 km. Complicating the picture, again, is the lack of differentiation in date between the villas considered, even if the majority are likely to have been in existence around A.D. 300.

These figures roughly coincide with I. Hodder and M. Millet's observations that peak villa density occurs at distances of 8–10 kilometers from high status towns, and that the gradual fall-off of villas around Cunetio suggests that it may have served, for its size and status, a significant variety of administrative and commercial functions.[19] Indeed, falling after Silchester, Verulamium, Colchester, and Dorchester (Dorset), yet before Winchester, the fall-off of villas around Cunetio is more typical of that around cantonal capitals, *coloniae,* and *municipia* than that of small towns, and the evident attraction of the *"ager Cunetionus"* for villas cannot be explained by market forces alone. On the other hand, the average mean distance of villas from Cunetio seems to diverge from M. Gregson's analysis of mean distances of villas from lesser walled towns over time: from c. A.D. 50–99 through c. 350–400, villas stand at a mean distance of c. 16 km or over, which only thereafter diminishes to c. 10 km.[20] The avoidance of the area within c. 6 km of towns may have been the result of farming from within the urban centers; likewise the greater mean distance of villas from cantonal capitals suggests that some may have served as "minor service centres. . . ."[21]

Distance to Roads and Trackways

The accessibility of villas is demonstrated by their proximity to the known and/or assumed route of major established roads.[22] On average, the villas around Cunetio were established 2.81 km from known or assumed major roads (as the crow flies). Eight, or one third, of the villas were located within 1 km of a major road leading to Cunetio.[23] Thus, ease of movement and the transport of products were obviously essential factors in villa site selection. The breakdown of the distances of villas from major roads leading to Cunetio is:

Distance to Major Road (km)	Villas	Percentage
0–0.99	8	33.33%
1.00–1.99	5	21.83%
2.00–2.99	2	8.30%
3.00–3.99	3	12.50%
4.00–4.99	0	0.00%
5.00–5.99	3	12.50%
6.00–6.99	0	0.00%
7.00–7.99	1	4.17%
8.00–8.99	1	4.17%
9.00–9.99	0	0.00%
10.00–10.99	0	0.00%
11.00–11.99	0	0.00%
12.00–12.99	1	4.17%

Thus, it appears that eighteen (75%) of the twenty-four villas or possible villas are located within 4 km of a known or assumed major road, and the distance to a secondary road would probably be considerably less. These distances agree remarkably well with those calculated by K. Branigan for villas in the southwest, where 73% lie within 4 km of a road.[24] The relatively large number—six (25%)—of villas located at distances greater than 5 km from major roads would, in some instances, raise questions about the economic basis—pastoral as opposed to arable?—of villas at greater distance from town. It is not clear that villas lying at greater distances from Cunetio were necessarily farther from major roads.

Efforts to determine the distance from villas to Cunetio via secondary trackways connecting to major roads are limited by lack of knowledge. Still, measuring assumed movement along major roads, paths of significant waterways, and geographical features such as valley bottoms added an average of only 2.47 km to the journey from villa to Cunetio (vs. as the crow flies).

The examination of the distance of Romano-British settlements and buildings to Cunetio and to major roads yields similar results. The average distance to Cunetio from known settlements and buildings is 11.66 km. Thirty-one percent of buildings/settlements are found less than 2 km from a major road, with the average distance to established roads being 4.01 km.

Proximity of Villas to Villas and Other Romano-British Sites

The significance of the proximity or lack of proximity of villas to each other and to other buildings and settlements is difficult to assess without a knowledge of land tenure, in light of varied terrain, and without more reliable chronological data on the contemporaneity of the various sites. With these problems in mind, villas generally appear to be located in fairly close proximity to one another, with the average distance between them being 3.27 km. The breakdown of distances from villa to closest neighboring villa is:

Distance from Villa to Nearest Villa (km)	Villas	Percent
Less than 1.0	0	0. %
1.0–2.0	3	12.50%
2.0–3.0	10	41.66%
3.0–4.0	3	12.50%
4.0–5.0	2	8.00%
5.0–6.0	4	16.67%
6.0–7.0	0	0. %
7.0–8.0	0	0. %
8.0–9.0	0	0. %
9.0–10.0	1	4.00%
10.0–11.0	1	4.00%

Similarly, the average distance between a villa and its closest neighboring building or settlement is 2.68 km. The problem of the relationship between villas neighboring settlements of differing morphology remains, as ever, problematic, particularly when many or even most Roman period sites that could be successive remain undated. Close proximity, as is the case with the settlements, kilns, buildings, and midden surrounding the possible villa at Draycot Farm (Wilcot), or Upper Upham villa (Aldbourne), surrounded by small likely settlements and buildings, would certainly suggest dependent sites and activities. It is, however, proximity rather than morphology that suggests this dependency, because other areas with no apparent villa contain similar settlements (farmstead, "corn-drier," small settlement, building).[25]

Thus, in most respects the villas surrounding Cunetio appear to conform to the general pattern as it is currently known in the southwest. Only the region to the southeast of Cunetio, within which the villa at Castle Copse is located, appears to be an anomaly, as is discussed below (chap. 4.19).

Notes

1. Most of the sites mentioned have not been seen by the authors; the data plotted are based primarily on the databases of the Sites and Monuments Record for the particular portions of the counties of Wiltshire, Berkshire, and Hampshire, through 1986. We are grateful to H. Cave-Penny, D. Hopkins, M. Hughes, P. Robinson, and B. Eagles for their assistance.

2. When many sites and/or finds cluster, it has been necessary to graphically "explode" the groupings on the maps.

3. On problems of settlement hierarchy and analysis, see chapter 3.1, n. 9.

4. This compares with thirty-three total from the Iron Age and thirty-four from the Saxon periods, though such figures may only reflect a strong preservation bias. Expressed in percentages, the proportions are: Iron Age 23.7%, Roman 51%, and Saxon 24.4%.

5. Particularly the northeast, northwest, southeast, and southwest, terrain not in all certainty falling within the territory of Cunetio. If certain outlying sites were eliminated and the area around

Cunetio were considered as a circle rather than extended more east-west along the Kennet Valley, the density would increase.

6. Not unexpectedly, both Iron and Saxon period settlements are considerably less frequent. In the Iron Age sites occur as: hillforts (13) 1/76.92 km²; settlements (20) 1/50.00 km²; and hillforts and settlements (33) 1/33.30 km². The thirty-four early Saxon sites, excluding the centers of Ramsbury and Lambourn, occur 1/29.41 km².

7. C. Young (1986: 60) notes that, on the Thames gravels to the west of Dorchester, "settlements are space at intervals of one to one-and-a-half kilometers . . ."; and over the whole of the civil zone, M. Gregson (1988: 33) has suggested a density of 0.25 villas per km².

8. Phillips and Walters 1981: 46.

9. Branigan 1985: 101.

10. Bonney 1968: 32.

11. For Wiltshire, by contrast, D. J. Bonney (1968: 32) concludes: "The bulk of the known Iron Age settlement sites is restricted to the Chalk while over one-third of all the Romano-British sites lie off it. . . . Villas and other substantial buildings, which clearly indicated a measure of Roman influence on the settlement, are far more numerous off the Chalk than on it. On the Chalk, the majority of Romano-British settlements are in the native tradition and many of them are on sites occupied during, and sometimes continuously since, the Iron Age."

12. J. C. Richards 1978: 49.

13. On the masking and destruction of valley-bottom settlements, whether Iron Age or Roman, see Bowen and Fowler 1966: 62.

14. Branigan 1977a: 29–30; and Bonney 1968: 33.

15. Branigan 1977a: 24–25; and 1976: 120–22.

16. Bonney 1968: 36.

17. Miles 1988: 65.

18. These figures are only approximate, due to the lack of locational accuracy for some sites.

19. Hodder and Millet 1980: 69–76. Gregson (1988: 24), however, suggests that a more gradual fall-off away from "high status" towns may indicate a "preference for siting villas away from urban influence." For a discussion of both, see Millett 1990: 189–97.

20. Gregson 1988: 31, fig. 3.3.

21. Gregson 1988: 32. See, too, Reece 1976: 66, on the difficulty of identifying what land belonged to walled Roman towns.

22. It is readily acknowledged that several sections of major roads are not certainly identified, and that specific individual distances from villa/settlement/building-to-road may err slightly.

23. Again, such figures will be inflated by those villas, buildings, and settlements lying on the outermost edges of the area under consideration, which may also or primarily have interacted with neighboring towns or secondary rural markets.

24. Branigan 1977a: 25–27.

25. On the problem, see Hingley 1989: 24, 103–110.

CHAPTER 4

The Romano-British Villa at Castle Copse, Great Bedwyn

4.1 SITING

ERIC HOSTETTER

The geological and topographical setting and the hydrological resources of the region in which the villa is located are described by D. Keefer (chap. 1), who emphasizes the natural advantages of the villa's position, its strategic location with respect to defense and transportation, its situation close to a rich variety of soils, and the site's potential for water supply.

Somewhat unusual is the villa's hilltop location, a position occupied by relatively few villas in the southwest. Although it is doubtful whether defense was a consideration in the choice of the villa's location, the site nevertheless dominates the primary passage to the southwest along the valley of the Bedwyn Brook (Figs. 2, 5–6, 11). The villa was, however, built across the Bedwyn Valley from Chisbury hillfort, whose builders clearly were concerned with defense. If a native settlement preceded the villa, then the latter's strategic location may be owed to Bedwyn Brail's earlier inhabitants—even if the hillfort was no longer occupied—and to the site's excellent water supply. This notion may be further supported by the manner in which Walbury hillfort, to the east, controls the divide east of the Vale of Shalbourne, and Fosbury hillfort, to the south, dominates the southern approach to the western divide (see chap. 1).

The villa is also advantageously located in relation to the regional and local road systems (see chap. 3.2) (Figs. 2, 25). A secondary road or trackway almost certainly ran along the Bedwyn Brook (Fig. 6)—still today the route of the Cornwall Express and the Kennet and Avon Canal—and would have joined the trunk road between Cunetio and Venta Belgarum, less than two kilometers from the villa itself.

4.2 TOPOGRAPHY, GEOLOGY, AND HYDROLOGY OF THE VILLA

DAVID K. KEEFER

The purposes of this section are to describe the topography, geology, and hydrology of the villa site itself and to discuss possible effects of these environmental characteristics on the construction and development of the villa complex.[1]

Topography and Vegetation

The villa complex is on Bedwyn Brail, an elongated ridge approximately 55 m high, 3.5 km long, and 1 km wide (Fig. 7a-b). This ridge is crescent-shaped in plan view, concave to the west, and its long axis trends north-to-northeast. The north flank of Bedwyn Brail slopes down into the valley of Bedwyn Brook, and the south flank slopes down into the Vale of Pewsey.

A gentle swale, 1 km north of the southern margin of Bedwyn Brail, separates a round, southern knob from the main part of the ridge and provides gently sloping access to the crest. The villa complex is on the broad, rounded crest of the main part of the ridge, 1.2 km north of the swale, at an elevation of 162 m above O.D. The highest point on Bedwyn Brail has an elevation 170–75 m O.D. and is 0.9 km south of the villa complex. The ridge flanks slope moderately, with inclinations of 5–20%, and are incised by small channels, typically less than 5 m deep, containing ephemeral streams.

Except where land has been recently cleared, as around the villa complex, the main, northern part of Bedwyn Brail supports a dense forest with thick undergrowth. In forest clearings ferns, nettles, and dock weed are abundant. The southern knob and lower flanks of the ridge are currently cultivated for grain.

Geologic Materials and Features

The distribution of bedrock, Quaternary deposits, and other geological features is shown in Figures 7b, 10 and 12. Geologic features and contacts between different materials in Figure 7b were located in the field using pace-and-compass traverses and plotted on the Ordnance Survey Sheet SU 26 SE, 1:10,000 scale, topographic map. Because bedrock is not exposed anywhere on Bedwyn Brail, except in pits and other excavations, geologic contacts were inferred primarily from changes in soil character and topography. Because of the inaccuracies involved in pace-and-compass traverses in densely wooded terrain, the uncertainties in location of individual features shown in Figure 7b are estimated to be as much as 100 m. Features other than contacts between different materials are shown only where encountered during the traverses; many other similar features may also be present, hidden by the dense vegetation. In particular, earthwork embankments were not traced systematically through the forest.

BEDROCK MATERIALS AND SOILS

The two types of bedrock underlying Bedwyn Brail are Chalk and Reading Beds-London Clay.[2] The Chalk underlies the lower slopes of the main, north part of Bedwyn Brail, the southern knob, and the valleys surrounding the ridge. This unit consists of a soft, white, uniform, microporous limestone containing flints and minor bands of clay; the limestone is 97–98% pure calcium carbonate throughout most of its volume.[3] This bedrock unit is part of the main aquifer, or source of ground water, for northeast Wiltshire and adjacent regions. Regional maps separate the Chalk into three units—Upper, Middle, and Lower Chalk (see Chapter 1)—but local evidence for making this distinction was not found during the field survey. The limestone making up the Chalk is dissolved by contact with percolating subsurface water, and the contact between the Chalk and overlying materials is thus typically irregular and characterized by filled depressions and sinkholes.

Soils developed on the Chalk normally consist of residue from the 2–3% of insoluble impurities (primarily flints and clay), mixed with pieces of unweathered limestone rubble, windblown silt and sand, and sediment transported downslope from overlying formations by water or slope-movement processes. On and adjacent to Bedwyn Brail, Chalk soil consists of very dark grey, crumbly and moderately plastic, sandy, clayey silt containing coarse pieces of unweathered limestone and flint, some of which are larger than 25 cm in diameter. On the slopes of Bedwyn Brail, this soil is typically only a few centimeters thick, but pits in the swale between the main part of the ridge and the southern knob expose soil as thick as 2.4 m.

The upper slopes and crest of Bedwyn Brail north of the swale, including the site of the villa complex itself, are underlain by sediments of the Reading Beds and London Clay. These sediments consist of soft, poorly consolidated clays, silts, sands, and gravels. These materials typically occur in layers and lenses a few centimeters to a few meters thick, exhibiting significant lateral variations in composition over short distances. Three stratigraphic sections of these sediments near the villa complex were described above in Figs. 16-18. On Bedwyn Brail and elsewhere, these sediments hold local bodies of groundwater "perched" on top of impermeable clays. This perched groundwater produces many springs, ponds, marshes, and ephemeral streams on the ridge (Fig. 7b).

Except in pits and excavations, the Reading Beds and London Clays on Bedwyn Brail are everywhere covered by soil. This soil consists predominantly of silts and very fine-grained sands, which contain variable amounts of clay and 5–10%, by volume, egg-shaped flint pebbles as large as 5 cm in diameter. These pebbles are concentrated on the ground surface and in channels of ephemeral streams, probably owing to selective removal of finer material by erosion. The soil matrix is generally mottled; colors are most commonly shades of brown, but are occasionally brownish yellow, yellowish red, or reddish yellow. Consistency of soil ranges from nonplastic to moderately plastic, and the soil is typically crumbly when dry and moderately soft and structureless when wet. This soil was presumably formed by in situ weathering, accompanied by local downslope transport of materials by such processes as soil creep, overland flow, and flow of ephemeral streams. Because systematic variations in soil properties or other features that would allow differentiation of the Reading Beds from the London Clay could not be mapped during field studies, Figure 7b shows these materials as "Reading Beds-London Clay-undifferentiated."

The Chalk, Reading Beds, and London Clay have all been folded subsequent to deposition (Figs. 15, 19). The main fold structures in the region around Bedwyn Brail have axes that trend east-southeast. The axis of a downwarp, or syncline, passes through Bedwyn Brail approximately 0.5 km north of the villa complex. Bedding in the Chalk, Reading Beds, and London Clay under most of the ridge, which is south of this axis, thus dips generally north-northwest. Because of the northward dip, perched groundwater in the Reading Beds and London Clay probably flows primarily northward from the highest part of the ridge toward the villa complex.

QUATERNARY DEPOSITS

Quaternary deposits on Bedwyn Brail include artificial fill and landslide deposits (Fig. 7b). Artificial fill denotes the presumed archaeological material in and around the villa complex excavation. The smaller landslide deposit is on the eastern flank of the ridge, and the larger is on the western flank, downslope from the villa complex.

The landslide deposits are characterized by irregular, hummocky surfaces and probably formed originally no more than a few thousand years ago. Features in the southern part of the larger deposit appear relatively fresh and unmodified by erosion. Intermittent, slow (a few millimeters to centimeters a day) movement of the landslide material could be continuing at present and could have been occurring also at the time the villa was inhabited. The landslide does not encroach on the villa complex itself, but slope material upslope from large landslides are typically susceptible to cracking, settlement, and downslope creep. A ditch and embankment that follow the upslope margin of the landslide deposit are undisturbed, indicating both that the landslide originally formed prior to the date of ditch-and-embankment construction and that significant upslope encroachment of the landslide has not occurred since construction.

OTHER FEATURES

Other features include terraces, pits, sinkholes, earthwork embankments, springs, marshes, and ponds (Fig. 7a-b). Terraces are anomalously flattened areas on the ridge flanks, typically rectangular and a few to tens of meters on a side; they were probably of human construction, and are possibly the remnants of field systems. Pits are also human-made, presumably the remains of small local excavations. Sinkholes are natural depressions in the ground surface, formed by dissolution of the Chalk limestone by water infiltrating the ground. They occur along the channels of ephemeral streams on and near the contact between the Chalk and Reading Beds-London Clay sediments.

Other human-made features on Bedwyn Brail include earthwork embankments. Some of these dam springs and ponds; such embankments are as high as 3 m. Longer embankments, with parallel and adjacent ditches, are as high as 1 m. Both types of embankments have rounded crests and gently-to-moderately sloping flanks. Embankments are abundant on Bedwyn Brail, but a systematic survey of their locations was beyond the scope of the present study.

Bedwyn Brail contains many springs, ponds, and areas of marshy ground, which evidence groundwater levels at or near the ground surface (Figs. 7b, 19). These features were observed up to an elevation of 170 m, near the highest point on the ridge and 8 m higher in elevation than the villa complex. Springs occur on all flanks of the ridge, and at least two springs and one pond are present within 100 m of the villa complex. Damming of several springs by embankments of human construction indicates that they were used for water supply at some time in the past.

Springs on Bedwyn Brail typically feed ephemeral streams. Several springs were seeping or flowing during both the 1983 and 1985 field seasons, but streams were flowing only during the 1985 season, when rainfall was exceptionally high. Observations by G. Gould, former gamekeeper of Bedwyn Brail, suggest that many of the springs flow in all but the driest conditions.

Hydrology, Water Supply and Foundation Conditions

As described above, (chapter 1) the bedrock comprising Bedwyn Brail contains two groundwater systems, a deep system in the Chalk (and underlying Upper Greensand) and a shallower and more accessible system in the Reading Beds and London Clay (Fig. 19). The deeper Chalk-Upper Greensand system is far more extensive, but the water table in this system is approximately 40 m deep beneath the villa complex and probably was little, if any, higher when the villa complex was inhabited. Thus, water from this system was probably not directly accessible to the villa complex itself. This system, however, does feed year-round springs at Wilton Water, 2–3.5 km southwest of the villa complex. Water could have been transported from these springs to the villa complex, but such water transport probably would not have been necessary if shallower groundwater, present in the Reading Beds and London Clay, was exploited.

This shallower, perched groundwater is present because clays within the Reading Beds and London Clay retard downward percolation of water, while the sands within these sediments are much more permeable to groundwater flow. Thus, water from precipitation onto Bedwyn Brail that infiltrates into the Reading Beds and London Clay flows predominantly northward, parallel to the bedding.

In and around the villa complex, several features indicate that the water table is at or near the surface. In particular, groundwater was encountered at a depth of 40–50 cm in the villa complex excavation during the 1985 season; a pond is present less than 100 m east of the villa; and a spring is present 70 m north of the villa. Thus, shallow wells within the villa complex itself could probably have provided water for the inhabitants.

The quantity of water available from the Reading Beds and London Clay is much less than from the deeper Chalk-Upper Greensand system. Nevertheless, the available shallow supply would almost certainly have been adequate for a rural estate, under most conditions. One estimate of groundwater availability near the villa complex was provided by measurements of flow from a group of springs 70–200 m north of the villa complex. The measurements were made on June 19, 1985, after several days of heavy rain, and are thus representative of wet conditions. The average measured flow was 14,300 l/day.

Merely for comparison, the average modern, domestic water use in the United States is 75–300 l/day per capita,[4] and at these rates, the spring could supply water for 48–190 people.

Another, more general estimate of groundwater availability can be made from the potential volume of groundwater in storage and potential groundwater recharge in the Reading Beds-London Clay sediments on Bedwyn Brail. The catchment area for this shallow groundwater upslope from the villa complex is approximately 24 hectares. Assuming that the average Reading Beds-London Clay thickness is 12 m (Figs. 15, 19), that 40% of these sediments are sands (Figs. 16, 18), and that the average porosity, or specific yield, of the sands is 35%,[5] the potential total ground-water storage is 400 million liters. With the average annual precipitation of 700–1,000 mm (see above), total annual recharge of this groundwater is probably several tens of millions of liters. Assuming a per capita domestic consumption of 300 l/day (110,000 l/year), 10 million l/year of recharge would provide for approximately ninety people. Thus, the estimated annual recharge could supply water for several hundred people (or for fewer people, with supply for livestock and other nondomestic water uses), and the potential storage is several times the annual recharge, providing a substantial reserve.

In addition to providing a local water supply, however, the soft Reading Beds-London Clay sediments and near-surface water table under the villa complex would have made foundation conditions soft, wet, poorly drained, and, possibly, locally unstable. Owing to the clays within the sediments, the ground in and around the villa complex is poorly drained, and during rainy periods surficial soils are soft, wet, and locally flooded. These conditions may have led to the placement of a pebble fill in the courtyard area of the villa. Such a fill, composed of egg-shaped flint pebbles common in the soil on Bedwyn Brail, would have provided excellent drainage and a dry pavement for the courtyard.

In addition, the soft, wet clays under the villa complex would probably have locally compressed and settled from the weight of heavy buildings. Because parts of the villa complex encroach on the ridge flank upslope from a large landslide, small and localized downslope movements may also have occurred under parts of the foundation. One potential response to such conditions would have been to place relatively substantial foundation elements, such as the large sarsen found in Sector C and others found elsewhere in the excavation (Fig. 37), under parts of the complex.

NOTES

1. This section is based on field surveys conducted from 24 July 1983 through 5 August 1983, and from 9 June 1985 through 21 June 1985 and on data from published geologic maps and other literature: H. White 1907; Jukes-Browne 1908; IGS 1947 and 1975; Barron 1976; IGS and TWA 1978.

2. Regional characteristics of these geologic units are discussed in more detail in chapter 1.

3. Limbrey 1975; and Barron 1976.

4. Leopold 1974: 134.

5. Davis and Deweist 1966: 375; and Peck, Hanson, and Thornburn 1974: 13.

4.3 STRATIGRAPHY

THOMAS NOBLE HOWE AND ERIC HOSTETTER

Introduction

Excavation of the villa (see Appendix 2) began in 1983, when Sector A was opened as a 20 x 20 m square on the site of W. C. Lukis's presumed excavations and the apparent north edge of the platform (Fig. 9). In 1984 Sector A was expanded with four more five-meter squares at the southwest corner, and Sectors B and C were laid out as 5 x 25 m strips to transect the presumed west and south wings of the villa respectively. Sector B was subsequently widened by four five-meter squares on its north side.

In 1985 excavation continued in all three sectors, C being narrowed to a 1 x 25 m strip, while Sector D was opened on the site of Pole's excavations. C was carried down onto and into the natural clay soils, while Sector D was investigated down to the top of undisturbed Roman layers. Both trenches were then backfilled.

In 1986 Sector A was reduced in extent to more or less the north half of the sector to approximately the N 515 line; the remaining area was carried down to natural. A small amount of further work was carried out on Sector B to complete the investigation to the top of Roman levels, and then both sectors were completely backfilled.

Other major operations during the four-year project included a preliminary resistivity survey in the summer of 1984 and an attempt to produce a full resistivity survey map of the open site and meadow in March of 1985 (Fig. 87). In the summer of 1985 a series of ten 1 x 2 m evaluation trenches was sunk on various parts of the site, in order to test the results of two resistivity surveys that suggested the limits of the main villa and the presence of outbuildings (Appendix 4).

In 1986 a 1 x 10 m trench was laid outside the wall of the close of the parish church of Great Bedwyn to evaluate premedieval levels, of which none were found.

Various field and geological surveys were carried out in all four summers, and in 1987 further study was carried out on regional boundaries. In addition, four members of the team conducted a winter-time field survey of both brails in March 1985.

Sector A: The Villa North Wing

Sector A was excavated down to natural over most of its area. In the last season of excavation, the area of the lower layers of excavation was reduced (cf. Figs. 32–33).

Phase

   I Beam-slot buildings, earliest ditch
       c. A.D. 50–70, through late second century (by pottery)
   II Terrace Gravel Dump
       Mid/late second century, possibly early third (by pottery)
  III Smaller Posthole Alignment, Phase I; Stakeholes?
       Late second–early third century
  IV Smaller Posthole Alignment, Phase II
       Late second–early third century
   V Larger Posthole Structures, Phase I
       Post A.D. 198 (coin)
  VI Larger Posthole Structures, Phase II
       Late second–early third century
 VII Construction of Aisled Building I
       Mid-third century (pottery)
VIII Occupation of Aisled Building I
       Mid-/later third century (pottery)
  IX Construction of Aisled Building II
       Later third/early fourth century (pottery)
   X Aisled Building II as Open Area
       Early fourth century through post–A.D. 330 (coin)
  XI Subdivision of Aisled Building II, habitation as luxury apartments and service;
       second phase of hypocaust backfill and redecoration
       After A.D. 330–31 A.D. (coin in Phase X), backfilling and second phase of deco-
       ration A.D. 340s or later, continuing in use to late fourth/early fifth century
       (approximately datable coins, pottery)
 X/XI Exterior of Aisled Building II
       Fourth century through A.D. 375 or later (coins), contemporary with X or XI
XI/XII Corridor (Unification of Aisled and Exterior Buildings)
       Early fourth century, extended post–A.D. 330–331, in use A.D. 353–360 or later,
       contemporary with later X or XI
 XIII Decay, Abandonment, Robbing
       Early fifth century and later (post–A.D. 388–402, coin)
 XIV Drainage Ditch
       Possibly eighteenth century (reference)
  XV Antiquarian/Modern
       Nineteenth/twentieth centuries

PHASE A:I: DITCH, BEAMSLOTS, POSTHOLES (FIGS. 33, 43–45, 63)

The earliest features cut into the natural clay soils on the site are a V-shaped ditch
(cut/fill A970=972/965=966–69=971); a series of beamslots belonging to a single structure (cut/fill: A803=882/802=881, A616/615, A667/666, A848/847, A817/816,

A933/932, A946/947); a scatter of postholes (cut/fill: A866/865, A804/653, A813/812, A815/814, A533/532, A513/512, A545/544, A494/493, A496/495, A507/506, A953/948, A945/944, A943/942); and possibly a linear cluster of stakeholes (considered under Phases A:III, IV). These features have no stratigraphic relationship to each other apart from some of the postholes having cut beamslot fills. All of these features are sealed by the gravel dump of Phase II.

The beamslots were visible as discolorations in the soil, and upon excavation the fills (A653, 666, 816, 847, 932, 946) yielded significant amounts of clean, high quality, carbonized barley seeds. These and the form suggest the identification of the building as a granary. Compacted surfaces to the north of the beamslots may distinguish the outside of the building from the uncompacted areas under the building (see chap. 4.4).

Date: The phase is well dated by substantial amounts of pottery in the ditch fills (A965, 966, 967, 968, 969). These contexts contained early Oare and Savernake wares, other Belgic wares, and some Terra Nigra dating to about A.D. 50–70. A single sherd of Highgate poppyhead beaker, which may be intrusive, raises the date of the deposit to A.D. 90. One of the postholes (fill A865), which cuts a beamslot, contained a Nauheim derivative fibula dating to the first century A.D. (**104**).

The date, the nature of most of the material, and the form of the ditch are identical to the ditch in Sector C (cut C59) and argue that the ditches in the two sectors are contemporary and part of the same habitation.

PHASE A:II: TERRACE GRAVEL DUMP

A 0.10–0.20 m-thick layer of dark brown redeposited gravel was found over all parts of the sector and is interpreted as part of a deliberate grading operation that may have covered the entire villa platform (see chap. 4.4). It was most clearly identified in Sector A where it survived as several islands cut by later structures.

Date: Pottery deposits, which are primarily Savernake wares and include South Gaulish "samian" (*terra sigillata* or red-slipped ware), and residual sherds of Oare and Silchester flint-tempered, indicate a date in the second half of the second or early third century A.D. The mid-third century is represented by Rhenish and New Forest sherds. The early pottery in the group tends to be highly abraded. The later pottery could easily have been deposited during the surface's use, since it remained an unsealed working surface for some half century or more.

PHASES A:III AND A:IV: SMALL POSTHOLE ALIGNMENTS, STAKEHOLES? (FIGS. 32–33, 43, 64)

The first structure cut into the terrace gravel is a line of postholes that probably ran across the entire width of the sector; those in the eastern end are truncated or removed by the later hypocaust of the Aisled Building II. This ought to be the structure for which the terrace gravel was laid.

The postholes are in two phases: postholes of the first phase were generally packed with flint (cut/fill: A540B/539B; A482/483; A525/524; A454/453; A450/451; A519/518; A515/514) and those of the second phase with greensand (cut/fill: A540A/539A; A478/477; A442/441; A448/447; A444/443; A446/445; A517/516; A511/510; A531/530; A527/526; A490/489). One of the later postholes cut the fill of one of the early ones, showing that the later posts were replacements for the earlier ones. The later posts were placed between the earlier ones and slightly farther south (Figs. 32, 42). The postholes showed no signs of post-pipes, the fill having slumped into the bottoms, implying that they were deliberately withdrawn. The postholes were about 0.60 m in diameter, but some preserved the impression of a timber c. 0.25 m².

A shallow, square-bottomed ditch (A363=536, under the later Mosaic Corridor, from 360/511 to 363/513) may be from these phases, although it could be from as late as A:X/XI.

The dense linear concentration of stakeholes was detected only after the removal of the terrace gravel (and so would appear to belong to Phase A:I), but the stakeholes prob-ably belong to these phases. Their fill would have been indistinguishable from the matrix of the gravel. They clearly postdate the ditch of Phase A:I, since several of them cut the bottom of that ditch as well as its fill. The reason for placing them here is architectural: they are adjacent and parallel to the small posthole alignments and not to the Phase A:I ditch or beamslots. Another group of eleven stakeholes (A547A–K) running north–south (Fig. 32; 357/518 to 358/520) may also be part of these phases and of this structure, or they may belong to the next (A:V–VI).

Date: No datable pottery or artifacts were recovered from the postholes. The date is probably late second/early third century, like the terrace gravel.

PHASES A:V, A:VI: LARGER POSTHOLE STRUCTURES (FIGS. 32–33, 42–43, 65)

The first phase of larger postholes (Phase A:V) consists of three large postholes (cut/fill: A474/473; A476/475; A471/433) running approximately east-west (from 356/519 to 359-519; Figs. 32–33) and two others approximately 1 m to the south (cut/fill: A480/479; A485/484) appear, by similarity of size, shape, and character of fill, to be one phase. Posthole A474/473 cuts one of the stakeholes of Phase:IV (A540B) establishing that the large posthole structures were built after the small posthole structures were removed.

The second phase (A:VI) is marked by two postholes (cut/fill: A470/469; A472/457) on the northern line that cut the fills of the two eastern postholes (A476/475; A471/433), again implying a replacement. The alignment of these postholes over this very short section appears to be almost due east-west, or about 30° counter-clockwise of the smaller posthole alignments. The two postholes of Phase A:VI preserved the impres-sion of circular-section timbers c. 0.30 m D.

Date: A plated denarius of Septimius Severus (**29**, post–A.D. 198) was found in the fill of a posthole of A474/473:V, giving a *terminus post quem* for the removal of the post and Phase A:VI. A small amount of pottery was recovered from the postholes of both phases and generally gives a date of later second or early third century A.D.

PHASES A:VII, A:VIII: CONSTRUCTION AND OCCUPATION OF AISLED BUILDING I (FIGS. 32, 47, 66)

The first aisled building is the first clearly attested masonry building in the sector, although some earlier contexts do contain small amounts of tile, implying the earlier presence somewhere on the site of partial masonry or at least tile-roofed timber build-ings.[1] The southwest corner of the first aisled building (A466/393B) cuts the fill of one of the pits of Phase A:VI (A470/469).

The preserved features of Aisled Building I are the west wall (cut in two sections by the eighteenth-century ditch: A537=500=460=397 to the north and A466=393B to the south), the north wall (cut by ditch A92), and two rows of holes for "stylobates" for timber columns. A thin layer of coarse *opus signinum* lay up against the outside of the south wall (A395=396).

The lowest interior floor (Phase A:VIII) was a layer of orange clay c. 0.10–0.12 m-thick (A614=542=915=876=877=957=920), recognized almost everywhere in isolated islands within the putative area of Aisled Building I. Certain contexts (A542) were fairly rich in pottery. Above this was laid a second surface of dark, compacted pebbly gravel and clay-silt (A574=522=439=874=875=954). A clay-lined bowl furnace (A502) was cut into this surface (at c. 362/523–25) and was surrounded by soft black ash and large pieces of charcoal and burnt daub. This furnace was in turn cut by a large pit (cut/fill: A458/431).

Outside the building (in 5-m grid 355/515), a pebbly silt surface (A439) developed over the earlier postholes during this phase.

Date: Most of the pottery from the floors is later second-century and is residual, but the forms of Black Burnished Ware bowls indicate a third-century date. The coin of Septimius Severus (**29**, post–A.D. 198) gives a *terminus post quem*. Hence, the first masonry structures, at least in this sector, were probably built in the middle of the third century A.D. The date is refined by the arrival, during Phase A:VIII, of wares typical of the mid-third century.

PHASES A:IX, A:X: CONSTRUCTION OF AISLED BUILDING II AND OCCUPATION AS OPEN AREA (FIGS. 31-32, 41-42, 67)

Aisled Building I was razed to the tops of its foundations and replaced by a building of almost identical dimensions, with some minor changes in technique. The second aisled building shares the same orientation as the first, but was moved almost 5 m east and 4 m south, so that there was no reuse of foundations. This might seem to imply that there was a period of time between the destruction of Aisled Building I and the construction of Aisled Building II, the first aisled building being invisible when the second was built, but the stratigraphy does not support this; the construction of Aisled Building II seems to have followed immediately upon the destruction of its predecessor.

The entire course of the west wall and a large section of the north and south walls can be traced within the sector, as robbing trenches, truncated foundation cuts with traces of the greensand footing, or, in the case of the north wall, the entire wall to above floor level. The column footings were in various states of preservation, from partially robbed to fully preserved. The original construction also may have included two short spur walls connecting the outer walls with the second column from the west on the north and south (A381 on the north and robber trench A180, fill A166 on the south). The north spur wall was not clearly bonded with the north wall but seems to have been built immediately afterward, as it overlies the third column base from the west and is apparently sealed by a chalk floor (A646). Aisled Building II was, therefore, originally an open area with two short spur walls in the aisles originally or shortly afterward.

The first floor of Aisled Building II was a deep deposit of clean chalk (A897=940= 896=939=760), which was patched with chalk and mortar only a few times before the process of subdivision and conversion of the building began. These floors were laid

directly over the stylobate pits of Aisled Building I, and the rotting of the sawed-off timbers caused subsidence quite early and were patched in this phase. This subsidence, plus
the fact that the north wall was founded in part on the stylobate pits, caused major structural problems in Phase A:XI (Fig. 57).

Date: Pottery associated with the construction and initial floors indicates a date
from the later third to early fourth century. A coin of Constantius II (**55**, A.D. 330–31) in
a mortar floor patch (A575) moves the date of continued use toward mid-century.

PHASE A:XI: SUBDIVISION AND OCCUPATION OF AISLED BUILDING II (FIGS. 31–32, 41, 68–70)

The sequence of events in the south aisle, and perhaps for the entire phase, begins with
the complete demolition of the south wall and its reconstruction about 0.5 m farther
south, with its footing laid in the ditch (cuts A328, 339) that had been cut against the
exterior face of the first south wall. The footing was a crude deposit of reused Pennant
stone rooftiles (some with nails still in them) and a deep bed of poor mortar. Nothing
was preserved of the upper wall (material was preserved only as remains in robbing
trench A76=124 cut into the fills A287=327 of ditch A328=339). Approximately the
same sequence is noticeable and better preserved at the north wall, with the difference
that here the entire wall was not removed but apparently only buttressed, since part of
the north wall I is still preserved to above floor level. Again, a footing of Pennant sandstone rooftiles and poor mortar (A156, 159, 89, 88) was laid in a cut in the fill of ditch
A92; some of the mortared flint rubble of the wall was preserved. This material both
sealed part of the wall and was laid up against part of its face. The north wall clearly
needed to be buttressed, since one edge of it had been laid on the footings of the Aisled
Building I columns and was tipping into the ditch (Fig. 57; see chap. 4.4). The technique of the replacement and bracing of the north and south walls seems to be the same,
but, because there is no stratigraphic relationship, they are only notionally contemporary
operations. Only the moving of the south wall has a stratigraphic relationship with the
subdivision operations.

In the south aisle (Rooms 1 and 2), the floor was lowered about 0.4 m for the insertion of pila hypocausts, and in the west room of the nave (Room 3), a channel hypocaust
was inserted. In the south aisle, the south wall was robbed out to the bottom course of
its greensand footings before the construction of the hypocausts and dividing walls. The
robbing trench was filled, and the whole surface was covered with a thin intermittent
layer of mortar (possibly only construction debris); over this a 0.10 m-thick chalk floor
was laid, which served as the floor of the pila hypocausts. Rooms 1 and 2 and their
hypocausts may have been either one room or two; the spur wall between Rooms 1 and
2 blocking the south aisle, built presumably in the previous phase, creating rooms open
to the nave, is indicated by a robbing cut (A166:X). The wall was clearly robbed out
before the hypocausts were backfilled (in later Phase A:XI), but it may still have been
standing when the hypocausts were inserted. A long, arcing cut (A161) passes under
Room 3 and must have served as the main feeder flue for the hypocausts in Rooms 1, 2,
and 3. Since it forks over the second stylobate pit in the south row, that column must
have been removed when this hypocaust was in use (see chap. 4.4).

There apparently was no wall blocking the two intercolumniations between Rooms

1 and 3. The cut itself was never revetted. If there was a wall separating Room 1 from Room 3, it would have had to have been on top of the cut to the north, therefore standing proud of the columns rather than between them. Therefore, it is possible that there was no wall, as well as no column, here, and that Rooms 1 and 3 were a single heated chamber the two parts of which were heated by two forms of hypocaust (see chap. 4.4). There were clear traces of a wall (A425) separating Room 4 from Room 2.

It is not clear when the Mosaic Corridor was attached. The foundation cut for its west wall abuts the first south wall of Aisled Building II; therefore, its first phase may be contemporary with later A:X, i.e., with Aisled Building II as an open area. The extension of that corridor to the west and the subdivision and insertion of the hypocaust in the Greensand Quoin Building may be contemporary with the rebuilding of the south wall (A:XI), but this conjecture is based on architectural reasoning, since the crucial stratigraphy was cut away here by the eighteenth-century ditch.

Both hypocausts (in Rooms 3 and 1–2) subsequently went out of use. In the south aisle the small blocking wall was robbed (cut A166); its robbing was sealed by a small crucible pit (cut A151, fill A149); and the entire hypocaust was filled with mortary rubble (A69). In the east end of the nave the channel hypocaust was filled (A261=276=315=336) and a plain checkerboard mosaic (A48=63=70, 6) was laid over a mortar and chalk bedding (A315=324=329) (A65=67=68=71=72=109). There was no indication of the nature of the floor in the filled-in south aisle, nor was there an indication of the latest activity in these rooms, because these were the two areas most thoroughly destroyed by Lukis in 1853 and 1854. Finds in the fills of these hypocausts provided a large bulk of the wall painting and mosaics; some of it may represent the decoration of the early part of Phase A:XI (see chaps. 4.5 and 4.6).

The stratigraphy in the east room of the nave (Room 4) is completely isolated from the other rooms. It consists of an accumulation of some 116 identifiable floors or floor patches, in which layers of burning alternate with mortar or chalk floors or patches that built up to a depth of about 0.25 m. The sequence begins immediately after the construction of the dividing wall in the nave (A552, between Rooms 3 and 4, built shortly after the insertion of the hypocaust in Room 3) and the laying of one more floor shared by Room 4 and the north aisle (A549) before these are separated by walls A423 and A424. The sequence continues without change of character until two final mortar and chalk floors (A129, 10) re-cover the whole room; these are then immediately sealed by the debris of wall-robbing operations. All these floors respect a tile threshold in wall A552 into Room 3. No particular pattern of furniture emerges from the patterns of these patches and floors, other than a rectangular cut at the northeast corner of the room near the end of the sequence. There are a few stakeholes at various levels, but in general it seems as if the burning or hearth operations constantly moved about the room. These floors were very rich in animal and bird bones and oyster shells. The roof of this room may have been open to the sky because of the desirability of a smokehole. Finds of owl pellets in these layers support this conjecture.

In the north aisle, floors A346, 347, 331, and 323 open to the nave built up between walls A381:X and A353:XI. The north aisle was cut off from the nave by the insertion of wall A269 between Rooms 3 and 6, immediately following the insertion of the hypocaust in Room 3, and by walls A423 and A424 separating Room 4 from Rooms

7 and 8; the east end of the nave and the north aisle share only one floor (A549) before they are separated.

After the separation of the nave from the north aisle, a series of mortar floors and silt layers was laid in Room 6 (A223, 291, 330, 229, 353, 219, 217). The silt layer A217 sealed the west wall A353, apparently making Rooms 5 and 6 a single chamber. This was paved by tile floor A99 and its mortar bedding A211. This tile floor either coexisted with industrial operations at the east end of the room or, more likely, was cut away at the east end by a shallow pit (A214) filling most of Room 6 and filled with burn silt with dense deposits of bone and oyster (A209). This was followed by more mortar layers that were again cut away and filled with burn, with deposits of bone, oyster, coins, and other matter (A207, 206, 204, 202). One of the last events in the north aisle was the construction of one more dividing wall (A212, between Rooms 7 and 8). This was a poorly built wall of small facing flints and rubble bonded in mud mortar. It was followed by three more mortar floors to the west (A198, A195, A189), the last of which sealed the next dividing wall to the west (A381). To the east, one more mortar floor was laid (A75). The last event in the phase was the digging of an industrial (?) pit through this floor (cut A85), which consisted of alternate layers of burn, sealed by linings of clay or mortar. These were sealed by rubble from the collapse or robbing of the structure.

Date: The *terminus post quem* for the beginning of the alterations of this phase is given by a coin (**55**) of A.D. 330–331 in the floor (A575) of the previous phase. The *terminus post quem* for the backfilling of the hypocausts is given by a coin of A.D. 335–340 (**65**) in the fill of the crucible pit (A149) sealing the robbing of the blocking wall of the south aisle and coins (**48, 63, 69, 71**) of A.D. 332–340 in the fill of the hypocaust itself. The second-to-last floor in the north aisle (A195) and about two-thirds of the floors in Room 4 have to have been laid after A.D. 353 (**74**, in A195; **73** in A356). Several coins of the A.D. 330s and 340s (**61, 47, 70, 50, 59, 36, 74**) were found in the floors of the north aisle rooms (mainly Room 6). Much material is residual (e.g., iron fibula, **164**, first-century, in floor A549, which has to be mid-fourth century).

A coin of Gratian (**79**, A.D. 375) and a quantity of late fourth/early fifth century Overwey pottery was found in the Pennant tile footing of the bracing of the second north wall (A88). If one accepts, on architectural grounds, that the north and south walls were rebuilt at the same time, this would be the *terminus post quem* for the entire phase of subdivision and its alterations. However, it is more likely that it results from a later deposit when the ditch was in use or when the wall was robbed out.

It is not possible to determine the end of the occupational use of the building. The pottery from almost all layers of this phase is exclusively fourth-century and early fifth, most of it wares common for this period and region, such as Oxfordshire and New Forest. In general, later fabrics such as Wessex Grog-tempered and late fourth/early fifth century Overwey appear in the stratigraphically later floors: (A204) in Room 4 (A223) and the fill of the ditch extended around the Mosaic Corridor (A121), found with a coin of A.D. 353–60 (**60**). However, in the east room of the nave, several contexts come from the middle of the stratigraphic sequence, as well as later: A204, 223, 229, and 209. As mentioned above, most of the floors in Room 4 have to date after A.D. 353–360. An unstratified coin of Arcadius was found in the overburden (A1:XV, **85**, A.D. 388–402). If one can assume, as seems probable, that this was deposited on the site sometime during A:XI, rather than during the robbing operations, then the occupational activity must continue into the first, and probably the second, decade of the fifth century. Whether or not it continues later depends upon some of the fundamental methods by which one dates post-Roman material in Britain.[2] In general, there is very little change in the technology or character of the occupation of the site until the very last events: the mud-mortared wall in the north aisle and the burn on the mosaic in the Mosaic Corridor. The nature of the occupation of the site seems technologically and culturally Roman throughout.

Carbon-14 dates (see Appendix 7) for material in the last deposit in the pit in the north aisle (A77) yielded dates of A.D. 265–440 within 68% certainty or A.D. 240–560 within 95% certainty. Material from the third to last floors in Room 4 (A191) yielded dates of A.D. 140–335 to 68% certainty and A.D. 90–400 to 95% certainty. By stratigraphy, the former must date to after A.D. 340; the latter, to well after A.D. 353.

In summary, the alterations began in the A.D. 330s or later, and the backfilling of the hypocausts in the A.D. 340s or later; and occupation of the site and use of the building probably continued essentially in unaltered manner into the first decade of the fifth century and possibly later. From the generally good condition of the coins minted in the A.D. 320s and A.D. 330s and the sudden increase on the site in coins from that date onward, the initiation of this phase probably does not date from long after A.D. 330.

PHASES A:X/XI, A:XI/XII: EXTERIOR SURFACES AND EXTERIOR BUILDINGS ASSOCIATED
WITH THE SECOND AISLED BUILDING (FIGS. 31–32, 67–71)

Phase A:X/XI refers to activities outside the main building contemporary with either the use of Aisled Building II as an open area (A:X) or its later subdivision (A:XI). Phase A:XI/XII refers to the addition and extension of the Mosaic Corridor. There are no stratigraphic relationships between the interior of Aisled Building II (Phases A:X, XI) and A:X/XI, A:XI/XII. The early phase of the Mosaic Corridor (early Phase A:XI/XII) is probably contemporary with the later use of Aisled Building II as an open area (later Phase A:X); the extension of the Mosaic Corridor (later Phase A:XI/XII) is contemporary with the subdivision of Aisled Building II (Phase A:XI).

Probably the first event was the cutting of two deep V-shaped, square-bottomed ditches directly against the north and south walls (cut A92/fills A169, 91 on the north wall; cuts A339=328, fills A287=327 on the south wall) and extending to the west (downhill).[3] Presumably, they ran along the entire outer faces of the north and south walls of Aisled Building II. Both the north ditch and north wall were identified in evaluation trench 10 at 401/519, 21 m farther to the east.

To the west, a small independent building (the Greensand Quoin Building) was constructed. Its southern wall (cut A279, wall A278=277) slightly cuts the south ditch (A339). Therefore, the Greensand Quoin Building probably postdates the construction of Aisled Building II, as well as the ditch in front of the aisled building.

The Greensand Quoin Building was originally an oblong extending beyond the western limits of the sector; the original floors were apparently a series of clay or silt with pebble layers (A374, 388, 389=384). This building was subsequently subdivided by a north–south wall (cut/fill A390/411 from 367/517 to 368/520; fig. 18); a radial channel hypocaust was inserted and a short corridor (first phase of Mosaic Corridor) built on the front (south, from 357/515 to 366/513) to connect it to Aisled Building II. The internal subdivision, hypocaust, and external corridor are notionally contemporary, because the west wall of the corridor aligns with the interior subdividing wall. To build the corridor, the west end of ditch A339 was filled, and a shadowing ditch (cut/fill A144/121) was carried around the corridor to the south.[4] This ditch contained a considerable number of artifacts, including a bone sword hilt guard (**467**).

The corridor was later extended to the west beyond the limits of the sector and with shallower foundations, and a mosaic (A8=178, **5**) was laid. This is the mosaic discovered and drawn by W. C. Lukis in 1853; the nails he used to draw it were found in situ. It is possible that the first version of the corridor also had a mosaic; six mortared tesserae (A293) were found under the bedding of mosaic A8=178, but they lay almost directly on the earth floor and were probably not in situ.

To the north of the Greensand Quoin Building (c. 363/523) was a large burn pit (cut A486; fills A499, 504, 546, 427). It is associated with no architectural remains and could be the remains of a *praefurnium* that was so heavily truncated that no walls survived. It is placed to feed both the radial hypocaust in the Greensand Quoin Building and the hypocausts in Aisled Building II.

To the south of the corridor in the open courtyard (at 353/507), a lump of chalk and mortar was found in a pit cut into the terrace gravel. This could be a mixing pit for chalk and mortar, rather than a structural feature.

The latest phases of use seem to be marked by filling in the radial channel hypocaust and localized burns on the mosaic (A8=178), suggesting industrial activity. To the north the "praefurnium" pit was sealed by a longitudinal north–south cut (A426, fill A418), sealed again by a thick chalk floor (A326). This may represent some industrial activity after the hypocausts went out of use. These were then sealed by rubble scatters of A:XIII.

Date: Pottery from these phases generally dates through the fourth century. A coin (**38**) in the ditch against the north wall (cut/fill A92/91) dates to A.D. 322 and a coin (**60**) in the fill of the ditch shadowing the Corridor (cut/fill A144/121) dates to A.D. 353–360. A coin of A.D. 375 (**79**) was found in A88, the sandstone footing of the bracing for the Aisled Building II north wall, but is probably intrusive from the ditch and records its continued use rather than its construction. This implies that the ditches (which are notionally contemporary) were both in use in the third quarter of the fourth century and almost certainly stayed in use into the fourth quarter of the century. There is no clear date for the Mosaic Corridor, other than that it is clearly after the construction of Aisled Building II (later third/early fourth century), and its extension (which included the mosaic **5**) was probably built after the subdivisions of Aisled Building II (*terminus post quem* A.D. 330–331) (see chap. 4.4, n. 28).

PHASE A:XIII: DECAY, ABANDONMENT, AND ROBBING

Rubble from wall-robbing operations seals the latest occupation floors in all areas. In only one context does the rubble appear to be collapse, rather than robbing detritus (A52). Robbing operations were very thorough, removing virtually all solid structures down to their footings, except the north wall and two column bases. Several of these operations probably follow fairly immediately after the abandonment of the villa, since the rubble lies on occupation floors without any noticeable buildup of silting on the floors. There is no clear indication as to whether the bulk of robbing operations was contemporary or occurred over a long period; there are numerous deposits that cut and interleave with one another, and many of the deposits were disturbed. There is some indication of burnt occupation debris (A36) among the rubble, but otherwise almost no indication of a general destruction by fire. The building appears to have been disman-tled, rather than destroyed by catastrophe.

Date: The *terminus post quem* for robbing operations is given by the Overwey pot-tery in the occupation floors of Phase A:XI (late fourth, early fifth century) and, at the earliest, the coin of Gratian, which is probably intrusive, in the footings of the second north wall (**79** in A88, A.D. 375). There is no clearly identifiable medieval material in the robbing debris. It is probable that much of the robbing was sub-Roman and immedi-ately followed the abandonment of the villa, but it also seems likely that robbing contin-ued through the medieval and modern periods (see Introduction).

PHASE A:XIV: DRAINAGE DITCH
A ditch (A4) and bank running from the meadow (465/380 to 100/760) was cut across the site and leads downhill into the forest. This could have been either a boundary ditch or a ditch to drain the top of the hill, which does not drain well.

Date: References suggest mosaics and, perhaps, a lead cistern were found on the site in 1779 or 1780, possibly when a ditch was dug.[5]

PHASE A:XV: ANTIQUARIAN AND MODERN (FIG. 30)
The excavations of W. C. Lukis were apparently concentrated in the area of Sector A, as shown by the correspondence of the mosaic (**5**, A8=178) to drawings preserved in the Devizes Museum. Lukis emptied the room in the east end of the nave (Room 3) and cut away a great deal of the hypocaust backfill in the south aisle (principally in Room 1), as well as much of the stratigraphy in the area of the Greensand Quoin Building and the Mosaic Corridor (cut A17=43=44=73, fill A13=19=35=40=95). Some robbing operations clearly postdate the eighteenth-century ditch (cut A60=100, fill A54=97), the robbing of the north wall of the Mosaic corridor, and A47, fill of robbing of the southwest corner of Aisled Building II. Since these robbing cuts are in the area where the eighteenth-century ditch cuts Aisled Building II, they may mark the point of the original discovery of walls and mosaics in c. 1780—Lukis therefore having started to dig at the point of the earlier discov-ery, rediscovering the mosaics for the second time (and this excavation for the third). There is no clear indication of robbing that is stratigraphically later than Lukis's excavations.

Date: 1853 or 1854 to present.[6]

Sector B: The Villa West Wing

Although this sector was excavated only to the top of Roman occupation levels, several robbing cuts and two small evaluation trenches revealed earlier phases. The sequence begins with a beamslot structure and a dump of terrace gravel revealed by the evaluation trenches; then there is a gap in our knowledge of the activity in the sector until the con-struction of a masonry building. The masonry building is then structurally altered; after that alteration, there seems to be another arrangement (hypocausts are backfilled and the final mosaics laid). There follows a clear decline in the status of the use of these heated and decorated rooms with the insertion of industrial activities. Finally, primitive structures are built in the courtyard after robbing of part of the masonry building. Description of events and features before the occupation of the altered masonry building (Phase B:V) is tentative, as it is based on surface observation, rather than excavation.

    I   Beamslot structure in Courtyard (unexcavated)
         Unknown, probably before A.D. 150–200, by comparison with Sector A
   II   Terrace Gravel Dump (unexcavated)
         Unknown, probably A.D. 150–200, by comparison with Sector A
  III   Early Villa West Wing (unexcavated)
         Unknown, third or fourth centuries (after c. A.D. 200), by comparison with
           Sector A
  IV   Later Villa West Wing, Alterations (unexcavated)
         Fourth century
   V   Roman Occupation of Late Villa West Wing.
         Fourth century (Late Roman)
  VI   Occupation in Courtyard associated with Later Villa West Wing
         Contemporary with B:IV, V, or VII (Late Roman)
 VII   Stakehole structure in Villa West Wing
         Contemporary with or later than B:V (Late or Post-Roman)
VIII   Major Robbing
         Late or Post-Roman
  IX   Late Construction and Occupation in Courtyard
         Late or Post-Roman
   X   Destruction over Villa West Wing and Courtyard
         Post-Roman
  XI   Overburden and Modern Disturbance
         Modern

PHASE B:I: BEAMSLOT STRUCTURE (UNEXCAVATED) (FIGS. 35, 72)

The earliest feature on the site is a beamslot structure cut into the natural clay-soil and revealed under the terrace gravel by a small evaluation trench at 339/478. The dimensions and orientation (approx. 103°) are approximately the same as those of the beamslots in Sector A. The beamslots were distinguishable from the natural clay-soil by the darker fill.

    Date: Unknown. Since these remained unexcavated, no finds were recovered. Because of the similarity to the beamslots in Sector A, it is likely that they are contemporary, meaning that they pre-date the laying of the terrace gravel in the second half of the second century A.D.

PHASE B:II: TERRACE GRAVEL DUMP (UNEXCAVATED)

The next event seems to be a deposit of clayey gravel that apparently covers the whole sector. It is visible under all the construction deposits and masonry structures in the courtyard and, presumably as the same layer, in an evaluation cut behind the west wall (at 318/470). Since the first phase of the masonry villa was not excavated, we cannot say with certainty what its relationship to this terrace gravel is, but it is probably cut into the terrace gravel.

    Date: There is no excavated material associated with this phase. If it is regarded as part of the same event as the deposit of terrace gravel in Sector A, it should date to the second half of the second or early third century.

In the evaluation cut behind the west wall (at 318/470), a darker clay-soil (B123) overlay the presumed terrace gravel. This layer was clearly cut by the second west wall (Phase B:IV). It is not clear if this layer precedes or succeeds the first west wall. It could therefore be another part of the gravel-dumping operation (Phase B:II) or part of a later levelling for either the earlier or later Villa West Wing (Phases B:III or IV). The small amount of pottery recovered from this deposit appeared to be later first- and second-century, and a coin of Hadrian (**28**, A.D. 119) was recovered from it. Such Hadrianic coinage commonly circulated into the third century in Gaul and Britain. Therefore, it seems likely that the second half of the second or the early third century A.D. is the date of the laying of the first gravel dump in Sector B, as it is in Sector A. The second dump may be a part of the same operation as the first, part of the preparation of the earlier or later villa west wing, or it may be a phase of occupation and construction between the terrace gravel dump and the masonry villa west wing.

PHASE B:III: EARLIER VILLA WEST WING (UNEXCAVATED) (FIGS. 35, 73)

At several points under the latest preserved Roman building (Phase B:IV), there are unexcavated but clear indications of earlier constructions partly to a plan different from those visible in Phase B:IV. Under the southern half of the robbed-out east wall (east wall of Room 1, from 333/470 to 334.5/474.5) are three sarsens that are unrelated to the mortar pads later placed in front of that wall, hence, presumably from an early phase of the porticus. From just north of the northern sarsen in that wall, a wall can be seen running west under the mosaics of Rooms 2 and 3, until it is visible in the face of the pit cut in Room 3 (B80, from c. 334/476 to 326/477). The wall lies just north of the later east–west wall between Room 2 and the vestibule to Room 3 and supports the remaining fragment of white mosaic **8** in Room 2. This may mark the northern end of an early unattached building. Room 2 and the northern half of Room 3 appear to be additions. The northern continuation of the footings of the east wall on the courtyard (from 334/475.5 to 335/480) appear to abut against the point where they would have been built against this removed east–west wall as if they had been laid against it with their footings cut slightly lower. The later east corridor continues this arrangement since it clearly does not run the whole length of the facade but is cut off by the added Room 2 in the manner of a winged corridor villa.

The first west wall was of mortared greensand. A small pit in Room 5 (B113) revealed a mortar surface, which may be associated with the first west wall; the clay makeup through which the pit was cut may be a levelling for the floor associated with the second wall (Phase B:IV).

Date: There is no stratigraphically recovered datable material from this phase. The *terminus post quem* is the early third century, based primarily upon the presumed date of the gravel dump (Phase B:II) based upon the parallel to the terrace gravel dump in Sector A (Phase A:II).

PHASE B:IV: THE LATER VILLA WEST WING (UNEXCAVATED) (FIGS. 35, 50, 74)

The plan of this wing is still not completely understood, because excavation terminated at the top surfaces of this phase. The position or existence of certain walls is still obscured by late occupation debris and upcast from robbing operations.

There seem to be five discrete rooms (as in Figs. 28, 74). The front corridor (Room 1) is paved with an interlaced box mosaic 7 (B18=33), which clearly does not extend across the full length of the courtyard front. Part of the north wall that terminates the corridor is still preserved (at 330/476 to 332/475.5). There is no clear indication as to whether or not a door led from the front corridor (Room 1) into Room 2 through this wall. The east wall of Room 1 may have been an open porticus or a colonnade on a low parapet, the bedding of the interlaced box mosaic seals part of the robbed foundations of the front wall, and irregularly spaced rectangular mortar pads, presumably footings for Bath stone blocks (like those found in Sector D), are laid against those foundations as if to support a colonnade. This colonnade seems to continue into Sector D. The mosaic is heavily worn.

In the early part of this phase, Rooms 2 and 3 may originally have been a single room, heated by a hypocaust which was later filled, then subdivided and covered by mosaics. The fill on both sides of the north–south wall between Rooms 2 and 3 is identical, and pilae are visible in the faces of the robbing cuts for the east wall of Room 2 and pit B80 in Room 3. There is no indication as to the location of doors. The entirety of Room 2 was apparently paved with a white mosaic (**8**).

The Cantharus Mosaic Room (Room 3) is a large square chamber, with an extension in the manner of an entrance vestibule on the southeast corner. The vestibule was entered from the front corridor (Room 1) through a double door whose sandstone threshold and contiguous tiled panel are preserved (Fig. 52). The vestibule was also entered from the south (from Room 4) through a cruder threshold of clay and crushed greensand (at 329/472.5), but this may be a later door cut through the south wall. The entire room and vestibule were paved with white mosaic, with a central emblem of a cantharus framed by an interlaced box octagon and a rectangular stepped meander (**9**, B19=20=23=32=33=36). There are clearly preserved areas of high wear, particularly at the southeast corner (c. 329/474 and c. 326/474), which preserve the trace of the traffic entering Room 3 through the vestibule. There are areas of lesser wear at the northeast corner, tentatively suggesting a door into Room 2 from there. The heavily trafficked areas in the southeast corner were crudely patched with mismatching *tesserae* cut from terracotta rooftiles (Fig. 103). Large quantities of wall painting were found in the robbing disturbance overlying this room, which included large pieces of red-painted plaster (see chap. 4.6).

The western half of Room 3 is taken up by a large (c. 3.35 x 2.95 m), neatly cut rectangular pit (cut B80), revealing a surface of rammed chalk and flint packed around sarsens and serving as a footing for a bedding of *opus signinum* (Figs. 35, 50). It seems to be centered on the emblem of the Cantharus Mosaic and coincides with the width of the patterned frame. The two features, therefore, may be related, the pit being the robbing cut for something like a hydraulic feature (a fountain or a plunge bath) aligned with the mosaic. No trace was found of actual hydraulic features. A channel, again a robbing cut, leads out of the pit to the northwest. Since the pit is a robbing cut, we cannot be certain that the feature in the pit is contemporary with the Cantharus Mosaic or that it is contemporary with the earlier hypocaust.

The position of the west wall of Room 3 (the presumed back wall of the villa west wing) is not known. It may continue the line of the west wall in 316/470, or it may jog west. There is also no clear indication of the existence or absence of a wall separating Room 3 from Room 5 (the rear corridor).

Room 4 was paved with a checkerboard mosaic framed by a broad tesselated border (**10**, B29=37=70). In its latest phase, it was entered from the vestibule of Room 3 by the greensand and clay threshold. The east wall cutting it off from the east corridor is a later addition, so that the room may for awhile have been open to the east corridor (Room 1). There is no indication within the sector as to whether or not there was a door in the east wall leading into the eastern corridor. On the north wall it abuts preexisting painted plaster, and on the west it is sealed by a quarter round mortar wall base moulding.

Room 5, by its shape and position, appears to be a corridor along the back of the villa west wing. As mentioned, there is no clear indication as to the existence or absence of a north wall separating it from Room 3. The rear wall, built of flints in alternate layers of chalk and mortar packed around sarsen foundation anchors, is a complete reconstruction of the predecessor from Phase B:III. The preserved surface of the room is a sandy, mortary layer with building rubble (B113) which is probably the levelling makeup for a now robbed floor. This seems to be approximately the same kind of matrix as the back-filled hypocausts in Rooms 2 and 3, but here it is shallower and overlies clay soil; its stratigraphic relationship to the makeup under the Cantharus Mosaic is unclear. It contained small lenses of ash and a fair number of small finds: pottery, a few glass sherds, shell, nails, and other metal objects, including ferrous slag.

Date: As for the preceding Phase B:III, the only stratigraphic *terminus post quem* is in the early third century, which is given by the presumed date of the laying of the terrace gravel and the deposit A123, which contained the Hadrianic coin (**28**). It also contained first- and second-century pottery. B123 is sealed by the subfloor to Room 5 (B113) and the second west wall (B115). This *terminus post quem* may be pushed back by a century by the small amounts of pottery from the subfloor for Room 5 (B113), which ranged from the second to the fourth century.

Therefore, the stratigraphic evidence makes it clear that there was activity in the area of Sector B in the second and third centuries, but does not indicate whether the main phase of the construction of the masonry west wing (Phases B:III and IV) dates to the third century or, like Sector A, to the fourth.

In the destruction debris over the main building (Phases B:VII through XI), some twenty-seven coins were recovered. Some of these coins date to the 260s or 270s (**33, 35, 31**), and some are generically third century (**87–88**); there are no further coins from the later third or early fourth century until a considerable group from the A.D. 320s, 330s, and 340s (**40–42, 45–46, 49, 51–54, 58, 64, 68**). This increase in coins from the 320s to the 340s may suggest a major phase of activity in Sector B contemporary with the building and alteration of Aisled Building II in Sector A. The later third-century coins may be contemporary with Aisled Building I.

Therefore, the stratigraphic evidence does not independently clarify whether the masonry phases of Sector B are contemporary with the comparable phases of Aisled Building II in Sector A in the mid- and later fourth century, or if their initial phases precede them and are contemporary with the more modest industrial or agricultural use of

Aisled Building I in the later third century. The pottery in occupation deposits in B83:V confirms that they stayed in use through the fourth century.

PHASES B:V AND B:VI: OCCUPATION IN THE LATER VILLA WEST WING; OCCUPATION IN THE COURTYARD ASSOCIATED WITH THE LATER VILLA WEST WING (FIGS. 34–35, 74)
There are a number of traces of later use of the villa west wing before its radical alteration or abandonment. The patching of the Cantharus Mosaic in Room 3, the clay and greensand threshold between the vestibule to Room 3 and Room 4, and the west wall of Room 4 have already been mentioned. There are also a number of occupation deposits within the west wing and in the courtyard that may be associated with this phase. Like the mosaic patches and the greensand threshold, they also may be early indications of the building's decline; many of these deposits seem to contain residual occupation debris scraped up from elsewhere (possibly in the process of alteration or robbing) and deposited as surfaces, particularly in the courtyard. They are, however, occupation deposits and not robbing debris. There is no stratigraphic relationship between the deposits in the courtyard (Phase B:V) and those within the villa west wing (Phase B:VI).

Those within the building are more likely associated with decay and partial robbing or alteration. In the rear corridor (Room 5), there is a patch of burning (B110) on the subfloor makeup (B113:IV, presumably robbed of its pavement) sealed by a patch of mortar, clay, and building detritus (B83); the patch of clay and mortar contained artifacts of metal and pottery and bone and shell fragments. On the sloping exterior surface to the west of the west wall, there was an extensive layer of mortary silt (B98) with assorted metalwork, bone, shell, and pottery.

The principal deposits in the courtyard were a series of thin irregular layers (B122, 124–126, 128, 130–133, 135b, 136b, 140–145). These layers were of two types: mixed pebbles and building rubble with silty matrices, and natural accumulations of surface silts. Both were consistently compacted and irregular in shape, with merging horizons.

Therefore, at any given time the courtyard surface seems to have been a series of thin patches and dumps; there seems not to have been a general laid courtyard surface, unless it was removed and succeeded by these patches and silt deposits. The foundation for such a general laid surface may be two large, unworn layers (unexcavated) visible underneath these deposits, one of chalk across the south half of the courtyard and another of greensand in the southeast corner (at c. 339/472–4).

About 3.5 m to the east of the east wall and parallel to it ran a linear flint scatter in two sections, which has the character of a built feature (B137=138, from c. 337.5/476 to 338.5/480, Fig. 35). The flints are large and are laid in one course without mortar, with flatter surfaces upward. The feature lies roughly in the middle of the stratigraphic sequence of the courtyard deposits.

The last layer before the extensive chalk surface that formed the foundation for all later constructions in the courtyard (B109:IX) was a layer of clayey silt with small inclusions of building detritus, which may mark a limited area of disuse or abandonment (B116). This was the uppermost deposit in the courtyard to contain well-preserved finds of quality (including a rectangular fibula with silver cording and a finger ring, 107, 120). Contexts B141 and B144, from early in the stratigraphic sequence for the courtyard, also yielded significant items of quality.

Date: Pottery from B83 in Room 5 ranges from the second to the fourth century and pottery from B98 to the exterior of the west wall from the second and third centuries (Phase B:V). Pottery from most of the occupation deposits in the courtyard, including the earliest, ranges from the second to the fourth century (Phase B:VI). Almost all of this pottery consists of small and badly abraded sherds of residual material and material from used surfaces. Therefore the early fourth century seems to be the general *terminus post quem* for these phases, and, considering the residual nature of the material, all of this activity could date to the later fourth century or later.

PHASE B:VII: LATE STAKEHOLE CONSTRUCTION (ROOM 4) (FIGS. 35, 51, 75)

In this phase, which is a stratigraphic event isolated to Room 4, the central section of the mosaic 10 was cut away, and stakeholes, industrial pits, and slots were cut into the mortar bedding and filled with slag, nails, and other burned deposits.

Stakeholes were scattered throughout the mortar bedding of the mosaic. One group of twenty (B92) clustered in an oval pattern approximately 1 m wide (at 328.5/472). These probably are the first features after the removal of the mosaic and are distinct from all other stakeholes.

This may have been contemporary with or succeeded by two narrow parallel slots (B76=77, B78) cut parallel to the north wall and cut from the west wall to the center of the room. The slots have closely spaced stakeholes cut into their bottoms, as if for the withe frame of a wattle-and-daub wall. The manner in which these compartmentalize the room makes it clear that the walls were still standing.

Both slots are truncated by irregular pits. The eastern end of the north slot is cut by a roughly rectangular pit with shallow sloping sides (B82=86). Seventeen small stakeholes are cut around the rim, although some are present in the basin. An oblong pit (B74) cuts through the south slot and disappears under the balk.

The fills of the slots (B57, N. slot; B64=73, S. slot) date from their use or the removal of the stake structures in them and contain pottery, nails, and slag, the south slot also containing shale fragments, bone, and shell. The fill of the pit truncating the north slot (B72=85) contained ferrous slag, a few fragments of shale, and small inclusions of mortar, flint, and chalk. The pit truncating the south slot had three fills: a lower fill (B67) of blackish charcoal silt, containing metal slag, three nails, a small copper hemispherical object, probably a terminal for furniture attachment (144) and inclusions of tile, mortar and chalk; a middle fill (B65) of orange/red fine sandy clay with flecks of crushed tile, containing metal slag; and an upper fill (B60) of brown/black sandy charcoal silt, containing pottery, five nails, metal slag, and shell. Sealing both the linear slots and the irregular pits was a dark grey/black layer of burning (B31), covering most of the central part of the room. It contained five nails and metal slag (540.5 g).

The cluster of stakeholes (B92), the two slots (B76=77, B78), and the two pits (B74, B82=86) all appear to involve nail manufacture and other forging processes, perhaps iron smelting. The slots may form compartments within this industrial room; they may be only parts of the forging furniture; or they may be stalls or some other sort of compartment which was removed when the room was further converted to forging activities.

Date: Stratigraphically, this activity in Room 4 may be contemporary with the late occupation in Room 3 (Phase B:V), including the patching of the mosaic, or later; it may be contemporary with the late occupation in the courtyard (Phase B:VI), or later. It certainly precedes some of the wall robbing of Phase B:VIII. It could be contemporary with the late mud-mortared constructions in the courtyard (Phase B:IX), but it probably is earlier, since the east wall of the Villa West Wing was robbed out before some of those constructions (see below, Phase B:IX).

Pottery in this phase is all residual and runs from the second to the fourth centuries. The only *terminus post quem* is the mosaic in Room 4. Therefore, the date is generically late or post-Roman.

PHASE B:VIII: MAJOR ROBBING

A fair amount of the robbing of the building seems to have taken place in the late or post-Roman era, possibly while parts of the building were still in use and certainly while occupation layers and constructions were still being laid down in the courtyard.

The robbing cut (B135a) and fill (B114) of the central section of the east wall was sealed by a shallow trench (B108) filled with a linear tile spread (B104) parallel to the line of the wall. The north section of the east wall was robbed significantly later (Phase B:X).

Other robbing operations are stratigraphically the first events on the site after habitation in the individual area, and therefore may be either contemporary with later use of parts of the building or the late courtyard constructions, or they may be spread over a very long time, into the medieval or the modern period. They are distinguishable from the modern overburden and disturbance.

The robbing trench for the wall between Rooms 2 and 3 demonstrates that the wall was cut into a uniform fill. The latest west wall (B115) was robbed in trench B74, and the cut (B59) and fill (B54) to the north (at 312/475) may be an extension of that wall.

The robbing of the feature in the square pit (cut B80) was complicated and shows that it was destroyed in stages. Along the eastern and northern edges the earliest phase of the robbing was two shallow cuts (B90, 134), later truncated by the major cut B80. Two robbing trenches may be associated with the feature in the pit. A broad and deep cut (B129) runs north and west from the pit into the balk and another (B84) cuts from the southeastern corner south through the wall between Rooms 3 and 4 and through the forging features of Phase B:VII. The first (B129) precedes the robbing of the pit feature; the second (B84) follows it. If the pit feature is a hydraulic feature, these could be robbing trenches for drain and feed pipes, the drain pipe having been discovered first outside the villa west wall, then followed to the pit feature itself, then the feed pipe followed from the pit through the floors to the south in Rooms 3 and 4.

The robbing fills contain a wide variety of material of Roman date: pottery, large numbers of nails, a bracelet, an iron knife blade, an iron punch, bone, shell, two glass beads, two third-century coins (**33, 35**, c. 270), and one fourth-century coin (**66**, A.D. 347–48).

Date: All the material from these fills is residual and probably better dates the walls and occupation layers which were disturbed by the robbing than the robbing itself. The clearest *termini post quem* are the coin (**66**) of the House of Constantine (A.D. 347–348) and the fourth-century mosaics and pottery. Therefore, the date is probably late fourth century or post-Roman.

PHASE B:IX: LATE CONSTRUCTION AND OCCUPATION IN THE COURTYARD (FIGS. 34, 53–54, 76)

In the last phase of occupation of the site a number of occupation layers and laid surfaces were put down in the courtyard, some of which clearly postdate the robbing of part of the east wall, and among them there are also some constructions of a radically more primitive character than the main Roman villa, including the mud-mortared flint footing for a wall. Stratigraphically, the late surfaces and constructions in the courtyard are isolated from the events in the building itself. However, one group of events (the laying of a tile "drip gulley" B104, and successive deposits) in this phase seals an early robbing of part of the east wall (B135a, 114), and the fill of a later robbing of the east wall (B103) seals the first chalky levelled surface B109. Therefore it is probable that these constructions, laid surfaces, and occupation layers are contemporary with some robbing operations (Phase B:VIII). We cannot tell if they are contemporary with or later than the stakehole structure and forging operations inserted into Room 4 in Phase B:VII.

The notional beginning of this phase is an extensive densely packed chalky layer (B109), which forms a graded surface for all later activity in the courtyard and seals a deposit of silt and detritus (B116:VI). It extends from the southern to the northern balk and is approximately parallel to the villa east wall. It is cut by the later robbing trench for the east wall B106 but does not have a relationship to the earlier robbing trench B114, B135a. It is, however, immediately sealed by a tile construction (B104, 107, 108), which also seals the earlier robbing trench of the east wall (B114, 135a), and therefore the chalky layer and most of the succeeding events in the courtyard are probably contemporary with a partly robbed main building. Since it seals a layer of detritus (B116) and possibly succeeds some robbing, it appears to be an attempt to clean up the courtyard surface at a time when the main building was in decline. The chalky layer contained significant amounts of pottery (286 g), shell (562 g), and bone (140.4 g).

The linear tile feature B104 was c. 0.4 m wide and was set immediately in front of the northern section of the east wall between two of the mortar pads (from c. 335/375 to 335.5/474). It consisted of large unworn fragments of rooftiles which were set in a shallow trench (B104) that sealed the cut and fill of part of the robbing of the east wall (B135a, 114). The sandy silt in the trench under the tiles (B107) contained residual pottery, bone, shell, slag, glass, plaster, nine nails, and other debris.

The large chalk surface B109 was sealed by a series of amorphous layers of different sizes and matrices, many of which were compacted and worn. Two of these layers immediately precede the courtyard constructions. One (B105) appears to be an occupational layer of sandy mortary silt covering much of the eastern end of the exposed courtyard area. Its western edge is sealed by another large layer of mortary chalk (B102) running from the southern to the northern balk and along the eastern edge of the lower chalky layer (B109).

This chalky layer (B102) is the uppermost in a series of graded surfaces and forms the footing, and possibly associated interior floor, of a mud-mortared flint wall (B55). The wall is made of medium-sized flints and runs at an orientation different from the villa building (Figs. 33, 52–53, 75). The southern end of the wall was interrupted by a threshold of two phases—the first of small Pennant sandstone fragments and heavily worn (B42), and the second of clean, crushed, hard lower chalk and largely unworn

(B39). This kind of chalk fragment has the appearance of the tailings from mosaic manufacture.

The thresholds do not follow immediately upon the construction of the wall, but are interposed by apparent thin occupation deposits. A silty clay layer (B50) sealed the east side of the mud-mortared flint wall and was sealed by the thresholds. On the wall's west side, a large and worn rubbly surface with a chalky silty sandy matrix (B45) sealed the chalk footing surface B102 of the wall and was also sealed by the thresholds; its western edge sealed the fill B103 of the later robbing trench B105 of the east wall, showing again that some construction (in this case the thresholds) is stratigraphically later than some robbing operations. (This robbing trench in turn is earlier than some of the other courtyard constructions, since its fill (B103) seals the earlier large laid chalky surface B109.)

At least one wall (B47) appears to lie against the mud-mortared flint wall (B55) (at its northern end, from c. 339/479 to 340/477.5), but in this case too a clay silt layer with residual occupational debris (B49) is laid down between the construction of the wall (B55) and this wall.

It is nonetheless possible that the mud-mortared flint wall B55 was the eastern wall of a building of at least two chambers (whose shadow can be seen in Fig. 34; see reconstruction, Fig. 76). The chalky layer B102 which serves as the footing for the wall lies under the wall and to the west. Most of the occupation layers which succeeded this surface lay to the west of the wall: the worn rubbly layer B45; a worn pebble and rubble surface B99; a linear spread of worn terracotta tile fragments, many laid edges up (B71), overlain by silt B68, which in turn was overlain by a similar linear spread of sandstone tiles (B63, at c 335.5/478); the silty clay layer abutting the wall B55 (B50). To the east of the mud-mortared flint wall B55 there are few indications of either constructed or worn surfaces or of occupation layers, though there are a few dumps of sandy clay silt mixed with chalk, shattered flints, and gravels (e.g., B94 along the eastern balk, overlying the first chalk surface B109, but underlying the second B102).

If this mud-mortared flint wall was part of a building of two chambers or more with interior surfaces to the west, one aspect of its character, if not its plan, is that the outer wall (wall B55) was primary and the inner (or lean-to) walls were secondary, added, like the thresholds, in the course of its use.

Date: All datable material is residual, providing only a general *terminus post quem* in the later fourth century (**52**, A.D. 347–48; pottery from later second through later fourth century). However, the residuality of virtually all the artifactual material and the crude character of the construction give an impression of an occupation period or a level of occupation that does not have access to the major technologies of Roman culture.

Furthermore, this phase of occupation, while clearly contemporary with robbing operations, does not appear to have been particularly short. Occupation layers are constantly put down between construction events: a silty layer (B105) succeeds the laying of the first chalk surface B109 and precedes the construction of the second (B102), which supports the mud-mortared flint wall; deposits intervene between the wall and additions to it (the thresholds, the supposed abutting walls); linear tile features are laid down and replaced (B63, 68, 71, 104). In short, the site is maintained and altered over a number of operations at a consistent level of technology, that is, with residual material and simple construction.

This phase is stratigraphically almost certainly the last occupation phase in the sector. It is possible that it is contemporary with the insertion of the stakehole construction and forging activity in Room 4 (Phase B:VII), but it probably is later; no wall robbing can be shown to be earlier than the stakehole and forging of Phase B:VII, the stakehole construction of phase B:VII relates to standing walls, and the late construction in the courtyard of phase B:IX seems in general to be concomitant with several robbing operations and does not relate to standing walls. The date, therefore, is late Roman or post-Roman.

PHASE B:X: DESTRUCTION OVER THE MAIN BUILDING AND THE COURTYARD

The distinction between the robbing operations of Phase B:VII, some of which are contemporary with the latest activity in the courtyard, and the later destruction over the main building and courtyard is somewhat arbitrary. Most of the deposits notionally placed in this phase are broad deposits of loosely mixed rubble, as opposed to the clear robbing trench cuts and fills or thinner deposits placed in Phase B:VII.

Toward the rear of the villa west wing, where the platform falls away (Room 5), these rubble deposits alternate with clayey gravels (e.g., B48) that are similar to the redeposited clay gravels of the platform levelling (B:II). Beneath many of the coarser upper rubble spreads lay cleaner mortary layers, apparently the result of leaching out of mortar while the rubble was exposed. Both the clay gravels and the mortar layers between the rubble spreads suggest that the rubble spreads were each exposed to the weather for a long time, implying that the individual robbing operations continued over a long period.

Rarely did the rubble layers reflect the character of the room underneath. One exception was a sandy, mortary clay silt layer (B24) over Room 4, which yielded one hundred fifty nails and an iron strip. Debris deposits in the courtyard differed from those over the building, in that they contained more chalk and less mortar and were composed of greensand, flint, and sandstone building materials of smaller dimensions (i.e., more broken up). Several such layers overlie the east wall. If such materials bespeak the nature of the late courtyard constructions of Phase B:IX, i.e., those built with unmortared residual materials, they suggest that the destruction of the courtyard building may have continued later than the destruction of the main building. On the other hand, further robbing of the main villa continued at a very late date; the robbing of the foundations of the northern end of the east wall (cut B14, fill B10) is stratigraphically later than most of these events.

Objects from this phase were recovered mostly from deposits over the main building and are consistent with the relatively high level of its original occupation. This once again suggests that coins, luxury metal objects, industrial ojects, and most of the pottery appearing in the occupational deposits of Phase IX is largely residual, dug up and redeposited, like this material, in the process of robbing operations of the main fourth-century villa building, and not dating to, or characteristic of, the activity of Phase:IX. Pottery was often of the finer wares. There were several pieces of copper alloy jewelry, an assortment of metal implements and nails, a pin (**468**), thirteen coins dating from the third century (**88**) to 387–388 (**84**), and various deposits of bone and shell.

Date: Probably entirely post-Roman.

PHASE B:XI: OVERBURDEN AND MODERN DISTURBANCE

Five layers of overburden and modern disturbance were distinguished (B1, 2, 4–6), consisting of humic soil mixed with rubble, mortar, and chalk. The uneven surface contours and the mixed composition of these layers demonstrated considerable modern activity from tree-root action, earthworms, animal burrowing, and antiquarian or robbing operations. The rubbly layer B5 immediately west and south of the presumed hydraulic feature in the square pit B80 in Room 3 was clearly upcast from a relatively recent robbing. Finds included ten coins from the third century (**87**) to A.D. 375 (**80**), pottery, metal, glass, fragments of bone artifacts, including a triangular bone weaving card (**480**), and diverse bone and shell.

The artifactual material from Sector B is generally of higher quality than that from A and certainly C, and the bulk of it comes from robbing operations.

Date: Modern.

Sector C: The Villa South Wing

    I Early Ditches
        c. A.D. 50–70
   II Laid surfaces (terrace gravel dump)
        Later second–early third centuries
  III Masonry building: construction and early use
        Fourth century
   IV Later use of masonry building
        End of fourth, early fifth centuries
    V Latest construction in courtyard, partial dilapidation
        Early fifth century or later (contemporary with or later than Phase C:IV)
   VI Abandonment, collapse, and robbing
        After early fifth century

PHASE C:I: EARLY DITCHES (FIGS. 36–37, 55, 77)

The first features cut into the natural clay soil are two ditches, apparently unrelated, or at least without stratigraphic relationship.

The first (cut C63) was a V-shaped ditch lying more or less under the later north wall (at c. 349/435-350/435) and approximately parallel to it, although the 1 m width of the excavation trench was too short to evaluate the alignment precisely. The ditch appeared to have been about 3 m wide and 1.5 m deep, and thus was similar in dimensions and alignment to the ditch in Sector A (A969=971:I). It contained several fills, the bottoms of which were of silty sand with concentrations of charcoal and a dense deposit of pottery, including Oare, south Gaulish "samian," Terra Rubra, and Silchester Flint-tempered wares, some with deposits of ochre in them.

The other ditch (cut C66) is a shallow, square-bottomed ditch at the southern end of the sector at the point where the platform begins to slope downward (at c. 350/420-423; Fig. 37). It is less clearly defined as a proper ditch and seems to be about 3 m wide and 0.4 m deep.

As mentioned, there is no stratigraphic relationship between the two, but the second ditch (C66) is probably later than the first (C63), since its fill was part of the gravel layer dumped over the whole site, while the first ditch acquired several fills before the gravel layer was laid. A small deposit of rubbish (C41) including pottery and sheep scapulae accumulated on the surface near the second ditch and was also sealed by the gravel dump.

Date: The V-shaped ditch is securely dated by pottery to c. A.D. 50–70. The pottery in the rubbish dump C41 is also generally later first century A.D. The shallow square-bottomed ditch does not have an independent fill, but the gravel which fills it (Phase C:II) contains residual first- and second-century pottery.

PHASE C:II: LAID SURFACES (TERRACE GRAVEL DUMP)

The existence of a general levelling dump of redeposited clay sand gravel is not as clearly attested in Sector C as it is in sectors A and B; there are, however, a number of surfaces of redeposited natural soil which cover almost the entire exposed excavation sector (C36 in the courtyard, C33 and 35 in the interior of the later masonry building, C37 on the exterior to the south). These surfaces are relatively thin (0.1–0.2 m) and are relatively clean of building material, which suggests that there was no masonry or tile building on the site when they were deposited.

Stratigraphically, these surfaces immediately precede the construction of the masonry building and seem to have lain exposed for part of the time when the building was in use, or were reexposed (through Phases C:III and C:IV). The surface to the south was both cut by the south wall and sealed by its collapse, with only two small deposits intervening.

Date: Much of the material in these layers must have been pressed into their surfaces while they lay exposed and, therefore, is contemporary with the use of the building. The bulk of the pottery is largely later third- and fourth-century; there is also abraded residual later first- and second-century material. Therefore, like the terrace gravel in A:II, this gravel could have been laid in the later second or third century and remained exposed through the main activity in the building in the third and fourth centuries A.D.

PHASE C:III: THE MASONRY BUILDING (FIGS. 36–37, 55, 78)

The villa south wing as built in this phase consists of a narrow wing one room deep; the walls have the same orientation as the masonry buildings in Sectors A and B. The north wall was built into the fills of the ditch C63, and the still visible depression acquired two more fills laid against the north wall after its construction (C52, 42). The contemporary floors no longer exist, as in Phase C:IV they were cut away to the level of the gravel laid in Phase C:II, but they are indicated by a line of *opus signinum* on the top of the first free-standing course of the north wall.

As mentioned above, the exterior surfaces both to the north and the south were the gravels laid in Phase C:II. About 6 m to the south of the southern wall, a concentrated pebble surface (C17) was laid on the terrace gravel, possibly serving as a path.

The wing may have had a porticus of light construction on its north side, facing the courtyard. The only indication for it is a series of laid surfaces about 5 m wide in front of the north wall, whose northern edges are parallel to the north wall. The first of these, a pea-grit and clay-with-flints-and-pebbles (C53), seals the fill C52 in the top of the ditch depression against the north wall, implying that the first porticus followed the construction of the north wall by enough time to allow for further subsidence of the ditch. The next surfaces were a thin layer of clean clay (C40) and a very thin surface of crushed chalk and mortar (C23). These did not extend all the way to the face of the north wall; they may originally have done so, but their southern halves were destroyed or obscured by a dump of building rubble (C31) that filled up the southern half of the presumed porticus.

A relatively clean deposit of clay sand (C21), very similar to the clay gravel of the courtyard dump, seems to have built up continuously in the courtyard throughout this phase and also through Phases C:IV and C:V; it eventually covered the chalk and mortar surface C23. It is notionally assigned to Phase C:V when it was sealed by the last courtyard construction. An ambiguous deposit or construction, a small concentration of flints (C24), was placed in the courtyard on the terrace gravel dump C36 and was covered by the accumulation of the clay sand C21 in this phase.

Date: The pottery in the first fill laid against the north wall (C52) contained third- and fourth-century south Gaulish, "samian," Silchester Flint-tempered, Savernake, Alice Holt, Black Burnished, and Midland Calcite-gritted wares. The pottery in the pebble surface on the exterior to the south (C17) is early fourth-century. There was no pottery from construction deposits and there were no coins. The masonry building was therefore probably built in the early fourth century. The pottery in the exterior surfaces which were exposed throughout the building's use indicates use throughout the fourth century.

PHASE C:IV: LATER USE OF INTERIOR (FIGS. 36–37, 55, 78)

In the last occupational phase in the interior, the floor was cut away to below the level of the exterior, reexposing the gravel layer laid before the south wing was built. This surface was directly overlain by patches of concentrated burning and grey silt with burning (C32, 37). These surfaces were then all neatly cut by a square-bottomed pit, laid against the inner face of the north wall (C55). The lower fill of this pit was a clean silty sand (C65), making the bottom of the pit bowl-shaped; it could be either a silt deposition or a deliberate lining. The upper fill (C64) was mixed with slumped debris from the earlier burning patches on the floor and had more rubble and debris.[7] The pit fill C43 contained a bone comb (**465–466**), a wood-, bone-, or antler-handled iron tool (**168**), substantial deposits of late cooking ware and coins of Constantius II and Arcadius (**59, 86**).

This activity is stratigraphically isolated from activity on the exterior of the building and is the last occupation activity in the interior before the rubble deposits C28, 26, and 22 indicate partial or complete dilapidation of the building.

The pottery from this phase, particularly from the pit fills C43 and 64, strongly suggests that this wing was a service wing. The clearest assemblage of utilitarian cooking wares on the site, the recovered sherds are unabraded and from contemporary wares and from relatively few vessels, with little or no residual material.

Date: The pottery from the industrial pit fills C43, 64, and 65 included Wessex Grog-tempered, Midland Calcite-gritted, and Overwey wares from the mid- and later fourth century to the early fifth. The moderately worn coin of Arcadius (**86**, A.D. 388–402) from the pit fill C43 gives a *terminus post quem* of the first decade of the fifth century.

PHASE C:V: LATE COURTYARD FEATURE (PORTICUS OR LEAN-TO?): (FIGS. 36, 79)
The latest phase of the courtyard feature, or presumed porticus, was a single course of small mud-mortared flints and other building rubble (C15, 16, 18), which repeated the north edge of the earlier layers in front of the north wall. At the time this was laid, the earlier surfaces in front of the north wall were buried by the build-up of silty clay (C21) in the courtyard.

The architectural, or built, character of the mud-mortared flint feature is ambiguous; on the one hand it appears to be a wall with irregularly spaced buttress-like projections, but on the other, it does not appear to be clearly distinguished from an accidental scatter of rubble. The area between this feature and the north wall was filled with rubble in a silty matrix (C19) and had several small finds.

It is not certain whether the north wall was still standing when the mud-mortared flints were laid; it is possible that some of the rubble in the presumed porticus (C19) seals part of the robbing of the north wall (the eastern end), but it is also possible that this rubble slumped over the north wall after it was robbed. The western end of the wall clearly was still standing when C19 was deposited.

It is possible that there was a timber partition within the presumed porticus, its position indicated only by the sharp edge of a rubble dump within it (C13, west edge from 348.5/437 to 349/438.5).

Date: This phase is stratigraphically isolated from activity in the interior. However, the rubble and silty clay C19 within the porticus, which appear to seal part of the robbing of the eastern end of the north wall, appeared almost continuous with the top layer of rubble within the building (C20). This in turn probably postdated the collapse of the south wall. It is possible that, if C19 and C20 are continuous, in its last phase the porticus was a free-standing structure that survived, standing against the north wall even after the south wall had collapsed, since C19 respected the north wall and line of the porticus, while C20 sealed the collapse of the south wall. The survival of the presumed porticus, if not necessarily its construction, would then postdate the fill of the industrial pit (early fifth century). Otherwise, we cannot tell if construction of the last phase of the presumed porticus preceded the industrial pit in the interior, was contemporary with it, or succeeded it.

The datable material from this phase, most of which is from the rubble dump on the porticus floor C19, appears to be residual. C19 appears to be a redeposited fourth-century habitation layer.

PHASE C:VI: COLLAPSE, DISTURBANCE, ROBBING
In the interior, a number of small rubble deposits pre-date the collapse of the south wall. The deposits are compact and differentiated, as if deposited by human action, but do not have the character of purposeful levelling.

The south wall was found largely as it collapsed to the south, the coursed flints of the outer facing lying at the bottom (C5). The collapse sealed the exterior surface into which the wall was built, with only a deposit of Pennant rooftiles (C29) and what appeared to be decayed mudbrick (C30) in between.

Then follows a series of large amorphous deposits of rubble that seal the south wall, but at most only part of the northern one (C20, 10). Some of the rubble deposits (C20, 19, 13) respect the lines of the north wall and the porticus and hence were probably dumped against them when they were still standing and possibly still in use. The distinction between the top two layers of rubble (C3, 2) repeats the line of the north edge of the porticus, but buries the north wall.

The last two layers of rubble are preceded by a number of other individual robbing operations, including the eastern end of the north wall (cut C12, fills C11, 8, recut, C7, fill C6).

Date: Fifth century to modern. A modern horseshoe in C9, sealing C10, demonstrated that much of the disturbance is very recent.

Sector D: The Villa West Wing (Southwest Corner)
(Figs. 38–39, 56, 80–81)

Sector D was laid out over part of the area of excavations conducted by E. R. Pole in 1936–37 at the southeast corner of the villa platform.[8] At the time of the current excavations, the limits of Pole's excavations are clearly visible as an irregular depression surrounded by mounds; two ashlar blocks of Bath stone lie on the surface. The current excavations removed only the layers disturbed by Pole, presumably backfill and slump, and treated them as a single context.

   I Roman building, earlier constructions (unexcavated)
      Roman (Late Roman?)
  II Roman building, alterations (unexcavated)
      Roman (Late Roman?)
 III Roman occupation layers (unexcavated)
      Late Roman
 IV Overburden and disturbance
      Modern

PHASE D:I: ROMAN BUILDING, EARLIER CONSTRUCTIONS (UNEXCAVATED) (FIGS. 38–39, 80)
It is clear that the villa west wing in its latest phase (Phase D:II) was the result of some alterations of earlier constructions (D:I). The indications of these alterations are traces of reflooring and alterations to the porticus. In area J of Pole's excavation (Figs. 38–39, probably at c. 324/455, outside the area of current excavation) was found "a level-surfaced layer of hard mortar . . . below the filling of loose stone supporting the mortar assumed to be the bed of former tesselated paving. . . . [This] strongly suggests an early building of which it formed part of the floor. The same layer was found projecting northwards 12" from under wall H for its whole length."[9] Differences in flooring sequences were also noticed in robbing cuts in the northern end of the sector during the current excavations. At c. 328.8/456.7 the sequence was flints, *opus signinum,* mortar, chalk, mortar, and mosaic (presumably Pole's pavement B); slightly to the west (at c. 327/457) the sequence was yellowish clay, chalk, mortar, chalk, mortar, and mosaic.

Therefore, at all three points there are at least two finished floors, as indicated by mortar layers. It is not clear, however, if there were major alterations (e.g., new walls) or if there was a totally different earlier building. There are indications of major alterations to the east wall or porticus.

Date: Roman. The architectural technique broadly suggests the third or fourth century.

PHASE D:II: ROMAN BUILDING, LATER ALTERATIONS (UNEXCAVATED) (FIGS. 39, 56, 81)
The latest Roman phases were still partly obscured by the overlying unexcavated occupation and destruction layers. Only one feature of the plan is moderately clear: the existence of the east wall, which appears to be a continuation of the porticus in front of Sector B. There is tentative indication that a wall cut the presumed porticus into two rooms north and south, and the plan published with Warren's report indicates a third room beyond.

The schematic plan published with Warren's report (Fig. 39) seems to record the line of the presumed front wall or porticus (the alignment of blocks F and C) more or less correctly (in actuality rotated some 15° further clockwise). The oblique orientation of the tesselated pavement B is not correct; these tesserae were reexposed in the current excavations and are aligned with the front wall. Therefore, the oblique orientation of the walls G and H, which lay outside the excavation sector, is also suspect. All constructions in Sector D are probably orthogonal and had the same orientation as all other Roman walls throughout the site.

The front wall can be traced either as a structure or as surface stratigraphy across the entire sector (from 326.5/445 to 330/458). It is flint founded on greensand and sarsens, and near its southern end has an ashlar of Bath stone embedded in it. Without excavation we cannot tell if the ashlar was an integral part of the wall or if the flint sections were infill built against the blocks.

This wall was apparently altered by a line of blocks placed in front of it, as in Sector B (although again without excavation the stratigraphic relationship is unproven; Fig. 56). One is in situ (at 328/445.5); two probably lay on either side of the robbing cut in the middle of the sector (no longer in situ but indicated by blocks F and C in Pole's plan); and another possibly lay in an oval robbing cut against the north balk. If these ashlars represent a colonnade, it would be one with very irregular spacing; the same situation holds for the presumed late colonnade added to the front of the east wall in Sector B. The unusually large sarsens in the bottom of the robbing cut in D would probably indicate some sort of large construction at this point; sarsens of this size appear on the Castle Copse site only as foundation anchors of very solid walls. It is possible that the entire front wall, in one of its two phases, is founded on sarsens of this size, revealed only in this cut.

The internal arrangements are ambiguous. The space behind the east wall or colonnade may have been divided into two rooms by a wall preserved as only a few flints at 326.5/451.6. The room to the north was paved with a mosaic, Pole's pavement B. The pattern is not identified by Warren and is preserved in only a few chalk and sandstone fragments. As mentioned above (Phase D:I), the last floor overlies earlier ones, and the sequence is different in two places; at c. 328.8/456.7 the sequence was: flints, *opus sig-*

ninum, mortar, chalk, mortar, and mosaic; slightly to the west (at c. 327/457) the sequence was: yellowish clay, chalk, mortar, chalk, mortar, and mosaic. The room to the south is covered with mortar and therefore may well also have been mosaic-paved. The sequence here was simpler: clay, chalk, and then mortar, as if the reflooring occurred only north of the putative wall.

Warren's plan, with some interpretation, allows one to conclude that there was a room (or a range of rooms) behind the front ones, separated by the walls G and H. The interior of this room (to the west of walls G and H) preserved a pavement of terracotta tesserae "with spaced lozenges of white tile."[10]

The area to the east of the eastern wall, the presumed courtyard, is covered by an extensive layer of graded chalk overlying mortar. There were chalk and mortar spreads in the courtyard in front of the porticus in Sector B, but those in D were much more solid. It is possible that this is, in fact, an interior surface. Its northern edge is obscured by overlying building detritus.

Date: Since there is no excavated material, the date is again only loosely describable as Roman or late Roman, based mainly on the character of the architecture. There are no signs of a sub-Roman level of technology.

PHASE D:III: ROMAN OCCUPATION AND LATER LAYERS (UNEXCAVATED)

The chalk surface in the courtyard to the east of the east wall carried disturbed scatters of greensand, mortar, chalk, flints (some of which showed signs of burning), terracotta and sandstone tile fragments, and other detritus mixed with oyster shell. Many of these layers strongly resemble those associated with late activity in the courtyard of Sector B (B:IX).

In the extreme northwest corner of the sector, untouched by Pole, lies a layer of mortary silt (D2), truncated by a linear greensand feature facing the exterior of the east wall.

Date: Since again there are no excavated finds, there is no independent evidence for a date. If this is a parallel to the similar activity in Sector B, the date could be late Roman or post-Roman.

The material recovered from the humic layers (Phase D:IV) may give some indication of a late Roman date. Material included shale, glass, nails, slag, and an assortment of iron and copper alloy fragments, as well as bone and shell. Two coins were recovered: an antoninianus of Tetricus I (**34**, A.D. 270–273) and an AE 3 of Valens (**78**, A.D. 375–378). Pottery spanned the entire period of occupation on the site and usually took the form of small abraded sherds, implying that the deposition of residual pottery continued here for some time, as in Sector B. Dates run from the second half of the first century through the fourth, and include both Oare and Overwey fabrics. Finds from Pole's excavations included pottery, bones, and metalwork and are consistent with those recovered by the current excavations.[11]

PHASE D:IV: OVERBURDEN AND MODERN DISTURBANCE

All the layers of this phase comprised Pole's backfill, slump, and accumulated humic soil. Some clear traces of Pole's activity are still preserved: in the northern part of the porticus, the mortar bedding of the mosaic is pitted by the marks of Pole's picks, and the shallow oblique trench in the chalk surface in the courtyard seems to be the result of

Pole's inter-arboreal burrowing methods. Two ashlar Bath stone blocks lay on the surface before the start of excavation. These presumably are Warren's blocks F and C and were therefore removed from their positions by the excavators or by vandals.

Date: Modern.

NOTES

1. See chap. 4.4.

2. E.g., Esmonde Cleary 1989b: 131–61, on the interpretation of archaeological material and the dating of the end of Roman material culture. Esmonde Cleary prefers a low dating (c. A.D. 430) for the end of the culture, based on these technologies. By contrast, Frere (1983a: 214–26) extends the well-known sequence for Verulamium Insula XXVII to A.D. 475+.

3. It is possible that the sequence is the reverse—that the walls were cut into the fills of already existing ditches, whose separation coincided with the new building's width, but a small part of the fill of the north ditch does appear to seal the footings of the north wall.

4. This further argues that ditches A92 and A339 were cut against the outer walls of Aisled Building II and were meant to be in use while that building was standing.

5. If they were not from the villa between the Roman "station" and the road; see Introduction; Ward 1860: 261; Goddard 1913: 188.

6. See Introduction for early activity on-site.

7. The pit was excavated in two halves, the fill treated first as one context, C43, and then recognized as upper and lower fills C64 and 65.

8. Warren 1938: 318–20.

9. Warren 1938: 319–20.

10. Warren 1938: 319.

11. Warren 1938: 320.

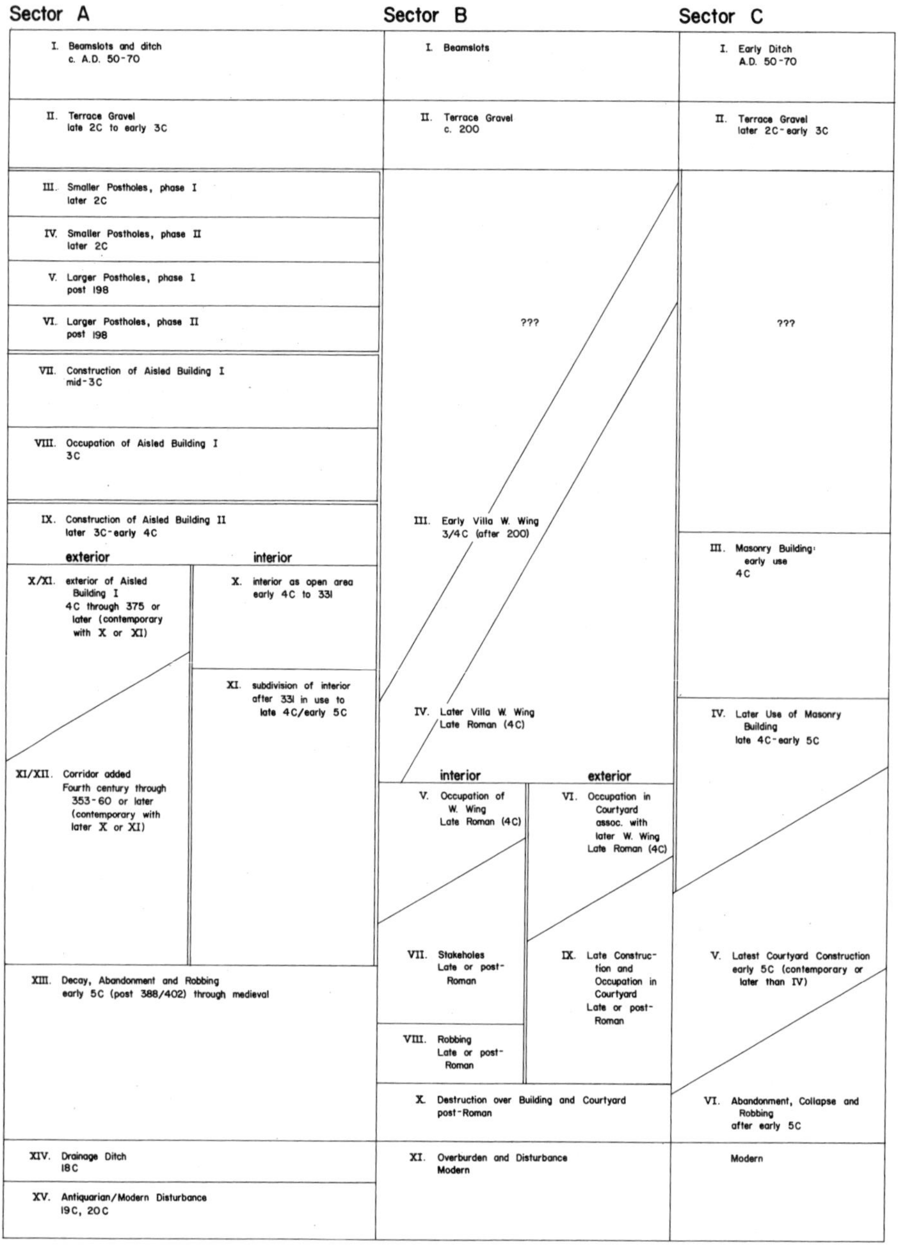

Sector A

I. Beamslots and ditch
   c. A.D. 50-70

II. Terrace Gravel
    late 2C to early 3C

III. Smaller Postholes, phase I
     later 2C

IV. Smaller Postholes, phase II
    later 2C

V. Larger Postholes, phase I
   post 198

VI. Larger Postholes, phase II
    post 198

VII. Construction of Aisled Building I
     mid-3C

VIII. Occupation of Aisled Building I
      3C

IX. Construction of Aisled Building II
    later 3C-early 4C

exterior | **interior**

X/XI. exterior of Aisled Building I 4C through 375 or later (contemporary with X or XI)

X. interior as open area early 4C to 331

XI. subdivision of interior after 331 in use to late 4C/early 5C

XI/XII. Corridor added Fourth century through 353-60 or later (contemporary with later X or XI)

XIII. Decay, Abandonment and Robbing early 5C (post 388/402) through medieval

XIV. Drainage Ditch 18C

XV. Antiquarian/Modern Disturbance 19C, 20C

Sector B

I. Beamslots

II. Terrace Gravel
    c. 200

???

III. Early Villa W. Wing 3/4C (after 200)

IV. Later Villa W. Wing Late Roman (4C)

interior | **exterior**

V. Occupation of W. Wing Late Roman (4C)

VI. Occupation in Courtyard assoc. with later W. Wing Late Roman (4C)

VII. Stakeholes Late or post-Roman

IX. Late Construction and Occupation in Courtyard Late or post-Roman

VIII. Robbing Late or post-Roman

X. Destruction over Building and Courtyard post-Roman

XI. Overburden and Disturbance Modern

Sector C

I. Early Ditch
   A.D. 50-70

II. Terrace Gravel
    later 2C-early 3C

???

III. Masonry Building: early use 4C

IV. Later Use of Masonry Building late 4C-early 5C

V. Latest Courtyard Construction early 5C (contemporary or later than IV)

VI. Abandonment, Collapse and Robbing after early 5C

Modern

Figure 26. Concordance of stratigraphic phases, Sectors A–C.

Figure 27. Sector A, room numbers.

Figure 28. Sector B, room numbers.

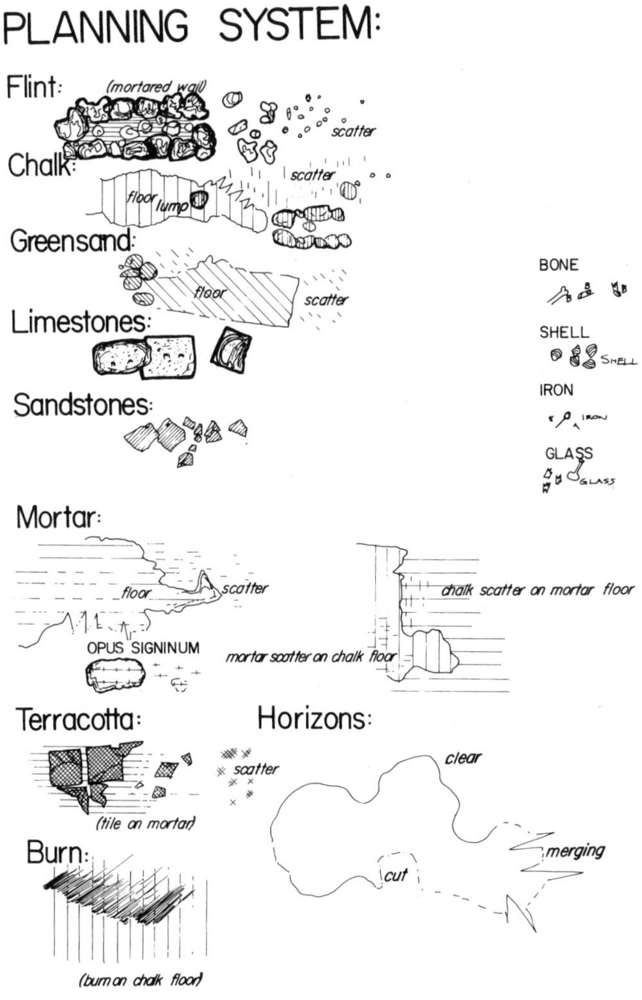

PLANNING SYSTEM:

Flint: *(mortared wall)*

scatter

Chalk:

scatter

floor lump

Greensand:

floor

scatter

Limestones:

Sandstones:

BONE

SHELL

SHELL

IRON

IRON

GLASS

GLASS

Mortar:

floor

scatter

chalk scatter on mortar floor

OPUS SIGNINUM

mortar scatter on chalk floor

Terracotta:

scatter

(tile on mortar)

Horizons:

clear

merging

cut

Burn:

(burn on chalk floor)

Figure 29. Graphic code for planning system.

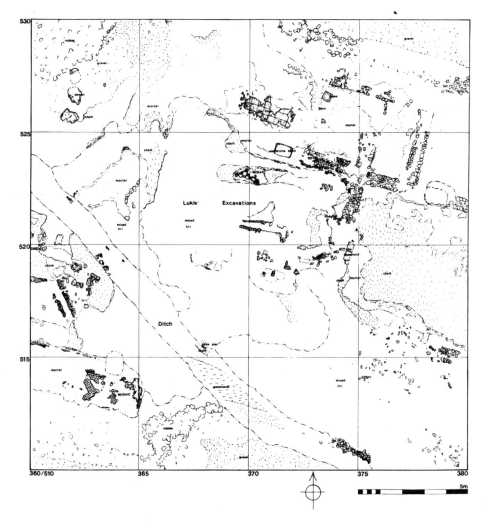

Figure 30. Sector A, state plan 1983.

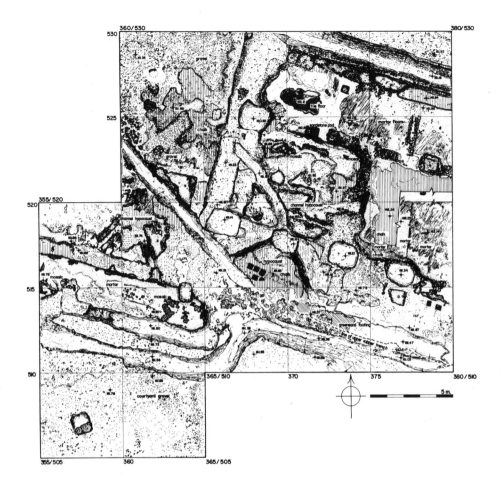

Figure 31. Sector A, state plan 1984.

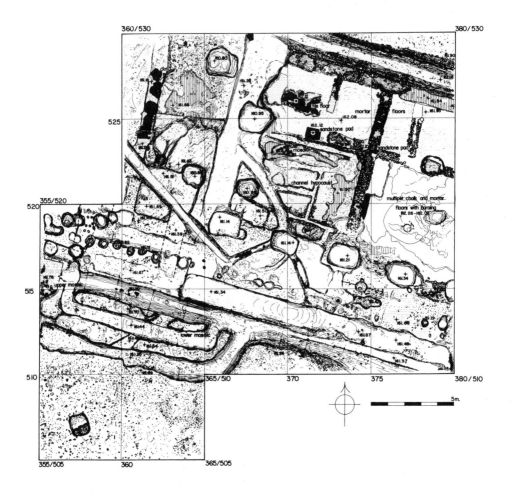

Figure 32. Sector A, state plan 1985.

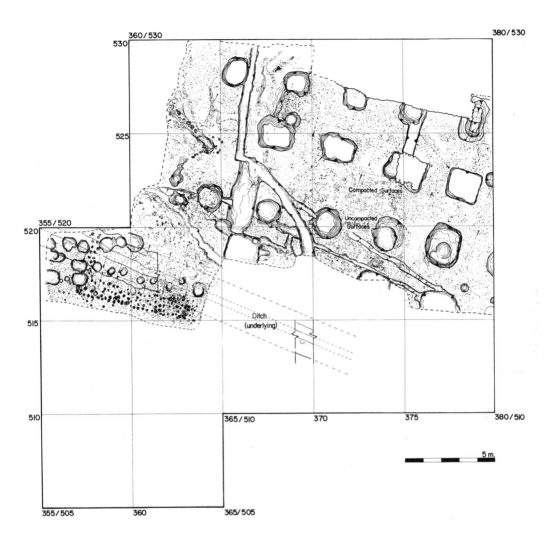

Figure 33. Sector A, state plan 1986.

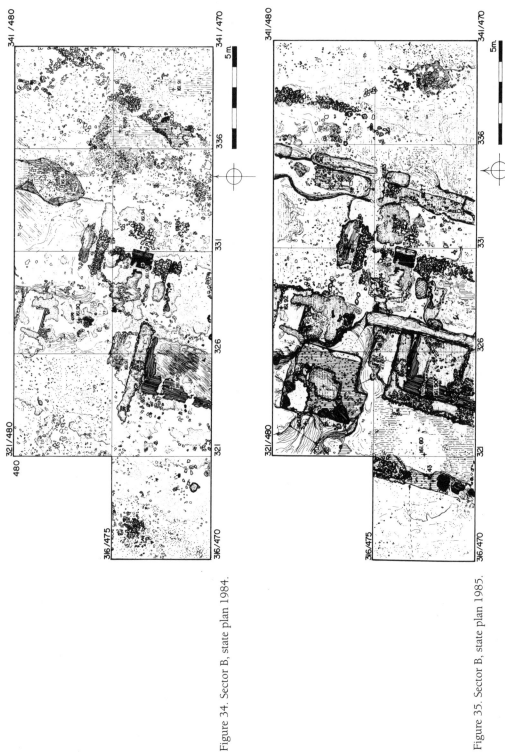

Figure 34. Sector B, state plan 1984.

Figure 35. Sector B, state plan 1985.

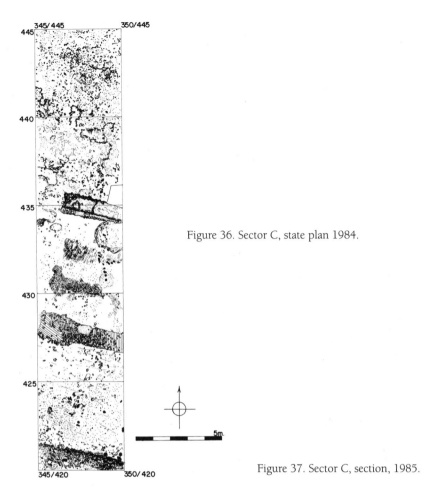

Figure 36. Sector C, state plan 1984.

Figure 37. Sector C, section, 1985.

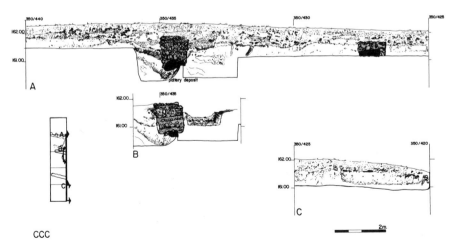

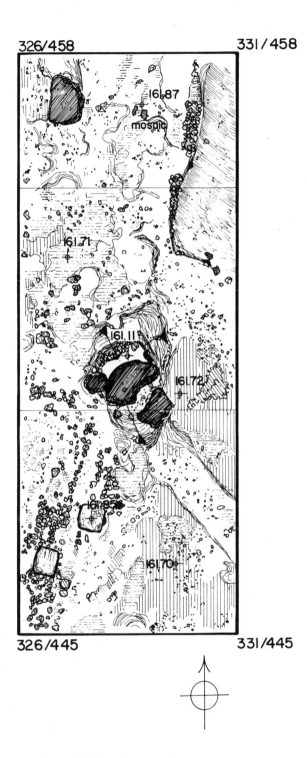

326/458   331/458

161.87

mosaic

161.71

161.11

161.72

161.85

161.70

326/445   331/445

Figure 38. Sector D, state plan.

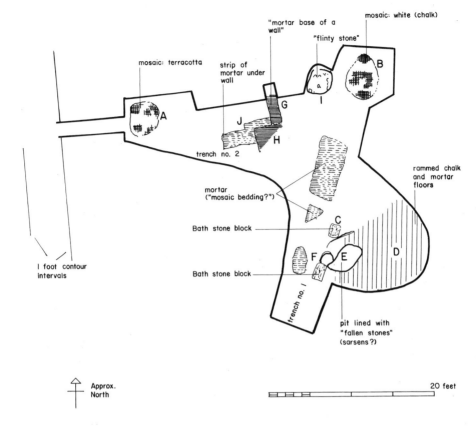

Plan of E.R. Pole's 1937 Excavation, redrawn after C.H. Diggory,
WAM 48 (1937-39) 318-20.

Figure 39. Sector D, plan of E. R. Pole's 1937 excavation. (Redrawn after C. H. Diggory [Warren 1938: figure opposite 318].)

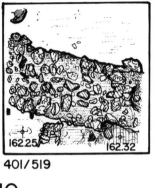

401/519

CC-10

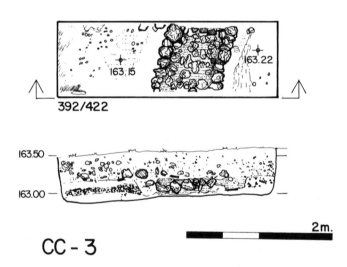

392/422

163.50

163.00

2m.

CC-3

Figure 40. Evaluation trench 3, state plan and section; evaluation trench 10, state plan.

Figure 41. Sector A, west end of Aisled Building II, with channel hypocaust (Room 3) and stylobate pits. (J. Crawford)

Figure 42. Sector A, toward east, with smaller and larger posthole structures. (J. Crawford)

Figure 43. Sector A, Stakehole structure and smaller and larger posthole structures. (J. Crawford)

Figure 44. Sector A, beamslots. (J. Crawford)

Figure 45. Sector A, first-century ditch. (J. Crawford)

Figure 46. Sector A, pit A85, with multiple layers of burn and chalk, and south walls A423 and A424 of Rooms 7 and 8. (J. Crawford)

Figure 47. Sector A, Aisled Building I stylobate pit. (J. Crawford)

Figure 48. Sector A, Aisled Building II stylobate pit. (J. Crawford)

Figure 49. Sector A, Aisled Building II N. wall. (J. Crawford)

Figure 50. Sector B, general view from west. (J. Crawford)

Figure 51. Sector B, Room 4, stakeholes cut through mosaic bedding. (J. Crawford)

Figure 52. Sector B, threshold between Rooms 1 and 2. (J. Crawford)

Figure 53. Sector B, courtyard feature (mud-mortared wall footing). (J. Crawford)

Figure 54. Sector B, courtyard feature (threshold). (J. Crawford)

Figure 55. Sector C, general view. (J. Crawford)

Figure 56. Sector D, presumed footings of porticus (Pole's blocks E and F). (J. Crawford)

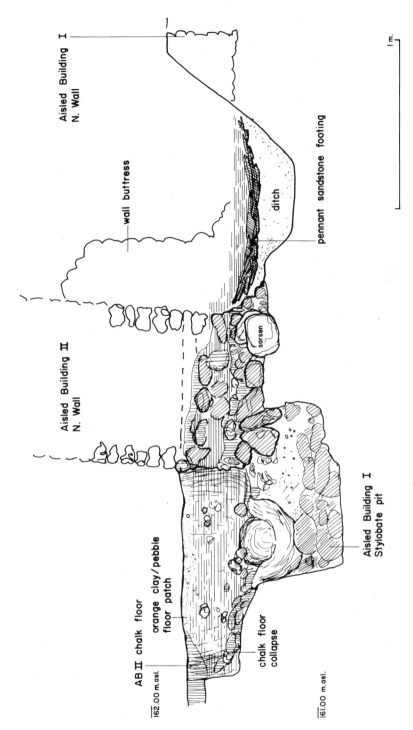

Aisled Building I
N. Wall

wall buttress

pennant sandstone footing

ditch

Aisled Building II
N. Wall

sarsen

Aisled Building I
Stylobate pit

AB II chalk floor

orange clay/pebble
floor patch

chalk floor
collapse

162.00 m.asl.

161.00 m.asl.

1 m.

Figure 57. Sector A, section of Aisled Building I stylobate pit and Aisled Building II N. wall.

4.4 ARCHITECTURE

THOMAS NOBLE HOWE

Architectural Phases

The Castle Copse site possesses four major architectural phases between the mid-first century A.D. and the fourth century A.D. They are: 1) early ditches and beamslot structures (late first through late second century); 2) earthfast post constructions built on a levelled gravel terrace (late second through mid-third century); 3) a masonry courtyard villa built on the same alignments (mid-third through end of the fourth/early fifth century; and 4) Late or sub-Roman squatter habitation (end of fourth/early fifth century).

1. EARLY DITCHES, BEAMSLOT, AND POST STRUCTURES (FIGS. 45, 63, 72, 82)

Phases A:I, B:I, C:I: mid- to late first century A.D.

The ditches, beamslots, and postholes that are the traces of structures of this phase have no stratigraphic relationship with one another. They may be successive or contemporary.

There are two very similar ditches in Sectors A and C that seem to be part of the same construction (Figs. 37, 45). Both are about 3 m wide, 0.9 m deep, V-shaped with flat bottoms and parallel to each other although separated by 85 m (Figs. 33, 82). They have a slightly different alignment from all of the structures that postdate the gravel dump. The fills are also contemporary.

There are traces of beamslot structures in Sectors A and B. The fill of the slots in A yielded significant amounts of clean, high quality carbonized barley seeds (see chap. 4.17). In Sector B the traces were discovered in a small evaluation trench that was sunk to evaluate the character of the first features cut into the natural, and they were left unexcavated.

In both sectors the beam width seems to have been about 0.25–0.3 m, and in A the depth was about 0.20–0.25 m. In Sector A there were slots with a tie beam between two of them. They must represent the north side of a building, the rest of which lies in an unexcavated part of the sector to the south. Immediately after trowelling, there was a clear difference between the uncompacted surface around the beamslots and the compacted surfaces to the north. The compacted surfaces to the north of the beamslots appear to represent the trodden exterior surface, and uncompacted soil around the slots represents the soil under the raised building. Two of the slots are not parallel: the spacing varies from 0.85 m to 1.3 m. In Sector B the spacing is about 0.8 m, and there is again a tie beam. There appear to be impressions of posts in the bottoms of several of the slots.

Two to three postholes lie around each end of the beamslots. At least one of the postholes has what appears to be a spade cut on one side, implying that the post was deliberately withdrawn.

The form of the slots in Sector A and the grain found in them suggest that this building was a long granary raised on posts placed on sills that were set into slots cut into the soil, or on densely spaced posts set into trenches. The depth and narrow spacing of the slots and the lack of postholes next to trenches seem unlike typical Celtic building practices.[1]

If this is a timber granary, it would be of the type that is called military even when it occurs on civilian sites.[2] The irregularity of the layout seems not to be typical of military wooden architecture, but examples of careless layout do occur.[3] The spacing of the trenches (c. 0.8 m) is about half that which is typical of military granaries (c. 1.5 m or 5 Roman ft),[4] but this still may be laid out using half the common military module of 5 Roman ft. The normal Iron Age granary is short and compact (rarely more than 3 m) and set on posts set into individual holes (four to nine).[5] Military granaries are long and narrow; the present building is at least 12 m long. Setting posts in trenches seems to be derived from military practice.[6] Sill beams do become an increasingly common technique in late pre-Roman Celtic Europe,[7] but these trenches are too deep for normal sill beams. Therefore, if this is a "military"-type granary, it is probably a private building[8] adapting ideas from Roman military building.

The two V-shaped ditches in Sectors A and C could be equally Celtic or Roman.[9] They are not necessarily too small for military ditches.[10] Since they are parallel, although widely separated, the site may have been set out by military surveyors, but structures and ditch enclosures on pre-Roman Celtic sites often adhere fairly closely to a single orientation over a large compound.[11] If this is a ditched compound, the granaries would appear to be on the outside, or the ditches are not perimeter ditches.

Too little is preserved of the other postholes to propose a reconstruction. Those near the ends of the slots may be typical of the isolated postholes for porches, which are common on the short ends of granaries.

Thus, the first phase of architecture could be from a Celtic non-villa settlement (although dating to after the conquest), but it appears that the architecture was in some way partly Romanized in the course of this period.

2. TERRACE GRAVEL, POSSIBLE STAKEHOLES, SMALLER AND LARGER POSTHOLE STRUCTURES (FIGS. 33, 42–43, 64–65, 83)

Phases A:II–VI, B:II, C:II: later second century

A shallow layer of clay gravel seals the earliest features and seems to represent a shallow terracing or grading operation over the entire "platform" of the villa site. These operations are followed by stakehole and posthole structures, in evidence only in Sector A. These structures determined the orientation of the subsequent masonry villa structures on the site.

Terrace Gravel: Phases A:II, B:II, C:II; later second–early third century. The terrace gravel is redeposited natural orange clay and pebbles, turned brown by oxidation on exposure to air and by mixture with topsoil. The contour maps of the site (Figs. 8–9) suggest that the western half of the villa site may be a levelled platform, with the terracing dump as deep as 1 m at the southwest corner. The actual evidence of terracing in Sectors A, B, and C shows a layer rarely more than 0.2 m deep. The grading or scraping operation, therefore, may not have been done with a surveyor's level or with the intent of creating an accurately levelled platform, although principal floor levels within Sectors A, B, and C are within 0.10 m of each other.

The Stakeholes; The Smaller Postholes: Phases A:III, IV; later second century (Figs. 33, 43). A dense, L-shaped cluster of stakeholes was discovered under the terrace gravel of Phase A:II, but they are tentatively placed here, after the laying of the terrace gravel.[12]

The stakeholes are about 0.05 m in diameter and spaced 0.05–0.15 m apart. The stakes on the south and west sides of the cluster are closely spaced and seem to form a front "edge" or face. Behind these the stakes seem not to be arranged in rows. Thus the south and west sides appear to be the exterior of a corner; the north and east sides, the interior reentrant.

A series of "smaller" postholes seems to cross almost the entire excavated sector in a straight line. The east end was truncated by the Aisled Building II hypocaust, and the holes that are visible on the state plan (Fig. 31) are probably only a small part of those remaining. The western end may terminate just inside the corner of the stakehole construction. The posts are in pairs, but each pair represents two phases; the holes of the first phase were generally packed with flints, and those of the second phase were packed with greensand. The postholes are about 0.60 m in diameter. In the bottom of some were preserved impressions of timbers about 0.25 m². The fills preserved no signs of post-pipes, implying that the posts were deliberately withdrawn.

The stakeholes themselves are very unusual structures. Normally, stakeholes support wattle and daub, but wattle-and-daub walls usually require only a single line of stakes, at most two. The depth and the dense cluster seem to imply a much heavier structure, or a retaining function, but even in examples of *murus gallicus,* or "box ramparts," a single line is sufficient to retain a berm or a face.[13]

If the stakeholes and the postholes are one structure, one may imagine the stakes (and wattle) to be retaining earth and to be tied back to the posts on the inner face of the wall. This would imply that the remains form the south and west wall of a structure, with only the south wall having earthfast posts, the west (gable?) end being a light non-load-bearing wall built on two lines of stakes and wattle. This building might correspond to the area and location of the two masonry aisled barns of the third and fourth centuries. However, there is no sign of another line of postholes to the north, and this kind of construction has no precise similarity to known rampart, house, or boundary construction. Normally, houses built of earthfast posts with wattle have a single or double line of stakes running just in front of the postholes or between the posts.[14]

Therefore, we propose no specific reconstruction for these features. They could be parts of two separate enclosure structures, or they could be associated as two phases of a single structure that would extend to the east and north, like the later aisled buildings.

The Larger Postholes: The first phase of postholes consists of two short rows of postholes, an east–west row of three and, 1 m to the south, a row of two. The second phase is a replacement for the first. Some of the posthole cuts preserve impressions of round timbers c. 0.30 m in diameter.

Remains of other postholes associated with this structure must lie under the balk to the north and west. The densely spaced pattern of the excavated section would make the structure similar to a small rectangular four-post or nine-post granary.[15]

Evaluation: The post and stake structures, visible only in Sector A, are apparently the structures for which the "terrace" was levelled. While we cannot identify the building type of any of the structures, they do not seem to be specifically Roman, military or otherwise. Roman sites, particularly military sites, make extensive use of levelled terraces, but not uniquely so, and this shallow grading operation is not on the scale of major projects like the Flavian palace at Fishbourne, which could have been executed only with the peculiar technical expertise of Roman surveyors.[16] The preparation of a terrace is also common on Celtic hilltop farmsteads and settlements as early as the Late Bronze Age.[17] Numerous pre-Roman patterns of building persist on farmsteads or villa estates in Roman Britain through the second century and later.[18]

Therefore, the traces of architecture visible from this late second-/early third-century phase could be equally in the tradition of Celtic multifamily farmstead or partly Romanized timber architecture.

The entire site must have been prepared for this phase at one time. The extent of that site, however, was probably determined by the preceding first century A.D. ditched compound (ditches in A:I and C:I). The shape and extent of that compound continued to be reflected in the extent of the masonry villa. The finds indicate that the surfaces on which these timber buildings were built remained open working surfaces until the middle of the third century. There is a possibility that some of these timber buildings may have had terracotta rooftiles and plastered walls, or that there were masonry buildings contemporary with the timber ones.[19]

3. THE MASONRY VILLA. MID-THIRD CENTURY TO THE END OF THE FOURTH OR EARLY FIFTH CENTURY

In Sector A the excavation recovered the sequence of all masonry structures from the mid-third century A.D. onward. In Sectors B, C, and D, investigation was limited to the latest phases of use of the masonry villa and revealed only tentative indications of the existence or form of early phases of the masonry villa, which might be contemporary with the third-century phases of Sector A.

The treatment of the masonry villa is divided into four parts: plan, technique, reconstructions, and a discussion of the evolution from timber buildings to masonry villa.

Plan:

The North Wing (Sector A).

Aisled Building I (Figs. 32–33, 66)

Phases A:VII–VIII: mid-third through early fourth century.

Aisled Building I immediately succeeds the removal of the timber structures of A:VI.[20] It is a conventional undivided aisled barn or hall with two rows of columns on isolated foundations.[21] The walls were flints and mortar on greensand footings; the column footings are greensand dumped into a pit without mortar. The columns were timber, buried below floor level and packed in clay. There is no indication as to the location of the exterior doors.

The floors were earthen, with burn traces of industrial activities. The first interior floor was a layer of orange clay about 0.10–0.12 m thick. Above was a second surface of dark, compacted pebbly gravel. Close to the west wall of the nave a clay-lined bowl furnace was cut into this surface. There is no indication of interior walls; therefore, Aisled Building I was either an open area or interior divisions must have been in perishable material, such as wattle and daub. It was apparently dedicated to industrial and agricultural use.

There is no indication in Sector A of other structures associated with or contemporary with Aisled Building I. Outside the building, a pebbly silt layer developed over the earlier posthole structure during this phase.

Aisled Building II as an Open Area and Exterior Buildings (Figs. 32–33, 67–68).

Phases A:IX–X: later third/early fourth centuries; and earlier parts of Phases A:X/XI–XI/XII: later third/early fourth centuries

Aisled Building II was built immediately after Aisled Building I was razed to the tops of its foundations. It is of almost identical dimensions and has some minor changes in technique and plan.[22] Aisled Building II is on the same orientation as the first, but was placed some 5 m east and 4 m south.[23]

In its first phase, Aisled Building II was a large, flint-built, aisled barn with a chalk floor. It was freestanding, closely bordered on its long walls by drainage ditches and separated by a small gap from a small building (the Greensand Quoin Building) to the west. There is no masonry collapse or scatter to aid in the reconstruction of the elevation, nor is there any indication of the location of exterior doors.[24]

Two of the internal masonry walls of Aisled Building II were built soon after the main building—those connecting the third columns from the west to the outer walls—creating open chambers facing the nave (Fig. 68).[25] There is no trace of other internal divisions. The first floor was a deep deposit of clean chalk, which was patched only a few times before the process of subdivision began.

The first event on the exterior after the construction of Aisled Building II was the cutting of V-shaped ditches directly against the north and south walls. The ditches contributed to undermining both the north and south walls, but they indicate that there was considerable concern for draining the damp clayey hilltop site.[26]

The ditches were probably followed by the construction of a freestanding building (the Greensand Quoin Building), which was originally an undivided oblong extending beyond the western limits of the excavation. Its first preserved floors (or subfloors) were a series of clay with silt and pebbles. The northeast corner was preserved to two courses of neatly trimmed greensand quoins.

At sometime before the major subdivisions of Aisled Building II, the Greensand Quoin Building was subdivided by a crossing wall and connected by a short corridor to the Aisled Building. The ditch flanking the south wall of the Aisled Building was diverted around the corridor and continued in use.

The Subdivision of Aisled Building II and Development of Neighboring Buildings (Figs. 31–32, 41, 48–49, 69–70)

Phases A:X/XI, XI, XI/XII: After A.D. 330–331 with refurbishment, including backfilling of hypocaust, in the A.D. 340s or later;[27] in use until the end of the fourth century or the beginning of the fifth.

This conversion project created two areas within Aisled Building II: a suite of heated and decorated rooms in the west end and south aisle, which also included the Mosaic Corridor and Greensand Quoin Building, and an apparent service or industrial area in the east end and probably all of the north aisle. Within this phase there was a second phase of redecoration, which may at first glance appear to constitute the beginning of a decline, since the hypocausts were backfilled, but the backfilled hypocausts were again paved in mosaic and the distinction of areas maintained.

The major subdivisions in Aisled Building II began with the complete displacing of the south wall some 0.5 m outward[28] and the bracing of the north wall. A channel hypocaust was inserted into Room 3, and the floors of Rooms 1 and 2 (the south aisle) were lowered 0.4 m for the insertion of a pila hypocaust. Dividing walls were placed between most of the columns.[29]

The plan of the building underwent minor changes between the earlier and later parts of Phase XI. In the south aisle, Rooms 1 and 2 may have been two separate rooms when the pila hypocaust was functioning; they clearly were one room after the hypocaust had been backfilled, since the backfilling seals the robbing of the dividing wall (Figs. 69–70). One of the oddities of the plan is that Room 3 may have been open to Room 1, creating one large heated room with two types of hypocaust; the column between the two rooms (the second column from the west in the south row) had been removed before the hypocaust channel was put in, and there there is no trace of a wall between the remaining columns.[30]

There is no indication of the nature of the first floors in Rooms 1, 2, and 3, i.e., those covering the hypocausts, but they presumably were paved with mosaic. After the hypocausts were backfilled, Room 3 was paved with the checkerboard mosaic (**6**), and Rooms 1 and 2 may also have been repaved, although there is no indication of the nature of the floor there. There is also no *in situ* indication of the nature of the wall painting of this phase, although Rooms 1, 2, and 3 must have had painted plaster. The fragments of painted plaster in the hypocaust backfill could give some indication of the first decoration of these rooms, although that material could have come from elsewhere on the site.[31] The wall painting of the later part of A:XI (after the backfilling and presumed repaving) might be represented in the material in A:XIII and later.

During this phase, the east end of Aisled Building II was an industrial area and remained so throughout the entire use of the west end as decorated apartments. The floor of Room 4 is a series of 116 mortar and chalk surfaces or patches. They begin to build up immediately after the insertion of the dividing wall between Rooms 3 and 4. Room 4 appears to have been a kitchen or an industrial butchery. There are stakeholes in various places in the floor, but in general there is no indication of permanent furniture in the room; it seems as if the hearth operations moved around the room. There was direct access from Room 4 to Room 3 across a tile threshold.

In the north aisle, Rooms 5 and 6 were divided by a light wall shortly after the major subdivisions, with industrial floors (silt and mortar) building up in Room 6 (Fig. 69). The wall was later removed, making 5 and 6 a single room; this was then paved with a tile floor (Fig. 70). The floor was later cut away by further industrial burning activity. Rooms 7 and 8, on the other hand, were originally one room and stayed so through most of the period, apparently serving the "kitchen" in Room 4; that room was separated from Room 4 almost immediately after the process of subdivision began (Room 4 shares only a single surface with Rooms 7 and 8). One of the last events in the sector was the construction of the light dividing wall between Rooms 7 and 8, a mud mortar and rubble construction. Shortly after the wall between 6 and 7 was removed, making 5, 6, and 7 one room and 8 another (Fig. 71).

On the exterior, the Mosaic Corridor was extended to the west and paved (or repaved) with a new mosaic (5). It is possible that in the same operation the radial channel hypocaust was inserted into the Greensand Quoin Building.

There is no indication of the location of an exterior door for Aisled Building II or of exterior paths or roads.

The West Wing (Sectors B and D).

Early Phases of the Villa West Wing (Figs. 73, 80, 84)

Phases B:III, D:I: third or fourth century

In Sector B the earlier phases are unexcavated. There are, however, two floor levels and earlier structures of slightly different plan which are visible in robbing cuts for the later walls (see chap. 4.3). The principal difference is that the wall at the north end of the corridor (between Rooms 1 and 2 of the later phase) is slightly farther north and seems to be the north end of the building. Therefore, B:III may be a series of rooms behind a corridor, which make it similar to a "corridor villa." There seems to be an earlier and later porticus in both Sectors B and D, and an earlier and later west wall in Sector D. Otherwise, in Sector D, the only indication of earlier phases is the existence of multiple floor levels.

There is no independent date for this phase, except that it is after the early third century A.D., that is, after the laying of the terrace gravel across the entire site.

Later Phases of the Villa West Wing (Figs. 34–35, 38–39, 50, 52, 56, 74, 81, 85).

Phases B:IV, D:II: fourth century

The new construction in Sector B added one range of rooms to the north end of the wing, terminating the porticus (Sector B, Room 2 and part of Room 3). This, in effect, converted the plan into what appears to be a winged corridor villa (although strictly speaking the wings do not project beyond the facade of the corridor), with the southern end to the south of Sector D. Room 5 in Sector B may represent a rear corridor.

In Room 1 (the porticus) irregularly spaced mortar pads (2.5–2.8 m on center) may have supported Bath stone stylobate blocks like those in Sector D (Fig. 38). A sandstone threshold leads through a double leaved door to the "vestibule" of the Cantharus Mosaic Room (Room 3), and a later threshold (of compressed clay and greensand) leads from that vestibule to Room 4. The wall separating Room 4 from the porticus is a later addition. Room 4, therefore, may originally have been open to the corridor, or the wall may represent only a late blocking of a door. The only features of the plan which are unclear are the location of doors into Room 2 and whether or not the rear corridor (Room 5) was separated from Room 3 by a door or wall. Traffic patterns on the Cantharus Mosaic indicate a door into Room 2 near the balk (at 329/479).

The wall that crosses Sector D is apparently the continuation of the porticus colonnade in B. There are very tentative indications of one crosswall to the west. It is difficult to correlate the drawing of E. R. Pole's 1936 excavation (Figs. 38–39),[32] but it appears that his plan, taken with ours, indicates that there was a large room behind the "porticus," paved with terracotta tesserae, and that there was some sort of wall between.[33] The porticus was paved with white mosaic and dark Pennant tile, as in Sector B, and there was a surface of chalk in front of it, also as in Sector B.

In this phase of Sector B there were two major phases of decoration and general fitting out: in the first, Rooms 2 and 3, and possibly the rear corridor 5, seem to have had pila hypocausts; in the second the hypocausts were backfilled and paved with mosaics (7–10). Large fragments of red painted wall plaster (as much as 0.25 m across) came from the robbing disturbance over Room 3, and may therefore be from that room. In Room 4 a quarter round molding seals the mosaic tesselated border of the checkerboard mosaic and earlier painted wall plaster.

In the middle of the west side of Sector B, Room 3, a large robbing pit (c. 3.25 x 2.95 m, c. 1 m deep) has tentatively been interpreted as a hydraulic feature. The hole is neatly cut and shares the same orientation as the architecture. The floor of the cut consists of a layer of *opus signinum* (D. = 0.07–0.10 m), which rests on a layer of rammed chalk and flints packed around sarsen fragments (D. = c. 0.15 m), implying that the robbing removed the lining (tile or metal?) of a tank. Two channels, both robbing cuts, which lead from the pit out of the room to the northwest and the south, may be the line of a drain and a supply pipe. No actual trace of hydraulic features was found. The discovery of a large lead cistern reported to have been found c. 1780 in Brail Wood may refer to this robbing operation, if the discovery was not, rather, at a second, smaller villa nearby (see Introduction); but it may also refer to something found when the ditch was dug across Sector A.[34] Much of the wall plaster found in the destruction layers over this area had been painted over several times, possibly implying rooms with unusually high humidity.

The courtyard seems to have had no special laid surface during the main phases of occupation of the west wing. The excavation distinguished two types of layer: mixed pebbles and building rubble with silty matrices; and natural accumulations of surface silts. The unmortared north–south alignment of flints visible in the lower state plan (Fig. 35) may be from a courtyard feature contemporary with the main use of the west wing.

The Villa South Wing (Sector C) (Figs. 36–37, 55)

Phases C:III, IV: fourth century, in use to early fifth century

This consists of a single narrow wing one room deep. The floors contemporary with the construction are cut away and are indicated only by a line of *opus signinum* on top of the first course of flints above the footing. The excavated sector revealed no internal divisions. There may have been a door in the south wall where it passes into the west balk. There may have been also a porticus of light construction on the north side facing the courtyard (in timber?). It is indicated only by the shadow of its interior floor surface; there is no trace of structure.

The original function is not known, since the original floor was cut away. The later function (Phase C:IV) was clearly industrial, since after the floor was cut away a deep pit with burn layers was inserted. This pit represents the last activity in the wing before the beginning of delapidation and may date to the late fourth or early fifth century. The lack of wall painting and fluetiles in the destruction overburden supports the identification as a service wing.

Again, there was no special courtyard surface, only the gravels laid in the terracing of Phase C:II. There may have been a pebble path outside the villa to the south, partway down the shallow slope.

Technique: Masonry Villa

The construction techniques for the masonry villa are consistent in all phases.[35]

Wall foundations are generally trench-built. The bottom courses, those below floor or ground level, were normally coursed flints or greensand with rammed chalk as a binder, often packed around moderately large sarsens (c. 0.4 to 0.9 m across).[36] In some walls soft greensand is used as a binder, and some use both, as if greensand was a regular alternative to chalk. The sarsens seem to have been intended as foundation anchors, apparently to try to stabilize the foundations against slippage in the notoriously unstable London/Reading clays.[37]

The flints or greensand of the footings generally rise two or three courses within the trench and then are levelled with a layer of rammed chalk.[38] In the deeper foundations they may rise another two or three courses and again be topped with a layer of chalk at or near floor level.[39] If part of the foundation rises above ground level, those courses will generally be flints and mortar, although they again will be topped with a levelling layer of chalk as a footing for the upgoing wall. In Aisled Building II the second levelling layer of chalk seems continuous with the first chalk floor that covers the entire building.[40] Foundations are generally as wide as or wider than the walls.[41]

A different foundation is found in the footings of the second north and south walls of Aisled Building II, where a raft of reused Pennant sandstone rooftiles in poor mortar was dumped into a partly filled ditch.

Columns, large and small, had isolated foundations, usually mortared rubble dumped into a pit and supporting a stylobate block. In Aisled Building I the columns rested directly on the unmortared greensand packing of the pit (below floor level); the upper part of the pit was then packed with orange clay, apparently the same clay as that of the first floor. The column was a square section timber, about 0.35 m on a side (Fig. 47).[42] The stylobate foundations for Aisled Building II had deep pits filled with densely packed flints and mortar, topped by an *opus signinum* bedding, on which was laid a hard greensand stylobate block, whose top surface was at floor level (Fig. 48).[43] Columns were presumably of wood; there are no setting marks on the blocks. The porticus of the west wing apparently had a colonnade resting on pads of mortar (c. 0.9–1.6 m) set in a continuous shallow trench. The pads presumably supported blocks that served as stylobates, probably represented by the two Bath stone blocks that were found by Pole, apparently in situ, in 1936.

Most of the major exterior walls and interior structural walls are sunk to depths of about 1 m; interior walls or small structures are in shallow trenches or sometimes laid on the existing surfaces.[44] Interior walls have deep foundations only if they are major structural walls.[45] Small buildings also seem to have had shallow foundations. The Mosaic Corridor and the Greensand Quoin Building had footings set into narrow square-bottomed trenches which could have been only about 0.2–0.3 m deep below contemporary ground level.

There is much evidence of structural problems caused by bad placement of foundations. The north wall of the south wing was built into the fill of the first-century A.D. ditch, causing it to lean into the ditch (Fig. 37). The south wall of the south wing may have collapsed (after abandonment). Similarly, one edge of the north wall of Aisled Building II rested on the stylobate footings of Aisled Building I, and this, together with the ditch cut against its north face, caused the wall to lean into the ditch and threaten collapse (Fig. 57). The south wall apparently did collapse, or at least was totally replaced. These repeated failures may be taken to confirm the "impression . . . of a provincial profession occasionally out of its depth," noted in an evaluation of architectural expertise in Roman Britain.[46]

Walls are mortared flints facing a roughly coursed rubble core. The outer flints are usually larger, and there is some effort to lay them with flat or split faces outward. In two places in Aisled Building II (the crosswall between Rooms 3 and 4 and the outer face of the north wall), the facing flints are set in a herringbone pattern. No wall is preserved to a height that would demonstrate whether there were tile levelling courses. The cores are fairly clean, and there is little other material (greensand, tile fragments) in them, except in some of the later walls. There is one use of quoins, the greensand blocks in the northeast corner of the Greensand Quoin Building.

Wall widths were usually 0.7–0.8 m; the outer walls of Aisled Building II are about 1.00 m; those of the south wing, 0.90 m. Interior walls are usually about 0.7–0.8 m. Some interior walls also show larger flints in the facing (wall in the nave of Aisled Building II); some apparently do not (walls in the west wing, Sector B).

There is no evidence of slots for half-timbering. It is probable that, in this phase of the villa, the walls were flint masonry for their full height, not just stone sills for timber or cob, although some walls may have been a combination of flints and mudbrick. In the south wing, the south wall collapsed on a spread of rooftiles, leaving the flints of the outer facing lying face downward. The mortared rubble seemed to be mixed with mudbrick material.

All paved floors, other than those over hypocausts, are laid on mortar beds which lie directly on earth or makeup dumps. In mosaic floors there is no use of the layer of coarse rubble aggregate (*rudus*) under the main mortar bed (the *nucleus*); also, the mortar bedding, usually about 0.10–0.15 m deep, is soft yellow to whitish mortar.[47] Utilitarian floors within the masonry buildings were often of earth.[48]

Floors normally are laid at the level of the first freestanding course of the wall above the footing. They were therefore often at the same level or only a few centimeters higher than the contemporary exterior natural surface.[49]

There is little indication of special preparation of exterior surfaces in the courtyard. In the late phases of the use of the courtyard in Sector B, there are surfaces of Pennant tile scatter and apparently a laid chalk surface. No trace of a road or track was found, with the possible exception of a pebble concentration to the south of the south wing, which may have been a footpath.

The site has both channel hypocausts (in the Greensand Quoin Building and Aisled Building II, Room 3) and pila hypocausts (in Aisled Building II, Rooms 1 and 2, and the west wing, Room 2, unexcavated). The channel hypocausts are cut into the standing earth fill and revetted with greensand and flints, the floor of the channels prepared with a thin mortar screed. Part of the channel revetment in Room 3 is laid in herringbone pattern. The floor of the pila hypocaust in Aisled Building II was a deposit of rammed chalk (D. = c. 0.10 m) on a thin mortar screed spread over the natural clay. The feeder flue which runs under the brick pila hypocaust is revetted with cut tiles. In neither case is the floor which they supported preserved.

In Aisled Building II three separate hypocausts were served by a single *praefurnium* or stokehole. In Room 3 the main feeder flue passes under the channel hypocaust, while feeding it through three outlets; it then forks into two channels over the position of the removed column in the south colonnade and runs under the floor of the pila hypocaust for some 3.5 m. It probably vented into the subfloor space through openings in the middle of rooms 1 and 2. The same *praefurnium* or stokehole probably also served the channel hypocaust in the Greensand Quoin Building.

These hypocausts must have been vented mainly by box tile flues embedded in the walls. One remains in situ at the head of the east end of the north channel of the hypocaust of Room 3 (at c. 374.5/522.5). There must have been a considerable number in the building, as in some of the later contexts of the destruction debris the volume of box tile fragments equals or exceeds the volume of rooftiles.[50]

There is very little use of cut stone on the site. Only two fragments of decorative cut stone were recovered: a small colonnette capital (**1**) and a base (**2**). Neither was found in situ. The only likely origin for the capital would be the small colonnade from the villa west wing. The only other cut stone blocks on the site are threshold or stylobate blocks.

The excavation recovered no evidence for the existence of ashlar walls, nor is there any clear evidence of any architectural marble from the site, with the exception of a few fragments of Purbeck marble from destruction layers.

Roofs were both terracotta tiles (pan and cover tiles) and Pennant stone slates. There is only one type of terracotta tile and two sizes of Pennant slates (see below). No distinction can be made as to which buildings or types of buildings used which roofing material, with the exception of the south wing, where the apparent collapse of the south wall rested on a dump of Pennant tile, as if, in the process of decay, the tiles had slid off the roof before the wall collapsed. It might imply that Pennant tile was used in service buildings; terracotta, in others.

Small amounts of tile are found in very early phases on the site. Some are found in the construction fills of earlier layers of the first masonry buildings (Phases A:VII, B:IV). There are even small amounts of tile fragments from the gravel dumps of Sectors A and B and the beam slot building of Sector A (Phases A:I and II, C:II), but much of this material must be intrusive, pressed into earlier layers when they were still open as working surfaces.

There are too few preserved built edges in the remains to support metrological study.[51] The lack of simple or repeated foot dimensions in the measurable features does not support the use of modular design.[52]

The similar orientation of the buildings and the shallow terracing of the platform raise the question as to whether the platform was surveyed and levelled. The buildings in Sectors A, B, and C all have principal floor levels within 0.10 m of each other, but if the terrace was levelled by instruments, it would have had to be for the earthfast timber buildings of Phases A:III–VI. Similarly, if surveyed, it would have been for the same timber buildings, since they seem to determine the orientation of the rest of the masonry buildings in Sector A. The degree of levelling and alignment indicated so far is not inconsistent with vernacular building. Aisled Building II is the only building well enough preserved to allow evaluation of the precision of the construction tolerances, and there adjacent stylobates are out of level by 0.02 m (162.10 and 162.12 m O.D.) and the bottoms of stylobate pits vary from 160.95 to 161.34 m O.D.

3. GENERAL RECONSTRUCTIONS

Upper Stories

There is no evidence for an upper storey anywhere on the site (including the existence of stairs). The amount of material from the *in situ* collapse of the south wall of the south wing suggests a one-storey structure, and the relative strength of the walls and foundations throughout gives ambiguous indication of higher vs. lower walls. The thickest walls were those of Aisled Building II, but this was also the highest space and may have had to bear lateral thrust from a large roof. If the relative strength of walls is any indication, the lesser thickness of all other walls would indicate that the rest of the complex was one storey.

The Ensemble and Outlying Areas

The buildings in the excavated sectors give the impression of a conventional "courtyard" villa[53] of the type which consists of a winged corridor villa and one or more aisled buildings (e.g., Halstock, Llanwit Major, Winterton, Mansfield Woodhouse, Sparsholt, Rockbourne, Gadebridge Park).[54] This is distinct from the type that forms a single coherent block, the wings being a "development" of the wings of a winged courtyard villa (e.g., North Leigh, the main block at Bignor, Woodchester, Spoonley Wood, Chedworth, Rockbourne),[55] even though some of these may also include aisled buildings somewhere in the compound (e.g., Rockbourne, Llanwit Major).

The west wing is tentatively reconstructed as a winged corridor, because in Sector B the corridor is terminated by a mosaic paved chamber (Room 2) in the fashion of the corner room of a winged corridor.[56] The earlier phase of the west wing, without Room 2, would have been a corridor villa. The rear of both phases of the west wing may have had a corridor.

In the north wing, Aisled Building II is reconstructed with at least ten bays and a length of at least 38 m[57] because of the spur wall found in evaluation trench 10 at the position of the tenth column from the west (Figs. 40, 85). Probably only the west end had accommodations for apartments; the chalk and mortar floors found in the evaluation trench indicate that the rest of the building had cruder floors similar to Room 4. It clearly did not have a front corridor or corner towers.

The south wing may be reconstructed as a single range of rooms without porticus, or with a light lean-to porticus, which probably extended across the entire south end of the platform. Its probable extent is indicated by surface scatter and is supported by phosphate sampling and resistivity survey (Figs. 87–88, Appendix 3). The interpretation as a service wing is reinforced by the lack of flue tiles in the destruction overburden, which is in sharp contrast to Sectors A and B.

There does not seem to be any clear social distinction between Aisled Building II and the west wing. If Aisled Building II was the house of estate laborers, then their status and accommodation must have been raised late in the villa's history, or they were displaced to make more space for the principal inhabitants. Functions seem to have remained mixed; the south wing and the eastern end of the north wing, both facing the main courtyard, seem to have remained utilitarian areas.

Theories of villas serving extended family groups can usually be studied effectively only when larger amounts of a villa's plan are recovered.[58] At Castle Copse, however, the idea that the creation of an "upper end" in Aisled Building II represents an early stage in the evolution of "new rights within the family group"[59] by the headman does not seem particularly tenable, since the insertion of luxury apartments is a late phase in the creation of Romanized apartments. The number of rooms is large enough to be a separate apartment for a family "unit," but the plan (e.g., of A Rooms 1, 2, 3) does not correspond to the type of arrangement Smith proposes for villas that accommodate the unit system type of estate tenure.[60]

There may be two other building blocks on the main platform: one might be part of the west wing, lying to the north of Sector B at c. 340/500; the other might be a block at the southeast corner of Aisled Building II, at c. 405/490. The presence of buildings here is suggested mainly by surface scatter and tentative results of resistivity survey (Fig. 87). If the complex included a separate bath block, these two places would be typical locations, on the north side of the complex and between major habitation units. Evaluation trenches at the latter failed to confirm structures.

There probably was no east wing, though there probably was a wall closing the east side, as indicated by a wall in evaluation trench 3, at 392/422 (Fig. 40). This tentatively suggests that there was a perimeter wall around the entire complex.[61]

The small areas of the courtyard that were excavated did not reveal any special surfaces or constructions for gardens, trackways, or water features (excepting the drainage ditch in Sector A).[62] The middle of the courtyard was not investigated.

The only documented connection between buildings is the Mosaic Corridor between the Greensand Quoin Building and Aisled Building II. Since there clearly was no corridor in front of Aisled Building II, it is likely that the main building blocks were freestanding rather than unified by a continuous corridor or porticus facing the courtyard.

Outbuildings or trackways outside the main building platform were not located. Resistivity (Fig. 87) and phosphate sampling (Fig. 88) recorded high concentrations corresponding to the area of the buildings on the platform.[63] Both types of testing also indicated two areas of higher concentration in the field to the southeast (at c. 500/380 and 400/340), but evaluation trenches (see Appendix 4) failed to find traces of structures or floors in these areas. Ostensibly Roman tile material has been found in this area in the years before the current excavation,[64] but field survey by the current excavation failed to locate a clear concentration of ancient material.[65] The sole area where ancient material was found was in a spring in a gully to the northwest of the aisled building.[66]

Fieldwalking over the entire Brail woods and the plowed fields around them produced only a few sherds of Roman material and no obvious indication of structures other than field terraces and a few earthworks.[67]

The field terraces visible in the small clearings in the forest on the east side of Bedwyn Brail (Fig. 7) seem to be earlier than most of the ditches and banks in the Brail woods and may be associated with the villa.[68] It is also possible, however, that they are an extension of the Wilton Down "Celtic" field system. In any case, they indicate at least one period when the extent of the forest cover was less than at present.

Evolution from Timber Buildings to Masonry Villa

The overall development of the compound appears to be as follows:

A possible ditched compound of timber buildings was laid out in the decades immediately following the Roman Conquest and was in use through the late second century A.D. Its function was at least partly agricultural, and its architectural tradition was mixed, including a probable granary building whose form and technique may have been influenced by Roman military granaries. In the later second century, the entire area was graded and terraced, and more posthole timber buildings were laid out on a slightly different orientation.

The overall extent of the eventual masonry villa and the general orientation of its buildings may have been established by the two timber phases, or at least the later of the two. There is no indication of a phase of destruction or abandonment between the first and second timber phases or between the second timber phase and the masonry phase.[69] There may have been buildings with terracotta roof- and fluetiles on the site contemporary with the timber buildings, although some of that material may be intrusive. There clearly was a building with wallplaster somewhere on the site before the building of Aisled Building I.[70]

An aisled building replaced timber buildings on the north side of the compound in the mid-third century A.D. and was rebuilt in the late third or early fourth century. Tile and plaster in the construction layers of the first aisled building tentatively indicate that the construction, and partial demolition (or remodelling?), of another masonry building may have preceded the construction of Aisled Building I.[71] The most probable candidate is the west wing. Therefore there is tentative indication that the corridor house of the west wing, and its possible remodelling into a winged corridor, may have preceded the construction of Aisled Building I. If this is so, it is likely that for a period (in the third century) the compound had both masonry and timber buildings.

The final fourth-century arrangement of the buildings and activity areas is reasonably certain. The compound consisted of free-standing building blocks around three sides of a wall courtyard. The largest residential building was the winged corridor of the west wing. The north wing was an "undivided" aisled building, which, after A.D. 331, evolved into a "developed" aisled building, with contemporary residential and "industrial" activity; it underwent further remodelling in the A.D. 340s or later.[72] The south wing appears to have been service and, possibly, industrial in character. There is no indication when the south wing was built relative to the others; all three wings were in use together, and all stayed in use until the first or second decade of the fifth century A.D.

This evidence tentatively argues for continuity between the timber and masonry phases of the site. The main arguments are the lack of identifiable destruction or abandonment layers in Sector A and the maintenance of the same extent and orientation of the compound from the beginning of the timber phases through the end of the fourth century.[73]

If the "timber" phases (including A:I) are a "native" settlement or farmstead, the historical development of the Castle Copse villa corresponds either to Branigan's Model 3 (a native farm established shortly after the conquest [or at Castle Copse, perhaps before?], which moves rapidly to the appearance of a villa house by the later first/mid-second century), or even more to Model 4 (a native farmstead founded shortly after the conquest, but moving to a villa house only much later in its history).[74] In both cases Branigan envisions these as projects of the "tribal nobility" who were "successful native craftsmen or businessmen." The image in these paradigms is that of native landowners or headmen founding new farmsteads or estates (or better, estate centers) as a response to the Roman Conquest, in order to adapt to or capitalize on the new order, but that the degree of use or adaptation of Roman ways was variable.

One of the most notable post-conquest changes in the local landscape around Castle Copse may have been the building of the Roman road that crosses the rise of Bedwyn Brail slightly less than 2 km to the southwest. Connecting Cirencester and Cunetio to Winchester, this road may have been pressed through very early after the conquest, possibly in the mid-first century A.D., just before the first ditches and presumed granary of Phase A:I.[75]

If, as seems likely, the Castle Copse villa represents the establishment of a new estate center in the half-century after the conquest on the hilltop near the road, then the architectural tradition of that estate appears rather mixed until approximately the mid-third century. The rectangular or subrectangular ditched compound would have been similar to several of the early "native" farmsteads that underlie later villas; these are often rectangular or subrectangular, even when they have circular huts.[76] The presumed granary, on the other hand, may make use of approaches taken more from Roman military tradition than from Celtic.

The opposed concepts of native and Roman therefore seem inadequate to explain the architectural development at Castle Copse; the timber phases may represent a selective use of Roman building techniques and forms, mainly those of the army, perhaps by a native landowner/headman in the layout of a new estate center that exploits the post-conquest situation.[77]

Similarly, the third-century development of this timber estate into a masonry villa may not represent a radical or sudden change of ownership;[78] rather, it may represent the kind of gradual replacement of timber buildings with stone, which is paralleled in both the large and small towns in second-century Roman Britain.[79] At Castle Copse, as elsewhere, the aisled building is not the necessary transitional phase in the evolution from "native" farmstead to "Roman" villa.[80] Here it is quite clear that the insertion of heated and decorated apartments into Aisled Building II was an expansion of luxury habitation and not the first step toward conversion from a Celtic native farmstead. Furthermore, it may not represent a radical change of cultural orientation: if both the corridor villa and the aisled hall are arguably forms of architecture that are native evolutions rather than imported or imposed,[81] then the pattern of replacement of timber buildings with masonry ones at Castle Copse—although it amounts to a substantial change in the architectural character of the compound—may indicate continuity or evolution within a class of owners from the same, but steadily changing, culture group.

4. DECLINE AND ABANDONMENT (FIGS. 34, 36, 41, 53, 71, 75–76, 79)

Phases A:XIII, B:VI–X, C:V–VI: later fourth and early fifth centuries

Architectural evidence exists for three types of decline on the site. The first represents attempts to maintain the villa as a residence with some luxuries, but with technology inferior to the original construction of the villa. The principle evidence for this is the crude patching of the traffic areas of the Cantharus Mosaic in Sector B (9) with tesserae cut from rooftiles (Fig. 103). There is also wall painting, not in situ, which lacks intonaco layers. The backfilling of the hypocausts in Sectors A (Rooms 1 and 2) and B (Room 2) does not necessarily constitute this kind of decline, since the backfilled hypocausts were again paved with mosaics in at least two rooms (A, Room 3, B, Rooms 2 and possibly 3). The last dividing wall constructed in the industrial area of the north aisle of Aisled Building II (between Rooms 7 and 8) is such an example of decline in technique, since it is made of mud-mortared flints and tile detritus in a shallow trench in the floor.

The second kind of decline is represented by traces of industrial activity in rooms which were previously decorated apartments. The Corridor Mosaic in Sector A shows substantial traces of burning. In Sector B much of the mosaic of Room 4 was cut away, and trenches and stakeholes for smithing operations were inserted (Fig. 51).[82]

The third represents constructions of a primitive or rustic nature, which either are built lean-to against the standing masonry villa or succeed the masonry villa's partial destruction. In Sector C there is a feature whose very existence as architecture may be doubted (C15–16, 18) (Fig. 37). It appears to have been a porticus or chamber built against the northern side of the west wing and consists of a single layer of small flint and tile detritus in mud mortar. It is preserved as a linear scatter in three compact islands that give the impression—or illusion, owing to an accident of preservation—of three buttress-like supports, spaced about 2.5 m apart.

In the courtyard in Sector B, there appears to be a two-chambered structure built on a different alignment from the west wing and lying on a number of occupation layers that seem to postdate the robbing of the east wall (Figs. 34–35, 53–54, 76). The clearest feature is its east wall (B55), c. 0.9 m wide, of medium-sized (c. 0.10 m) mixed flints in mud mortar. This wall has a threshold in two phases (B42, 39), the lower of worn Pennant stone, the upper of hard lower chalk. This wall is associated with other flint scatters and surfaces on its northwest side, giving the impression of two end-to-end chambers approximately 2.5 m wide. However, the walls suggested by the flint scatters seem smaller than the main wall, and the main wall runs beyond the "chambers" to the north, so that an alternate interpretation is that these layers actually represent two lean-to structures lying against the northwest side of an enclosure wall.

Both these features may be footings for cob walls. As a technique it appears in some early Saxon architecture,[83] but there is nothing in the form or the finds here to suggest association with any particular cultural group.

Thus, the last phase of the site at Castle Copse represents two types of habitation. The first shows a decline in the status of the villa, but of the sort that indicates either the maintenance of luxury habitation with inferior technique or the transformation of some of the luxury habitation to rural industry. The second suggests "squatter" habitation, built against standing walls or over robbed structures or inserted into the spaces in between. In the former case, the buildings may still have been functioning as a Roman villa; in the latter, the primitive construction is of a character not normally seen in the main spaces of a Roman villa until after their abandonment.[84]

SUMMARY

The Castle Copse site possesses four major architectural phases between the mid-first century A.D. and the fourth century A.D. The first is a series of ditches and beamslot and posthole structures. They may or may not be contemporary (mid-late first century A.D. through second century). Not enough has been excavated to suggest a firm reconstruction for any of them, with the exception of one (in Sector A), which is tentatively suggested to be a granary. It is ambiguous whether the remains represent Roman or pre-Roman Celtic architecture.

The second is a series of earthfast posthole structures built into a gravel terrace. The posthole structures are in evidence only in Sector A, but the gravel terrace seems to be in evidence in Sectors A, B, and C. The date is late second or early third century A.D. No reconstruction can be suggested from the small area excavated and no clear suggestion made as to the function of the site, whether native farmstead, military site, or Roman villa. The finds are clearly Roman. The site may represent the steady Romanization of a "native" farmstead or estate.

The third phase is the major masonry villa, consisting of wings on at least three sides of the levelled platform. The north wing was clearly an aisled building; the west wing may have been a winged corridor villa; and the south wing seems to have been a single range of service rooms. It is unlikely that there was an east wing, though there may have been an eastern perimeter wall. In the partially explored west wing, there is a phase earlier than the latest fourth-century one, and that phase is presumably third century. It is tentatively suggested that the west wing preceded the construction of the first aisled building (I). The later phases of the west wing date to the fourth century and include hypocausts and mosaics. In the north wing the first masonry aisled building was built in the mid- or later third century. In the late third or early fourth century the north wing was totally rebuilt, again as an aisled building (Aisled Building II), and used as an open area. In the second quarter of the fourth century (after 331), the Aisled Building II was subdivided so that the west end and adjacent building ("Greensand Quoin Building") were equipped with hypocausts and mosaics; the east end was clearly a service area, perhaps a kitchen. The use of the south wing as a service area is also datable to the fourth century. In all parts of the site, this masonry villa seems to stay in use until the later fourth century, possibly even into the early fifth.

The fourth phase consists of three types of evidence of decline. The first shows attempts to maintain the luxury accommodations, but with substandard Roman technique, and consists of crude patching of mosaics and wall paintings. The second consists of the insertion of industrial activities in the former residential areas. The third consists of traces of crude light structures of timber or cob on a thin flat socle, all insufficiently preserved to suggest reconstructions. These constructions probably date to the early fifth century. There is no evidence of medieval construction on the site.

Architectural Fragments

CARVED FRAGMENTS

1. Capital. A58:XIII (Fig. 58)

D. shaft=c. 0.23–0.24; W. abacus=0.38

"Tuscan" capital of oolitic limestone (Bath stone)[85] preserves abacus, high cushion (asymmetrical quarter round), and necking (stretched scotia); broken at connection with shaft. Presumably from a small monolithic colonnette. Found in disturbed building collapse layer.

2. "Ionic" base. A121:XI/XII (Fig. 59)

H.=0.076; D. reconstructed column=0.35; D. reconstructed torus=0.42.

Single torus with oblong dowel hole and pour channel in upper surface. Symmetrical stretched scotias top and bottom; upper surface with traces of saw cut-marks. Found in fill of ditch A144, deposited after A.D. 353–360.

ASHLAR BLOCKS

The only other sizable blocks of fragments of cut stone found are two different series of blocks, all to different dimensions. All the squared stones found on the site appear to be supports (stylobates) for columns or piers: there is as yet no evidence for ashlar wall construction on the site.

Type A: Stylobate blocks (Sector A) (Fig. 48)

Hard greensand, roughly trimmed with a pick or hammer on bottom and side surfaces, trimmed to a flat surface with a toothed chisel on top

Two blocks preserved in situ: Block 1 (at 372/524) L.=0.78–0.81; W.=0.52–0.57; Th.=0.28. Lifted; Block 2 (at 375/523) L.=0.48; W.=0.46–0.47; Th. obscured. Left in situ. Both are from Aisled Building II, later third century.

Type B: Four ashlar blocks (Sector D) (Fig. 56)

Oolitic limestone, traces of tool-working largely effaced by erosion, possibly finished with a drove. Top surfaces dressed, sometimes side surfaces appear to have been dressed to a plane, which may imply that some blocks were meant to be set next to other ashlars. Block 1 (surface find) L.=0.48; W.=0.31; Th.=0.20; Block 2 (surface find) L. 0.59; W. 0.57; Th. 0.17; Block 3 (in situ) L.=0.51; W.=0.50; Th.=0.25. Cutting for lewis in top surface; Block 4 (in situ) L.=0.59; W.=0.44; Th. obscured.

BRICKS[86]

Although most of the terracotta was preserved in fragments so small as to make it impossible to distinguish bricks from rooftiles, about forty pieces were well enough preserved to show that true bricks were used on the site. They appear to have been produced in three thicknesses and approximate the size of a sesquipedalis, pedalis, and bessalis.[87] All were found in later third- or fourth-century A.D. contexts (A:VII and later). Most material was in fragments too small to be identified by type.

A sesquipedalis is usually thicker than other bricks and most often is used in bonding courses,[88] but on this site some of the thinnest bricks are sesquipedales and are used as thresholds. The in situ pilae in Sector A were pedales.[89] There is evidence of round column bricks on the site,[90] although no indication of whether they were used for freestanding columns or hypocaust pilae.

No evidence exists on the site for triangular bricks, brick bonding courses, or stamped bricks. There are some tentative raked patterns on some of the sesquipedales, and one 0.06 m thick bessalis has a curious conical hole (D.=0.04) drilled almost entirely through it while the clay was still leather hard.

The dimensions for bricks at Castle Copse are:

Bricks of Th. 0.025–0.030:

> Sesquipedalis: L.=0.39–0.40; W.=0.26–0.27 (two of which used as door thresh-
> old in Sector B)
>
> Bessalis: L./W.=0.20

Bricks of Th. 0.035–0.045:

> Sesquipedalis: L. 0.043; W. 0.30–0.31
>
> Pedalis: L./W. 0.270
>
> Bessalis: L./W. 0.170–0.185

Bricks of Th. 0.045–0.050:

> Sesquipedalis or pedalis: W=0.31
>
> Pedalis: L./W.=0.27
>
> Bessalis: L./W.=0.20

Column brick:

> Two fragments (from B117, Evaluation Trench 10). Th.=0.040–0.060; D.=c.
> 0.240

PAN TILES (TEGULAE) (FIG. 60)

There seems to be only one type of pan tile on the site, with some five varieties of cutting the bottom edge flange and two of cutting the top flange. No fragment preserves the entire length measurement;[91] widths and thicknesses seem fairly standard for Roman Britain.[92] W.=0.290–0.300.; Th.=0.020–0.030; Th. flange= c. 0.040–0.060.

Several tiles preserve nail-holes near the top edge (D.=0.070–0.100), but other tiles lack nail-holes. So few large fragments are preserved that the presence or absence of nail-holes (proportion c. 1:1) is insignificant.[93] A few tiles have concentric raked patterns on the bottom (visible) edge of the top surface.

COVER TILES (IMBRICES) (FIG. 60)

There seem to be only two distinguishable forms of *imbrices* in the fragmentary material.

> Type A: Flattened curve and tapered plan. L. and W. top not preserved; W. bot-
> tom=c. 0.017–0.018
>
> Type B: Segmental (circular section) curve; apparently not tapered. L. and W. not
> preserved, but latter approximately 0.015)

There are no clear examples of nail-holes. The upper surfaces are commonly raked in a variety of patterns.

OCTAGONAL/HEXAGONAL TILE

One tile fragment has two adjacent 135° corners, and hence it must be octagonal or hexagonal. Because it is of the size and form of the smaller of the two types of Pennant sandstone roof slates it is probably a terracotta equivalent of the sandstone slates.[94]

> L. preserved side=0.13; L. reconstructed=c. 0.26–0.27

FLUE TILES (FIG. 62)

About half the volume of the terracotta material on the site was clearly identifiable as flue tiles, most with traces of scorching.[95] Almost all of the material is broken into such small fragments that it cannot easily be assigned to conventional types. No single tile preserves a clear indication of its complete form or a full set of dimensions—or, often, even any significant dimensions.

One clear distinction in the material is between tiles with squared and tiles with rounded vertical edges. Most of the material with squared edges appears to be half-box tiles, though some are clearly also *tubuli,* and it is possible that all of the material with rounded edges represents *tubuli.* Much of the material cannot be identified one way or the other.[96]

HALF-BOX TILES

Several fragments of half-box tiles preserve the full lateral flange with an indication of a finished edge; the front (or back) surface (and often the lateral flange) always has a raked or combed pattern, usually a cross or an X framed at the edges. Combs usually have five or six tines, with a width of 0.030–0.035 m.

Dimensions: L. variable, from 0.095 to 0.15+,[97] W.=0.14–0.17+, 0.15 average; Th. (depth of flange) rarely attested; few examples vary from 0.025–0.05.

Proportions: Most seem to have been square; those with shortest length were horizontally oblong.

Types: Few forms identifiable:
A. Triangular flange, probably on one end only, similar to G. Brodribb's Type E.[98] L. flange=0.05.
B. Shallow solid flange, similar to Brodribb's type A or D, but with no hole cut in the center of the flange.[99] L. flange=c. 0.025–0.03.

ROLLED HALF-BOX TILE (?)

A few fragments are very similar to the rolled *tubuli,* except that they preserve a finished edge, and hence cannot be rolled *tubuli.* Thus, they are almost indistinguishable from *imbrex* type A, except that they are scorched on the inside, and the combed X-pattern on the outer surface is common to flue tiles and not to rooftiles.[100]

L. not preserved (0.015+); W. (reconstructed)=0.015.

SQUARED TUBULI

Some of the pieces with combed faces and squared corners are clearly *tubuli* and not half-box tiles, since the full depth of the lateral side is preserved and several have the lateral sides perforated with the characteristic square and round holes.[101] The lateral faces normally seem not to have been combed.

L. not preserved; W. (of front face) not preserved; Th. (depth of lateral face)=0.095–0.105.

ROLLED TUBULI

This material is identified as *tubuli,* because none preserves an unbroken flange with a finished edge, and in a few cases one face preserves two rounded corners and the adjacent face is longer and/or has raked patterns, meaning that the shorter face must be the lateral face of a *tubulus* made by wrapping or rolling a sheet of clay into a rough oblong box shape. These tiles are hand-formed and very irregular in execution and there is little indication of the use of a former or mold. (Inner edges are also rounded.) Combed patterns are generally hastier and broader than on the half-boxes or squared *tubuli*; combs of five or six tines are about 0.05–0.07 wide. Rolled *tubuli* occur only in the later contexts. They first occur in very small amounts in A:XI (post 331) and then are about 10% of the identifiable material in later contexts. Hence, they seem to be used on the site only from about the second quarter or middle of the fourth century.

Dimensions: L.=0.012–0.015, 0.020+ (only attested dimension); W.=0.015 avg., up to 0.020; Th. reconstructed (depth of lateral face)=0.012.

Types: The material is too fragmentary clearly to associate the range of measurements into individual types. However, it does seem that there are (possibly among others) two types, a smaller and a less common larger. There is little variation in form other than proportion. The smaller size seems to be combed on front and lateral faces; the larger size, on front only.

> Type A. This is the most common type and is probably either square or short. L. (height of front face)= either 0.12 or 0.15; W.=0.15; Th. (depth of lateral face)=c. 0.10.
>
> Type B. Larger Type. L.=0.20+, W.=0.20+, Th.=0.12.

ROOF SLATES (FIG. 61)

About half the volume of preserved roofing material is Pennant sandstone.[102] The slates are of two colors—the more common dark purple red and a small amount of light grey—but they seem all to be of the same material and from the same quarries, since some slates represent both materials. All slates are stretched hexagons (i.e., with the lateral corners 45° and the bottom 90°), although top edges are very roughly cut and do not often complete a neat hexagon. Apparently all slates had nail-holes, usually in one of the upper corners, but location is very irregular and often is virtually in the center. There was no clear example of an in situ nail in a full tile, so it is uncertain if the method was to lay them in a left-handed or right-handed pattern, or both.[103] This type of roof apparently was laid directly on open battens with no decking.

There are two sizes of slate:

> Type A: L. (from upper corner to bottom tip)[104]=0.26–0.28; W.=0.26–2.27. Batten spacing estimated at 0.15–0.16. Load 108 kg/m². This is by far the most common size, representing about 95% of the material.
>
> Type B: L. (from upper corner to bottom tip)=0.18; W.=0.18–0.19. Batten spacing estimated at 0.10.

NOTES

1. Audouze and Büchsenschütz 1992: 44–55, 56–84. Sleeper beam construction, when it does occur, tends to be shallower.

2. Manning 1975; Morris 1979: 29–39. Another use of beamslot construction on a civilian site, but not a granary building, exists in an oblong building at the Honeyditches villa: Miles 1977: 113, Figs. 6, 7. On Roman granaries, Rickman 1971.

3. E.g., Old Kirkpatrick: Manning 1975: 118. On stone military granaries, see Gentry 1976.

4. Manning 1975: 106.

5. Manning 1975: 121.

6. Manning 1975: 121.

7. Audouze and Büchsenschütz 1992: 61–62, 76–77.

8. Civilian granaries of military type are known at Whitton and Mucking. Manning 1975: 121.

9. According to some, V-shaped ditches are most common in early Celtic sites, and flat-bottomed ditches appear to become more common in Late Iron Age Celtic architecture without displacing the earlier form: Audouze and Büchsenschütz 1992: 89.

10. E.g., Cawdor, where a ditch at the corner of an encampment is 3.60 m wide: Frere 1988: 425–26.

11. Several examples include square ditched enclosures (Zeijen, farmsteads in the Landshut region), farmsteads and settlements in which all the buildings retain more or less the same orientation across the site (Goldberg, Baden-Württemburg; Grønthoft and Hodde, Denmark), all in Audouze and Büchsenschütz 1992: 212–42. E.g., sites which continue into Roman Britain: Lowbury Hill (Berkshire): Collingwood and Richmond 1969: 178. Even the normally rounded enclosed farmsteads of Iron Age and Romano-British Wales include several nearly rectilinear compounds: C. A. Smith 1977: Figs. 1, 2.

12. The reasons for placing them here rather than in the phase preceding the laying of the terrace gravel are, first, that the fill is identical with the terrace gravel and hence the holes would have been undetectable when the terrace gravel was being excavated and, second, the stakeholes are parallel to the later posthole features and not to the features of Phase I.

13. On types of fortification construction: Collis 1984: 107–109; Audouze and Büchsenschütz 1992: 90–94, Fig. 49. According to the analysis presented in Fig. 49, by O. Büchsenschütz, there is one type of Celtic rampart (in two variations) that uses wattle to retain the outer face of a berm: "box ramparts," with a berm retained between two rows of paired earthfast timbers, spaced about 1 m apart in each face, and the interstices filled with wattle; and Hod Hill type, more or less the same with the inner timbers no longer earthfast. At Nitriansky Hradok (Slovakia), the rampart is retained solely by light wattle, without the use of large posts; the outer face has two rows of wattle on stakes, the inner only one. Audouze and Büchsenschütz 1992: Fig. 51.

14. As in Zippelius 1953: Abb. 5, types A through F, or the byre houses at Feddersen Wierde: Audouze and Büchsenschütz 1992: Fig. 41.

15. On small earthfast post huts vs. granaries: Audouze and Büchsenschütz 1992: 62–67.

16. de la Bédoyère 1991: 13.

17. Audouze and Büchsenschütz 1992: 182.

18. de la Bédoyère 1991: 182; Hingley 1989: 31.

19. Small amounts of tile of all types were found in all of the early pre-masonry phases of Sector A (I–VI), and wall plaster and painting fragments were found in several (II and VI–VII). Some may be intrusive, but those from A:VII are sealed.

20. The foundations cut one of the pits of the posthole structures. The building is preserved in foundation and robbing trenches, which have small amounts of material in them, and in the stylobate pits, some of which are almost completely preserved. A section of the footing of the north wall is preserved on the north side of the ditch cut against the north wall of Aisled Building II.

21. Since there are no preserved built edges, dimensions are approximate. The total width of the building is about 13 m (on center dimensions), the aisles about 3.25 m and the nave about 6.5 m. The length of the building is unknown. The spacing of the colonnade is about 3.1–3.3 m.

22. The column stylobates are at floor level and are hard greensand blocks resting on mortared flints in a pit, rather than greensand rubble in a pit. The only difference in plan is that the pair of columns at the end stand just proud of the wall, rather than a full bay away.

23. Its foundations were laid directly over foundations of the earlier Aisled Building I, which later caused substantial structural problems and possibly even a wall collapse. The wood columns of the first building seem to have been sawn off and left in place and were then covered with the makeup of the floors of the second building. When the columns rotted, they created voids in the subfloor and caused subsidence in the floor surfaces, which are repeatedly patched and filled (Fig. 57).

24. The building was about 14.5 m wide (on center dimensions, c. 13.7 m clear span), the aisles 3.9 m (3.3 m clear span), and the nave about 6.7 m (c. 5.7–5.8 m clear span). The spacing of the colonnades was c. 3.6–3.7 m. The overall length of the building was at least 38 m, since the continuation of the north wall and north-south spur wall abutting it were found in an evaluation trench to the east. The spur wall would mark the position of tenth pair of columns from the west end. See note 63.

25. These spur walls may also date only to the beginning of the process of subdivision, that is, at the time the hypocaust is inserted into the south aisle.

26. The south ditch was displaced and maintained when the Mosaic Corridor was added, which confirms that the ditches and Aisled Building II were conceived of as functioning together.

27. The date of the entire subdivision may be some decades later than the A.D. 330–331 *terminus post quem* proposed here. A coin of A.D. 353–360 (**60**) was found in the fill (A121) of ditch A144, which was diverted around the Mosaic Corridor. This is a continuation of the same ditch that lies next to the south wall of Aisled Building I. The ditch next to the Aisled Building appears to have been filled in when the south wall was rebuilt, initiating the entire process of subdivision. Therefore, if the section of the ditch next to the Mosaic Corridor was filled in at the same time as the section next to the Aisled Building, the subdivision began about A.D. 360. Also, a coin of A.D. 375 (**79**) was found in the foundation dump A88 for the north wall bracing (in ditch cut A92). If the moving of the south wall, which begins the entire process of subdivision, and the bracing of the north wall are contemporary, this would put the entire process of subdivision remarkably late, to after A.D. 360 or even A.D. 375. However, the coin was probably deposited in ditch A144, as it remained open after the construction of the Mosaic Corridor; and the coin in A88 also would more likely have been deposited during the use of the ditch after the construction of the bracing structure for the north wall or during its robbing, rather than during its construction.

28. An alternate interpretation for the history of the south wall of Aisled Building II is that the rebuilding of the wall is contemporary with the backfilling of the hypocaust in the south aisle, rather than its construction, although this contradicts some of the observations of the stratigraphy.

29. The major dividing walls (inserted directly between the columns) were probably almost all contemporary, and their construction followed very quickly upon the insertion of the hypocausts.

30. The hypocaust feeder channel runs across the robbed foundation pit. On the other hand, a light wall could have stood north of the line of columns just inside Room 3.

31. The makeup layers in phases A:IX (construction of Aisled Building I) and XI (subdivision) contained large amounts of painted plaster and fragments of mosaic, but these do not necessarily come from the north wing. Both the mosaics and the wall paintings on the site show a presumed higher quality series and a lower quality series, not necessarily "earlier" and "later"; the latter series of mosaics more or less matches the mosaics in situ in A and B. All of the higher quality—and supposedly earlier—mosaics on the site come from phase A:XI; the fragments of higher quality wall painting, mainly from B:VI and X. They were found in what amount to makeup dumps and destruction debris. The earliest deposits with plaster were A960:VII (unpainted) and A287, 760, and 872:IX and B113:IV (painted).

Since the phases earlier than A:XI are essentially barns, it is unlikely that the earlier series of painting and mosaics comes from the earlier phases of the aisled building, but rather from other parts of the site, probably the west wing. Makeup dumps are commonly generated on parts of sites other than where they are used. Thus it is possible that the material represented in these layers in Sector A, and in the later west wing (B:IV), was carried from the west wing during its rebuilding (the existence of an earlier phase—B:III—in the west wing is certain, its date is not) and that this material represents the decoration of the first phase of the west wing.

This would also indicate that the construction of the west wing precedes Aisled Building II (A:IX), or possibly even Aisled Building I (A:VII), since decoration from what might be the first phase of decoration of the west wing is found in construction layers of Aisled Building I (A960:VII) and use layers of Aisled Building II. The painted plaster in A:VII may also indicate that some of the buildings of the timber phase were plastered.

32. Warren 1938: 318–320, illustration opposite 318. The drawing appears to be rotated

some 82° clockwise, with north at the right. In our surface plan of the area (Fig. 38), his Trench 2 is the oblong contour running out to the edge of the terrace. His Pit E, "a circular hollow . . . about 1ft. 6 ins. deep, lined with large stones, but blocked with large stones in its eastern half," is probably the pit with one particularly large sarsen in the middle of the state plan for Sector D.

33. The orientation on his plan of walls is probably inaccurate, since the wall was robbed out and recorded in only a short section of mortar. The 1985 excavation demonstrated that the mosaic tesserae are laid parallel, not obliquely, to the line of the porticus, as his plan shows.

34. Goddard 1913: 188.

35. I.e., there are very few instances where two different technical approaches are applied to the same type of problem (e.g., the stylobate foundations of Aisled Buildings I and II).

36. Sarsen foundation anchors are attested in the north and south walls of the south wing, the east and west walls of both phases of the west wing, and the west wall of Aisled Building II. They do not seem to have been used in Aisled Building II, although a sarsen was found in the robbing trench of its west wall. The footings of the north wall contain a few sarsens, but they are the same size as the Greensand blocks.

37. Builders in London had the same problem, so this kind of problem was widely recognized: de la Bédoyère 1991: 11–16.

38. In the south wing, the lowest layer of the footing is three courses of soft greensand packed around sarsens (H.=0.75 m), the next is two or three courses of flints in mortar (H.=0.45 m), topped off with a thin (H.=0.05 m) layer of chalk. The upgoing wall then rests on that, the wall being narrower than the footing. In the Aisled Building I north wall the footing is shallower: two courses of greensand in rammed chalk (H.=0.25 m), with the flint and mortar wall rising on that. In Aisled Building II, the foundation of the north wall is considerably deeper; the lower foundation spreads considerably and is one course of large greensand lumps (L.=c.0.15–0.2 m; H.=c.0.25 m) and occasional small sarsens and chalk lumps in rammed chalk, topped with a layer of clean chalk. Above that, and stepped back on the outside some 0.3 m, are two more courses of greensand and flints in mortar, topped by another layer of clean chalk. The rising wall rests on this level, which is the equivalent of the interior floor.

39. These chalk courses might be attempts to restrict the rising damp, although examples of such are very rare in Roman Britain: de la Bédoyère 1991: 19.

40. Reading the seam between two deposits of chalk that abut may sometimes be impossible, since the semifluid masses have a tendency to fuse. Hence, this upper chalk layer may mark the intended height of the interior floor, but the interior floor may have been laid after the entire wall went up.

41. As mentioned (n. 38), the lower footing of the Aisled Building II north wall is 0.3 m wider on the outside than the upper footing. It appears that the lower footing was laid in a trench and then brought to ground level, then the upper footing was laid and the earth was raised to its level. The wall was then stepped back from the edge of this surface some 0.1 m and the floor laid against the first course of the wall. In the west wing, the east wall rests on a shallow footing of chalk lumps and rammed chalk that is about 0.25 m wider than the wall.

42. The pits were rounded rectangles, c. 1.0 x c. 1.6 m with several courses of large greensand lumps (0.2–0.3 m, depth c. 0.3–0.45 m). The column rested directly on the greensand and was packed with orange clay and pebbles that filled the rest of the pit (depth c. 0.15–0.2 m). The clay preserved the approximate impression of the timber column; the holes were squarish, sometimes as large as 0.9 x 0.7 m, but normally more like 0.45 x 0.4 m. This implies columns of squared timbers about 0.35–0.40 m across.

43. The pits were relatively square cut (c. 0.9 x 1.6–1.8 m, depth c. 0.7–1.3 m). *Opus signinum* bedding (depth c. 0.10–0.15 m). The blocks were of nonstandard dimensions, but their upper surfaces were well trimmed with a tooth chisel. They were fairly well levelled, but not laid out with the precision of monumental architecture (the two preserved blocks are adjacent and have top surfaces at 161.10 and 161.12 m O.D.). The upper parts of the pits were again packed with flints and mortar. The upper surface of the stylobate blocks seems to have determined the main level of the floors, or stood a few centimeters above them.

44. The outer walls of the south wing go to about 1–1.2 m below ground surface. The walls of

Aisled Building I are shallower than those of Aisled Building II (c. 0.4–0.8 m vs. c. 0.6–0.9 m). In the unexcavated west wing, the robbing pit for the presumed hydraulic feature shows some kind of foundation materials at a depth of 1 m. The west wall shows a chalk-and-flint footing at about 0.8 m. The later west porticus seems to have a very shallow footing of only c. 0.2–0.3 m.

45. One set of interior walls with very deep foundations is the two spur walls connecting the outer walls of Aisled Building II to the third pair of columns from the west end. These go down almost the full depth of the stylobate and outer wall foundations and seem to be early additions, hence probably seen as bracing structures, not just divisions.

46. de la Bédoyère 1991: 14–16.

47. This not the layer of tile and lime (*nucleus*) recorded by Vitruvius (7.1.1); Moore 1978: 57–68. The sequence in Vitruvius, and in most practice, is: *statumen*, i.e., the building structure; *rudus, nucleus,* then the *tesserae.* Moore asserts the existence of a "supernucleus," a layer of fine mortar on top of the nucleus which is the actual mortar into which the tesserae are pressed. In the second phase of the Mosaic Corridor, the mortar bedding for mosaic **5** is laid directly on earth, including a ditch fill. In Room 3 of Aisled Building II, the checkerboard mosaic (**6**) is laid on a 0.10 m bedding of yellow mortar, which lies on the chalk floor surface which had served as the first floor of Aisled Building II. In the west wing (Sector B), all of the in situ mosaics seem to be bedded on a similar mortar layer, which rests directly on hypocaust backfill.

48. The first and second floors of Aisled Building I were thin layers of orange clay and brown clay gravel (both redeposited natural, 0.10–0.12 m, and c. 0.15 m, respectively). The first floor of Aisled Building II was a chalk surface (0.10–0.20 m deep) laid over the entire interior surface at the time of the construction, directly lying on the floors of Aisled Building I. The floors of the presumed "kitchen" of Aisled Building II (Room 4) were scores of chalk and mortar patches. The working surface normally was soft rammed chalk. Rooms 5–8 in the north aisle had similar surfaces, with the exception of a surface of rooftiles laid between utilitarian floors in Room 5.

49. E.g., chalk floor of Aisled Building II at 161.97 m O.D., exterior gravel 161.95 m O.D.; mosaic floors in the west wing 161.92–161.98 m O.D., late courtyard surface, slightly built up, 161.97 m O.D.

50. In the layers of overburden or destruction (Phases A:XIII, XIV, B:X–XI), which produced the largest volume, there is a larger volume of flue tile than pan tile. Most of the pan tiles were apparently removed intact as usable material during the lengthy and thorough process of robbing building material; the flue tiles are preserved only in very small fragments and are the result of the breaking up of the walls in which they were embedded. There is very little material for flue tiles from Sector C, which reinforces the impression that C was the service wing and had no hypocaust-heated rooms.

51. Using a foot of 0.296 m (Walthew 1982: 15). Two of the Bath stone blocks from D show a dimension of 0.59 m (2 ft). The interaxial spacing of the columns of Aisled Buildings I and II are 3.3 and 3.6 m, respectively (c. 11.25 and 12.25 ft). The best-preserved dimension is the width of Aisled Building II (between wall faces): c. 14.5 m on center, (49.15 ft). The nave is approximately twice the width of the aisles (6.7 m and 3.9 m, respectively). The width of the south wing is about 6.35 m (21.45 ft). The west wing is 12.2 m wide (41.25 ft).

52. Walthew 1982: 15–35; Millett 1982: 315–20.

53. Richmond 1969: 49–70.

54. Hingley 1989: 64–71, figs. 29, 31, 33; Neal 1974, plans facing page 6. Richmond (1969: 146) calls the type the "improvement of a farmyard surrounded by buildings into a more elegant and unified structure," as opposed to the "development . . . of a corridor house with deep lateral wings."

55. Hingley 1989 51–54.

56. This type is often classified among corridor villas (cf. Downton, Wymbush) although the room terminating the corridor must function more or less in the same way, whether it projects or not: Hingley 1989: 45–47.

57. The resistivity suggests that Aisled Building II does not extend far beyond the evaluation trench at 401/519. If the placing of the spur walls in the east is similar to the west end, this might mean two more bays, for a total length of c. 45.6 m.

58. J. T. Smith 1963: 4, 12–17 and 1982: 321–36. On the unit system in Iron Age Glastonbury and its continuity into Romano-British villas, D. L. Clarke 1972: 801–69.

59. Hingley 1989: 42.

60. The common feature of most types of unit system plan is that each unit comprises a row of two or three rooms that runs from front to back of a wing. The larger rooms cross the full width of the wing; one of the narrower is divided into front and back chambers, the front one of which is a "lobby," either to a porticus or to a large shared room between two dwelling "units": J. T. Smith 1978a: 157; and 1982: 325–26, plans.

61. Enclosing perimeter walls were the norm for British villas: Hingley 1989: 56–57.

62. J. T. Smith 1978a: 349–56, on courtyards.

63. Extensive resistivity survey was conducted in the winter of 1984–85 by C. Gaffney and C. Heron of the Department of Archaeological Sciences, University of Bradford. The survey covered the villa platform and the field to the southeast, taking readings in every 1 m square. In 1985 the results of the resistivity were used to locate ten 1 x 2 m evaluation trenches (see chapter 4.3), of which only two revealed structures (Fig. 40). Resistivity failed to find buildings perhaps because, on this site, buildings are often preserved only as empty foundation trenches covered with broad spreads of destruction rubble; areas of higher resistivity therefore often record only scatters of building material. Also, because the clayey soil was wet and did not drain well, resistivity contrasts registered only large areas of damp vs. dry. For comments on locating villa outbuildings by excavation, see Goodburn 1978: 73–102.

64. Communication from B. Walters.

65. Field survey was conducted in the summer of 1984, when the field was in hay and had not been plowed since the late 1970s. Most of the material found at the time of the field survey was from the rubble of a nineteenth-century cottage that had stood near the pond and had been razed earlier in the century, the material having been dragged across the field and dumped into the forest.

66. At c. 315/605. The material consisted of a dense spread of small terracotta chips, either from brick or tile. It could either be washed or dumped down from the Aisled Building or, perhaps, represent the trace of a spring house, as it is located by the source of a small stream which drains the clay terrace and which flows downhill to the northwest into a sinkhole in the chalk.

67. In March 1985.

68. In the few places where they intersect other ditches or banks, they seem to be cut by them.

69. Cf. native sites with clear discontinuity between the end of the native farmstead and the establishment of a Roman villa: Collingham, Radwell, Stanton, Thenford, Frocester Court, Rudston—all cited by Branigan (1982: 92). Latimer villa demonstrated a twenty-five-year period of abandonment, with the posts of the timber villa being pulled and the ground levelled for the masonry villa. In spite of that, the masonry villa was built on precisely the same alignment as the native timber farmstead: Branigan 1971: 56–60, 169–70; and 1982: 93.

70. There is now clear evidence for the use of wall plaster, even painted plaster, on timber buildings in Roman Britain: Blagg 1991: 10.

71. If the mosaics and wall painting, which are found in makeup layers in A:IX and XI, in fact come from Sector B, then it is possible that the first phase of the west wing predates the construction of Aisled Building II in the late third or early fourth century. If fragments of plaster in A:VII (in the foundations of Aisled Building I) are not from timber buildings, then the first phase of the west wing may predate Aisled Building I. See note 31.

72. Hingley 1989: 41–42. The construction of Aisled Building I in the later third century is therefore typical of the appearance of aisled buildings in Roman Britain, which do not become common until the second half of the second century: Applebaum 1967: 227.

73. Although see note 69.

74. Branigan 1982: 87–92; however, whether newer argicultural techniques were adopted is unknown.

75. Margary 1973: 90–91, no. 43, who argues that the major roads were built soon after the conquest to a coherent plan and that construction of the major roads of the overall system probably reached the line of the Fosse Way by A.D. 47–50. He further argues (1973: 224–25) that some

of the earliest roads on the south coast would have been those pressed inland from the coastal ports, and that road no. 43 would have been among them, from Winchester to Old Sarum, and soon extended to Cunetio, Wanborough, and Cirencester.

76. At Gargrave and Brixworth, rectilinear compounds surround circular huts: Woods 1972; and Goodburn 1976: 317. Langton and Settrington are examples of sites that are founded soon after the conquest as rectangular ditched enclosures and are converted to villas only much later. At Barton Court Farm a trapezoidal compound with timber buildings of the first and second centuries develops into a compound with a small corridor villa in the third century: Miles 1986: 4–19.

77. There is increasing evidence that military engineers may have been influential in shaping the hasty establishment of the infrastructure of the province of Britannia in its early decades, but that infrastructure was largely timber. "It might be argued that it was in timber rather than stone construction that the army's assistance was influential in the towns.": Blagg 1991: 4. Frere (1972:10–11) suggests that military carpenters may have aided in the construction of structures with sleeper beam construction in Verulamium Insula XIV.

78. As in the villas supposedly created by the flight of Gallic capital in the later third century, as posited in D. J. Smith 1969a: 114–16; Rivet 1969: 208–209; Percival 1976: 48; Applebaum 1966: 104; and Branigan 1973: 82–95; 1976: 47; but see chap. 3.1., note 101.

79. Esmonde Cleary 1989: 68; J. H. Williams 1971a: 169.

80. Cf. Sparsholt, with an undivided aisled hall (second century), replaced by a developed hall (c. A.D. 200), with a winged corridor added in the fourth century; with Mansfield Woodhouse, with a late second-century corridor house, with aisled building added in the early fourth: Hingley 1989: 69.

81. Hingley 1989: 40, 50. On the concept of the winged corridor being a result of immigration of landowners from the continent: Applebaum 1967: 132.

82. The pattern of the reoccupation of villas in Gaul of the later third and early fourth centuries is supposedly similar to some types of late use in Britain: villas continue to be used, but at a lower economic level, and rural industrial activities move into the former residential buildings, rather than rebuild the less solid outbuildings: Percival 1976: 48, 169; Branigan 1976: 99–100.

83. E.g., a hut with a footing of flint scatter as at Dorchester: Addyman 1972: 276; Rahtz 1976: 56.

84. Addyman (1972: 276) suggests a similar initial type of layout in the initial "Germanic" habitations in Portchester and Canterbury, where the buildings may have been built into the spaces between the surviving Roman buildings.

85. J. H. Williams 1971b: 99–105.

86. A sample of all types of terracotta elements is in the Devizes Museum. The remaining bulk from the site (c. one cubic meter) was deposited in the northeast corner of Sector B during backfilling.

87. Normal range for a pedalis—L. 0.026–0.027, and for a bessalis—L./W. 0.0170–0.0235, average 0.198: Brodribb 1987: 34.

88. Brodribb 1987: 37.

89. Bessales are normally more common for pilae: Brodribb 1987: 34.

90. Round bricks are supposedly rare in Roman Britain and are usually used for hypocaust pilae: Brodribb 1987: 35, 56.

91. Brodribb (1987:11) reports varieties of dimensions from 0.310 x 0.270 to 0.570 x 0.380 m. The variation at Castle Copse seems much less, as if using only a single standard type in all periods.

92. Brodribb 1987: 11.

93. Brodribb (1987: 11) reports that at Beauport Park only one in five pan tiles has a nail-hole.

94. Brodribb 1987: 17–18, fig. 8.

95. In most phases in Sector A, 45–66% would be flue tiles, 10–17% pan and cover tiles, and 12–15% bricks. The large proportion of flue tiles may be due to the almost complete robbing of building material, in which rooftiles and most bricks could be removed easily, but in which flue tiles, being embedded in the walls, were probably shattered into unusable sizes.

96. There is no evidence of *tegulae mammatae* or spacer bobbins.

97. This is the longest clearly attested length; other fragments demonstrate longer tiles.

98. Brodribb 1987: 65–66.

99. Brodribb 1987: 65–66.

100. *Imbrices* are sometimes used for makeshift flues. Brodribb 1987: 26.

101. Brodribb 1987: 73, 75, figs. 32, 33.

102. A mix of tile and Pennant sandstone roofs is common in the villas in the area. Current opinion is that Pennant slates would have come overland from the Mendips or the Forest of Dean: J. H. Williams 1971a: 178.

103. Two examples of nails were found in fragmentary tiles, one in the dump which constituted the footing of the second outer wall of Aisled Building II and one in the collapse of the south wall of Sector C.

104. This is the only consistent length dimension, since the upper "triangle" of the "hexagon" is always roughly cut and to various dimensions.

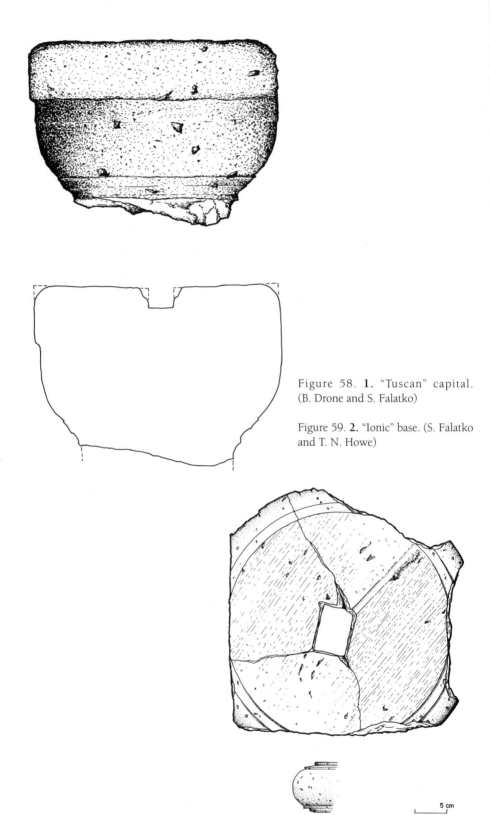

Figure 58. **1.** "Tuscan" capital. (B. Drone and S. Falatko)

Figure 59. **2.** "Ionic" base. (S. Falatko and T. N. Howe)

5 cm

Figure 60. Terracotta roof tile system. (J. Crawford)

Figure 61. Pennant sandstone roof slate system (J. Crawford)

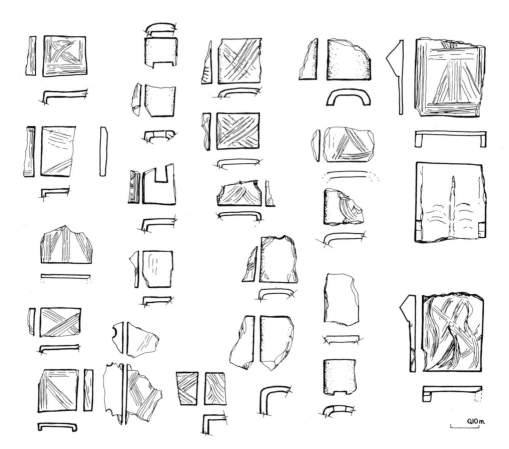

Figure 62. Flue tiles. (T. N. Howe)

0.10 m.

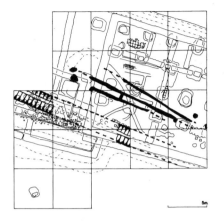

Figure 63. Sector A, Phase I, ditch and beam-slot structure/granary (late first century through second century A.D.).

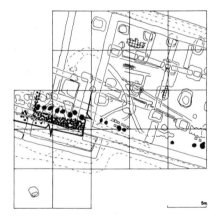

Figure 64. Sector A, Phases III–IV (stakehole and smaller posthole structures (later second century A.D.).

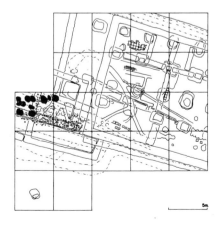

Figure 65. Sector A, Phases V and VI, larger posthole structure (later second, early third centuries A.D.).

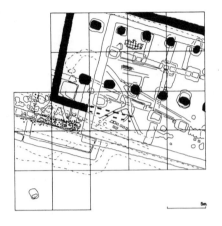

Figure 66. Sector A, Phases VII, VIII, Aisled Building I (mid-third century).

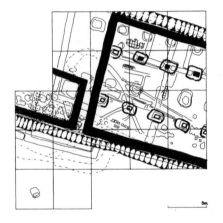

Figure 67. Sector A, Phases IX, early X, X/XI, Aisled Building II as open area, Greensand Quoin Building, flanking ditches (later third–early fourth centuries).

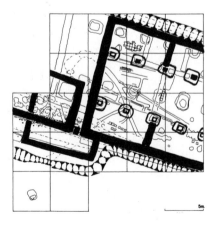

Figure 68. Sector A, Phases later X, X/XI, early XI/XII, Aisled Building II, with first phase of Mosaic Corridor (later third–early fourth centuries).

THE
BRITISH
MUSEUM
FRIENDS

Since starting in 1968 the Friends of the British Museum have made grants of over £2.5 million. The Department of Prints and Drawings, which is responsible for the exhibition *Albrecht Dürer and his legacy*, is just one department that has greatly benefited from this support.

Benefits of membership includes free entry to all exhibitions. Join today and we will refund the cost of your exhibition ticket.

For an application form contact the Friends desk in the Great Court or complete the form below and return it to:
The British Museum Friends
Freepost LON14119
London WC1B 3BR

Mr ☐   Ms ☐   Mrs ☐   Miss ☐   Other ☐

Full Name

Address

Postcode

Daytime Telephone

Email

Registered Charity Number: 1086080

Figure 69. Sector A, early Phase XI, XI/XII, Aisled Building II, early phase of subdivisions, with hypocausts and extension of Mosaic Corridor (after 331 A.D.).

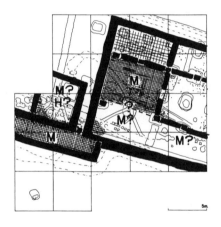

Figure 70. Sector A, later Phase XI, XI/XII, Aisled Building II, later phase of subdivisions, with mosaics on backfilled hypocausts (after A.D. 331 through late fourth century A.D.).

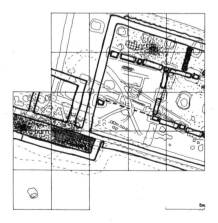

Figure 71. Sector A, later Phase XI, Aisled Building II, insertion of industrial activities into decorated areas.

Figure 72. Sector B, Phase I, beamslots (first–second centuries A.D.).

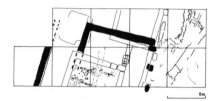

Figure 73. Sector B, Phase III, early phase of the west wing (third–fourth centuries A.D.).

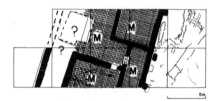

Figure 74. Sector B, Phase IV, later phase of the west wing (fourth century A.D.).

Figure 75. Sector B, Phase VII, insertion of industrial activities into decorated areas (later fourth century A.D. or later).

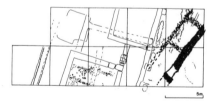

Figure 76. Sector B, Phase IX, later occupation in courtyard (later fourth or early fifth century A.D.).

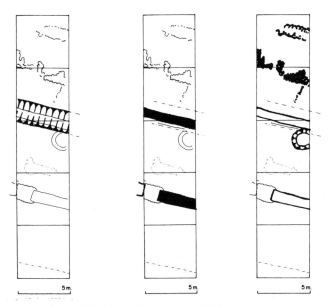

Figure 77. Sector C, Phase I, ditch (later first century A.D.).

Figure 78. Sector C, Phase III (fourth century A.D.).

Figure 79. Sector C, Phase V, latest constructions in courtyard (later fourth or fifth century A.D.).

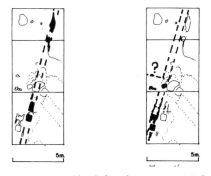

Figure 80. Sector D, earlier construction (third–fourth centuries A.D.).

Figure 81. Sector D, later construction (fourth century A.D.?).

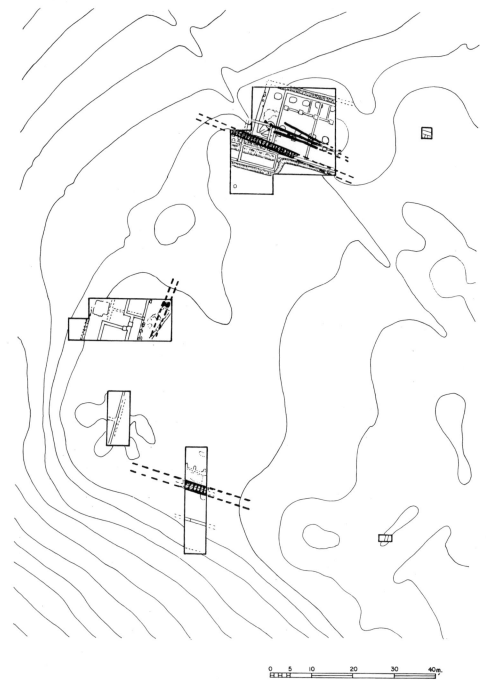

Figure 82. Early ditches and beamslot structures (late first century A.D. through later second century A.D.).

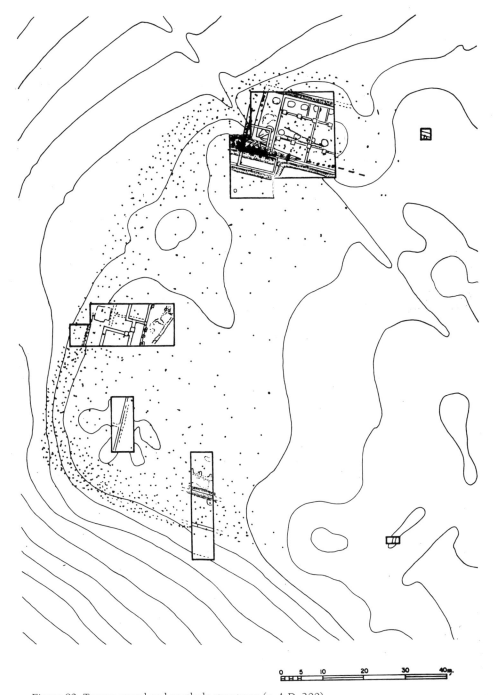

Figure 83. Terrace gravel and posthole structures (c. A.D. 200).

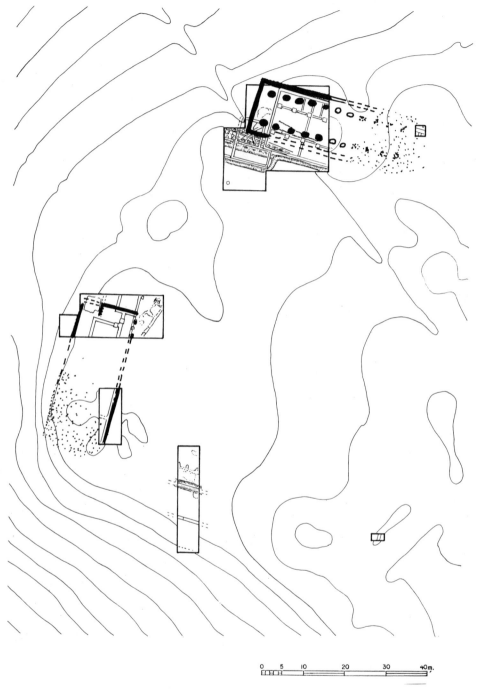

0 5 10   20   30   40m.

Figure 84. Early masonry buildings: Aisled Building I, early phase of west wing (mid-/later third century A.D.).

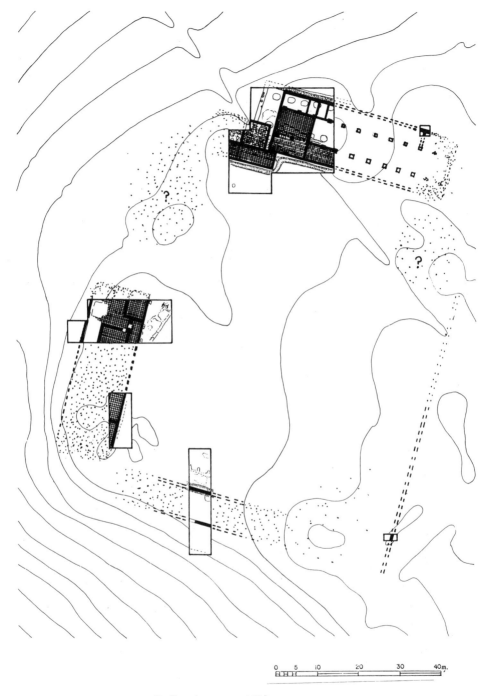

Figure 85. Later masonry villa (fourth century A.D.).

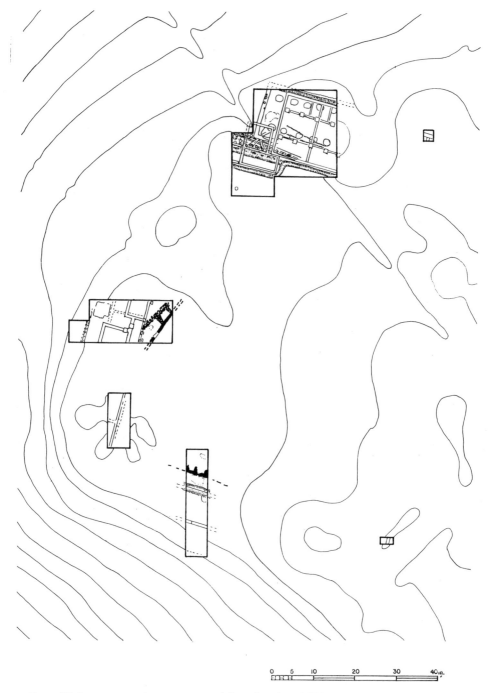

Figure 86. Late constructions in courtyard (later fourth and fifth centuries A.D.).

0 5 10   20   30   40 m.

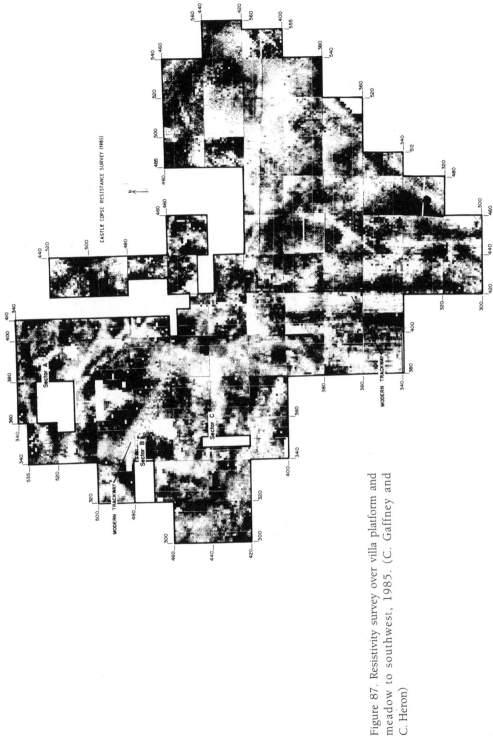

Figure 87. Resistivity survey over villa platform and meadow to southwest, 1985. (C. Gaffney and C. Heron)

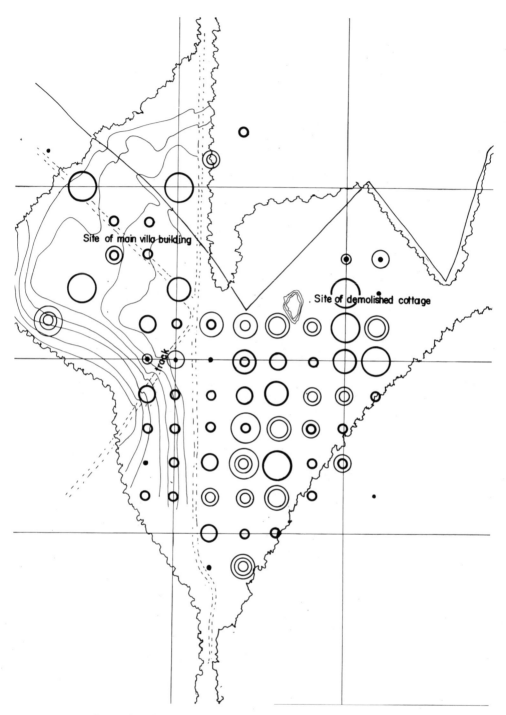

Figure 88. Relative phosphate intensity over villa platform and meadow to southwest, 1985. (K. L. Gleason and G. C. Mees)

4.5 MOSAICS

JOHN F. KENFIELD

Mosaics were found in the Castle Copse villa in both Sectors A and B (Figs. 89–90). These mosaics seem to fall into two groups in terms of chronology and style. The evidence for the earlier series is limited to fragments found in A and for the most part was found incorporated into the matrix of later floors. With one important exception, these fragments are too small to allow a reconstruction of the motifs, but they are remarkable for the tiny size of their tesserae, as small as 0.005 x 0.005 m, and for their broad color range. These characteristics mark them as significantly different from their in situ successors in both Sectors A and B, approaching the technical level of Neal's Grade 1, a refinement of technique rare in Roman Britain.[1]

All of the contexts in which these early mosaic fragments were found appear to belong to A:XI, the remodelling of Aisled Building II, or later.[2] This indicates that the earlier mosaics formed pavements contemporary with A:IX, the early Aisled Building II, although not necessarily in that building. No fragments of this early series were found in Sector B, the west wing, though B underwent modifications similar to those in A.[3]

The evidence for the later series of mosaics in both Sectors A and B is much more complete.[4] Several fragments are in situ. The closest parallels are with many of the mosaics in the complex of buildings at Lydney Park, and there are strong resemblances with the mosaics in many of the villas in central southwestern Britain, most notably at Box, Wellow, Whittington, and Withington.[5] What is especially interesting about this relationship between the mosaics from the villa at Castle Copse and those at Lydney Park is the dating evidence provided by the Castle Copse series. According to the results of excavations conducted by P. J. Casey at Lydney Park in 1980 and 1981, it now seems certain that the Guesthouse, Abaton, and Baths were built in the late third or early fourth century A.D., considerably earlier than originally suggested by Wheeler.[6] The argument for the dating of the mosaics in these buildings revolves around whether the mosaics are contemporary with the building or replacements for earlier floors. Cookson states that, with the exception of the interlaced squares mosaic in room XVIII of the Guesthouse, "all [the mosaics at Lydney] now remain difficult to assign to a period after c. 340."[7] The numismatic evidence at Castle Copse, however, suggests that the comparable mosaics in A:XI and XI/XII and the construction of the Mosaic Corridor probably postdate A.D. 331.

The later mosaics are composed of large, relatively coarse, occasionally ungrouted and unpolished tesserae that display a limited palette. The later series of mosaics in the villa at Castle Copse is, with one important exception in Sector B (**9**) (Figs. 100–104), devoid of representational images and specific iconographic references.

Earlier Series[8]

Most of the findspots of this series give no indication of the original location. Many fragments were found in the series of chalk and mortar floors of Sector A, Room 4 (e.g., **3**, Fig. 91), which was presumably a kitchen or industrial area. Many of the fills of the channel hypocaust of the Greensand Quoin Building contained mosaics of similar dimensions, but they are not necessarily from the floor above.

3. Three fragments in four colors with straight and curved linear patterns. Sector A, Room 4, A141:XI (Fig. 91).

Max. L.=0.007. Color and dimensions of tesserae: white (7.5YR 8/2): chalk 0.009 x 0.009–0.007 x 0.006; black (7.5YR N4/): Lias limestone 0.009 x 0.009–0.007 x 0.006; red, (10YR 5/4): terracotta 0.009 x 0.009–0.007 x 0.006; greyish green (10YR 7/2): Pennant stone 0.009 x 0.009–0.007 x 0.006.

4. Fragment with possible interlaced square. A364:XI (Fig. 92)

Color and dimensions of tesserae: white (10YR 8/1): chalk 0.006 x 0.0057; grey (5Y 6/2): Pennant stone 0.007 x 0.007; red (10YR 5/4): terracotta 0.007 x 0.007; purplish red (5R 4/4): Pennant stone 0.007 x 0.009.

This fragment provides the clearest indication of the kind of motif of the early series. The fragment shows a section of a straight band filled with a stepped meander in black, grey, red, yellow, and white tesserae. This band is bordered by an angle of c. 55° in white tesserae and contains a fragmentary design in black, grey, red, and white tesserae. The fragment appears to come from one of the sides of a rotated interlaced square, whether a single pair or in multiple pairs as the central motif,[9] and preserves part of the filler design between the side of the square and the rectilinear frame that encloses the central interlaced squares motif. Because of the degree of the angle, it is assumed that the interlaced squares were rotated according to Cookson's Types B or D, either paradigm providing a late third-/early fourth-century A.D. date, if the revised dating of Lydney is accepted.[10] It is also possible, given the degree of the angle, that the fragment derives from a central motif using radiating panels in a hexagonal or octagonal pattern.[11]

Later Series

5. Corridor Mosaic. Sector A. A8=178:XI/XII (Figs. 93–96).

L. (reconstructed)=11.20+; W.=(reconstructed) c. 1.90.

Three rectangular mats (5a–c) from east to west: guilloche mat; a running pelta; another guilloche mat with inner meander frame, all with continuous tesselated border. Approximately 1.0 m² of guilloche mat preserved at eastern end, 0.5 m² of meander frame at western end, only a few tesserae of central pelta panel.

5a. Corridor Mosaic: Guilloche Mat. Lifted in 1983 and now in Devizes Museum.

L. unknown, W.=1.16.

Color and dimensions of tesserae: grey border (5Y 6/2): Pennant stone 0.04 x 0.025–0.025 x 0.0175; grey of guilloche (5Y 6/2): Pennant stone 0.015 x

0.0125–0.0125 x 0.01; white (10YR 8/1): chalk 0.02 x 0.02–0.015 x 0.01; red (10YR 5/4): terracotta, 0.02 x 0.0125–0.015 x 0.01

The guilloche mat, or basket weave, motif occurs often as a border or filler motif in Romano-British mosaics.[12] Its use as the central design is rare and limited to Woodchester, Lydney Park, and Kings Weston.[13] The use of the guilloche mat as a sequential motif in a corridor occurs at Woodchester and Withington, both in southwestern England and dating to the fourth century.

Mid-fourth century A.D.

5b. Corridor Mosaic: Pelta Panel

L. unknown; W. (reconstructed)=1.16

Color and size of tesserae: Several mosaic fragments consisting of five or more tesserae were discovered that appear to derive from the original running peltae panel. Red (10YR 5/4): terracotta 0.02 x 0.125–0.015 x 0.01; grey (5Y 5/1): Pennant stone 0.015 x 0.0125–0.0125 x 0.01; grey border (7.5YR N4): Pennant stone 0.04 x 0.025–0.025 x 0.0175; white (7.5YR 8/2): chalk 0.02 x 0.02–0.015 x 0.01.

Discovered by W. C. Lukis and later destroyed.[14] From the evidence left in situ, it would appear that whoever was responsible for the antiquarian digging in the Mosaic Corridor had lifted at least a section of the central panel. A section of what appears to be the Mosaic Corridor's pavement was drawn by Lukis's team at the time of excavation and is now in the library of the Devizes Museum.

The watercolor in Devizes shows the following motifs: a design of peltae in red, grey, and white arranged in rectangles and squares, the entire panel outlined again first with a thin frame of white, two tesserae in width, succeeded by a thick grey frame in coarser tesserae. To the west, presumably, the peltae are followed first by a meander frame in red, grey, and white. This meander is an inner frame around the westernmost of the motifs of the Mosaic Corridor, another rectangular guilloche mat/basket weave panel in red, grey, and white. This meander is simple in form on the short sides and converts to a swastika meander on the long sides. The entire series of three panels, including the meander around the westernmost guilloche mat, appears, in turn, to have been bordered by a plain grey frame of large pennant stone tesserae.

Several observations can be made on the basis of the comparanda.[15] First, the use of the pelta motif is largely confined to southwestern Britain. Second, in those excavations in which firm dating evidence was discovered, the pelta mosaics seem to date to the fourth century A.D. In none of these examples, however, are the peltae defined by rectangles in squares as they were at Castle Copse, at least according to Lukis's watercolor. Of the comparanda listed (n. 15), the closest parallels again seem to be with Lydney Park, where the pelta motif is used in rectangular panels, both a primary motif in Room XXXV of the Bath frigidarium, and as one of a series of motifs in a corridor, as in Room XI of the Guesthouse. The third example at Lydney Park is in Room LXV of the Temple, where it occupies a corridor-like position. The Whittington Court example, also in Gloucestershire, is one of a sequential series of motifs decorating the pavement of a corridor. The running pelta motif is used similarly in the villas at Box and Wellow. The Lydney Park examples may be secondary and therefore date to the second half of the fourth century A.D., a date that accords well with Whittington Court and Castle Copse.

Mid-fourth century A.D.

5c. Corridor Mosaic: guilloche mat with meander frame

L. unknown, W. reconstructed=c. 1.10–1.20

Color and size of tesserae: red (10R 5/4): terracotta 0.02 m. x 0.0125–0.015 x 0.01; white (7.5YR 8/2): chalk 0.02 x 0.02–0.015 x 0.01; grey meander (5Y 6/2): Pennant stone 0.015 x 0.0125–0.0125 x 0.01; grey frame (10YR 7/2): Pennant stone 0.04 x 0.025–0.025 x 0.0175.

According to Lukis's watercolor in the library of the Devizes Museum, the pelta mosaic was succeeded to the west by another rectangular guilloche mat in red, grey, and white. Thus, it would appear that the pelta panel was sandwiched between two guilloche mat panels. Unfortunately, nothing remains in situ of this western guilloche mat, but it seems to have corresponded to that at the eastern end of the Mosaic Corridor, except that it was narrower because of the surrounding meander frame. Portions of this meander frame have survived in situ, showing that it, too, was set within the same grey, tessellated frame as the other motifs of the corridor. The meander frame border also has form and dimensions on the panel's short sides different from those on the panel's long sides. The long sides are bordered by the swastika meander, which, because of its more complex design, is broader than the simple meander at the short ends of the panel. The swastika meander marches to each corner of the panel, and then, as it marches through the final crossing of the swastika and turns the corners to form the short sides of the border, it becomes a simple meander. Such is the appearance of the fragments in situ which preserve the southwest corner of this border. Such is the appearance, too, of the watercolor in Devizes of the mosaic discovered at Castle Copse by Lukis. The colors of the meander border are red, grey, and white.[16]

The guilloche/basket weave mat[17] in the Guesthouse at Lydney Park is not used in a corridor, but is instead the central motif in a room that lies immediately to the east of the large central room in the northeastern wing of the building. Otherwise, the Lydney Park mosaic is the same as the eastern guilloche mat of the Mosaic Corridor at Castle Copse, including the surrounding frame which consists of three bands, the outer being a grey frame of large tesserae.

An exact parallel had yet to be found for a meander border surrounding a guilloche mat, as in the western panel of the Mosaic Corridor. Fragments of a similar meander border have been found around the cantharus *emblema* in Room 3 of B. Meander borders are common. The closest parallel in terms of geographical proximity and probable date is the broad meander border used in Room VIII of the villa at Box. The unusual interlocking-squares or brick motif found in Room 1 of Sector B also has its closest parallel with Room XX in the villa at Box. Though no unimpeachable dating evidence is available for the mosaics of the villa at Box,[18] the strong similarities of the late mosaics of the villa at Castle Copse with the mosaics at both Lydney Park and the villa at Box suggest that the mosaics at all three sites are roughly contemporary and products of the same *officina*.

Mid-fourth century A.D.

6. Checkerboard mosaic. Sector A, Room 3. A48=63=70:XI (Fig. 97)

L. (reconstructed)=c. 8.4; W. (reconstructed)=5.5 (full area of Sector A, Room 3): L. fragment=1.20; W. fragment=0.50.

Color and dimensions of tesserae: white (7.5YR 8/2): chalk 0.025 x 0.02–0.015 x 0.01; red (7.5R 5/6): Pennant stone 0.035 x 0.03–0.025 x 0.02; grey border (5Y 6/2): Pennant stone 0.04 x 0.025–0.025 x 0.0175.

Several fragments lie in situ and several red sandstone border tesserae also lie in situ in the northeast corner of Room 3.[19] Since all of the fragments lie toward the periphery of the rooms, it is uncertain whether or not the checkerboard pattern was an inner frame surrounding a central motif. In Sector A, Room 3, the checkerboard extends almost as far as the wall, whereas in Room 4 of Sector B, a broad tesselated frame surrounds the checkerboard fragments. Given the crude workmanship of these checkerboard mosaics, it seems most likely that it was the single decorative motif within the surrounding outer frame.

Though the majority of the comparanda[20] are in the southwest of Britain, it is clear that this motif enjoyed popularity throughout Britannia, both as a framing device and as a central motif. The comparanda date from the second to the fourth century. Hurst, Dartnall, and Fisher say of the example in the villa at Box, "In its materials and cruder workmanship (tesserae c. 0.02 m across or larger, more irregularly shaped than in the other floors), it stands apart from the other floors just described and it might be tempting therefore to regard it as later."[21] The same comments might be made about the checkerboard mosaics in Sectors A and B, but their cruder workmanship seems due to their secondary importance rather than to a date relatively later than the other in situ fourth-century mosaics.

After A.D. 331.

7. Interlocking box corridor mosaic, Sector B, Room 1. B:IV (Figs. 98–99).

L.=5.40+; W.=2.10. Largest preserved fragment c. 0.90 x 1.80 at 332/473.50; 161.885–161.940 O.D.

Color and dimensions of tesserae: white (10YR 8/1): chalk 0.022 x 0.014–0.011 x 0.01; dark grey or black (7.5YR N4): Pennant stone 0.022 x 0.014–0.011 x 0.01.

Heavily worn. Interlocking boxes in black lines against a white ground. The tesserae are set into a bed of *opus signinum*. Photographs of Pole's 1936–37 excavations, now housed in the library of the Devizes Museum, seem to show that the southern end of this corridor, Sector D, Room 1, was paved with a similar motif.

There is no exact parallel[22] for mosaic 7. The closest examples are a mosaic at Box and another apparently Flavian example in Room 21 at Fishbourne Palace. Given the geographical and chronological proximity, as well as the other similarities of the mosaics at the Castle Copse and Box villas, it is probable that they were produced by the same *officina* and share a similar date in the fourth century A.D.[23]

Fourth century A.D.

8. White Pavement, Sector B, Room 2. B:IV

Room 2 measures c. 4.20 x 4.60, exposed. A single expanse of white mosaic is preserved in the southern half of the room (c. 1.95 x 0.80 at 331.50/476.40; 161.980–161.993 O.D.).

Color and dimensions of tesserae: white (10YR 8/1): chalk 0.025 x 0.02–0.015 x 0.01.

The tesserae are ungrouted and unpolished and are set into a bed of *opus signinum* (161.776–161.879 O.D.) which is in turn spread over a coarse flint packing.

White tesselated floors are common in Roman Britain from the first century.[24] Since the tesserae are similar in material and size with the white tesserae used in the other in situ mosaics in Sectors A, B, and D, it is probable that Sector B, Room 2 mosaic is contemporary with the others.

Fourth century A.D.

9. Cantharus Mosaic, Sector B, Room 3. B:IV (Figs. 100–104).

L. Room 3 reconstructed 6.3; W. Room 3 reconstructed 6.0

Color and dimensions of tesserae: white (10YR 8/1): chalk 0.025 x 0.025 (outside *emblema*), 0.0125 x 0.01 (within *emblema*); offwhite (7.5YR 8/2): Bath stone 0.015 x 0.0075 and smaller red (10YR 5/4): terracotta 0.015 x 0.015–0.0125 x 0.01; dark grey (7.5YR N4): Pennant stone 0.02 x 0.018–0.012 x 0.012; light grey (5Y 5/1): 0.017 x 0.015–0.012 x 0.01m.

Many areas of the mosaic display considerable wear, particularly in the vestibule where the plain white pavement has twice been patched with sandstone and terracotta border tesserae of mismatching colors and sizes. Damage has also been caused by floor subsidence. In the vestibule this subsidence may be due to an underlying robber trench, as the slumping follows a linear north-south alignment; elsewhere it is more random, perhaps reflecting the earlier hypocaust in the northern half of Room 3 and beneath adjacent Room 2. A quarter round molding of *opus signinum* (B34=35) overlies the white tesselation of the mosaic along the east wall of the room, perhaps associated with the apparent replasterings and repaintings of Room 3.

All of Room 3 was paved with a high quality, white mosaic of relatively small, carefully prepared, highly polished tesserae, set in an *opus signinum* bedding. The mosaic, like the room, is irregular in shape with a large nearly square central space and an offset entrance vestibule in the southeast corner. The east half of the nearly square central chamber is embellished with a polychrome fluted cantharus *emblema* in tesserae considerably smaller than the surrounding white field. The inner frame that immediately surrounds the fluted cantharus was circular and filled with a stepped meander design. The octagonal outer contour for this inner frame is formed by the inner contours of two interlaced squares, the interiors of which are filled with a cable or simple two-strand guilloche. The space between the inner circular frame and the octagonal middle frame formed by the two interlaced squares is filled with white tesserae. These interlaced squares are not rotated. Thus one of the two interlaced squares has its four sides parallel with the sides of the swastika meander that forms an outer rectangular frame around the interlaced boxes; the other is rotated at 45°. The rectangular outer frame is very fragmentary, but enough remains to show that its long sides (the eastern and western sides) were swastika meanders, of which the two marching lines are black and grey, and each is two tesserae in width (c. 0.025 m). It would appear that the eastern and western points of the interlaced squares set at 45° would have intersected these swastika meanders, but the mosaic is too fragmentary to provide any evidence as to how this intersection was accomplished. The swastika meanders completed the four corners of the outer frame, but, then, the short sides between the corners were formed by some other decorative motif, again too fragmentary to reconstruct. The fragments of these panels do contain right-angled triangles in white and grey, and a small portion of a curvilinear design in red terracotta and offwhite tesserae set against a grey field. These panels in the short sides of the outer frame are bordered, certainly to the outside, and presumably to the inside as well, by the parallel grey and black lines of the swastika meander. Otherwise, the entire floor is paved with white tesserae. The white tesserae outside the swastika meander frame are three times the size of the tesserae of the swastika meander frame and the motifs within it. The outer frame lies c. 1.10 m from the north and south walls of the room, but is extremely close to the east wall and the pit in the west half of the room. The cantharus motif faces and is axially aligned with the pit, emphasizing the relationship between the two features.[25]

Both of the main central motifs—the interlaced squares and the enclosed volute crater or cantharus—are motifs that are relatively common in the repertory of Romano-British mosaics.[26] The meander frame is also well-known in Romano-British mosaics.[27] There appear to be no swastika meander frames that are quite as high quality as this example. The closest parallel for this meander again appears to be with several mosaics in the villa at Box, where, among others, a swastika meander against a white ground appears in the almost square Room VIII, framing a simple box motif containing a quatre-foil guilloche or knot.[28] The particular combination of elements present in Mosaic **9**, though, appears to be unique.

The square pit cut through the mosaic and centered on the cantharus *emblema* (Fig. 104) may be the robbing out for a hydraulic feature such as a plunge bath or fountain. The close similarities between the mosaics in the villas at Castle Copse, Box, and the complex at Lydney Park lead to the impression that they are all more or less contemporary and by the same *officina*, a supposition strengthened by the fact that the Baths at Lydney Park contain the only other cantharus mosaic in a bathing context in Roman Britain.[29] Of the interlaced square mosaics at Lydney Park, however, the closest in style to that at Castle Copse is that in Room XVIII of the Guesthouse. The interlaced squares of this example are filled with a cable or two-strand guilloche like that at Castle Copse, and the squares are not rotated, a feature said by Cookson to be typical of the second half of the fourth century and perhaps a characteristic of an *officina* based at Lindinis (Ilchester).[30]

Fourth century A.D.

10. Checkerboard Mosaic, Sector B, Room 4. B24=34=70:IV (Fig. 105)

L. Room 4=5.90; W. exposed=3.80; 161.38–161.915 O.D.

Color and dimensions of tesserae: white (7.5YR 8/2): chalk 0.022 x 0.014–0.011 x 0.01; dark grey or black (7.5YR N4): Limestone 0.020 x 0.015–0.01 x 0.009; red (1OR 5/4): terracotta 0.035 x 0.03–0.025 x 0.02.

Fragments of large red terracotta border tesserae set into an *opus signinum* bedding survive around the northern and western edges of the room. At c. 0.90 m from the west wall (at 324.70/472), there survive small fragments of two lines of alternating black sandstone and white chalk tesselated squares (c. 0.11 x 0.11 m). None of the surviving tesserae were grouted or polished. A single quarter round *opus signinum* molding (B30) (L.=c. 0.34 x W.=0.10 x H.=0.06 at 323.45/470.80; 161.96 O.D.) sealing the edge of the mosaic is preserved along the west edge of the room, whereas, in the north, the mosaic abuts a preexisting plaster surface. The central part of the checkerboard was destroyed by a series of scattered stakeholes and two parallel beam slots. Since these later structures destroyed the greater portion of the mosaic and its entire center, it is impossible to know if the checkerboard motif covered the entire floor within the outer border, or whether the checkerboard pattern served as an inner frame around a central pattern.

The checkerboard motif occurs throughout the province from the Flavian period on,[31] usually in borders, but occasionally as a central motif in the context of a corridor or a vestibule.[32] The checkerboard motif is most often found in a large room as a peripheral panel in a frame around more important central motifs (Fig. 105). Since Room 4 in Sector B is neither a corridor nor an ancillary room, there is no way of knowing whether the scraps of checkerboard pattern present in mosaic **10** represent traces of the overall pattern used on the floor or traces of an inner frame around a more complicated central motif. The tesserae, however, are large and irregular, and they remained ungrouted and unpolished, perhaps suggesting late production. The lesser importance of Room 4 suggests the lack of a central motif. Though mosaic **10** may be late, there is no evidence to suggest that it is other than contemporary with the other in situ mosaics in Sectors A and B.

Fourth century A.D.

11. Mosaic (Interlocking Box?), Sector D, Room 1.[33]

Dimensions uncertain.

Room 1 was paved with mosaic preserved only in a few small chalk and limestone fragments (e.g., at 328.80/456.70, 161.862 O.D. and at 328.40/458.00, 161.858 O.D.). In the eastern part of the room, the scattered tesserae are bedded in mortar which, in turn, overlies chalk, mortar and *opus signinum,* with the scattered flint nodule. To the west the sequence appears to be mosaic over mortar, chalk, mortar, chalk, and yellowish clay. Much of the exposed mosaic mortar bedding in Room 1 is pocked by a series of small diagonally-oriented holes, the marks of the pick of Pole's excavators. The pattern is not identified by Warren in his report nor could it be identified in the 1985 excavations. Three photographs of Pole's 1936–37 excavations housed in the library of the Devizes Museum appear to show the unearthed mosaic of Pavement B or details thereof.[34]

Though it is difficult to discern the design shown in these photographs, they appear to show a series of straight dark (black or grey) lines some of which are parallel and some which intersect others at right angles, all set against a white background. These dark lines seem to have a width of two tesserae, whereas the stripes of white background are three and sometimes four tesserae in width. In addition, a watercolor of a mosaic fragment discovered in Pole's excavations in the Devizes Museum shows a line of black tesserae five cubes in width separating rows of stepped triangles both above and below the line against a white background. Unfortunately it is not known whether the fragment shown in this watercolor belongs with the fragments shown in the photographs.

Various features were discovered in the excavation of Sector D that suggest that Room 1 is the southern end of a long colonnaded corridor running along the courtyard facade of the western wing (see chapter 4.4). The interlocking box mosaic in Sector B, Room 1 preserves another section of the pavement of this corridor. Indeed, the mosaic fragments shown in Pole's photographs of Sector D appear to belong to the same pattern. Thus, it would appear that this interlocking box motif paved the entire corridor and that, at least at the southern end of the corridor, the interlocking box motif was framed by a series of black and white bands containing the stepped triangles. Since the periphery of the mosaic in Sector B, Room 1 is destroyed, it is impossible to know if the interlocking box motif at the northern end of the corridor was framed in a similar fashion. The interlocking box motif[35] is unique to Roman Britain, though it does resemble various patterns sometimes called "brick work" that appear to have been common throughout the Empire.

The banded frame containing stepped triangles is also common throughout the Late Roman Empire.[36] In Britain, as elsewhere, the motif is used most often around more complicated motifs at both the periphery of mosaics and as a filler motif on interior frames.[37]

Fourth century A.D.

12. Room 3, Sector D (Fig. 39).

Dimensions uncertain

Room 3 of Sector D is of uncertain form, since it lay outside the 1985 excavations and is known only from Diggory's plan as published by Warren. It lies to the west of Room 1, and is separated from it by the mortar base of a northwest-southeast wall (Feature G) which turns a corner towards the southwest (Feature H). The floor within and along the walls' angle is described as having been paved with mortar, presumably a mosaic bedding,[38] while a mosaic fragment c. 4.0 m to the west and presumably that labelled A on Diggory's plan preserved a tesselated pavement of terracotta tesserae "with spaced lozenges of white tile."[39]

It is impossible to know from this brief description what part of the pavement is being described, and whether, for that matter, the pavement was a combination of *opus tessellatum* and *opus sectile*. Lozenges are unusual, but not unknown, in end-to-end rows in the outer frames surrounding larger and more complex central motifs.[40] At Thruxton, Winterton, and Brantingham the lozenges of the outer frame are enclosed by rectangles. At both Winterton and Aldborough the lozenges are concentric. If either had been the case in Room 3 of Sector D, it seems reasonable to assume that it would have been mentioned by Warren.

As a motif in the central designs of tesselated pavements, the lozenge is almost ubiquitous as the unit of eight-pointed perspective stars, and as a filler motif in many complex designs.[41] It would seem from Warren's description that the portion of a tesselated pavement found in Room 3 of Sector D was probably a frame. The known instances of the use of the lozenge as a border and/or corridor motif in Roman Britain all seem to date to the fourth century A.D.; and that at the Whittington Court, probably to that century's third quarter.

Fourth century A.D.

NOTES

1. Neal 1981: 21, 34–35; Rainey 1973: 12–13. Rockbourne: Hewitt 1969: pl. IV; Harpham: Cookson 1984: 88–89, pls. 86–87. Both the Rockbourne and Harpham mosaics appear to date to the early fourth century, which accords well with the dating evidence for A:IX, the phase during which the early series of mosaics was presumably laid. The high quality of these mosaic fragments for the early phases of the monumentalized stone villa at Castle Copse may be indicated, too, by the wall painting fragments, many of which are in "Egyptian" blue, said to be a costly imported pigment reserved for only the most magnificent of buildings.

2. A287 is the fill of the ditch on the south side of Aisled Building II. It may date to A:IX, but more probably belongs to A:XI. See n. 8.

3. Sector B did provide a finer series and a coarser series of wall paintings, presumably earlier and later, respectively, both found as residual material in later layers.

4. The few traces of mosaic found in Sector D are probably part of the same mosaic as in Sector B, Room 1.

5. Cookson 1984: 46–99; Neal 1981: 19–20; D. J. Smith 1969a: 95–102; and 1969b: 235–45. Similarities exist also between the mosaics at Castle Copse and those in northeastern England. These similarities appear first in the early series and the mosaics in the villa at Harpham (Yorkshire) in work that approaches Neal's Grade 1. The fourth-century mosaics in northeast England show a propensity for meander and stepped triangle frames, guilloche mats, and peltae panels, all prominent features of the later series at Castle Copse: Cookson 1984: 78–99.

6. Wheeler and Wheeler 1932: 66 for a late date. Casey 1981: 30–32; and Cookson 1984: 55–57 for the earlier dating.

7. Cookson 1984: 56.

8. Only the two largest fragments of this earlier series of mosaics from Sector A have been included in the following catalogue. The other contexts in which the tesserae from this earlier series were found include A287:IX (or XI), A348, 556–559:XI, A196:XI/XII, A15:XIII, A1–2, 21, 24, 40:XIII–XV. Among the tesserae of these uncatalogued fragments, only one color is found (in A15:XIII) that does not appear in the two catalogued fragments, yellow 10YR 8/1: chalk 0.007 X 0.008 m.

9. Cookson 1984: 55–58. Rotated interlaced squares: Bathurst and King 1879: pl. VII; Wheeler and Wheeler 1932: 66, pl. XXI; Cookson 1984: pls. 48, 50, 54, 79; Neal 1981: 69 and 104–105, nos. 36 and 63; Johnson 1982: pl. 35. Multiple rotated interlaced squares: Cookson 1984: pl. 49, 56, 63b; Lysons 1817: pl. V; Rainey 1973: pl. 13B; Neal 1981: no. 58; Lysons 1817: pl. XXVIII.

10. Cookson 1984: 55–57.

11. Neal 1981: 31–33, figs. 10 and 11. Radial octagon panels: Neal 1981: 104–105; Johnson 1982: pls. 30 and 43; Johnson 1982: pl. 30; D. J. Smith 1969a: pls. 3.3–4.

12. Guilloche mat mosaics, parallels at: Woodchester, Room 3; Withington; Kings Weston; Lydney Park, Guesthouse, Room XIV; Cirencester: Lysons 1797: pls. XI, XIII; Lysons 1817: pls. XIX, XXII; Boon 1950: 5–58, pl. IIIa; Bathurst and King 1879: pl. XV; Wheeler and Wheeler 1932: pl. XXIIb: Neal 1981: nos. 23, 28–29.

13. Its use as a central motif occurs on a fourth-century mosaic from Carthage in the British Museum: Hinks 1933: fig. 129 = no. 38.

14. Lukis and Ward 1860: 261.

15. Pelta comparanda: Ilchester Mead; Wellow, Room A, pelta panel used in border, central medallion of interlaced squares contains guilloche and surrounds circular guilloche, corridor mosaic, Room C, and border, pavement E, corridor M; Fullerton Manor, Wherwell, corridor; Wiggington, border of pelta and meander; Horkstow; Scampton, corridor; Chedworth, Room 14; Lydney Park, Room LXV, Temple, Side Chapel, Room XXXV of Bath frigidarium, Room XI of Guesthouse; Box, corridor; Whittington Court, corridor II, north end; Llanfrynach; Dorchester/Somerleigh Court; Frampton, Room A, Room B; Bancroft Villa, Room 12 (fourth-century addition); Thenford; Aldborough, corridor: Neal 1981: nos. 6, 79; Lysons 1813: i, pl. VII, iii, pls. IV, V, VI; D. J. Smith 1969a: pls. 3.22. 3.27; Cookson 1984: pl. 58a, 84; Wheeler and Wheeler 1932: pls. I, XXa, XXIIa; Brakspear 1904: 245, 344, fig. 2; Hurst, Dartnall, and Fisher 1987: fig. 5; O'Neil 1953: 13, pls. II, IV.

16. For a general discussion of meander patterns, Neal 1984: 33–34.

17. Parallels for meander border at: Box, corridor IV, Room VII, Room XX; Wellow; Combe St. Nicholas; Withington; Woodchester, corridor 2, Room 10, Room 15, Room 18; Micklegate Bar; Stonesfield; Newton St. Loe, Room 4; Walton Heath; Great Witcombe, mosaic 1; Chedworth, Rooms 5 and 10; Cirencester, Ashcroft House, mosaic 1 and Dyer St., Seasons Mosaic; Barton Farm, mosaic 6; Rudston; Aldborough, Muses Mosaic: Brakspear 1904: 247, 249, 344 fig. 1; Lysons 1779: p. XI, XIIa, XIX, XVII, XVIII; Lysons 1817: pls. XIX, figs. E and G, XX; Cookson

1984: pls. 40, 46, 47, 57a, 58b, 64, 93b, 81; Rainey 1973: pls. 12A, 3A; Smith 1969a: pls. 3.12, 3.14, 3.15a; Smith 1975: pls. CIX.2, CXXV, CCCX; Smith 1986: figs. 138–35; Neal 1981: 53–54, nos. 3, 19; Johnson 1982: pl. 30.

18. Hurst, Dartnall, and Fisher 1987: 23–25 present a new, if brief, discussion of the mosaics. Since no independent dating evidence was discovered in these most recent excavations, there is a heavy reliance on comparanda, with advice from D. J. Smith, in arriving at a late third/early fourth-century A.D. date. The Castle Copse mosaics suggest that the Box mosaics may be somewhat later.

19. There is a similar pavement in Room 4 of Sector B.

20. Verulamium, Insula IV, building X, corridor; Newton St. Loe, Room 1, Room 6; Lippen Wood, West Meon, Aisled Building, Room P; Bignor, Room 55; Fishbourne, N2 (Room 54), N7, Room 3–border, N13, Room 10; Newport, Room 5; Cirencester, Ashcroft House; Brislington, mosaic 1, frame; Hadstock; Greatwell Fields; Colchester, under "People's Hall"; Lydney Park, Room LXIV of the Temple, Abaton, Room L, inner frame; Woodchester, Room 19, Room 19; Dewlish, Rooms 1 and 4; Dorchester, Glyde Path Road; Colliton Park, Dorchester, Building I, Room 13; Lenthay Green, Sherbourne; Pit Meads, outer frame; Withington, both panel and corridor; Whittington, Room 10 and corridor; Box, Room IX, corridor; Ebor Brewery Site, checkerboard panel in vestibule; Malton, inner frame: Wheeler: 1936, pl. XLVIIIb; Lysons 1797: pl. XXII, fig. 1; Lysons 1817: pls. XXIX, XIX, fig. B, XXI, 2; Neal 1981: no. 31; Cunliffe 1971a: pls. LVIa, LXXXVIa, XLVII–LIII, LXXXIII, LXXXVIII, XLIII, and LXXXIV; Cookson 1984: pls. 65, 79, 89, 105; Hull 1958: pl. XXIVa; Wheeler and Wheeler 1932: pls. XIXbm, XXI; Bathurst and King 1879: pls. VII, IX; D. J. Smith 1965: fig. 13; D. J. Smith 1969a: pl. 3.31; Johnson 1982: pl. 44; and Hurst, Dartnall, and Fisher 1987: 25, fig. 4.

21. Hurst, Dartnall, and Fisher 1987: 25.

22. Box, Rooms VI, XX, and XXX; Cirencester, The Avenue, Insula I; Fishbourne Palace, west corridor, Room 62, W6 Room 70, N12 Room 11; Fullerton Manor, Wherwell, mosaics b and g; Cherry Orchard; Yeovil/Westland, Rooms 3 and 10; Winchester, Middle Brook St.: Brakspear 1904: 248, 344, fig. 1; Goddard 1897: pls. facing 407; Neal 1981: nos. 47, 55, 57; and Cunliffe 1971: pl. LXXXVII, XXVb, XXIV, LXXVIII, XVIb, LXXIV, LXXXII.

23. Brakspear 1904: 249; Goddard 1897: pls. facing 407.

24. Johnson 1982: 13, 26; and Rainey 1973: 13.

25. Some of the finest wall painting fragments of the villa at Castle Copse were found in destruction layers over Room 3, including the only fragments that can be securely identified as figural.

26. Neal 1981: 12–13. Hutchinson 1986: 427–34, counts 24 examples of canthari in known Romano-British mosaics.

27. Neal 1981: 33.

28. Brakspear 1904: 249.

29. Hutchinson 1986: 431.

30. Cookson 1984: 56, pl. 76.

31. For a partial list of comparanda, see **6**.

32. E.g., the vestibule of Room LXIV of the Temple at Lydney Park: Bathurst and King 1879: pl. X; Wheeler and Wheeler 1932: fig. 3, pl. XIXb.

33. Warren 1937–39: 318–20. Only layers disturbed by Pole's 1936–37 excavations, primarily backfill, were excavated in 1985, so that the portions exposed were visible only in their latest form. Warren claims that two fragments of mosaic were found. The first lay at the eastern end of the irregular Trench 2, designated Pavement B on Diggory's plan (Fig. 39), and in the northern part of Sector D, Room 1. The other fragment lay at the western end of Trench 2, is designated Pavement A on Diggory's plan, and is located to the west of Sector D, Room 3. Room 2, at the south end of Trench 1 on Diggory's Plan, was paved with mortar, evidently the bedding for a mosaic of which no tesserae were preserved in 1985, nor presumably in 1936–37, since Warren has nothing to say about it.

34. These photographs and the watercolor do not, in any event, show the other pavement described by Warren (ms. account of excavations to the Great Western Railroad Archaeological Society, 15 September 1937) as a tesselated pavement of terracotta tesserae "with spaced lozenges

of white tile," a description presumably referring to Pavement A on Diggory's plan at the western end of Trench 2 in Sector D, Room 3.

35. For comparanda of the interlocking box motif, see mosaic 7.

36. E.g., the use of bands and stepped triangles as an outer frame for corridor mosaics. See Stern 1965: 329, figs. 6, 7; and Smith 1965: fig. 18.

37. Parallels at: Newton St. Loe, Rooms 2 and 5; Frampton; Cirencester, Building XIII, Hare mosaic; Lydney Park, Room XVIII of Guesthouse; Fullerton, Mars mosaic; Fifehead Neville; Hinton St. Mary; Colchester; Horkstow; Winterton, Providentia mosaic; Hovingham; Malton; Aldborough; Beadlam; Brantingham: Rainey 1973: pl. 12b; Johnson 1982: pl. 33; Cookson 1984: pl. 35a–b, 72, 88–89, 97; Neal 1981: nos. 1, 9, 12, 25a–c, 41, 45, 62, 88; D. J. Smith 1965: figs. 1, 9; and D. J. Smith 1969a: pl. 3.18. Strong connections with the mosaicists in northeastern England are again indicated. The only other examples in Britain in which stepped triangles are extensively used in a corridor, albeit as an interior motif, are: Great Weldon, Northamptonshire (Lysons 1813: iv, pl. VII; and D. J. Smith 1969a: pl. 3.21) and Brantingham, North Humberside (Neal 1981: no. 13).

38. Warren 1938: 319.

39. Warren, ms. account of excavations to the G.W.R. Archaeological Society, 15 September 1937.

40. Parallels at Newton St. Loe, Rooms 2 and 3; Gloucester; Woodchester, great pavement; Gadebridge Park; Verulamium; Rapsley; Wigginton; Thruxton; Winterton; Aldborough; Brantingham: Rainey 1973: pl. 12b; Neal 1981: nos. 12–13, 51, 65, 74–75, 78, 83, 87a–b; D. J. Smith 1969a: pls. 3.9, 3.17; and Cookson 1984: pls. 84–85.

41. Parallels at Newton St. Loe; Whittington Court, corridor II (north end); Bancroft; Cirencester; Colchester; Eccles, gladiator mosaic: Cookson 1984: pls. 40; Neal 1981: nos. 7, 22, 25a–b, 39, 43.

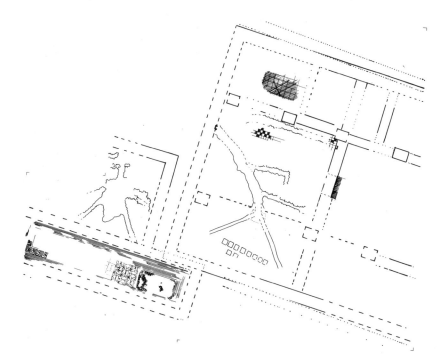

Figure 89. Sector A, location of mosaics in rooms.

Figure 90. Sector B, location of mosaics in rooms.

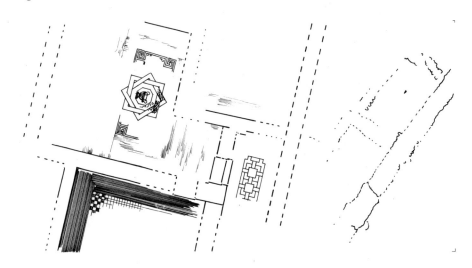

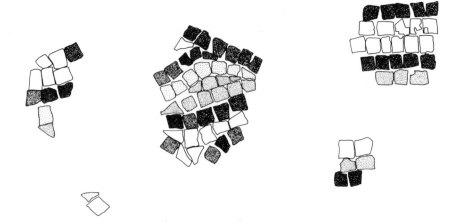

Figure 91. **3**. Mosaic fragments in four colors. A141 (1:1).

Figure 92. **4**. Fragment with possible interlaced square. A364.

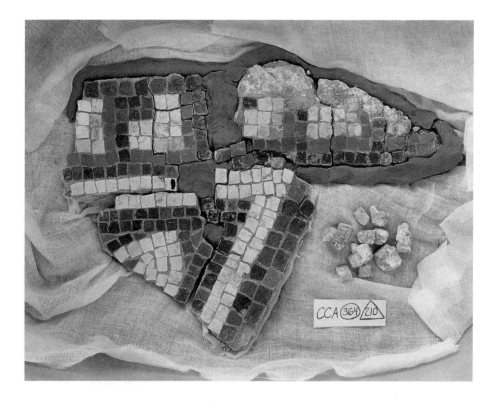

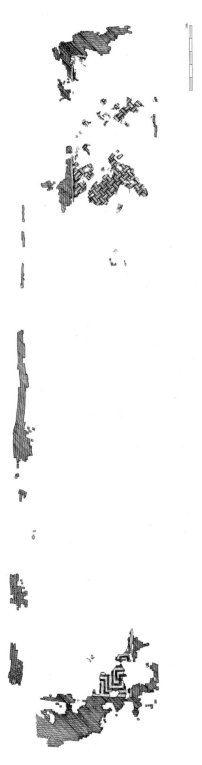

Figure 93. 5. Corridor Mosaic. A8=178.

Figure 94. **5**. Corridor Mosaic, in situ. A8=178.

Figure 95. **5**. Pelta mat, watercolor from W. C. Lukis's excavations. A8=178. (Photo courtesy of The Museum, Devizes.)

Figure 96. Swastika meander, watercolor from W. C. Lukis's excavations. (Photo courtesy of The Museum, Devizes.)

I m.

Figure 97. **6**. Checkerboard mosaic. A48=63=70.

Figure 98. **7**. Interlocking box corridor mosaic. B.

Figure 99. **7**. Interlocking box corridor mosaic. B.

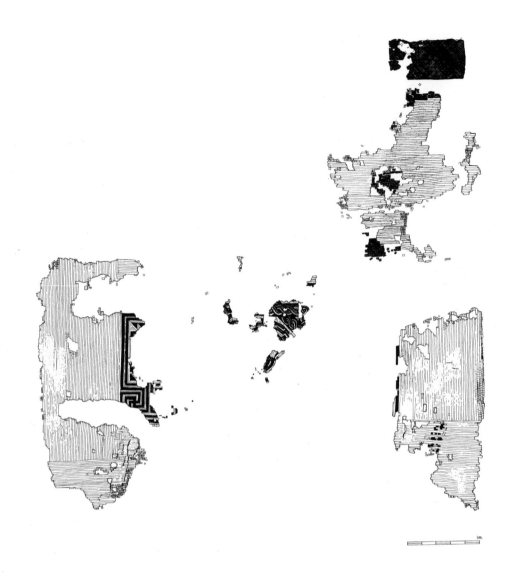

Figure 100. **9**. Cantharus Mosaic. B.

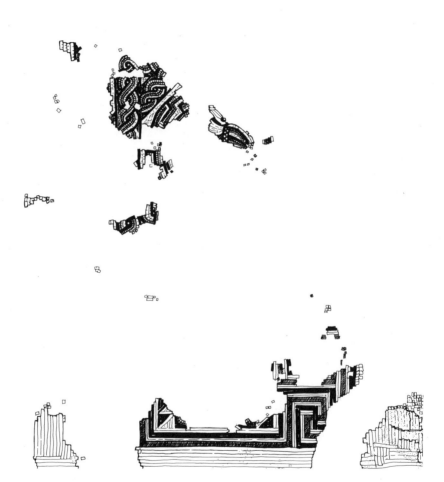

Figure 101. **9**. Cantharus Mosaic, detail. B.

Figure 102. **9**. Cantharus Mosaic. B.

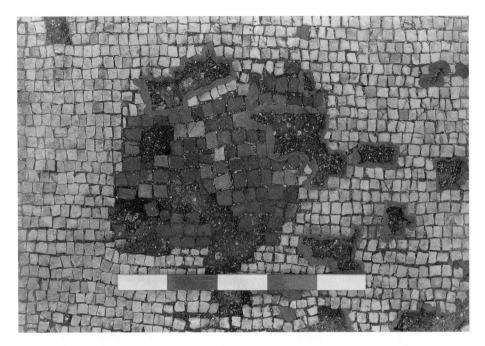

Figure 103. **9**. Cantharus Mosaic, floor patch. B.

Figure 104. **9**. Pit in Room 3 and Cantharus Mosaic. B.

Figure 105. **10**. Checkerboard mosaic. B24=34=70.

4.6 WALL PAINTING

JOHN F. KENFIELD

The Castle Copse site produced several hundred wall painting fragments, almost exclusively from sectors A and B. The paintings appear to belong to two series, an earlier and a later. The two series seem to have been executed during the two masonry phases of the villa; the earlier would be the initial mid-third-/early fourth-century phase (A:IX and B:III), for which our only evidence is a few fragments from B, and the later would be the fourth-century remodeling (A:X, XI, XII; B:IV), for which material is abundant in both sectors. As with the mosaics, the few fragments of the earlier series are enough to show that the technique was especially fine for Roman Britain.[1] The more abundant evidence for the later series shows that it, like the later mosaic series, was competent, but lacked the finesse of the earlier series, and certainly did not make use of the same rare and costly materials.[2] The majority of fragments for both series are sufficiently similar in colors and plaster to suggest that they were executed at the same times and by the same *officinae*.

Chronology

In Sector A, unpainted plaster fragments that were found in sealed contexts (A960:VII, the stylobate packing for Aisled Building I, and A76:IX, the first floor of Aisled Building II) suggest that somewhere on the site there were buildings with undecorated plaster before the first Aisled Building (mid-third-century). A few other painted fragments were found in contexts that predate Aisled Building II, but they were not in sealed deposits.

The earliest excavated context in sector B containing painted plaster is B113:IV (Room 5, the later Villa W. Wing, fourth-century). This material, therefore, may represent painting from the previous phase B:III (the early Villa W. Wing, third/fourth centuries), although formally it belongs to the "later" series.

In any case, this evidence demonstrates that there was white plaster somewhere on-site before the construction of Aisled Building I, painted plaster before Aisled Building II, and painted plaster also before the later phase of the west wing.

The Early Series

The evidence for the "early" series actually comes from late deposits (B144:IV, late occupation in the courtyard, and B58:X, destruction after building and courtyard). Hence, walls with "early" and "late" paintings may have been standing until the abandonment of the villa, and "earlier" and "later" are not necessarily stratigraphically sequential.

Wall paintings of this series used expensive pigments such as Egyptian blue and bright red made from pure cinnabar imported from Spain.[3] They are thought to be earlier mainly because pigments typical of this series are reused in the other series of wall paintings. The principal evidence for an early wall painting series comes from Sector B (B58:X and B144:IV), where fragments contain calcite in the *intonaco* layer and in the pigmentation.[4]

The Later Series

Some of the wall painting fragments of this series show evidence of overplastering and repainting. Others show painted plaster with high quality pigments, presumably from the earlier series, ground up and incorporated into the mortar of later painted walls (A198, 224; B10, 8).

A fragment from B13:X (**25**) seems to show a process of repeated replastering and repainting. The original wall was plastered and painted, and then replastered and repainted two more times, in each instance using the same buff mortar as that of the original wall. Finally, a fourth coat of plaster was applied, this time with the addition of water-resistant terracotta dust, and repainted. Such fragments were also found in B52, 61, 65, 91, and A7. If B Room 3 really did include a plunge bath or tank, then this fragment may be typical of the kind of replastering that is common in bathing rooms.

Perhaps the most interesting instance of reuse of pigments occurs in A224:XI, where the red pigment is composed of crude cinnabar or costly pure cinnabar that was scraped off the earlier walls, mixed with red ochre and terracotta dust, and then reapplied to later walls. Thus the evidence for these later series of wall paintings, apparently executed during the remodeling in A:XI, presents a picture similar to the earlier and later series of mosaics.

The major deposits of both the earlier and later series of wall painting fragments occurred in the later phases (B:X, VI; A:XII, XIII). Some wall painting fragments in B lack an *intonaco* layer, and this substandard technique may be parallel to the inexpert patching of the Cantharus Mosaic (**9**, B Room 3) with terracotta. This evidence suggests that there was a decline in the technique of the maintenance of the villa in the last decades of use.

A:XIII contained a good number of contexts that yielded wall painting fragments. These fragments agree in color and plaster with those from A:XI and no doubt represent further decay of the building into the late fifth century A.D. This decline and destruction is apparently the result of abandonment and decay, rather than a conscious conversion of interior space from one use to another as was the case with A:XI. B:VIII, the major robbing phase, in which a large percentage of the West Wing's wall painting fragments were found, probably corresponds to A:XIII. B:X yielded a sizable percentage of fragments. This again argues that the bulk of the painted material comes from walls that were standing at the time of the villa's abandonment (i.e., walls built and painted in A:XI, XII, B:IV).

Schemata

Almost all of the wall painting fragments from A and B either are monochromatic red or show a series of colors juxtaposed along straight, ruler-drawn lines. Such fragments seem to imply that the background color for most walls was red, and that the walls were further divided, above a red dado course, into a series of square or rectangular panels framed by the straight lines of varying widths and colors which form concentric boxes around these panels. Each panel may have contained decoration in the form of organic motifs, vegetable, or figural. It would appear, too, that the background color of the interior of these panels against which these motifs were painted was different than the basic red of the walls outside the panels. Between the tops of the multiple framed panels and the juncture of the wall with the ceiling would probably lie an architrave course in the same red as the rest of the wall surrounding the panels.[5]

Of the several hundred fragments of wall painting, only a very small percentage displays curvilinear lines drawn freehand. Of these, only a single fragment from Sector B (B95, **22**), again from Room 3, can be associated with a recognizable form: the three outer fingers of a right hand, perhaps extended palm up, cupping something black, and its joining wrist enclosed by a sleeve, the folds and shadows of which are represented in reddish brown (Figs. 106, 108).[6] The hand is modelled in three tones.

A number of fragments from contexts of Room 3 in Sector B (B52, 61, 91, and 95) are in the basic red of the walls and have bevelled edges. The edge at which the facets meet is usually marked by a ruler-drawn white stripe, 0.01–0.015 m wide, and overdrawn on the red ground of the wall. These bevelled fragments are from those portions of the walls that surrounded window frames and door jambs, and occur in Sector A as well as B.

Colors

The colors or pigments present among the wall painting fragments from the villa at Castle Copse are made from the following earth minerals:

Red: red ochre, hematite, crushed terracotta (silica with amorphous iron compound), cinnabar (imported from Spain)
        Munsell: 2.5R 6/4, 2.5R 6/8, 2.5YR 4/6, 2.5YR 5/4, 2.5YR 5/6, 2.5YR 5/8, 2.5YR 6/4, 2.5YR 6/6, 2.5YR 6/8, 5R 4/3, 5R 4/4, 5YR 4/4, 5YR 5/4, 5YR 6/6, 5YR 7/4, 5YR 8/4, 7R 5/6, 7.5R 3/2, 7.5R 4/2, 7.5R 4/4, 7.5R 4/6, 7.5R 5/4, 7.5R 5/6, 7.5R 6/6, 7.5R 6/8, 10R 3/2, 10R 4/1, 10R 4/3, 10R 4/4, 10R 4/6, 10R 5/4, 10R 5/6, 10R 5/8, 10R 6/4, 10R 6/6, 10R 6/8

Yellow: yellow ochre
        limonite
        Munsell: 2.5Y 7/6, 2.5Y 8/4, 2.5Y 8/8, 7.5YR 7/6, 7.5YR 7/8, 10YR 7/6, 10YR 7/8, 10YR 8/2, 10YR 8/3, 10YR 8/4, 10YR 8/6, 10YR 8/8

Black: carbon from charcoal or soot
        Munsell: N4/, 7.5YR N4/, 10YR 3/1, 10YR 5/1

Green: green earth
        glauconite (occasionally containing Egyptian blue)
        Munsell: 5Y 4/2, 5Y 5/3, 5Y 6/3, 5Y 8/1, 5Y 8/2, 5G 7/2, 5GY 6/1, 5GY 7/1

White: pure lime (used as the *intonaco* coat)
        Munsell: 2.5Y N8/, 2.5Y 8/2, 5YR 8/1, 5YR 8/2, 7.5R 6/6, 7.5YR 8/2, 10YR 8/1, 10YR 8/2

Orange: red and yellow ochre
>Munsell: 5YR 3/3, 5YR 5/1, 5YR 5/2, 10YR 6/6

Blue: crushed faience
>Munsell: 5B 6/1, 5B 7/1, 5BG 6/1, 5BG 7/1, 5G 7/1, 5GY 7/1

Other colors present in the wall paintings—purple, pink, brown, and grey—are combinations of the minerals listed above.

Purple: Munsell: 2.5YR 3/4, 5R 3/3, 5R 6/3

Pink: Munsell: 5R 6/2, 5R 6/3, 5YR 8/3, 7.5YR 8/2

Brown: Munsell: 5YR 3/3, 5YR 5/1, 5YR 5/2, 10YR 6/6

Grey: Munsell: N4/, 2.5YR N4/, 2.5YR N6/, 5Y 6/1, 5YR 4/1, 5YR 6/1, 5YR 6/2,
>5YR 8/1, 10R 5/1, 10YR 5/1, 10YR 6/1, 10YR 7/1, 10YR 7/2

Most of the minerals were probably obtained locally, but both Egyptian blue and, though to a lesser degree, the bright red produced by cinnabar are rare in Roman Britain. Pure cinnabar occurs once at Castle Copse (in A224:XI, **18**); the context also contained fragments painted with crude cinnabar, a pigment in which pure cinnabar is mixed with red ochre and clay. G. C. Morgan suggests that pure cinnabar is used earlier than crude cinnabar. The crude cinnabar in A224, **18** (as well as A198, B10, and 89) appears to be scraped off earlier paintings. The scavenged pure cinnabar was then recycled into the later wall paintings and stretched by mixing it with red ochre and terracotta dust. G. C. Morgan says this crude cinnabar technique is typical of the later fourth century A.D.

Mortar

There is little difference among the plaster types, with only the slight variations in the chalk and flint content. These ingredients appear to have been made from the local chalk deposits. Most fragments also have a coat of white lime *intonaco* between the pigments and the mortar. This *intonaco* coat, originally a layer of wet lime c. 0.001–0.003 m thick, is necessary for true fresco work; its absence on a few fragments suggests rather poor, very late work. The use on some fragments, however, of imported calcite or crushed marble in both the *intonaco* coat and the pigmentation to increase light reflectance is exceedingly rare in Roman Britain.[7]

Catalogue

SECTOR A

Wall painting fragments are found in the following contexts and phases of Sector A:

A:II Terrace Gravel Dump, mid- to late second century into possibly early third century A.D. Wall painting fragments probably intrusive.
>A523

A:VI Post Structures, late second into third century A.D. Wall painting fragments probably intrusive.
>A418, 463

A:VII Construction of Aisled Building I, third century A.D.
>A960

A:IX   Construction of Aisled Building II, later third/early fourth centuries A.D.
A287, 760, 872

A:X/XI   Exterior of Aisled Building II, early 4th century through A.D. 375 or later
A91, 150, 159, 213

A:XI   Subdivision of Aisled Building II and Habitation as Luxury Apartments through
Aisled Building II's Early Decline, post–A.D. 330–331
A10, 65–66, 71, 75, 79, 81, 107, 129, 142, 148, 189, 191, 198, 200, 202,
207–209, 212, 217, 224, 248, 261, 276, 285–286, 288, 291, 307, 325, 336,
353, 355–356, 358, 377

A:XIII   Decay, Abandonment, and Robbing, fifth century A.D. A6, 7=15=51, 9, 24=49,
41, 105, 114, 125, 140

A:XV   Antiquarian and Modern Disturbances
A1, 19, 35, 39.

13. Two fragments plaster. A960:VII (stylobate packing of Aisled Building I)
No color preserved.

14. Two fragments in two colors. A287:IX (fill of ditch with mortar-packed debris).
Two small fragments: one shows blue field with white stripe; the other, light red
field with white stripes meeting at a right angle.

    Munsell: blue   5BG 7/1
                white   7.5YR N8
                red   2.5 YR 5/6

15. Three fragments in white. A760:IX (chalk floor, earliest surface in Aisled Building II)
Three small fragments in white.

    Munsell: white   10 YR 8/2

16. Fragments in three colors. A872:IX (burn pit/hearth)
Many tiny fragments that juxtapose red and white or red and yellow along a straight
line. Red overpainted with yellow on one fragment.

    Munsell: red   10R 4/4
                white   10YR 8/2
                yellow   10YR 8/8

17. Fragments in eight colors. A198:XI (mortar patch) (Fig. 106)
Reused painted plaster in the mortar. Many fragments in eight colors from probable
large expanses of wall in yellow, bluish green, reddish brown. Preserved fragments include:

    Fragments with yellow field with framing lines of white or reddish brown. Curvilinear
    forms in yellow surrounded by outline of reddish brown and bordered above and
    below by straight lines of reddish brown succeeded by lines of white.

    Fragment with yellow field overpainted with curvilinear forms in dark reddish
    brown, light reddish brown, and olive green.

    Palimpsest fragment with a yellow field on faceted surfaces of mouldings, which
    was later replastered and repainted.

    One fragment of yellow with a light red line running through it.

    Fragment shows a yellow field juxtaposed with olive green along a straight line.
    Olive lines appear in three shades bordering a field of pink or mauve.

    Fragment with two facets that meet at a right angle, one facet in yellow, the other in
    light reddish brown.

Fragments with a red field overpainted with curvilinear forms in olive or a red field
  bordered by straight lines, sometimes in white, sometimes olive, succeeded by
  yellow.
Fragments with yellow field overpainted in dark red curvilinear forms.
Fragment with greenish blue field overpainted in dark red.

Munsell:	yellow	10YR 8/6
	reddish brown (dark)	5YR 3/3
	reddish brown (light)	10R 4/4
	white	5YR 8/1
	olive green (dark)	5R 4/2
	olive green (medium)	5Y 5/3
	olive green (light)	5Y 6/3
	pink	5YR 8/4

18. Fragments in six colors. A224:XI (mortar floor patch)

Mortar contains reused painted plaster. Many fragments in six colors. Some fragments painted with both pure and crude cinnabar. Some lumps of this mortar contain
fragments of painted wall plaster of various colors and combinations of colors. Some fragments, too, seem to show evidence of replastering and repainting. Many large fragments
are monochromatically painted in red, green, blue, and brown, showing that fairly large
expanses of the wall were painted in these colors. Examples of mouldings in blue, brown,
and red, which appear to have been plastered over later. Preserved fragments include:
Fragment with curvilinear juxtaposed brushstrokes in grey, green, and blue.
Fragment with two faces meeting at a 45° angle.
Fragment with two faces meeting at a right angle;
Fragment with two blue faces meeting a torus moulding that is now broken away;
  then upper angle blue surface partially painted over and painted red.
Fragment with two faces of blue meeting at a 45° angle.
Fragment with two faces of red meeting at a 45° angle, then overpainted in white
  and bound below in greyish black.
Fragment combining blue and black curvilinear brushstrokes.
Fragment with grey and white on one side; red, blue, and white on the other.
Fragment with two faces meeting at acute angle shows reddish brown, grey, and
  white on one side, and red, grey, white, and yellow on the other.

Munsell:	olive green	5GY 6/1
	sky blue	5BG 7/1
	red	7.5R 6/8
	white	5YR 8/2
	brown	5YR 5/2
	grey	5YR 4/1

SECTOR B

In Sector B wall painting fragments are found in the following contexts and phases:

B:IV   Late Villa West Wing, probably after A.D. 200; late Roman in latest form.
       Unexcavated.
       B113

B:VI   Occupation in the Courtyard (associated with late villa west wing), late Roman.
           B144

B:VII   Late Stakehole Structure in late villa west wing, late/post-Roman.
           B85

B:VIII   Major Robbing Phase, late/post-Roman.
           B54, 61, 81, 89, 91, 95, 101, 114, 117, 121, 127, 145

B:IX   Late Constructions and Courtyard Occupation, late/post-Roman.
           B103, 107, 112

B:X   Destruction over Main Building and Courtyard, post-Roman.
           B7, 9–11, 13, 22, 24, 26, 44, 52, 58, 69

B:XI   Overburden and Modern Disturbance, modern.
           B1–2, 4–5

19. Fragments in two colors. B113:IV (subfloor of Room 5)

Two small fragments of blue and grey juxtaposed along a straight line.

Munsell:	grey	N4
	blue	5B 7/1

20. Fragments in four colors. B144:IV

Calcite in *intonaco* layer and pigmentation. Sixteen small fragments in two shades of red, white, and yellow. Several fragments show freehand red and white lines converging.

Munsell:	red	10R 4/4
	red	10R 5/6
	white	10YR 8/2
	yellow	10YR 7/6

21. Fragments in five colors. B89:VIII (fill of robbing cut B84 Room 4)

Mortar contains reused painted plaster. Many fragments solidly colored in one of two shades of red, or solidly in white. One fragment preserves red and yellow juxtaposed along a straight line. One small fragment in light blue.

Munsell:	red (dark)	7.5R 3/2
	red (light)	2.5R 6/8
	white	10YR 8/2
	yellow	10YR 8/6
	blue	5B 7/1

22. Figural fragments in seven colors. B95=61:VIII (fill of B80, Room 3) (Figs. 106, 108)

Overplastering in four separate coats. Many fragments. Two preserve red fields separated by a white stripe c. 0.01 thick. One fragment shows red field succeeded by a white stripe c. 0.015 thick, this in turn succeeded by a red stripe c. 0.01 thick, succeeded by white field containing freehand brushstrokes. One fragment juxtaposes red and yellow along a straight line. One large fragment shows a field of yellow succeeded by a white stripe overpainted on red and c. 0.015 thick. This white stripe is succeeded by a red stripe c. 0.01 thick, which is in turn succeeded by a white figure field. Figure field contains a fragment of figurative painting: dark red squiggly lines that appear to represent the folds in the sleeve of a garment. An undergarment projects from the end of the sleeve in orange-red and blue. Two fingers of the right hand, turned palm-up, are painted in the Hellenistic tonal tradition in three colors: parts in the shadow are red, succeeded by pink as the rounded form gets closer to the light source, with the parts of the finger closest to the light source overpainted in white. The hand appears to be cupping something black with a yellow highlight at the top of the fragment. Another fragment preserves freehand brushstrokes in blue, red, and green, but cannot be seen as any recognizable form. Other fragments preserve red overpainted by a greyish-green. The large majority of the fragments are solid red.

Munsell:	red	7R 5/6
	red	10R 5/6
	white	10YR 8/2
	yellow	7.5YR 7/8
	yellow	2/5Y 7/6
	blue	5BG 6/1
	grey	2.5YR N4/

23. Eleven fragments in seven colors. B7:X

One fragment juxtaposes red and white along a straight line; another juxtaposes two shades of yellow along a straight line; and a third juxtaposes red and yellow along a straight line.

Munsell:	red (light)	2.5YR 6/4
	red (dark)	10R 4/6
	red	10R 5/6
	white	10YR 8/2
	yellow (light)	10YR 7/8
	yellow (dark)	10YR 8/2

24. Six fragments in three colors. B10:X (fill of robbing cut B14)

Mortar contains reused painted plaster. Two fragments juxtapose red and white along a straight line, and another juxtaposes dark red and light red along a straight line.

Munsell:	red (light)	2.5YR 6/4
	red (dark)	10R 6/6
	white	2.5Y 8/2

25. Fragments in six colors: B13:X (Fig. 107)

Varied fragments include:

Fragment preserving two fields of red separated by a white stripe c. 0.01 thick.

Fragment with fields of white and yellow separated by a line of blue c. 0.005 thick.

Fragment preserving two superimposed layers of plastering and painting: the lower has a light red field bordered by a dark red stripe c. 0.005 thick, succeeded by a white stripe c. 0.01 thick, followed by a broad field of white. Upper painted surface preserves white juxtaposed along a straight line.

Two large fragments in red, preserving parts of moldings from around door jambs or window sills.

Fragment preserving freehand brushstrokes in red, white, yellow, and green that seem to converge and probably derive from some figurative panel.

Munsell:	red (light)	2.5R 6/4
	red (dark)	7.5R 5/4
	white	7.5R 6/6
	blue	5B 6/1

yellow	2.5Y 8/8
green	5GY 7/1

26. Three fragments in two colors. B58:X

Calcite in *intonaco* layer. Two fragments painted solidly red; the third and largest preserves two red fields separated by a straight white line c. 0.005 in breadth.

Munsell:	red	7.5R 4/6
	white	5YR 8/1

27. Fragments in eight colors. B4:X (Fig. 107)

Most fragments painted solidly red in varying shades, of which one preserves two painted surfaces meeting at right angles. Three fragments show freehand, curvilinear brushstrokes in blue, green, grey, and purple, and one shows red and white juxtaposed along a straight line.

Munsell:	red	10R 5/6
	red	10R 5/4
	red	10R 6/6
	white	5YR 8/4
	blue	5B 7/1
	green	5GY 7/1
	grey	10YR 7/2
	purple	2.5YR 3/4

NOTES

1. On wall painting in the western provinces, Liversidge 1982.

2. The author thanks G. C. Morgan, Senior Curator, Archaeology Department, University of Leicester for a pigment analysis of representative samples of wall painting fragments. The samples were from: contexts A35, 85, 189, 198, 200, 224; B10, 13, 22, 26, 61, 89, 95, 117, and water separation samples, B1, 10, 13, 58, 114, 144. Three principles guided the selection of these samples: the variety and strength of the colors of the fragments from a particular context; any context in which the fragments seemed in any way unusual; and the general applicability of the fragments in a sample, i.e., the fragments from a context in Sector A appeared similar to the fragments from one or more contexts in Sector B and vice versa. The pigments were identified using microchemical tests and confirmed using x-ray diffraction. Mortar or plaster analysis was attempted on a few wall painting fragments from: contexts B7, 85, 198, 200. Generally, the samples were too small for mortar analysis, and, indeed, the analysis was complicated by the fact that the aggregate, being composed of local materials, is mainly calcareous. Thus separation of the lime and aggregate was not possible with traditional methods.

3. G. C. Morgan has ascertained fifteen occurrences of pure cinnabar in Britain within the last three years, making it somewhat more common than was formerly thought, but still expensive since it had to be imported. Egyptian blue, although more common than cinnabar, is also thought to have been imported and expensive: Forbes 1955: 205–28; Liversidge 1969: 128–29; Plesters 1963: 337–41.

4. Pliny *N.H.* 33.115–123; 35.30; Vitruvius 7.11–12. Both authors mention the use of calcite in the very best fresco painting as a means of increasing reflectance. G. C. Morgan (pers. comm.) says that at this time, calcite has been found in the painted plaster from only one other site in Roman Britain, the hitherto unpublished excavation at Fenchurch Street, London.

5. Ling 1985: 21–38, especially 31–33; Davey 1972: 251–68; Liversidge 1969: 127–53; 1977:

75–103; Davey and Ling 1982. It is from these same contexts (B52, 61, 91, 95) that Sector B's palimpsest fragments derive, showing that in the case of Room 3 of Sector B—if all the fragments came from that room—the walls were plastered and painted four times.

6. Hutchinson 1986: 427–34. For Lydney Park, see Rainey 1973: 120; Wheeler and Wheeler 1932: pl. 19c; and Casey 1981: 30–32.

7. G. C. Morgan has told us that the only other occurrence in Roman Britain is at the unpublished site in Fenchurch Street, London.

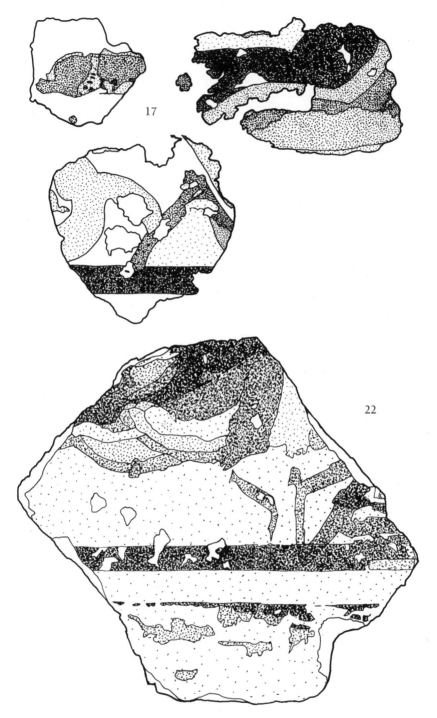

Figure 106. Fragments wall painting: **17.** A198; **22.** With fingers, B95=61. (1:1)

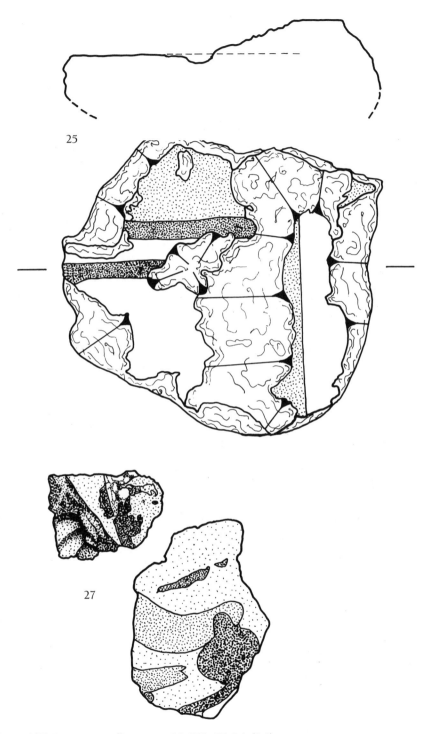

25

27

Figure 107. Fragments wall painting: **25.** B13; **27.** B4. (1:1)

Figure 108. **22.** Fragment wall painting with fingers.

4.7 COINS

THEODORE V. BUTTREY

The seventy-four coins from the Castle Copse excavation include, as one would expect, no gold and very little silver. In Reece's categorization the identifiable pieces fall as below.[1]

Date	Genuine		Imitations		Illegible	
	AR	AE	AR	AE	AR	AE
to A.D. 41						
41–54						
54–69						
69–96						
96–117						
117–138		1				
138–161						
161–180						
180–192						
193–222	1					
222–238						
238–260						
260–275	6					
275–296						
296–317						
317–330		6				
330–348		25		4		
348–364		2		2		
364–378		8.5				
378–388		1.5				
388–402		2				
					2	13
	7	46		6	2	13

Plainly, this is the smallest of small change. Of the silver coins, the only one produced prior to the middle of the third century is a contemporary plated counterfeit (**29**), while the others are classed as silver only by convention since the alloy of the antoninianus had by this time become almost entirely bronze (**30–35, 87–88**).

This is also quite a small number of coins from which to draw any conclusions about circulation patterns in the area, but their distribution does allow us to suggest something about the occupation of the site. What is interesting is as much what is missing as what has been found. There is nothing Celtic, Roman Republican, or first-century A.D., in contrast to the nearby site of Chisbury Hill. The earliest piece is the second-century sesterce of Hadrian (**28**), the only large bronze of the group. Its condition, Fine, shows that it had been in circulation for some time before loss.[2] There is no way of saying how long it had been, but it is well known that imperial sesterces of the second century circulated in Gaul and Britain well into the third century and were even overstruck by Postumus (c. A.D. 259–268). On purely numismatic grounds, therefore, it is possible that the coin represents either a second-century or a third-century loss, although its rather nice condition suggests an earlier rather than a later date.

The third-century coins begin with a plated denarius of Septimius (**29**), an ancient counterfeit. Its production should date roughly from the period of circulation of the original which it copies, say the early years of the third century. There is then a gap of over fifty years before the appearance of a few base antoniniani, presumably losses of the A.D. 270s; then nothing for almost another half-century.

There has been much speculation about the nature of third-century circulation in Britain.[3] The Castle Copse coins are too few in number to contribute much to that discussion; but the evidence from elsewhere illuminates the particular conditions at Castle Copse. It is obvious that the third-century pieces are relatively thin compared to those of the fourth. There is no example from the reign of Claudius II, otherwise so common in Britain, or any other of the later third-century emperors of the Central Empire. Comparison with other nearby finds shows that coins of these reigns really did circulate here in quantity. The most dramatic indication of local circulation is the composition of the giant Cunetio hoard from Mildenhall, just five miles away from Castle Copse on the Roman road that lay below the villa.[4] It extended to Aurelian, and included twenty-five thousand coins of Valerian–Gallienus and over two thousand of Claudius II.

Again, there are in the finds at Castle Copse only two pieces of the Gallic Empire (**34–35**) although coins of Postumus, Victorinus, and Tetricus I and II occur by the thousands in the hoards; the hoard from Aldbourne, nine miles north of Castle Copse, contained 3,336 pieces of the Gallic Empire.[5] The British Empire of Carausius and Allectus is completely unrepresented. The subsequent reform of Diocletian leaves no mark in the late third and early fourth centuries, whereas a notable hoard of Diocletian's bronze has been found at Upavon, only ten miles to the southwest of Castle Copse.[6] In the Blackmoor (Hampshire) hoard, buried A.D. 296, over 22,000 coins survive. The coins of Claudius II–Diocletian are two and a half times as common as those of Gallienus, while those of the Gallic Empire constitute no less than 73% of the total.[7]

During this period, then, there was always some quantity of coin available in the area, but very little activity at Castle Copse that required the handling (and losing) of coins, at least on this part of the site. It is only in the mid-320s, to judge from the condition of the losses, that coins begin to appear in any quantity. By date and mint, the identifiable pieces are distributed as follows:

Date	London	Trier	Lyons	Arles	Aquileia	uncertain
317–320		1				
320–325	2	2				
325–330		1				
330–335		4	2			1
335–341		2	3	3		5
341–348		2		1		2
348–350		1				
350–364			1			
364–378			3	3	1	1
378–402						4

The distribution by mint is in accordance with the British evidence generally: London has closed by c. A.D. 326; Trier is at first the major supplier, with Lugdunum and Arles taking over.[8]

Dates of production, of circulation, and finally of loss are not necessarily very closely connected. But the small group from the 320s are in lovely condition: BEATA TRANQVILLITAS (37 XF, 38 VF+, 43 XF) and the contemporary or slightly later SARMARTIA DEVICTA (39 VF+) and CONSTANTINVS AVG (40 VF). Whether they represent a compact lot of money which reached Castle Copse at one time, or are the kind of coin which percolated through gradually, they had circulated only a few years before their loss, probably A.D. 325 and shortly after. A hoard of just such material, described as not having seen circulation, was found about a mile from Cunetio. Stretching from Licinius I to Constantius II Caesar, it was particularly rich in Constantine I and II (also Crispus, not represented at Castle Copse), and in the BEATA TRANQVILLITAS, SARMATIA DEVICTA and wreath reverses that figure on the nearly uncirculated pieces of the excavation. The hoard, buried c. A.D. 326, presumably related to military pay, and the excavation pieces may well derive from the same shipment.[9]

In A.D. 330 the mints introduced the type GLORIA EXERCITVS, which was to be struck over the next decade from Lugdunum to Alexandria and to achieve wide currency over the Empire. This type, with the contemporary Wolf and Twins follis, constitutes about a third of the entire Castle Copse finds. Two pieces of the two-standards variety are in unusually nice condition, which argues for a fairly early loss, perhaps by the middle of the decade (44 VF+, 48 VF+); four pieces of the one-standard variety are also in VF condition, and must have been lost in the early A.D. 340s.

The large proportion of GLORIA EXERCITVS in the finds does not of itself guarantee the presence of an unusual amount of money at Castle Copse during the A.D. 330s; the type was a common one, and some of the more eroded examples may have continued to circulate into the next decade or even after, to be lost then: the type appears in hoards buried as late as the A.D. 370s, in very small quantities even as late as the end of the century.[10] However if the excavation specimens of the GLORIA EXERCITVS and the subsequent VICTORIAE DD AVGGQ NN types were still circulating as late as the A.D. 350s, one would expect to find them accompanied by examples of the really very common series of the 350s, the FEL TEMP REPARATIO coinages. A hoard from Easterton, about seventeen miles southwest of Castle Copse, consisted very largely of the several FEL TEMP REPARATIO types and included nothing before the GLORIA ROMANORVM of 350.[11] But the FEL TEMP REPARATIO occur at Castle Copse in only two examples, plus two imitations. It should be valid to conclude that the coins struck in the A.D. 330s were largely or wholly lost before FEL TEMP REPARATIO began to appear c. A.D. 348, and that whatever it was that caused so much coin to be available to be lost in the 330s and 340s, the same conditions did not hold in the 350s.

The chronology of the GLORIA EXERCITVS and FEL TEMP REPARATIO imitations is not entirely certain, and in the catalogue the most conservative dates have been suggested on the assumption that the imitations are most likely to have been excited by simultaneous circulation of the original types. Reece has argued, however, that they were produced somewhat làter, when official coinage was in short supply: c. A.D. 341–344 for GLORIA ROMANORVM, c. A.D. 353–364 for FEL TEMP REPARATIO.[12]

A relatively more vigorous loss of coin occurs after the mid-360s for the roughly twenty years of Valentinian, Valens, and Gratian, which produced nine pieces. The condition of some suggests that they might have continued to circulate even into the fifth century and beyond Roman occupation. Two pieces of Arcadius close the finds. Any of the later fourth-century material could well have been used by post-Roman inhabitants of the site, since nothing was struck after the withdrawal of Roman authority in the early fifth century, and it is clear from numismatic finds generally in Britain that no further consignments of imperial coin were transmitted to the now abandoned province. What lay to hand was what was used. A late Roman or even a post-Roman hoard from Chisbury Camp contains small bronzes attributable (largely by fabric) to Arcadius and Honorius, but contains one piece as early as the VRBS ROMA issue (cp. **46–47**), A.D. 330–335, and one FEL TEMP REPARATIO Falling Horseman (cp. **60**).[13]

Finally, we turn to a comparison of Castle Copse against other sites. No comparison should be pushed very far, given that the number of coins found at Castle Copse is so small: half a dozen more or less could have a large impact on percentages and proportions of the whole. As indicated above, some nearby hoards include issues of coin which do not appear among our finds at all. Nonetheless, a general comparison with other local villa site finds, based on Reece's helpful collection of the material, shows that they are in general accord chronologically with those of Castle Copse. Graph 1 (Fig. 109) displays two curves, the one illustrating the Castle Copse finds, the other a compendium of six villa sites from the same area of western England, namely Atworth (Reece no. 105), Barnsley Park (93), Chedworth (91), Frocester Court (94), Rockbourne (97), and Shakenoak (99). The graph is laid out according to Reece's fourteen periods (numbered as now in n. 14). Find totals have been adjusted to a base of 1,000 in each case, to make the two curves comparable.

It would appear that all these villas fall into a generally similar pattern of occupation and coin usage. The other villas report some first-century coins, where Castle Copse does not—though excavation strategy may bias the sample here—and more second-century; but their numbers are still insignificant compared with the later issues in which all villas abound. Castle Copse is unusual, in that period 14 is missing entirely (examples occur in each of the other six villas), while period 17 is unusually rich. It is difficult to derive large significance from within the limits of just 59 coins, and conversion to base 1000 distorts the mountains and valleys of the curve; similarly the ratios of A/B, etc., generated by Reece,[14] are not likely to be reliable informants in such a small body of material. Still, the general profile of our finds accords well with that illustrated by the finds at other villas of this area.

It is the case that coin finds all over Britain exhibit some of the features illustrated here, notably the large representation of period 17, the decline in 18, and the renewed strength of 19. At the same time it does not follow that *any* site will provide the same results. The finds from some eastern villas fall into quite a different pattern for the same period of occupation: Graph 2 (Fig. 110) compares Castle Copse with Gestingthorpe (Reece no. 95) in Essex. Non-villa sites, too, can vary: Graph 3 (Fig. 111) sets the finds from Castle Copse against those from the shrine of Apollo at Nettleton (Reece no. 131), at the western edge of Wiltshire. The fourth-century predominance in both is clear, but within that period the percolation of coins into each site must have been motivated quite differently.

Catalogue

LRBC = R. A. G. Carson, P. V. Hill and J. P. C. Kent, *Late Roman Bronze Coinage.* London, 1965.

RIC = Harold Mattingly and Edward A. Syndeham, et al. *Roman Imperial Coinage.* London, 1923–.

Hadrian, A.D. 117–138
28. sestertius. B123:IV-II (318.45/470.68) Rome   A.D. 119   F
PONT MAX TR POT COS III SC   RIC 2.411.563.a
Felicitas stg. 1.

Septimius Severus, A.D. 193–211
29. denarius A473:V   —   Post-A.D. 198   VF
RESTITVTOR VRBIS   cf. RIC 41.108.140
Septimius sacrificing l.

Gallienus, A.D. 260–268
30. antoninianus. A217:XI (dry-sieved) Rome   A.D. 260–268   F
AEQVITAS AVG   RIC 51.144.159
Aequitas stg. left with scales and cornucopiae
31. antoninianus. B68:IX (336.78/479.55)   [ ]   A.D. 260–268   VF
[Illegible]   ——

Claudius II, *postumus,* A.D. 270–
32. antoninianus. C19:V (348.40/435.50)   [ ]   A.D. 270–   VF
CONSECRATIO   RIC 51.233.259
Altar aflame
33. antoninianus. B95:VIII (332.90/479.23)   [ ]   A.D. 270–   F
CONSECRATIO   RIC 51.234.265
Eagle to left

Tetricus I, A.D. 270–273
34. antoninianus. D1:IV   —   A.D. 270–273   VF
HILARITAS AVG   RIC 52.408.79–81
Hilaritas stg. left with palm and cornucopiae
35. antoninianus. B81:VII (324.61/474.05)   —   A.D. 270–273   VF
LAETITIA AVGG   RIC 52.408.87
Laetitia stg. left with wreath and anchor

Constantine I, A.D. 306–337
36. follis. A212:XI (377.40/524.43)   Trier, S   A.D. 319   VF
VICTORIAE LAETAE PRINC PERP   RIC 7.183.216,222
Victories vis-à-vis holding shield on altar
37. follis. C5:VI (345.90/426.90)   Trier, P   A.D. 321   XF
BEATA TRANQVILLITAS   RIC 7.190.303
Globe on altar
38. follis. A91:X/XI (376.53/523.41)   London, P A.D. 322   VF+
BEATA TRANQVILLITAS   RIC 7.194.341
Globe on altar
39. follis. A1:XV (361.45/513.13)   London, P A.D. 323–324   XF
SARMATIA DEVICTA   RIC 7.115.290
Victory right spurning captive
40. follis. B2:XI (326.09/477.65)   Trier, P   A.D. 326   VF
CONSTANTINVS AVG   RIC 7.209.485
Wreath above legend
41. follis. B2:XI (324.88/470.67)   [   ]   A.D. 330–334   F
GLORIA EXERCITVS   —
Two soldiers with two standards

Constantine I, *postumus,* A.D. 337–340
42. follis. B10:X (334.24/479.36)   Lyons, [ ] A.D. 337–341   F
AETERNA PIETAS   RIC 8.206.41
Constantine stg. right

Constantine II, Caesar, 316–337
43. follis. C19:V (348.96/437.30)   London, P A.D. 323–324   XF
BEAT TRANQLITAS [*sic*]   RIC 7.115.287
Globe on altar
44. follis. A39:XV (370.96/513.24)   Lyons, P   A.D. 330–331   VF+
GLORIA EXERCITVS   RIC 7.138.244
Two soldiers with two standards

Constantine II, Augustus, A.D. 337–340
45. follis. B7:X (339.98/479.36)   —   A.D. 337–340   F
[e.g., GLORIA EXERCITVS, but obverse brockage]   —

VRBS ROMA

46. follis. B6:XI (324.79/470.42)   Trier, P   A.D. 332–333   VF
    Wolf and Twins left   RIC 7.217.542
47. follis. A217:XI (372.48/524.76)   Trier, S   A.D. 332–333   F+
    Wolf and Twins left   RIC 7.217.542

Constans, Caesar, A.D. 333–337
48. follis. A69:XI (371.90/514.50)   Lyons, P   A.D. 332   VF+
    GLORIA EXERCITVS   RIC 7.138.255
    Two soldiers with two standards
49. follis. B13:X (323.99/477.01)   Trier, P   A.D. 333–334   F/VF
    GLORIA EXERCITVS   RIC 7.218.552
    Two soldiers with two standards

Constans, Augustus, A.D. 337–350
50. follis. A209:XI (374.37/520.32)   Lyons, [ ]   A.D. 337–340   F/VF
    GLORIA EXERCITVS   RIC 8.178.16
    Two soldiers with one standard
51. follis. B1:XI (339.47/474.36)   Arles, [ ]   A.D. 337–340   F
    GLORIA EXERCITVS   RIC 8.205.23
    Two soldiers with one standard
52. follis. B103:IX (wet-sieved)   Arles, [ ]   A.D. 347–348   VF/F
    VICTORIAE DD AVGGQ NN   RIC 8.209.87
    Victories vis-à-vis, each holding wreath and palm
53. follis. B1:XI (329.54/470.64)   Trier, S   A.D. 347–348   F
    VICTORIAE DD AVGGQ NN   RIC 8.152.205–6
    Victories vis-à-vis, each holding wreath and palm
54. follis. B1:XI (334.10/470.44)   Trier, P   A.D. 348–350   F
    FEL TEMP REPARATIO   RIC 8.154.228
    Phoenix on mound

Constantius II, Caesar, A.D. 324–337
55. follis. A575:X (376.63/516.86)   Trier, P   A.D. 330–331   VF
    GLORIA EXERCITVS   RIC 7.215.528
    Two soldiers with two standards

Constantius II, Augustus, A.D. 337–361
56. follis. C19:V (349.95/438.00)   Trier, P   A.D. 337–340   VF
    GLORIA EXERCITVS   RIC 8.143.50,58
    Two soldiers with one standard
57. follis. A202:XI (375.82/524.96)   Lyons, [ ]   A.D. 337–340   F+?
    GLORIA EXERCITVS   RIC 8.178.8
    Two soldiers with one standard
58. follis. B7:X (337.82/476.32)   Arles, [ ]   A.D. 337–340   VF
    GLORIA EXERCITVS   RIC 8.205.2
    Two soldiers with one standard

59. follis. C64:IV (348.82/433.91) Arles, P A.D. 337–340 VF
GLORIA EXERCITVS RIC 8.205.12 VF
Two soldiers with one standard
60. AE 3. A121:XI/XII (365.96/570.00) Lyons, P A.D. 353–360 VF
FEL TEMP REPARATIO RIC 8.191.189
Falling horseman

Delmatius, Caesar, A.D. 335–337
61. follis. A223:XI (dry-sieved) Trier, [ ] A.D. 335–337 VF
GLORIA EXERCITVS RIC 7.223.588
Two soldiers with one standard

[House of Constantine]
62. follis. A2:XIV (370.20/511.75) [ ] A.D. 335–340 F?
GLORIA EXERCITVS —
Two soldiers with one standard
63. follis. A69:XI (372.62/514.77) [ ] A.D. 335–340 —
GLORIA EXERCITVS —
Two soldiers with one standard
64. follis. B7:X (331.95/471.98) [ ] A.D. 335–340 VG
GLORIA EXERCITVS —
Two soldiers with one standard
65. follis. A149:XI (373.40/514.66) [ ] A.D. 335–340 F
GLORIA EXERCITVS —
Two soldiers with one standard
66. follis. B89:VIII (328.81/475.36) Trier, [ ] A.D. 347–348 —
VICTORIAE DD AVGGQ NN RIC 8.152.207–211
Victories vis-à-vis, each holding wreath and palm
67. follis. A9:XIII (378.28/525.32) [ ] A.D. 347–348 F
VICTORIAE DD AVGGQ NN —
Victories vis-à-vis, each holding wreath and palm
68. follis. B7:X (328.62/472.92) [ ] A.D. 347–348 —
VICTORIAE DD AVGGQ NN —
Victories vis-à-vis, each holding wreath and palm

House of Constantine, imitations
69. follis. A69:XI (373.53/515.02) post–A.D. 330 F?
type of GLORIA EXERCITVS, two standards —
70. follis. A209:XI (374.21/526.10) post–A.D. 330 —
type of GLORIA EXERCITVS, two standards —
71. follis. A69:XI (372.80/512.27) post–A.D. 335 F?
type of GLORIA EXERCITVS, one standard —
72. follis. A156:X/XI (375/525) post–A.D. 335 VF
type of GLORIA EXERCITVS, one standard —
73. follis. A356:XI (327.30/519.05) post–A.D. 353 VF

type of FEL TEMP REPARATIO, falling horseman —

74. follis. A195:XI (dry-sieved)   post–A.D. 353   —
type of FEL TEMP REPARATIO, falling horseman —

Valentinian, A.D. 364–375

75. AE 3. B22:X (330.26/474.44)   Lyons, [   ] A.D. 364–375   VF+
GLORIA ROMANORVM (8)   LBRC 2.279, etc.
Emperor right, dragging captive

76. AE 3. B2:XI (328.00/472.81)   Arles, P   A.D. 367–375   VF
GLORIA ROMANORVM (8)   LBRC 2.525
Emperor right, dragging captive

Valens, A.D. 364–378

77. AE 3. B7:X (328.65/473.48)   Arles, S   A.D. 367   F
SECVRITAS REIPVBLICAE   LRBC 2.496
Victory striding left, with wreath and palm

78. AE 3. D1:IV (328.93/455.00)   Lyons, P   A.D. 375–378   VF+
SECVRITAS REIPVBLICAE   LRBC 2.365
Victory striding left, with wreath and palm

Gratian, A.D. 375–383

79. AE 3. A88:XI/XII (377.59/527.81)   Arles, [   ] A.D. 375   G+
GLORIA NOVI SAECVLI   LRBC 2.503 etc.
Emperor stg. right

80. AE 3. B1:XI   Aquileia, P. A.D. 375   G+
SECVRITAS REIPVBLICAE   LRBC 2.1022
Victory striding left, with wreath and palm

81. AE 3 B7:X (328.62/473.38)   [   ]   A.D. 375–383   F
[   ]

82. AE 3. A18:XIII   Lyons, [   ] A.D. 364–375   F
SECVRITAS REIPVBLICAE   —
Victory striding left, with wreath and palm

[Valentinian, Valens, or Gratian]

83. AE 3. B7:X (330.60/472.91)   [   ]   A.D. 364–378   VG/F
GLORIA ROMANORVM (6–8)   —
Emperor right, dragging captive

Flavius Victor, A.D. 387–388

84. AE 4. B7:X (331.46/476.58)   [   ]   A.D. 387–388   F
SPES ROMANORVM   —
Camp gate

Arcadius, A.D. 383–408

85. AE 4. A1:XV (365.31/527.20)   [   ]   A.D. 388–402   VF
VICTORIA AVGG   —

Victory left, with palm and wreath

86. AE 4. C43:IV (wet-sieved)   [ ]   A.D. 388–402   F
VICTORIA AVGG   —
Victory left, with wreath and palm

[Illegible]

87. antoninianus. B4:XI (323.65/479.39)   3d century   F
[ ]

88. antoninianus. B12:X   3d century   F
[ ]

89. follis, AE 3. B9:X   4th century   —
[ ]   —

90. follis, AE 3. B1:XI (329.24/472.59)   4th century   F
[ ]   —

91. follis, AE 3. B7:X (333.86/472.82)   4th century   VG
[ ]   —

92. AE 4. A75:XI (374.21/523.10)   4th/5th century   —
[ ]   —

93. AE 4. A101:XIII (356.42/519.33)   4th/5th century   —
[ ]   —

94. AE 4. A202:XI (374.21/525.13)   4th/5th century   —
[ ]   —

95. AE 4. A348:XI (327.35/518.42)   4th/5th century   —
[ ]   —

96. AE 4. A355:XI (dry-sieved)   4th/5th century   —
[ ]   —

97. —. A24:XIII   —   —
[ ]

98. —. A202:XI (wet-sieved)   —   —
[ ]

99. —. A223:XI (364.47/525.85)   —   —
[ ]

100. —. A355:XI (dry-sieved)   —   —
[ ]

101. —. B95:VIII (323.80/478.34)   —   —
[ ]

Notes

1. Reece 1991a; with which should be read his 1991b: 253–260.

2. In the catalogue, the condition of each coin has been assessed in dealer's terms, as a general guide to their state of wear at the time of loss. It is a special hazard of excavation specimens such as these that some have suffered badly from corrosion, so as to obscure not only their identification, but their condition at the time of loss. The judgment is subjective to some extent, but it does pro-

vide a relative reading for the whole group: UNC., fresh from the mint; Extra Fine, XF, showing the lightest wear on the highest points; Very Fine, VF, some evident wear, but all elements clear; Fine, F, considerable wear, but all major elements of type and legend legible; Very Good, VG, some parts obliterated by wear; Good, G, widespread obliteration by wear.

    3. C. E. King 1981: 89–126.

    4. Besly and Bland 1983.

    5. Besly 1984: 63–68.

    6. Burnett and Robinson 1984: 89–99.

    7. Bland 1982.

    8. Reece 1978: 138, fig. 1.

    9. Soames 1890: 282–84; and 1892: 39–41.

    10. Kent 1981: 78–89. "Most hoards of copper coins deposited around 400 contain up to two per cent of coins struck between 330 and 348, still in recognizable condition" (Reece 1972: 276).

    11. Moorhead 1984: 41–49.

    12. Reece 1978: 130.

    13. Burnett 1983: 144–45.

    14. Reece 1991a: Tables V–VII; and 1991b: 256–58.

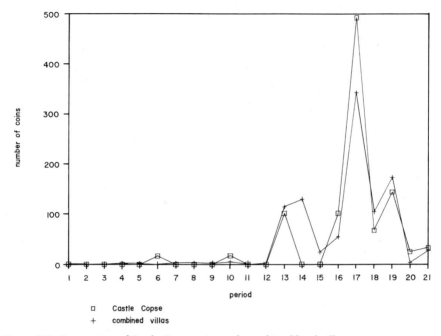

Figure 109. Comparison of Castle Copse coins with combined local villas.

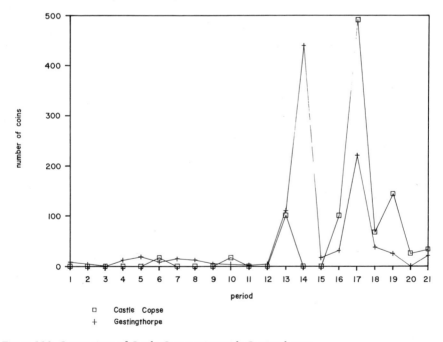

Figure 110. Comparison of Castle Copse coins with Gestingthorpe.

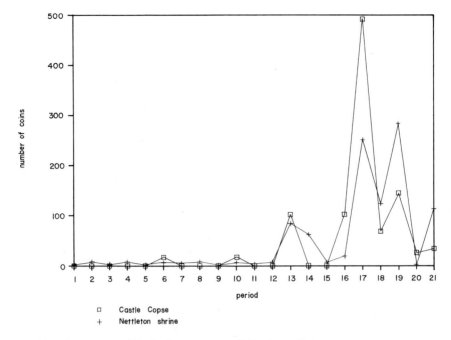

Figure 111. Comparison of Castle Copse coins with Nettleton Shrine.

4.8 OBJECTS OF METAL

BRADLEY AULT AND VALERIE HUTCHINSON PENNANEN

The assemblage of metal objects is comprised of a statuette fragment, items of dress and adornment, furniture and architectural fittings, and varied types of tools and hardware. The catalogue includes all significant metal artifacts recovered; in the case of nails, tacks, and shoe cleats, representative examples of individual types have been selected.[1]

The precise dating of individual pieces is difficult because of the nondiagnostic character of many of the objects and the character of the stratigraphy from which many were recovered. The majority of finds come from disturbed contexts or levelling layers deposited significantly later than the period during which the objects were in use, and are therefore residual. Unless precisely dated parallels are cited, the dates assigned are relative; no date is given if the piece can be identified only as being Roman in date.

Past discoveries (c. 1780) and excavations (c. 1853–54 and 1936–37) at and near the villa yielded a variety of metal objects, including: a gold finger-ring inscribed with an "X" (Fig. 112); four additional rings, pins, a fragment of a bracelet, the bowl of a spoon, a figurine in the form of a cockerel (Fig. 112), and a steelyard weight in the form of a female head (Fig. 112), all in copper alloy; an iron stylus; and a large lead cistern.[2] A decorated clay fragment, probably to be associated with bronze "casket ornament," was also reportedly found at the villa (chapter 4.10, Fig. 125).

With the exception of the concentrated debris from smithing operations in the very late occupation phase (B:VII) in the villa west wing, only the provenances of the objects of personal adornment shed light on the character of the villa wings. Their findspots, by phase and sector, are as below:

Provenance of Principal Jewelry Types by Sector, Phase, and Context

Sector	A		B		C	
	Catalogue		Catalogue		Catalogue	
	No.	Context:Phase	No.	Context:Phase	No.	Context:Phase
Fibulae	104	865:I	103	144:VI		
	105	129:XI	106	141:VI		
	164	549:XI	107	116:VI		
			163	144:VI		
			108	7:X		
Bracelets	115	337:XI	116	144:VI	112	19:V/VI
	110	121:XI/XII	119	144:VI	109	26:VII
			111	95:VIII		

			117	105:IX		
			113	7:X		
			114	7:X		
Rings	123	129:XI	120	116:VI	127	43:IV
	126	377:XI	121	99:IX	124	28:VI
	130	15:XIII	125	49:IX	128	28:VI
			129	7:X		
			122	2:XI		

Clearly, the concentration of items of jewelry in the villa west wing in its late Roman occupation and late or post-Roman phases (B:VI–XI) further confirms the luxury character of that wing.

Objects of Copper Alloy

STATUETTE

102. Statuette fragment. A1:XV (Fig. 113)
    L.=0.019, W.=0.025; Th.=0.005
Drapery fragment with three linear ridges on exterior, roughly textured interior, and jagged edges.
    From large hollow-cast statuette or small statue.

FIBULAE (BROOCHES)

Six copper alloy fibulae or fragments thereof were recovered. Two (**106–107**) are relatively unusual enamelled types, and one of these (**106**) is probably continental in origin.[3] All but one (**104**) are residual. Two iron Nauheim derivative fibulae were recovered (cf. **163–164**).

103. Nauheim derivative. B144:VI (Fig. 113)
    L. pin=0.042; L. bow=0.037
Narrow triangular bow decorated on top of foot with eight transverse incisions. Tip of catch-plate broken.
    A popular type during the first century A.D. through the Flavian period (cf. **104–05**).[4]
    First century.

104. Nauheim derivative. A865:I (Fig. 113)
    L.=0.058, W. bow=0.004
Form as **103**. Pin missing, one edge of bow chipped. Incised transverse line across middle of bow with nine notches along edges between mid-bow and head. Casting seam running length of bow's underside.
    First century.

105. Sprung-pin. A129:XI (Fig. 113)
    L.=0.026; D. coils=0.006
Double-coiled spring and bent pin.
    From a Nauheim derivative fibula?
    First century?

106. Enamelled plate fibula. B141:VI (Fig. 113)

L.=0.033; W.=0.016; Th. plate=0.002

Trapezoidal plate decorated with three parallel rectangular cells filled with enamel, blue in the middle, ivory on the sides. Horizontal curved molding decorated with incised notches, surmounted by lower third of fragmentary notched ring at apex of plate. At base, horizontal concave molding with incised notches on upper and lower borders, ends in punched circlets. Shaft finial in form of triple reel and spool projects below. Hinge, with traces of ferrous corrosion, projects at right angle from back of notched ring, catch-plate from profiled shaft. Pin missing.

The best parallels come from Germany and have been dated to after the mid-second century.[5] An example from Heddernheim, recovered in a deposit containing first- and second-century material, is extremely close, save for red enamel contained in its lower horizontal molding.[6]

Bibliography: Hostetter and Howe 1986b: 42 (incorrectly labelled cloisonné, rather than champlevé).

Mid-second century.

107. Enamelled plate fibula. B116:VI (Fig. 113)

L. plate=0.024; W. plate=0.012, Th. plate=0.001 (with cording 0.002)

Rectangular plate decorated with silver cording (partially missing), U-shaped in section, and applied with tin-lead solder, along borders and in form of a dolphin. Green enamel dolphin with two rows inlaid copper chips on blue, cracked and friable enamel field. Faint roundish impression with traces of tin-lead solder in the center of dolphin. Reverse bears catch-plate and two lugs holding sprung-pin.

Laboratory analysis has revealed that two compositions of bronze were used in the manufacture of the piece, one for the fibula and another for the pin, which shows a greater tin content.[7] The fibula proper was cast in one piece and trimmed with a file, while the sprung-pin was pulled through a drawplate and the pinpoint filed sharp.

This type of fibula is of British manufacture, and can be distinguished from continental plate fibulae by its combined use of the sprung-pin and the presence of decorative work in appliqué white metal, a technique apparently confined to Britain.[8] Similar examples, especially a rectangular plate fibula from Old Sarum, bearing an animal (dog?) and traces of silver "plating," have been considered second- or possibly early third-century A.D.[9]

Second–early third century.

108. Terminal from crossbow fibula. B7:X (Fig. 113)

D.=0.017; H.=0.018

Irregular sphere with ring molding and traces of lead solder at base.

Similar terminals are a typical feature on the head or wings of crossbow fibulae.[10]

Late Roman.

BRACELETS

Four bracelets and fragments of seven others were recovered. With one exception (**109**), all are made of copper alloy and represent types common in later Roman Britain.[11] A late Imperial date would also accord with the provenance of most of the Castle Copse examples.

109. Strip bracelet. C26:VII (Fig. 114)

D.=0.047; W.=0.005; Th.=0.003

Strip, rectangular in section with tapering ends, broken at tips, bent into approximately circular form. One end has partially preserved hole at break, remains of eye to receive hook or clasp. Outer face decorated with incision: shallow notches, regularly spaced and oblique.

A nearly identical bracelet is known from Hadstock, Essex.[12]

Bibliography: Hostetter and Howe 1986b: 43.

Late Roman

110. Strip bracelet. A121:XI/XII (Fig. 114)

D.=0.051; W.=0.004

Flat strip, bent into approximately circular form. Pierced at one end, tapered at other, and bent into hook. Outer face decorated with incision: short notches clustered at middle and ends, placed between two lines running length of strip.

A similar bracelet, from a robber trench at Frocester Court Villa, is thought to be of late Roman date. A like hooked terminal, including similarly placed incised decoration, comes from Gadebridge Park.[13]

Late Roman

111. Strip bracelet. B95:VIII (Fig. 114)

D.=0.059; W.=0.003

Flat strip with hook-and-eye clasp; tip of pierced end missing. Outer face decorated with incision: seven clusters triangular notches (nine to twelve per cluster) cut along alternate edges. Two pairs of transverse parallel notches near each terminal.

The triangular notched motif is common on Romano-British bronze bracelets and finger-rings.[14]

Late Roman

112. Strip bracelet. C19:V/VI (Fig. 114)

D.=0.030; W.=0.003

Flat strip with looped eye clasp; hooked tip missing. Outer face decorated with incision: six clusters of six triangular notches cut on alternate edges.

The small size suggests that it belonged to a child. On decoration, cf. **110-111.**

Late Roman.

113. Strip bracelet fragments. B7:X (Fig. 114)

L. (each fragment)=0.020 and=0.010; W. (both)=0.003

Two fragments, one bent, flat strip. Outer face of longer fragment decorated with incision: clusters of two transverse lines between opposing triangular notches. Between each cluster are two more opposing triangular notches. Second fragment similar.

A similarly decorated strip bracelet comes from Gestingthorpe.[15]

Late Roman

114. Strip bracelet (or finger-ring) fragment. B7:X (Fig. 114)

L.=0.014; W.=0.003

Flat, tapering strip, roughly rectangular in section. Bent and broken at both ends (?). Outer face decorated with incision: two longitudinal and five transverse lines.

Late Roman.

115. Strip bracelet (or finger-ring) fragment. A377:XI (Fig. 114)

L.=0.023; W.=0.004

Strip, lentoid to rectangular in section; broken at both ends, cracked and bent. Outer face decorated with irregularly positioned, stamped circles with central dot. Small triangular notches cut along both edges between circles.

Probably from a bracelet of common strip type. Similar ring-dot decoration is found on bronze bracelets from Gadebridge Park and Braintree; however, the same general type of decoration appears also on bronze finger-rings from Gestingthorpe and Brigstock.[16]

Late Roman.

116. Strip bracelet fragment. B144:VI

L.=0.035; W=0.003

Flat, tapering to plain terminal; one end broken.

Late Roman.

117. Double coil fragments. B105:IX (Fig. 114)

L. (longest)=0.026; D. (each)=0.002

Three fragments wire, "D" in section, with pairs of coils. Identification as bracelet is based on more complete examples from South Shields and Gadebridge Park.[17]

Late Roman.

118. Terminal hook from bracelet (?). Surface (Fig. 114)

L.=0.028; D. (base)=0.004

S-hook, squarish in section, with flat strip wrapped twice around broken base.

The dimensions suggest a bracelet terminal. Compare a hooked clasp on a bracelet from Chichester.[18]

119. Chain with glass beads. B144:VI (Fig. 114)

L. longest section=0.028; L. links (each)=0.002; D. beads=0.003

Numerous short segments of chain of tiny links of bronze wire, alternating with round, fluted, pale-yellow glass beads, four links between every two beads. Links through beads each made of single wire fashioned into elliptical loop wrapped around itself near base (to prevent bead from sliding) and inserted through hole in bead, with similar loop made at other end of wire. Intervening links of circular type.

A similar chain, with blue glass beads, comes from Bignor.[19] A more elaborate example, with beads in five different colors, comes from Gadebridge Park and has been identified as a necklace.[20] The diminutive size of both beads and chain links in the Castle Copse example may, however, suggest a bracelet.

RINGS

Of eleven examples, seven are finger-rings, while four are of uncertain use. The finger-rings are of well-known types; some (**121–122, 125**) date to the third and fourth centuries, but others (e.g., **127**) are impossible to date. Decoration, where present, is simple, usually confined to incisions on the bezels. However, inexpensive settings also occur (**122–123**).

120. Finger-ring. B116:VI (Fig. 115)

D.=0.019; Th. hoop=0.002; L. bezel=0.007, W. bezel=0.003

Oval ring, approximately circular in section, except where flattened into bezel. Bezel in form of rectangle crowned by four small rectangular projections (one chipped), and flanked by single indentations with transverse incisions. Bezel decorated with incision: "V" roughly bisected by vertical line, within rectangle.

A bronze (?) "key-ring" with similar decoration, likewise designed to be worn on the finger, is published by J. Ward, but without date or provenance.[21]

121. Finger-ring. B99:IX (Fig. 115)
L.=0.014; D. bezel=0.007; Th. bezel=0.002
Fragment sheet bronze, with raised oval bezel and sloping shoulders. Incised decoration: on bezel, two S-shaped zigzags; on shoulders, pairs of converging lines.

Corresponds to Henig Type VIII, dated to the third century.[22] Compare examples from Colchester and Portchester Castle, of "white metal" and silver, respectively.[23]

Third century.

122. Finger-ring. B2:XI (Fig. 115)
L.=0.017; W.=0.010; D. bead=0.005
Fragment of flat strip sheet bronze, widening toward bezel, bent to form faceted hoop; abraded, blue glass setting.

Parallels have been dated to the later Empire; the type is probably third-century.[24]

Bibliography: Hostetter and Howe 1986b: 43.

Late Roman.

123. Setting from finger-ring. A129:XI
L.=0.017; W.=0.008
Oval fragment sheet bronze, folded to enclose squarish inlay (green enamel?).

Possibly the bezel of a finger-ring.

124. Finger-ring. C28:VI (Fig. 115)
D.=0.019; Th.=0.002
Polygonal ring, probably hexagonal.

Poorly made. Compare an example in silver "with bevelled shoulders" from Rapsley, Ewhurst.[25]

125. Finger-ring. B49:IX (Fig. 115)
D.=0.020; Th.=0.003
Fragment octagonal ring, with two adjacent faces wider than others.

A common type, particularly in the third and fourth centuries.[26]

Late Roman.

126. Finger-ring. A377:XI (Fig. 115)
D.=0.017; W.=0.003; Th.=0.001
Bent, circular strip, rectangular in section; rounded pierced end overlaps opposite rectangular end. Outer face decorated with incision: transverse parallel notches near each end and longitudinal line down middle.

Expanding finger-rings of this type have been found at Gadebridge Park and South Shields.[27]

Bibliography: Hostetter and Howe 1986b: 43.

127. Finger-ring. C43:IV (Fig. 115)
D.=0.015; Th.=0.001
Wire, rectangular in section, twisted into two parallel coils with ends overlapping. Incised decoration: nicks along edge of wire.

Possibly a child's ring (cf. **128**). Parallels range from Iron Age to Saxon in date.[28]

Since **127** was recovered from a pit deposit in association with a coin of Arcadius (**86**) and a bone comb (**464**), a late or post-Roman date is probable.

128. Ring. C28:VI (Fig. 115)

D.=0.020; Th.=0.002

Plain ring of circular section.

Small ring from a chain or simple finger-ring.

129. Ring. B7:X (Fig. 115)

D.=0.019; Th.=0.001

Similar to **128**. One-quarter missing; minor chipping.

Ring from chain, ear-ring or finger-ring.

130. Ring. A15:XIII

D.=0.014; Th.=0.002

Similar to **128**. Half missing; worn or flattened at one end.

ORNAMENTAL PINS

131. Pin. A191:XI (Fig. 115)

L.=0.027; D. (head)=0.007

Domed head; bent shaft of rolled sheet bronze. Surface spotted (decoration?).

Delicate construction; probably ornamental.

132. Chain with ring and pin. A9:XIII (Fig. 115)

L. (longest chain segment)=0.038; L. links=0.015; L. pin=0.025

Fragments chain of figure-8 links, associated with fragmentary ring and pin. Figure 115 combines three fragments in a possible reconstruction.

Chains with attached rings and pins (hair pins?) are known in Britain, from both the Roman and Anglo-Saxon periods.[29]

Late Roman?

BUCKLES

133. Buckle loop. A209:X/XI (Fig. 115)

L.=0.035; W.=0.023; Th.=0.007

Oval loop, D-section, open at one side.

Buckles with similarly shaped loops, and with oval plates, have been dated to the second half of the fourth century.[30] The context of this piece, found among the burnt floor debris in the aisled building, would support such a date.

Late Roman.

134. Buckle loop. C19:V/VI

D.=0.030; Th.=0.004

Fragment round-sectioned ring; notch on inner surface.

Similar round-looped buckles have been dated from the second half of the fourth to the fifth centuries.[31]

Late Roman.

135. Buckle loop. C5:V (Fig. 115)

L.=0.024; Th.=0.003

Fragment ring, triangular in section.

Probably from a small buckle.

BELT ATTACHMENT

136. Belt attachment. A218:X/XI (Fig. 115)

L.=0.022; W.=0.011

Rectangular piece sheet bronze, pierced by two rivets at ends, one bearing irregularly shaped washer. Outer face decorated with: punched dot within two concentric rings on cross-shaped motif with arms elaborated by triangular notching.

Parallels from both Britain and the continent support the identification as a belt fitting.[32]

Late Roman?

BOSSES

For examples in iron, see **179–183**.

137. Boss. B113:IV (Fig. 116)

D.=0.025; H.=0.009. Sheet bronze disk, cracked in center and on edge, which slightly curls under.

To judge by parallels, probably for attachment to wood or leather.[33]

138. Boss. B75:X (Fig. 116)

D.=0.024

As **137**. Fragmentary.

139. Boss. B7:X (Fig. 116)

D.=0.015; H.=0.007

Convex disk with domed center. Base of missing shank round in section.

Probably for attachment to wood or leather.

140. Boss. A310:XI (Fig. 116)

D.=0.031; H.=0.012

Convex disk with jagged edges pierced by iron nail with shank missing. Ferrous corrosion.

Probably for attachment to wood or leather.

141. Boss. B144:VI

D.=0.018; H.=0.011

Three bent fragments of convex sheet bronze disk; base of missing shank square in section. Fragments organic material (leather?) cling to underside.

HANDLES, FINIALS, AND FURNITURE ATTACHMENTS

142. Handle/Finial. B7:X (Fig. 116)

L.=0.031; D.=0.015

Solid cast, elongated, profiled conical knob with fragmentary iron dowel projecting beneath.

Terminals of this type are fairly common and may have served a variety of purposes, most frequently as knobs or handles on furniture.[34]

143. Handle/Finial. A393:IX (Fig. 116)

L.=0.020; D=0.024

Profiled, bell-shaped finial with fragmentary iron dowel visible above and below encasing bronze collar. As **142**.[35]

144. Terminal. A67:XI (Fig. 116)

D.=0.015; H.=0.014

Hemisphere of cracked sheet bronze with iron core. Shank missing.

Furniture foot or decorative stud?

145. Terminal. C18:V/VI

D.=0.015; H.=0.014

As **144**. Shank missing and bronze sheathing cracked. Ferrous corrosion.

IMPLEMENTS

146. Spoon. C19:V/VI (Fig. 116)

L.=0.112; W. bowl=0.031; Th. handle=0.004

Bent oval bowl, two-thirds missing, with bent handle, rectangular in section, tapering to blunt point. Notch in top of handle near join with bowl.

Similar examples from Gadebridge Park, Portchester Castle, and Verulamium suggest a Late Roman date.[36]

Bibliography: Hostetter and Howe 1986b: 43.

Late Roman.

147. Nail-cleaner. B144: VI (Fig. 117)

L.=0.062; Th.=0.003

Forked shaft, rectangular in section, profiled handle, divided into two sections decorated with incised oblique lines, terminates in pierced disk.

A nail-cleaner of the type seen in "pocket-sets" of toilet instruments, often hung on a small ring together with tweezers and "ear-scoop." Close parallels come from Gloucester and Nettleton.[37]

148. Spatulate implement (?). A223: XI (Fig. 117)

L.=0.086; W. (spatulate end)=0.008

Elongated S-shaped shaft, rectangular in section, flattened and rounded at one end. Narrow end pierced below rod terminal. Three transverse notches on upper surface. Spatula from toilet set (cf. **147**); or handle, with hole for attachment by means of a pin?

149. Profiled handle. A382: XI (Fig. 117)

L.=0.057; D.=0.008

Profiled shaft, circular in section, decorated with beads and double reels each bearing oblique slashes in alternate directions. Pointed tang (broken?) projects at one end.

Possibly from a small spoon, fork, or cosmetic implement?[38]

150. Handle/Pin (?). C18:V/VI (Fig. 117)

L.=0.076; Th.=0.002

Bent, tapering shaft, squarish in section, broken at both ends.

Probably from a cosmetic implement: e.g., ligula or ear pick, or a straight pin.[39]

151. Pin/Ligula head. B12:X

D.=0.005

Irregular sphere with fragment of missing shaft.

Probably the head of pin or olivary enlargement from ligula.

152. Pin/Ligula head. C10:VI

D.=0.004

Irregular sphere with indentation for missing shaft. As **151**.

MISCELLANEOUS

153. Decorated strip. B9:X (Fig. 117)

L.=0.047; W.=0.002

Bent, flat strip, one face with incised decoration: four clusters of four shallow notches.

Probably a decorative staple or edging, as for a box.

154. Staple. B113:IV (Fig. 117)

L. back=0.035; L. tangs=0.015

Plain strip, ends tapered and bent.

From furniture tacking? Compare an example from Silchester.[40]

155. Tack or stud head. A355:XI (Fig. 117)

D.=0.011; H.=0.008

Cracked, bronze-sheathed iron head of tack or stud; shank missing.

156. Tack head. A191:XI (Fig. 117)

D.=0.009

Conical head of sheet bronze; shank missing.

From furniture?

157. Sheathing. A18:XIII

L.=0.024; H.=0.014

Fragmentary dome-shaped sheet bronze with traces of lead (?) and burnt organic material.

Possibly from boss or steelyard weight?

158. Sheathing. A355:XI (Fig. 117)

L.=0.021; D.=0.006

Fragmentary, semi-cylindrical hollow "tubing" of thin sheet bronze.

Function unknown.

159. Rivet. B85:VII (Fig. 117)

L.=0.009; D.=0.006; Th. shank=0.002

Sheet bronze folded to form head and shank with broken tip.

Probably from small fitting, as for a belt. Compare rivets on **136.**

160. Link. A191:XI (Fig. 117)

L.=0.016

Fragment figure-8 chain link, flat in section.

161. Strap with split pin. B144:VI

L.=0.097; W.=0.017

Bent, fragmentary, rectangular strip with one end rectangular and spatulate, the other pierced and joined to a split pin.

Possibly from a type of loop-hinge best known in iron (see below, "Hinges").[41]

162. Double interlocking pin-rings. A121:XI/XII (Fig. 117)

L.=0.057

Bronze split-pin linked to iron split-pin (?).

Possibly from a small loop-hinge.[42]

Objects of Iron

FIBULAE

163. Nauheim derivative. B144:VI (Fig. 118)

    L. bow=0.022, W. spring=0.008

    Sprung-pin fibula; catch plate, portion of bow and pin missing.

    Such simple fibulae are common in iron as well as bronze (cf. **103**).[43]

    First century.

164. Nauheim derivative. A549:XI (Fig. 118)

    L. pin=0.029; W. spring=0.014

    As **163**. Catch plate, bow, and portion of pin missing.

    First century.

TOOLS

Four tools appear to reflect the working of metal, wood, and leather. Three of these—a nail-heading tool (**165**), chisel (**167**), and awl (**168**)—were recovered from late/post Roman activity debris in each of the three villa wings. Their presence in these contexts reflects the changing functions of villa rooms in their latest phases, as workshop activities took place within areas formerly reserved for living or other service needs.

165. Nail-heading tool. B67:VII (Fig. 118)

    L.=0.162; Th.=0.012, D. disk=0.047

    Broken (?) shaft, rectangular in section, ends in disk recessed on top and pierced by hole.

    Similar tools come from other Romano-British sites, including Silchester.[44] The Castle Copse example is notable for having been recovered in a late or post-Roman context in association with ferrous slag and other traces of ironworking. For analysis, see Appendix 5.

    Late Roman.

166. Punch. B95:VIII (Fig. 118)

    L.=0.137; D.=0.018

    Cylindrical shaft, tapered into squarish blade.

    For metalworking; numerous other examples are known.[45]

167. Chisel. A209:X/XI (Fig. 118)

    L.=0.118; W. tip=0.025; Th. tip=0.010, D. socket=0.021

    Two fragments. Slightly convex blade with rolled socket and flared tip. Traces of wood in socket.

    Probably for woodworking, the rolled socket and curved blade correspond to Manning's classes of firmer and mortise chisels.[46] Found upon a floor surface within the aisled building among burnt debris, including two coins dating after A.D. 330 (**50** and **70**) and a probable fourth-century buckle (**133**), a late date is likely.

    Late Roman

168. Bone-handled awl. C64:IV (Fig. 118)

    L.=0.119; Th. bone handle=0.014

    Shaft, squarish in section, tapers toward missing point below; above, pointed tang with hafting of bone or horn, much of which is missing.

For leatherworking, this would seem to correspond to Manning Type 4 awl.[47] Recovered from a pit in association with a coin of Arcadius (**133**) and a bone comb (**465**), a late date is probable.

Late Roman

CUTTING IMPLEMENTS

Seven cutting tools range in date from early to late Roman.[48]

169. Razor or knife. B144:VI (Fig. 118)

L.=0.166; W.=0.016; D. handle ring=0.015; Th. blade=0.002; Th. handle=0.006

Of one piece: handle, rectangular in section, with looped butt for suspension; thin, straight blade.

Corresponding to Manning Type 1a, the piece is probably a razor, rather than a knife.[49] An example from Verulamium is especially close.[50]

First or second century.

170. Knife blade. A377:XI (Fig. 119)

L.=0.109; W.=0.031; Th.=0.008

Two joining fragments, complete (?).

Tang in S curve and squarish in section; subtriangular blade with cutting edge offset from tang.

Probably of Manning Type 23 or 24, although the characteristic "markedly upturned tip" is not so apparent here, possibly due to breakage.[51] Derived from Iron Age precursors, known examples are dated to the first and early second centuries.

First–early second century.

171. Knife blade. A40:XV (Fig. 119)

L.=0.135; W.=0.020; Th.=0.004

Tang broken (?), blade in several joining fragments with tip missing. Centrally projecting, broken (?) tang, square in section below narrow blade, in several joining fragments, with straight back and cutting edge with slow curve.

Possibly of Manning Type 15, the most common of all knife forms and used throughout the Roman period.[52] For analysis, see Appendix 5.

172. Knife blade. A7:XV (Fig. 119)

L.=0.078; W.=0.020; Th.=0.004

Broken tang, flat and rectangular in section, below blade with slow downward curvature and missing tip.

Possibly corresponding to Manning Type 14,[53] it is among the most common knife forms and has a long period of use. The form of the blade may have been modified by sharpening.

173. Knife blade. C19:VII (Fig. 119)

L.=0.039; W.=0.016; Th.=0.004

Narrow blade in four joining fragments (only two shown in Fig. 119); tang missing. Straight cutting edge, back angled to meet slightly upturned point.

Possibly corresponding to Manning Type 14 (see **172**). For analysis, see Appendix 5.

174. Knife blade. B89:VIII (Fig. 119)

L.=0.124; W.=0.031; Th.=0.002; L. tang=0.042

Centrally projecting tang, squarish in section, angled slightly. Broad, fairly symmetrical blade with curving edges.

Of Manning Type 21, the form is late.[54] Examples not cited by Manning are known from Portchester Castle, Nettleton, and Barnsley Park. The latter comes from a late fourth-century context.[55]

Late Roman.

175. Cleaver. A919:VIII (Fig. 119)

L.=0.226; W.=0.059; Th.=0.008; D. socket=0.030

Two joining fragments. Rolled socket slightly offset from blade's back edge and wholly from cutting edge; back of socket in same plane as blade, rolled portion projects laterally. Blade forms elongated right triangle.

Corresponds to Manning Type 3 cleaver, and is especially close to a first-century example from Alchester.[56]

First century.

SPEARHEAD

176. Spearhead. A35:XV (Fig. 119)

L.=0.095; W.=0.020; D. socket=0.007

Three joining and other miscellaneous fragments; rolled, angular (as preserved) socket broken. Triangular head, flat on one face, low central ridge on other.

The broken socket would have considerably extended the length of the piece and supports its identification as a spearhead.[57] For analysis, see Appendix 5.

KEYS

177. Latch-lifter (?) fragment. B144:VI (Fig. 120)

L.=0.140; W.=0.018; Th.=0.005

Stem broken, tip missing. Handle and stem flat and rectangular in section; handle end rounded.

A simple form of key found in both the Iron Age and Roman period. Typically the handle is perpendicular to the stem and bears a suspension loop.[58] For analysis, see Appendix 5.

178. Lever-lock key. A91:X/XI (Fig. 120)

L. shaft=0.075; D. shaft=0.009; L. plate=0.025; W. plate=0.023; Th. plate=0.006

Shaft, round in section, terminates in ring-handle and plate with meander pattern; teeth probably project from bottom of plate, but corrosion obscures. Handle missing.

The type is common.[59]

BOSSES

Five examples were recovered (cf. **137–141** for examples in copper alloy).

179. Boss. B10:X (Fig. 120)

D.=0.036; H.=0.027

Domed head with jagged edge above plain disc rim; shank, rectangular in section and with tip missing, projects below.

Probably for attachment to wood.

180. Boss. A139:XIII (Fig. 120)

D.=0.039; H.=0.012

Domed head above jagged disc rim with toothed cuttings; square nail-hole in center. Probably for attachment to wood or leather. For analysis, see Appendix 5.

181. Boss. A217:XI (Fig. 120)

D.=0.050; H.=0.055

Dome-shaped head with shank, square in section and missing tip, projecting below. Attachment for wood.

182. Boss. A7:XIII (Fig. 120)

H.=0.037; L.=0.045; W.=0.033

Portion of plate, tip of nail missing.

Flat fragmentary rectangular plate pierced by dome-headed nail; shank, square in section, bent at angle and missing tip.

Attachment for wood.

183. Boss. A140:XI cleaning pass (Fig. 120)

H.=0.051. L.=0.078; W.=0.046

Lozenge-shaped, fragmentary plate with concave sides and elongated tips; center pierced by hole with molding on back of plate, dome-headed nail survives in place. Shank, squarish in section, bent back toward plate.

Attachment for wood.

HINGES

In addition to the two examples here, two possible loop-hinges in copper alloy (**161–162**) are discussed above. Simple hinges could also be fashioned using looped spikes (cf. below **196–202**).[60]

184. Drop-hinge. C43:IV (Fig. 121)

L.=0.178; W. across loop=0.035; W. sides=0.040; Th.=0.005

Long, thick, rectangular plate, forming U-shaped loop open at one end. Two large Manning Type I nails (cf. below, "Nails") pass through both arms of loop, near open end, and at midpoint; nail points hammered back against face of arm.

This type of hinge is typically used upon doors, frequently in conjunction with L-shaped staples (as **191**), but is also found with bindings on chests or coffins.[61] One arm is generally longer than the other.

Late Roman.

185. Loop-hinge. B141:VI (Fig. 121)

L.=0.051; W.=0.040

Fragmentary. Heavy corrosion and incrustation. Rectangular plate with rounded corners; hooked loop bends back from middle of short side.

This small loop-hinge may have been used on a box lid or window shutter. A similar example is known from Bignor.[62]

BINDINGS

Such bindings were typically used for reinforcement by fastening pieces of wood together (as on a door or box).[63]

186. Binding. C19:V/VI (Fig. 121)

L.=0.054; W.=0.020; Th.=0.003

Rectangular strip, flat in section, with slight curvature and broken ends; squarish nail-hole near end.

Architectural (?) fitting.

187. Angle-binding. C5:VI (Fig. 121)

L.=0.067; W.=0.060; Th.=0.003

Bent and fragmentary flat rectangular strip; wide and rounded end bears two squarish nail-holes, broken end has central notch.

Function uncertain, though architectural bindings of this sort are common. A mid-first-century example from Hod Hill is very similar.[64]

188. Binding or fitting. B7:X (Fig. 121)

L.=0.077. W.=0.024; Th.=0.004

Strip, flat in section, with preserved end rounded and slightly bent, the other missing.

Possibly from a binding or other fitting. For analysis, see Appendix 5.

189. Angle-binding or other fitting. A355:XI.

L.=0.060; W.=0.030; Th.=0.003

Trapezoidal plate in three joining fragments, flat in section, terminating in disk end pierced with squarish hole.

Probably a fragmentary angle-binding with identical half now missing, but a portion of a door fitting or a loop for attaching a drop-handle remain possibilities.[65]

JOINER'S DOGS

These common cleats for joining timbers were manufactured in a variety of sizes.[66]

190. Joiner's dog. C19:V/VI (Fig. 121)

L.=0.095; L. tangs=0.050 and=0.042; H.=0.052; Th.=0.012

Blunt tangs, one missing point, descend from horizontal bar, square to rectangular in section.

191. Fragmentary joiner's dog or L-shaped staple. B7:X (Fig. 121)

L.=0.038; L. tang=0.051; H.=0.054; Th.=0.010

Blunt tang, rectangular in section, decends from horizontal bar; half of bar and other tang missing.

A joiner's dog (?), or possibly an L-shaped staple of the type often used with a drop-hinge like **184**.[67]

192. Joiner's dog. A121:XI/XII (Fig. 121)

L.=0.067; L. tang=0.028; Th.=0.007

Smaller version of **190**. Fragmentary.

193. Joiner's dog. C23:III

L.=0.105; L. tangs=0.053; H.=0.054; Th.=0.010

Large version of **190**.

194. Joiner's dog. A874:VIII

L.=0.100; L. tangs=0.049 and=0.045; H.=0.050; Th.=0.009

Similar to **190**. Point of one tang missing.

195. Joiner's dog. A425: XI

L.=0.068; L. tangs=0.059 and 0.047; H.=0.060; Th.=0.010

Smaller version of **190**. Point of one tang missing.

LOOPED SPIKES

These fittings were a common means of attaching a loop to building materials.[68]

196. Loop-headed spike. B52:X (Fig. 122)

L.=0.101; D. loop=0.026; Th. loop=0.012

Disk head, flat in section; spike, rectangular in section, tapering and curving. For analysis, see Appendix 5.

197. Loop-headed spike. A7:XIII (Fig. 122)

L.=0.090; D. loop=0.017; Th. shaft=0.008

Looped head, flat in section; spike, square-rectangular in section, tapering.

198. Loop-headed spike. B64:VII (Fig. 122)

L.=0.065; D. loop=0.19; Th. shaft=0.008

Looped head, square in section; spike, rectangular in section, tapering.

199. Double-spiked loop with ring. A7:XIII (Fig. 122)

L.=0.175; D. ring=0.076; Th. ring=0.012; L. spiked loop=0.111; Th. single spike=0.006

Ring, squarish in section, through looped head of double spike. Spikes, rectangular in section, taper to points which, near ends, bend outwards. For analysis, see Appendix 5.

200. Double-spiked loop. A121:XI/XII (Fig. 122)

L.=0.096; D. loop=0.030; Th. single spike=0.008

Looped head, flat in section; spikes, rectangular in section, taper to points (one missing) which, near ends, bend outwards. For analysis, see Appendix 5.

201. Double-spiked loop. A121:XI/XII (Fig. 122)

L.=0.107; D. loop=0.044; Th. single spike=0.005

Two joining fragments. Thick looped head, flattened and rectangular in section; spikes, square in section, tapering and bent. For analysis, see Appendix 5.

202. Double-spiked loop. A104:XI (Fig. 122)

L.=0.062; D. loop=0.021; Th. single spike=0.003

Looped head, square in section. Spikes, square in section, bent out below head; tip of single surviving spike bent back upon itself.

This would seem to correspond to Manning's "anomalous forms" of double-spiked loops from Hod Hill.[69] Function uncertain.

SHOE CLEATS

Used for reinforcing the soles and heels of shoes and boots, the type is common.[70] In addition to the three examples catalogued and illustrated below, another sixteen shoe cleats were recovered from various levels at the site.

203. Shoe cleat. B3:X (Fig. 123)

L.=0.031; W.=0.012; Th.=0.005

Ovoid disk, flat in section, with two tangs, one missing point, projecting laterally.

204. Shoe cleat. C5:VI (Fig. 123)

L.=0.026, W.=0.010; Th.=0.005

As **203**, but with shorter tangs, one missing point.

205. Shoe cleat. A91:X/XI (Fig. 123)

L.=0.025; W.=0.014; Th.=0.005

As **203**. One tang and point of other missing.

HORSESHOES

Horseshoes from the Roman period in Britain are now securely attested, the more common "hipposandal" having been used for unshod animals when on paved surfaces.[71] Neither of the Castle Copse horseshoes comes from securely Roman contexts.

206. Horseshoe. C9:VI (Fig. 123)

L.=0.115; W.=0.035; Th.=0.005

Elliptical shoe with one end missing, flat in section with two rectangular nail-holes. One preserves rectangular-sectioned nail.

Roman?

207. Horseshoe. A21:XV

L.=0.078; W.=0.104; Th.=0.005

Fragmentary shoe, flat in section, with irregular curvature; three rectangular nail-holes with three nailheads survive. For analysis, see Appendix 5.

Roman?

MISCELLANEOUS

208. Wallhook. A39:XV

L. hooked arm=0.037; L. shank=0.034

Right-angled wallhook with both nail shank and bent hook rectangular in section.

Other small wallhooks frequently bear a knob on hooked end, presumably for hanging garments. Similar examples have been found at Gadebridge Park, Hod Hill, and Verulamium, among many other sites.[72]

209. Hook. B4:XI (Fig. 123)

L.=0.191; D.=0.009

Shaft, round in section, carries ovoid disc, flat in section and pierced with squarish hole at one end, and tapers to hook at other.

The hook was probably intended to be nailed to a beam; a nearly identical example comes from Great Wakering, Essex.[73]

210. Hook or T-clamp. B7:X (Fig. 123)

L. pierced strip=0.043; L. attached arm/shank=0.052

Fragmentary (?), bent, flattened strip pierced near ends with two nail-holes; shaft, squarish in section and bent, projects from center.

Possibly a wallhook, although the form does not correspond to the most ubiquitous type (cf. **208**). May also be a small T-clamp, but none of the examples catalogued by Manning show the pierced head.[74]

211. Pierced triangular object. B83:V (Fig. 123)

L.=0.050; Th.=0.005

Roughly triangular piece with corner missing, flat in section, pierced by squarish hole.

Possibly a washer, or fragment of a considerably larger object (e.g., a binding). For analysis, see Appendix 5.

212. Shaft with disc terminal. A101:XIII (Fig. 123)

L.=0.064; D. disc=0.039; D. shaft=0.017

Upturned disc end, flat in section, pierced by hole; thick, broken shaft, round in section.

Function uncertain, possibly an architectural fitting or part of the mechanism to a large lock.[75]

NAILS AND TACKS

Over 2,700 nails have been recovered from the villa at Castle Copse.[76] The vast majority, as is usual on Romano-British sites, belong to Manning Type I (chart; **213–19**).[77] Virtually all of the Type I nails from Castle Copse, whether large or small, have square-sectioned tapering shanks and flattened heads hammered into a roughly square-to-circular shape. Occasionally these heads are offset to one side of the shank (**218–219**), due to careless workmanship or breakage, rather than design.[78] Complete examples have a maximum length of 0.132, with a head 0.029 in diameter and shank 0.015 thick (tapering to less). Approximately 36% of the total number of Type I nails probably measured between 0.05 and 0.10 in length, while roughly 27% measured less than 0.05. Almost none (less than 1%) were longer than 0.10. The remaining 37% of Type I nails were too fragmentary for their original lengths to be estimated.

Given the great quantity of nails needed in the construction of the villa complex, traces of ferrous smithing slag present throughout excavated levels, and the recovery of a nail-heading tool (**165**), it is assumed that Type I nails were made on the site (see chapter 4.9). The distribution of Type I nails among sectors and by size is shown in the first chart below. The second chart shows the phase distribution of all nails and makes clear that the majority were recovered as residual finds in disturbed levels. Of note, however, is the large number of nails from Sector C (Phase IV), primarily from the fill of the late or post-Roman pit.

Distribution of Type I nails by sector and size.

Sector	<0.05	0.05–0.10	0.10–0.15	Omitted*	Total
A	497	461	2	238	1198
B	154	355	0	481	990
C	61	153	0	261	475
D	35	21	0	15	71
Tests	3	7	0	9	19
Total	750	997	2	1004	2753

*due to breakage

Distribution of nails by phase.

Sector	A		B		C	
	Phase	Number	Phase	Number	Phase	Number
	I	9	I	(unex.)	I	1
	II	16	II	(unex.)	II	15
	III	0	III	0	III	35
	IV	3	IV	7	IV	165
	V	3	V	43	V	6
	VI	8	VI	143	V/VI	54
	VII	17	VII	24	VI	212
	VIII	21	VIII	83		

IX	29	IX	120
X	12	X	364
X/XI	135	XI	101
XI	229		
XI/XII	79		
XII	0		
XIII	275		
XIV	22		
XV	349		

Four Manning Type II nails have also been identified (**220–222**). These have squarish shanks crowned by triangular heads, which lie in the same plane as the shaft. The largest and smallest of these Type II nails measure 0.157 and 0.085 in length, respectively, with maximum shank thicknesses of 0.012 and 0.009.

Several variants on the two main classes of nails also occur at Castle Copse. One example with a flat, lozenge-shaped head measuring 0.027 in length and 0.019 in width (**223**), may correspond to Manning Type VII (see above; note 77). It very likely served some decorative purpose.

The shanks of five nails do not have offset heads, but are instead flattened and flared at the top, so that their heads resemble the blunt tips of styli (**224**).[79] The smallest example of this type (**224**), probably from the same object, shows its head bent at a 90° angle to the shank, presumably as a result of hammering. Similar to this last, but lacking the distinctive flared head, are three nails, still encrusted with traces of wood, which show only a slight enlargement of their rectangular section at the head (**225**).

Finally, some sixty iron tacks and hobnails were recovered. Averaging 0.020 in length, the majority have domed heads (**226**), while others have heads more conical in shape (**227**). Their shanks vary from square to round in section. Manning Type I nails include:

213. A15:XIII (Fig. 123)
   W. head=0.012; Th. shank=0.004
214. C34:IV (Fig. 123)
   L.=0.053; W. head=0.018; Th. shank=0.005
215. C34:IV (Fig. 123)
   L.=0.078; W. head=0.018; Th. shank=0.006
216. A522:XI (Fig. 123)
   L.=0.112; W. head=0.025; Th. shank=0.01
217. A121:XI/XII (Fig. 123)
   L.=0.127 (tip missing); W. head=0.029; Th. shank=0.017
218. A91:X/XI (Fig. 124)
   L.=0.04; W. head=0.001; Th. shank=0.005
219. A41:XII (Fig. 124)
   L.=0.04; W. head=0.02; Th. shank=0.006
Manning Type II nails include:
220. A19:XV (Fig. 124)
   L.=0.085; W. head=0.021; Th. shank=0.009

221. A1:XV (Fig. 124)

L.=0.098; W. head=0.019; Th. shank=0.008.

222. A110:XIII (Fig. 124)

L.=0.157; W. head=0.023; Th. shank=0.012

Variant nail types include:

223. B83:V (Fig. 124)

L. head=0.027; W. head=0.019

Manning Type VII?

224. B83:V (Fig. 124)

L.=0.045; W. head=0.011; Th. shank=0.005

225. Three nails with wood. A19:XV (Fig. 124)

L.=c. 0.075; W.=c. 0.03

Hobnails and tacks include:

226. Hobnail or tack. B15:X (Fig. 124)

L.=0.012; W. head=0.009; Th. shank=0.002

227. Tack. B12:X (Fig. 124)

L.=0.024; W.=0.012; Th. shank=0.002

Objects of Lead

In addition to the two objects catalogued here, a number of small lead fragments and drippings from melted lead were found in disturbed levels on the site.

228. Perforated disc. A445:IV (Fig. 124)

D.=0.017; Th.=0.005

Disc-shaped, one face flat, sides and other face rounded. Center pierced by hole, which tapers in diameter from flat to rounded face.

Probably a weight, perhaps for a loom or fishing net.[80]

229. Strip C43:IV (Fig. 124)

L.=0.133; W.=0.061; Th.=0.009

Bent and roughly rectangular in shape.

This strip was presumably cut for scrap from a larger object. It recalls the 1860 mention of a large lead tank (?) found at the villa.[81]

NOTES

1. Unidentifiable finds, such as small corroded lumps of bronze, iron and lead have been omitted.

2. Cunnington and Goddard 1911: 51–52, pl. 22:8, 25:5–6, 27:1 and 1934: 196–197, figs. 30–31, pl. 70.1; and Grinsell 1957: 73; both with further references to these finds. The steelyard weight in the form of a female head is not certain to be from the villa site. Several other of the objects are now lost or destroyed.

3. On fibulae and enamelling: Hattatt 1982, 1985, and 1987; Hull and Hawkes 1987: especially 1–3 on terminology; Mackreth 1973; Bateson 1981; and Butcher 1977: 41–70.

4. On type, see Hattatt 1982: 57–59, fig. 17; and Mackreth 1973: 11, fig. 3.

5. Exner 1939: 55–56, for a discussion of the type and its date, and 86–88, Taf. 9, for examples.

6. Fischer 1973: 92–94, no. 15, Abb. 19.15.

7. Alloy analysis (XRF) and microscopic examination were kindly carried out by C. Mortimer and E. Cameron (Research Laboratory for Archaeology and History of Art, Oxford University); this and other technical information is based on their report.

8. These observations are owed to the kindness of D. F. Mackreth.

9. Hattatt 1985: 163, no. 586, fig. 67:586; see, too, Hattatt 1985: 162, nos. 584–585, fig. 67:584–585; and 1987: 200–202, nos. 1097–1098, fig. 63.1097-1098. On manufacture and dating, D. F. Mackreth, pers. comm.; see also Mackreth 1983: 58–59, fig. 4:11 (with additional references); Mackreth 1986: 64, fig. 40:6; and Hattatt 1982: 43, Table I.

10. For comparison, see Hattatt 1982: 122, no. 104, fig. 53:104, dated to the fourth century.

11. E.g., Waugh and Goodburn 1972: 120, nos. 33–34, fig. 32:33–34 (both from late Imperial contexts); Webster 1975: 205–209, with comments on typology and decoration (209); and Wheeler and Wheeler 1932: 82–83, fig. 17 (most examples of presumed later fourth-century date).

12. Liversidge 1968: 142, fig. 55b.

13. Frocester Court: E. Fowler 1970: 53, no. 15, fig. 12:15; Gadebridge Park: Neal and Butcher 1974: 139, no. 171, fig. 61:171.

14. E.g., bracelet: G. Webster 1982: 107, no. 20, fig. 24:20 (from context dated 375–80); finger-ring: Wedlake 1982: 214, fig. 91:30 (probable fourth-century date).

15. Henig 1985: 29, no. 34, fig. 10:34.

16. Gadebridge Park: Neal and Butcher 1974: 139, no. 155, fig. 60:155; Braintree: Pratt 1976: 17, fig. 11:5 (from mid-fourth century context); Gestingthorpe: Henig 1985: 33, no. 64, fig. 12:64 (dated third century); Brigstock: Greenfield 1963: 228–63, 243–47, 247, no. 13, fig. 6:13 (fourth century?).

17. South Shields: Allason-Jones and Miket 1984: 134–36, nos. 3:271, 3:275; Gadebridge Park: Neal and Butcher 1974: 139, nos. 164–70, fig. 61:164-170.

18. Down 1981: 169, no. 22, fig. 8.31:22.

19. Grew 1982: 179, no. 9, fig. 26:9.

20. Neal and Butcher 1974: 133, no. 75, fig. 58:75.

21. Ward 1911: 240, fig. 76Q.

22. Henig 1978: 35, fig. 1:VIII.

23. Crummy 1983: 49, no. 1791, fig. 52:1791; Webster 1975: 210, no. 49, fig. 112:49.

24. M. Henig, pers. comm. Cf. Toynbee 1982: 143–49, 148, 9.iii, fig. 63:7, pl. 23.a (from late fourth-century floor level); and Henkel 1913: 59, no. 428, Taf. 22 (from Mainz; form dated to the third century).

25. Hanworth 1968: 33, no. 13, fig. 14:13.

26. Cf. Goodburn 1984: 31; and Henkel 1913: 219–21. For additional parallels, see Rennie 1971: 81, no. 18, fig. 6:18; Henig 1985: 33, no. 63, fig. 12:63; Wright 1970: 246–61, 257–59, fig. 7 (three examples of probable late fourth-century date); Ward 1911: 270, fig. 76.I (in silver, from Rushmore); Allason-Jones and Miket 1984: 122, no. 3:166, fig. 166.

27. Neal and Butcher 1974: 147, no. 257, fig. 65:257; Allason-Jones and Miket 1984: 122, no. 3:164, fig. 164.

28. Henig 1985: 33, no. 66, fig. 12:66. Henig notes the longevity of the type citing: Wheeler 1943: 266, nos. 10–17, fig. 86:10–17 (dated c. 25 B.C.–A.D. 50) and Kirk and Leeds 1952–53: 70, Grave III, find (h), fig. 29:14 (late fourth or early fifth century).

29. Cf. Waugh and Goodburn 1972: 124, nos. 77a and 80, with 127, fig. 36:77a and 80; and Jessup 1953: 103, nos. 6 and 8, pl. 9:6 and 8 (from a barrow, Breach Down, Kent).

30. See Clarke 1979: 270–72, fig. 34, nos. 27, 122, 421; and Henig 1985: 29, no. 17, fig. 9:17.

31. D. Brown 1975: 267–94, 290–94, 292, fig. 8 (dated second half of fourth–fifth centuries); and Neal and Butcher 1974: 129, no. 38, fig. 55:38 (from a fourth-century context).

32. E.g., from Shakenoak: Brodribb, Hands and Walker 1968: 92, 100, no. 58, fig. 32:58; and from Altenstadt in southern Bavaria: Keller 1971: 68, Abb. 23.15 and Taf. 34:9; and 67, Abb. 23:13, Taf. 35:4 (belt fittings from graves dated second half of the fourth century).

33. See Curle 1911: 163, pl. 25:1–36; Droop and Newstead 1931: nos. 3–4, 133, cat. nos. 21, 23, pl. 46:21, 23 (one from an Antonine deposit); and Wheeler and Wheeler 1928: 111–218, 168, no. 4, pl. 32, fig. 2:4 (from a Flavian deposit).

34. For similar examples, see Allason-Jones and Miket 1984: 216, nos. 3:733–3:736, figs. 733–736; and Flight and Harrison 1978: 42, nos. 4–5, fig. 7:4–5.

35. For select parallels: Bushe-Fox 1916: 26, no. 22, pl. 17:22 (linch-pin); Henig 1985: 41, no. 128, fig. 15:28, with additional cross-references (terminal for use with lock-pin); and, from Bignor, Grew 1982: 179, no. 13, fig. 27:13.

36. Neal and Butcher 1974: 135, no. 81, fig. 58:81; Webster 1975: 212, nos. 58–59, fig. 133:58–59; and Goodburn 1984: 21, no. 9, fig. 4:9 (silver, fourth century).

37. Hassall and Rhodes 1974: 66, no. 28, fig. 26:28; and Wedlake 1982: 219, fig. 94:5–6 {from third–fourth century levels).

38. For similar handles see: Ward 1911: 209, fig. 59:J; Grimal 1963: ill. 220, between pp. 280–81 (handle of two-pronged fork).

39. For select parallels: Bushe-Fox 1914: 13, no. 8, fig. 5.8 (ear-pick); Milne 1907: 77–78, pl. 18 (ligulae); and MacDonald and Curle 1929: 556, fig. 116 (long pin with baluster-head).

40. Cotton 1947: 145, no. 9, fig. 9:9.

41. See Manning 1985b: 126, fig. 31:2, for a discussion of examples in iron.

42. Ibid.

43. For select parallels: Mackreth 1976: 25, no. 3; Manning 1985a: 27, no. 2, fig. 8:2; and Wheeler 1943: 262, nos. 33–34, fig. 85:33–34.

44. For examples from Silchester, now in the Reading Museum, McWhirr 1982: 20, pl. 12, also illustrated with discussion in Manning 1976b: 151–152, fig. 259.

45. E.g., Down 1978: 310, no. 166, fig. 10.42:166; and Down 1979: 155, no. 13, fig. 47:13; Manning 1985b: 9–11, nos. A23-A32, pls. 5–6, nos. A23–A32; Manning 1985a: 46, no. 156, fig. 20:156; and Manning 1976a: 150, fig. 255 (examples from Silchester).

46. Manning 1985b: 21, 22–24, nos. B31, B33–B37, fig. 4:4, pl. 10.B31, B33–37. See also Down 1979: 155, no. 12, fig. 47:12; and Piggott 1953: 48, no. B.40, fig. 13.B.40.

47. Manning 1985b: 39, 40–41, nos. E9–E17, fig. 9:4a-b, pl. 16:E9–E27.

48. For a thorough treatment of cutting implements, see Manning 1985b: 108–23, fig. 28, pls. 53–57. Manning's types are adopted for the Castle Copse examples.

49. Manning 1985b: 108, fig. 28:1a, and 110, no. Q1, pl. 53:Q1 (type dated first to second century A.D.).

50. Manning 1972: 176, no. 41, fig. 65:41 (from a context dated A.D. 140–150).

51. Manning 1985b: 118–19, nos. Q66–Q85, fig. 29:23–24, pl. 56:Q66–Q85.

52. Manning 1985b: 114–16, fig. 28:15, nos. Q48-Q54, pl. 55:Q48–Q54.

53. Manning 1985b: 114–15, fig. 28:14.

54. Manning 1985b: 117, fig. 29:21.

55. Webster 1975: 237, no. 198, fig. 126:198; Wedlake 1982: 228, no. 13, fig. 99:39; and Webster 1982: 107, no. 15, fig. 23:15.

56. Manning 1985b: 122, no. Q100, fig. 30:3, pl. 57:Q100; Iliffe 1932: 35–67, 65, no. 9, pl. 18:1.

57. See Manning 1985b: 160–170, pls. 76–81, for a discussion (with I. R. Scott) of spear-heads, most of which are early in date.

58. For discussion, see Manning 1985b: 88–89, nos. 01–020, pls. 37:01–39:020.

59. On lever-locks and lever-lock keys, see Manning 1985b: 94, nos. 060–062, pl. 42:060–062. Nos. 061–062 (from Great Chesterford) are especially close.

60. See Manning 1985b: 126, fig. 31, for a brief discussion and illustration of the major hinge types.

61. Examples include: Brampton: Manning 1966b: 29, no. 38 (dated late Roman); Ickling-ham: West with Plouviez 1976: 74, no. 1, fig. 37:1 (late Roman, c. 350); Ilchester: Leach 1982: 257, nos. 32–38, fig. 124:32–38 (tie bindings from coffin); and Lakenheath: Manning 1985b: 126–127, nos. R8–R9, pl. 58:R8–R9 (Late Roman).

62. Grew 1982: 181, no. 25, fig. 28:25.

63. For a discussion of bindings, see Manning 1985b: 142–43; and 1972: 188, 190.

64. Manning 1985b: 142, no. S110, pl. 69:S110.

65. Angle-bindings: Manning 1984b: 91–174, 139–52, 149, nos. 48–49, fig. 35:48–49; door-fittings: Cleere 1958: 59, fig. 4; handle-attachment loop: Piggott 1953: 32, no. C.11, fig. 8:C.11 (dated first century A.D.).

66. For a discussion, Manning 1985b: 131.

67. Cf. Manning 1985b: fig. 31:1a–b.

68. Examples in Manning 1985b: 129–31, pls. 59:R27–R33, 61:R34–R51.

69. Manning 1985b: 130, nos. R49–R50, pl. 61:R49–R50 (mid-first century).

70. For a brief discussion, including examples from Rushall Down (Wiltshire) and other sites, see Manning 1985b: 131, nos. R54–R64, pl. 61:R54–R64.

71. See Manning 1976b: 31; and 1985b, 62, especially n. 1.

72. Manning 1974: 165, no. 373, fig. 70:373; and 177, nos. 522–523, fig. 75:522–523; Manning 1985b: 129, nos. R23–R26, pl. 59:R23–R26 (from Hod Hill, dated mid-first century); and Manning 1972: 184 no. 86, fig. 68:86 (from levels dated A.D. 130–140).

73. Manning 1985b: 129, no. R21, pl. 59:R21.

74. Manning 1985b: 131–32, nos. R69–R72, pl. 62:R69–72.

75. For a similar object identified as part of a lock mechanism, see Manning 1972: 181, no. 69, fig. 67:69, from a context dated A.D. 280–315.

76. The term "nail" is here applied in a generic sense only; some ten to twelve of the more robust examples (**216–217, 222**) might well be described as spikes.

77. Manning 1985b: 134–37, fig. 32, pl. 63.

78. See comments in Manning 1985a: 58.

79. Cf. Jarvis and Maxfield 1975: 244, fig. 13:9, where a similar example is identified as a Type I nail.

80. Cf. Cunliffe 1971b: 144, nos. 8–9, fig. 66:8–9.

81. Ward 1860: 261.

Figure 112. Gold finger ring, cockerel, and steelyard weight in form of female head from 1853–54 excavations at Castle Copse. (Redrawn from Cunnington and Goddard 1934: 196–97, figs. 30–31, pl. 70.1.) (1:1)

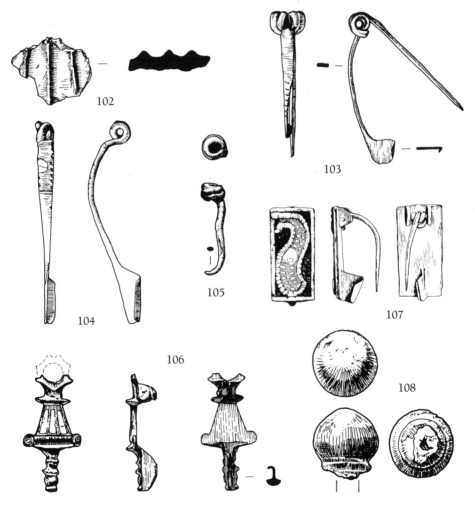

Figure 113. **102.** Statuette fragment. A1. **103–108.** Fibulae. B144, A865, A129, B141, B116, B7. (1:1)

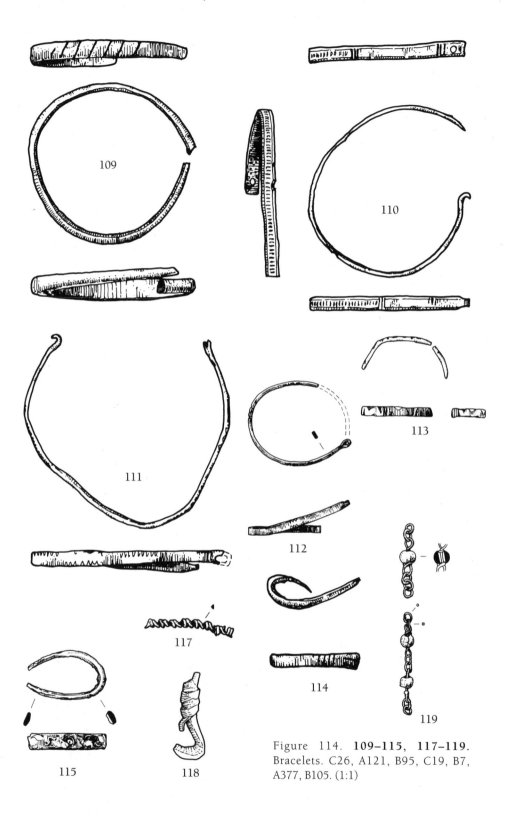

Figure 114. **109–115, 117–119**. Bracelets. C26, A121, B95, C19, B7, A377, B105. (1:1)

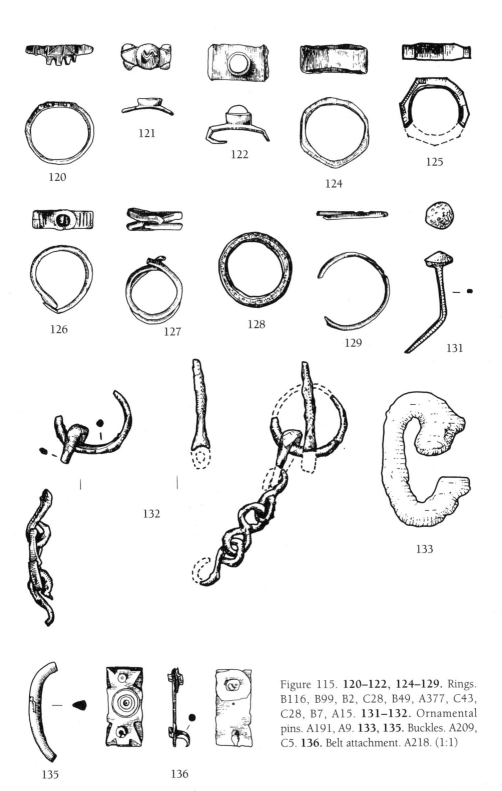

Figure 115. **120–122, 124–129.** Rings. B116, B99, B2, C28, B49, A377, C43, C28, B7, A15. **131–132.** Ornamental pins. A191, A9. **133, 135.** Buckles. A209, C5. **136.** Belt attachment. A218. (1:1)

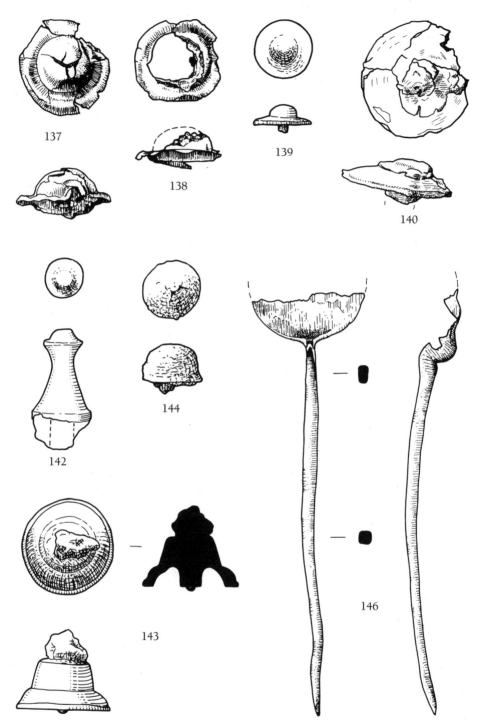

Figure 116. **137–140.** Bosses. B113, B75, B7, A310. **142–144.** Handles/finials. B7, A393, A67, C18. **146.** Spoon. C19. (1:1)

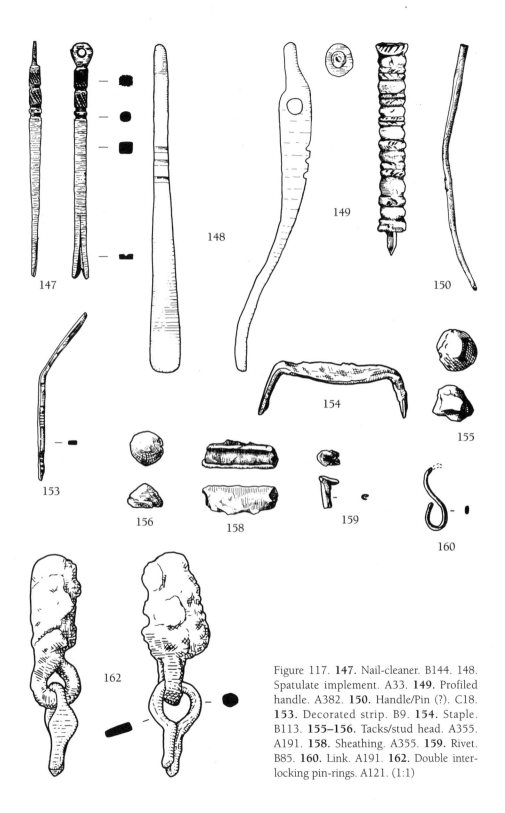

Figure 117. **147.** Nail-cleaner. B144. **148.** Spatulate implement. A33. **149.** Profiled handle. A382. **150.** Handle/Pin (?). C18. **153.** Decorated strip. B9. **154.** Staple. B113. **155–156.** Tacks/stud head. A355. A191. **158.** Sheathing. A355. **159.** Rivet. B85. **160.** Link. A191. **162.** Double interlocking pin-rings. A121. (1:1)

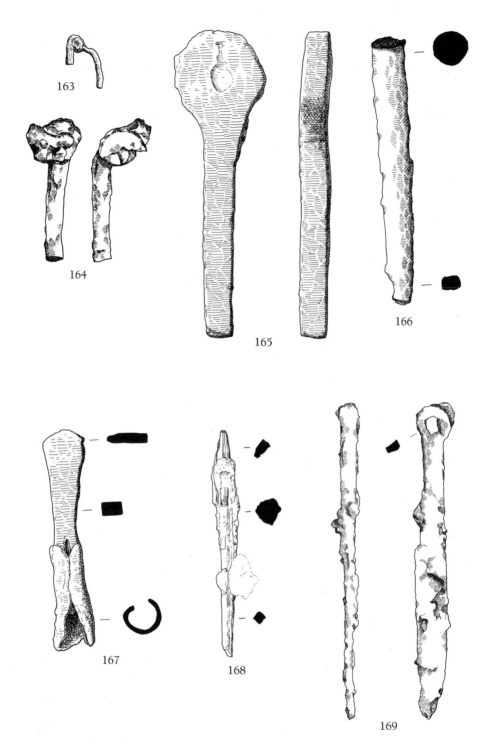

Figure 118. **163–164.** Fibulae. B144, A549. **165.** Nail-heading tool. B67. **166.** Punch. B95. **167.** Chisel. A209. **168.** Bone-handled awl. C64. **169.** Razor or knife. B144. (1:2, except 164 at 1:1)

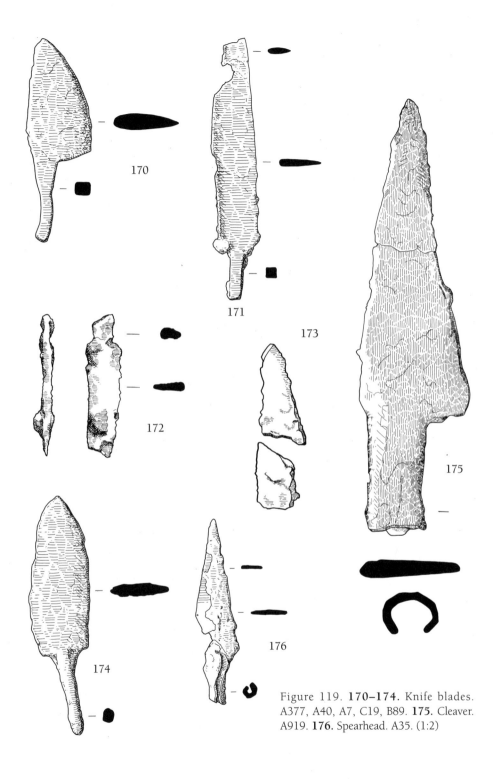

170

171

173

172

175

174

176

Figure 119. **170–174.** Knife blades. A377, A40, A7, C19, B89. **175.** Cleaver. A919. **176.** Spearhead. A35. (1:2)

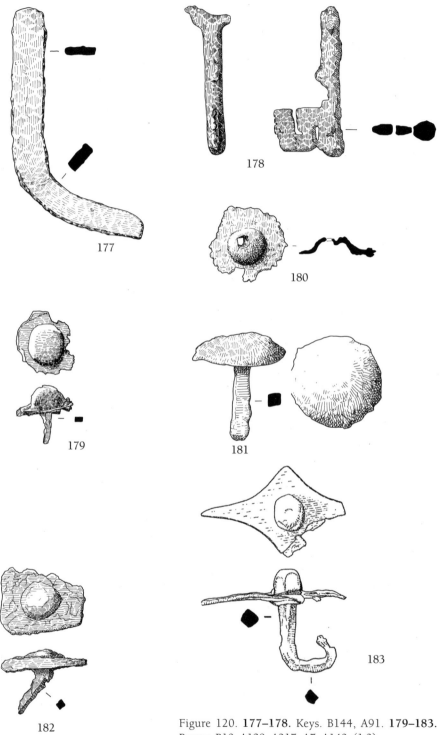

Figure 120. **177–178**. Keys. B144, A91. **179–183**. Bosses. B10, A139, A217, A7, A140. (1:2)

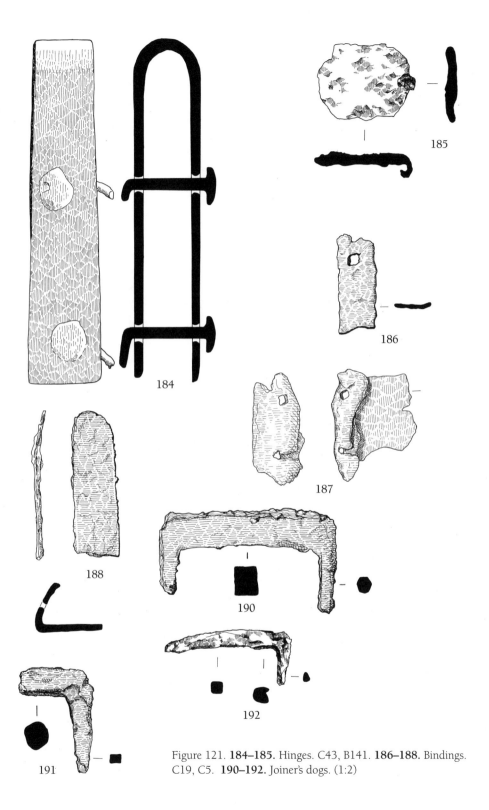

Figure 121. **184–185.** Hinges. C43, B141. **186–188.** Bindings. C19, C5. **190–192.** Joiner's dogs. (1:2)

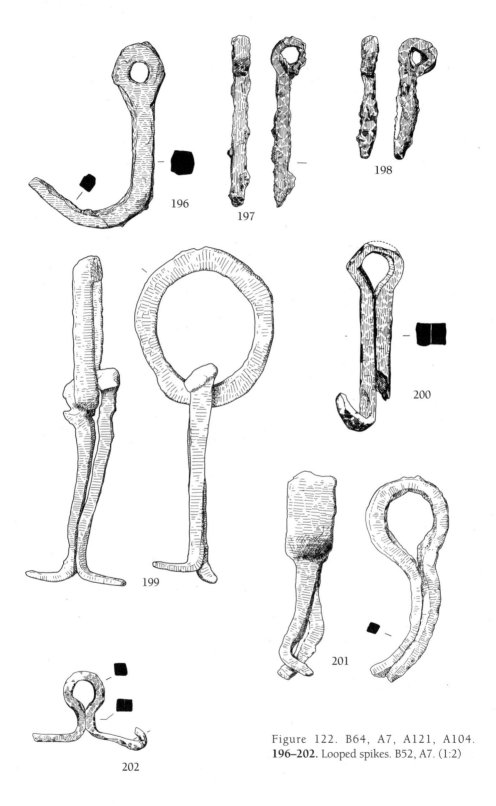

Figure 122. B64, A7, A121, A104.
196–202. Looped spikes. B52, A7. (1:2)

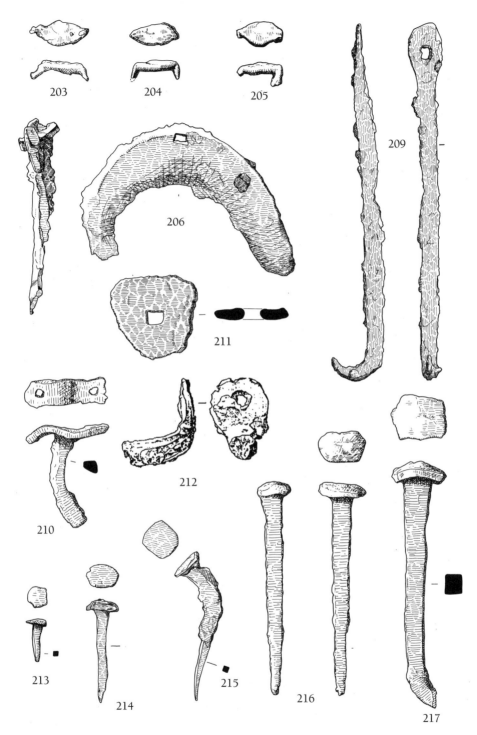

Figure 123. **203–205.** Shoe cleats. B3, C5, A91. **206.** Horseshoe. C9. **209–210.** Hooks. A39, B4, B7. **211.** Pierced triangular object. B83. **212.** Shaft with disc terminal. A101. **213–217.** Nails (Manning Type I). A15, C34, A522, A121. (1:2)

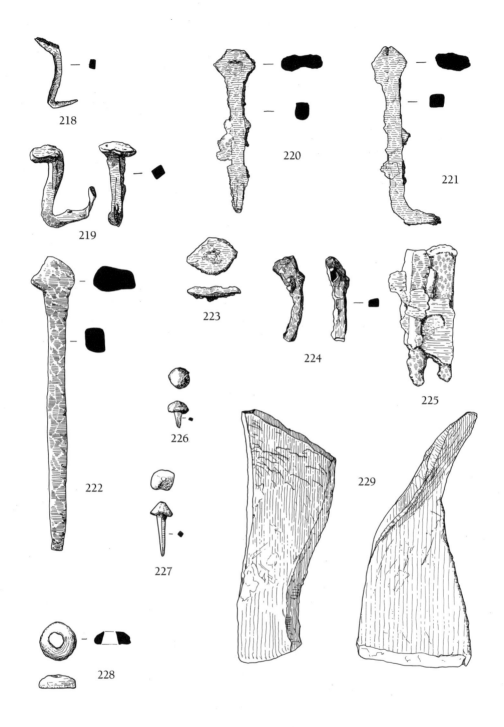

Figure 124. **218–219.** Nails (Manning Type I). A91, A41. **220–222.** Nails (Manning Type II). A19, A1, A110. **223–225.** Variant nails. B93, A19. **226–227.** Hobnails/tacks. B15, B12. Lead: **228.** Perforated disc. A445. **229.** Strip. C43. (1:2)

4.9 ANALYSIS OF THE IRON ASSEMBLAGE

ROBERT M. EHRENREICH

The iron assemblage was metallurgically analyzed to determine the level of sophistication attained by the blacksmithing community supplying the site and the reliance of the inhabitants of the villa on local iron sources.[1] Fifty iron artifacts, ten grams of slag, and three grams of magnetic particulates were analyzed.[2]

Analysis

A small wedge was removed from each of 50 of the 350 iron artifacts recovered. Each sample was then embedded in Alplex, a clear plastic resin, and polished to a mirror finish for metallurgical examination with an optical microscope, Vickers hardness tester, and electron microprobe. Of the fifty artifacts sampled, forty-seven yielded sufficient metal to be analyzed; the remaining three were too corroded (see Appendix 5).

OPTICAL METALLOGRAPHY

The grain structures of the Castle Copse samples were examined under an optical microscope to determine whether advanced blacksmithing techniques (i.e., annealing, carburization, quenching, and tempering) were practiced. Predominantly, the results indicated that the artifacts were simply and rapidly produced. Seven of the forty-seven samples analyzed had elongated grain structures caused by cold-working, eight had non-equiaxed grains produced by forging at temperatures below the recrystallization point of the iron, and six had spheroidized cementite indicative of excessive heating during smithing. These grain structures could have been rectified during the Roman period by using finishing techniques such as annealing.[3] The fact that the grain structures of nearly half of the objects sampled were not corrected, however, would suggest that these artifacts were either manufactured by unknowledgeable blacksmiths or unworthy of lengthy finishing techniques.

The data obtained from the optical metallographic examination of the Castle Copse assemblage implies that the advanced ironworking techniques of carburization and quenching were not understood until late in the occupation of the site.[4] Carburization produces the harder alloy of steel, and quenching greatly increases the hardness of steel, but also drastically reduces its toughness.

Seventy-five percent of the artifacts sampled had low carbon content. Thirty-five of the forty-seven objects etched had carbon concentrations of below 0.4%. Eight samples had carbon contents of between 0.4% and 0.6%. Four samples had carbon concentrations exceeding 0.6%. Of the four samples with high-carbon concentrations, however, just one appears to have been deliberately and expertly heat-treated. The undated Roman blade (**171**) from the overburden in Sector A (A40:XV) was properly carburized and quenched to enhance its function. The increased hardness of the blade resulting from quenching would have allowed it to have a finer, more wear-resistant cutting-edge. The existence of only one advanced artifact among those sampled implies that carburization and quenching were rarely practiced by the blacksmiths supplying the villa, at least in the late period of habitation, from which most sampled objects derived.

TRACE ELEMENT ANALYSES AND HARDNESS TESTING

The samples were analyzed with an electron microprobe to determine the quantities of phosphorus, sulfer, and cobalt contained. Like carbon, small concentrations of phosphorus increase the hardness of iron. For example, the average hardness of the Castle Copse low-phosphorus iron objects is 148.0 HV, while the average hardness of the Castle Copse high-phosphorus (i.e., exceeding 0.080%) ironwork is 176.8 HV. Phosphoric iron is produced when naturally phosphorus-rich iron ore is smelted. Unlike carbon, however, high phosphorus content restricts the diffusion of carbon in iron and causes the metal to be brittle at sub-zero degree C. temperatures. However, a society incapable of producing steel may have sacrificed low-temperature reliability for the advantages of a harder alloy. Phosphoric iron does appear to have been preferentially selected during the late Iron Age for the production of tools and weapons because of its enhanced hardness.[5]

Although the phosphoric ironwork from the villa at Castle Copse is harder than the low-phosphorus iron artifacts, phosphoric iron does not seem to have been used with any consistency. Thirty-one of the forty-seven samples suitable for microprobe analysis had phosphorus concentrations of below 0.080%, and only sixteen had high phosphorus contents. Phosphoric iron apparently was also not used to enhance the properties of specific products at the villa. Cleats and horseshoes were the only objects that tended to be more commonly produced from phosphoric iron, but these are inconsequential artifacts that would not have benefited from being made from high-phosphorus iron.

The sulfer concentration of the ironwork was determined, because sulfur content exceeding 0.035% causes iron to be brittle and unusable. The sulfer concentrations of the Castle Copse ironwork were generally low: only two pieces of scrap out of the forty-seven samples analyzed with the electron microprobe had high sulfur concentrations. The remainder of the assemblage had sulfur contents of well below 0.035%. This absence of high-sulfur, finished iron artifacts at the villa indicates that high-sulfur iron could be identified and its use eliminated.

Iron with cobalt concentrations exceeding 0.1% was available during the Roman period only from the Devon-Cornwall region.[6] No high-cobalt artifacts were identified at Castle Copse, however. The highest cobalt content registered was 0.062% (nail from B144: XI), which is well below the 0.1% concentration used to distinguish high- from low-cobalt iron. The absence of high-cobalt iron at the villa indicates that the site was not relying on the Devon-Cornwall iron manufacturers, but on the closer iron producers of the low-impurity sources of the Weald and the Forest of Dean, and the phosphoric sources of the Jurassic Ridge region.

Ironworking By-Products

Two ironworking by-products were discovered at the villa at Castle Copse: approximately four kilograms of slag and three grams of coarse magnetic dust. The method by which these by-products were produced can yield information regarding the range of metalworking processes executed on-site.[7]

SLAG

Although slag is usually associated only with smelting, smithing can produce small amounts of slag in two manners. First, the slag inclusions commonly trapped within iron from initial smelting can melt while the iron is being heated in preparation for forging. This molten slag will collect along the bottom of hearths and must be periodically cleaned out. Second, a slaggy material can also be formed when small pieces of iron fall into the forge and burn. Thus, the discovery of slag on a site does not necessarily indicate that iron was smelted there. Unfortunately, it is difficult to distinguish smelting slags from smithing slags, since both have basically the same composition.

The source of the slag discovered on a site can be inferred from the quantity recovered. Approximately 10.5 kg of slag is formed when 1.1 kg of iron is smelted.[8] Since slag is a durable substance and an undesirable commodity, the quantity produced on a site usually does not decrease with time.[9] The quantity of slag recovered from the late or possibly post-Roman phase in the west wing of the villa (B:VII) is far less than the amount expected from the smelting of iron. Large quantities of slag could have been removed from the site and placed in middens, but the lack of corroborative evidence for smelting at the villa (e.g., ore, charcoal, roasting pits, or furnace structures) and the existence of forging tools (i.e., nail-header **165**, smith's punch **166**) suggest that the metalworking residues found were blacksmithing waste.

MAGNETIC PARTICULATES

The magnetic particulates discovered were analyzed with an x-ray diffractometer. The results revealed that the particles consisted of magnetite, wüstite, calcite, quartz, and hematite. This composition would indicate that the substance is hammer scale, a ubiquitous by-product of forging, produced by one of three methods. First, forging iron causes small segments of its exterior to fragment. Second, hammering heated iron also expels trapped slag from the metal.[10] Third, welding ejects small globules of molten, flux-enriched oxide;[11] the calcite and quartz discovered with the magnetic particles could be either flux from welding or contaminates from excavation.

BLACKSMITHING DURING THE ROMAN PERIOD

The metallurgical examination of the Castle Copse assemblage implies that the inhabitants of the site were generally not able to, or neglected to, obtain carburized or quenched ironwork. No artifacts sampled, apart from the undated Roman knife blade (**171**) from the modern phase A:XV, were carburized, quenched, or even enhanced by the preferential selection of naturally harder phosphoric iron alloys.

There are several potential reasons for the scarcity of advanced carburized and quenched ironwork on the site. The results of the metallurgical examination could have been biased by the rudimentary types of artifacts predominantly sampled and the preponderance of objects sampled from the later period of occupation at the site. Few tools were recovered from Castle Copse, and fewer still were sufficiently robust to be sampled. The blacksmiths supplying the villa may have disregarded heat-treating the nails, cleats, door-hinges, and other basic artifacts analyzed from the site, because these artifacts were too common to warrant time-consuming finishing techniques, and the increased hardness caused by heat treatments would have adversely affected their reliability. Thus, more carburized and quenched artifacts may have been discovered from earlier phases of inhabitation at Castle Copse if more objects worthy of time-consuming heat treatments could have been analyzed. The blacksmithing remains recovered from Castle Copse come from phases associated with late or possibly even post-Roman occupation (e.g., nail-header **165**). This activity may have been principally for the care of animals.[12] and for the manufacture of small hardware—nails, hinges, etc.—rather than for satisfying all the material requirements of the site.

IRON PRODUCTION CENTERS

The limited quantity of slag discovered, the absence of corroborative smelting remains (e.g., furnace linings, ore supplies, roasting pits), the presence of forging by-products (i.e., hammer scale), and the discovery of a nail-header and smith's punch (**165–166**) at the villa of Castle Copse suggests that blacksmithing was the only metalworking process performed on the site. This is not unexpected, because smelting was not usually performed on smaller sites in Britain. Since the Middle Iron Age, only one settlement site (i.e., Gussage All-Saints) and a few villas (e.g., Brislington, Lansdown, and Gatcombe) have shown evidence of smelting. The villas were all associated with the iron production centers of the southwest;[13] and the inhabitants of the Middle-Late Iron Age settlement of Gussage All-Saints were manufacturing chariot hardware for trade.[14] Thus, the smaller sites producing their own iron were probably doing so to support metal-based exchange systems and not to satisfy the normal materials requirements of the sites.

Furthermore, it would have been superfluous for the inhabitants of Castle Copse villa to manufacture their own iron, since the site was situated so near the large iron production centers of southern Britain. The Wealden ore sources were annexed and enlarged by the Romans in the first century A.D., and the indigenous iron production sites in Northamptonshire and the Forest of Dean were expanded during the second century A.D.[15] The cobalt-rich iron ore sources in the Devon-Cornwall region were not enlarged by the Romans, probably because the supply of iron from the Weald, the Forest of Dean, and Northamptonshire was sufficient to support the requirements of southern Britain. This chronology for the expansion of the British iron production centers during the Roman period is discernable in the results of the trace element analysis of the Castle Copse iron assemblage. Two-thirds of the iron from Castle Copse had low phosphorus concentrations and low cobalt contents, showing that the site obtained metal from the low-impurity iron producers of the Weald and the Forest of Dean. The sixteen high-phosphorus iron artifacts discovered within the Castle Copse iron assemblage confirm that iron from Northamptonshire was also being imported. The fact that the inhabitants of the villa were able to import iron from three large iron production centers and disregard the high-cobalt metal produced in the Devon-Cornwall region implies that they were able to obtain all of the iron required from trade and would not have needed to smelt their own metal.

NOTES

1. For summaries of Roman iron-making and smithing techniques, see Cleere 1976 and Manning 1976a: 127–53. On ironworking in the Iron Age, Ehrenreich 1985 and 1986.

2. By the writer at the Conservation Analytical Laboratory, Smithsonian Institution, Washington D.C. The author expresses his appreciation to L. van Zelst and J. Olin of the C.A.L.; R. Clarke, Jr. and E. Jarosewich of the Museum of Natural History, Smithsonian Institution; C. McGill of the British Council: and K. M. Zwilsky of the National Materials Advisory Board, National Research Council.

3. I.e., heating iron above 750°C. and allowing it to cool slowly.

4. Carburization is the process of adding carbon to iron by heating the metal to a temperature in excess of 750°C. in a reducing atmosphere. Quenching is the technique of rapidly cooling steel with a carbon content exceeding 0.3% from above 750°C. to room temperature by plunging it in a liquid medium (e.g., water).

5. Ehrenreich 1985: 82.

6. Ehrenreich 1985: 97.

7. For ironworking by-products from another Roman site, see Greenough 1987: 25–27.

8. Salter and Ehrenreich 1984: fig. 10:1.

9. Archaeological slag has occasionally been collected: the Romans used slag for metalling roads, and eighteenth-century metalworkers resmelted slag in blast furnaces. In both cases, however, it was the large slag piles associated with the major Iron Age and Roman production centers that were destroyed, not the small quantities from settlement sites and villas. Thus, while some slag may have been removed, the quantity of slag discovered at Castle Copse should probably be considered representative.

10. J.R.L. Allen 1986: 97.

11. Welding occurs when two clean iron surfaces come into contact: flux is placed along the surfaces of the heated iron to be welded to reduce the melting point of the oxides. When the bars are hammered together, the flux and molten oxides are expelled, permitting the two, clean, iron surfaces to come into contact and weld. Two common fluxes are fine sand and borax.

12. According to Branigan (1977a: 81), ironworking remains discovered on villas in Britain have been associated with horse stables.

13. Branigan 1977a: 84.

14. Spratling 1979: 144.

15. Cleere 1981: 187.

4.10 TRIANGULAR IMPRESSED CLAY FRAGMENT (LOST)

RUTH MEGAW AND VINCENT MEGAW

L. intact side=c. 0.003 or 0.0035 maximum; L. side of enclosed triangle=0.0025: measurements after published photographs.[1] Corner missing; abraded. (Fig. 125)

This piece was first referred to by Ward (1860),[2] as coming from the site of a Roman villa at Great Bedwyn. In 1902 it was exhibited at the Society of Antiquaries as being from this same site, together with other material such as a small finger-ring and the bronze figure of a cock.[3] In 1911 it appeared in the Devizes Museum catalogue as "from Great Bedwyn," and there is a reference to "a Romano-British settlement in and about Bedwyn Brail Wood within a short distance of the site of the villa."[4]

Description

The original photograph republished here (Fig. 125) shows the actual object on the left and an impression taken from it on the right. The fragment is obviously a piece of fired clay of near-triangular shape with two rounded corners and with the third corner broken off; Goddard describes it as brownish earthenware.[5] On the clay is an incised triangle with a tripartite design revolving around a central incised small circle. Each arm of this design appears to be a broken-backed S-scroll, with three dots added at the end of each element; the design is a not-quite-perfect broken-backed triskel.

Function

The object has been described as a "small triangular stamp of earthenware for producing a pattern in relief,"[6] or as a die block.[7] It seems unlikely that it could have been used directly as a die block because of the fragile nature of clay if used to impress harder metal or leather. It seems more probable that this was a mold for the creation of a die-stamp for so-called casket-ornament, or even a trial piece on which a metal stamp had been tried out. It is generally assumed that metal stamps were used to create casket-ornament and the associated brooches in the period following and immediately before the Roman Conquest.[8] The metal die for a strip from Wroxeter[9] and the tab-shaped die, perhaps for a disc-brooch cover from the Santon hoard, with its vaguely animalistic triskel (Fig. 126),[10] are examples. Stamps, possibly of metal, apparently were occasionally used for pottery in Britain in the post-Roman-Conquest, but pre-Flavian, period.[11] The possibility of using metal stamps for the production of designs on the thin copper (more probably bronze) sheet used for disc-brooch covers has recently been challenged by Kilbride-Jones,[12] who asserts that wooden, rather than metal, molds were used, because wood has more "spring" than metal.

Since the object itself is now lost, it is impossible to ascertain whether it was made from the type of clay generally used for Iron Age molds, or whether any remaining traces of metal remained in it from casting or stamping.[13] If indeed the piece was a mold, it is not one for lost-wax casting, which necessitates the breaking open of the mold to extract the cast metal object. Rather, it is an open flan mold, or, just possibly, part of a two-part mold.

The triangular form of the fragment is, so far, unique among known pieces of die-stamped casket ornament and would make it difficult to create a continuous design using the pottery piece or metal cast from it as a die, except by the time-consuming method of constantly reversing its orientation. Nor is it of the right shape to produce a disc-brooch cover. A stamped bronze triangular object from the Roman temple and cult site of Woodeaton, Oxfordshire—which was in use from perhaps pre-Roman days until the late Roman period[14]—is, however, known. This bears a design of an ithyphallic figure with a border of dots following the edges of the triangle, and is very different from the Castle Copse mold.[15]

Style

The closest parallels are certainly to examples of casket-ornament. "Casket-ornament" was first defined by Cyril Fox as "repetitive ornament in relief, curvilinear on narrow strips or squares of thin bronze . . . widespread in Belgic and Celtic Britain in the last century before independence."[16]

Megaw and Merrifield note that most of the then known forty or so pieces of casket-ornament came "from sites in the southern half of England with evidence of occupation dating to or continuing into the period of Roman occupation," and comment on the combination of die-stamping with continued use of repoussé work.[17] MacGregor sees a close relationship between the designs of casket-ornament proper and the bow and fantail and disc brooches.[18] Findspots are mainly southern and generally from settlements, though there are also four hoards and seven or eight Belgic burials. MacGregor also sees the Marlborough and Aylesford buckets as ancestral to casket-ornament in their repoussé (not die-stamped) decorative bronze strips attached to wooden objects. Certainly, the use of wooden formers to shape the bodies of the Basse-Yutz and Dürrnberg flagons, if not the repoussé designs on such material, is probable from as early as the La Tène A period in the fifth century B.C.[19]

The triskel is one of the motifs characteristically used in the casket-ornament style and especially on disc-brooches.[20] More specifically, from Castle Copse, we have an example of a broken-backed triskel, where each arm bends back upon itself at a sharp angle.[21] While Kilbride-Jones sees the origins of broken-backed scrolls in such Irish pieces as the Lough Crew, Co. Meath bone flakes,[22] he sees the broken-backed triskels as originating in Britain, possibly, specifically Wales. He points particularly to the non-engraved shield mount from Tal-y-llyn, Gwynedd, Wales,[23] to a bronze mount from

Alnwick Castle, and to the "eared" lyre-loop on the carved ash wood (?) mold or stamp from Lochlee Crannog, Tarbolton, Stratchclyde (Fig. 127) as examples. It is nonetheless worth pointing out that the scroll and the triskel, both broken-backed, appear side-by-side on the same piece from Lochlee Crannog, which casts doubt on the theory of entirely separate origins for these motifs. Raftery sees the broken-backed curve as "otherwise" than at Lough Crew "absent in Ireland but . . . well represented in Scotland. . . . Though the motif was only partly understood by the Irish craftsman, it is likely that renderings such as that on a beaded torc from Lochar Moss in Scotland, or that on a scabbard from Mortonhall in the same country, could have provided the inspiration for the Irish veneration of the design."[24]

The ring-and-dot centered triskel standing in relief on the Lochlee wood block is probably even later—from the second century A.D.—and is very similar to the triskel on the Castle Copse clay object;[25] the full potential of the broken-backed triskel was not reached until the second half of the first century A.D.[26] Even closer in outline is the lost shield mount from Moel Hiraddug, Clwyd, Wales (Fig. 128), where the broken-backed triskel revolves around a central double ring.[27] It is different in that the Moel Hiraddug triskel is contained in a circle, itself placed within a square border; it is "keeled," and the enclosing circle is composed of trumpet shapes, which are lacking on the Castle Copse example, which is, of course, smaller and appears to be less carefully executed. It is worth noting that Fox thought that Moel Hiraddug was perhaps created by copying a piece of carved Celtic woodwork or, more likely, "wrought . . . on an iron die."[28]

The apparent disintegration of the triskel on the Castle Copse fragment may be interpreted in one of two ways. It may be due to the characteristically La Tène tendency to dissect designs into their component parts and reassemble them;[29] or it may be due to the design being imperfectly understood by its creator, an interpretation which is perhaps strengthened by the absence of trumpet shapes on this particular piece.

Date

The Castle Copse object was reportedly found in a Roman villa, which in itself suggests a post-conquest date. Such a date is borne out by the stylistic comparisons for the piece. Although Savory has persistently argued for an early date of about 200 B.C. for material found in Wales (especially Tal-y-llyn)[30] and for a Welsh place of manufacture for pieces from the important Iron Age hoards found there, including those from Moel Hiraddug, his arguments have not met with wide acceptance, largely because of metallurgical problems involved.[31] Claimed early material from Tal-y-llyn is brass, containing a high proportion of zinc together with the tin and copper which constitutes the usual bronze of the pre-Roman Iron Age. Such brass did not apparently appear in Britain until after the Roman conquest.[32] The Moel Hiraddug plaque was recorded, before its loss, as tinned, once more a technique not elsewhere found in pre-Roman Britain. The similarity of the Castle Copse object to the design of the Moel Hiraddug plaque cannot, therefore, be used to argue for an early date, and indeed suggests a date after the Roman Conquest and, thus, the latter part of the first to the second century A.D. So, too, does the occurrence of the broken-backed arms of the triskel, a style which is generally late, mostly from the later part of the first century A.D. into the following century.

NOTES

1. Goddard (1908: 406) gives its dimensions as 1-3/8 inches on the side and 3/8 of an inch thick.
2. Ward 1860: especially 261.
3. Goddard 1902; see also Goddard 1908.
4. Cunnington and Goddard 1911: 51–52, no. 401, pl. 22:8. The Devizes Museum catalogue of 1934, however (Cunnington and Goddard 1934: 302, fig. 34), while preserving the previous catalogue number, firmly puts it at North Wraxall, which is some distance removed from Great Bedwyn, but which also has a Roman villa and contains a Castle Combe; confusion may have arisen since North Wraxall followed directly after Great Bedwyn in the 1911 Devizes catalogue (Cunnington and Goddard 1911: 53–55). The North Wraxall attribution was followed by M. MacGregor (1976: 157), where she refers to it as a clay die-block for casket ornament, like the metal one from Wroxeter. Grinsell (1957: 73) locates the object in Brail Wood, but gives a map reference that clearly puts Brail Wood in Great Bedwyn. It is therefore to be presumed that an error was made in the 1934 Devizes catalogue followed by MacGregor, and that the object comes, in fact, from Brail Wood at Great Bedwyn. At some time since its accession in the Devizes Museum, the object has apparently been lost.
5. Goddard 1908: 406.
6. Cunnington and Goddard 1911: 52.
7. M. MacGregor 1976: 157.
8. Fox 1958: 105; Megaw 1970: 172; Megaw and Merrifield 1970: 156–58; Spratling 1972: 269; M. MacGregor 1976: 125, 156; and Hattatt and Webster 1985.
9. Atkinson 1942: 216–18, pl. 52:12; Fox 1958: 105; Megaw 1970: 172; Megaw and Merrifield 1970: pl. 16c; and M. MacGregor 1976: 157.
10. R.A. Smith 1908–09: 149–50, fig. 3; Megaw 1970: 172; and Megaw and Merrifield 1970: 158, here photographed for the first time.
11. Rodwell 1988: 107, 109–10.
12. Kilbride-Jones 1987.
13. As well as our own observations, we have sought the opinions of I. M. Stead and V. Rigby of the Department of Prehistoric and Romano-British Antiquities at the British Museum, and P. Northover of the Department of Metallurgy and Science of Materials, Oxford University.
14. Kirk 1949; Goodchild and Kirk 1954.
15. M. J. Green 1976: 178–79, pl. 6f; 1983: 13, pl. 6; and 1986: 212. The shape and material also call to mind terracotta antefixes, which were often elaborate and decorated; these were mostly used by the legions, but are also found in lesser numbers on civilian sites. They are, however, usually much too large for comparison with the Castle Copse fragment, with sides of about 0.015 m. See Webster 1985: 136, n. 1; and Toynbee 1964: 428–31, pls. 98–99.
16. Fox 1958: 105; see also Fox 1946: 21–23, 89, fig. 11 (map). He adds that the die-stamped pieces generally have "little merit," though he devotes some space to the "baroque" Elmsworth plaque, which combines stamped and repoussé work.
17. Megaw and Merrifield 1970: 156. See also Spratling 1972: 239–40, nos. 431–457; and Megaw and Megaw 1989: 231–35.
18. M. MacGregor 1976: 156–59, 173–76, map 22.
19. Megaw and Megaw 1991, especially chap. 5.
20. Megaw and Merrifield 1970: 157–58, fig. 1.
21. Such designs are identified and illustrated by Leeds (1933: 56–60, figs. 22–23).
22. Kilbride-Jones 1980: 87–91. See also Megaw 1970: no. 256; Raftery 1983: no. 668 and 1984, 251–63, especially fig. 129:2; and Megaw and Megaw 1989: 206 ff.
23. Megaw 1970: no. 267; Savory 1976a: fig. 12.
24. Raftery 1984: 261.
25. Munro 1882: 133–35, figs. 149–50; and M. MacGregor 1976: no. 337.
26. As is pointed out by M. MacGregor (1976: 24).

27. Fox 1958: pl. 45b; Megaw 1970: no. 268; Savory 1976a: pl. 2b; Megaw and Megaw 1986: pl. 41; and id. 1989: 232–33.

28. Fox 1958: 117.

29. As can be seen in the adaptation of classical and Hellenistic prototypes for Celtic coinage.

30. Savory 1964; 1966; 1971: 69–75; 1973; 1976a; 1976b.

31. Spratling 1966; and 1972: 314–17; Savory 1976a: 48–50; and 1976b: 199; Frey with Megaw 1976: 61; M.L. Jones 1984: 229; Megaw and Megaw 1986: 45–46; Northover 1988; and Megaw and Megaw 1989: 200.

32. Although there is a high natural occurrence of zinc in some Welsh copper deposits, it apparently takes special and sophisticated techniques to retain the zinc during smelting.

Figure 125. Clay mold fragment (lost) from Castle Copse villa. (Photo courtesy of the Devizes Museum; drawing after Cunnington and Goddard 1934: 202, fig. 34.) (1:1)

Figure 126. Tab-shaped bronze die from hoard found at Santon, Norfolk, or Santon Downham, Suffolk, and impression made from it. L.=0.590 m. (Cambridge University Museum of Archaeology and Anthropology.)

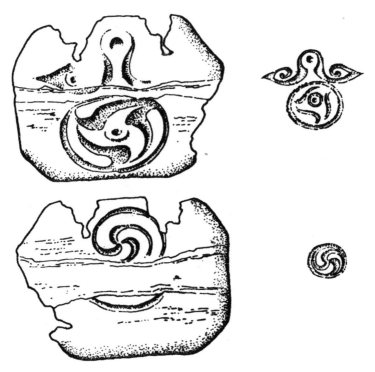

Figure 127. Carved ash wood block. Lochlee Crannog, Tarbolton, Strathclyde, Scotland. c. 0.128 x 0.128 m. Cast in Royal Museums of Scotland, Edinburgh. (Redrawn after MacGregor 1976: fig. 337.)

Figure 128. Tin-plated bronze (?) shield mount (lost). L. side=0.153 m. From Moel Hiraddug, Clwyd, Wales. Formerly Powys Museum, Welshpool. (Drawing: National Museum of Wales, Cardiff.)

4.11 POTTERY

ANTHONY R. WILMOTT

Introduction

The pottery from the villa at Castle Copse has been studied with a number of aims in mind.[1] These are primarily internal to the study of the site: dating the phases of activity represented in the areas excavated and suggesting functional divisions among parts of the villa at large. An analysis of the sources of pottery and their relative importance at various times during the Roman period has proved less satisfactory, due to the lengthy break in domestic occupation represented within the area excavated and also the general paucity of pottery recovered.[2]

The ceramic assemblage from Castle Copse was, on the whole, small and of very poor quality, contrasting strongly with the quality of the structural and stratigraphic evidence. Given the nature of the excavation and the strategies adopted in the four sectors, this could have been expected, and it is useful briefly to review these strategies and their effect on the collection of pottery.

Sectors A and D were sited to coincide with the areas disturbed by Lukis and Pole, respectively (see chapter 4.3). Any pottery derived from the excavation trenches of these operations would clearly be of little use for analytical work, because it must be assumed that the material had already been sorted through, and pottery deemed worthwhile in antiquarian terms removed from site.

As excavation continued in Sector A, it became clear that Lukis's trench had cut into earlier flint robbing trenches, as well as the drainage works associated with a nearby cottage (now demolished). Pottery from these deposits also has a very limited usefulness. Sector A is, however, the only substantial area to have been totally excavated, and consequently the only area from which a complete sequence of pottery from the earliest to the latest periods could have been recovered.

In Sector B, the aim of excavation was to examine the building at its floruit, and to dissect carefully the structures and deposits of the periods of decline. This meant that the early development and construction phases of the building were not investigated. The sparse pottery groups from within the villa west wing reflect the luxury and high quality of the buildings, which are of such a nature that they would have been kept clean at all times. Pottery does not enter the building until late in its life, and much of this appears to have been residual at the time of its deposition.

Sector C, which is situated in the south wing of the villa, provided some of the best assemblages from the site. This was the case despite the fact that only a small portion of the sector was totally excavated.

Sector D, the area of E. R. Pole's excavation, was opened down to the top of the extant architecture. Pottery was, therefore, previously sorted material from topsoil only and is not included in this report.

Methodology

The pottery has been studied within its stratigraphical groups.[3] Though all of the pottery has been examined in the preparation of the report, not all is published. This is due to the large proportion of the material recovered from antiquarian trenches and late robbing deposits. The unpublished groups are listed in Appendix 6.

Except for the groups recovered from the early ditches in Sectors A and C, which are sufficiently similar and important to demand separate treatment, the material is published by sector, beginning with Sector A.

The production of a vessel form type series has not been attempted. It was believed more useful to publish illustrations of all forms in the significant groups only, though this effectively means that every vessel form represented on the site has a sample illustration. The fabrics have been classified, however, as there are relatively few, and they present a substantial overlap between groups. The production of a set of fabric descriptions at the head of the report obviates the need for tedious repetition in the catalogue. Classification of fabrics is based on macroscopic observation only.

Quantification has been based on the assessment of the minimum number of vessels represented by any given group. The weight of pottery has not been considered, as much of the material is from the heavy Savernake wares, a fact which would distort any comparison of quantities. This method of quantification has other advantages in that it yields useful information on the character of deposits. The closer the number of sherds to the minimum number of vessels, the more likely a group is to have been disturbed. Where the ratio is even, it can be deduced that the material has moved a long distance from its primary breakage sites. Conversely, the presence of many sherds from a single vessel would suggest that the material is more nearly in situ. Quantification is expressed in terms of tables (Tables 1–13), and a table is presented for each relevant phase.

The incidence of joining sherds between scattered deposits has been examined in an attempt to describe the patterns of movement of material both spatially and stratigraphically. This exercise has proven almost completely fruitless, which further attests to the disturbed nature of the pottery deposits.

Fabrics

Fabrics 1–35 are listed in order of their appearance within the stratigraphical sequence in Sector A. Fabrics 36–37 do not occur in Sector A, and are listed as they appear in Sectors B and C. No division is made between fine and coarse wares, as the former are very rare on the site. In the tables, the expression "Misc. Sandy Grey Wares" is used for those sherds that fit into no clear fabric category.

1. *Oare Fabric 1*. Described by Swan.[4] Hard, fine blue-grey to grey-buff paste tempered with crushed ironstone, flint, and grog. Occasionally there is a sandy feel. The tempering produces a distinctive speckled appearance. Most vessels are wheel-thrown.

2. *Oare Fabric 2.* Described by Swan.[5] Dark, coarse and gritty, normally black or dark brown in section and black on the surfaces. Sometimes grog and hematite are found in the inclusions, but the predominant tempering is flint. Vessels in this fabric are usually handmade.

3. *Silchester Flint-tempered Ware.* This distinctive ware is recognized as an early fabric at Silchester. The dense, but irregular, crushed flint tempering is unlike any other Castle Copse fabric, with the possible exception of Fabric 13.[6]

4. *Local Butt Beaker.* Used for the manufacture of butt beakers, a buff, sandy micaceous fabric, fine-grained but crumbly in fracture.

5. *Terra Rubra (TR3).* The Terra Rubra fabrics, which are very rare at Castle Copse, occurring only in Sector C, Phase I, have been classified by Rigby in her analysis of Gallo-Belgic material from Skeleton Green, Herts.[7] Fabric 5 is equivalent to her TR3 classification "very fine grained paste, smooth in fracture, highly polished self colored paste."

6. *Terra Rubra (TR2).* Orange paste, self-colored red surfaces, equivalent to Rigby TR2 classification.[8]

7. *Terra Nigra (TN1).* White paste with dark blue-grey slip, equivalent to Rigby TN1 classification.[9]

8. *Gloucester-type Sandy Ware.* Hard fabric tempered with abundant, well-sorted quartz-sand, giving a "sandpaper" feel. Appears in oxidized and reduced versions. The fabric is thought to derive from the Gloucester area, and has been found in large quantities in the early military site at Kingsholm.[10]

9. *Highgate C. Ware.* Well-finished, sometimes burnished fine, hard grey sandy ware. Temper is very fine and well-sorted sand.[11]

10. *Savernake Grog-tempered Ware.* Grog-tempered Savernake Wares are here defined as very coarse sherds, mostly from large storage jars. These are a subset of Fabric 12, below.[12] The fabrics are often patchily fired, grey and orange in color, with lumpy surfaces, due to the large inclusions of ill-sorted grog and flint. Some of the vessels reported upon below may be from the production center at Purton.[13]

11. *Samian Wares* (i.e., *terra sigillata,* red slip or red gloss ware). Glossy red pottery, the ubiquitous imported fineware of Roman Britain; for this, see almost any Romano-British pottery report. Surprisingly rare at Castle Copse.

12. *Savernake-type Grey Wares.* Standard Savernake fabric, similar to, and thought to descend from the Oare Wares (Fabrics 1 and 2 above).[14] Hard, mostly light-mid grey in color, containing particles of dark ironstone, flint, and grog. The coarseness, proportions, and abundance of these inclusions vary enormously between vessels, and Fabric 10, above, is a subset of this fabric. The finer fabrics are like those from Whitehill Farm (Fabric 23, below); it is possible that products of that industry have been identified under this head.[15]

13. *Hard Sandy Flint-tempered Ware.* Hard sandy fabric with frequent large, ill-sorted inclusions of dense angular dark or white flint. Surfaces are orange-red with a blackish core.

14. *Black Burnished Ware 1.* Well-known dense black fabric tempered with medium-coarse quartz sand, described by Farrar and Williams.[16]

15. *White-slipped Redware.* Fine sandy ware with sparse chalk grits: cream slip is applied to red surfaces. A Gloucester product found in first- and second-century deposits at Cirencester.[17]

16. *New Forest White Ware.* Hard, fine, white fabric.[18]

17. *New Forest Color-coated Ware.* Fine, hard, iron-rich fabric, sometimes achieving the hardness of a stoneware with red-brown to purple color coats.[19]

18. *Hard Grey Sandy Ware.* Moderately fine, hard fabric tempered with well-sorted moderate sand, giving a slightly rough, soapy feel. The ware is similar to Savernake products, though it may be from elsewhere.

19. *Severn Valley Ware.* Orange or red fabric, often with a reduced core. Fabric is fine and sandy.[20]

20. *Lower Rhineland Fabric 1.* White, very fine fabric with black or red-brown color coat.[21]

21. *Alice Holt/Farnham Ware.* Fine grey sandy ware, with a varying proportion of quartz sand.[22]

22. *Ironstone-tempered Grey Ware.* Fine, hard, and dense grey sandy fabric. The appearance of the fabric is lightly speckled with small particles of abundant, well-sorted black ironstone and quartz.

23. *Whitehall Farm Ware.* A finer and harder fabric than the standard Savernake fabric of Fabric 12 above. The fabric is sandy, containing small ironstone particles.[23]

24. *Dressel 20 Amphora.* Hard buff fabric, gritty with abundant quartz.[24]

25. *Oxfordshire Red Ware.* Sandy oxidized ware, the Castle Copse examples are predominantly of types with a white color coat.[25]

26. *Wessex Grog-tempered Ware.* Medium hard, black or dark brown fabric containing ill-sorted inclusions of red, brown, and black grog. Fulford has identified a distribution throughout Hampshire and south Wiltshire, and Castle Copse is on the edge of this distribution area.[26] The crude handmade products of this industry sit alongside far finer wares, for example, those from the New Forest kilns from the late third century through the fourth.

27. *White-slipped Sandy Grey Ware.* Indistinguishable from the fabric of the Whitehill Farm products (Fabric 23, above), but with a thin cream slip applied to the outer surfaces. The slipped surfaces have traces of burnishing. A very infrequent fabric on the site.

28. *Hadham Ware.* Hard fine sandy ware, red in color, with vertical burnishing. There are very few sherds from Castle Copse, and all are from flagons. The ware is common in London from the mid-fourth century, though known in the Hertfordshire and Essex areas long before this.[27] The Castle Copse sherds are outliers to the general distribution, though Hadham Ware has been found at Littlecote.[28]

29. *Nene Valley Color-coated Ware.* Moderately fine white fabric with some small ironstone inclusions.[29]

30. *Rhenish Ware.* Red-orange, fine sandy fabric with a dark brown-black color coat. An Upper Rhineland, product, described by Anderson.[30]

31. *Oxfordshire White Ware.* Sandy white fabric with translucent flint trituration grits.[31]

32. *Soapy Sandy Ware.* Soft fabric of pinkish-orange color, tempered with medium-fine quartz sand. Grey surfaces, and the outer surfaces are finely burnished giving a characteristically soapy feel.

33. *South Midland Shell-gritted Ware.* Black fabric, occasionally with lighter surfaces. This ware has a soapy feel, and contains a high proportion of ill-sorted shell inclusions.[32]

Vessels are often rilled. Manufactured from the late third century onwards, it has a wide currency in the Midlands during the fourth century.[33]

34. *North Wiltshire Color-coated Ware.* Hard, fine, sandy grey fabric, with quartz and ironstone inclusions. The color coat is black and glossy[34] and is applied to all surfaces. Sometimes large fillers cause a lumpy appearance to the interior.

35. *Overwey Ware.* Grey-buff paste with buff-creamy yellow surfaces. Very sandy and fairly rough. The source of this fabric was identified by Lyne and Jeffries,[35] though it is still sometimes referred to by its earlier common name of Portchester "D" Ware.[36] The most common products of this industry are the rilled jars, and rilling is characteristic of the products of the industry found at Castle Copse.

36. *North Gaulish Fabric 2.* Very fine and soft fabric containing red ironstone inclusions. Glossy dark brown color coat.[37]

37. *Oxfordshire Color-coated Ware.* Hard, red, sandy, micaeous fabric with a glossy dark brown color coat.[38]

Pottery Supply—Preliminary Observations

Only a summary outline of pottery supply is possible, given the paucity of site evidence, and the only useful sequence of pottery is from Sector A.

The earliest pottery at Castle Copse, from Sectors A:I and C:I, consists of Belgic types of Fabrics 1–2, Oare fabrics. The Oare industry was local, and is the obvious source for pottery supply for the mid-first century. The more exotic Gallo-Belgic finewares, traded from abroad, are rare, but more widespread insular trade covers the south of England, from Silchester (Fabric 3) and even London (Fabric 9) in the east to Gloucestershire (Fabric 8) in the west. The site is about equidistant from these areas, and this central southern location is mirrored in pottery supply throughout the occupation of the site.

The long gap between Phases I and II of Sector A represents a period during which pottery was supplied from a variety of industries (Table 2), and it is clear that the Savernake industries, developing as they did from the Oare industry, were by far the most important suppliers (Table 2, Fabrics 10 and 12).[39] The traditional supply center thus was still operating during the entire period that the area of Sector A may have been peripheral to the focus of settlement on the site, in the second and early third centuries. By the later third century, Phase A:VIII, when the first aisled building in Sector A was in use, it is clear that the Savernake industries were suffering considerable pressure from the Dorset producers of Fabric 14 (Black Burnished Ware 1) and also increasingly from the New Forest and Alice Holt/Farnham material, although this never enjoyed a large market on the site.

In the third century, the broad spread of supply already noted is represented by the arrival of pottery from Oxfordshire, the Severn Valley, and the Hertfordshire Hadham Ware kilns. The coarse Wessex Grog-tempered fabric also appears around this time, and the site appears to have been on the fringes of the distribution areas of several of these regional wares.

There are two specifically fourth-century wares from the site. Pots of Fabric 33, South-Midland Shell-gritted Ware, arrive during Phase X of Sector A, and seem to occur from the beginning of the phase. At the same time, Wessex Grog-tempered Ware, never frequent, almost disappears. Though the South Midland pottery was manufactured throughout the fourth century, it seems that it came into this area during the later part of the century, as it did at Cirencester.[40] The latest ware to arrive on the site is Fabric 35, Overwey Ware, which appears in the latest floors of Phase XI, Sector A. This is characteristic of the very late fourth century onwards, and occurs frequently with the South Midland products. In pit fill C43 of Sector C—the best evidence on the entire site for very late activity—the ware is contemporary with the coin of Arcadius (86) (A.D. 388–402). This association is in accord with the discovery of Overwey Ware in quantity in contexts associated with the construction of the riverside defense wall in London, an event which cannot have begun before A.D. 388.[41]

Given the quality of the site, it seems odd that finewares are very uncommon throughout. Perhaps this is due to the generally poor sample present. This phenomenon is particularly marked in the lack of samian ware, a lacuna that may be explained by the fact that during the second century, when samian enjoyed its period of greatest use, the areas excavated may have been on the edge of the site. It is very noticeable that where samian occurs, its surfaces are weathered and abraded, and, indeed, throughout the study of the pottery the presence of samian in a context suggests a high residuality factor.

Pottery Groups

SECTORS A:I AND C:I. EARLY DITCH FILLS (TABLE 1)
Though spatially far apart, the Phase I deposits in Sectors A and C were of remarkably similar character, in terms of both the context and composition of the groups. Both are large groups recovered from the fills of ditches of similar shape and dimension, and probably similar purpose (chapter 4.3), which were the earliest features excavated in the respective sectors. In the limited range of fabrics in these assemblages, Fabrics 1 and 2 (Oare Fabrics 1 and 2) are overwhelmingly predominant, though a few other wares are also present. Of some interest is the presence of Gallo-Belgic wares in this assemblage, as is the total absence of samian wares.

V. Swan suggests a date c. A.D. 50–70 for the groups from Sector C, while those from Sector A have a slightly later terminal date (c. A.D. 50–90) as a result of the presence of a single sherd of a Fabric 9 (Highgate C) poppy-head beaker. The large groups suggest deliberate rubbish deposition in the boundary ditches of a pre-villa hilltop settlement.

C59: Bottom Fill of Ditch
Fabric I. Oare Fabric 1 (Figs. 129–130).
Carinated Bowl:
230. Fine carinated bowl, originally pedestalled. Burnished on exterior and inside rim.[42]
    Bead rim bowls or jars:[43]
231. Coarse fabric, burnished over rim onto the shoulder.
232. Fine fabric with dark surfaces. Burnished on rim and shoulders.
233. Coarse fabric with thick rim.
234. Fine fabric, smoothed on inside and burnished on the exterior.
235. Fine fabric. The bowl has a very slight rim and a high shoulder.
236. Fine fabric. The rim has a square bead, approaching cornice shape.

237. Fine fabric, smoothed inside and out. The vessel is large and bulbous, with a small rim.
238. Fine fabric, burnished inside and out.
239. Medium fine fabric, burnished over the pronounced rim and onto the shoulder.
240. Fine fabric, smoothed on the exterior.
241. Fine fabric, with wipe marks on the interior and a burnished exterior. The beaded rim is very slight.
242. Fine, sandy fabric.
243. Very fine fabric, smoothed on the exterior.
244. Medium-fine fabric, smoothed on the exterior.
245. Fine fabric, burnished on shoulder and exterior of rim.
246. Fine fabric, burnished on all surfaces. Barely perceptible beaded rim.
247. Fine fabric, smoothed inside and out.
248. Medium fabric, smoothed on exterior, pronounced rim.
249. Straight-necked bowl or jar.[44] Complete vessel in fine fabric, burnished on the outside and smoothed inside.
250. Platter,[45] Fine fabric, densely burnished on all surfaces. Swan divides platters into two groups,[46] and this vessel is typical of her Group B, without a foot-ring. The heavy burnishing is intended to copy Gallo-Belgic vessels.
     Lids:[47]
251. Medium-fine fabric, smoothed on both sides.
252. Fine fabric, burnished on top, with marked seat.
     Butt beaker:
253. Butt beaker. Fine fabric, smoothed on the outside, with zone of burnished cross-hatching.
     Fabric 2. Oare Fabric 2 (Figs. 130–131)
254. Bead-rim bowl or jar.[48] Fine fabric, burnished on the shoulder and rim, with a smoothed interior.
255. Strainer. A jar in coarse fabric, with smoothed surfaces, with three holes in the base. The size of the holes (D.=0.01) might suggest use for straining large material, such as vegetables. The wide opening at the top precludes use as a watering pot.
     Fabric 3. Silcester Flint-tempered Ware (Fig. 131)
256. Large bead-rim bowl, burnished on the rim and deeply over the shoulder. Wiped on the inside to reveal flint tempering.
257. Bead-rim jar, smoothed on the outside, the interior wiped to reveal flint tempering.
     Fabric 4. Local (Fig. 131)
258. Butt beaker. Smoothed on the inside and painted on the exterior with a pinkish-buff slip. The slip is burnished over.
     Fabric 5. Terra Rubra (TR3) (not illustrated)
259. Beaker body sherds. Fabric is not used for any other class of vessel.[49]
     Fabric 6. Terra Rubra (TR2) (Fig. 131)
260. Butt beaker with notched scroll decoration.[50]
     C57: Upper Fill of Ditch
     Fabric 1. Oare Fabric 1 (Fig. 131).

261. Straight-neck jar.[51] Fine fabric, smoothed on the inside and burnished over the shoulder. Burnished rays on lower body.
     Fabric 2. Oare Fabric 2 (Fig. 131)
     Straight-neck bowls or jars.[52]
262. Medium fabric, smoothed on exterior.
263–264. Coarse fabric, smoothed on exterior.
     Fabric 8. Gloucester-type Sandy Ware (Fig. 131)
265. Flat-rimmed bowl with pronounced foot-ring and burnished zigzag on the outside. Pieces of this vessel were also found in context C52.
266. Flat-topped lid (not illustrated).
267. Small jar or bowl with pronounced bead-rim.
268. Bowl with flat, everted rim. Linear burnished decoration on the wall of the vessel.
     A965–971: Ditch Fill
     Fabric 7. Terra Nigra (TN1) (Fig. 131)
269. Small platter with slightly beaded rim.
     Fabric 1. Oare Fabric (Fig. 132)
     Bead rim bowls or jars:[53]
270–272. Medium to fine fabric, smoothed on the inside and burnished over the rim.
273–275. Medium fabric, smoothed on the inside.
     Straight-neck bowls or jars:[54]
276. Fine fabric, smoothed on the inside and burnished on rim and shoulder.
277. Fine fabric, smoothed on inside and outside.
278. Lid.[55] Slightly domed lid, smoothed on both sides.
     Fabric 2. Oare Fabric 2 (Figs. 132–133)
     Bead rim bowls or jars:[56]
279–281. Medium fabric, smoothed on all surfaces and burnished over rim and shoulder.
282–284. Fine-medium fabric, smoothed on all surfaces.
     Straight-neck bowls or jars:[57]
285. Fine fabric, smoothed on the exterior.
286. Fine-medium fabric.
     Lids:[58]
287. Medium-fine fabric, with burnished surfaces.
288. Fine black fabric, with burnished surfaces (as **287**; not illustrated).
289. Medium fabric, smoothed surfaces.
290. Pedestal from pedestal bowl. Black fabric, with burnished surfaces.
291. Strainer. Fine fabric, smoothed on all surfaces.
     Fabric 3. Silchester Flint-tempered Ware (Fig. 133)
292. Bead rim bowl. Fine fabric with few inclusions.
     Fabric 9. Highgate C Ware (Fig. 133)
293. Poppy-head beaker.[59]
     Fabric 8. Gloucester-type Sandy Ware (Fig. 133)
294. Lid with smoothed surfaces.
295. Bead-rim bowl with smoothed exterior surfaces.

SECTOR A:II–XII

Discussion

Because Sector A is the only complete ceramic sequence excavated at Castle Copse, any glaring gap in this sequence must represent a genuine break in occupation in that area. A clear gap can be seen between the A.D. 90 terminal date of Phase A:I (above) and the Phase A:II levelling of the site. The character of the pottery suggests that there must have been occupation on the hilltop during the second century, but that the major operation of levelling did not occur until the later part of that century, or the early third. The levelling probably took the form of scraping material together from the whole hilltop.

The earliest features after the levelling were the four phases (A:III–VI) of postholes. The earliest of these phases (A:III) is given a *terminus post quem* of A.D. 211 by a Severan coin (**29**), and the latest (A:VI) includes mid-late third-century pottery. It is clearly possible that during the third century post-built structures were replaced or remodeled, as is suggested not only by the character of the features, but also by the tiny volume of pottery recovered. This situation did not change until the erection of the first aisled building during Phase A:VII. The occupation of this building again yielded little pottery, though the material does go on until the later third century.

The first aisled building appears to have been replaced soon after its construction. A small amount of pottery was found in the Phase A:X undivided second aisled building, but only in the chalk floors, which can give evidence of dating for the construction of the building. This material is mid-third century, and therefore residual. Residuality is further proved by the discovery of a coin (**55**) of A.D. 330–331 in a floor patch of the occupation phase of the undivided building. This coin is the *terminus post quem* for the occupation of the subdivided building of Phase XI, and the pottery demonstrates uninterrupted activity to the end of the period of production of Fabric 35, Overwey Ware c. A.D. 420; there is no reason to believe that it did not continue beyond that.

SECTOR A:II. TERRACE GRAVEL DUMP (TABLE 2)

Contexts A509, 541, 582, 629, 927, 964.

All sherds from context A964 are small and abraded, and very few join. There is a high probability of residuality for much of this material. The character of the deposit is of material deposited in bulk in one levelling operation, and the condition of the pottery is consistent with this. The deposit is difficult to date closely, though Fabric 14, Black Burnished Ware 1 cooking pots (**310–311**) suggest a generic second-century date. V. Swan comments that the presence of the stabbed tazza (**315**) and some sherds of Fabrics 16 and 17, New Forest Whiteware and New Forest Color-coated Ware, weights the group toward the early third century; this is confirmed by the appearance of Fabric 21 (Alice Holt/Farnham Ware) in some quantity.

Fabric 10. Savernake Grog-tempered Ware (Fig. 133)

296. Large storage jar in coarse, lumpy fabric. A927.

297–298. Straight-sided jar. A964, 927. Similar form to the Oare vessels 40–45.[60]

299. Storage jar with pronounced lid seat. A964.

300–301. Jars in coarse fabric, lumpy on the inside, but with smoothed exterior. A964.

296–301 are all forms which occur in corpora from Savernake kilns 1–2[61] and 7.[62]

Fabric 12. Savernake Ware (Fig. 134)

302–306. Four jars and small platter. A964.

307. Wide-mouthed jar. A541.

Fabric 13. Hard Sandy Flint-tempered Ware (Fig. 134)

308. Large storage jar. A509.

309. Domed lid. A927.

Fabric 14. Black Burnished Ware 1 (Fig. 134)

310–311. Cooking pots of second-century form.[63] A964.

312–313. Domical lids. A629, 927.

Fabric 15. White-slipped Redware (Fig. 134)

314. Jar fragment with crosshatched decoration. A964.

Fabric 16. New Forest Whiteware (Fig. 134)

315. Thin-walled jar. A964.

Fabric 17. New Forest Color-coated Ware (Fig. 134)

316. Fragment of beaker with stabbed triangle decoration. A964.

Fabric 18. Hard Grey Sandy Ware (Fig. 134)

317. Fragment of stabbed tazza. A964.

Fabric 19. Severn Valley Ware (Fig. 134)

318. Bead-rim bowl. A629.[64]

Miscellaneous Sandy Grey Wares (Fig. 134)

319. Jar or flagon neck. A964.

SECTOR A:V. POST STRUCTURES I (TABLE 3)

One counterfeit denarius of Septimius Severius (**29**) was found in one of the postholes (A473) of Phase V and dates to after A.D. 198. These postholes follow immediately upon the laying of the terrace gravel of A:II and the two earlier post alignments. The importance of this coin lies in the fact that Phases A:III–VI are not dated by any other means, pottery being extremely limited, and the coin provides a useful *terminus post quem* for the construction of the first aisled building in Phase VII.

    A433: Posthole fill.

Fabric 14. Black Burnished Ware 1 (Fig. 134)

320. Cooking pot of early to mid-third-century form.[65]

SECTOR A:VI. POST STRUCTURES II (TABLE 3)

This phase comprises replacements to the Phase V posts. Pottery gives a similar early third-century date for the phase, based on the form of Black Burnished Ware 1 and New Forest White Ware in the single useful group.

    A462: Slot fill.

Fabric 10. Savernake Grog-tempered Ware (Fig.135)

321. Lid.

Fabric 12. Savernake-type Grey Wares (Fig. 135)

322–323. Bead-rim bowls or jars.

Fabric 14. Black Burnished Ware 1 (Fig. 135)

324. Cooking pot. Early to mid-third-century form.[66]

Fabric 16. New Forest White Ware (Fig. 135)

325. Ring-neck flagon. Fulford Type 12.1 is the nearest in the New Forest corpus.[67]

Fabric 20. Lower Rhineland Fabric 1 (Fig. 135)

326. Beaker.

Fabric 21. Alice Holt/Farnham Ware (Fig. 135)

327. Jar.[68]

SECTOR A: PHASE VII. CONSTRUCTION OF THE FIRST AISLED BUILDING (TABLE 4)

The latest pottery in this phase again dates to the early to mid-third century. New fabrics during this phase are Fabric 22, Ironstone-tempered Grey Ware, and, recognizably, Fabric 23, Whitehill Farm Ware. In the latter industry, third-century products imitating Black Burnished Ware forms were common.[69] The small amount of pottery present is in accord with the coin evidence (see above) in giving a *terminus post quem* of this date to the building.

A397: Wall Construction; A960: Stylobate Packing

Fabric 12. Savernake-type Grey Wares (Fig. 135)

328–329. Jars. A960, 397.

Fabric 21. Alice Holt/Farnham Ware (Fig. 135)

330. Jar. A397. Of a type dated to A.D. 270+ by Lyne and Jeffries.[70]

SECTOR A:VIII. OCCUPATION OF FIRST AISLED BUILDING (TABLE 5)

The largest pottery group from Phase A:VIII was from the latest floor surface of the aisled building. This surface comprised packed gravel, but was separated from the Phase A:II terrace gravel by a thin band of orange gravel, which is interpreted as the earliest floor of the building. This phase is significant in including an influx of new fabrics, probably reflecting a rise in status and certainly suggestive of date. Fabrics 25 (Oxfordshire Red Ware), 26 (Wessex Grog-tempered Ware), and 28 (Hadham Ware), all begin to achieve wide currency in the mid-third century, while Fabrics 25, 28 and 30 (Nene Valley Color-coated Ware) are finewares, which are hitherto very rare on the site. The latest group, which is published in full below, is typical of the phase as a whole.

A552, 574, 874, 954: Gravel Floor of Building.

Fabric 10. Savernake Grog-tempered Wares (Fig. 135)

331–339. Jars of various forms and sizes. **331–333** from A522, **334–335** from A574, **336–339** from A954; **339** as **338** (not illustrated). Some may be Purton products.[71]

340. Lid.

Fabric 12. Savernake-type Grey Wares (Fig. 136)

341–347. Jars of various forms and sizes. **341–342** from A874, **343–347** from A954.

Fabric 14. Black Burnished Ware 1 (Fig. 136)

348–357. Cooking pots of a number of forms. **348–349**, **350–352** from A395; **350**, **363** from A522; **355–357** from A954. All but **350–351** are residual in this phase. **350–352** are late third century in date.[72]

Fabric 16. New Forest White Wares (Fig. 136)

358. Jar.[73] A954.

Miscellaneous Sandy Grey Wares (Fig. 137)

359–365. Jars and bowls of various forms. **359–361**, **364–365** from A954; **362–363** from A874. The range of forms is similar to that of the identifiable wares.

SECTOR A:IX. CONSTRUCTION OF SECOND AISLED BUILDING

SECTOR A:X. SECOND AISLED BUILDING BEFORE SUBDIVISION (TABLES 6–7)

The pottery from A:X is derived from the chalk floors of the building, and the construction phase of the building produced no illustratable groups. That all of the material was residual when deposited is shown by the presence of a coin (**55**) of A.D. 330–331 in a floor patch of the occupation phase of the undivided building. The latest vessels are of mid-third-century or later forms and fabrics. No new fabrics occur, except Fabric 32, Oxfordshire White Ware. This is an accident of recovery, as this ware has the same date as its counterpart, Fabric 25, which occurs in the preceding phase.

A10, 646, 760, 897, 939: Chalk floor of building.

Fabric 10. Savernake Grog-tempered Wares (Fig. 137)

366. Large bead rim jar. A760.

Fabric 12. Savernake-type Grey Wares (Fig. 137)

367. Jar. A939.

Fabric 14. Black Burnished Ware 1 (Fig. 137)

368. Cooking pot. A760. Mid-third-century form.[74]

Fabric 15. White-slipped Redware (Fig. 137)

369. Beaker with exaggerated cornice-type rim. A760.

Fabric 21. Alice Holt/Farnham Ware (Fig. 137)

370. Jar. A760. Mid-third-century form.[75]

SECTOR A: PHASE X–XI. EXTERIOR OF SECOND AISLED BUILDING (TABLE 8)

This phase contains contexts which are contemporary with the use of the second aisled building in all its phases up to Phase XII. As such the phase includes material of wide-ranging dates, which can be refined somewhat within the aisled building, where Phases X and XI are divided. The important aspect of the agglomeration of new fabrics in these phases is the appearance of the mid-fourth-century Fabric 33, South Midland Shell-gritted Ware. This material is absent in Phase X, though it is present in Phase XI. It seems to have made its appearance on-site during the occupation of the subdivided aisled building, the *terminus post quem* for which is provided by the coin of A.D. 330–331 (**55**) mentioned above.

A88: Fill of Foundation Trench A89

Fabric 8. Gloucester-type Sandy Ware (Fig. 137)

371. Straight-sided dish.

Fabric 12. Savernake-type Grey Wares (Fig. 137)

372–373. Jars with square rims and rilled decoration.

374. Bowl with plain rim and decoration of burnished irregular strokes on inner and outer surfaces.

Fabric 14. Black Burnished Ware 1 (Fig. 138)

375. Plain-rim dish with burnished strokes on the outside.

Fabric 33. South Midland Shell-gritted Ware (Fig. 138)

376. Flanged bowl with rilled body.

A91: Fill of Ditch A92 on North Side of Aisled Building

Fabric 10. Savernake Grog-tempered Ware (Fig. 138)

377. Large bead rim jar.

Fabric 14. Black Burnished Ware 1 (Fig. 138)

378–379. Flanged bowls.

380. Cooking pot. Late third-early fourth-century form.[76]

Fabric 21. Alice Holt/Farnham Ware (Fig. 138)

381. Bowl. Mid-third-century form.[77]

Fabric 26. Wessex Grog-tempered Ware (Fig. 138)

382. Plain rim bowl, with roughly burnished stripe around outside.

SECTOR A:XI. SUBDIVISION AND OCCUPATION OF SECOND AISLED BUILDING (TABLE 9)

Most of the pottery relating to this phase is in the form of small scrappy groups, primarily containing body sherds only. These are derived from floors, particularly from the complex of floors and occupation debris in the easternmost room defined in Sector A. The fabrics include fourth-century types in all contexts, and it is not possible, due to the limited volume of material, to date these floors any more narrowly. It is notable, however, that the only significant new fabric of this phase, the late fourth-century Fabric 35, Overwey Ware, occurs only in the later floors, such as A229. The assemblage from context A377, which is of some importance because of the quantity of animal bone recovered from a totally dry-sieved context, produced a large number of small sherds only, which were primarily Black Burnished Ware 1.

Fabric 17. New Forest Color-coated Ware (Fig. 138)

383. "Castor Box" form[78] in fine New Forest fabric, with faint feathered decoration. A355.

384. Indented beaker with stabbed decoration above the indents. The vessel is of a late third- to mid-fourth-century form,[79] and may have been old when broken. Sherds of this pot were found in A198 and A208, both floor layers in the same room.

Fabric 35. Overwey Ware (Fig. 138)

385–386. Hook-rim jars. A355, 229. Dated A.D. 330–420.[80]

SECTOR A: PHASE XI–XII. UNIFICATION OF AISLED BUILDING II AND CONTEMPORARY STRUCTURES (TABLE 9)

This phase is chiefly represented by the ditch, pottery from whose fill (A121) is catalogued below. This ditch contained sherds of all current late Roman wares, including the latest, Fabric 35, Overwey Ware.

A121: Fill of Ditch A144

Fabric 10. Savernake Grog-tempered Ware (Fig. 139)

387. Large, everted rim jar.

Fabric 12. Savernake-type Grey Ware (Fig. 139)

388. Flagon or jug.

Fabric 19. Severn Valley Ware (Fig. 139)

389. Flagon or jug.

Fabric 21. Alice Holt/Farnham Ware (Fig. 139)

390–391. Two jars with partial hooked rims.[81]

Fabric 23. Whitehill Farm-type Ware (Fig. 139)

392. Single-handled flagon in overfired fabric.

Fabric 25. Oxfordshire Red Ware (Fig. 139)

393. Mortarium.[82] There are faint traces of the white color coat originally applied to this vessel.

Fabric 31. Oxfordshire White Ware (Fig. 139)

394. Mortarium. Dated from the late third and throughout the fourth centuries.[83]

Fabric 35. Overwey Ware (Fig. 139)

395–399. Hook-rim jars in rilled fabric, dated A.D. 330–420.[84]

Sector B

DISCUSSION

There are eleven phases in the stratigraphical sequence for Sector B. The pattern of pottery deposition during the whole history of the sector shows very little material within the Roman building, and large amounts from the courtyard. The successive courtyard deposits consist of dumps of debris intended to patch and build up the surface. Most of the pottery within these groups comprises small, abraded sherds with no joining fragments, dating from the first to the fourth century. It has the aspect of material scraped together from all over the hilltop for levelling purposes.

Within the building, all surfaces had been kept clean during the Roman period, and no pottery was forthcoming. Even the later features within the Roman building itself yielded very little pottery. There is no way of dating the post-mosaic features, except by a *terminus post quem* from the fourth-century mosaic itself. Most of the pottery came from deposits of Phases VII–XII, and, even during these periods of decline and destruction, a very limited amount of pottery came from within the building. The material from the sector at large includes pottery covering the entire Roman period, with the earlier wares predominating. All material should be regarded as residual and disturbed, and is therefore considered only in summary in this report where it coincides with actual structural phases.

SECTOR B:III. EARLY VILLA WEST WING (TABLE 10)

This is the earliest ceramic phase in Sector B, and represents the limited evidence for the construction of the main building. This comprises a group of three sherds of Samian and Savernake wares. The coin of Hadrian dated to A.D. 117 (**28**), derived from the same deposit (B123), provides a far better *terminus post quem* for the phase. The pottery, for what it is worth, does not contradict a date generally in the second century. Comparison with Sector A on structural grounds, however, suggests that the phase is probably third-century.

Fabric 12. Savernake-type Grey Wares (Fig. 139)

400. Small jar of a form similar to mid-second-century Black Burnished Ware 1 types.[85]

SECTOR B:IV. LATER VILLA WEST WING (TABLE 10)

SECTOR B:V. OCCUPATION VILLA WEST WING

These phases relate to the villa west wing and its occupation. Little pottery was recovered, probably due to the inhabitants' desire to keep the building clean. There are, however, two reasonably large groups, both of which contain largely residual material.[86]

B113: Subfloor, Room 5
Fabric 12. Savernake-type Grey Wares (Fig. 140)
401. Storage jar.
Fabric 19. Severn Valley Ware (Fig. 140)
402. Flagon neck.[87]
Fabric 20. Lower Rhineland Fabric 1 (Fig. 140)
403. Beaker.
B98: Mortar spread
Fabric 2. Savernake Grog-tempered Ware (Fig. 140)
404. Large storage jar.
405. Small jar.
Fabric 8. Gloucester-type Sandy Ware (Fig. 140)
406. Jar.
Fabric 12. Savernake-type Grey Wares (Fig. 140)
407. Wide-mouthed jar of form similar to a second-century vessel from Whitehill Farm.[88]
408–410. Jars of various forms.
Fabric 14. Black Burnished Ware 1 (Fig. 140)
411. Plain-rim bowl.[89]
412. Lid.
413. Grooved-rim bowl.[90]
414. Jar of third-century form.[91]
415–416. Jars.
Fabric 22. Ironstone-tempered Grey Ware (Fig. 140)
417. Flat-rim bowl.
Fabric 36. North Gaulish Fabric 2 (Fig. 140)
418. Cornice-rim beaker with rustication of clay pellets under a fine, glossy color coat.

SECTOR B: PHASE VI. COURTYARD SURFACES ASSOCIATED WITH MAIN BUILDING (TABLE 11)

Phase VI consists of courtyard surfaces associated with the Roman building. The phase has a *terminus post quem* derived from B148, the earliest excavated layer in the courtyard, which contained Fabric 26, Wessex Grog-tempered Ware, dating from the late third to the fourth century. None of the material is illustratable.

Sector C

DISCUSSION

Six stratigraphic phases were defined during excavation in Sector C. The latest clearly Roman period occupation phase (C:IV) in this sequence included the best very late Roman pottery from Castle Copse. The deposits associated with the collapse of the south wall of the Roman building in Phase V and every subsequent deposit, unlike the contexts of Phase IV, contain a wide range of mixed and entirely residual material, originating from all earlier periods. For this reason, pottery of Phases C:V–VI, undatable in ceramic terms, is not included here.

Phase C:I is the period of the ditch with its large quantities of Oare Ware, described above which leaves the Roman Phases C:III–IV to consider. Phase C:IV, the latest certain activity in the building, is defined in ceramic terms most markedly by the presence of Fabric 33 (South Midland Shell-gritted Ware) and the later fourth–fifth-century Fabric 35 (Overwey Ware). Of particular interest are the sealed pit groups C43 and C64; the former, in particular, contained a good group of contemporary wares with few vessels, unabraded sherds, and little or no residual material. The pottery is contemporary with the coin of Arcadius (**86**, A.D. 388–402).

SECTOR C:III. ROMAN BUILDING (TABLE 12)

The pottery of this phase, representing the occupation of the building, was found in both interior and exterior surfaces. Despite a large residual component of first- and second-century sherds, some of the wares present give a firm third–fourth century date for the phase.

C37. Exterior surface

Fabric 10. Savernake Grog-tempered Ware (Fig. 141)

419. Bead rim storage jar.

420. Storage jar with everted rim.

Fabric 14. Black Burnished Ware 1 (Fig. 141)

421. Deep, straight-sided bowl.

422. Cooking pot.

Fabric 31. Oxfordshire White Ware (Fig. 141)

423. Mortarium.[92]

424. Mortarium.[93] Dated to the latter half of the fourth century.

Fabric 33. South Midland Shell-gritted Ware (Fig. 141)

425. Flanged bowl.

SECTOR C:IV. LATE ACTIVITY IN BUILDING (TABLE 13)

See above; the material below is derived from the late pit groups.

C43. Pit group.

Fabric 33. South Midland Shell-gritted Ware (Fig. 141)

426. Jar. Apparently, though not certainly, one vessel in rilled fabric.

Fabric 35. Overwey Ware (Fig. 141)

427. Hook-rim jar in rilled fabric.[94] The vessel has joining sherds in contexts C43 (pit) and C2 (topsoil).

NOTES

1. The author would like to thank P. Austen, L. Hird, S. Moorhouse, R. Perrin, A. Vince, and, especially, V. Swan for their help and comments in the preparation of the pottery reports. S. Rushton undertook the pottery illustrations.

2. Detailed analysis of regional pottery supply will have to await the publication of material from more extensively excavated sites nearby, such as Littlecote villa.

3. The pottery analysis leading to the publication of this report has been recorded on pro forma worksheets, based on those currently (1987) in use by the West Yorkshire Archaeology

Service. These sheets form the archive on this work, following the guidelines laid down by the Directorate of Ancient Monuments and Historic Buildings (Young 1980). They will be deposited with the sherds themselves in the Devizes Museum.

4. Swan 1975: 42.
5. Swan 1975: 42.
6. For full description, see Fulford 1984: 135.
7. Rigby 1981: 159.
8. Rigby 1981: 159.
9. Rigby 1981: 159.
10. Hurst 1985: 78–79.
11. Cf. C. M. Green 1980: 54.
12. A. S. Anderson 1980a: 13.
13. A. S. Anderson 1980b: 52.
14. Swan 1975.
15. A. S. Anderson 1980a: 13.
16. Farrar 1973; and D. F. Williams 1977.
17. Rigby 1982: 160, fabric 71B.
18. Fulford 1975b: 26, fabric 2b.
19. Fulford 1975b: 24, fabric 1a.
20. Tomber 1985.
21. A. C. Anderson 1980: 14.
22. Lyne and Jefferies 1979: 18.
23. A. S. Anderson 1980a: 13.
24. C. M. Green 1980: 40.
25. Young 1977: 117.
26. Fulford 1975a: 286–92.
27. Harden and Green 1978: 171.
28. Pers. comm., B. Walters.
29. Howe, Perrin, and Mackreth 1980: 14.
30. A. C. Anderson 1980: 26.
31. Young 1977: 56.
32. Cf. Woodfield 1983: 75, fabric 44d.
33. Brodribb, Hands and Walker: 1971: 68.
34. A. C. Anderson 1980: 11.
35. Lyne and Jefferies 1979: 37.
36. Fulford 1975a: 299.
37. A. C. Anderson 1980: 33.
38. Young 1977: 123.
39. Swan 1975.
40. Keely 1986: 163.
41. Parnell 1985: 30, 58.
42. Cf. Swan 1975: fig. 2, no. 20 for identical vessel, probably by the same hand.
43. Cf. Swan, 1975: fig. 3, nos. 23–34.
44. Cf. Swan, 1975: fig. 4, nos. 40–46.
45. Cf. Swan, 1975: fig. 2, nos. 12–17.
46. Swan 1975: 50.
47. Cf. Swan, 1975: fig. 2, nos. 35–39.
48. Cf. Swan, 1975: fig. 3, nos. 23–34.
49. Rigby 1981: 159.
50. Cf. Rigby, 1981: 172, fig. 78: 39a–b.
51. Cf. Swan, 1975: fig. 4, nos. 40–45.
52. Cf. Swan, 1975: fig. 4, nos. 40–45.
53. Cf. Swan, 1975: fig. 3, nos. 23–34.
54. Cf. Swan, 1975: fig. 4, nos. 40–45.

55. Cf. Swan, 1975: fig. 2, nos. 35–39.
56. Cf. Swan, 1975: fig. 3, nos. 23–34.
57. Cf. Swan, 1975: fig. 4, nos. 40–45.
58. Cf. Swan, 1975: fig. 2, nos. 35–39.
59. Cf. C. M. Green 1980: fig. 28, no. 153.
60. Swan 1975: fig. 4.
61. Annable 1962a.
62. Devizes Museum 1961.
63. Gillam 1976: types 1 and 3.
64. Cf. Hurst 1980: fig. 31:216.
65. Cf. Gillam 1976: fig. 1:6.
66. Cf. Gillam 1976: fig. 1:6.
67. Fulford 1975b: 48.
68. Cf. Lyne and Jefferies 1979: Type 1.20.
69. A. S. Anderson 1980a: 13.
70. Lyne and Jefferies 1979: Type 1.32.
71. A. S. Anderson 1980b: 55.
72. Cf. Gillam 1976: fig. 1:9–11.
73. Cf. Fulford 1975b: type 97.1.
74. Cf. Gillam 1976: type 9.
75. Cf. Lyne and Jefferies 1979: 75.22, type 1:31.
76. Cf. Gillam 1976: type 11.
77. Cf. Lyne and Jefferies 1979: type 6B: 3.
78. Howe, Perrin, and Mackreth 1980: 24, no. 89. The form does not appear in Fulford's (1975b) corpus.
79. Fulford 1975b: 52, type 27:11.
80. Lyne and Jefferies 1979: type 3C:11.
81. Cf. Lyne and Jefferies 1979: type 3c:20.
82. Cf. Young 1977: type WC7.
83. Cf. Young 1977: type M22.
84. Cf. Lyne and Jefferies 1979: types 3C:11–14.
85. Gillam 1976: type 2.
86. See Table 10. Group B95=61 from the fill of cut B80—though stratigraphically seemingly from the major late robbing phase (B:VIII) of the villa west wing—also comprises residual material, an early/mid-third-century assemblage of Black Burnished Ware 1 (Fabric 14), comprising: flanged bowls (cf. Gillam 1976: type 45); flat-rimmed bowl, whose groove around the top of the rim makes this a transitional form between flat-rimmed and flanged bowl; jar of the early/mid-third century (cf. Gillam 1976: type 7); and jar.
87. Tomber 1985: type 22.
88. A. S. Anderson 1980a: fig. 8:3.
89. Gillam 1976: type 83.
90. As Gillam (1976) type 52, but smaller and lacking crosshatched decoration.
91. Gillam 1976: type 6.
92. Cf. Young 1977: type M3.
93. Cf. Young 1977: type M23.
94. Cf. Lyne and Jefferies 1979: type 3C:13.

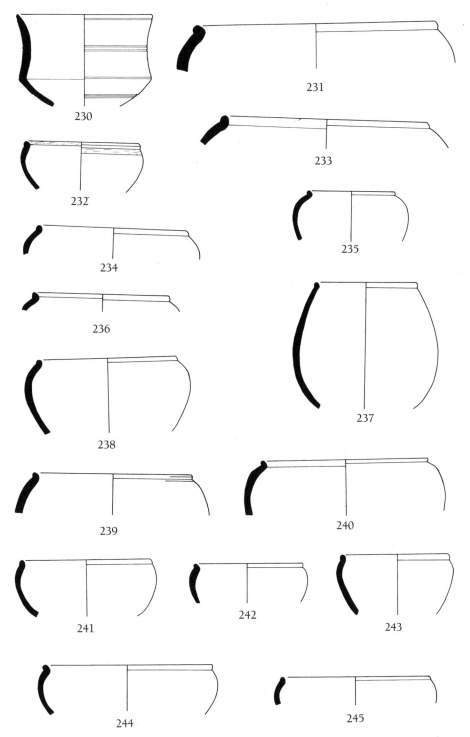

Figure 129. **230–245.** Fabric 1, Oare Fabric 1. C59. (1:4)

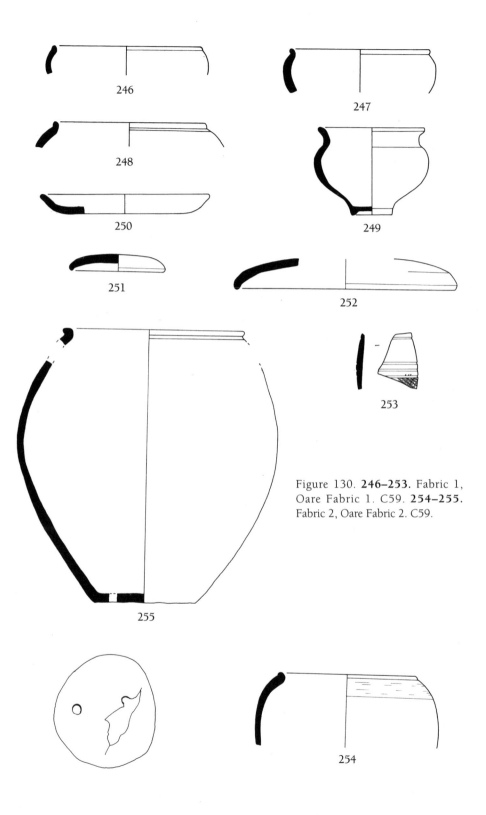

246

247

248

249

250

251

252

253

Figure 130. **246–253**. Fabric 1,
Oare Fabric 1. C59. **254–255**.
Fabric 2, Oare Fabric 2. C59.

255

254

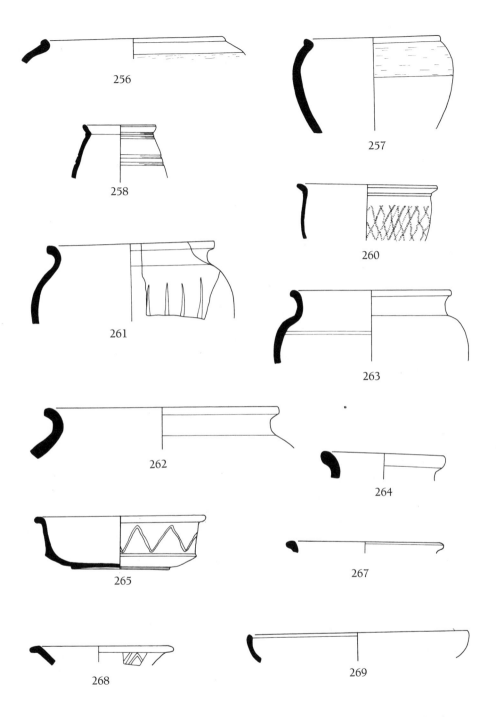

Figure 131. **256–257.** Fabric 3, Silchester Flint-tempered Ware. C59. **258.** Fabric 4, local. C59. **260.** Fabric 6, Terra Rubra (TR2). C59. **261.** Fabric 1, Oare Fabric 1. C57. **262–264.** Fabric 2, Oare Fabric 2. C57. **265, 267–268.** Fabric 8, Gloucester-type Sandy Ware. C57. **269.** Fabric 7, Terra Nigra (TN1). A965–971. (1:4)

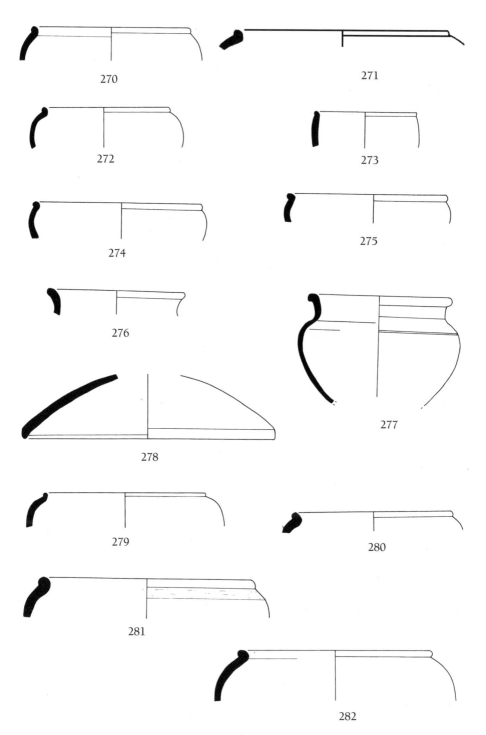

Figure 132. **270–278.** Fabric 1, Oare Fabric 1. **279–282.** Fabric 2, Oare Fabric 2. A965–971. (1:4)

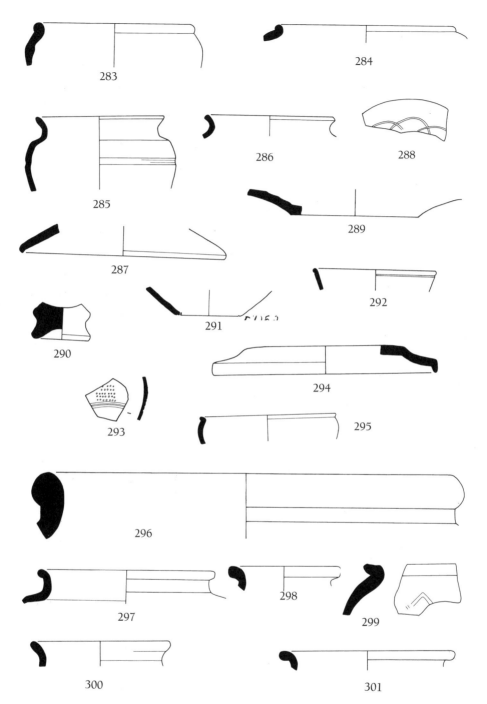

Figure 133. **283–291**. Fabric 2, Oare Fabric 2. A955–971. **292**. Fabric 3, Silchester Flint-tempered Ware. A965-971. **293**. Fabric 9, Highgate C Ware. A965–971. **294–295**. Fabric 8, Gloucester-type Sandy Ware. A965–971. **296–301**. Fabric 10, Savernake Grog-tempered Ware. A927, 964. (1:4)

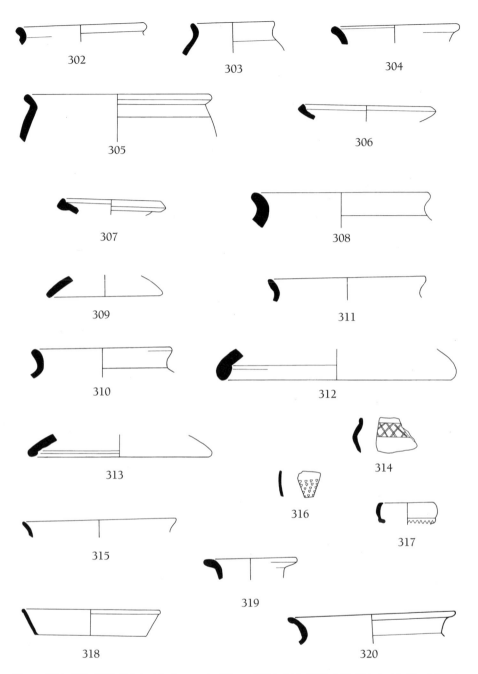

Figure 134. **302–307.** Fabric 12, Savernake Ware. A964, 541. **308–309.** Fabric 13, Hard Sandy Flint-tempered Ware. A509, 927. **310–313.** Fabric 14, Black Burnished Ware 1. A964, 629, 927. **314.** Fabric 15, White-slipped Red Ware. A964. **315.** Fabric 16, New Forest White Ware. A964. **316.** Fabric 17, New Forest Color-coated Ware. A964. **317.** Fabric 18, Hard Grey Sandy Ware. A964. **318.** Fabric 19, Severn Valley Ware. A629. **319.** Miscellaneous Sandy Grey Wares. A694. **320.** Fabric 14, Black Burnished Ware 1. A433. (1:4)

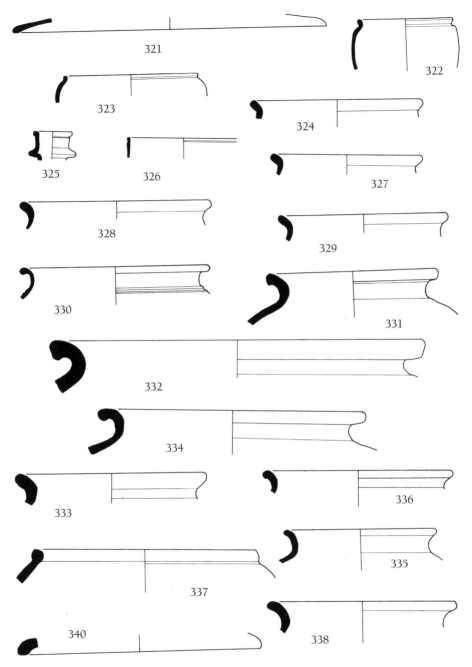

Figure 135. **321.** Fabric 10, Savernake Grog-tempered Ware. A462. **322–323.** Fabric 12, Savernake-type Grey Ware. A462. **324.** Fabric 14, Black Burnished Ware 1. A462. **325.** Fabric 16, New Forest White Ware. A462. **326.** Fabric 20, Lower Rhineland Fabric 1. A462. **327.** Fabric 21, Alice Holt/Farnham Ware. A462. **328–329.** Fabric 12, Savernake-type Grey Ware. A960, 397. **330.** Fabric 21, Alice Holt/Farnham Ware. A397. **331–338, 340.** Fabric 10, Savernake Grog-tempered Ware. A522, 574, 954. (1:4)

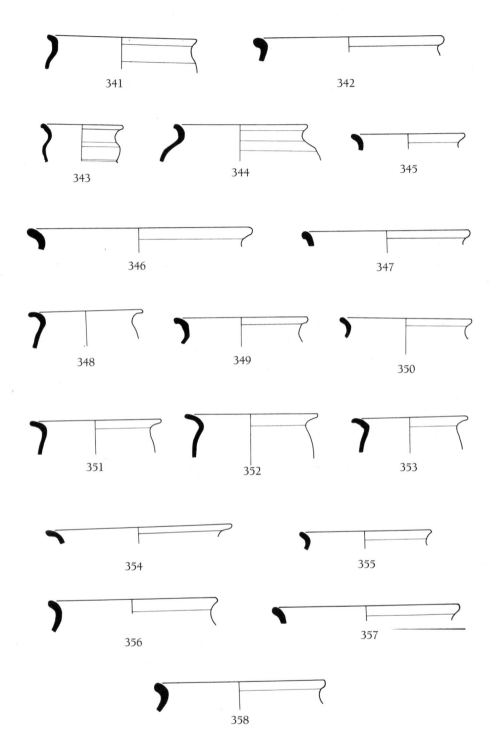

Figure 136. **341–347.** Fabric 12, Savernake-type Grey Ware. A874, 954. **348–357.** Fabric 14, Black Burnished Ware 1. A395, 522, 954. **358.** Fabric 16, New Forest White Ware. A954. (1:4)

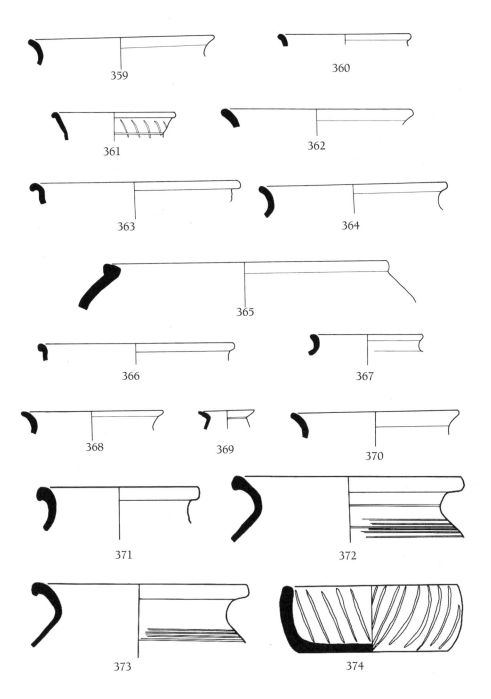

Figure 137. **359–365.** Miscellaneous Sandy Grey Ware. A954, 874. **366.** Fabric 10, Savernake Grog-tempered Ware. A760. **367.** Fabric 12, Savernake-type Grey Ware. A939. **368.** Fabric 14, Black Burnished Ware 1. A760. **369.** Fabric 15, White-slipped Red Ware. A760. **370.** Fabric 21, Alice Holt/Farnham Ware. A760. **371.** Fabric 8, Gloucester-type Sandy Ware. A88. **372–374.** Fabric 12, Savernake-type Grey Ware. A88. (1:4)

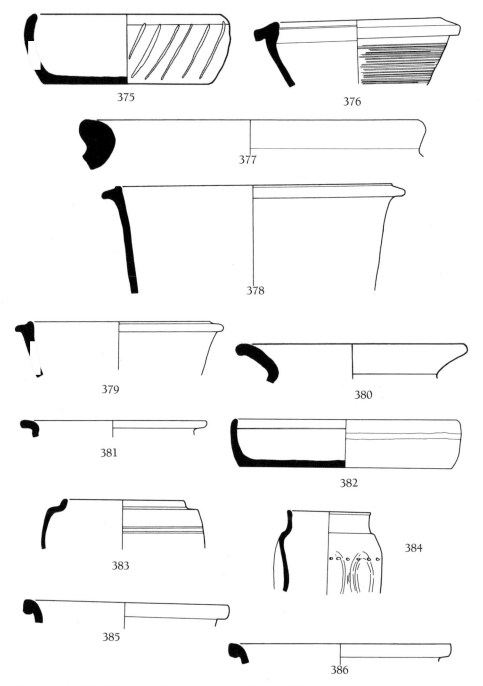

Figure 138. **375.** Fabric 14, Black Burnished Ware 1. A88. **376.** Fabric 33, South Midland Shell-gritted Ware. A88. **377.** Fabric 10, Savernake Grog-tempered Ware. A91. **378–380.** Fabric 14, Black Burnished Ware 1. A91. **381.** Fabric 21, Alice Holt/Farnham Ware. A91. **382.** Fabric 26, Wessex Grog-tempered Ware. A91. **383–384.** Fabric 17, New Forest Color-coated Ware. A355, 198, 208. **385–386.** Fabric 35, Overwey Ware. A355. (1:4)

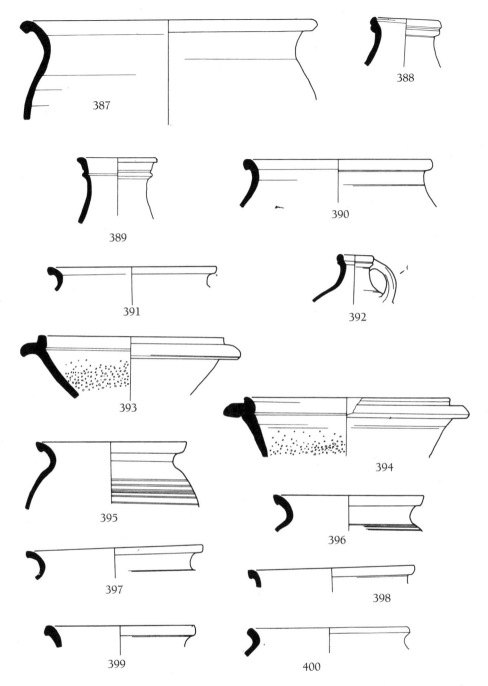

Figure 139. **387.** Fabric 10, Savernake Grog-tempered Ware. A121. **388.** Fabric 12, Savernake-type Grey Ware. A121. **389.** Fabric 19, Severn Valley Ware. A121. **390–391.** Fabric 21, Alice Holt/Farnham Ware. A121. **392.** Fabric 23, Whitehill Farm-type Ware. A121. **393.** Fabric 25, Oxfordshire Red Ware. A121. **394.** Fabric 31, Oxfordshire White Ware. A121. **395–399.** Fabric 35, Overwey Ware. A121. **400.** Fabric 12, Savernake-type Grey Ware. B123. (1:4)

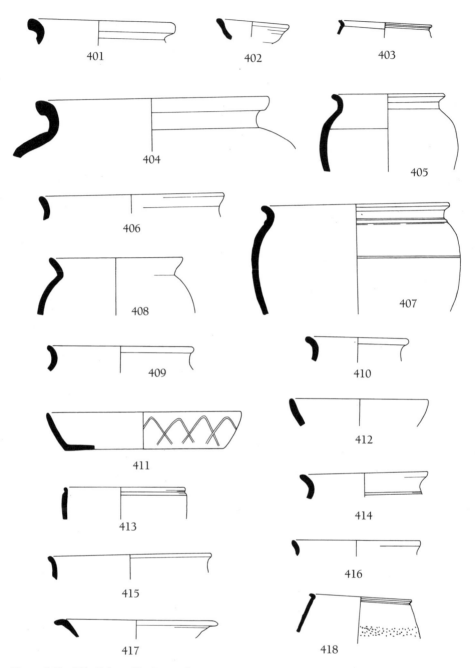

Figure 140. **401.** Fabric 12, Savernake-type Grey Ware. B113. **402.** Fabric 19, Severn Valley Ware. B113. **403.** Fabric 20, Lower Rhineland Fabric 1. B113. **404–405.** Fabric 2, Savernake Grog-tempered Ware. B98. **406.** Fabric 8, Gloucester-type Sandy Ware. B98. **407–410.** Fabric 12, Savernake-type Grey Ware. B98. **411–416.** Fabric 14, Black Burnished Ware 1. B98. **417.** Fabric 22, Ironstone-tempered Grey Ware. B98. **418.** Fabric 36, North Gaulish Fabric 2. B98. (1:4)

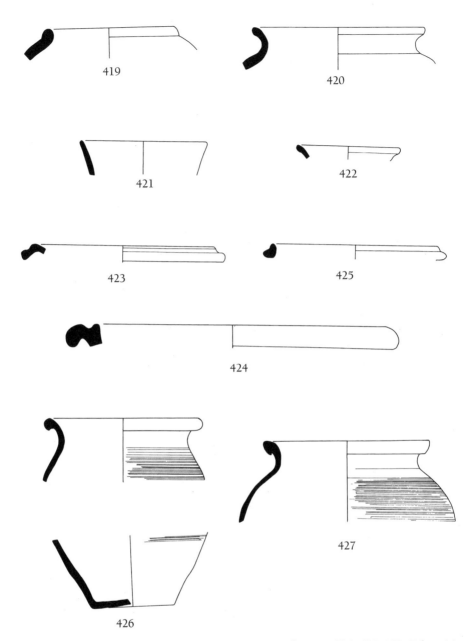

Figure 141. **419–420.** Fabric 10, Savernake Grog-tempered Ware. C37. **421–422.** Fabric 14, Black Burnished Ware 1. C37. **423–424.** Fabric 31, Oxfordshire White Ware. C37. **425.** Fabric 33, South Midland Shell-gritted Ware. C37. **426.** Fabric 33, South Midland Shell-gritted Ware. C43. **427.** Fabric 35, Overwey Ware. C43. (1:4)

4.12 GLASS VESSELS AND OBJECTS

DAVID FREDERICK GROSE

Approximately nine hundred tiny fragments of vessel and window glass were recovered from Sectors A, B, and C.[1] With few exceptions, the vessel fragments were once part of thinly-blown, undecorated domestic wares, principally drinking vessels, either bowls or beakers. The majority are naturally colored and share a distinctive, transparent green color, a hue characteristic of much of the utilitarian glass of late Roman and post-Roman date in Britain and elsewhere in transalpine Europe. Most of these vessels also display numerous spherical or elliptical bubbles and blowing spirals. A smaller percentage of the finds are from different fabrics, as is suggested by their colors: some are greenish-yellow, pale olive, or light yellow; a few are colorless (**433–434, 439**) (Fig. 142), the result of antimony and/or manganese added during manufacture to neutralize the effects of iron and other oxides present in the sand of the batch; and several, including **429** (the rim of a Roman prismatic bottle) (Fig. 142), are natural bluish-green, the color associated with much of the blown glass of the first century A.D. Finely made or decorated pieces are surprisingly absent, given the architectural evidence for the villa's prosperity in late Roman times, but two fragmentary facet-cut bowls (**437–438**) were discovered in late Imperial contexts. Also, from the period before the establishment of the villa, is a body sherd of a cast, polychrome mosaic ribbed bowl (**428**), a find that helps corroborate the suspicion that the Roman army may have briefly fortified the site following Vespasian's advance into Wiltshire or, more likely, that a native settlement existed at Castle Copse during the first century. Among the finds there are no discernible examples of palm cups, conical and bag beakers, or other vessels typical of the early Anglo-Saxon and Frankish glass industries.

Considering the damp climate of the region, the glass finds are in unusually good condition, with little evidence of iridescence, pitting, and other weathering products. Several remelted and deformed fragments (unpublished) are the result of accidental exposure to intense heat and are not evidence for glassmaking on the site.

Although none of the glass was recovered from closely dated deposits, the diagnostic fragments (almost entirely rims), supported by the pottery, numismatic, and general stratigraphic evidence, suggest two broad periods that saw glass in use at the site. The earlier belongs to the mid- to late first century A.D.; the later, to the third through fifth centuries A.D., roughly coincident with the principal occupational phase of the courtyard villa. The window glass (**440–442**) can also be attributed to the later period.

Early Imperial Cast Vessels (Fig. 142)[2]

The earliest dated vessel is a fragment of the side and bottom of a medium-sized mosaic ribbed bowl in a marbled pattern with opaque white rods set in a purple ground (**428**). Such vessels were manufactured by fusing scores of small, disk-shaped sections cut from mosaic canes into a flat circular blank, which, in a second stage of production, was sagged over a hemispherical "former mold" to achieve the shape of a bowl.[3] During manufacture the softened cane sections flowed together, thereby distorting the white rods and creating the appearance of random veining or marbling. The intent was to imitate semi-precious bowls laboriously cut from banded agate or other variegated stones.

Mosaic ribbed bowls constitute their own class of early Imperial Roman glass and, together with fifteen other classes of cast monochrome or mosaic vessels, represent much of the earliest production of the Romano-Italian glass industry of the Augustan and Julio-Claudian periods.[4] Closely related to the mosaic ribbed bowls are the far more numerous monochrome colored, natural colored, and decolorized ribbed and pillar-molded bowls that are found in profusion on almost all Mediterranean and western European archaeological sites. Whereas the manufacture of mosaic ribbed bowls is confined to the Augustan through Neronian eras, the monochrome versions continued in circulation (at least in the provinces of the Roman West) until the close of the first century, or even a little later.

In Britain, mosaic ribbed bowls, like all other classes of Roman mosaic glass, first occur in Claudian and Neronian levels, obviously the result of the Plautian conquest of the island. On Italian, Gallic, and German sites, however, they first appear in late Augustan and Tiberian strata, indicative of when the class was first devised. Their close association with legionary encampments, whether Camulodunum in Britain, Magdalensberg in Austria, Vindonissa in Switzerland, or Valkenburg in Holland, suggests that the Roman army or its suppliers, whether official or unofficial, were initially responsible for their wide dissemination outside Italy.[5] On the other hand, mosaic ribbed bowls were also sold, traded, or presented as gifts to the local populations, both within and beyond the frontiers of the empire.[6] In Britain the following military, urban, and rural sites have reported examples of mosaic ribbed bowls: Camulodunum, Wroxeter, Richborough, Caerleon, Fishbourne, Southwark, Leicester, Stanwick (unpublished), Greenhithe (Kent), Kingsholm (Gloucestershire), Brandon Camp (Herefordshire), Radnage (Buckinghamshire), Whitton (South Glamorgan), Dinas Powis (South Glamorgan), and Traprain Law (Scotland), in addition to Castle Copse.[7]

428. Fragment bowl. B1:XI.
Th.=0.003.
Fragment of lower side and bottom of medium-sized mosaic ribbed bowl. Purple ground with opaque white rods. Convex curving side; slightly concave bottom. On the exterior, the lower ends of two narrow ribs extend to the junction of the side and bottom. Cast from sections of mosaic cane; rotary-polished on the interior, fire-polished on the exterior.

Early Imperial Blown Vessels (Fig. 142)

Following the invention of the blowpipe and related inflation technology toward the close of the first century B.C., the nascent Roman glass industry quickly adopted the new technique to mass-produce glass tablewares and storage wares.[8] Among the most common classes to emerge in the mid-first century A.D. was the mold-blown prismatic bottle, which in section might be square, hexagonal, cylindrical, or multi-sided.[9] Roman prismatic bottles became a hallmark of the Flavian glass industry in Italy and in the provinces of the western Mediterranean. Especially common are square bottles in a natural bluish-green fabric, with applied hip-handles on the shoulder and rim, and geometric patterns or raised inscriptions on their bottoms. On occasion they were reused in the early Imperial period as cinerary urns. The example at Castle Copse (430) belongs in all likelihood to such a bottle. Its profile, natural color, and thick walls further identify it as a mold-blown bottle of the second half of the first century. Possibly from the same period is 431, a greenish-yellow two-handled jar with a rounded body.[10] Although jars of comparable shape continue to be made in the second and third centuries, the fabric and context of this piece suggest an earlier date.

429. Fragment jug or bottle. B12:X.

D.=0.060; Th.=0.005.

Fragment or rim, neck, and shoulder of large jug or prismatic bottle. Natural bluish-green. Solid, downward sloping rim, triangular in cross section; cylindrical neck; almost horizontal shoulder. Thick-walled. Blown and tooled; body possibly blown in a mold.

430. Fragment jug or jar. A9:XIII

H. handle=0.097; W. handle=0.025; Th. body=0.002

Fragment of body and most of handle of a jug, or more likely, a two-handled jar. Natural greenish-yellow. Rounded convex upper body; tall, three-ribbed strap handle attached to the upper body and rim; the handle arches above the level of the rim. Blown and tooled.

Early to Late Imperial Undecorated Blown Vessels (Fig. 142)

Undecorated bowls and beakers, either naturally colored or colorless, comprise the bulk of the identifiable glass present at Castle Copse. Although relatively few of the tiny fragments from the site are sufficiently large to permit their reconstruction, (431–437) suggest the varieties of utilitarian tablewares once present at the site. They range from medium-sized bowls with tubular rims of a sort manufactured from the first through fifth centuries (431), to broad shallow bowls (432) and smaller beakers (435–437) with offset rims, which were ubiquitous in Britain and the western provinces in late Imperial times.[11] Also found are colorless beakers with fire-polished rims (433) and the base of a naturally colored conical beaker or lamp of the fourth or fifth century (437).[12]

431. Fragment bowl. C33:III

D.=c. 0.016; A. Th.=0.002

Fragment of rim and side of medium-sized bowl; natural bluish-green. Upright tubular rim, folded outward and downward; convex curving side. Blown and tooled.

432. Fragment bowl. A287:IX

D.=c. 0.150; A. Th.=0.002

Fragment of rim and side of medium-sized bowl; colorless. Offset rim; convex curving side. Blown; polished at the rim.

433. Fragments beaker. B58:X

D.=c. 0.110; A. Th.=0.001

Seven joining and nonjoining fragments of beaker; colorless and free of bubbles. Solid, thickened rim; convex curving side. Blown and tooled.

434. Fragments beaker. A101:XIII (not illustrated)

D.=c. 0.100; A. Th.=0.002

Two nonjoining fragments of rim and side of beaker; colorless with slight greenish tinge. Slightly offset rim; nearly straight side, tapering downward. Blown; polished on the top and outside of the rim.

435. Fragment beaker. A1:XV (not illustrated)

D.=c. 0.090; A. Th.=0.002

Fragment of rim and side of beaker; natural yellowish-green with blowing spirals. Slightly offset rim; nearly straight side, tapering downward. Blown; polished on the top and outside of the rim.

436. Fragment beaker. A1:XV

D.=c. 0.090; A. Th.=0.001

Fragment of rim and side of beaker; natural light green with tiny bubbles. Slightly offset rim; nearly straight side, tapering downward. Blown; polished on the top and outside of the rim.

437. Fragment beaker or lamp. A35:XV

D. bottom=0.030; A. Th.=0.003

Fragment of side and bottom of small beaker or conical lamp; natural bluish-green, possibly incompletely decolorized. Straight side, tapering downward to a right-angled basal curve; pointed concave bottom.

Late Imperial Decorated Blown Vessels (Fig. 142)

Two fragmentary faceted and cut beakers in good colorless glass (**438–439**) are perhaps the finest glass objects recovered from the excavations at Castle Copse. Both are representative of a large class of drinking vessels in widespread use throughout the transalpine provinces in the first half of the century.[13] All share the same bulbous-to-spherical form and have slightly out-splayed rims that were knocked off the blowpipe, then lightly ground to smooth the rough edges.[14] Bottoms are uniformly convex, but often have a single circular facet on the underside that serves as a stable resting surface. Walls are fairly thick, to accommodate the needs of the cutter, and the fabrics are carefully decolorized in order to enhance the visual effect of the faceting. On the exterior, the decoration is disposed in four or five horizontal zones reaching from the shoulder to the bottom, usually with a single pattern of cuts repeated in a symmetrical fashion in each zone. Typical patterns include rows of circular, oval, or grain-shaped facets; straight horizontal or vertical strokes forming a diamond or an "I" motif; or shallow crosshatching. Although two pieces rarely enjoy identical decoration, all share sufficient elements in common to identify these beakers as part of a single class, at least conceptually.

In Britain comparable cut beakers have been found at many sites, including London, York, Wroxeter, Richborough, Silchester, Canterbury, Lullingstone (Kent), Abingdon (Oxfordshire), and above all, Verulamium, where six were discovered in the cellar of Building XIV in contexts dated from A.D. 280–315 or 300–315.[15] Similar dates in the early to mid-third century are assigned the many examples known from Cologne, where Fremersdorf believes the class to have been manufactured,[16] and to an equally large group found on the military camps of Aquincum, Intercisa, and Brigetio in Pannonia.[17] Further afield are additional colorless cut beakers of this general type found at Dura Europos, also in levels that must date before the abandonment of the site in A.D. 256.[18] Given the wide distribution of these beakers, a single center of production is unlikely. Rather, it would appear that factories and/or glass cutters at several centers were responsible for the class and its variants.[19]

438. Fragment beaker. B52:X

D.=c. 0.110; A. Th.=0.250

Fragment of rim and side of bulbous beaker; colorless with a slight yellow-green tinge. Slightly outsplayed rim, knocked off and ground smooth; convex curving side. On the exterior, three partly preserved horizontal registers of grain-shaped facets, short straight cuts, and crosshatching. In the uppermost register below the rim are two parallel rows of exceedingly narrow grain-shaped facets flanking a central row of broad grain-shaped facets, all set end to end; below, a register of broad, intersecting straight strokes forming contiguous diamond-shaped areas, within which is shallow crosshatching; above and below the diamonds are broad grain-shaped facets set end-to-end; below this, a register of broad, grain-shaped facets set vertically and alternating with narrow grain-shaped facets, also disposed vertically. Blown and cut; polished on the interior and also on the top and outside of the rim.

439. Fragment beaker (?). A101:XV

Small fragment of side near rim of beaker or other vessel; colorless. Slightly outsplayed rim; convex curving side. On the exterior, four parallel horizontal rows of grain-shaped facets set end-to-end; two rows are composed of exceedingly narrow facets, two of broad facets. Blown and cut. This fragment may be part of the same vessel as **438**.

Imperial Window Glass

Over half of the glass finds at Castle Copse were once part of windowpanes or quarrels used in the various rooms of the courtyard villa. All examples are of the common matte/glossy variety and occur in a light green, bubbly fabric, indicative of regional man-ufacture in the third through fifth centuries.[20] While no example preserves a finished edge longer than 7.5 cm, the panes appear to have been rectangular units of much larger size. Window glass was the invention of the Romano-Italian glass industry at the close of the first century B.C./early first century A.D., and its initial function was to provide bath complexes with the means of admitting light, while conserving heat. In the colder climate of the transalpine regions, window glass was used for general glazing purposes in public buildings and domestic quarters. It is commonly found on Romano-British sites.[21]

440. Fragments windowpane. A121:XI/XII

Max. L=0.073; Max. W.=0.041; A. Th. edge=0.003; A. Th.=pane 0.002

Eighty-two joining and nonjoining fragments of a pane, with one beveled edge preserved; natural light green. Numerous small bubbles. Uneven, shiny upper surface; flat, matte underside with numerous striations.

441. Fragment windowpane. A69:XI

Max. L.=0.059; Max. W.=0.042; A. Th. edge=0.005; A. Th. pane=0.002

One fragment of a pane with one beveled edge preserved; natural light green. Numerous oval bubbles with stress marks. Uneven, shiny upper surface; flat, matte underside. Tooling mark along beveled edge.

442. Fragments pane. A35:XV

Max. L.=0.075; Max. W.=0.047; A. Th.=0.003

Five nonjoining fragments of a pane; natural light green. Numerous tiny bubbles and striations. Uneven, shiny upper surface; flat, matte underside. One grozed edge preserved.

NOTES

1. I wish to thank E. Hostetter for inviting me to publish the glass from Castle Copse and to acknowledge gratefully the assistance and offprints provided by J. Price, Durham University. Finally, I wish to acknowledge my debt to J. P. Gillam, University of Newcastle upon Tyne, and G. Webster, Cambridge University, who many years ago introduced me to the history and archaeology of Roman Britain while I spent a year of study in Britain on a Fulbright-Hays Fellowship.

2. In this glass catalogue, L., W., and H. represent preserved dimensions, and D. the estimated diameter. Th. represents thickness, and A. Th. represents average thickness.

3. On the proposed technique of manufacturing mosaic ribbed bowls, see the discussion and illustrations in Grose 1989: 31–33 and 244–49; also Cummings 1980: 26–29.

4. For the early history of the Romano-Italian glass industry and the various families and classes of cast tablewares, both monochrome and mosaic, that it is thought to have produced, see Grose 1989: 241–62, and specifically 244–49 concerning ribbed bowls.

5. For mosaic ribbed bowls on transalpine sites, see the discussion with references in Czurda–Ruth 1979: 26–28; Berger 1960: 9–18; and van Lith 1979: 12.

6. Price and Cool 1985: 41–42; and Price 1981: 152.

7. See citations in Price and Cool 1985; and Price 1981: note 5; also in Harden 1947: no. 18; Harden 1963: 178; and Charlesworth and Price 1987: 220.

8. On the invention of the blowpipe and the proliferation of glassblowing in the Roman world, see Grose 1977: 9–29; and Grose 1984: 25–34, especially 32–34.

9. On Roman prismatic bottles, see Isings 1957: 63–67 (Form 50); Charlesworth 1966: 26–40; and Charlesworth 1972: 200–202, where it is noted that their period of greatest use was between A.D. 70–120, but that they first occur on Italian and continental sites a decade earlier. In fact, small mold-blown prismatic bottles are present at Cosa (Italy) in contexts as early as A.D. 40–45; see Grose 1974: nos. 35–39, 45–47, and 51.

10. Isings 1957: 32–34 (Form 15).

11. See examples and citations in Charlesworth 1972: 210–212, where additional pieces from Silchester, Wroxeter, Corbridge, Traprain Law, and the Rhineland are noted. Still others are discussed by Price 1979: 43–44; and Price 1983, which mentions beakers with similar rims from Portchester, Shakenoak, Caerwent, Corbridge, and the New Market Hall, Gloucester.

12. Isings 1957: 101–103 (Form 85), for colorless beakers with fire-polished rims. On the possibility that some of the beakers may in fact have been used as lamps, see Charlesworth 1972: 212.

13. Isings 1957: 113–16 (Form 96), with numerous references; Charlesworth 1972: 206 and 208–19 (beakers with zoned decoration); Fremersdorf 1967: pls. 55, 57, 60–62, 66–70; Barkoczi 1986: 166–90; and 1988: 64–66.

14. A deeper form with a true base also exists; see Charlesworth 1972: 209, no. 52.

15. Charlesworth 1972: 210, with citations to examples from other sites; Charlesworth and Price 1987: no. 12, 222, with a context of A.D. 290–320; the Abingdon reference kindly supplied, along with other information, by J. Price.

16. Fremersdorf 1967: 82–83.

17. See references in note 12.

18. Clairmont 1963: especially 70–72, pl. 26.

19. It would appear that several common styles of decorated glass in the third century were produced at multiple production centers, possibly owing to peripatetic glassmakers or glass cutters. Snake-thread and related appliqué decoration is another example.

20. On the invention and early use of window glass, see Grose 1989: 357–58.

21. Harden 1958: 39–63; Boon 1966: 41–47.

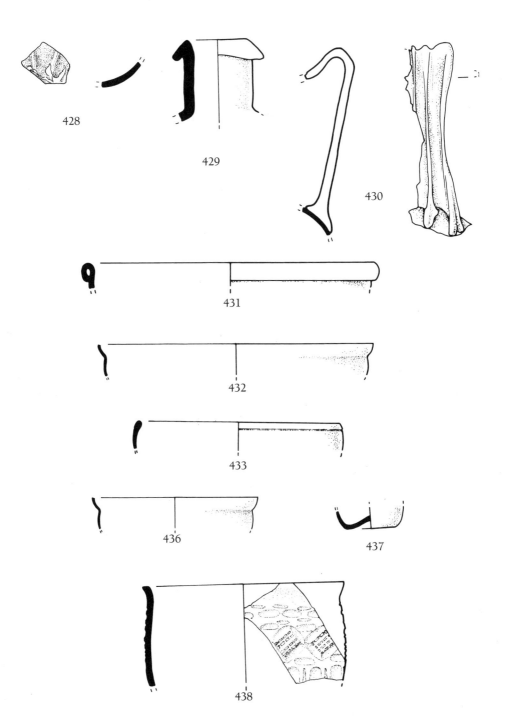

Figure 142. **428.** Fragment bowl. B1. **429.** Fragment jug or bottle. B12. **430.** Fragment jug or jar. A9. **431.** Fragment bowl. C33. **432.** Fragment bowl. A287. **433.** Fragments beaker. B58. **436.** Fragment beaker. A1. **437.** Fragment beaker or lamp. A35. **438.** Fragment beaker. B52. (1:2)

4.13 BEADS

MARGARET GUIDO

The presence of one native Iron Age bead (**443**) might suggest that the occupation of the villa began in earlier Roman times, even if it was a survival out of context. The remaining beads are fairly common late Roman types.[1]

Eight beads were recovered in Sector A:

443. Large gold-green annular bead. C21:III/IV (Fig. 143)

D.=0.021; Th.=0.009

Possibly Iron Age from nearby Chisbury.[2] This bead has been tested, and Dr. Julian Henderson reports that the analysis is consistent with an Iron Age date.[3]

444. Fragmentary turquoise green translucent segmented bead.

A415:XI (Fig. 143)

D.=0.005

Probably fourth–fifth century A.D.

445. Small green biconical bead. A400:XI (Fig. 143)

D.=0.005; H.=0.003

Very common late Roman type lasting into fifth century.

446. Green bead (?). A257:XI (Fig. 143)

D.=0.003; L.=0.003

Originally almost surely part of a translucent green segmented bead (as **445**).

447. Emerald crystal bead. A22:XIII (Fig. 143)

D.=0.010; L.=c. 0.008

The hexagonal shape is natural, and it has been skillfully bored. It is not possible to date closely. This stone was much valued in the Roman period, and was regarded as having talismanic and medicinal properties. Possibly from India. It suggests that some rich person was for a time living in the villa.

448. Two wound semi-translucent bluish green bead(s). A222:XI (Fig. 143)

Bead A: D.=0.004; L.=0.004. Bead B: D.=0.003; L.=0.004

These two beads may once have joined and so made a segmented bead. Likely date A.D. 350–450.

449. Metal-in-glass bead. A437:XI (Fig. 143)

D.=0.002; H.=0.002

May have originally been a segmented bead from which this one element may have broken off. These occur throughout the Roman period, but the great majority of them belong to the sixth century A.D.

450. Cylinder segment. A437:XI (Fig. 143)

D.=0.005; H.=0.003

Green, nearly opaque glass bead. Perhaps imitating emerald. Probably late fourth–fifth century A.D.

Four beads are from Sector B:

451. Translucent mid-blue, square-sectioned bead. B9:X (Figure 143)

D=0.003; L.=0.005

Probably fourth century A.D. or slightly later.

452. Semi-translucent, greenish, long oval wound bead. B117:VIII (Fig. 143)

D.=0.004; L.=0.013

Probably late Roman.

453. Globular bead, originally segmented "black" glass. B117:VIII (Fig. 143)

D.=0.003; L.=0.003

Broken at collar. These generally date from the fourth–fifth centuries A.D.

454. Annular bottle glass translucent bead. B144:VI (Fig. 143)

D.=0.011; L.=0.003

Small perforation. Not closely datable.

NOTES

1. See Guido 1978: 95–100.
2. Guido 1978: 65–69, group 6.
3. At the Institute of Archaeology of Oxford.

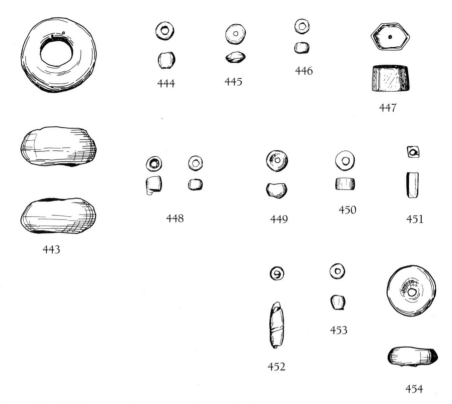

Figure 143. **443.** Large gold-green annular bead. A21. **444.** Fragmentary turquoise green translucent segmented bead A415. **445.** Small green biconical bead. A400. **446.** Green bead (?). A257. **447.** Emerald crystal bead. A22. **448.** Wound, semi-translucent, bluish green bead(s). A222. **449.** Metal-in-glass bead. A437. **450.** Green cylinder segment. A437. **451.** Translucent mid-blue, square-sectioned bead. B9. **452.** Semi-translucent, greenish oval wound bead. B117. **453.** Globular bead, segmented "black" glass. B117. **454.** Annular bottle glass bead. B144. (1:1)

4.14 OBJECTS OF STONE

MARYLINE PARCA

Relatively few objects of stone were recovered at Castle Copse. Those that were are all common pieces on Romano-British sites.

Whetstones (Fig. 144)

Five whetstones were recovered. With the exception of **455**, all are probably late Roman in date. It is of interest that three (**456–459**) were recovered in the villa west wing, the more luxurious area of the villa.

455. Whetstone. C5:I

    L.=0.058; W.=0.018–0.012/0.013; Th.=0.014

    Fragmentary elongated sandstone, broken at thick end. Grey with rust stains. Worn.

    From the fill of an early ditch in Sector C which contained pottery dating to A.D. 50–70, this piece probably dates to the first century A.D.

456. Whetstone. A207:XI

    L.=0.048; W.=0.021–0.019; Th.=0.010–0.009

    Broken sandstone, slightly tapering. Bluish grey with white flecks and veins. Well worn.

457. Whetstone. B83:V.

    L.=0.092; W.=0.019 (tapering to 0.014); Th.=0.009

    Broken sandstone in three fragments, grey with white flecks and rust stains. Well worn.

458. Whetstone. B121:VIII. (not illustrated)

    L.=0.043; W.=0.043; Th.=0.011

    Trapezoidal greyish brown and grainy sandstone, whose shape may have been derived from natural form. Heavily abraded.

459. Whetstone (?) B52:X

    L.=0.052; W.=0.047–0.042; Th.=0.010

    Fragmentary trapezoidal grey sandstone with white flecks and veins. Well worn, with rounded edges.

Objects of Shale (Fig. 144)

One spindle whorl, two bracelet fragments, one possible bracelet fragment, and one amorphous fragment were recovered.

460. Spindle whorl. C21:III/IV

D.=0.029; H.=0.022; D. hole=0.010–0.011

Squat tapering cylindrical form, flattish on top and bottom and hole in middle. Two faint parallel lines around middle.

From the "service" south wing of the villa, the shale spindle whorl is probably late Roman, although it was recovered in the same context as the residual Late Iron Age bead **445**.

461. Fragment bracelet. A69:XI

L.=0.051; H.=0.006; Th.=0.003

Curved fragment shale, squarish in section with outer edge rounded, inner more faceted. Estimated diameter of complete bracelet is c. 0.060.

Recovered from the backfill of the hypocaust of phase A:XI, the bracelet is late Roman.

462. Fragment bracelet. A278:X/XI

Curved fragment shale, subrectangular in section. Late Roman.

L.=0.019; H.=0.007; Th.=0.004

463. Fragment bracelet (?). C5:VI

L.=0.021; H.=0.006; Th.=0.002

Probable fragment bracelet.

464. Fragment shale. A473:V

L.=0.032; W.=0.026; Th.=0.004

Roughly triangular fragment with one worked facet. Recovered from the fill of a posthole of phase A473, the piece dates after A.D. 198.

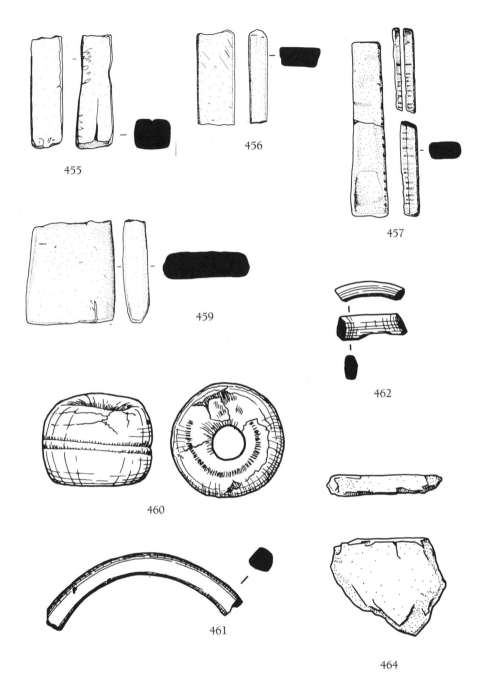

Figure 144. **455–457, 459**. Whetstones. C5, A207, B83, 52. (1:2) **460**. Shale spindle whorl. C21. (1:1) **461–462**. Shale bracelets. A69, 278. **464**. (1:1) Fragment with worked facet. A473. (1:1)

4.15 BONE AND ANTLER OBJECTS

ROSEMARY J. PAYNE

Combs (Fig. 145)

465. Composite double-sided antler comb. C43:IV
L.=(0.111); W.=(0.070); Th. end plate=0.0035; total Th.=0.0090
Estimated original L. at c. 0.145, original W. at 0.090[1]

Most of a composite, double-sided antler comb with two widely spaced pairs of flat connecting plates.[2] Dove-tailed between each pair of connecting plates is a thin pierced strip of antler, displaying a sheet of metal through the holes. At each end the pierced strips are held in position by a small rectangular piece of antler secured to the end plate by an antler peg. Only one of the end plates survives, too damaged for its original shape to be seen, but its decoration included two small round holes. There are four tooth plates (three reasonably complete, one just a fragment), two wider ones in the center flanked by narrower ones next to the end plates. There is, as usual, one row of coarse teeth and one of finer teeth. There were approximately forty-eight coarse teeth (traces of thirty-six survive) spaced 5.2 per cm, and approximately sixty-three fine teeth (traces of only thirty-one survive) spaced at 6.8 per cm. There are also a number of loose teeth which could not be joined to the plates, but which clearly belonged to this comb.

The comb is held together by ten iron rivets, five through each pair of connecting plates, evenly spaced so that the outer two pierce the end plates while the inner three are precisely on the junctions between the tooth plates, presumably to reduce the risk of splitting the plates. This even spacing provides four panels on each connecting plate for decoration. Each panel has a pair of vertical parallel lines at each end, with a diagonal cross between them, again made of pairs of parallel lines. Unusually, the connecting plates are flat; they are stepped around the outer edges.

The thin strips of antler dovetailed between the pairs of connecting plates are pierced by thirty-two neat round holes, four sets of four of which have been joined to form cruciforms. Sandwiched between each pierced strip and the solid zones of the tooth plates is a sheet of lead-tin alloy.[3] When the comb was new the metal would have shone like silver through the holes. The pegged rectangles which hold the ends of the pierced strips have oblique inner edges as if for dovetailing, although the ends of the pierced strips themselves are cut straight, so that the pegged pieces merely prevent them from moving lengthwise. They are flat on top, stepped to match the connecting plates, and decorated with parallel incised lines.

The comb was recovered, together with South Midland Shell-gritted Ware and Overwey Ware, in the fill (C43:IV) of a pit deriving from late occupation in Sector C.

Bibliography: R. Payne 1989: 101–102, no. 62.

466. End Plate fragment. C43:IV

L.=0.017; W.=0.009; Th.=0.003

Small fragment of the outer corner of the end plate of a composite comb, and fragments of fifteen fine teeth, all with tips burnt black. The end plate fragment preserves a small section of original edge, decoratively curved as is common in Roman combs, but it is too small a piece to allow any useful reconstruction.

This is probably not part of the same comb as **465**, although it came from the same stratigraphic unit (C43). It is noticeably thinner (less than 0.003 as against 0.0035), the unburnt parts are a noticeably different color, and there is no trace of burning on **465**.

Double-sided antler combs were common in the northern provinces of the Roman empire, particularly in the late third and fourth centuries A.D., but they are normally much simpler, with only one pair of connecting plates.[4] Only seven Roman combs with two pairs of connecting plates, all from the late fourth century, are known to this writer: from Beadlam[5] and Langton[6] Roman villas in Yorkshire, from Altenstadt[7] and from Jakobwüllesheim[8] in Germany, from Steinfort[9] in Luxembourg, and from Vermand and Abbeville in France.[10] On all seven of these combs the pairs of connecting plates are widely spaced and the solid zones of the tooth plates are decoratively pierced; the Beadlam, Jakobwüllesheim, and Steinfort combs are so closely similar that it has been suggested that they came from the same workshop, if not the same craftsman.[11] The Altenstadt comb has linked circles forming cruciforms on this central portion, very like the pattern on the central strips of the Castle Copse comb. The drawings of the French combs suggest that they have frames around the central sections, with separate end pieces similar to the Castle Copse pegged rectangles, but it is not clear from the drawings whether they also have separate central strips. In no case is there any mention of a sheet of metal.

The use of metal revealed through decoratively pierced bone or antler from the Roman period is unknown to the author, but in the early Middle Ages the technique was used occasionally on caskets and on some composite combs, mostly from Scandinavia (e.g., medieval Tommarp),[12] but also one from York.[13] Five loose teeth of the comb were therefore directly dated by the Oxford Laboratory by accelerator radiocarbon dating (see Appendix 7). The result was a date of 1690±80 (OxA–1353), which, when calibrated, gives a date range at 2ς (95% confidence) of c. A.D. 135–545. This confirms the late Roman stratigraphic date given to the comb, and its place among the small group of unusually elaborate double-sided combs of the late fourth century.

Sword Hilt Guard (Fig. 145)

467. Sword Hilt Guard. A121:XI/XII

L.=0.077; W.=0.036; Th.=0.021; L. slot (hilt side)=0.027; L. slot (blade side) =0.057; Th. slot=0.008

The guard, which is complete, is a flattened ellipse of solid antler, with a slot cut through from one flat surface to the other shaped to fit the shoulder of the sword, sloping from the broad blade to the narrow tang. The shape of the slot on the hilt side, with a narrower portion at each end, indicates a flat, rectangular tang with a small flange on each edge. The guard is well polished and used, though the original marks of manufacture (by grinding) are still visible in places. The only decoration is a groove round the outer surface close to the flat (sword) side, lost at one end of the ellipse where the antler is more cancellous.

Bone or antler hilt guards are known from Romano-British sites, but they are not common. Greep lists nine;[14] the only close parallel comes from Caister-by-Norwich.[15] It also is made of antler (the others being of bone or ivory), and is a flattened ellipse of similar size, though the ends of the ellipse are more pointed, and the slot for the tang is shorter and broader, particularly on the hilt side. It is similarly decorated, having two grooves round the outer surfaces, close to the edges. The Caistor hilt guard was a surface find and is thought to be late Roman rather than from the Saxon cemetery.

Hair or Fastening Pins (Fig. 146)

The pin typologies follow those of Crummy.[16]

468. Pin. B52:X

L.=(0.038); D.=0.003

Complete head and part of shaft. Conical head, with two grooves just below it, the lower groove not quite meeting accurately. Broken shaft, tapering slightly from maximum diameter at head. Lightly polished.

Crummy, Type 2.

469. Pin. B141:VI

L.=(0.027); D.=0.003

Complete head and part of shaft. Conical head, with two fine grooves below it, the upper groove not quite meeting accurately. Broken shaft, tapering slightly from maximum diameter at head. Lightly polished.

Crummy, Type 2.

470. Pin. B116: VI

L.=(0.044); D.=0.006

Chipped head and part of shaft. The head was probably conical, with two grooves below it, each forming a complete ring. Broken shaft, tapering from maximum diameter at head. Lightly polished.

Probably Crummy, Type 2.

471. Pin. C40:III

L.=(0.043); D. head=0.007; D. shaft=0.003;

Complete head and part of shaft. Conical head, with a single reel. Broken shaft, much narrower than head, swelling slightly to maximum diameter at the break.

Crummy, Type 5.

472. Pin. B144:VI

L.=(0.061); D.=0.003

Two joining shaft fragments, round in section, tapering gently. Lightly polished.

473. Pin. B144:VI

L.=(0.043); D.=(0.003)

Shaft fragment, round in section, tapering gently. Lightly polished.

These long, slender pins are commonly found on Roman sites; they were probably used as hair pins or to fasten clothing. Their heads vary from plain flat or conical to highly decorated, and frequently have the grooves seen on the Castle Copse examples. Their shafts are round in section, and either taper slightly from the head or swell gently in the middle of the shaft. Crummy has established a bone pin typology based mainly on 342 pins from Colchester.[17] Of the four pins from the villa which still have most of the head, two (**468–469**) and probably a third (**470**) fall into Crummy's Type 2, which is common at Colchester (sixty-three examples), but absent from the later site of Portchester. Crummy dates this type from c. 50 to c. 200 A.D. The fourth headed pin (**471**) from Castle Copse belongs with Crummy's Type 5, which she dates to the fourth century A.D. The three pins of the earlier type all come from Sector B, Phases B:VI and X (occupation of the courtyard associated with the late Roman building or later), whereas the example of the later type comes from Sector C, phase B:III (early use of the masonry building, fourth century A.D.).

Handles

474. Handle. A69:XI

L.=0.101; W.=0.022

Complete, made from a sheep metatarsal. The distal epiphysis is only just fused, the line of fusion being clearly visible. Cylindrical hole pierced from front to back though each condyle. The proximal end of the bone has been cut off, and the cut end of the shaft ground flat. The outside of the shaft has been slightly shaped with long facets from the cut end and has a definitely used appearance, but the medullary canal shows no sign of the wear one would expect if a metal tool had been inserted into the bone; even traces of the residual lamella between the third and fourth metatarsals are still clearly visible.

A number of metapodials pierced at the distal end and with the shaft cut straight across have been found from Roman sites; they are commonly decorated with ring and dot patterns as at Bourton on the Water[18] and Richborough.[19] Undecorated handles of this type may be more common then they appear from the literature, as they are more easily missed during excavation; the Castle Copse example was not recognized in the trench, but found in the bone batch. A closely similar undecorated handle from the Lankhills cemetery[20] has a tang (probably of a knife) in the shaft and several have iron stains, but none has been found with the complete tool in place. They should not be confused with the more common "spindles," which are also made from sheep or goat metapodials, but use the proximal end of the bone, and are pierced across the middle of the shaft and often longitudinally through the articulation of the bone as well.[21]

475. Handle. B144:VI

L.=(0.045); W. at shoulder=0.010; Th.=0.005

Part of a handle, probably made from antler, drilled lengthwise to hold tang of a metal tool. Split in half along drilled hole and broken across its length, so only one corner survives. Unbroken end has a sharply projected shoulder; sub-rectangular in section. The surface is decorated with grooves along the whole length, continuing across the top of the shoulder. The tang hole is stained with iron for only about 0.030 m from the shouldered end, which is therefore likely to be the tool end of the handle, the shoulder acting as a thumbrest or guard.

A single piece of bone, drilled to hold a tang, was frequently used for the handle of a small knife or other metal tool. Longitudinal grooving is not a very common form of decoration. It is found on "spring clip" knives[22] (but the Castle Copse example lacks the characteristic waist that holds the clip), and on a larger subrectangular handle, also made of antler, from Langton Roman villa in Yorkshire,[23] which also spreads at one end, though into a less marked shoulder than the Castle Copse piece.

Counters (Fig. 146)

476. Counter. A221:XI

    D.=0.014; Th.=0.006

Complete but battered. Small piece of long bone roughly shaped to a disc; one side retains natural surface, the other has two lathe-turned rings grooved around a central dot, but the counter has been shaped by rough faceting of the edges so that the rings are not centrally placed on finished object.

477. Counter. A69:XI

    D.=0.016; Th.=0.005

Very battered and partly burned. Very similar to **476**, but a little larger and thinner.

Gaming counters are commonly found on Roman sites (e.g., York),[24] and these two fit easily into Type 2 of Kenyon's typology from Jewry Wall Leicester,[25] although they are more crudely made than many, and slightly smaller and thicker.

Pin Beaters (Fig. 146)

478. Pin beater. B7:X

    L.=0.127; W.=0.009; Th.=0.008

Complete. From a strip of long bone worked to a sharp point at one end and a blunter tip at the other, the point of maximum width being closer to the blunt end. Section varies from nearly round to subrectangular. Grinding marks from manufacture just visible in facets on the well-polished surface.

479. Pin beater. A35:XV

    L.=(0.080); W.=0.011

One end broken; made from a strip of long bone tapering from broken end to stout sharp point. Section is close to round near tip, but retains natural concavo-convex shape at broken end. Grinding marks visible under polished surface.

A number of these cigar-shaped pin beaters are known from Romano-British sites, but not from well-dated contexts. Continental ones are, however, more securely dated,[26] and there is no real reason to doubt their Roman provenance, although the type is more commonly found on Saxon sites. It is generally accepted that they were used as weaving tools to press down the weft or pick up individual threads, and some, but not the Castle Copse examples, have the transverse wear grooves that would be likely to result from prolonged use of this sort.

Weaving Tablet

480. Weaving tablet. B5:XI (Fig. 147)

L.=(0.026); W.=(0.013); Th.=0.002

Corner fragment only of a thin flat triangle, broken through a hole pierced equidistant from the two original sides.

Thin, flat triangular or square pieces of bone, with a hole close to each corner, were used for weaving narrow braids. They usually have rays grooved around each hole, caused by the wear from the threads, but the Castle Copse piece lacks these marks.

Furniture or Casket Inlay Mounts (Fig. 147)

481. Seven mounts. A191:XI.

	L.	W.	Th.
a.	0.025	0.009	0.001
b.	0.025	(0.010)	0.002
c.	0.020	0.009	0.001
d.	0.018	0.010	0.001
e.	0.034	(0.010)	0.002
f.	0.021	0.011	0.001
g	(0.044)	0.015	0.002

Seven narrow, flat, trapezoidal strips made from ribs, recovered from both trowelling and wet- and dry-sieving. **a**, **e** and **f** are complete; **c** has one corner chipped; and **b** and **d** are each broken along one long edge. Decoration: **a–e**—two parallel lines close to the long edges. **f**—three parallel lines. **g**—two concentric rings with a central dot and two diagonal lines touching the outer ring to give a scroll effect. This piece is pierced with a small round hole, and would have been held in place with a small peg. The other pieces must have been glued.

482. Two mount fragments. A80:XI

a. L.=0.015; W.=0.014; Th.=0.002. **b.** L.=0.023; W.=0.006; Th.=0.002

Two flat fragments, both made from ribs, recovered from flotation. **a**—square, divided by grooves into four smaller squares, two of which are divided by diagonal crosses. One corner broken off along one of the diagonal grooves. **b**—narrow trapezium, complete. Two parallel lines close to long sides. Decorated side well polished.

483. Mount. B144:III

L.=0.020; W.=0.007; Th.=0.003

Leaf-shaped with ring-and-dot at widest point. Unusually thick for inlay.

484. Mount. C5:VI

L.=(0.021); W.=0.005; Th.=0.002

Very narrow strip, broken at both ends, and slightly curved. These thin, flat geometric pieces, usually cut from long, narrow, straight-sided strips (but not always; cf. **483**) and decorated with grooved lines or ring-and-dot motifs, are very common on

Roman sites. They were used to decorate caskets and furniture, particularly couches and stools.

Worked Antler (Fig. 147)

485. Fragment worked antler. C5:VI

L.=(0.073); W.=0.051; Th.=0.046

Piece of antler beam with two sawn surfaces, one removing a tine, the other cutting across the beam.

This is the only indication that bone- or antler-working may have been carried out on the villa site.

NOTES

1. In this catalogue, if an object is broken, the affected measurements are given in parentheses.

2. Terminology follows Galloway (1976), except for "tooth plate" and "end plate" for her "tooth segment." Since the Castle Copse comb is, at least at present, unique in its complexity, I have not tried to introduce more terms that could be of general application, but merely to describe the extra pieces.

3. I would like to thank Dr. J. A. Charles, Department of Metallurgy and Materials Science, Cambridge University, and Dr. J. Bayley, Ancient Monuments Laboratory, English Heritage, for analyzing samples of the metal sheet.

4. The excavation is grateful to Dr. A. MacGregor of the Ashmolean Museum for examining the comb shortly after its discovery in 1985 and alerting us to its unusual characteristics.

5. Stead 1971: fig. 10.

6. Corder and Kirk 1932: fig. 20. Fragments of only two of the four connecting plates survive on the Langton comb, both of which have swivelled through 90° on the connecting rivet. It is not clear from the illustration that it is one of this group of combs, but on examination it was obvious that there were originally four connecting plates, and that the central portion of at least the end plate was pierced. My thanks are due to P. Wiggle and the management board of Malton Museum for permission to examine the Langton comb.

7. Keller 1971: pl. 33:2.

8. Haupt 1970: pl. 31:4.

9. Haupt 1970: pl. 31:3.

10. Pilloy 1879: 177 ff.

11. Galloway and Newcomer 1981.

12. Thun 1967: fig. 28:g.

13. Waterman 1959: pl. XVIII.2.

14. Greep 1983.

15. Myres and Green 1973: 42, fig. 64:7.

16. Crummy 1979: 157–63.

17. Crummy 1979: 157–63.

18. Donovan 1934: fig. 10:7.

19. Bushe-Fox 1928: pl. XIX:31.

20. G. Clarke 1979: 251, fig. 83.

21. Wild 1970.

22. Greep 1982.

23. Corder and Kirk 1932: fig. 19:11.

24. A. MacGregor 1976: fig. 3.

25. Kenyon 1948: 266, fig. 91.

26. Wild 1970.

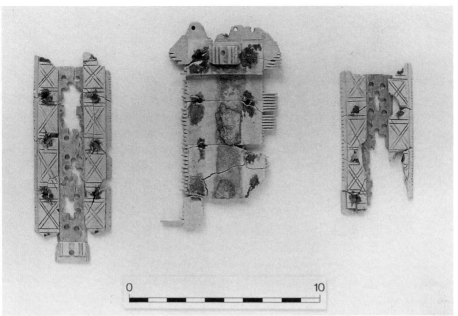

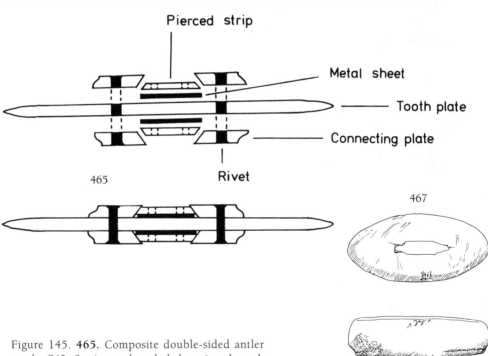

Pierced strip

Metal sheet

Tooth plate

Connecting plate

Rivet

465

467

Figure 145. **465.** Composite double-sided antler comb. C43. Section and exploded section through comb. (1:1) **467.** Sword hilt guard. A121. (1:2)

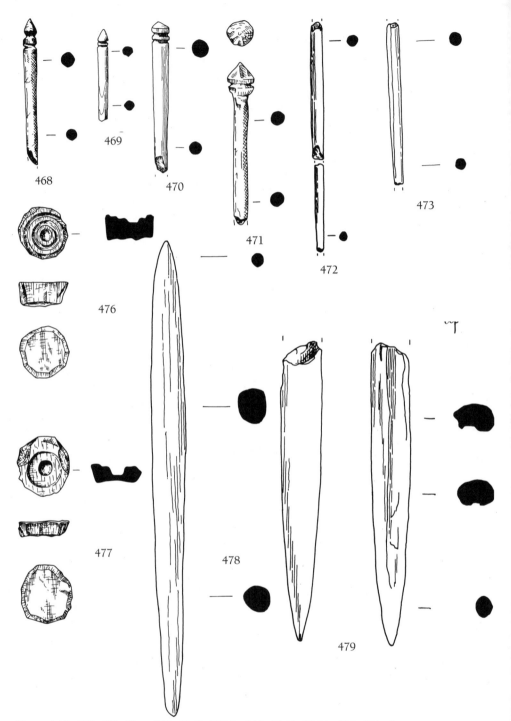

Figure 146. **468–473.** Pins. B52, B141, B116, C40, B144, B144. **476–477.** Counters. A221, A69. **478–479.** Pin beaters. B7, B35. (1:1)

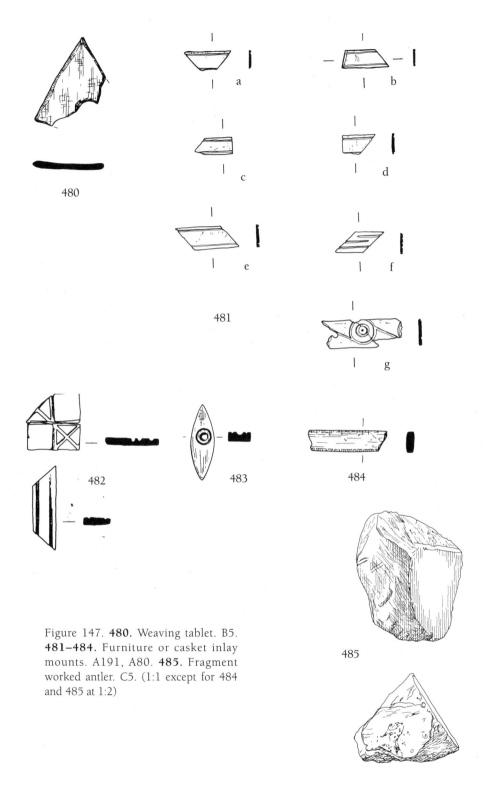

Figure 147. **480.** Weaving tablet. B5. **481–484.** Furniture or casket inlay mounts. A191, A80. **485.** Fragment worked antler. C5. (1:1 except for 484 and 485 at 1:2)

4.16 ANIMAL REMAINS

SEBASTIAN PAYNE

Introduction

A study of the animal bones[1] from a site such as Castle Copse has two main purposes. The first is to learn about hunting and stock-keeping, butchery, diet, and refuse disposal at the site, and to contribute to answering more general questions about the site's environment, status, and function. The second purpose is to record and describe the animal bone collection so as to contribute data toward broader syntheses in the future.

Animal bones were found throughout the Castle Copse excavations, but in large concentrations only in the Phase A:XI deposits within the second aisled building in Sector A. As available funding did not permit detailed study of all the animal bones, and as the assemblage from Phase A:XI appeared to be of unusual interest, we decided to concentrate first on a detailed study of this assemblage and those from the earlier phases of Sector A.

All the bones that were seen during excavation were recovered. Most of the contexts were excavated by trowelling; some were dry-sieved. In addition, earth samples, usually of around ten liters of earth but sometimes larger, were taken for water-sieving. It had originally been intended to treat the trench-recovered and water-sieved bone assemblages separately, using the water-sieved assemblage as a control for bias in the trench-recovered assemblage. This was, however, not possible because the bones from the water-sieved samples had not always been kept separate from the trench-recovered bones; and, when they had been kept separate, it seemed clear, especially from the absence of larger bones in the water-sieved bone samples, that these samples were incomplete. As a result, and as the quantities of water-sieved bones were not large, the counts and other data for trench-recovered and water-sieved bones have been combined in this report. Interpretation of the results has, therefore, to take into account that the assemblages are of trench-recovered bones, recovered to a better-than-usual standard, with the addition of a small and variable proportion of water-sieved bones.

As is usual from inland sites in Britain, the bulk of the bone was mammal bone—over 90% by weight in every phase (Table 14). The mammal bones are described below. Bird bones were relatively scarce (less than 1% by weight) in Sector A, Phases A:I–IX, increasing to an unusually high 5.4% by weight in Phase A:XI; they have been examined by Enid Allison (below). Fish bones are 0.1% by weight or less in every phase: they have been examined by Andrew Jones (below). Reptile and amphibian bones were generally very scarce, except in one context which produced a number of frog bones; they were examined by Terry O'Connor (below).

Oyster and other seashells were also common, especially in Sector A, Phase A:XI (below).

Larger Mammals

Table 15 gives a general summary of the identified larger mammal bones. As this shows, there is a considerable contrast between Phases A:I–X, in which about 40% of the identified bones are of cattle and 30% of sheep/goat, and A:XI, in which nearly 70% of the bones are of pig. Horse, red and roe deer, hare, rabbit, dog, fox, cat, badger, and a small mustelid (stoat or weasel) were also found.

SECTOR A: PHASES I–X ASSEMBLAGE

The assemblage from Sector A, Phases A:I–X is not very large—just over 200 identified bones, of which about 40% are cattle, 30% sheep/goat, and 20% pig, with a few horse, red deer, roe deer, hare, and dog bones (Table 15). The single definite rabbit bone is taken to be intrusive (below). Condition is generally moderate—-the bones are basically solid, but surfaces are often slightly battered. Two groups of sheep bones, from A942:I and A953:I, are treated separately.

More detailed information on the relative representation of the different parts of the skeleton is given in Figure 148 and Table 16, from which several points of interest emerge.

First, the proportion of teeth and jaws is relatively high. There are, for instance, thirty-six isolated cattle teeth, together with a further twenty-seven cattle teeth in jaws, in a total of ninety-seven identified bones; the thirty-nine lower molars must come from at least seven individuals, which is almost twice as many as indicated by the commonest postcranial part of the skeleton (the proximal metatarsal). Similarly the thirty-three sheep/goat lower molars indicate more individuals than any of the postcranial parts of the skeleton, and pig teeth and jaws are again relatively common. This, together with the relative scarcity of weaker parts of the skeleton, such as proximal humeri, proximal and distal femora, and proximal tibiae, suggests considerable destruction of bone.

Second, counts are, as so often, low for the smaller parts of the skeleton, suggesting loss by poor recovery: there are far fewer incisors and premolars than molars, for instance, and relatively few carpals, smaller tarsals, and phalanges.[2]

Once the effects of preservation and recovery bias have been taken into account, the data in Figure 148 and Table 16 include two features which deserve further comment:

Cattle: There are many fewer upper teeth than lower teeth: only four upper molars and premolars as compared with fifty lower molars and premolars.

Red deer: Though samples are small (but see also Phase A:XI, Table 17) the absence of teeth (and of skull and jaw fragments) is noteworthy in view of the relative abundance of teeth of cattle, sheep/goat, and pig.

SECTOR A: PHASES I–X BONE GROUPS

A942:I: Most of the skeleton of a sheep was found in A942, the fill of a small pit. The bones found include the left maxilla and mandible, a few vertebrae, the right distal humerus, the right and part of the left radius, three of the right carpals, both metacarpals, part of the right innominate, the left distal femur, the left distal tibia, the left astragalus, both naviculo-cuboids, the left metatarsal, the right distal metatarsal, and parts of at least four first phalanges, four second phalanges, and a third phalanx. Cut-marks show that this was not just a dead animal buried in a convenient pit: light cut-marks on the astragalus and both naviculo-cuboids indicate skinning (the alternative, that they suggest disarticulation, is less likely since both metatarsals are found in the pit), while heavier chop-marks on the right ischium suggest jointing and/or the removal of meat. Perhaps this was a sheep that was killed for consumption and defleshed without being disarticulated, leaving a more or less complete skeleton for disposal. The missing bones suggest either that only part of the skeleton was dumped in this pit, or that the pit contents may have been subsequently disturbed; a calcaneum, which may be from this animal, was found in A932 (also A:I).

A953:I: A partial skeleton of a second sheep was found in 953 (fill of posthole A948). Its bones include loose teeth, the axis and atlas vertebrae, parts of two more cervical vertebrae and some caudal vertebrae, the left and part of the right humerus, the right distal radius, five carpals, parts of the left femur, the right proximal and the left distal tibia, and some distal metapodial fragments. Both lower third molars and an upper first/second molar show pronounced growth arrests. Most of the bones are slightly burnt, and the left proximal humerus had several cut-marks on the trochanter major, again suggesting jointing or the removal of meat. Again, the missing bones suggest either that only part of the skeleton was dumped in this pit, or that the pit contents may have been subsequently disturbed.

Also in the same context were many of the bones of a fetal sheep/goat: these included parts of both scapulae, both humeri, both radii, an ulna, an innominate, both femora and tibiae, one calcaneum, four metapodials, and several phalanges. The size and state of development of the bones suggest that this fetus was less than a month before birth.

SECTOR A: PHASE XI ASSEMBLAGE

The assemblage from Sector A, Phase A:XI is larger than that from Phases A:I–X. There are over 1600 identified "countable" larger mammal bones (Table 15), of which nearly 70% are of pig, nearly 20% of cattle, and 7% of sheep/goat, together with small numbers of horse, red and roe deer, hare, dog, and cat. A number of rabbit bones and parts of three fox skeletons are probably intrusive (below).

Carbon–14 determinations (see Appendix 7) of a bone fragment and a pig metapodial from A77:XI (OxA 1892) and A191:XI (OxA 1893), respectively, yielded dates of 1645 ± 70 and 1780 ± 60, the calibrated (2ε) age ranges for these two dates A.D. c. 240–560 (OxA–1892) and A.D. c. 90–400 (OxA 1893) (see Appendix 7) confirming a Late Roman date for the assemblage.[3]

The condition of the bones was generally rather better than in Phases A:I–X, though still variable; and the larger numbers of smaller teeth and phalanges suggest that recovery may have been better: as the contexts concerned were inside a building, overlay mosaic floors, and were full of smaller bones, they were generally excavated relatively slowly and carefully, sometimes with dry-sieving.

The pig bones could be separated into two rather distinct groups: bones and teeth of very young piglets with deciduous premolars that are either unworn or only just entering wear, suggesting animals up to 2–3 months old, and bones and teeth of sub-adults and adults, which deciduous premolars either very worn or replaced by the permanent premolars and long-bones either fused or, if unfused, already close to adult size.

A similar but less clearly marked division seemed to exist between the younger and older sheep and goats; and while the older sheep/goat bones that could be identified to species were all of sheep, more of the younger milk teeth that could be identified[4] were of kids than of lambs.

More detailed information on the relative representation of the different parts of the skeleton is given in Figure 148 and Table 17, from which several points of interest emerge:

Cattle: Phalanges are strikingly abundant: there are 78 in a total of 110 bones (in Phases A:I–X, by contrast, there are thirteen phalanges out of ninety-seven cattle bones). Even once allowance has been made for the numbers of phalanges in the skeleton, long-bones are clearly underrepresented in relation to phalanges, and teeth are also notably scarce.

Pig and sheep/goat: Reasonably good preservation is suggested by the relatively large numbers of very young postcranial bones, especially of pigs.

(a) Older pig phalanges and metapodials are clearly overrepresented in relation to long-bones and teeth: on a minimum numbers of individuals basis, for instance, at least twenty-three older pigs are indicated by the metapodials against no more than 6 by the teeth and three by the commonest long-bone ends (Fig. 148). The lower counts for phalanges than for metapodials, and for lateral phalanges than axial phalanges, might well reflect recovery bias. Harder to understand, however, are the higher counts for lateral than for axial metapodials, and for incisors relative to molars.

(b) In contrast, the piglet bones show no such bias: long-bones are relatively common. The relative scarcity of phalanges, carpals and tarsals of piglets, and of some of the smaller teeth, can probably be accounted for by a combination of destruction and recovery bias.

(c) The lamb and kid bones show a pattern which is similar to that of the piglet bones, except that long-bones are relatively scarcer.

(d) Among the older sheep/goat bones, the greater abundance of upper teeth as compared with lower teeth requires explanation, as, among the lower teeth, does the relatively large number of incisors (in most unsieved assemblages sheep/goat cheek-teeth, and especially molars, are much commoner than incisors, which usually fall out of their sockets and are small and easily lost). The more robust parts of the forelimb, such as the distal humerus and proximal radius, are relatively common; while the similarly robust distal tibia appears to be less common. Phalanges are relatively scarce.

Red deer: As with the cattle, phalanges are strikingly abundant, making up nineteen of the twenty-one red deer bones; and again, as in Phases A:I–X, there are no teeth.

For an unusual deposit of this kind, which might have been produced by a single incident or during a limited period, it is of particular interest to try to determine how many animals were involved. Crude minimum estimates can be produced (Fig. 148) by dividing the counts of commoner elements by the frequencies of those elements in the skeleton. On this basis, the assemblage contains the remains of at least one horse, four cattle, four young kids and three young lambs (on the basis of the numbers of deciduous fourth premolars), eight older sheep/goats, seventeen young piglets (on the basis of the number of deciduous lower fourth premolars), twenty-three older pigs, one red deer, one roe deer and three hares. But these estimates are no more than a minimum, assuming near-complete preservation and recovery of the parts of the skeleton on which the estimates are based; the more bone that has been lost, the higher the original number of animals must have been.

One way of trying to estimate whether more animals were involved is to attempt to match up right and left pairs.[5] In practice, this is an uncertain procedure, as it is rarely completely clear whether right and left bones are pairs from the same animal; an attempt to try to pair the juvenile pig lower deciduous fourth premolars led to considerable uncertainty and no useful result. An attempt to pair the young lamb and kid lower fourth premolars gave more useful results. There are fourteen of these teeth in early wear in this assemblage, eight right and six left. Close examination of these showed that there were only two possible pairs, and neither of these was very convincing. This shows that there must have been at the very least twelve lambs and kids (as compared with the original crude minimum of seven), and that there may have been considerably more. If, as I think likely, none of these teeth are in fact a pair, not only must there have been fourteen animals but, as Krantz points out, if there were only fourteen animals, the probability of randomly selecting fourteen non-pairing teeth is very low, and the original number is likely to have been substantially higher; one estimate, the Peterson index $(L+1) (R+1)$, produces an estimate of sixty-three animals.[6] If similar loss and destruction rates have affected the other parts of the assemblage, the total number of animals involved was probably fairly large, and it is hard to see this deposit as the refuse from a single event.

SECTOR A: PHASE XI BONE GROUPS

A261: Fox bones found in this context include parts of at least two adults and one cub. Though many of the bones are missing, the completeness of many of the bones and their unusually pale colour suggests either that these are intrusive (perhaps buried in a collapsed earth), or that they might be animals that were killed and disposed of rapidly. No cut-marks were seen; this, together with the excavator's interpretation of A261 as a hypocaust channel backfill, makes it more probable that they are intrusive.

A229: A group of rabbit bones are probably intrusive: they are pale, relatively complete, and show no butchery marks.

BONE MODIFICATION: BUTCHERY, BURNING, GNAWING, ARTIFACTS (TABLE 18)

Cut-marks: Relatively few of the bones from Castle Copse show cut-marks. They are commoner on the bones of larger animals than on the bones of smaller animals: thus 10% of the Castle Copse cattle bones show cut-marks as compared with only 2% of the pig and sheep/goat bones, and none of the hare bones showed definite cut-marks. Most of the cut-marks were relatively fine marks of the sort most probably made by a knife, often in parallel or subparallel groups; a smaller number of heavier chopmarks might have been made by a cleaver or an axe, but could also have been made with a heavy knife used as a chopper.

Some of the marks appear to have been made during disarticulation, others in cutting meat off the bones, and others during skinning.

Of particular interest are clear cut-marks on the proximal tibia of a horse (A121: XI/XII): four fine cut-marks on the higher of the intercondylar eminences were almost certainly made during disarticulation of the stifle joint (which corresponds to the knee in man). In the same context, a horse distal metapodial had several possible cut-marks on the distal articulation.

Burning and gnawing: Relatively few of the bones have been burnt or gnawed. Bones probably gnawed by dogs include a number of the pig metapodials from A:XI; only four bones that had been gnawed by rodents were noted.

Bone and antler artifacts: Bone and antler artifacts were relatively scarce (see above); there is a single antler offcut (**485**) from Sector C.

CATTLE: AGE, SEX, MEASUREMENTS, PATHOLOGY, AND NON-METRIC VARIATION
The number of cattle bones is fairly small; they are treated here as a single assemblage.

Age: As Tables 16 and 17 show, loose teeth generally outnumber teeth in jaws. Only four mandibles have complete molar tooth rows, which, using Grant's system of wear stages and scores,[7] give mandibular wear stages between 31 and 51 (Table 19).

Rather more information is given by considering the wear stages of individual teeth (Table 19). These clearly indicate that most of the cattle were killed as subadults and young adults. Thus, nearly all the M_1s and M_2s are between stages f and m, most of the M_3s are in early wear stages, and there are relatively few dP_4s. Converting these data into age estimates is problematic, but reasonable estimates suggest that the youngest animal (with its dP_4 at b/c) is likely to have been a calf of around 2–4 months, and that most of the cattle were probably killed between 2 and 5 years.

Epiphysial fusion data are more likely to be biased against younger animals, as unfused bones are weaker and more likely to be destroyed than fused bones. Long-bone ends are relatively less abundant than teeth in this assemblage: there are 18 M_3s, while the commonest long-bone ends, proximal radii and distal tibiae, are only about half as frequent. Nonetheless, the fusion data (Table 20) are in broad agreement with the picture given by the teeth: few of the early-fusing epiphyses are unfused, suggesting that few animals were killed before 18 months, while over a third of the late-fusing group are unfused, suggesting appreciable kill-off before 3–4 years.

Sex: Too few of the cattle bones could be sexed to give any useful indications.

Measurements (Appendix 8): There is some variation in the size of cattle during the Roman period in Britain. In some areas, such as the southwest, cattle remained fairly small, like those of the Iron Age (e.g., Exeter);[8] but in the midlands and southeast, Roman cattle tended to be larger, and there is clear indication of size increase during the Roman period.[9] The number of bones from Castle Copse that could be measured was fairly small; Figure 149 and (Table 21) indicate that they are fairly large, but it should be remembered that the scarcity of older adults suggests that a high proportion may have been male.

Pathology: In keeping with the relative scarcity of older animals, only two pathological specimens were noted. An ankylosed naviculo-cuboid and second and third tarsal (A477:IV) presumably represent an early stage of spavin, a condition in which the bones of the hock joint fuse together and the joint loses mobility. A first phalanx

(A427:X/XI) has a small proximal exostosis. Both conditions are thought to be common in draft animals; but no special significance should be attached to two minor cases.

Nonmetric variation: Two M_3s out of a total of eighteen have reduced third pillar: the two are probably from the same animal (A965 and A969, both Phase A:I). Another of the M_3s (A233:X/XI) lacks the lingual cusp of the second pillar, and the third pillar is somewhat displaced toward the missing cusp.

"Notches" on the proximal articulations of the third phalanges were noted in six out of twenty-eight cases. These notches run medio-laterally across the articular ridge; their cause is unknown, and their frequency appears to vary from site to site.

SHEEP/GOAT: AGE MEASUREMENTS AND PATHOLOGY

In view of the presence of a relatively large number of very juvenile sheep and goat teeth and bones in Phase A:XI, ageing data are given in a way that makes it possible to compare the Phase A:XI assemblage with that from Phases A:I–X. For other purposes the sheep/goat bones from all studied phases at Castle Copse (A:I–XI, X/XI and XI/XII) are treated as a single assemblage.

Age: As in the case of the cattle, loose teeth generally outnumber teeth in jaws. Details of all mandibles with molars, dP_4 or P_4 are given in Table 22: the proportion of mandibles with milk teeth in early wear is relatively high, especially in Phase A:XI, and there are no mandibles with advanced wear on M_2 or M_3 (stages H and I). A similar picture is given when loose teeth are taken into account. The number of dP_4s in early wear (stage 13 or sooner) is relatively high, and most of them (13/14) are from Phase A:XI; only one of the 51 $M_{1/2}$s is in later wear (i.e., beyond stage 9), and most (15/17) of the M_3s are in early wear (before stage 11). This suggests consumption of animals mostly less than five years old and, especially in Phase A:XI, frequent consumption of lamb and kid less than six months old. The predominance of sheep among identifications of older (fused) postcranial bones suggests that nearly all the older teeth and jaws are of sheep, rather than of goats; older goats probably rarely figured on the menu.

Younger animals appear to be underrepresented in the epiphysial fusion data (Table 23), presumably because unfused bones are more easily destroyed.

Sex: Too few of the sheep and goat bones could be sexed to give any useful indications.

Measurements (Appendix 8): As in the case of cattle, Roman sheep are generally larger than Iron Age sheep, especially in central and southeastern England, where there is also evidence for size increase between the first and the fourth centuries (e.g., Colchester[10] and Chichester,[11] but at Exeter there is only a slight increase in size over the same period.[12] while the number of available measurements is small, Figure 150 and Table 24 indicate that the Castle Copse sheep bones are comparable in size to those from other later Roman sites in central and southeastern England. The sheep skeleton from A942 contributes a number of the largest measurements.

Pathology: Pathological specimens were uncommon. Growth arrests and enamel abnormalities were noted on four teeth, three of which belonged to the sheep skeleton found in A953:I (see above). A distal humerus from A425:XI has a small lateral exostosis, of a sort that might reflect a condition such as "penning elbow."

PIGS: AGE MEASUREMENTS AND PATHOLOGY

In view of the unusual nature of the Sector A, Phase XI assemblage, data are given separately where relevant.

Age: Details of mandibles and mandibular teeth are given in Table 25, and details of epiphysial fusion in Table 26. As these both show, and as is commonly found, adult pigs are relatively scarce. In Phase A:XI, milk teeth of piglets only a few weeks old are common—about two-thirds of the dP_4 are still at wear stage a, while fusion data for the older pigs in A:XI suggest that many of these were killed between twelve and thirty months—few of the second phalanges are unfused, while few of the lateral metapodials are fused.

Measurements (Appendix 8): These are compared in Figure 151 with a standard based on Turkish wild boar.[13] The Castle Copse pigs are generally smaller than the Turkish wild boar: log ratio values peak between –0.07 and –0.11. The asymmetry of the distribution suggests that a few of the larger specimens may be wild boar, but this must be regarded as a tentative conclusion in the absence of better comparative data from other English sites.

Pathology: A few of the teeth showed minor growth arrests on the enamel of the crowns.

Husbandry: Probably as a result of the water-sieving and generally good recovery, a fairly large number of deciduous third incisors and canines were found. Some are unworn, some in early wear; nearly all are unbroken. This is of interest because it is common practice today to break them off in order to prevent piglets from harming their litter-mates; clearly this was not the practice at Roman Castle Copse, and it would be interesting to learn when this practice first appears.

OTHER SPECIES (MEASUREMENTS IN APPENDIX 8)

Horse: A number of the teeth could definitely be identified as horse, not donkey; there is no indication that either donkey or mule was present.

Deer: Red and roe deer are both present.

Dog: Dog is represented by only a few bones from Castle Copse. A number of bones had been gnawed by some fairly large carnivore, presumably dog (Table 18), and a badger phalanx (see below) was corroded in a manner consistent with having passed through the gut of a dog.[14]

Cat: Cat is represented by a few bones; none was particularly large or heavy.

Other carnivores: Badger is represented by a second phalanx from A430:X/XI, and a juvenile mustelid (probably stoat) by a mastilla from the same context. A group of fox bones from A261:XI (above) may be intrusive.

Hare and rabbit: Over thirty hare bones were present in the Castle Copse assemblage, mostly from Sector A, Phase A:XI. Though none had definite cut-marks, most of them were broken, were found singly rather than as associated groups, and were usually stained like most of the other bones. In contrast, the rabbit bones were often unbroken, usually paler in color than most of the other bones, and often found as associated groups: one in A229:XI; (see above), another in A103:X/XI, and another of a very young animal in A430:X/XI. It seems likely that the Castle Copse rabbit bones are all intrusive, and it is generally thought that rabbits were not introduced to Britain until after the Roman period.[15]

Smaller Mammals

Most of the small mammal remains were recovered by water-sieving; they presumably represent only a small fraction of the small mammal bones that were present in the deposits (brief summary in Table 27).

Common shrew (*Sorex araneus*), pygmy shrew (*Sorex minutus*), bank vole (*Clethrionomys glareolus*), short-tailed vole (*Microtus* cf. *agrestis*), wood mouse/yellow-necked mouse (*Apodemus sylvaticus/flavicollis*) and house mouse (*Mus musculus/domesticus*) were identified.

Few contexts produced more than one or two bones, but a group of small mammal bones from A729:IX included the remains of at least three common shrews, one bank vole, one field vole and one *Apodemus,* and may either be from a natural pit-fall trap or from a group of decayed owl-pellets.

Birds
BY ENID ALLISON

A total of 1641 fragments of bird bone were submitted for identification.[16] Where possible, all bones of domestic fowl, dove, goose and mallard were measured following the system of von den Driesch (data in Appendix 9).[17]

Much of the bird bone is fragmentary and rather abraded. Many fragments show signs of rodent gnawing, especially at the articulations, an indication that at least some of the bone debris had lain on the surface for a time rather than being buried immediately after deposition. Twenty percent of the total fragments were unidentified. These are mainly small fragments recovered by wet-sieving. A full list of all species identified and number of fragments recorded from each phase is given in Table 28.

SECTOR A: PHASE I–X

Little can be said of the very small bird assemblages from A:I–X, except that the species recorded are typical of those found in food debris from Roman occupation sites, with domestic fowl (*Gallus gallus*) being represented by the greatest number of fragments. Other species recorded are mallard (*Anas platyrhynchos*) and another species of duck, golden plover (*Pluvialis apricaria*), woodcock (*Scolopax rusticola*), a small wader, a large raptor, dove (*Columba* sp.), and blackbird (*Turdus merula*). A few bones of small passerines could not be identified to species.

Three large raptor bones (shafts of a humerus and a tibiotarsus, and a badly damaged proximal half of a femur) were recorded from Phase A:IX. All features on the bones correspond with the available reference specimens of goshawk (*Accipiter gentilis*). The size of the bones from Castle Copse is intermediate between the sizes of reference material of the two sexes, however.[18] For this reason, and because of the lack of articular ends on the bones recovered, the identification of goshawk is rather tentative, although available modern reference specimens of other similarly sized raptors are unlike the bones from Castle Copse. When raptor bones are found in an archaeological context they are often considered unlikely to have been the remains of food. This is particularly true in medieval deposits, as falconry is known to have been a popular activity during that period and hawks and falcons were therefore valuable birds. The Romans, however, are not known to have indulged in hawking, so it may be more likely the raptors were eaten if they were caught, although they would not have provided a great deal of meat. Perhaps the most likely explanation of the presence of hawk on site is that it was killed to prevent it preying on domestic poultry. Varro, for example, describes a simple trap using birdlime for this very purpose.[19]

SECTOR A: PHASE XI

The majority of the bird bones (93% of the total examined) are from this phase. The range of species is again typical of Roman food debris and dominated by domestic fowl, which accounted for 55% of the total fragments. A large proportion of the fowl fragments are badly abraded, and some had also been gnawed by rodents. Detection of knife-marks was consequently difficult and they were observed on only ten bones. Most of these are on the distal articulations of tibiotarsi, caused during the removal of the lower legs and feet which provide no meat. A humerus with knife-marks on the proximal end was noted as well as a femur with knife-marks on the distal articulation. Knife-marks may also be present on the distal end of an ulna. The positions of these marks suggest the cutting of limbs into portions at the joints, but since too few of the bones actually show knife-marks, fowl was probably more commonly torn apart for eating than cut up.

Domestic fowl: The domestic fowl show a size range very like that observed on other Roman sites, with the majority being of a size similar to bones of bantam versions of modern Mediterranean breeds, and a few fragments indicating the presence of much larger and particularly small birds. For bones where a reasonable number of measurements were available, there seems to be a division into two main size groups (Figs. 152–153). These probably correspond to males and females, and the size difference between the groups is of the order that would be expected if this were so. The larger bones are the more numerous—this might be expected, as more cockerels than hens would be eaten if the latter were also required to produce eggs. Hens past their egg-laying prime might have ended up in the pot. Medullary bone, the presence of which indicated a laying female, was observed in only five bones: a coracoid, two femora, and two tibiotarsi, although only femora and tibiotarsi were systemically examined for medullary bone.[20]

Tarsometatarsi are not as well represented as the other leg bones (Table 29), but again there is the basic division into two size groups. All of the large tarsometatarsi possess spurs or spur socket primordia, which develops in young birds and to which the spur core, which is ossified separately, eventually fuses.[21] One of the smaller tarsometatarsi also possesses a spur. Spurs do develop in some otherwise normal hens, some reaching the length of those in normal cocks,[22] so it is possible that this bone belongs to a hen. Spurred hens may have been more likely to end up in the pot than unspurred individuals: spurs generally, though not always, develop in older birds, and egg-laying ability declines with age. Columella advised that spurred hens should not be chosen for breeding, one of the reasons being that spurs would tend to damage eggs.[23] Some small spurred bones from tenth–thirteenth century deposits at the Coppergate site in York are believed to have come from spurred females.[24] The general form of the small spurred bone from Castle Copse suggests, however, that it was from a small cock. Several distinct "breeds" of fowl which had been developed in different regions were known to the Romans, including a bantam form,[25] although it is not known whether any particular breeds were present in Roman Britain. The spurs on four of the tarsometatarsi, including that which is presumed to be from a small cock, are long and composed of dense bone, an indication that they are from mature cocks. These may originally have been used for breeding. The spurs of the younger cocks are composed of much less dense bone, which is easily abraded.

Eighteen percent of the total fowl bones from this phase are incompletely ossified, i.e., from young birds under about 4–5 months of age.[26] Of these bones, 9% are from very small individuals. This greatly contrasts with the age of a few weeks at which the majority of chickens are consumed today.

Healed fractures were noted on the shaft of a humerus and on a furcula, but no other pathological features were seen. An unusually short humerus is of interest, however. This bone is morphologically normal, apart from shortening of the shaft (Fig. 154). Similar bones have been recorded from three archaeological sites of Anglo-Scandinavian to postmedieval date in York, where it was suggested that they were the result of the presence of a particular mutation.[27] The semidominant creeper gene causes shortening of the long bones in the limbs, particularly in the legs.[28] Except for the tibiotarsus and fibula, the morphology of the limb bones is unaffected. The condition is lethal to homozygotes.[29] The gene varies in expression, but fowl possessing it generally have such short legs that they appear to be sitting down even when standing! It has now been incorporated as the distinguishing characteristic of several modern breeds of fowl in different parts of the world. The short humerus was compared with others from Castle Copse with similar breadth measurements, but normal shaft lengths. This showed that there had been a reduction in shaft length of 17–18%. Landauer[30] showed that the long-bones in limbs of males with the creeper gene were shorter than those of their normal siblings by 18–31%, with the higher values being for the leg bones.

Duck: Ducks are well represented, and their remains make up 10% of the total fragments. Mallard (*Anas platyrhynchos*) is by far the most important of the ducks, and its remains account for 79% of the duck bones from this phase. Teal *Anas crecca* was represented by several fragments. Fragments of at least one medium-sized duck species are also present, but none of these could be assigned to any species with certainty. Some of the duck bones bear knife marks, presumably caused during division of the carcasses for eating and in scraping meat off the bones. Roman agricultural writers have described the capturing of waterfowl from the wild and their maintenance in enclosures until required for the table. Whether ducks (and other wild fowl) were kept in or near this site in any way is a matter of speculation. No measurements of the archaeological material are sufficiently common to provide any useful statistics for a comparison of the archaeological mallard bones with modern specimens.

Goose: Goose bones account for only 2% of the total fragments. Such a low proportion is typical of Roman sites. In Britain, geese appear to have become of much greater economic importance from the Anglo-Saxon period onwards. All of the goose bones from Castle Copse are comparable in size with those of domestic goose, but since there is a large overlap in the size of the bones of domestic goose, its wild ancestor the greylag (*Anser anser*), and bean goose (*A. fabalis*), the presence of some bones of the latter two species cannot be ruled out. Shaft breadth measurements of the tarsometatarsus appear to be reasonably reliable for separating goose from other species,[31] but no tarsometatarsi were recovered from Castle Copse, probably because they were removed during preparation of goose carcasses for the table, and we have here the remains of the food rather than the waste from food processing.

Wading Birds: Wading birds of various kinds make up 7% of the total assemblage, the species represented by the greatest numbers of fragments being woodcock (*Scolopa rusticola*) and plover (*Pluvialis* sp.(p)). Many of the latter bones are referable to the golden plover (*P. squatarola*). Most the the limb bones of the golden plover are shorter than those of grey plover, but it is difficult to separate fragmentary material. The position of the site some distance inland makes the presence of the latter species (a winter visitor and passage migrant to coastal areas) less likely, however. Both woodcock and golden plover are frequently recorded from archaeological sites, and both appear to have been important game species throughout the centuries in Britain. Snipe (*Gallinago gallinago*) is represented by a single fragment.

Dove: The dove bones recorded could not be identified to species, but must be either stock dove (*Columba oenas*), domestic dove (*C. livia domestica*), or rock dove (*C. livia*), which are very similar morphologically and overlap in size. The differences in the proximal end of the tarsometatarsus figured by Fick[32] were not used to distinguish the species, as examination of modern feral pigeon material showed that these characters may be rather variable. Almost half the dove bones from Castle Copse are from young birds. Domestic doves are believed to have been kept in Britain during the Roman occupation, but it cannot be proved that they were widely bred.[33] Some structures on Roman sites have tentatively been identified as dovecotes,[34] but none have been definitely identified as such.

Passerines: Bones of small passerines are relatively numerous. Many of those are thrush (Turdidae) species, with bones of blackbird (*Turdus merula*) being the most numerous of those identified. Various species of thrush, caught by the use of nets, were kept and fattened in aviaries by Roman farmers in Italy. It is possible that the same thing also took place in the country districts of Roman Britain. Food for humans was not their only use: Varro considered that the best dung for fertilizer was from the aviaries of thrushes and blackbirds, and that it was also excellent food for fattening cattle and pigs.[35]

Unfortunately, due to the rather fragmentary condition of many of the bones of smaller species of passerine, and also to the lack of reference material, many could not be identified to species. House sparrow (*Passer domesticus*) was recorded, and a sternum fragment may be of a starling (*Sturnus vulgaris*). Although there is no reason why either of these species would not have been eaten, both are so commonly found around human dwellings that their remains may have become incorporated into the deposit in some other way.

Three species of corvid were represented: jay (*Garrulus glandarius*), either rook (*Corvus frugilegus*) or crow (*C. corone*), and jackdaw (*C. monedula*). The last species was represented by several fragments, including a pair of tibiotarsi, which contained large amounts of medullary bone, indicating that the female to which they belonged was in peak laying condition at the time of death. This strongly suggests that jackdaws nested in the building during this phase.

CONCLUSIONS SECTOR A: PHASE XI

The assemblages appear to have been chiefly the remains of food. The species recorded from Phase A:XI indicate that the deposits were waste from high-grade food, rather than refuse left by squatters. The building may have simply been used for dumping rubbish from other parts of the site. The presence of bones of a laying female suggests that jackdaws nested in the building during this period.

Domestic fowl was represented by the greatest number of fragments, as is usual on Roman sites, and this is probably a true reflection of its importance. Cocks appear to have provided the bulk of the food, while hens were probably kept primarily for egg production. It has been speculated above that wild birds (ducks, waders, and thrushes) may have been captured and kept in nearby aviaries until required for the table. Domestic doves and geese may be represented in the assemblage, but this is uncertain because of the difficulties of distinguishing bones of domestic birds from morphologically similar wild species.

Since most of the wild bird species were caught for food and may have been brought onto the site from some considerable distance, they are much less likely than the small mammals to reflect the immediate surroundings of the site. A variety of habitats appears to have been exploited by fowlers. Goshawk and jay are woodland species, and woodcock favors not too dense woodland with fairly wet areas for feeding and wide ridges or clearings.[36] Golden plover on the other hand occurs in much more open situations. Snipe are found in areas of impeded drainage, and the mallards and other ducks must have come from watery areas.

Fishes

BY ANDREW K. G. JONES

Two hundred ninety-four fish bones were examined, of which 147 (50%) could be identified to family or lower taxon (Appendix 10). Most of the bones are from Sector A deposits dated to Phase A:XI. However, all phases at the site produced broadly similar assemblages of fish remains.

Flatfish (Pleuronectidae) remains dominated the assemblage, with sixty-six bones, mostly vertebrae. Flatfish vertebrae are extremely difficult to identify to species and the only bone which was assigned to species was an epihyal of flounder (*Platichthys flesus*). All the other flatfish bones are consistent with flounder; it is, however, possible that other flatfish species are present in the assemblage. Measurements (Appendix 10) on precaudal vertebrae showed that most of the flatfish were between 30 and 45 cm total length, while smaller specimens were also present.

Other fish bones included eel (*Anguilla anguilla*) vertebrae. These bones indicate that eels of approximately 35–65 cm in length were brought to the site.

The family Salmonidae includes trout (*Salmo trutta*) and salmon (*S. salar*). Both species are present, although most of the bones were from trout ranging in size from approximately 20 to 35 cm total length.

It is interesting to note that one trout and two eel vertebrae (from A377:XI and A252:XI, respectively, were crushed in a manner consistent with having been passed through an animal (perhaps human) gut. Crushed vertebrae are commonly present in the feces of piscivores.[37]

Other freshwater fishes include at least one member of the Cyprinidae, but none could be identified to species.

Of considerable interest are bones of marine fishes which, although not abundant, are from a diverse selection of good quality food fish. Herring bones were the most common. Other marine fishes present included bass (*Dicentrarchus labrax*), gilthead (*Sparus auratus*) and horse mackerel (*Trachurus trachurus*), which were represented by small numbers of bones.

Clearly, it would be unwise to place great emphasis on the significance of such small numbers of bones; however it is most unusual to find an assemblage of this kind in archaeological deposits of Roman date in Britain. Generally, Roman deposits produce small numbers of fish remains, mainly from river fishes; occasionally sparid remains are present.[38] It is not possible to determine whether any of the fish arrived at the site as preserved fish, or whether they were all fresh.

There can be little doubt that the fish remains from Castle Copse were food debris. It is also clear that the remains were not simply a typical selection of the locally available fish. The presence of gilthead, bass, and other highly regarded food fish indicates that some specially selected fish were being brought to the site. It is tempting to suggest that some of the fishes were "high status" foods, which were presumably available only to relatively wealthy persons.

REPTILES AND AMPHIBIANS

A large group of frog bones (*Rana* sp., probably *R. temporaria*) from A208:XI, includes the remains of at least nine individuals of a range of sizes. Accumulations of dead frogs are often found in pits or wells, which act as pit-fall traps. In this case, the context is interpreted as refuse dumped against a wall; the frog bones may indicate that at least part of this refuse came from emptying out the fill of some place that acted as pit-fall, such as a pit or part of a disused hypocaust system.

Otherwise, the small number of scattered finds from Castle Copse includes more bones of frogs (*Rana* sp.), a large toad (?) humerus (?*Bufo* sp.), a lizard femur (cf. *Lacerta* sp.), and a slow-worm vertebra (*Anguis fragilis*).

SEASHELLS

Oyster (*Ostrea*) shells were abundant at Castle Copse, especially from Phase A:XI. Mussel (*Mytilus*) and whelk (*Buccinum*) shells were also found, but were very much less common.

General Interpretation

In his comparative survey of bones assemblages from Roman Britain, King[39] pointed to a number of generalizations and trends: that the relative abundance of sheep tends to decline during the Roman period, and the abundance of pigs and cattle to increase (especially on "Romanized" sites); that military sites tend to have high frequencies of cattle bones; that horse was not regularly consumed; that most assemblages have few horse bones; and that deer bones are more commonly found on later Roman sites than on early ones.

SECTOR A: PHASES I–X

The bone assemblage from Castle Copse Phases A:I–X fits reasonably well with these general expectations, and compares reasonably well with the general run of bone assemblages from Roman villas,[40] where cattle are generally between 40% and 60% (42% at Castle Copse A:I–X), sheep between 20% and 40% (33% at Castle Copse A:I–X) and pig between 10% and 25% (18% at Castle Copse A:I–X). The fairly low figure for cattle at Castle Copse may well reflect a better standard of recovery than at most excavations, whose assemblages are probably rather more strongly biased by poor recovery.

As one bullock provides more meat than a pig or a sheep, beef undoubtedly contributed much more to the diet than pork or mutton. Most of the meat was from sub-adults—the age at which meat is most economically produced—though some younger and older animals were also eaten.

The presence of most parts of the skeleton suggests that animals were killed and butchered on site; the scarcity of heavy butchery marks contrasts with bone assemblages from Roman towns, and suggests that the site was not large enough to support a full-time butcher with specialized equipment. Most of the discrepancies in the relative representation of the different parts of the skeleton can be explained by preservation and recovery bias, but the scarcity of upper teeth of cattle (Fig. 148, Table 16) may suggest that cattle skulls were removed from the site: cattle skulls are sometimes put on poles, for instance, and used as scarecrows.

The relatively small numbers of bones of deer and other wild animals suggest that hunting was of minor importance. The absence of red deer teeth and head bones may suggest that these were not brought back to the site; they may have been treated as trophies, or may have been discarded at the kill site as too heavy to be worth carrying back to the site. Birds and fish probably contributed relatively little to the diet, though their importance is likely to be underestimated as a consequence of recovery bias.

Whether horse was eaten is uncertain. Its bones are relatively scarce and, as commonly observed, less broken than the cow bones; but while only one horse bone (from Phase A:XI/XII) shows definite cut-marks, the proportion of cattle bones with cut-marks is not significantly greater (Table 18).

There is little suggestion of tidy or organized dumping of bones; the general abundance of bones suggests that they were disposed of rather haphazardly, while the abundance of teeth relative to postcranial bones, and of stronger parts of the postcranial skeleton relative to weaker parts (e.g., of distal humeri and tibiae as compared with proximal humeri and tibiae), suggests fairly high rates of bone destruction, indicating that the bones were dumped on ground surfaces, where they would have been accessible to dogs and rodents, and open to physical and chemical weathering, rather than being deliberately buried. The two groups of sheep bones in pits (above) appear to be isolated cases of tidier disposal—in each case it is clear that the animal concerned was butchered (and presumably eaten), and not just a dead animal dumped in a pit.

It is likely that this was both a "producer" and a "consumer" site. The presence of seashells and marine fish provides clear evidence for food being brought onto the site, and contributes to a picture of a relatively high standard of living, as does the relative scarcity of aged animals, while the late fetal sheep/goat bones in the pit in A953/948:I, are presumably either from an aborted fetus or from an animal killed in late pregnancy—likely only in the event of sudden sickness or accident, and suggesting keeping of animals at Castle Copse. Few of the mature animals that presumably made up the breeding stock, and were probably milked and provided wool and traction, have contributed to the assemblage; they may, together with surplus younger animals, have been sold to provide meat for urban markets.

The assemblage from Phase A:XI, on the other hand, is clearly unusual. The high proportion of pig (nearly 70%) is well outside Romano-British norms,[41] though it has slightly later parallels at Dinas Powys in South Wales[42] and at Saxon Wicken Bonhunt,[43] and Roman parallels elsewhere in Europe.[44] Equally unusual is the abundance of bones of very young piglets, lambs, and kids, the high proportion of bird bones, and the large numbers of pig foot bones and cattle and deer phalanges.

The assemblage comes from various rooms inside the second aisled building, and many of the bones were found in concentrated dumps. Preservation and recovery both seem to have been relatively good; nonetheless, some features of the assemblage (Fig. 148 and Table 17), such as the scarcity of piglet carpals, tarsals, and phalanges, or the scarcity of older pig lateral second and third phalanges in comparison with axial second and third phalanges, may well reflect a combination of destruction and recovery biases. Other features of the assemblage, such as the relative abundance of foot-bones of older pigs and phalanges of cattle and red deer, presumably reflect patterns of butchery and disposal. But none of these explain why older pig lateral metapodials (especially distal ends) are considerably commoner than axial metapodials, or why older pig incisors are commoner than molars; and if recovery bias accounts for the shortage of older pig lateral second and third phalanges, it is surprising that sheep/goat incisors are as common as sheep/goat molars. These observations suggest that some mechanism may have operated to remove some of the larger bones, such as pig and sheep/goat mandibles and pig axial metapodials, from the assemblage. One possibility might be that larger bones were collected and dumped outside the aisled building; another that the dumps that make up a large part of the assemblage might represent accumulations of smaller-sized rubbish from floor-sweepings, or the smaller bones that fell through gaps between planks in an upper floor.

The individual contexts, representing different dump areas and episodes, vary to some extent in the relative abundance of bird bones, older pig foot bones, piglet bones, lamb and kid bones, oyster shells and other components of the assemblage; but they are sufficiently mixed that there is no strong suggestion that they are different and unrelated components—rather, the suggestion is that they are variable parts of a single assemblage.

Some parts of this assemblage—the older pig's feet, for instance, and the cattle and deer phalanges—might be thought to be parts of the body cut off during an early stage of butchery and dumped as primary butchery debris, though Roman primary butchery dumps in urban sites usually include heads as well as feet, and it is usually cattle, and sometimes sheep, that are dealt with in this way, not pigs. Dumps of cattle and sheep foot bones are sometimes found in areas of medieval and later towns that have some association with tanning, but not pig foot bones; and sheep and cattle metapodials are found with the phalanges in these deposits (e.g., York and Dorchester).[45] Concentrations of pig metapodials and phalanges have been reported from some sites (e.g., Roman Exeter and Dorchester,[46] but the number of bones involved in each case is much smaller than at Castle Copse, and the assemblages concerned do not share the other unusual features of the Castle Copse assemblage.

Another possibility is that the foot bones result from some kind of specialized processing, perhaps making glue or gelatine. But this does not explain the other features of the assemblage, and the good condition of the foot bones does not suggest that they have been subjected to that kind of prolonged cooking.

The large numbers of piglets, lambs, and kids might suggest the disposal of natural mortalities. Some of the piglets are young enough for this to be a possibility, but the wear states of most of the lamb and kid dP_4s suggest animals of 1–3 months,[47] rather than newborn or very young animals.

An interpretation that accounts for more features of the assemblage is that the bones are food remains. The piglet bones could have been young sucking pig, and the lambs and kids would have been at a good age to eat. The abundant oyster shells and chicken bones add to the impression of luxury foods, as do the duck, woodcock and golden plover bones and the salmon, trout, and imported sea fish. In this light, the pig foot bones could represent a taste for pig's trotters cooked in some special way. It is clear from Apicius[48] that pork was particularly esteemed on the Roman table, and a number of his recipes describe special ways of cooking it, including parts that are not highly prized today, such as udder and stomach. Apicius mentions pig trotters in several recipes; he also gives a large number of recipes for cooking suckling pig, kid, and lamb, and recipes for cooking hare, chicken, a range of wild birds, and eels and other fish, often including oysters. The cattle and deer phalanges may also represent particular culinary specialties. The other pig, sheep, and cattle bones show that more everyday pork, mutton, and beef were also eaten; the relatively high frequency of pig and sheep teeth and jaws may suggest that pig and sheep heads were brought to the table.[49]

This, then, is the interpretation that is offered of this assemblage—that it is accumulated floor-sweepings or table-refuse from a dining area; but whether it represents the diet of a well-to-do family, a number of large and ostentatious feasts, or the food eaten at a gastronomic inn or club is unclear. No doubt the food was eaten elsewhere—probably in another building; at least parts of the aisled building may well have been in a half-ruined state, used as a dump and nested in by jackdaws (above). What are clear are the indications of luxury, high status, and the "consumer" nature of the assemblage,[50] though some of the food may have been produced locally—the presence of most parts of the skeleton suggests on-site killing and butchery at least for the main domestic animals, as in the earlier phases.

Environmental Conditions

The domestic cattle, pigs, sheep, and chickens which provide the bulk of the animal bone assemblages from Castle Copse tell us little about environmental conditions—these animals can be reared without difficulty almost anywhere in lowland Britain in conditions ranging from open grazing and arable fields to heavily wooded areas with limited clearings.

The presence of red and roe deer suggests at least some woodland or scrub cover around Roman Castle Copse, as does wild boar, if this is present. Woodcock suggests woodland glades or margins, while golden plover suggests open areas; and the duck and the fresh-water fish suggest ponds or rivers. But none of these animals is common, and, especially in Phase A:XI, they may have been brought in from some distance, as were the oysters and marine fish.

The small mammals (Table 27) again tell us relatively little. Short-tailed voles suggest open rough grassland, while bank voles and *Apodemus* suggest more scrub cover; but all might be found in an untidy garden or along field margins, and, as all live in burrows, there is no certainty that they are of Roman date. All the species of small mammal listed in Table 27 are probably to be found within a short distance of the site today, in the rough grassland of the clearing and the scrub around its edges.

NOTES

1. I am grateful to Eric Hostetter for inviting me to work on the Castle Copse animal bones; to members of the excavation staff for all kinds of help and information; to Enid Allison, Andrew Jones, and Terry O'Connor for looking at the bird, fish, amphibian, and reptile bones; and to Simon Davis, Bruce Levitan, Terry O'Connor, and Rosemary Payne for reading and commenting on earlier drafts of this report.

2. This is normal in unsieved assemblages; the standard of recovery at Castle Copse appears to have been good in comparison with most other Romano-British and medieval sites.

3. Hedges et al. 1989: 223–24. We thank Rupert Housely for making these arrangements.

4. S. Payne 1985.

5. E.g., Krantz 1968.

6. Fieller and Turner 1982.

7. Grant 1982.

8. Maltby 1979.

9. E.g., Luff 1982: Tables 3.13 and 3.14.

10. Luff 1982.

11. Levitan 1989.

12. Maltby 1979.

13. Payne and Bull 1989.

14. Payne and Munson 1985.

15. Sheail 1971.

16. Methods are described by Allison 1985.

17. von den Driesch 1976.

18. Sexual dimorphism is very pronounced in the hawks, of which females are the larger sex.

19. Hooper and Ash 1935: 465.

20. It is present in these bones in greater quantities than the other limb bones and is therefore more easily seen, if present.

21. Juhn 1952.

22. Kozelka 1933.

23. Forster and Heffner 1954: 327.

24. Allison 1985.

25. Forster and Heffner 1954:331.

26. Latimer 1927; Church and Johnson 1964.
27. Allison 1985.
28. Hutt 1949.
29. Landauer and Dunn 1930.
30. Landauer 1934.
31. Bramwell 1977; and Allison 1985.
32. Fick 1974.
33. Applebaum 1967.
34. Chambers 1920.
35. Hooper and Ash 1935: 263.
36. Sharrock 1976.
37. A. K. G. Jones 1984 and 1986.
38. A. K. G. Jones 1988; O'Connor 1988.
39. A. C. King 1978.
40. Cp. A. C. King 1978: fig. 3.
41. See A. C. King 1978: figs. 3–4.
42. Cornwall and Haglund-Calley 1963; Gilchrist 1988.
43. Macready 1976; P. Stevens, forthcoming.
44. A. C. King 1984.
45. York: O'Connor 1984; Dorchester: S. J. M. Davis 1987.
46. Exeter: Maltby 1979: 12 and Dorchester: Maltby 1990.
47. Cp. Deniz and Payne 1982: fig. 20.
48. Flower and Rosenbaum 1958.
49. The absence of older goat bones suggests that older goats may not have been eaten.
50. Compare the assemblage from the Roman legionary fortress baths at Caerleon described by O'Connor (1986).

Figure 148. Castle Copse, relative representation of the different parts of the skeleton of the more common larger mammals. In each case the counts given in Tables 16 and 17 have been divided by the frequency in the skeleton of the tooth or bone in question to give a crude measure of the minimum number of individuals represented for that part of the skeleton.

	CATTLE A:I-X	CATTLE A:XI	SHEEP/GOAT A:I-X	SHEEP/GOAT A:XI	juv.	older	PIG A:XI juv.	older
Maxilla	|	|	|	|	|**	|****	|***	
Mx. teeth: Incisor (di + I)						–	|***	
Canine							–	|***
Premolar (dP + P)	|*	|	|*	|****	|******	|***	|***	
Molar	|*	|*	|***	|	|********	|	|**	
Mandible	|****	|	|*****	|**	|****	|****	|***	
Md. teeth: Incisor (di + I)	|*	|*	|*	|**	|****	–	|******	
Canine						–	–	|***
Premolar (dp + P)	|****	|	|***	|*****	|****	|******	|****	
Molar	|*******	|*	|******	|*	|****	|	|**	
Mx./Md. (dc + di)					|****	–		
Scapula	|*	|	|	|*	|***	|******+		|*
Humerus proximal	|	|	|*	|	|*	|***+		|
Humerus distal	|**	|*	|*	|*	|*****	|***+		|
Radius proximal	|***	|*	|*	|*	|*****	|*****+		|
Radius distal	|**	|*	|*	|**	|**	|***+		|*
Ulna proximal	|**	|*	|*	|*+	|****	|*********		|***
Ulna distal	|*	|*	|	|+	|	|*		|*
Carpals	|	|*	|	|	|*	|		|**
Pelvis (acetabulum)	|**	|**	|*	|**	|**	|****+		|
Femur proximal	|*	|*	|	|	|**	|**+		|**
Femur distal	|	|*	|	|	|*	|*+		|
Patella	|	|*	|	|	|	|		|
Tibia proximal	|*	|	|	|+	|*	|***+		|
Tibia distal	|**	|	|**	|*+	|*	|***+		|***
Fibula proximal						|		|*
Fibula distal	|	|	|	|	|	|		|
Astragalus	|*	|*	|*	|*	|	|		|*
Calcaneum	|*	|***	|**	|*	|**	|****		|***
Other tarsals	|*	|	|*	|	|	|		|**
Metapodial proximal	|***	|*	|*	|*+	|****	|******+		|****************
Metapodial distal	|*	|*	|*	|**+	|**	|******+		|********
Lateral metapodial proximal						|*	|*	|**********************
Lateral metapodial distal						|*	|*	|******************
Phalanx 1	|**	|***	|*	|	|**	|*		|**********
Lateral phalanx 1						|*	|*	|**********
Phalanx 2	|*	|****	|*	|*	|*	|*		|********
Lateral phalanx 2						|*	|*	|**
Phalanx 3	|*	|****	|*	|*	|*	|*		|*******
Lateral phalanx 3						|*	|*	|**

crude minimum number estimate

0 5   0 5   0 5   0 5   0 5   0 5   0 5 10 15 20

Notes Data taken from Tables 16 and 17.

Animal bone groups have been excluded.

For cattle and sheep/goat, incisors include canines; for juvenile pigs maxillary and mandibular deciduous incisors and canines have been grouped.

+ = also some non-countable shafts.

Figure 149. Castle Copse cattle measurements compared with Exeter Roman mean standard (based on Maltby 1979: Table 65), using log ratio method (as in Payne and Bull, 1989).

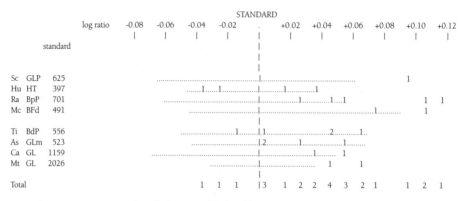

Note   The Exeter Roman ranges are shown by the extents of the dotted lines.

Figure 150. Castle Copse sheep/goat measurements compared with Exeter Roman mean standard (based on Maltby 1979: Table 79), using log ratio method (as in Payne and Bull 1989).

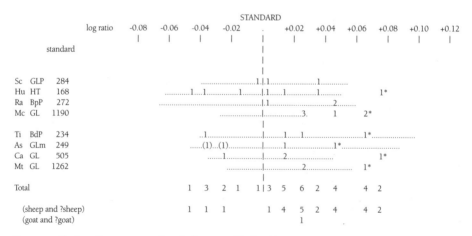

Notes   The Exeter Roman ranges are shown by the extents of the dotted lines.
    * = Measurements taken on the sheep skeleton in A942 (and on the calcaneum in A932, which appears to be from the same skeleton).
    ( ) = Measurements taken on juvenile astragali.

Figure 151. Castle Copse pig measurements compared with Kizilcahamam wild boar standard, using log ratio method (as in Payne and Bull 1989).

		standard	-0.14	-0.12	-0.10	-0.08	-0.06	-0.04	-0.02	STANDARD	+0.02
dP^4	WP	132	1	1 1	1	1					
M^1	WA	159				3	1				
M^2	WA	200			1	1 1	1	1			
M^3	WA	217			1		3		1		
dP_4	WP	101		2	7 5	5 6	2	1			
M_1	WA	119		1	1	1 1	1 2				
M_2	WA	157		1	1 3	1					
M_3	WA	183			3 2	2	1				
Hu	HTC	225					1				
Ra	BpP	342			1	1					
McIII	GL	896			1 3		1	1	1	1	
McIV	GL	915			2 1		1				
Ti	BdP	346			1	2		1			
As	GL1	487					1		1		
MtIII	GL	970				1	1				1
MtIV	GL	1051			1		1				
Total			1	1 7	17 18	15 14	8 4	3 1	3	1	1

Note   Metapodial GL standards are not given in Payne and Bull (1989); the standards given here are based on the same Kizilcahamam sample.

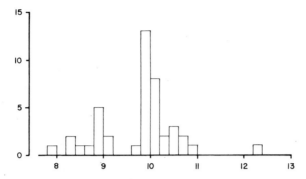

Figure 152. Ulnae of domestic fowl. Histogram showing distal diameter in millimeters.

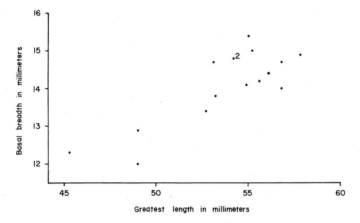

Figure 153. Scattergram of domestic fowl coracoid measurements, showing grouping of larger (presumed male) and smaller (presumed female) bones.

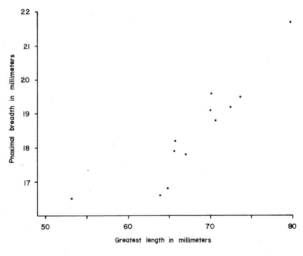

Figure 154. Scattergram showing variation in size of domestic fowl humer, including very short bone that may be the result of a genetic defect.

4.17 ARCHAEOBOTANICAL EVIDENCE

ALAN CLAPHAM AND KATHRYN L. GLEASON

Introduction

Excavation at Castle Copse villa has produced assemblages of plant remains from phases spanning early Roman to at least the fifth century A.D., primarily from building interiors.[1] In addition to contributing to the corpus of Romano-British plant remains, this study has three objectives. The first is to examine the plant remains for evidence of exploitation of different habitats surrounding Castle Copse by the inhabitants of the villa in different phases; the report is organized according to these habitats. The second objective, considering the interior location of most deposits, is to clarify wherever possible the functions of the excavated structures by establishing the character of carbonized plant assemblages. The final objective of the study is to document changes in the agricultural economy over time, particularly as the site entered the fifth century.

Methodology and Preservation

The evidence preserved at Castle Copse consists almost entirely of charred plant remains.[2] Occasional mineralized remains were encountered, and no waterlogged ones. The techniques for on-site sampling and recovery of the remains are discussed above (Appendix 11). For the laboratory analysis, eighty-three samples were selected: fifty from Sector A, twenty-one from Sector B and twelve from Sector C. Samples were chosen on the basis of a clearly definable context and the richness of the sample itself. While the preferred size for reliable interpretation is at least 100 seeds,[3] most samples from Castle Copse produced fewer components (Table 31).[4] The samples mostly have relatively low densities of charred material and relatively few identifiable items (Figs. 158–160).

Charcoal was identified only in the samples from Sector A chosen for the study of other plant remains, and of those, only fragments of reasonable size were examined. Some amorphous plant material thought to be soft parenchymatous tissue was also preserved, but no criteria have been established for the identification of such remains. Similarly, a large number of small, charred round objects, probably fungal sclerotia,[5] were present but not identified.

The plant remains from Sectors A and B are, on the whole, poorly preserved, preventing complete identification in nearly all cases. In all sectors, cereal grains are the most distorted and fragmented; in Sectors A and B, weed seeds are in similarly fragmentary condition, but are better preserved in Sector C. This situation is also true of the chaff remains, especially glume bases. As most fragments tend to be small and lacking most criteria for precise identification, only broad taxonomic categories are used in this report. Most charcoal fragments are well preserved, but again, too small for ready identification.

While most of the cultivated cereal remains are indeterminate, wheat and associated chaff are regularly present in the samples. Glume bases are most readily identified, the majority belonging to emmer (*Triticum dicoccum*). Some forms of chaff, such as spikelet and rachis fragments are rare, and of those found, few can be identified with any amount of certainty (Table 31).

Overall, there is a notable paucity of weed seeds in the samples. While the species list may seem quite comprehensive, most specimens occur either in single contexts of a given phase or appear only once. This has made it difficult to interpret the remains.

Modes of Arrival

Living representatives of most of the archaeological taxa can today be found in more than one of the area's habitats. It is difficult to be certain, however, that unprocessed crops were not brought from the broader region. Weeds from arable habitats may suggest local crops, but it is difficult to identify the specific crop and to determine whether the seeds arrived with the crop or are a product of a stage of crop processing.[6] The remains of edible fruits are likely to be the discarded parts of a meal or snack, harvested from either local wood- or scrubland.

Species from a grassland habitat are typically preserved on archaeological sites as remains of one or more of the following activities: as a component of hay gathered as fodder, preserved when discarded fodder was used as tinder or accidentally burned; as a source of tinder in the first place; through dung used as fuel; and as bedding. The contexts from which these remains were recovered, however, did not provide evidence for any particular uses.

Wasteland species often arrive attached to boots, hooves, clothing, or fur, becoming accidentally charred: the "welly-boot effect," often observed during excavations by those arriving at site after crossing fields and pastures.[7] The same may well be true for the wetland species represented, these arriving on the hooves or feet of domestic animals or in the drinking water.

Land Use and Habitat

Within a seven-kilometer radius of the villa buildings lies a landscape of richly varied soils, water features, topography, and the corresponding range of plant and wildlife habitats (see chapters 1, 4.2), and most of the agricultural and animal remains found on the site could have been supplied in this area. The information provided on the accompanying maps is drawn from the geology and soils of the area. The maps that accompany each section of this report contain information from supplementary studies of aerial photographs and historical documents.

Another contributing form of evidence is place names. While none of the field-names and few of the place names have received the systematic attention of place name specialists (see chapter 5)—and no examination was attempted here—it is impressive to observe the often close relationship between the place and field names recorded since A.D. 778 and the topographical features of landscape. For example, the distribution of names ending in -*leah* and -*tun* correspond with woodland and agricultural areas, respectively, while names ending in -*hamme* are found in the well-watered areas of the Vales of Ham and Pewsey. These names are noted on the habitat maps.

WOODLAND

In the region of the villa, there is a long history of woodland and forest on the chalk hills capped with Reading and London clays (Fig. 155).[8] The latter, especially, produces particularly heavy soils, unsuitable for agriculture or pasture. O. Rackham suggests that industry, with its fuel requirements, tends to protect woodland against the incursions of farmers.[9] If so, the presence of Roman pottery kilns in Savernake Forest may suggest the presence of managed woodland. The lighter Reading clays have a mixed history of woodland and agricultural uses, as is suggested by the field lynchets southeast of Bedwyn Brail (Fig. 156).[10] The remains of goshawk, jay, and woodcock identified at Castle Copse villa by E. Allison (see chap. 4.16) also suggest the presence of light woodland, and the presence of red and roe deer, identified by S. Payne, may suggest woodland and scrubland (see chapter 4.16).

Charcoal has been studied in Sector A (A223, 288, and 355). Only oak (*Quercus* sp.) was seen, species of which are present today in Savernake Forest, as well as on Bedwyn Brail. Carbonized nut remains of hazel are seen throughout the samples in all sectors. Other seeds add to the picture of woodland types. In Phase A:I, there is a predominance of knotgrass (*Polygonum* sp.) and members of the daisy family (Compositae). These represent wood/scrubland habitats similar to weed species found in Phase A:XI: sloe (*Prunus spinosa*), wood avens (cf. *Geum urbanum*), bramble (*Rubus fructicosus*), and hazel (*Corylus avellana*). Woodland is similarly represented by other woody species in phase A:II–X: sloe (*Prunus spinosa*), bramble (*Rubus fructicosus*), and elderberry (*Sambucus nigra*). As has been recorded in historical times, the types of woodland are likely to have been diverse.[11]

All of the woody species listed above were observed in a brief survey of the hedgerows in a two-kilometer radius of the villa.[12] Hedges are attested in the earliest historical records of the area (A.D. 778).[13] The plants were represented at the villa site by the remains of their edible fruits; the soft fruits of the bramble and sloe require rapid consumption, while hazel nuts can be stored.

Finally, Saxon documents also record the presence of bounded woods and the importance of hunting in the woods of this area in this period.[14]

ARABLE: CEREALS

The region around the villa offers a range of soils suitable for cereal production, from the well-drained loams of the greens and valleys to the chalk slopes, some enriched by runoff from the overlying clays, others thinly covering the steep slopes of the chalk downs (Fig. 156). All but the most intractable soils overlying the London Clays and the sterile Middle

Chalk slopes of the downs are arable and, therefore, it is not possible to designate the areas of the crops represented in the archaeological record. Recent work on the nearby Lambourn Downs suggests that some "Celtic" field systems on downland are in fact largely Roman in date.[15] Whether this is the case elsewhere, as with the ancient field systems on the Upper Chalk downs and hillslopes in the area of Great Bedwyn, which included the system visible in aerial photographs of the southeast slope of Bedwyn Brail, is not known.[16]

Although various artifacts typical of an agricultural villa were found during the excavations, these did not include the scythes, sickles, ploughshares, or other harvesting equipment that would contribute to an assessment of agricultural innovations over time. Nor can the evidence from the carbonized remains provide a complete picture; but in combination with an understanding of the resources of the area, they provide preliminary evidence for agricultural production at the villa.

Three species of wheat are found at Castle Copse. Emmer (*Triticum dicoccum*) and spelt (*T. spelta*) are glume wheats, while bread wheat (*Triticum aestivum*) is free-threshing. The glume wheats are hardier crops, resisting weed and insect infestation, spelt being the hardiest. Bread wheat is easily threshed and has a high yield potential, but the loose ear is vulnerable to birds and fungi, and the plant competes poorly with weeds. In terms of soil conditions, spelt is the most versatile; emmer responds best to light soils and dry conditions. Bread wheat responds best to heavy soils with high clay and silt content. Both conditions are present in the study area. The wheats also respond differently to climatic factors: emmer is frost-susceptible and is planted in the spring; spelt and bread wheat, being frost-hardy, can be sown in the autumn. Thus, cultivation of the three crops would allow farmers to use land more efficiently over the course of the year.

Spelt was favored by the Romans, although it had been present in England since the Neolithic and is well attested in Iron Age deposits. The flour has excellent milling and baking properties. Emmer, the principal wheat of the Neolithic and Bronze Age, is consistently secondary to spelt in the Roman and Saxon archaeological records, including that at Castle Copse. It is characterized by exceptionally high quality flour and was preferred for soup, being higher in protein than bread wheat. Bread wheat was introduced during the Neolithic, but, perhaps due to its growing requirements, did not gain prominence until Roman and Saxon times.[17] A small number of club wheat grains (*Triticum aestivo-compactum*) were also found in Sector C. This dense-eared form of bread wheat was popular in the Roman period; however, the economic significance of its genetic distinction from bread wheat is not known.

Due to the paucity of remains directly attributable to crop storage and processing, the excavation deposits at Castle Copse contain little information on crop management, but a few trends are seen. In the samples studied, spelt is the most common find in Sectors A and B, followed by emmer; only one grain of bread wheat was encountered. In Sector C, however, bread wheat predominates, the bulk of the remains coming from a pit (C64:IV); emmer and spelt were mainly represented by their chaff fragments, rather than their caryopses.[18] Emmer wheat may have become less popular as bread replaced porridge as the main staple food.

The presence of a large number of wheat glumes of spelt, emmer, and unidentifiable fragments suggests that the glume wheats were stored as spikelets, protecting the grain against rodent and insect attack.[19] Sprouting can occur in the ears of crops harvested in damp weather and insufficiently dried afterwards, but grain was also intentionally sprouted for malting, as at Catsgore.[20] Sprouted grains of wheat at Castle Copse are present but, unlike at Catsgore, in too small a quantity to conclusively indicate malting.

Barley (*Hordeum vulgare*) grows in diverse conditions throughout Britain, except in very acid or poorly drained soils.[21] The classical sources indicate that the grain was used for both humans and animals, and was popular for brewing. Usually a fodder crop for domestic animals, it was also a punishment food for disobedient soldiers.[22]

Barley is represented in Sectors A and B by hulled symmetrical grains and rachis fragments that suggest two-row barley. The large percentage of indeterminate fragments does not preclude the possibility of six-row barley, more readily identifiable in Sectors B and C.[23] Barley and wheat remains were found together at Castle Copse, which may suggest that the crops were grown together for some purpose such as animal feed, although they are first processed in different ways.

Rye (*Secale cereale*) is very hardy in most soil conditions, except heavy clays, and is present as a crop in the archaeological record as early as the Iron Age in Wiltshire. A small number of grains of rye were found in the early occupation phase (A:I) of Sector A and in no other contexts (Table 31).[24] The rye may have been a local crop or merely a contaminant in the wheat fields. The grains are edible and add to the yield of the crop, so they would not be removed during weeding or processing.

Cultivated oat (*Avena sativa*) is a crop that tolerates the acid and infertile soils of the highlands, though it prefers the moist conditions of deep loams or clay loams. It is not frost-hardy and thrives with a mild, moist growing season following a spring sowing. Oats are present in the archaeological record in Britain from the Iron Age to the Saxon period. An increase in the Roman period, notably in the highlands, has been linked to military demands for horse fodder; in the lowlands, increased evidence for oats and rye may indicate a disparity between "rich" farmers intensively working the fertile soils and "poor" farmers relegated to the marginal soils.[25] At Castle Copse, the remains of carbonized oats found in Phases C:III and C:IV of Sector C do not retain the "sucker mouth" scar of the floret necessary for identification as a cultivated species. The absence of any substantial evidence for oats and rye may simply fit the overall pattern of wealth evident at this villa throughout much of its later history.

Only one pea (*Pisum sativum*), from Sector A, has been identified, and its small size suggests that it may be a weed rather than a crop.

The beamslot building in Sector A, Phase I contained cereal assemblages (A816, A937, and A946:I) of particular interest (Tables 30–31). Wheat glume bases, spelt, and other wheat grains, barley grains, and some weed seeds are present. The remains appear to be of prime grain mixed with fine cleanings, although an important part of the chaff fraction (rachis fragments) is missing. Interpretation is difficult. The building may have been used as a store for both the fine cleanings and prime grains, which mixed; alternatively, the grain may have been damaged in some way (insect or fungal attack) and deliberately mixed with fine cleanings as feed for domestic animals. The resulting mixture was preserved through carbonization, although the source for the fire is not evident. As the remains were found in the beamslots, a third possibility is that several different activities carried on in the structure mixed together after the destruction of the building.

Also of interest is the sample from the fill of a late fourth-century pit in Phase C:IV of Sector C (C43, 64:IV; see chapter 4.3) a pit which cut through fills deposited after the Roman floor had been removed (Table 31). The plant remains appear to be similar throughout, the major difference being the quantity in each sample. Bread wheat is the dominant cereal, with little emmer or spelt. The very small quantities of the latter may be residual in nature. The weed seeds indicate a mixture of both ruderal and segetal habitats, suggesting that the remains may represent dumping in a general rubbish pit.

ARABLE: SEGETALS

Segetals, or arable weeds, are excellent indicators of habitats, crop types, and crop processing; however, despite the evident range of weed species at Castle Copse, they are too few in number to offer a full range of interpretation. Large weed plants, particularly the ubiquitous weed of Roman times, the corncockle (*Agrostemma githago*) are noticeably absent, and there may be several explanations for the general paucity of weeds at the site. Some of these may be that crops were weeded regularly or were harvested high enough up the straw to avoid the weeds (although a number of low-growing weeds are present); the first stages of crop processing took place elsewhere and only semi-cleaned grain was brought into the excavated areas; few weeds survived the charring process, although corncockle, much denser than other weed seeds that did survive, would then be expected; and lastly, more weeds are present but not in the samples studied.[26]

Segetals comprise the majority of weed seeds found at Castle Copse. Most are common to all sectors. Charlock (*Sinapis arvensis*) is common in Roman contexts, found in quantities at Catsgore and Wilderspool.[27] Other common arable weeds include chickweed (*Stellaria* cf. *media*), violet (*Viola* sp.), fat hen (*Chenopodium* cf. *album*), clover (*Trifolium* sp.), sheep's sorrel (*Rumex acetosella*), knotgrass (*Polygonum aviculare*), redshank (*Polygonum persicaria*), cleavers (*Galium aparine*) and scentless mayweed (*Tripleurospermum maritimum inodorum*). Cornsalad (*Valerianella dentata*) is an indicator of the calcareous arable land in the vicinity of the villa.

RUDERAL/PASTURE

Ruderal, or wasteland, habitats are represented by a large number of species. Overall, the area possesses a diverse range of habitats available for pasturing animals: downs and other calcareous grasslands, wet meadows, rough pasture, and wasteland (Fig. 157). No evidence for hay production has survived. In addition to the grass taxa, the ruderal species include corn spurrey (*Spergula arvensis*), usually present on sandy soils (limited at Castle Copse to the Bagshot beds atop the hills to the north and west of the site (historically, wastelands); violet; melitot (*Melitotus* sp.); stinging nettle (*Urtica dioica*); ribwort plantain (*Plantago lanceolata*); and nipplewort (*Lapsana communis*); as well as the grass taxa. One badly damaged find may be either tansy or feverfew (*Chrysanthemum vulgare* or *C. parthenium*). Many of these species can also be expected on continuously disturbed lands such as tracks, pathways, manure heaps, and rubbish tips. Stinging nettles, in particular, have an affinity for the high concentrations of nitrogen and phosphorus found in these areas. Pellitory of the wall (cf. *Parietaria diffusa*) was found in a dump of building material (which was perhaps once a wall).

Several species present at Castle Copse indicate the presence of nearby grasslands. Purging flax (*Linum catharticum*) is an indicator of calcareous grassland, while black knapweed (*Centaurea* cf. *nigra*) can be an indicator of grassland on clay soils. Other indicators of grassland environment include crane's bill (*Geranium* sp.), meliot, and ribwort plantain. Ox-eye daisy (*Chrysanthemum leucanthemum*) may indicate the presence of meadows. The grass taxa may also have derived from this habitat.

RIVERINE/WETLAND

Flax (*Linum usitatissimum*), a soil-exhausting crop, is frequently cultivated on the fertile lands of alluvial valleys, present along Bedwyn Brook and, more abundantly, in the Vales of Ham and Pewsey (Fig. 157). Such a location is ideal for fiber production. The retting process, in which fibres are released from the stem material, requires plentiful water.[28] The seed capsules are usually removed before this process and stored for the next sowing. Surplus is sold or used in gruel or porridge, a favorite dish of the Romans.[29] Flax is also grown for its oil, produced by pressing, and it is possible to grow the crop for both fibre and oil.[30] Linseed was found in all sectors from which samples were taken at Castle Copse, though in scant quantities.

Wetland is indicated by two water edge plants, spike-rush (*Eleocharis* sp.) and sedge (*Carex* sp.). *Eleocharis* sp. is generally an indicator of damp soils, either heavy or light, often in the presence of rivers.[31] The presence of this weed in a deposit of grain from the first century A.D. (A932:I) may indicate that even marginal lands were under cultivation, as has been noted during this period in the south in general.[32] Unexpected was the presence of greater dodder (*Cuscuta europaea*). Often a parasite on nettles,[33] it is also a serious pest of flax fields, as just two plants per square meter can destroy an entire crop.[34] These wetland species form a small minority of species identified from Castle Copse, although the site is less than a kilometer from the Bedwyn Brook.

Imported Exotic Species

Remains of olive (*Olea europaea*) and fig (*Ficus carica*) represent the importation of foodstuffs to Castle Copse, as neither are native to the British Isles. Olive was found in Sectors A:XI and C:IV. Although it is possible to see fig growing in English parks and gardens, they are parthenocarpic (non-fruitbearing), and any remains of especially well-developed seeds must be of foreign origin. Fig was imported in a dried state and is usually found in cess samples; at Castle Copse, the sole specimen of fig was recovered from the occupation of the first aisled building (A:VIII) in Sector A.[35]

Relative Components of the Different Sectors and Phases

In Sector A, Phases A:I (c. A.D. 50–70) and A:XI (after A.D. 331 to the late fourth/early fifth century) represent the first and one of the later Roman phases of occupations of the site, respectively. Both of these phases contain spelt wheat grains and glume bases, as well as those belonging to the *Triticum* indeterminate category. Hulled barley grains (*Hordeum vulgare*) are also found in both, as is cultivated flax (*Linum usitatissimum*). The weed seeds of fat hen (*Chenopodium* cf. *album*), clover (*Trifolium* sp.), ribwort plantain (*Plantago lanceolata*), sedge (*Carex* sp.), and rye grass (*Lolium* sp.) are common to both Phases A:I and A:XI.

Differences between the early and late phases of Sector A also exist: Bread wheat (*Triticum aestivum*) and emmer (*Triticum dicoccum*) are found in Phase A:I, but not in A:XI, as expected; however, rye (*Secale cereale*) and oat (*Avena* sp.) follow the same pattern, contrary to the model of increased usage currently accepted for Romano-British agriculture. Olive (*Olea europaea*) is found only in Phase A:XI, and fig only in Phase A:VIII, indicating overseas trade of these products in the late phase (see below).

In Sector B, there is no apparent pattern in the distribution of charred plant categories, although Phase B:II (late second–early third century A.D.) and Phase B:III (after A.D. 200) contain the largest proportion of preserved remains. Overall, the most frequent remains are those of spelt wheat grains, glume bases, and rachis fragments, along with indeterminate wheat grains and glume bases. Hazel is also frequently present. Most categories are common to all phases.

By far the richest phase in Sector C is C:IV (late fourth–early fifth century A.D.), due to the discovery and complete water flotation of the pit feature, C64, discussed above. Spelt wheat grains and glume bases, bread wheat grain, along with indeterminate cereals, are present in all phases of Sector C, as are hazelnuts, clover, and the small grasses. There do not seem to be any dramatic changes between phases with regard either to cereal types or habitats represented.

Comparison of Sectors A–C shows that most categories are common to all. Exceptionally, the weeds melilot (*Melilotus* sp.), stinging nettle (*Urtica dioica*), greater dodder (cf. *Cuscuta europaea*), black knapweed (*Centaurea* cf. *nigra*), crane's bill (*Geranium* sp.), and bent grass (*Agrostis* sp.) can be found only in Sector B, although with only a few examples of each.

Conclusions

The excavations at the villa at Castle Copse centered primarily on the interior of buildings. Thus, in the areas studied, domesticated plants appear to have been used after most stages of processing had been carried out elsewhere. Even pits and other refuse areas reflect this situation, suggesting that most early stages of crop-processing in all periods concerned took place outside the buildings excavated. Botanical evidence from the beam slot building in Sector A suggests a function as a storage facility for crop products or as a small barn; in general, however, the scant finds were well mixed before or after charring, preventing an interpretation of the activities represented.

The hypothetical model seen in Fig. 157, summarizing the previous discussion of archaeobotanical remains in conjunction with preliminary evidence of historical documents, place-names, and aerial photographs, suggests that the varied and rich resources of the local landscape can account for the botanical remains recovered in the excavations.

Within the limits of the evidence, it appears that crop types and habitat indicators changed little over time, though it is often proposed that a dramatic shift occurred in the range and type of crops cultivated: from one of mainly spelt, emmer, and bread wheat, with barley as a animal feed, to an agriculture dependent upon the cultivation of rye and oats.[36] At Castle Copse, Roman crop types continue into the fifth century, with bread wheat and the glume wheats in steady use. Similarly, the habitat range, with wild species dominated by ruderals and segetals, does not suggest dramatic changes. M. Jones has recently discussed how such changes can occur within a single region and time period, reflecting economic disparity.[37] The evidence from Castle Copse, admittedly less than conclusive, nevertheless offers little to support this theory. Indeed, the opposite is suggested, that is, over the roughly four centuries of occupation documented by the excavations, there appears to be remarkably little change in agricultural practices.

NOTES

1. In this section, K. Gleason has taken the final laboratory report prepared by Clapham and set it into the overall context of the site, as the latter joined the project only after the conclusion of fieldwork. G. Hillman kindly made some preliminary observations in 1983, while N. F. Miller has made numerous improvements and invaluable suggestions throughout the writing process.

2. The plant remains were identified using the modern seed reference collection at the Human Environment Department, Institute of Archaeology, London. Wood identification was carried out with a Wild Epi-illuminating Microscope.

3. G. E. M. Jones 1984.

4. The notable exceptions are: A205, A932, A942, A946; B110, B113, and C64.

5. I.e., the mycelia stored with reserve food that remains dormant until an opportunity for growth arises.

6. See Hillman 1984.

7. Hillman 1984.

8. The history of Savernake Forest, which has historically included the area of Castle Copse villa, is detailed in Ailesbury 1962. See also Brentnall 1941: 391–433.

9. Rackham 1990: 84–88, on the relationship of industry and woodland. On managed woodland, see M. Jones 1989: 128.

10. This system may have been preserved by a medieval wood, Lynley, mentioned in the perambulations in Savernake Forest between A.D. 1300–1350: Brentnall 1941: 427. Other lynchets are visible in the woods on the southeast slope of Bedwyn Brail.

11. For example, herbaceous species such as wood avens are found in woodlands, while melilot (*Melilotus* sp.) and smooth tare (*Vicia tetrasperma*) are more characteristic of scrubland.

12. A preliminary survey of hedgerows was carried out in 1983–84. While too incomplete for publication, it did record the species composition of hedgerows that have been removed. On hedgerows, see Rackham 1990: 60.

13. Grundy 1919: 151; and 1920: 76.

14. The charters for both Great Bedwyn and Little Bedwyn, for example, describe a *haga*, translated as a deer fence or game enclosure, just north of the villa: Grundy 1919: 151. Other boundary hedges, for fields or woods, are noted in the bounds of Great Bedwyn, A.D. 968: Grundy 1920: 74; Crawford 1921: 282–83.

15. Gaffney and Tingle 1989.

16. A study of crops marks and existing field boundaries carried out using GIS (Geographic Information Systems) software revealed no traces of Roman centuriation or any significant or conclusive relationships between field systems, roads, villa, or the cardinally oriented town of Cunetio.

17. Helbaek 1952; M. Jones 1981: 104.

18. In one of the samples (C37), the wheat glume bases appeared to be an intermediate form of spelt, with a slightly pronounced secondary keel. This pronounced keel was not so enlarged for the glume bases to be considered as being of emmer wheat, but was viewed as the effect of charring. Some spikelet forks and rachis fragments in Sector C were of a tetraploid wheat, most likely emmer, but positive identification was not possible.

19. Hillman 1981.

20. Hillman 1982: 138. "Corn-driers" were used to dry both malted grain and grain harvested in damp weather—it is difficult to distinguish between intended and accidental uses.

21. Moffet 1987.

22. Greig 1983. Its use as animal fodder is demonstrated at Lancaster, where horse dung was analysed: Wilson 1979.

23. Here the grains are twisted, a characteristic of six-row barley, which may, however, be the result of charring. A definite identification cannot be given due to the small number of grains found and the lack of intact rachis fragments.

24. Rye appears in Britain in the Iron Age, perhaps first as a weed, but becoming a staple by medieval times. It is found today on poorer and drier soils: Dimbleby 1978: 79.

25. M. Jones 1989: 133.

26. Hillman 1981: 148.

27. Hillman 1980; and 1982.

28. Clapham 1986.

29. Renfrew 1973.

30. Theoretically, the product for which the crop has been grown can be determined by accurate measurement of the seeds, the crop cultivated for fiber having the smaller seeds; however, the high oil of both types causes distortion during charring and prevents accurate measurement.

31. M. Jones 1981: 111–12.

32. M. Jones 1989: 129.

33. Rose 1981.

34. Clapham 1986.

35. Fig has also been found at York, Colchester, and London (Willcox 1977: 271).

36. Hillman 1981: 124. For a review of "shifts of emphasis" in agricultural practice and archaeological methods of analysis, see M. Jones 1981: 95. On barley as animal feed, see Greig 1983.

37. M. Jones 1989: 133.

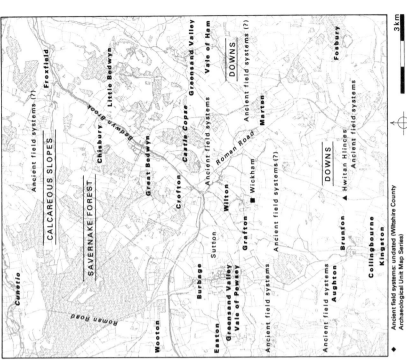

Figure 156. Map of agricultural resources in the area of the villa. Ancient field systems are indicated by bolder lines.

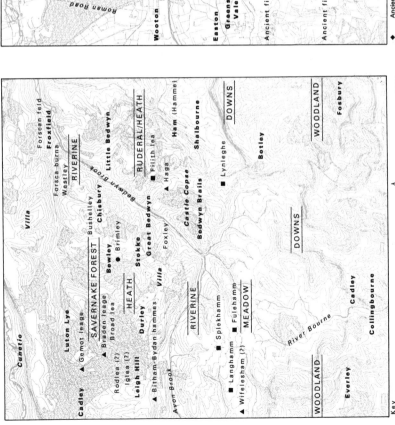

Figure 155. Map of woodland, ruderal, and riverine habitats.

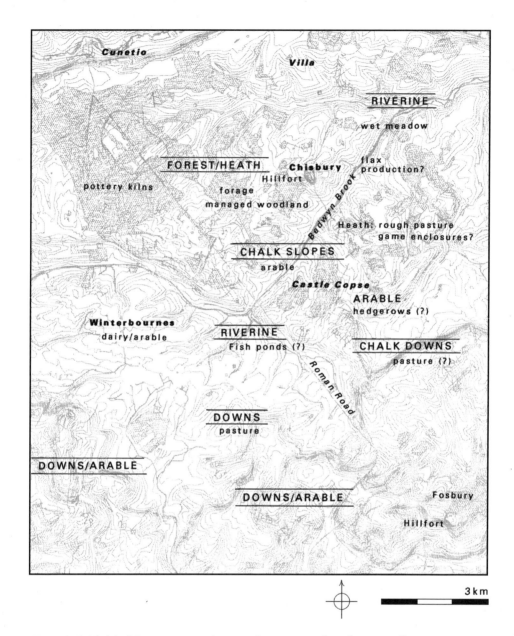

Figure 157. Model of the resources in the immediate vicinity of Castle Copse villa.

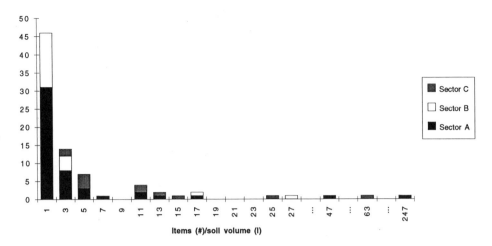

Figure 158. Botanical recovery Sectors A–C: items (number)/soil volume (liters).

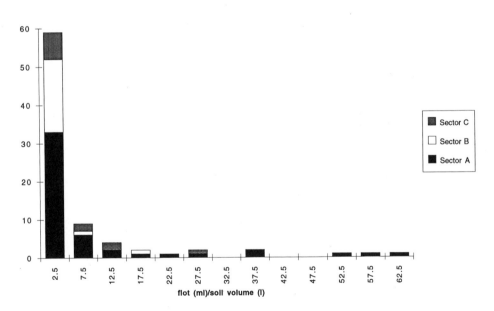

Figure 159. Botanical recovery Sectors A–C: flot (ml)/soil volume (liters).

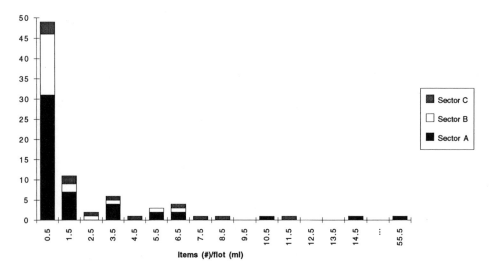

Figure 160. Botanical recovery Sectors A–C: items (number)/flot (ml).

4.18 OBSERVATIONS ON THE BEDWYN DYKE

THOMAS NOBLE HOWE AND ERIC HOSTETTER

As early as the second decade of the nineteenth century, it was suggested by R. Colt Hoare that a number of linear earthworks in the neighborhood of Chisbury hillfort could be an eastern extension of the Wansdyke, running from Savernake Forest to Inkpen Hill on the edge of Salisbury Plain (Fig. 2).[1] O. G. S. Crawford (1953), though initially referring to them as Wansdyke, suspected that they were only disjointed fragments and marked them so on the O.S. maps, calling the best-preserved section between Chisbury and Bedwyn Brail the Bedwyn Dyke.[2] A. and C. Fox (1960) concluded that they had no connection with the Wansdyke, and, like Crawford, gave serious regard only to the segment between Chisbury and Bedwyn Brail.[3]

The sections of dyke lying both to the east and west of Chisbury hillfort are without question different in character from the Wansdyke both in their scale (c. half the width) and the way they lie on the land. Moreover, as only small sections of dyke are well preserved, it cannot be proved that these sections formed part of any continuous barrier originating with the Wansdyke. However, based on a survey conducted in the spring of 1986,[4] it can be argued that a number of features previously dismissed or undiscovered might be associated by their dimensions or their lie on the land to form a single, more or less continuous, linear earthwork.

Description

The group of earthworks which might be associated as a Bedwyn Dyke "system" runs through the parishes of Little Bedwyn, Great Bedwyn, Shalbourne, Ham, and Inkpen (Figs. 2, 5, 161–162). The earthworks usually appear to consist of a single bank and ditch (although see below on the possibility of a counterscarp bank) with a total width usually very close to fifteen meters. The height is nowhere reliably preserved since most sections have been altered by plowing and virtually all sections run on clayey soils which have eroded. The "system" generally faces to the north or east and appears to seek to close gaps across open terrain between forested areas.[5] Like the Wansdyke, many sections run across high terrain, on or just below a ridge, and consistently parallel to the contours with the ditch downslope; unlike the Wansdyke, however, other sections jog suddenly at near right angles to run directly across a valley to the next ridge or feature. For this reason, sections of the "system" have been referred to as cross-valley dykes,[6] which constitute one of its most important features. Finally, again like the Wansdyke, sections which may be associated with the Bedwyn Dyke "system," both east and west of Chisbury hillfort, appear not always to respect parish boundaries, but cut across them to take advantage of the terrain.

To the west of Chisbury, three sections of earthwork, only one of which is clearly discernible today, have been claimed for the Bedwyn Dyke/Wansdyke (Fig. 2).

BIRCH COPSE—BELMORE COPSE.
The first seems to lie along the contour across a shallow combe facing downhill to the north between Birch Copse and Belmore Copse. While this section is not beyond argument presently visible, it appears to correspond to the easternmost section of Colt Hoare's map, and was claimed and later discounted by Crawford.[7]

SOUTHWEST OF CHISBURY LANE FARM.
Crawford also claimed and later discounted a section "250 yards SW. of Chisbury Lane Farm."[8]

CHISBURY WOOD (FIG. 161).
The third section is still plainly visible. It runs some 390 meters east-west in the northwest corner of Chisbury Wood across high terrain which gently slopes to the north.[9] This section seems to consist of a double bank and double ditch; the lower, smaller bank is very low, and at first glance eroded and hard to discern, but it clearly runs the whole length of the preserved section and lies downslope of the main bank in the manner of a counterscarp. The width of the principal bank and ditch is about 15 m, as in the rest of the "system," and the total width is about 30 m. Both ends of the section run up to the edges of the wood into arable, where no trace of it remains.

If the existence of the first two sections cannot today be ascertained, their validity should perhaps not be completely discounted. Both continue in a line from the section in Chisbury Wood that corresponds to the seeming method of laying the "system" on the land—although crossing nearly level ground, the ditch is always downslope. The section in Chisbury Wood, if continued to the east to Chisbury, would run along top of the highest descending ridge on the west side of the hillfort, hence the most logical position to attach an earthwork running west from the fort.[10] Finally, the line of these dykes seems roughly parallel to the boundary between the parishes of Little and Great Bedwyn, until the dyke continues east to Chisbury hillfort, while the parish boundary veers south. This may suggest that the posited dyke postdates the boundary.

CHISBURY HILLFORT—ROUND COPSE—VILLA AT CASTLE COPSE (FIGS. 2, 5, 161–162).
From Chisbury hillfort the "Bedwyn Dyke" cuts south/southeast directly across the Bedwyn valley and rises up the opposite slope into Jockey Copse. The section downhill of Chisbury is preserved today mainly in the form of a high (c. 3 m) lynchet, in which the field to the east has filled in up to the top of the bank from the outside (i.e., the northeast, hence filling the presumed ditch as well). Only at the very bottom, where the earthwork is crossed by the road to Little Bedwyn, does the profile of the bank and part of the presumed ditch appear to be preserved; while the profile of the ditch is slightly

truncated by the adjacent field (Figs. 2, 5, 161), the total width again appears to be about 14 m. On the other side of the valley, the earthwork is clearly traceable as a ditch and bank rising up the steep slope to Jockey Copse. It continues, though today rather ploughed out, across a field on high ground to Round Copse (Figs. 161–162), the ground being very nearly level, but the ditch still being downslope (to the northeast). In 1953, Crawford saw this section as a double bank and ditch.[11]

At the northeast corner of Round Copse, the "system" appears to—or may at least be argued to—branch: one fairly well-attested section (mentioned in the Anglo-Saxon charter of A.D. 778; see chapter 5) jogs southwest to cross the valley called Harandene and run toward Bedwyn Brail; the other turns east and, somehow, crosses Burridge Heath—or relies on the forests that may have existed there—to connect with the next well-preserved section near Eastcourt Farm.[12]

Through Round Copse the ditch and bank are clearly identifiable and appear to be about 15–18 m wide (Figs. 2, 161–162). They follow a descending ridge, generally keeping the ditch downslope. In the bottom of the Valley called Harandene, the line of the bank does not continue directly across the valley toward the nearest high ground in Bedwyn Brail, but jogs slightly and climbs obliquely up the slope; the bank no longer exists, but its line is still visible as a chalky mark when the field is freshly plowed.[13] There may have been a gate here, at least at the time of the Saxon charters,[14] and this jog allows the ditch to be somewhat more clearly downslope than the direct route would have allowed. Some 55 m south, this line again jogs west at near right angles and enters Bedwyn Brail. Within the Brail there is another little-noticed (although recorded on O.S. maps), but well-preserved, section with a great deal of chalk upcast on its surface (Fig. 161).[15] It clearly demonstrates features similar to those of the Bedwyn Dyke with a ditch and bank of a total width of about 15 m. The ditch is still on the same side of the bank (here to the south), but a peculiarity of this section is that the ditch is slightly uphill of the bank. This reverse slope is, however, so gentle as to be virtually negligible and is remedied as soon as the bank begins to rise up the steeper slope of the Brail. The ditch and bank can be followed for almost 200 m into the forest before they fade in the forest cover and softer clays just after they begin to curve southwest uphill. From this point, the line of the ditch can probably be followed farther uphill as a stream which has followed the line of the ditch and eroded deeply into the slope; this continues until it disappears in a ploughed field at a point slightly less than 200 m from the Castle Copse villa platform and in an area of small earthworks, probable paddocks, etc., and where two heavily abraded Roman sherds were recovered.

None of the earthworks identified in Bedwyn Brail can be associated with the Bedwyn Dyke "system"; all appear to be Celtic or Roman field terraces, postmedieval field boundaries, game park enclosures, or even, conceivably, parts of the Lord Protector Somerset's abortive constructions. No continuation of the Bedwyn dyke "system" south toward the downs or west into Wilton Brail has been identified.[16]

ROUND COPSE—BURRIDGE HEATH—BAGSHOT—EASTCOURT FARM (FIGS. 161–162).

At the point of the supposed branch of the Bedwyn Dyke "system" at the northeast corner of Round Copse, the Bedwyn Dyke appears to cut across the ditch and bank which serve as the parish boundary between Great and Little Bedwyn, and about 50 m to the south there is an intersection between the parish boundaries of Great Bedwyn, Little Bedwyn, and Shalbourne, with the Little Bedwyn–Shalbourne boundary (Figs. 161–162). However, the Bedwyn Dyke cannot definitively be said to cross the parish boundary, because at the intersection both the parish boundary and the dyke make a near right-angle jog. The short (c. 70 m) north-south section of the parish boundary is quite eroded, but is unusually broad (c. 15–18 m) and actually continues the line of the previous section of the Bedwyn Dyke. The ditch is to the same side as on the dyke and the adjacent sections of the parish boundaries seem to be smaller and much more typical of the proportions of parish boundaries. When this north-south section jogs east at the intersection with Shalbourne, it does so to follow a ridge across Burridge Heath, which is the usual siting method for the Bedwyn Dyke "system."

It is possible, therefore, that this section of the parish boundary is actually a continuation of the dyke and that the Bedwyn Dyke does not so much cross the parish boundary at this point as branch, one section going southwest to Bedwyn Brail and the other, following the parish boundary, continuing in a straight line 70 m south, and there, possibly, jogging east to cross the high ground in Burridge Heath. The terrain in Burridge Heath is highly irregular, but one of the most logical routes across it—that is, keeping the outside downslope—follows the parish boundary as far as a wood called the Dell, where it must turn at right angles to cross a stream valley and rise around the north side of the hill of Bagshot.

Colt Hoare covered this ground in 1813 and 1814 and, without complete conviction, concluded for a route somewhat farther to the south.[17] This route—if we correctly read his early plans—-appears somewhat peculiar, as it seems to avoid high ground, crosses as many valleys as possible, and often has the outside upslope. He did, however, notice a "very strong bank" near Bagshot and another near Polesdon Dairy (later discarded), which might have lain in plausible terrain for this connection. We have not been able to locate these.

From the northeast corner of Round Copse there is therefore a well-attested section of dyke to the southeast to Bedwyn Brail and one or two plausible routes for one to the east to Eastcourt Farm. The possibility remains, of course, that this latter section was closed by forest.

EASTCOURT FARM—OAK POLLARD—DANIEL'S LANE—MOUNT PROSPEROUS—SADLER'S COPSE (FIGS. 2, 161).

At a point near Eastcourt Farm, Shalbourne, a section of earthwork can be clearly recognized. Colt Hoare followed a section of it (northwest) of the Shalbourne stream into the wood called Oak Pollard; it can today be followed on the east side of the stream (southeast) as a ploughed-out field boundary (still marked on O.S. maps) and then across the Salisbury-Hungerford road in a hollow way called Daniel's Lane. From Daniel's Lane the "system" can be recognized or inferred as it runs east for some 3 km parallel to the slope of the ridge of Mt. Prosperous. In Daniel's Lane it is preserved as a hollow way with a steep lynchet on only one side (the southwest) and the track on the site of the presumed ditch to the northeast (Fig. 161). This line continues directly into the adjacent field of Mount Prosperous Farm, where it is still sometimes recognizable as a ploughed chalky mark.[18] It continues on Mount Prosperous Farm as an earthwork, then a high lynchet filling the bank from the north (Fig. 161), and then as a ploughed-out lynchet (Fig. 161). The ditch is not preserved anywhere on this section (unless in the form of the track in Daniel's Lane), but it was presumably to the north which is always downslope.

SADLER'S COPSE—RIVAR COPSE—OLD DYKE LANE—INKPEN HILL (FIGS. 2, 161).

Somewhere near SU 350644 (once Sadler's Farm), where this ridge begins to run out, the "system" probably makes a right-angle bend, crosses a broad valley (whose floor descends to the east or the "outside"), while running for some 2 km almost in a straight line to a projecting ridge on Inkpen Hill, called Rivar Copse. As it descends the hill to cross the valley a broad ditch and bank (width c. 15 m) are recognizable in "Old Dyke Lane," with the ditch (a track) to the east and slightly downslope of the bank (Fig. 161). Crawford thought he identified the continuation as a field mark extending straight south from the end of Old Dyke Lane.[19] While the field mark is clearly real, this line puts the outside slightly upslope; a more topographically consistent, if hypothetical, line branches slightly west and follows a field boundary bank which serves as both a parish boundary (between Ham and Inkpen) and a county boundary (Wiltshire and Berkshire). Inkpen Hill apparently forms the terminus of the "system," and from this point east, and easily as far as Walbury hillfort, the downs would have formed a clear and daunting boundary facing north. In Rivar Copse, where the presumed dyke "system" meets the downs, there are a number of tumuli.[20]

Constructional Method

At first glance the putative Bedwyn Dyke "system" appears very irregular and disjointed with, in its present state, several changes of scale, but the ditch and bank may actually be of consistent dimensions throughout, and they clearly follow a uniform approach in their positioning on the terrain. The sections of the "system" either run along high terrain parallel to the contours or jog at near right angles to follow a convenient ridge or run directly across a valley by the shortest possible route, except for the section from Round Copse to the meadow immediately east of the villa at Castle Copse. On high terrain the dyke sections run on or below a ridge, with the ditch always downslope and on the outside (i.e., approximately to the north and east) and with Chisbury hillfort, the villa site, and Great Bedwyn on the inside. When they jog to cross a valley they continue to try to keep the ditch downslope, usually by following a descending ridge.

This lie on the land particularly distinguishes the preserved or suspected sections of the dyke "system" from most field and parish boundaries which do not consistently follow high or descending ridges. The sections of the dyke "system" almost always keep the "outside" downhill and avoid running along low features.

Where recognizable and preserved, the main ditch and bank are consistently about 15 m wide. The original height cannot be estimated easily, since almost all sections of the "system" run on relatively clayey soils which have eroded steadily or have been plowed. Still, the probable dyke sections are higher and broader than conventional field boundaries: at Mount Prosperous and in Bedwyn Brail and the adjacent field, the ditch was dug deeply enough, through a meter or more of topsoil, to cast chalk up onto the bank.[21] If, as it suggested by the Wansdyke, an inclination of c. 30–40° is presumed, a bank c. 7–8 m in width would have been about 3–4 m high.

It is also possible that the "system" was meant to have a counterscarp bank. This profile is fairly clear in the section in Chisbury Wood and, as noted above, Crawford observed that the section in the field between Jockey Copse and Round Copse had the appearance of a double bank and ditch.[22] In most other locations the position where the low counterscarp bank would be expected is arable field and—if it ever existed—has been ploughed out. The only exception to this situation is in Round Copse where the dyke descends through what appears to be older forest; however, the forest cover and the heavy erosion of the profile make reading the terrain difficult, and in the lower, steeper part of the ridge some enigmatic surface features could as easily be interpreted as a disturbed double bank as a single one.[23]

Thus, if the dyke sections discussed above, especially from Burridge Heath eastwards, are in fact a part of one continuous "system"—and here detailed study of medieval documentary evidence may prove helpful—its purpose may have been to protect, from the northeast, the open terrain in the valleys between Savernake Forest and Inkpen Hill by a linked series of cross-valley dykes.

Lastly, the geological and topographic reasons for building a dyke "system" have been discussed by D. Keefer (chapter 4.2): essentially, Chisbury, Great Bedwyn, and Castle Copse villa derive their strategic importance from their location on the east-west trending upland between the Kennet River and the Vale of Pewsey, a natural defensive position between these two major valleys, which is further strengthened by the rough and broken nature of much of this terrain and by the presumed presence of dense woods, particularly on the Tertiary sediments and clay-with-flints soils. Keefer also notes that Chisbury hillfort, the villa at Castle Copse, and Great Bedwyn are at a convergence of four lines of transportation: the valley of Bedwyn Brook, which connects the Vale of Pewsey with the Kennet-Thames Valley; the upland divide connecting the Marlborough Downs to Salisbury Plain; the Roman road between Cunetio and Winchester; and the possible east-west line of dykes and hillforts on the most defensible upland terrain between the lowlands of the Kennet and Thames and the Vale of Pewsey.

Discussion

The possible Bedwyn Dyke "system" as presented here, can hardly have been a convincing work of defensive military architecture. It was only 7–8 m wide and 3–4 m high, and, even with a palisade on top, seems unlikely to have been a cross-country barrier meant to prevent penetration of a specific territory. Only half the size of the Wansdyke, it is usually—and vaguely—referred to as a "cross-valley dyke," perhaps to hinder small-scale raiding.[24] However small, it may still have been useful. Intruders moving through the clear terrain of valley bottoms could probably have been spotted from points of high ground. From Chisbury there is a good view over the Bedwyn Valley, and from the site of the villa at Castle Copse one can view arrivals from the southwest through the Vale of Ham and Harandene. Less likely, perhaps, is the possibility that it was intended solely as a political or cultural boundary.[25]

In the absence of archaeological evidence, various proposals have been made regarding the date of the Bedwyn Dyke. It could conceivably be wholly Iron Age in origin, connecting Chisbury hillfort and a possible native settlement underlying the later villa.[26]

Or, the "system" could be late or post-Roman and, if truly defensive rather than boundary in nature, intended to discourage Saxon incursions from the Kennet and Thames valleys. As the dyke crosses the Bedwyn stream and the presumed Roman secondary road that must surely have followed the course of the valley, does not, like the Wansdyke, respect parish boundaries[27] (and hence is unlikely to have been an estate boundary), and more generally blocks presumed lines of passage through the Vale of Ham and the Harandene and Bedwyn Valleys, a late or post-Roman date seems likely.

A. and C. Fox suggest that the Bedwyn Dyke was intended to defend Cissa's "metropolis," and J. Haslam has argued that Bedwyn was the focus of a Saxon *villa regalis* whose estate was based on earlier Roman boundaries.[28] If the Bedwyn Dyke does, in fact, throw out a branch from Round Copse toward the east, possibly as far as the downs immediately west of Walbury hillfort at Rivar Copse, it may have been intended to block not merely the Bedwyn Valley and a minor passage through the valley of Harandene, but also the somewhat larger area of a villa estate and its presumed Saxon successor.[29] On the other hand, as B. Eagles points out (chapter 5), King Cynewulf's charter of A.D. 778—which mentions the Bedwyn Dyke, though not by name—demonstrates that it does not lie wholly within a single Saxon estate, though royal control was nevertheless maintained.

If the successor to the Roman villa, whatever its precise form, sought in some fashion to protect or mark the boundary of a large land unit, the Bedwyn Dyke may have been part of that strategy. Even if the pattern of building truly defensive earthworks on Roman estates was not common in Roman Britain, examples are attested by A.D. 367, the date of the second phase of Bokerly Dyke.[30]

If the Bedwyn Dyke "system" was built at a time when the estate owners or their descendants were trying to maintain, at some level, both the villa site in Bedwyn Brail and the hillfort at Chisbury—in itself by no means certain—then the period may have been relatively short. Pottery and coinage from the villa demonstrate that it probably participated in the market economy until at least the late fourth century and perhaps slightly later, and continued to be inhabited, if at a significantly lower material level, into the fifth century and after the collapse of the market economy. The duration of this late habitation phase is unclear, but it may have been relatively brief, as there is to date no Saxon material from the site and the last occupation layers from the site are not particularly deep. And at Chisbury, at least for the moment, evidence is lacking for very late and post-Roman habitation (see chapters 2, 3.1, 4.19, 5).

Thus, if the Bedwyn Dyke is not Iron Age in origin, connecting hillfort to a possible settlement, the most likely time for its construction and use may be in the late fourth or fifth century. It cannot be known whether this occurred after Cunetio, a town which received some of the latest defensive walls (after A.D. 354–358) known in Britannia,[31] had fallen, or before the construction of the eastern Wansdyke in the sixth (?) century.

Whatever its date, the Bedwyn Dyke "system" may or may not have been essential to the success and continuity of a possible Bedwyn-Chisbury estate through the unstable times of the fifth and sixth centuries, but its mention in a Saxon charter of A.D. 778 (see chapter 5), may hint that it could at least have contributed to the durability of such an estate.

NOTES

1. Colt Hoare explored this area on horseback in 1813 and 1814: Colt Hoare 1819: 32. More recent attempts to argue for a continuous linear earthwork: Major and Burrow 1926: 116 and Burne 1953: 126–34. For other Wansdyke bibliography, see Green 1971: 129.

2. Crawford 1953b: 119–25.

3. Fox and Fox 1960: 20. More recently, H.S. Green and others have considered the Wansdyke in Somerset and Wiltshire to have served as a single defensive frontier, while allowing for possible earlier sections, and corrected Pitt Rivers's impression that the Wansdyke consisted of two periods: H. S. Green 1971: 129–46.

4. Undertaken by the authors, K. L. Gleason and D. M. Evans. We are grateful to D. M. Evans for sharing both his time and his considerable knowledge of landscape archaeology, and to B. Eagles for his many constructive and cautionary comments.

5. Although the openness of the terrain in antiquity may have differed. On the usefulness of forest, or the lack of need of running a cross-country dyke through a forest, see Fox and Fox 1960: 16–17, who suggest the Savernake as the eastern terminus of the Wansdyke.

6. Fox and Fox 1960: 18–20. The preference for this term is in part due to the opinion that the only valid sections of the Bedwyn Dyke system are those across the Bedwyn Valley, Harandene, and near Shalbourne, and hence were in fact disjointed "short lengths of barrier earthwork."

7. Crawford 1953b: 119–20. Colt Hoare 1819: pls. of Wansdyke. The Foxes (1960: 18) thought it to be an accidental product of levelling after surface quarrying.

8. Crawford 1953b: 119.

9. Both the Foxes (1960: 18) and Crawford (1953b: 119–20) considered this section doubtful. The Foxes describe it as "in a dense plantation"; now the plantation consists of large pine trees, whose litter has created a forest floor blanketed with needles and devoid of growth, which allows the surface undulations to be read. The continuity of the double bank and double ditch, running for some 390 m with one interruption, is very clear.

10. There is also a break in the fortifications at this point which may represent a passageway at the hypothetical point of attachment—if that break is original to this period and not, as is likely, of more recent origin. Colt Hoare's map shows some earthworks connecting at the south end of Chisbury; this is a much less likely location, since it is on lower terrain, with the outside distinctly uphill. Nothing is visible there today.

11. Crawford 1953b: 121.

12. Arguing for a continuation through Burridge Heath to Inkpen Hill: Colt Hoare 1819: 32; Major and Burrow 1926: 115; Burne 1953: 126–34.

13. Fox and Fox 1960: fig. 16, pl. VI B. Crawford mapped this section in 1921, but eliminated it from his later map of 1953 (1953b).

14. Crawford 1922: 281; Grundy 1919: 151–52; and 1920: 75–76.

15. R. H. Burne (1953: 128) claimed to have followed this section of dyke in a straight line some distance along the southeast edge of the Brail (as marked in Trowbridge maps, section SU 26 SE mon. 637), but in the Brail this is only a small gamepark bank; from the sharpness of its profile it must be relatively recent in date and can be followed in the same form around the entire perimeter of the Brail.

16. The only attempt to do so, by R. H. Burnes (1955) can largely be discounted, as many of his physical descriptions are, at best, vague. He hypothesizes an elaborate three-phase system, the first running from Chisbury to Bedwyn Brail to Wilton Windmill; the second, an added arm from Bedwyn Brail to Botley Copse; and the third, an added arm from Round Copse to Inkpen Beacon.

17. Colt Hoare 1819: 31–33.

18. Crawford 1953: 122–23, pl. opposite 122, shows the mark in an airphoto.

19. Crawford 1953a: 257; and 1953b: 123–24, pl. opposite 123.

20. On the importance of Saxon or other tumuli near linear earthworks: Bonney 1973: 470–79; and 1966: 25–30, who notes that the siting of pagan Saxon burials near parish boundaries was a deliberate practice and that that argues for their antiquity. Other tumuli near the Dyke

system are at the supposed section near Chisbury Lane Farm, south of Chisbury (shown in an engraving of W. Stukely), and near Sadler's Farm.

21. In contrast to the adjacent field boundaries, which do not normally have chalk upcast on them.

22. Crawford 1953b: 121–22.

23. Colt Hoare's plan shows a road following parts of this length of bank.

24. Fox and Fox 1960: 18–20; Cunliffe 1973: 458–59; and Bonney 1973: 479.

25. As may have been the case with the Bokerly Dyke, in existence since the Middle Bronze Age: Bowen 1990: 39–41.

26. Another local early dyke may be Grim's Ditch, running to the south and west around Fosbury hillfort. D. J. Bonney (1972: 181–83, fig. 22) suggests that there the ditch and dyke are built over earlier Celtic fields, but that the fields on either flank continued to be worked, that the dyke is earlier than the Roman road which also circles the camp, and that it might have served as a peaceful boundary related in some manner to Fosbury hillfort.

27. Bonney 1972: 176.

28. Haslam 1980: 56–64.

29. This possibility recalls Sidonius Apollonaris's description (*Letters* 5.14.1) of the estates of Aper, a wealthy Gallo-Roman of the later fifth century who managed to retain a number of large estates in Gaul by providing them with *montana castella* or, as P. Salway puts it (1984: 457), Aper simply "adapted to circumstances by providing his properties with suitable hillforts instead of villas—or perhaps as well as them."

30. Bowen 1990: 38–41, with earlier bibliography. Dating of Bokerly Dyke depends on "samian" pottery and coins as late as Gratian (A.D. 367–383); Bowen suggests that the Bokerly Dyke may well be post-Roman (in final form), but following a line that dates to the prehistoric period.

31. Burnham and Wacher 1990: 150.

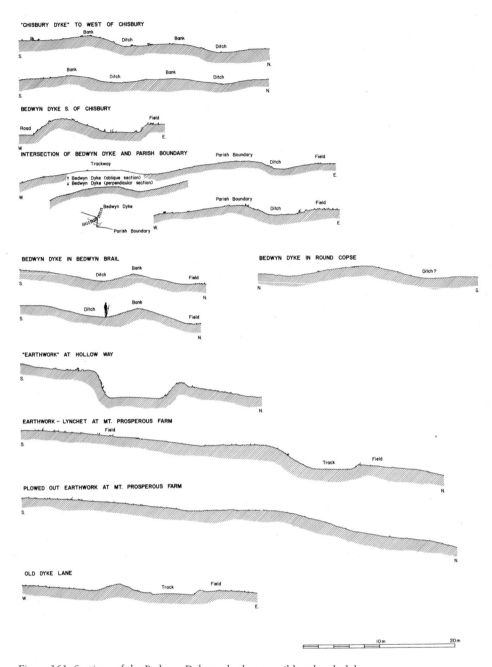

Figure 161. Sections of the Bedwyn Dyke and other, possibly related, dykes.

Figure 162. View of Bedwyn Dyke in Round Copse, toward southwest (SU26/16384291).

4.19 SUMMARY

ERIC HOSTETTER

The earliest evidence of habitation at Castle Copse is the series of ditches and beamslot and posthole structures (Fig. 82). In Sectors A (A965–971:I) and C (C57, 59:I), similar parallel ditches c. 85 m apart contained refuse-like deposits of Belgic types of Oare pottery (Fabrics 1–2) dating to between A.D. 50–90 and A.D. 50–70, respectively. The positions of the widely separated yet parallel ditches suggest the possible presence of constructions extending across the entire area of the later villa platform. On the evidence of associated carbonized cereal remains, the beamslot structure in Sector A may belong to an early granary. Both sets of constructions might represent either native or Roman habitation, or both.

Other evidence for early occupation, Celtic and Roman, includes the recovery, albeit from late Roman layers, of a gold-green annular bead (**443**) of Iron Age date and several Nauheim derivative fibulae of first-century date; while most were from later contexts, one (**104**) was recovered from the fill of an early posthole (A865:I) in Sector A and is of a type popular in the Flavian period.[1] South Gaulish first-century *terra sigillata,* including a fragment with the stamp of *Virtus,* was reported from Lukis's excavations.[2] Also originating from this period, although recovered from a later context, is the fragment of a first-century mosaic-ribbed glass bowl (**428**) of a class familiar from early military sites in Britain and the continent. This piece hints at, but hardly proves, the presence, however transient, of the Roman military at a possible native settlement either on site and/or at or near the neighboring hillfort at Chisbury. Further, the recovery of other sherds of mid- to late first-century Roman glass may also hint at the presence of an early site of some status. The reported discovery of a terracotta object with impressed triskelis at Castle Copse, perhaps an open flan mold or part of a two-part mold for producing "casket ornament"[3] of post-conquest date, perhaps in the latter part of the first into the second century A.D., further suggests the existence of an early settlement, and one which may be viewed as a "production" site manufacturing items of some sophistication.

The early material from Castle Copse is well compared with that from within and near Chisbury hillfort, which includes a modest amount of pottery and coinage of the late Republic, Augustan, and Tiberian periods, as well as two bronze pendants of types popular in the military in the second half of the first century A.D., from a presumed settlement west of the hillfort which may have failed after 60–80 A.D. (Fig. 23). Thereafter, limited evidence exists for renewed small-scale habitation within the hillfort, where storage pits have yielded Savernake Ware of the second half of the first century A.D. and other assorted "status" finds, including an *aureus* of Augustus, an amphora sherd, and a South Gaulish *terra sigillata* ware bowl.

Thus, although Castle Copse lacks the late Republican and early Imperial coinage found at and near Chisbury hillfort, the combined evidence of the two sites does suggest an early Roman presence, conceivably, but hardly certainly, military, at both.[4] If a native settlement or *oppidum* existed at Castle Copse, it may have been connected to Chisbury hillfort by the Bedwyn Dyke—unless the latter is, as seems likely, late or post-Roman in date.[5]

Excavation produced relatively few and generally small bone and plant assemblages of an early date, but mixed farming and animal husbandry are tentatively indicated. To the south, "Celtic" field systems have been identified at Wilton Down, and to the east, another undated field system is still discernible on the slope of Bedwyn Brail.

The Savernake pottery industry could conceivably also have been economically important for Castle Copse—as it was for the neighboring kiln site of Tottenham some three kilometers to the west on the road between Cunetio and Venta Belgarum[6]—even though, apart from the triskelis-impressed clay fragment, there is no evidence that Castle Copse was an "industrial" site.

In the late second or early third century, a gravel terrace was constructed, which extends across the entire site at Castle Copse (Fig. 83). A series of posthole structures is then built on this terrace gravel platform, parts of which (in Sector A) are linear in plan and may or may not represent some sort of earth-backed palisade or enclosure. The function of the structures and the culture to which it pertained—native farmstead or settlement, Romanized or Roman farmstead, or military site—remain ambiguous, but fragments of tile and plaster suggest that at least a few of the timber structures may have had plastered walls and terracotta roof tiles.

The pottery from the site during this period derived primarily from regional sources producing Savernake Wares, but increasingly from other, more distant regional manufacturers, a situation which reflects a steadily growing participation in the Roman market economy. The character of some pottery assemblages from this phase, perhaps formed during the construction of the platform, suggests occupation on the site in the second century, prior to the creation of the platform.

The origins of the site owner(s) remains unknown, but the model of a gradually Romanized site is as convincing as the imposition of Roman culture on native. It is also possible that control of the area during this period emanated from the site at Castle Copse, which, as a possible native settlement succeeded by a "villa," continued to develop, in contrast to Chisbury hillfort and its associated settlement(s), which apparently ceased to evolve.[7]

A masonry villa follows, probably in the third rather than in the second century (Fig. 84). This shift from timber structures to a masonry villa and the elaboration of the villa in the fourth century appear to reflect a process of gradual change and evolution within a single cultural group.

The stone villa's orientation is perhaps determined by the earlier timber buildings. The earlier phases of the partially explored west wing of the developed courtyard villa suggest that the villa may have originated as a winged corridor villa. These early masonry structures, associated with a residual second century sesterce of Hadrian (28), the only large coin from the site,[8] seemingly precede the construction of the first aisled building (I) in the later north wing. In its later phases, the west wing develops into the more luxurious, probably residential, quarter of the villa, with a possible bath, mosaics, and figural wall painting (Fig. 85).

In the north wing, the first aisled building, a flint structure with chalk floors, is erected in the mid- or later third century (Fig. 84), perhaps over a yet earlier structure of uncertain nature, following the removal of earlier timber structures. It is probably industrial in nature. In the later third/early fourth century the first aisled building is razed, and the second, with at least ten bays and thirty-eight meters in length or more, is built on the same alignment (Fig. 85). At first built as an open area, like its predecessor, after A.D. 331 it was subdivided so that the west end and adjacent building ("Greensand Quoin Building") were equipped with hypocausts and decorated with mosaics and wall painting. Late in its history, when slurried floors of mortar and chalk are associated with animal and bird bone, oysters, olive, and moveable hearths, this same area served as a service area, perhaps a kitchen. A smaller structure, the Greensand Quoin Building, is located immediately to the west, and at some point in the fourth century is connected to the second aisled building by a guilloche and pelta mosaic (5) corridor.

Though much disturbed, the south wing appears to have been a series of service rooms, an interpretation also suggested both by the lack of flue tiles and mosaics therefrom and the utilitarian character of the pottery recovered there (Fig. 85).

Other building blocks on the platform surely existed as part of the west wing, north of Sector B (at c. 340/500), and at the southeast corner of Aisled Building II (at c. 405/490) (Fig. 85). A perimeter wall may exist to the east, thus completing a large rectangular courtyard. The outbuildings, perhaps in the meadow to the southeast and elsewhere, were not located.

The villa reaches its floruit in the mid-fourth century, when it was a large courtyard complex whose west and north wings were luxurious quarters with hypocaust heating, imported Bath stone capitals, glass windows and, in the west wing, a possible plunge bath. Mosaics were laid in styles and patterns (5) familiar from other central southwestern villas, such as Box, Lydney Park, Wellow, Whittington, and Withington; and wall painting was executed in a variety of colors using local and imported pigments (including cinnabar and Egyptian blue) and, in the west wing, displaying half life-size figural work (22).

The prosperity of the villa is also reflected by the smaller objects recovered in the late phases. Bronze jewelry, including at least one enamelled plate fibula of likely continental origin (106) and others of first and second century date of British manufacture, which may have been handed down over generations (e.g., 103, 105–106, and possibly 107) are present, as is shale jewelry. An emerald bead (447), possibly from India, was recovered in a late burn layer of the north wing. Bone pins from the villa south and west wings are late Roman,[9] as is the ornate, composite bone comb (464), seemingly unique in its complexity, recovered in a late pit (C43:IV) in the south wing.

The vast majority of the seventy-four coins from the villa at Castle Copse date to the third and fourth centuries, and a few to the fifth century. Though first-century pieces are lacking, the coins otherwise roughly mirror the general patterns of use and loss of the combined coinage of six other villas in the southwest. The series ends with two bronzes of Arcadius (**85–86**).

As elsewhere in the south, increasing quantities of regional wares arrive on site in the third and fourth centuries. Curiously absent—as is also the case with glass—are significant amounts of the finer quality wares, a situation which, however, may reflect antiquarian disturbances and excavation strategy. The latest fabric on site appears to be Overwey Ware of the end of the fourth and probably early fifth centuries, contained in the latest slurried floor levels of the subdivided Aisled Building II (A:XI).

The economy of the villa at Castle Copse may have focussed on estate consumptions with a few products produced for market.[10] The fact that few of the larger iron farming implements were found suggests that excavation did not concentrate in areas where such would be found and that the architecture of the courtyard complex in this period, with the possible exception of the south wing, was devoted primarily to residential functions, with farming and industrial activities occurring in out-buildings elsewhere.

In its relative proportions, the animal bones from Phases A:I–X appears generally to conform to assemblages from villas elsewhere. Cattle were most important, followed by sheep, then pig, and most were probably butchered on site. Wild animal bones, including red and roe deer, were present if not in great numbers; birds and fish may likewise have been relatively unimportant in the diet. The presence of seashells and marine fish and the relative absence of mature animals suggest a relatively high standard of living.

The animal remains from A:XI, after A.D. 331, recovered amid late chalk and mortar floors of the second aisled building, constitute a particular assemblage, notable for its high proportion of pig; the abundance of young piglets, lamb, and kids; the high proportion of bird bones; and the large numbers of pig foot bones and cattle and deer phalanges. All are probable food remains from the table of the wealthy,[11] a view perhaps supported by the presence of imported olives from the same phase. Given the location and the unusual character of the pig bones, it is uncertain whether any specialization is indicated. Weaving implements, a weaving tablet (**480**) and two bone pin beaters (**478–479**) from late Roman phases suggest sheep raised for wool, while a fragment of worked antler (**485**) intimates the possible production of the same and other implements.

The limited plant remains from earlier phases suggest an emphasis on cereals, especially spelt wheat. Imported fig was recovered from the first aisled building (A:VIII), hinting at a certain level of wealth in the third century. Among crops of the later phases, cereals remain the most prominent.

Attempting to characterize the full nature and range of the late Roman villa economy on the basis of the data from four trenches in the villa proper, only one with a completely excavated sequence, would be unwise.[12] We note only that excavation data tentatively elicit a rather general and "orthodox" model of mixed farming, a view perhaps supported by resources available in the extremely varied geology and topography around the Great Bedwyn region, which included grassland, open grazing and arable fields, woodland, and riverine habitats (Figs. 155–157). On the basis of very limited evidence, it may be that the crop types changed relatively little over time, and that Roman crop types—bread wheat and the glume wheats—stayed in use into the fifth century. The late faunal evidence, limited by the study of only the distinctive assemblage in the north wing (A:XI), disallows comparison of the late phases in all three wings, as well as speculation regarding the relative importance of cattle and sheep in the late fourth century.[13]

The latest phases of the villa evidence decline and impoverishment (Fig. 86). Attempts are made to maintain the luxurious character of the villa, and industrial activities are introduced in formerly residential areas; both changes are particularly evident in the west wing, where mosaics are coarsely patched with mismatched tesserae, and smithing operations defile a mosaic floor in Room 4. Probably in the earlier fifth century, crude structures of timber or cob on a thin flint socle are built in the villa west wing and possibly in the south wing. The duration of this phase cannot be established. Thus, habitation on site continued in some form into the fifth century and after the collapse of the Roman market system, when the usual chronological indicators—mass-produced pottery and coinage—no longer enjoyed widespread circulation.

In the late or post-Roman period, the villa site may have been linked to Chisbury hillfort by the cross-valley Bedwyn Dyke, creating a barrier toward the Kennet Valley and the Vale of Ham, and perhaps serving to shield a tract of land to the southwest (Fig. 2).[14] Because the Bedwyn Dyke, like the Wansdyke, disregards both parish boundaries and Roman roads, it is likely to be of a late, post-Roman date.

Finally, the location of the villa at Castle Copse is curious for the relative paucity of surrounding villas, and indeed of Roman period buildings and settlements in the entire quadrant to the southeast of Cunetio in which Castle Copse is located (Fig. 24). This pattern of scarcity also appears to obtain for Roman period finds (Fig. 25), and emerges clearly in I. Hodder's study of the distribution of Savernake Ware.[15] Despite the fact that the major road towards Leucomagus and Venta Belgarum would seemingly offer a ready marketing avenue, Hodder initially attributed the absence of such ware to the southeast of Cunetio primarily to chance.[16]

The explanation may be geologic and topographic. The terrain to the southeast of Cunetio—or to the northwest of Castle Copse—is in large part broken and uneven, often comprises sandy soils overlying Bagshot Beds, has traditionally been relatively unproductive agriculturally and, at least partially (to the west), is covered by Savernake Forest. Thus, the area may have been less attractive for settlement than other tracts of land or, perhaps, the current, often dense vegetation has simply hindered recognition of archaeological features and material.

Or, perhaps the explanation is social. I. Hodder's subsequent (1979) study of the distribution of Savernake Ware suggested that tribal boundaries may have conditioned the distribution of Savernake Ware, tending towards Dobunnic territory to the northwest of Cunetio[17]—away from Castle Copse villa to the southeast—and P. Robinson, in his study of local Iron Age coinage, has posited the potential presence of an unrecognized local native group between the Dobunni and the Atrebates, perhaps centering on the area around Cunetio.[18] Together, these considerations at least suggest the possibility of a continuing social distinction between the area southeast of Cunetio and that to the west and north.

If, for the sake of argument, the relative absence of Roman sites and finds southeast of Cunetio is taken to mirror the domination of a land unit by a single authority—in this case by the villa at Castle Copse—then perhaps it is possible, as J. Haslam has suspected, that such an estate may have existed, in the preceding Iron Age, when it centered upon Chisbury hillfort and when there is also a relative paucity of sites and finds in the area,[19] as well as in the succeeding Saxon period, when it likely assumed the form of a *villa regalis* centering on Great Bedwyn, a secondary market town important enough to have minted its own coinage.[20] Perhaps, as elsewhere, such an estate may have derived from the nucleus of properties held by native rulers, in this case, from the territory controlled by Chisbury hillfort and the associated settlement(s), though, at least at present, the former seems not to have been occupied in the Late Iron Age.[21]

Smaller villas such as Tottenham, Rudge Manor, and Harrow and the unlocated but probable villa at Shalbourne could all be viewed as dependencies or, given their distance from Castle Copse, as villas lying beyond the limits of land associated with Castle Copse.[22] The documented villa closest to Castle Copse, Tottenham, roughly four kilometers distant on the road to Venta Belgarum, could have been a dependency or merely a neighboring villa whose property was bounded by the road and whose economic basis lay both in agriculture and in the production of Savernake Ware. The estate of the next nearest, a posited villa at Shalbourne, may well have centered on the head of the Vale of Ham and extended primarily toward the east.

The relative or seeming absence of Roman period native and non-villa settlements in the immediate environs of Castle Copse villa—apart from Chisbury hillfort and/or a possible extramural settlement(s) in the Bedwyn Valley—further supports this model. While not wholly unusual for villas in the area around Cunetio,[23] this nevertheless appears somewhat anomalous for the extensive area concerned and is certainly not the case with several other large villas in the southwest which have eight or nine associated native or non-villa settlements.[24]

In this admittedly speculative model, the various succeeding Iron Age, Roman, and Saxon settlements—Chisbury hillfort and associated extramural settlements; the possible native settlement preceding the Roman villa at Castle Copse and the villa itself; a hypothetical settlement of *coloni,* perhaps deriving from the earlier extramural settlement(s) below Chisbury, in the Bedwyn Valley, "Cissa's burh" or "metropolis" (Chisbury); the *villa regalis* focused on Great Bedwyn proposed by J. Haslam; and the Saxon town of Great Bedwyn (chapter 5)—may all reflect the possibility of varying degrees of continuity, probably more economic than social, characteristic of a nonurban, secondary market center. The fact that Chisbury hillfort lay roughly eight kilometers from Forest Hill hillfort, Castle Copse villa approximately the same distance from Cunetio (9 km), and Great Bedwyn a similar distance from Ramsbury (slightly over 7 km) and Marlborough (9.5 km) might support the notion of a long-established outlying, secondary rural market center.[25]

The undated Bedwyn Dyke, running from Chisbury hillfort to the site of Castle Copse villa is also of interest here. If the dyke is Iron Age in origin, it would seemingly enhance the status of the probable Iron Age settlement—more *oppidum* than farmstead?—which may have preceded the Roman "villa." Or, if it is of late or post-Roman date, it would suggest an organized response to protect a tract of land to the southwest or, at the very least, a desire to define and control the northeastern boundary of a specific territory. Either possibility strengthens the notion that the villa at Castle Copse and its associated settlements may in some manner have functioned as a modest rural *caput pagi,* that this status may have been inherited from the Iron Age, and that it may have endured, in whatever changing forms, into the Saxon period.

NOTES

1. The others, in bronze and iron, include: **103, 105–106, 163–164,** and possibly **107.**

2. Cunnington and Goddard 1934: 197, no. 406.

3. Reportedly from Castle Copse, with a reference to "a Romano-British settlement in and about Bedwyn Brail Wood within a short distance of the site of the villa": Cunningham and Goddard 1911: 51–52, no. 401, pl. 22:8.

4. Ditches villa (Trow and James 1989), possibly built in the first century A.D., may have some relationship with the *oppidum* at Bagendon some two or three kilometers away. Ditches, like Chisbury, produced metalwork (two objects) suggesting a Roman military presence.

5. *Oppida* of the south often display significant diversity, being of various sizes, enclosed or unenclosed with dykes, and sometimes connected with dyke systems: Haselgrove 1989: 10–12.

6. See Branigan 1988: 48–49. V. Swan (1984: 119) notes that "a large 'loom-weight' and a 'cubical object' found together in the earliest double-flued Savernake Ware kiln at Great Bedwyn are reminiscent of objects associated with Iron-Age camp-sites. . ." On pot, brick, and tile villa production, see Todd 1988: 19–20, who maintains that such industry developed where materials were close to hand, with few close to an urban center and many relatively remote.

7. Early villas often derive from native settlements, e.g., the courtyard villa at Fishbourne within the Selsey territorial *oppidum* and the courtyard villa at Woodchester near a possible territorial *oppidum* at Minchinhampton.

8. The rarity of the early coinage probably reflects the fact that earlier phases of this wing were not excavated.

9. According to Crummy's typologies, the latter three fall in the period 50–200 A.D., but the phases in which they were recovered (BB52:X, B116, 141:VI) suggest that they are late Roman— as indeed J. C. Beal's typology allows: Beal 1983: 202, AXX, 13, no. 710, pl. 36; and for the example from the south wing, cp. 200, AXX, 10, no. 705, pl. 36. I thank A. St. Clair for these references.

10. Or to K. Branigan's (1988:49) second level of villa economy specialization.

11. Other late Roman villa sites exist where pig bones in third- and fourth-century contexts are well above expected percentages; according to A. Grant (1989:141-42), these might indicate a high status diet familiar from the tables of the continental Romans.

12. As it has proved elsewhere on the basis of a good deal more evidence: Barker and Webley 1977, 198–211.

13. At Shakenoak, spelt wheat is the predominant grain, and cattle, followed by sheep, are the predominant animals (Young 1986: 61; Brodribb, Hands, and Walker 1978, 15–19). Branigan (1977: 80–83) suggests increasing importance of sheep on the Marlborough Downs in the late period.

14. One might note that to the east of the Bedwyn Dyke "system" the pattern of roads and field boundaries is today quite different from the area to the west "behind" the system: fields are small, highly irregular, in a pattern often suggested to be Saxon.

15. Hodder 1974a: figs. 4–5.

16. Hodder 1974a: 75–76.

17. Hodder 1979: 193–94.

18. Robinson 1977a.

19. At least as they are listed in the Ancient Sites and Monuments Record databases to 1986.

20. Haslam 1980: 60–64. One may also note that Tottenham villa, where mosaics were recovered in 1859, is interesting for its place-name (see chapter 5), which belongs to the *-ham* group of

Old English place-names, often considered to be of early date. Hence, the Bedwyn Valley may present a good candidate for an early Saxon settlement, perhaps developing from an earlier settlement of Roman *coloni,* after the villa at Castle Copse is abandoned.

21. There is no reason to suppose that the area around Castle Copse villa was imperially owned, though in other areas where imperial estates have been proposed—e.g., the gravel areas in Upper Thames Valley and in the Fenland—villas also often tend to be conspicuous by their relative absence. At Cranbourne Chase, Cunliffe (1973: 447) has seen the possibility of an Imperial estate created either as a punishment for opposition to Roman authority during conquest or as a manner to secure grain for the army. On Imperial *saltus,* Todd 1988: 14–20; Hingley 1989: 127–128. Salway 1981: 603–604, on the Fenland.

22. On the possibility that the sizes of estates were determined by peripheral distributions of dependent settlements, see Hingley 1989: 106–108; and Applebaum 1963: 2.

23. If the absense of systematic field-walking does not deceive.

24. E.g., Gatcombe or Woodchester: Branigan 1977b: 206; Hingley 1989: 107.

25. Chisbury hillfort lies c. 10.5 km from Walbury hillfort and roughly the same distance from Fosbury hillfort; the latter two lie 7.5 km from each other, though over rough terrain.

Hingley (1989: 114) suggests that peasants would walk c. 7–10 km to market (and back in the same day), thus markets tend to appear c. every 10 to 14 km. Hodder (1974: 74, fig. 5) speculates that some anomalies in the distribution of Savernake Ware—the presence of Savernake Ware in only a single cluster to the east (southeast) of Cunetio—may reflect market mechanisms other than purchase at Cunetio or sale along the main roads, perhaps the sale in a local rural market on a weekly basis.

CHAPTER 5

The Area around Bedwyn in the Anglo-Saxon Period

BRUCE EAGLES

Introduction

In the first part of this chapter,[1] there is a discussion of the evidence from a wide region for the period between the fifth and the seventh centuries, that is, from the time of the first arrival of the Anglo-Saxons in the area until their adoption of Christianity. This broad frame permits a consideration of a sufficient number of the earliest of their sites (which in most cases lie at some considerable distance from each other), for them to be placed in the context of the main developments of Anglo-Saxon settlement, and for the artifacts from them to be evaluated overall against those recovered elsewhere. Accordingly, for the purpose of this review of the evidence from this period, the geographical limits are taken to extend from the Ridgeway, which attains almost 300 m (900 ft) on Hackpen Hill, southwest of Barbury Castle, on the Upper Chalk, some 18 km (11 miles) northwest of Bedwyn, to the headwaters of the Avon and the Bourne, only some 8 km (5 miles) and 6 km (4 miles), respectively, from Bedwyn, in the south; at the east, sites as far as Kintbury in Berkshire are taken into account. This large area encompasses a quite variable geology and a correspondingly contrasting terrain. At the north there are the high chalklands of the Marlborough Downs. Farther south, the slopes of the Kennet Vale carry extensive spreads of clay-with-flints, particularly on the south in Savernake Forest; on the south bank too are the Eocene Beds, which offer poor soils of little use for agriculture. At the extreme southeast of the region, the chalk rises again to form the downs at Wexcombe, one of the Domesday manors which constituted a part of the Bedwyn estate. It is from the eighth century onward that land charters allow the Bedwyn estate itself to become the focus of attention.

Studies of the pagan Anglo-Saxons have traditionally relied heavily upon information derived from their cemeteries, which are readily distinguished in the archaeological record by the deposition of grave-goods to accompany the burials, a practice which was widespread, whether the interments were made by the rite of cremation or inhumation. In recent years, settlements of this period have been increasingly recognized and excavated, but in general it is true that understanding of them remains very limited. The chronology within the pagan period is also still only very incompletely determined. However, detailed studies of a wide range of objects, notably spearheads, swords, shield-bosses, and a number of the main classes of brooches, have provided the means to determine at least certain broad chronological phases of the period.

The Survival of the British Population

The British monk Gildas, writing, it is generally thought, in c. 540 A.D., vividly describes the slaughter of the Britons at the hands of the Saxons in the period before he was born, that is before c. 500 A.D.[2] In spite of this testimony, though, it is now widely considered that large numbers of Britons survived, even in eastern and central England. The prevalence of this view is due in no small measure to the influence of the work of K. Jackson. He has shown clearly that there was a period of bilingualism when, during a time of close contact, the Britons acquired a thorough knowledge of the language of the dominant English who, however, themselves assimilated only a very few words of Brittonic speech.[3] Nevertheless, varying numbers of British place-names and river-names did continue in use in almost all parts of the country.

In the area of this study, one river-name and the names of only a very few places have been shown to be of Brittonic origin. However, Wiltshire, unlike its neighbor Berkshire, has not been the subject of a recent survey by the English Place-Name Society, and the number of pre-English names which have been identified should be treated as minimal. Savernake is in origin a river-name, possibly of the Bedwyn stream, which was borrowed by the Anglo-Saxons from Primitive Welsh in the mid-sixth century.[4] The river-name of this group is that of a major tributary of the Thames, the Kennet. The Roman town of *Cunetio* presumably gained its name from the river.[5] It is situated in this valley immediately to the south of the present village of Mildenhall, a name first recorded as *Mildenheath* in a charter of Cynewulf (757–86 A.D.).[6] The Roman town was clearly a place of some significance, for villas surrounded it[7] and it was defended with a wall with contemporary external towers late in the fourth century. The date of these defenses is provided by a coin of 354–358 A.D. that was found in the primary silt of a ditch underlying the wall, indicating that the stone circuit is one of the latest in Roman Britain. A building, probably of winged corridor type and with an apse, in the northwest corner of the town was either contemporary with or later than the defenses.[8] The site has also produced a perforated buckle plate of a type which was attached to the *cingulum*, the broad belt which was part of the official uniform of army officers and civil servants; the piece dates to the period 350–80 A.D.[9] The valley was also a focus for early Anglo-Saxon settlement, as is shown below. The old English word *wealh*, which was used in Wessex to refer either to a Briton or, certainly by the later Anglo-Saxon period, to a slave,[10] occurs in *waeluueg* in a Bedwyn charter[11] and, in a slightly variant form[12] in another for Burbage,[13] both of which are discussed below.

The Earliest Anglo-Saxon Settlement

No settlement site of the pagan period has yet been identified in the area around Bedwyn. The earliest cemetery, with a number of fifth-century graves, is that at Collingbourne Ducis, in the valley of the south-flowing Bourne, a tributary of the Avon, to the south of Bedwyn. Thirty-four inhumation graves were excavated there in 1974–1975.[14] Notable objects include an oval buckle inlaid with transverse silver wires in grave 11; applied brooches decorated with six human masks, probably of the second half of the fifth century, in graves 20 and 23[15]; and an equal-armed brooch of the Nesse type, which has been repaired, in grave 6.[16] Inlaid metalwork is otherwise known in the region only farther south, at Salisbury.[17] Recent casual finds at Collingbourne Kingston,[18] the parish immediately to the north of Collingbourne Ducis, comprise a gilded copper-alloy saucer brooch decorated with five spirals (Fig. 163.1) and a fragmentary "pair" of very worn tinned or silvered disc brooches with ring-and-dot decoration (one of which has the remains of sheepskin adhering to it) (Fig. 163.2–3), which possibly indicates another cemetery of a similar date.[19] A saucer brooch (Fig. 163.4) with a star design from immediately northwest of Membury hillfort in Ramsbury parish may also belong to the fifth century.[20]

Certain other sites also appear to begin before 500 A.D. The cemetery at Blacknall Field (known locally as Black Patch), Pewsey lies about 13 km (8 miles) southwest of Bedwyn, in the upper part of the Avon Valley, south of the river itself and on the southern slopes of the Pewsey Vale. Excavations there between 1969 and 1976 uncovered 102 inhumations and 3 cremations. The earliest graves are recognizable from the presence in them of applied saucer brooches decorated with a star (grave 66), saucer brooches with five scrolls (grave 104), button brooches (graves 38, 44, 67),[21] and a spearhead of Swanton's group E1 (grave 16). The spearheads of this category, which are both widespread and numerous in England, are thought to date before rather than after the end of the fifth century.[22] The cemetery is discussed further below. Another example of the E1 type of spearhead[23] and the upper part of a cruciform brooch are recorded from Upper Upham, a hamlet situated on clay-with-flints, which overlies the Upper Chalk at 267 m (800 ft) above O.D. in Aldbourne parish, north of Ramsbury. This site has also produced Romano-British finds, including a late fourth-century dolphin-headed buckle with a long and narrow plate, a type which was produced in Britain.[24] The place-name Upham itself is also of interest. It is recorded as *Uphammere* in 955 A.D.[25] and belongs to the *-ham* group of Old English settlement names, many of which are considered to be of early date;[26] another name of this type occurs at Tottenham, in Great Bedwyn parish, where a tessellated pavement was uncovered in 1859.[27] Early Anglo-Saxon material recovered from other places in Aldbourne village comprises a saucer brooch[28] and a fragment of a small-long brooch from Holes Field (Fig. 163.5).[29] An inhumation grave located near Savernake Hospital contained a spearhead of group K1, of the late fifth or early sixth century.[30]

The cemetery at Blacknall Field, already noted, continued in use throughout the sixth century. Notable grave-goods include a francisca in grave 7 and silvered scabbard fittings in 22. Most of the graves were very shallow and had been badly damaged by modern ploughing. None of the burials was superimposed upon another, which perhaps indicates that they were originally defined in some way above the ground, although no trace of any grave marker was recovered. Where it could be determined, forty-four of the bodies were fully extended and a further thirty-seven laid with legs slightly flexed; another six were on their sides with the legs flexed. There was also one double burial, with an adult male and a female, and there were children's graves. One body had been placed in a prone position in the grave; in this case the left forearm had been amputated before death and had subsequently healed, and both feet and the distal ends of the tibiae and the fibulae had also been cut off at, or shortly before, death.

Most of the pagan period burials and casual finds in the area belong to the sixth century. In the Kennet Vale, an inhumation recorded at Mildenhall in 1827 was accompanied by a pair of saucer brooches with cruciform design, a bronze pin, a knife, a bronze ring, and twenty-one beads.[31] A loose find of another saucer brooch is also known from that parish[32] and there is a fragmentary one (Fig. 163.6) and also a plain disc (?) brooch (Fig. 163.7) from Ramsbury parish,[33] both now in Devizes Museum. A spearhead is recorded from Chilton Foliat.[34] To the north of the Kennet Valley, beside one of its tributaries, the River Og, there are recent records of a small-long brooch, conventionally of sixth-century date,[35] and a saucer brooch decorated with six spirals, from two locations at Ogbourne St. Andrew.[36] Sherds of organic-tempered pottery have been reported from an area of clay-with-flints on Round Hill Down, Ogbourne St. George.[37] Immediately to the east of Bedwyn, at Shalbourne, newly recovered finds of pagan and later Anglo-Saxon date include a small-long brooch and part of the head-plate of a gilded square-headed one of Kentish type, together with pins, strap-ends, a buckle, two sceattas, and a seventh-century gold thrymsa, attributed to Wessex (Figs. 164.1–164.8, 165).[38] Another small-long brooch, with a square head and a crescentic foot, is known from Wilton, in the parish of Grafton, which adjoins Bedwyn on the South.[39] At Easton, west of Grafton, a burial with a knife and a double-sided bone comb, in a wooden coffin, is probably of Anglo-Saxon date.[40]

Some burials and objects can be shown to belong to the later part of the pagan period. A spearhead of group G2, of the late sixth or early seventh century, was found together with a bronze buckle in a Bronze Age disc barrow at Great Botley Copse at East Grafton (see below).[41] Another spearhead of this date, but of group E3,[42] is from a burial on Hinton Down, Bishopstone (see below).

The area lacks the rich burials, apparently of princely status, of the seventh century, which are such a conspicuous feature of the archaeological record elsewhere in Wiltshire, for instance, at Roundway Down north of Devizes[43] and in the southern part of the county at Salisbury Racecourse, Coombe Bissett,[44] and at Swallowcliffe.[45] A late seventh-century gold pendant, however, has recently been recorded from Pewsey.[46]

There is, therefore, widespread evidence for the presence of pagan Anglo-Saxons in this region. Their cemeteries provide an indication of the general locations and environment of some of their earliest settlements, although it is known that burials may lie, apparently, on the boundary of a community's lands. In the area under present discussion, burials occur on an ancient parish boundary at Great Botley Copse.[47] In the chalklands, many of the earliest settlements may well lie, so far undiscovered, in the valleys, with a settlement pattern similar to that familiar in the medieval and later periods in this type of country. Indeed, it can be argued that the apparent concentration of sites around Mildenhall, discussed below, has as much to do with their easy access to the River Kennet as with their proximity to the Roman roads. However, in the earliest phases of settlements, at least, it is not necessary to suppose that the demonstrable presence of Anglo-Saxons in certain places implies their control of the region as a whole. It is possible that some settlement came about as a result of local agreements with British leaders, who themselves may have possessed no more than a regional power. In some circumstances, the British may have been able to recruit Saxon warriors, who received estates in exchange for military service. The Saxon presence at East Shefford,[48] Collingbourne, and around Salisbury[49] could have come about in this way. The sites at East Shefford and Salisbury are close enough to Roman roads to suggest that at those places there were strategic considerations at play, which could have been as relevant to any British tyrant[50] as to any Saxon leader.

In any area, the routes by which newcomers reached their destinations are by no means easy to define. The likely source of certain unusual types of early Anglo-Saxon objects may be indicated by their form and design, as mentioned above with regard to the inlaid buckle from Collingbourne Ducis, but it should be noted that singletons of any group are as likely to have arrived through trading as through the movement of people themselves. The finds in any one place rarely include a sufficient number of objects from a particularly distinctive source to provide a strong pointer to the origin of an incoming group. Warriors were, in any case, in a special category. Bede[51] says that young nobles from many different places attached themselves to the successful king Oswine of Deira. The nobles may have brought their own followers with them. Thus, at least during periods of fighting, there may have been some movement of this element in the population. The almost universal occurrence of spearheads as grave goods must surely indicate the presence of warriors in most communities. Weapon burial itself, however, appears to have been a rite accorded only to an individual or a family of a certain status, for skeletal evidence suggests that not all warriors were buried with arms, and weapons were certainly placed in the graves of children and the physically handicapped.[52]

The area had been easily accessible in Roman times. It is traversed by three major Roman roads, which are focused upon a crossing of the Kennet at Cunetio. One of these roads led from Wanborough (probably Durocornovium), 16 km (10 miles) away to the north, where it had left the route between the cantonal capitals of Cirencester (Corinium Dobunnorum) and Silchester (Calleva Atrebatum). A short distance south of Cunetio the road bifurcated, one branch leading south to Old Sarum (Sorviodunum), the other to the Southeast, to Winchester (Venta Belgarum). Winchester was the administrative center of the self-governing district of the Belgae, of which the area about Bedwyn was a part. The third road passed from west to east through Cunetio, linking Bath (Aquae Sulis) with the Cirencester-to-Silchester highway. A stretch of it has been recorded in Hens Wood, north of Puthall in the parish of Little Bedwyn, whose bounds in 778 A.D. make mention of the road—which suggests that at that time it was still recognizable—and whose northern boundary still lies close beside it.[53]

The known distribution of early Anglo-Saxon sites is, in the main, not particularly related to the network of Roman roads, although there are indications, as in the environs of Cunetio, that certain roads, at least in part, were still in use. Some of the evidence for Anglo-Saxon activity around Cunetio is unfortunately only generally located within the large parish of Mildenhall, including the burial and a record of a stray find from north of the village, already noted, and fused glass beads in Devizes Museum, obtained from the Brooke Collection in 1916. A second, and altogether exceptional, burial from Poulton Downs (Mildenhall) is of a woman who had been thrown into a Roman well. Objects found with her comprise a knife, two iron buckles, a bronze pin, and three beads which are dated to the sixth or early seventh century.[54] This site lies on Poulton Downs, some 450 m (1350 ft) to the west of the Roman road to Wanborough, and 2.5 km (1.5 miles) north of Cunetio. Finally, an inhumation burial, mentioned above, was found approximately 1.2 km (.75 mile) west of Cunetio, near Savernake Hospital. Altogether there is, therefore, considerable evidence for the presence of Anglo-Saxons in the area of Cunetio between the fifth and seventh centuries, and this is a pattern of occupation which might point to the continuing importance of the river crossing there. Elsewhere in the region discussed in this chapter, only one site, and that of only probable Anglo-Saxon date, lies close to a Roman road, and that is the burial at Grafton (noted above) near the route to Winchester. Some of the graves in a cemetery at Crofton, Great Bedwyn, near the same road, were laid out in a spoked-wheel arrangement.[55] They may be of Anglo-Saxon date. This unusual setting is paralleled at Potterne (an unpublished discovery of undated burials in the 1920s)[56] and at a few early Anglo-Saxon sites elsewhere.[57] The burial at Grafton is likely to date to the seventh century (above). The proximity of these graves to main Roman roads is a feature which they share with a number of other richly furnished, seventh-century burials in other parts of the country. An example of this phenomenon in Wiltshire is the grave, already mentioned, on Salisbury Racecourse, which lies beside the route leading southwestwards from Old Sarum to Badbury and on to Dorchester (Durnovaria Durotrigum) in Dorset. The burial at Swallowcliffe was beside a *herepath* referred to in a tenth-century charter.

The other important ancient route in the area is the Ridgeway (above). The Ridgeway is unmetalled, and its general, if not its precise, course is likely to be of prehistoric origin. The trackway enters Wiltshire from the northeast at Bishopstone. It was certainly well used in early Anglo-Saxon times, for the *Anglo-Saxon Chronicle*[58] records battles at hillforts along its course, and there are finds of pagan period objects from locations beside it, including Barbury itself.[59] In the region under consideration in this chapter, the *Chronicle* reports that fighting took place in 556 at Barbury Castle and again in 592 and 715 at Wodnesbeorg. The latter name was that given to the Neolithic long barrow now known as Adam's Grave, which lies only 1.5 km (1 mile) south of the point, at Red Shore, Alton Priors, where the Ridgeway passes through the only original gap as yet identified in the East Wansdyke,[60] a linear earthwork which is further considered below. There is an Anglo-Saxon single-edged battle knife from Barbury (Fig. 166).[61] At Liddington Castle, another hillfort on the Ridgeway in this area and approximately 6.5 km (4 miles) to the northeast of Barbury, limited excavations indicated some refurbishment of the ramparts, but this activity can be dated no more closely than to the Roman period or later.[62] Farther east along the route, an Anglo-Saxon saucer brooch has been recorded at Bishopstone.[63] At Bishopstone, too, on Hinton Down in the former parish of Little Hinton, Greenwell at some date between 1877 and 1889 opened a Bronze Age bowl barrow which produced an Anglo-Saxon inhumation with a spearhead.[64] The other place in the region on this highway where there is an early Anglo-Saxon site is at West Overton, where Bronze Age round barrows on Overton Hill, immediately east of the Ridgeway and above the River Kennet, were found to contain pagan Saxon secondary burials. One of those interments may belong to the fifth century, but others are certainly of sixth-century date.[65] Taken together, the historical and archaeological information thus points to the use of the Ridgeway throughout the early Anglo-Saxon period.

However, this record should perhaps be seen mainly in the context of the passage of armies across the region, rather than directly related to the establishment of settlements.

Reference has already been made to the Wansdyke. The Wansdyke (*wodnes dic,* Woden's dyke),[66] is recorded in various charters from 892 A.D. onwards.[67] The dyke falls into two parts.[68] The West Wansdyke is in Somerset and is separated from the eastern dyke by a 22-km (14-mile) stretch of the Roman road between Bath and Mildenhall. The East Wansdyke begins on Morgan's Hill some 10 km (6 miles) west of the Ridgeway, and continues eastwards to New Buildings, less than 1.5 km (1 mile) west of the present edge of Savernake Forest. Pitt-Rivers has shown that at Brown's Barn, Bishops Cannings, the East Wansdyke was built in the third century A.D. or later. A. and C. Fox[69] demonstrated that at Morgan's Hill it blocked the Roman road from Mildenhall to Bath, and Green[70] at New Buildings showed its construction there to be post-Roman. In chalk country the dyke is a massive barrier (up to 30 m [90 ft] across) to movement from the northeast, but on the mixed soils east of Shaw House, which is less than 1.5 km (1 mile) east of the Ridgeway, in the area here under discussion, the Wansdyke is of much smaller dimensions. It has been considered that the Wansdyke was continued farther to the east by other dykes in the parishes of Great and Little Bedwyn. The dykes in Little Bedwyn are recorded in a land charter of the eighth century,[71] which is further discussed below. However, they are otherwise undated and it has been pointed out that they have never been named Wansdyke; they are therefore, probably best regarded as of a different origin and serving a different function.

Great Bedwyn

The mention of the charters for Bedwyn brings the Anglo-Saxon estate there into focus for the first time (Fig. 167). The earliest of these land grants, which survives in a tenth-century copy,[72] by King Cynewulf to his *comes* and *minister* Bica is of 778 A.D. and relates to an area of thirteen *manentes in Bedewindan.*[73] The bounds of this charter make it clear that the grant corresponds to the parish of Little Bedwyn.[74] The name Bedwyn, however, was shared with Great Bedwyn, a vast Saxon estate adjacent to Little Bedwyn on the south (below), and with the Bedwyn Brook; and it therefore appears to have been given to all the land at the headwaters of this stream.[75] It has been suggested that the name, which seems to be of Old English origin, described a place where bindweed flourished.[76]

The parish of Little Bedwyn is dominated by the Iron Age hillfort of Chisbury "Cissa's burh,"[77] which is situated to the west of Little Bedwyn village. The *Historia Monasterii de Abingdon,* first compiled in the twelfth century, but elaborated in the thirteenth, ascribes the earliest endowments of that monastery to one Cissa, said to have been a king of the West Saxons.[78] The History also states that Cissa was the predecessor of Caedwalla (685?–688) and ruled Wiltshire and the greater part of Berkshire from his "metropolis" at Bedwyn. Bede (*Historia Ecclesiastica,* iv.12)[79] says that there was no centralized power in Wessex between the death of Cenwealh in A.D. 672 and the accession of Caedwalla, but that during that time the kingdom was subdivided among *subreguli.* The Abingdon tradition therefore accords well with Bede's view of the political conditions in the period in question, and, although Cissa himself is not recorded elsewhere, several strands of evidence within the *History* point to the incorporation within it, in however muddled a form, of a number of sources of seventh-century origin.[80] The *Anglo-Saxon Chronicle,* however, records a continuous succession of Wessex kings, at least one of whom, Centwine, other sources confirm was an able and strong ruler.[81]

Several dykes lie in the vicinity of Chisbury hillfort. The longest of them adjoins its defenses, in an as yet undetermined sequential relationship, at the southeast and thence falls from a height of 167 m (500 ft) above O.D. to cross and thereby block the Bedwyn Valley before rising to a comparable height on the far side; at its southern end, the dyke continues through a sharp westerly turn and, it may be noted, across the parish boundary with Great Bedwyn, to traverse the valley called Harandene and finally to rise again, today flattened and seen only as a crop- or soil-mark, until it enters and finally disappears in Bedwyn Brail.[82] The name "Borough (Burridge) Heath" appears on Andrews and Dury's map of 1773, and "West Borough" on other maps of 1792 and 1842[83] probably refers to the dyke. It has been suggested[84] that the dyke may have been built to strengthen the defenses of Cissa's "metropolis." The charter of 778 shows that, at least at that time, it was not considered necessary for the full length of the dyke to lie within a single estate: indeed it shows that the area where Chisbury itself and the greater part of the main dyke were situated could pass out of royal hands altogether. At some date in the ninth century, royal control was regained of Little Bedwyn[85] and thereby all the defensive works that were still considered effective; as will be seen below, King Alfred, in all probability, utilized Chisbury in his system of forts which defended Wessex against the Danes in the late ninth century. It should also be pointed out that the dyke, in any case, may be of solely Iron Age construction and if Cissa built any fortifications at all, they may have been only at the hillfort itself.

The reign of Cynewulf, the grantor of the Little Bedwyn estate, was a period of some significance in the history of Wessex. After the death of Aethelbald of Mercia (715–757), Cynewulf refused to recognize Mercian Supremacy—and indeed the Bedwyn charter makes no mention of any overlord. West Saxon control of Berkshire and North Wiltshire was reasserted and he controlled lands on either side of the Thames until the victory of Offa at Bensington in 779 A.D.[86] One of the series of silver sceattas[87] has been tentatively attributed to Cynewulf.[88] Individual specimens have been recorded at Axford in Ramsbury parish[89] and at Summerfield House, Marlborough College, most probably, and not near Clatford in Preshute parish.[90]

The likelihood of Alfred's reuse of Chisbury as a burghal fort, noted above, depends upon the occurrence in the *Burghal Hidage* of the name *Cissanbyrig,* which probably refers to Chisbury and which appears in that document's list of forts between the entries for Wilton in South Wiltshire and Shaftesbury in Dorset.[91] The extant text of the *Hidage* may date to the reign of Alfred's elder son and successor Edward the Elder (899–924) and may represent a revision of a list originally drawn up by Alfred.[92] The locations of the listed forts show that they were sited near main roads and that it was intended that most of the population should live within some twenty miles of any one of them. The *Hidage* states that seven hundred men were required to man its defenses; the figure was calculated on the basis of four men for every pole (5 m or 5-1/2 yards) of the defended circuit, each man to be provided from one hide of land. An interesting feature of the site which can be seen today is St. Martin's Chapel, possibly a successor to one which served the burh.[93] In

904, King Edward gained Stoke by Shalbourne, an addition to an already substantial land block, whose acquisition may be related to the establishment of the burghal fort.[94]

Bedwyn is among the estates which is mentioned in Alfred's will, in which the king bequeathed it to his elder son Edward.[95] At some date between 801 and 805, Little Bedwyn, along with Wooton Rivers, Mildenhall, and Foxfield, appears to have passed into ecclesiastical possession. This estate, if so it was, returned to royal hands at some date later in the century.[96]

The Great Bedwyn estate is first defined in a charter of 968 A.D.[97] This charter records the grant by King Edgar of a vast area at Bedwyn—which was presumably therefore the most important place—to Abingdon Abbey (the estate was soon in royal hands again).[98] The description of the bounds indicates that the territory included the ancient parish of Great Bedwyn (which until 1844 incorporated Grafton), the greater part of the former parish of Tidcombe, most of Burbage parish, and a part of the former parish of South Savernake. Although the precise location of many of the boundary markers is uncertain, the general course of the boundary is in little doubt. The least certain section lies at the northwest in Savernake Forest, where Crawford's delineation depends largely upon the identification of the present Thornhill Pond with Whalemore, a name still in use locally when Crawford checked the bounds. Grundy,[99] however, did not consider that it was possible to reconstruct the boundary in that area. Ancient boundaries in woodland appear to have been less static in general than those elsewhere.[100]

The importance of Great Bedwyn itself in the tenth century, already hinted at by the construction of a burghal fort nearby, is clear from evidence of a very different and surprising kind. A gospel-book, which is preserved at Berne, but was written in Celtic Britain in the early ninth century and had reached England by c. 900 A.D. when two poems on Alfred were added, also contains four other, tenth-century, manuscript additions in Old English, which were made at Bedwyn.[101] These four entries relate to the render of tithes, guild statutes, and two manumissions.[102]

Only the first part of the item on the tithes survives; it refers to the provision of two-thirds of the tithes from Bedwyn and Lambourn (in Berkshire, see further below) for the sevants of God in Bedwyn. The first obligatory tithe payments date between 926 and c. 930 A.D. in Aethelstan's reign, with the probable intention both to protect the revenues of old ministers and to endow new ones,[103] and the evidence for Bedwyn points to the existence there of a college of secular priests and therefore a minster church, a status which is confirmed by later sources. The financial and administrative arrangements for the minster here, as in many other places, were doubtless closely tied to those for the royal estate at whose center it was located.[104] In 1086 A.D. *Domesday Book* records that the priest Brictward held the church, with 1½ hides and land for one plough, that it was valued at 60 shillings, and that Brictward's father had held it before him in the time of King Edward.[105] The nature of this entry, with its separate mention of the church, its priest, a valuation, and an endowment in excess of one hide, again indicates a church of minster status—although the community of priests had apparently by now departed, as is known to have happened elsewhere by this date.[106] The minster often served a Hundred and lay at its core,[107] and this too was the case at Bedwyn, which in 1281 is recorded as the head of Kinwaston Hundred.[108] Later, there were dependent chapels at Marten and East Grafton (both of which lie in the nineteenth-century parish of Grafton) and at Knowle, Chisbury, and in Little Bedwyn village itself in Little Bedwyn parish.[109] This parish was created in the fifteenth century; some reorganization of tithing boundaries at this time may be implied by the contrast in the record of the population at Chisbury where there were eighty-seven poll-tax payers in 1377, but in 1428 the place had fewer than ten households.[110]

The guild statutes point to the status of Great Bedwyn as a "town," ill-defined as this concept was in Anglo-Saxon England.[111] These regulations define religious obligations and arrangements to be made on the death of a member, help to be given if a member's house is burnt down, and compensation to be paid if a guildsman has been accused of lying or cheating by one of his fellows. Further ground for recognizing the place's urban character is the existence there in the eleventh century of a mint, where coins were struck by the moneyer Cild; the mint is not mentioned in the Domesday survey, which only includes the one at Malmesbury in Wiltshire.[112] *Domesday Book*[113] records twenty-five burgesses on the royal demesne at Bedwyn. The rents that burgesses paid to the king were an important source of royal revenue.[114] The proximity of the Burghal Hidage fort at Chisbury (see above) may also have played a part in Bedwyn's development.[115]

Haslam[116] has argued that the role played by Bedwyn in the Burghal Hidage, which has been discussed above, and its development as an urban center, presupposes the existence there of a *villa regalis*. He has pointed out that "Cissa's burh" may originally have referred to Cissa's "fortified dwelling" and not to the hillfort itself and that place-names indicate similar royal residences at Ramsbury, and also at Kintbury and Lambourn in Berkshire, which are discussed below in other contexts.

It has been suggested (see above) that before A.D. 778 the Little Bedwyn estate was combined with that at Great Bedwyn, as defined in the charter of 968 A.D., to form a large tract of country in royal hands, whose northern border was shared with a similarly large royal estate at Ramsbury, which lay to the north of the Kennet.[117]

Important excavations carried out in the High Street at Ramsbury in 1974 have thrown considerable light on the place in the late eighth and early ninth centuries. The investigation revealed a thriving and major iron-working industry on the north bank of the River Kennet, whose advanced technology and scale of activities, in all probability serving regional, not merely local needs, had clearly required substantial capital investment. Rhenish lava querns, which had arrived at the site from the port at Hamwih, beside Southhampton on the south coast, point to long-distance contacts. Although the iron ore itself had to be imported, the industry also relied on abundant local timber, for which the numerous bones of beaver, deer, and pig are clear evidence. The fingers of clay-with-flints that reach down towards Ramsbury on the northern slopes of the Kennet Vale are a particularly likely location for woodland. Examination of the animal bones also showed the horses to have been under great strain, most probably as a result of pulling carts laden with the ore.

The iron industry at Ramsbury may well have been under royal control. Haslam considered that it is necessary to presuppose a *villa regalis* at Ramsbury to provide a context for the establishment of a bishopric there in 909 A.D. The see was reunited with that of Sherborne in 1058 and with Old Sarum (Salisbury) in 1078. The bishop of Sarum is listed in *Domesday Book* as the owner of the 90-hide estate of the manor and Hundred of Ramsbury. Haslam noted that the shape of Ramsbury Hundred suggests that it was formerly part of a vast royal estate that had included Aldbourne, the Ogbournes, Preshute, and Mildenhall.

Notable parallels may also be drawn between the Bedwyn and Ramsbury estates and two others, which were also very large and in royal hands—Kintbury and Lambourn, in West Berkshire. Kintbury was apparently a *villa regalis,* probably with a minster, by the early tenth century.[118] The whole of the Hundred of Kintbury was always a royal hundred.[119] Kintbury itself, as Ramsbury, lies in the Kennet Valley, and at both places there is evidence of a Roman villa nearby, a contiguity which, it has been thought, may suggest that the Saxon centers directly replaced Roman ones. Lambourn Hundred, too, it has been argued, may have been a discrete estate since even the Iron Age.[120] Like Bedwyn, Lambourn was referred to in Alfred's will; it was royal in *Domesday Book.*

There is, therefore, the possibility that in the late Saxon period there were four very large and contiguous royal estates which stretched across the Kennet Valley, all with their origins in the Roman period. It should be pointed out, however, that it is also possible that these large land units were brought together only after the Roman period, and did not correspond with earlier estates.[121]

Haslam[122] has drawn attention to the essentially complementary nature of the evolving roles of the Kennet vale settlements at Bedwyn, Chisbury, and Ramsbury at the end of the Saxon period. J. Chandler has pointed to the equally striking variety of function which appears to be indicated in the names of the places which formed parts of the Great Bedwyn estate of the tenth century, although the names themselves are of much earlier origin: Grafton, "the farm by the grove";[123] Wexcombe, probably "(bees) wax-valley";[124] and Wilton, "the farm where wool was prepared or kept."[125]

There is some archaeological evidence for occupation at one particular location at Marlborough in the Saxon period. Finds recorded at Summerfield House, Marlborough College, include the eighth-century sceatta already mentioned and a silver-gilt pin of the late ninth or early tenth century. Other probable late Saxon finds are two iron padlock keys that were recovered with the pin.[126] Marlborough apparently takes its name from The Mount (*Merleberge* [DB], "Maerla's barrow"),[127] which is thought to be of prehistoric origin and which was the site of the castle built by William I. The Mount lies near the River Kennet and some 600 m south of Summerfield. It is of interest to note that, when the parish of Marlborough was defined, its boundary excluded Summerfield, which became part of Preshute. The growth of Marlborough proved to be at the expense of Bedwyn and Ramsbury. William transferred the mint there from Great Bedwyn,[128] although Marlborough already had a moneyer of its own.[129]

Domesday Book provides information about the tenure of different estates and the extent of arable, meadow, pasture, and woodland on many of them at the end of the eleventh century. These statistics allow us to gain a general impression of the countryside at that time, although it can be difficult to identify some of the smaller holdings.

Little Bedwyn has one entry, under Chisbury, in the Survey,[130] which does not distinguish between the settlements at Chisbury (on the Reading Beds and the London Clay), Little Bedwyn, Knowle (on the chalk; late Saxon pottery [now in Devizes Museum] has been found there), and Puthall (also on the chalk; the place is mentioned in the charter of 778 A.D. and is now Puthall Farm). The great estate of Bedwyn that is described in the charter of 968 A.D. is divided into its constituent parts. (Great) Bedwyn was held by the king, as it had been by Edward the Confessor;[131] it had never paid tax, nor had it been assessed in hides, but it was subject to the ancient due of a "night's farm," that is, it was required to supply provisions for the king and his retinue when they were in residence. The terms of the tenure point to the great antiquity of the arrangements and, most probably, of the estate itself. King Edward held six very large manors in Wiltshire on these terms—in other counties similar dues fell on a group of estates.[132] There were three other holdings at Great Bedwyn; the largest one was at Crofton[133] (on the chalk); another went with the church (see above), and the third was at Harding (Haran Dene in 778 A.D. and now Harding Farm, also on the chalk).[134] Grafton was entered separately in the survey: five estates are listed there, but of these only Wolf Hall is identified by name; the others presumably relate to East and West Grafton (or Wickham; that name and Wick's Mead appear on maps of 1792 and c. 1810 near Manor Farm),[135] Wexcombe, and Wilton. Three holdings in Marten, in Grafton parish, also have a distinct mention. All the settlements in Grafton, apart from Wexcombe, which is on the Chalk, lie on the Greensand, where springs and streams are plentiful. At Tidcombe, there is reference to a single estate. Burbage, the other land unit encompassed by the tenth-century charter, had four estates, including a holding of one virgate, which went with the church.

The Domesday survey gives some interesting statistics about the extent of woodland in the region. On the estates mentioned above, the largest woods were in Great Bedwyn itself, where two woods each stretched for two leagues and were one league wide, and another was half a league long and three furlongs broad.[136] The survey uses the term *silva*, which generally describes continuous woodland, for the two larger woods in I.2 and refers there to the smaller one as *lucus*, but in 39.1 this too is called *silva*.[137] At Grafton one estate contained two "arpents" of woods; at Wolf Hall (a manor held by the Seymour family in the early fifteenth century) the woods were two furlongs wide and the same long; at Crofton they were three furlongs long and one wide;[138] Marten had no woodland. There were four acres under wood at Tidcombe. Burbage had three woods; one was four furlongs long, the others three furlongs, and all three of them were two furlongs wide. Little Bedwyn had forty acres of woods.

The exact location of the Domesday woodlands in unknown. Their great extent at Great Bedwyn, however, may well coincide, at least in part, with the eastern limits of Savernake Forest, which lay within Great Bedwyn parish. Before the deforestation of 1330, the forest had extended from East Kennet in the west to Hungerford in the east and from the River Kennet in the north as far as Collingbourne in the south.[139] Great Bedwyn itself lay near the center of this vast area, although it may be noted that the town was exempt from forest duties.[140] Local names around Bedwyn, however, attest the impact of forest management; the Castle Copse villa is situated in Bedwyn Brail, the brail being an enclosed deer park within the forest[141]—an indication, presumably, that the site of the Roman remains has lain in woodland at least since the medieval period.

There was another medieval forest, that of Barroc, which gave its name to the country of Berkshire,[142] to the east of Bedwyn. Its exact location is uncertain, but it has been suggested that it stretched from Enborne to Hungerford, its heart on the clays in the area of Kintbury.[143] Romano-British pottery kilns at Kintbury and Hamstead Marshall, as those at Savernake and elsewhere, point to a wooded environment at that time.[144] It seems likely, therefore, that Barroc and Savernake forests were almost continuous. Extensive woodland cover in southwest Berkshire in the early Anglo-Saxon period would probably have discouraged newcomers to the area, and, indeed, few sites of the pagan period are known there. Furthermore, study of the place-names has pointed to a marked survival of Brittonic names in that part of the country.[145] The list of names in this group includes Barroc itself, and in this connection it may again be noted that Savernake (Forest), too, is a pre-English name.

Summary

In the tenth century, the enhanced status of Bedwyn is clear from its possession of both a minster church and a guild: the place doubtless benefited from its proximity to the *burh* at Chisbury. The town's prominent position in the eleventh century is marked by a mint and the presence of burgesses, who are mentioned in the *Domesday Book*.

Other evidence indicates Bedwyn's importance at an earlier date. Charters of 961 and 968 A.D. define a great royal estate centered on (Great) Bedwyn, which place-names and the dependence of a chapelry at Little Bedwyn suggest had been combined with a royal estate there, before the latter's alienation in 778 A.D. The total extent of these estates appears to have approximated to that of the ancient royal fiscal unit of a hundred hides. The paramount position of Great Bedwyn in this area was retained until the thirteenth century, when it is recorded as the head of Kinwaston Hundred.

A tradition that is preserved in the *History of the Monastery of Abingdon* relates that in the seventh century Chisbury was held by Cissa, who is said to have ruled Wiltshire and much of Berkshire; dykes near the hillfort have been attributed to him. Pagan Anglo-Saxon burial sites known within the limits of the greater Bedwyn estate are so far few and none is of a high status. The Anglo-Saxons were certainly present in the general area in the fifth century, notably to the south of Bedwyn at Collingbourne and to the northeast at East Shefford in Berkshire. It is not clear, however, that, at an early stage of their settlement, the Anglo-Saxons controlled the whole territory, and it is by no means impossible that in the fifth century, at least, the Britons retained some influence. British resiliance is indicated by the survival of British place-names in both southwest Berkshire and Savernake, where extensive forests may well have inhibited Anglo-Saxon immigration.

Notes

1. The writer would like to express thanks to P. H. Robinson, who readily gave information about recent early and middle Anglo-Saxon finds, and kindly made available a copy of the typescript interim note by S. Hirst and P. Rahtz on the results of excavations at Liddington Castle. K. Annable generously sent details in advance of publication about his excavations at Black Patch cemetery at Pewsey. B. Yorke, J. Chandler, in particular, and A. Borthwick also kindly helped by providing references in the literature to the later Saxon period and to a number of matters relating to the history of the Bedwyn area. The illustrations have been prepared by N. A. Griffiths, and to him too I offer my warm thanks.

2. Gildas, *De excidio Britanniae*, cc. 23–26 (Winterbottom 1978).

3. K. Jackson 1953: 241–246.

4. Gover, Mawer, and Stenton 1939: 15; Jackson 1953: 294.
5. K. Jackson 1953: 302, 331, 555, 674, 676.
6. Finberg 1964: 71, no. 191.
7. Haslam 1980: fig. 25.
8. Burnham and Wacher 1990: 148–52.
9. Annable 1978a: 128, fig.1; and Böhme 1986: 481, 563 (list 1, no. 50a).
10. Faull 1975; and Gelling 1988: 93–95.
11. Sawyer 1968: no. 756.
12. Grundy 1920: 78.
13. Sawyer 1968: no. 688.
14. Gingell 1978.
15. Evison 1978: 266–68; and Böhme 1986: 548, 572.
16. Evison 1977: 133; and Böhme 1986: 571.
17. Evison 1965: map 2.
18. Information from P. H. Robinson.
19. Evison 1981: 137; and Dickinson 1991:55.
20. M. G. Welch 1976; Evison 1978: 261–62; and Böhme 1986: 547. Information from P. H. Robinson.
21. Avent and Evison 1982.
22. Swanton 1973: 79.
23. Swanton 1974: 87.
24. Hawkes and Dunning 1961: 45 and fig. 13g. The cruciform brooch is in Devizes Museum.
25. Gover, Mawer, and Stenton 1939: 293.
26. Gelling 1976: 815–19, following Cox 1972–73.
27. Ward 1860: 262.
28. Information from P. H. Robinson.
29. WAR 1987: 142.
30. Swanton 1973: 128; and 1974: 66.
31. Grinsell 1957: 89 gives a full bibliography.
32. Passmore 1934: 393, in the Ashmolean Museum.
33. Information from P. H. Robinson.
34. Wiltshire County Council Sites and Monuments Record.
35. Information from P. H. Robinson.
36. WAR 1988: 185.
37. P. J. Fowler 1966: 31–32.
38. Information from P. H. Robinson.
39. Burchard 1971: 178–79.
40. Grinsell 1957: 68.
41. Swanton 1973: 101; and 1974: 47.
42. Swanton 1973: 83; and 1974: 56.
43. Grinsell 1957: 188–89, 243 provides references.
44. Evison 1963: 42.
45. Speake 1989.
46. Youngs 1992.
47. Bonney 1966.
48. Evison 1965: passim.
49. Evison 1965: passim.
50. Gildas, *De excidio Britanniae,* cc. 19, 21 (Winterbottom 1978).
51. Bede, *Ecclesiastical History,* III. 14 (Colgrave and Mynors 1969).
52. Härke 1990: 36.
53. Crawford 1921: 296–97; and 1953a: 68–71.
54. Meyrick 1949–50. Information on beads.
55. Anonymous 1922: 312.
56. Information provided by P. H. Robinson.

57. Dickinson 1974: 3, 19–24.
58. Whitelock, Douglas, and Tucker 1961.
59. Bonney 1973: 469.
60. H. S. Green 1971.
61. In Devizes Museum; information from P. H. Robinson, correcting that given in references in Grinsell 1957: 94: the two spearheads listed by Swanton (1973: 81; and 1974: 31) are of Iron Age date.
62. Hirst and Rahtz 1976.
63. WAR 1980: 207, where the findspot is wrongly given as Wanborough.
64. Grinsell 1957: 159 gives a full bibliography.
65. Eagles 1986: but of R. H. White 1988: 17.
66. Gover, Mawer, and Stenton 1939: 17.
67. Bonney 1973: 478.
68. Fox and Fox 1958.
69. Fox and Fox 1958: 5.
70. H. S. Green 1971.
71. Crawford 1921: 295.
72. Edwards 1988: 59; and Dumville 1992: 82.
73. Sawyer 1968: no. 264.
74. Crawford 1921, 292–97; cf. Grundy 1919: 151–55; and Darlington 1955: 5.
75. Cf. Haslam 1980: 62.
76. Gover, Mawer, and Stenton 1939: 332.
77. Gover, Mawer, and Stenton 1939: 334–35.
78. Biddle, Lambrick, and Myres (1968) provide a discussion of the archaeological and written evidence for the foundation.
79. Colgrave and Mynors 1969.
80. Stenton 1913: 8–19.
81. Stenton 1971: 68.
82. Information from E. Hostetter and T. N. Howe.
83. Information from C. J. Chandler.
84. Fox and Fox 1958: 18–20.
85. Dumville 1992: 107.
86. Stenton 1913: 23–25; and 1971: 209.
87. *BMC* type 49.
88. Andrews and Metcalf 1984.
89. Rigold and Metcalf 1984: 246.
90. Robinson 1981: 59; Metcalf 1984: 37, 54, fig. 7; and Rigold and Metcalf 1984: 255.
91. Brooks 1964: 75–79; and Hill 1969.
92. Keynes and Lapidge 1983: 24–25, cf. 339–340.
93. Haslam 1984: 96.
94. Dumville 1992: 107–108.
95. Keynes and Lapidge 1983: 175.
96. Dumville 1992: 43, 107.
97. Sawyer 1968: no. 756; for interpretation of bounds, see Crawford 1921: 282–92; Grundy 1920: 75–80; and Darlington 1955: 97.
98. Darlington 1955: 98; and Dumville 1992: 109, 111.
99. Grundy 1920: 79.
100. Hooke 1988: 141.
101. Keynes and Lapidge 1983: 338; and Dumville 1992: 79–82.
102. Brentnall 1948; and Whitelock 1955: 559.
103. Blair 1985: 119.
104. Blair 1985: 116.
105. *Domesday Book* I. 23j (Thorn and Thorn 1979).
106. Blair 1985: 106, 114, 119.

107. Blair 1985: 118.

108. Cam 1944: 68; and Gover, Mawer, and Stenton 1939: map in end pocket, for position of Bedwyn at the geographical heart of the Hundred. The Kinwardstone itself is on the boundary between the present parishes of Grafton and Burbage.

109. Brentnall 1948: 363.

110. Beresford 1959: 309, 314. I owe this point to C. J. Chandler.

111. Pugh 1981.

112. Darlington 1955: 20.

113. Thorn and Thorn 1979: 1.2.

114. Wormald 1982: 153.

115. Brooks 1964: 78.

116. Haslam 1976: 23; and 1980: 63.

117. Haslam 1980, for this and other matters relating to Ramsbury that are discussed below, unless it is noted otherwise.

118. Peake and Cheetham 1924: 206, 216.

119. Peake and Cheetham 1924: 157.

120. Gelling 1976: 810.

121. Cf. Esmonde Cleary 1989b: 187.

122. Haslam 1984: 94–102.

123. Gover, Mawer, and Stenton 1939: 347.

124. Gover, Mawer, and Stenton 1939: 347.

125. Gover, Mawer, and Stenton 1939: 347.

126. P. Robinson 1981.

127. Gover, Mawer, and Stenton 1939: 297–98.

128. Stevenson 1983: 165.

129. Haslam 1984: 89.

130. Thorn and Thorn 1979: 29.1.

131. Thorn and Thorn 1979: I.2.

132. Darlington 1955: 61.

133. Thorn and Thorn 1979: 26.4.

134. Thorn and Thorn 1979: 68.6.

135. Information from C. J. Chandler.

136. Thorn and Thorn 1979: 1.2, 39.1.

137. Darlington 1955: 59.

138. Thorn and Thorn 1979: 26.4.

139. Ailesbury 1962: map on 10.

140. Ailesbury 1962: 9.

141. Gover, Mawer, and Stenton 1939: 332.

142. Gelling 1976: 801.

143. Hooke 1988: 150 (following Peake).

144. Swan 1984: 6–8.

145. Gelling 1976: 801–805.

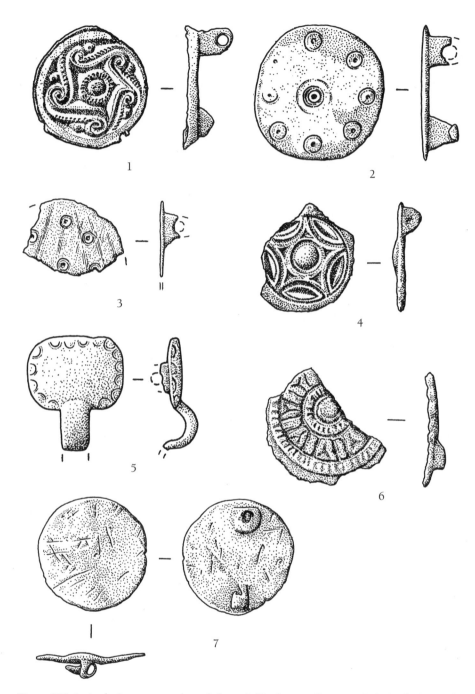

Figure 163. 1: Anglo-Saxon saucer brooch from Collingbourne Kingston. 2–3: Anglo-Saxon disc brooches from Collingbourne Kingston. 4: Anglo-Saxon saucer brooch found near Membury hillfort, Ramsbury. 5: Part of an Anglo-Saxon small-long brooch from Aldbourne. 6: Fragmentary Anglo-Saxon saucer brooch found at Ramsbury. 7: Back-plate of an applied brooch (?) from Ramsbury. (1:1)

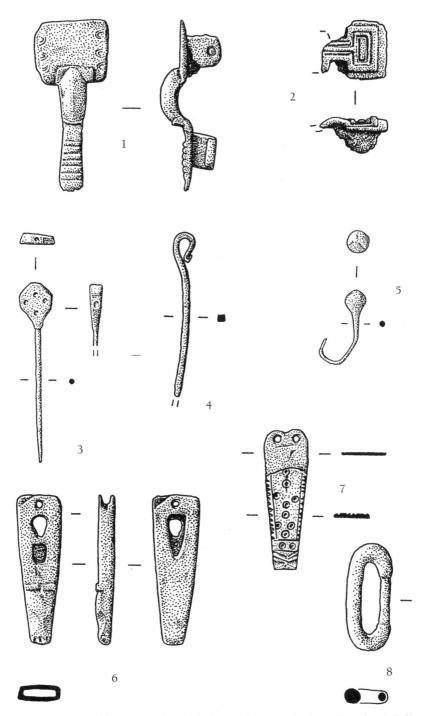

Figure 164. 1–2: Small-long brooches of early and later Anglo-Saxon date from Shalbourne. 3–5: Pins of early and later Anglo-Saxon date from Shalbourne. 6–7: Strap-ends of later Anglo-Saxon date from Shalbourne. 8: Buckle loop of Anglo-Saxon date from Shalbourne. (1:1)

Figure 165. Gold sceattas from Shalbourne.

Figure 166. Single-edged battle knife from Barbury Castle. (1:2)

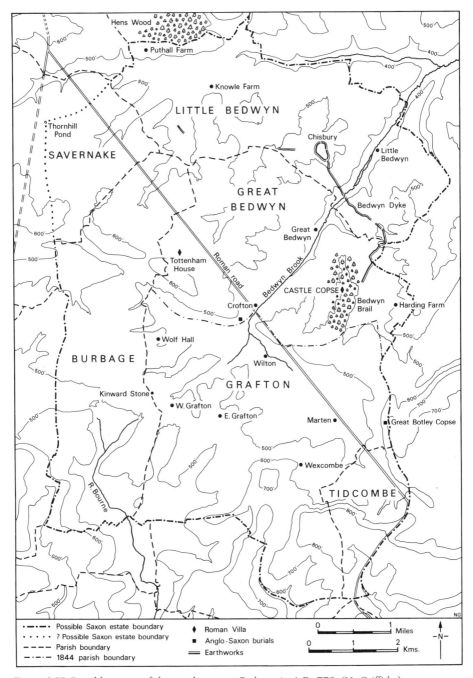

Figure 167. Possible extent of the royal estate at Bedwyn in A.D. 778. (N. Griffiths)

APPENDIX 1:
LIST OF ROMAN SITES AND FINDS PLOTTED ON AREA MAPS
(FIGS. 24–25)

ERIC HOSTETTER

This list of sites for the maps illustrating the area around Cunetio in the Roman period (Figs. 24–25) is based primarily on information contained in the databases of the Sites and Monuments Record for the concerned areas of the counties of Wiltshire, Hampshire, and Berkshire as of 1986, an area found on O.S. maps 173–174 (Second series Sheets 173 and 174; scale of 1:50,000).

Many of the sites have been identified only through sparse surface remains, and their classification is somewhat vague and subjective; industrial sites, for example, are not distinguished from buildings/settlements, and we have next to no knowledge of religious sites in the area concerned. The classifications and criteria (structural and associated finds) adopted here are:

Town: known urban center.

Villa or possible villa: substantial building debris with luxury features such as hypocausts, mosaic pavements and tesserae, painted plaster, and glass constitute certain villas. Possible villas have some indication of luxury features.

Buildings/Settlements: buildings and settlements, including earthworks, associated with habitation, industry, or other purposes and which do not have ready signs of luxury, as defined for villas.

Finds, as given in the Sites and Monuments Record, are plotted on the map in Figure 24, but are not listed here.

Walled Town
1. Black Field (Mildenhall) 217/695.

Villas or Possible Villas
2. Aldbourne Gorse (Aldbourne) 2625/7350.
3. North Farm (Aldbourne) 2512/7885. Villa or settlement.
4. Stock Lane/Hillwood (Aldbourne) 2363/7413. Villa (?).
5. Upper Upham (Aldbourne) 2281/7695.
6. Windmill Hill, S of (Avebury) 0841/7001.
7. St. James Church (Cherhill) 0385/7029.
8. South Farm (Chiseldon) 1912/7681.
9. Cuffs Corner (Clyffe Pyppard) 0814/7640.
10. Harrow Farm (Froxfield) 2789/6822.
11. Rudge Manor Farm (Froxfield) 2765/6995.
12. Fyfield House (Fyfield) 1489/6872.

13. Castle Copse (Great Bedwyn) 2835/6295.
14. Tottenham House (Great Bedwyn) 2475/6376.
15. Kennet and Avon Canal, S of Wilderness (Kintbury) 39410/67150.
16. Basset Down (Lydiard Tregoze) 1154/7996.
17. Manningford Bruce Churchyard (Manningford) 1402/5805.
18. Browns Farm (Marlborough) 1930/6785.
19. Forest Hill Farm (Mildenhall) 210/687. Villa (?).
20. Barton Down (Preshute) 1698/7045.
21. Littlecote (Ramsbury) 3000/7062.
22. Ramsbury, Manor Farm (Ramsbury) 2676/7148. Villa or farmhouse.
23. Tockenham, N of village (Tockenham) 0392/7963.
24. North Field (West Overton) 1251/7001.
25. Draycot Farm (Wilcot) 1460/6320.

Buildings/Settlements
26. Woodsend (Aldbourne) 2265/7590. Settlement (?).
27. Allington, NE of (All Cannings) 0732/6330. Settlement (?).
28. Knap Hill (Alton) Enclosed settlement.
29. West Stowell (Alton) 1377/6190. Building.
30. Avebury Trusloe, N of (Avebury) 0841/7016. Farmstead (or villa?) (see no. 6).
31. Silbury Hill, SE of (Avebury) 1010/6830. Settlement, both sides of Roman road.
32. Finches Farm (Baydon) 2874/7806. Farmstead (?).
33. Wilsford, SE of (Charlton St. Peter) 108/567. Building (?).
34. Buff Barn, N of (Chiseldon) 1795/7890. Settlement.
35. Burderop Down (Chiseldon) 1630/7713. Settlement with square huts, stone floor tiles.
36. Summer Down (Collingbourne Kingston) 2160/5550. Settlement (?).
37. Pans Lane (Devizes) 008/607. Settlement, 2 inhumations.
38. Everleigh, E edge of Barrows (Everleigh) 1850/5604. Village within squarish earthwork, field system.
39. Wroughton Copse, NE of (Fyfield) 1405/7140. Small settlement.
40. Tottenham House, SW of (Great Bedwyn) 248/635. Kilns.
41. Wood Copse (Ham) 349/626. Settlement or farmhouse.
42. North Hidden Farm, N of (Hungerford) 34600/72770. Settlement within enclosure.
43. St. Michael's Church, S of (Inkpen) 35600/63400. Possible settlement, roof and box tiles, pilae.
44. Kennet and Avon Canal (Kintbury) 39460/67130. Settlement (?).
45. Baydon, SE of (Lambourn) 2922/7738. "Corn-drier" (see nos. 46–47).
46. Baydon Overbridge (Lambourn) 29200/77400. Possible small settlement on both sides Roman road.
47. Membury, Cheynes Meadow (Lambourn) 30900/76050. Probable Roman building, dressed mortared flints.
48. Row Down (Lambourn) 29960/79590. Settlement (?).
49. Chisbury hillfort (Little Bedwyn) 2790/6595. Two settlements?

50. Marden earthwork, S of (Marden) 0877/5781. Settlement, Iron Age and Roman.
51. Marlborough (Marlborough) 195/690. Possible building or trackway (?).
52. Marlborough, The Gasworks (Marlborough) 1928/6910. Settlement.
53. St. Margarets Mead (Marlborough) 196/688. Settlement.
54. Summerfield (Marlborough) 1850/6909. Building, roof tiles.
55. Poulton Down (Mildenhall) 2041/7155. Villa or farmhouse (?), building debris, well with female Anglo-Saxon (?) skeleton.
56. Milton Hill (Milton Lilbourne) 191/583. Building, brick, stone, and terracotta tile.
57. Southend (Ogbourne St. Andrew) 1921/7311. Building, slight mound: stone and terracotta tiles, flints.
58. Chase Woods, Ogbourne Hill (Ogbourne St. George) 2162/7550. Two buildings, one with chalk blocks.
59. Round Hill Downs (Ogbourne St. George) 214/754. Settlement.
60. Martinsell Hill (Pewsey) 1750/6385. Settlement with kiln debris.
61. Hodds Hill, below (Ramsbury) 2864/7526. Settlement (?) with platforms and enclosures.
62. Leigh Hill, N of (Savernake) 2224/6497. Seven kilns.
63. Savernake Forest (Savernake) 222/650. Savernake Ware kiln.
64. Sheepwalk Plantation, N of (Wanborough) 2444/7937. Settlement with huts, smelting area.
65. Sugar Hill (Wanborough) 2362/7925. Settlement (?).
66. Overton Down (West Overton) 1312/7009. Settlement with hut platforms.
67. Overton Down, S of (West Overton) 131/705. Settlement, Iron Age to Roman.
68. Pickledean (West Overton) 1304/6981. Enclosed settlement, huts with chalk floor.
69. Pickledean (West Overton) 133/697. Settlement.
70. Bethnal Green, NE of (Wilcot) 1663/6255. Building, stone tiles.
71. Wilcot, NW of (Wilcot) 139/612. Settlement.
72. Withy Copse (Wilcot) 1721/6429. Midden with Iron Age and Roman sherds, kiln debris.
73. Barbury Castle, N of (Wroughton) 1499/7678. Rectangular earthwork with wall foundations.

Burials
74. Allington, NE of (All Cannings) 0732/6330. Infant bones in well.
75. Honey Street (Alton) 1025/6140. Inhumations (?).
76. Knap Hill (Alton) 121/636. Inhumation (1): gravegoods.
77. Avebury, Avenue to Beckhampton (Avebury) 093/693. Inhumation (1): child with gravegoods.
78. Silbury Hill, E of (Avebury) 1037/6855. Inhumation (1): gravegoods.
79. Weir Farm, N of (Broad Hinton) 115/772. Cemetery, probably cremations: sarsen slabs, gravegoods.
80. Southgrove Farm (Burbage) 227/582? 225/585? Inhumation (1): gravegoods including animal bones, iron and bronze work, whetstone.
81. Whyteways, The Street (Cherhill) 0400/7030. Inhumation (2): Savernake sherd with human bones; second skull with color-coated ware.

82. Broad Town Field (Clyffe Pyppard) 095/774. Inhumations (3): 3 skeletons beneath sarsens; sherds, coin of Marcus Aurelius, part of brooch, stone spindle whorl.
83. Cuffs Corner (Clyffe Pyppard) 080/764. Inhumations (9): interments beneath sarsens.
84. Nursteed Road (Devizes) 0122/6087. Inhumation (4): one stone, one lead, two wood (?) coffins with grave goods, including coins of Maximianus and Carausius.
85. Pans Lane (Devizes) 008/607. Inhumation (2), grave goods.
86. Wayside Farm (Devizes) 0140/6055. Inhumation (1): gravegoods.
87. Rudge Manor Farm (Froxfield) 2675/6995. Skeletons (4–5) in well (see no. 11).
88. Upper Lambourn (Lambourn) 31780/79990. 3 inhumations, 2 male, 1 female with RB pottery and hobnail.
89. Knowle Barn (Little Bedwyn), NE of gravel-pit against parish boundary 254/675? Inhumation (1): skeleton, pottery and fibula; separate excavation yielded pottery, nails, sandal cleats.
90. Granham Hill (Marlborough) 1823/6813. Bowl barrow (doubtful): RB sherds.
91. St. Margarets Mead, Colemans Mead (Marlborough) 196/691. Inhumations (numerous): grave goods including coins Diocletian and Antoninus, *terra sigillata,* and New Forest sherds.
92. Black Field (Mildenhall) 2173/6920. Inhumation (1): lead coffin.
93. Forest Hill Farm (Mildenhall) 2089/6872. Cremation (1): Roman (?), urn under Roman brick arch (see no. 19).
94. Clatford Bottom (Preshute) 147/714. Inhumation (1): Decapitated (?) female, grave goods.
95. Manton House, NE of (Preshute) 1592/7093. Inhumation (2): wealthy gravegoods, including 26 *siliquae* Julian II to Honorius.
96. Littlecote (Ramsbury) 3000/7062. Inhumations: baby burials within villa.
97. Roundway, The Folly (Roundway) 017/626. Inhumation (1): lead coffin.
98. Overton Hill (West Overton) 1192/6835. Primary cremation (1): in bowl barrow, surrounded by ditch with postholes. Saxon (?).
99. Overton Hill (West Overton) 1192/6833. RB tomb (1?): in bowl barrow, with secondary burials.
100. Overton Hill (West Overton) 1193/6837. RB cremation (?) (1?): in doubtful bowl barrow, with secondary Saxon burials.

APPENDIX 2:
EXCAVATION RECORDING AND FINDS PROCESSING

ERIC HOSTETTER, THOMAS NOBLE HOWE, MARYLINE PARCA, AND ARCHER ST. CLAIR.

Excavation and Recording

Trenches were laid out on even one-meter or five-meter intervals of the O.S. grid. The recording system was derived from that of the Museum of London and Littlecote Roman villa, with contexts recorded as positive features, layers, and negative features. Each layer was defined horizontally and the outline and levels of its top surface were planned (in "context plans") at 1:20 before removal, usually by trowel, often by complete dry-sieving, rarely by pick and shovel. Each context was described individually on a context sheet and its finds listed on a finds sheet and in the *Finds Recording Book*. Day-to-day operations were also recorded in *Field Journals* for each sector. Diagrammatic matrices presenting the stratigraphic sequence were also kept. At various intervals (usually two to four times a season), excavation was stopped in an entire sector at an approximate stratigraphically uniform level, and all surface features were planned together in detail at 1:20 ("level plans," published here as state plans). Many contexts were dry-sieved in whole or in part, and environmental samples were taken from almost all contexts and processed by flotation.

Finds Processing

Excavated material was sorted into the following categories: stone building material, stone (other), ceramic building material, plaster, mosaic, pottery, glass, iron, copper alloy, bone, shell. Each object was marked in ink with its site, sector, and context number, the latter in a circle. For special finds, a "small find" number was also assigned and marked in a triangle, and all "small finds" were logged in a *Finds Recording Book* and upon individual forms. The overall contents of each context were also recorded and described by class and one or more of the following criteria—number, volume, and weight—in a *Finds Summary Book,* along with quantity and/or weight, thus enabling an understanding of the contents of each context following washing.

APPENDIX 3:
PHOSPHATE ANALYSIS
KATHRYN L. GLEASON AND FERN FRYER

In 1984, G. Mees directed a series of simple visual analysis soil phosphate tests on the unexcavated portions of the building platform and adjacent field, with the hope of locating trackways, paddocks, gardens, graves, and other features and activities that contribute large quantities of phosphates to the soil.

A soil corer was used to remove four cores from each location. From each core, a sample was taken at a point approximately 0.25 m below ground level. Fifty mg of soil from each sample was placed on filter paper and treated with two drops of acid ammonium molybdate solution, followed two minutes later by two drops of .5% ascorbic acid solution. The subsequent reaction produced a blue stain on the paper in proportion to the amount of phosphate in the sample. This color was fixed by rinsing the paper in a 33% sodium citrate solution for two minutes, after which the filter papers were dried and arranged in four categories, according to the relative density of the stain. These densities are indicated by the size of the circles in Fig. 88.

Unexpectedly, the highest concentrates of phosphate were found in samples taken directly over the areas of known masonry walls, rather than areas of organic debris (Fig. 88), suggesting that the mortar used in the buildings retained high levels of inorganic phosphate.[1]

Phosphate tests in the large field east of the villa platform to detect the presence of other associated buildings yielded inconclusive results (Fig. 88). Nonetheless, the highest densities matched areas of intensive activity located in the resistivity survey (Fig. 87) and the site of the razed nineteenth-century brick cottage. Very low readings were found in the adjacent woods, leaf litter preventing the corer from taking a sample of comparable depth to those taken in the open.[2]

NOTES

1. Similar results were obtained at the Herodian palace at Jericho, Israel, where the building materials indicated higher levels of phosphate than areas known (by the presence of flowerpots and domestic debris) to be fertilized gardens.

2. Mees, pers. comm.

APPENDIX 4:
LOCATION OF CASTLE COPSE EVALUATION TRENCHES

Evaluation Trenches No.:
> Southeast corner of

1. 375/453
2. 501/436
3. 392–422 Wall (Fig. 40): Wall suggesting an eastern perimeter wall.
4. 398/464
5. 458/340
6. 520/399
7. 520/446
8. 538/450
9. 400/493
10. 401/519—Aisled Building II: At position of tenth column from west (Fig. 40).

APPENDIX 5:
ANALYSIS OF IRON ASSEMBLAGE
ROBERT M. EHRENREICH

Columns one through three are self-explanatory; columns four through six present the percent of cobalt, phosphorus, and sulfur contained in each sample. Some concentrations presented are below the detection limits of the microprobe used (i.e., 0.020%); these numbers were used to facilitate the computerized manipulation of the data, and should not be considered accurate readings. Column seven presents slag inclusion density per sample in terms of "L" for low (under 2%), "M" for medium (2 to 4%), and "H" for high (over 4%). Column eight lists the hardness of the samples as determined by a Leitz Hardness tester with a 500 g weight. The ninth column lists the relative grain size of the artifacts in terms of small, medium, or large. The final column presents carbon concentration. Carbon contents divided by a "/" indicate samples that exhibited definite divisible areas of differing carbon concentrations. The carbon contents divided by a "–" indicate that the sample contained carbon concentrations varying within that range. Objects are listed in order of context numbers in Sectors A–D.

Cat. no.	Object	Context	Co	P	S	Slag	HV	Grain	Carbon
199	Loop, two-spiked	A7	.022	.058	.007	M	89.5	L	None
207.	Horseshoe	A21	.027	.212	.012	H	186.5	M	None
176.	Spearhead	A35	.018	.051	.008	M	94.7	L	None
171.	Blade	A40	.017	.059	.009	M	324.4	S	0.6
—.	Shaft, disc-ended	A101	.016	.115	.017	H	158.7	L	None
201.	Loop, two-spiked	A121	.022	.012	.011	H	168.5	L	None
200.	Loop, two-spiked	A121	.035	.078	.013	L	170.0	M	None/0.8
180.	Boss, small	A139	—	—	—	—	—	—	No metal
—.	Nail	A196	.021	.031	.007	M	92.6	L	None–0.2
—.	Nail	A223	.021	.125	.011	M	146.5	L	None–Low
—.	Nail	A223	.016	.040	.016	H	194.0	M	None–0.2
—.	Sheet	A265	.014	.295	.008	H	191.8	S	0.3/Low
—.	Cleat, small	A265	.009	.049	.005	M	197.3	M	None
—.	Nail	A323	.021	.053	.006	M	117.8	M/L	Low/0.2
—.	Nail	A355	.025	.078	.014	M	103.1	L	None
—.	Scrap	A378	.008	.368	.053	L	137.6	M	None
—.	Cleat, small	A395	.014	.081	.006	H	158.0	S	Low–0.1
—.	Nail	A397	.018	.071	.008	M	256.6	M	None/0.7
—.	Nail	A427	.021	.045	.006	L	166.9	S	0.3
—.	Nail	A443	—	—	—	—	—	—	No metal
—.	Nail	A473	.019	.130	.011	H	127.5	M	None–Low

—.	Bar fragment	A475	.014	.101	.008	M	159.5	L	None–Low
—.	Nail	A520	.026	.015	.004	L	210.4	M	0.4/0.6
188.	Binding/fitting	B7	.009	.069	.008	M	109.8	L	None
—.	Nail	B31	.008	.043	.007	M	147.6	L	None
—.	Nail	B42	.024	.030	.009	H	128.5	S	0.1
—.	Nail	B47	.019	.020	.015	M	122.0	L	None
—.	Spike, loop-headed	B52	.004	.077	.005	M	162.6	L	None–0.1
—.	Nail	B55	.018	.112	.011	M	176.1	S	None–0.2
—.	Nail	B57	.007	.031	.005	L	131.1	M	0.3
165.	Nailheader	B67	.012	.039	.004	H	169.2	L	None
—.	Plate	B98	.005	.126	.043	M	128.5	L	None–Low
—.	Cleat, small	B99	.008	.085	.008	H	247.0	S	0.3–0.7
—.	Cleat	B109	.008	.032	.005	M	152.5	M	Low/0.5
—.	Nail	B110	.021	.046	.005	H	153.2	S	None
—.	Nail	B112	.021	.079	.010	H	206.7	M	Low–0.7
—.	Nail	B144	.016	.060	.013	L	119.1	M	None–0.2
—.	Nail, large	B144	.062	.149	.012	L	238.4	S	0.1–0.4
177.	Latch-lifter	B144	.001	.067	.004	H	161.2	M	None–0.4
206.	Horseshoe	C9	.001	.227	.010	H	217.5	M	None
173.	Blade fragment	C19	—	—	—	—	—	—	No metal
190.	Cleat/joiner's dog	C19	.007	.102	.007	L	130.6	L	None
—.	Brad/nail	C43	.008	.054	.007	M	197.0	M	None–0.2
—.	Plate	C43	.003	.043	.004	H	80.0	L	None
—.	Spike, large	C43	.004	.056	.003	M	83.9	L	None
184.	Drop-hinge	C43	.003	.085	.006	L	155.7	M	None–0.3
—.	Nail	C64	.018	.008	.005	M	157.0	S	0.3/0.6
—.	Nail	C64	.036	.083	.006	M	268.8	S	Low–0.4
—.	Nail	C64	.016	.075	.006	H	192.7	S	0.3–0.5
—.	Nail	C64	.028	.043	.013	M	104.1	L	None

APPENDIX 6:
POTTERY EXCLUDED FROM ANALYSIS
ANTHONY R. WILMOTT

1. Contexts later than latest dated occupation phases containing only residual material.

Sector A:	B:		C:	D:
1–5	1–7	99	2	1
13–14	9-13	103	4–5	
16-17	22	107	10	
19	24–28	109	13	
21	48	117	15	
35	52	121	18–22	
39–40	58	149	26	
42–47	61		28	
54	69		30	
60	81			
73	89			
95–97	93			
100–101	95			

2. Pottery groups from occupation phases comprising less than five body sherds.

Sector A:				B:	
9	252	423	800	8	135
10	254	433	812	15	148
74–75	257	445	847	43–44	150
87	261	451	849	46–47	
93	264–265	453	865	49–50	
104	296	473	873	56–57	
108	301	475	887	60	
113–114	309–310	477	900	68	
118	325–326	482	908	71	
129	336	487	910–911	75	
189	346	495	914	77	
194	348	508	922	79	
198	353	521	947	88	
202–203	356	523	958	94	
205	360	545		100	
207	372	575		102	
210	382	585		105	
219	388	600–601		112	
221	390	653		120	

Sector A: B:

223   394   666   122
228   403   700   128
231   415–416   723   130
242   725   133

APPENDIX 7:
RADIOCARBON DATES

The following accelerator dates were obtained through the kind assistance of Rupert Housely at the Research Laboratory for Archaeology and the History of Art at Oxford University in 1988 (1) and 1989 (2–3) (Hedges et al. 1988: 298; and 1989: 223–24). Dates are expressed in radiocarbon years before A.D. 1950, using the half-life of 5,568 years (calibration: Stuiver and Kra, *Radiocarbon* 28, 2B, 1986: 805–38).

1. Double-sided composite comb (**465**). C43.
   OxA-1353   1690 ± 80
   One Σ (68% confidence): cal A.D. c. 240–425
   Two Σ (95% confidence): cal A.D. c. 135–545

2. Bone from sealed burn fill. A77
   OxA-1892   1645 ± 70
   One Σ: cal A.D. c. 265–440
   Two Σ: cal A.D. c. 240–560

3. Pig metapodial. A191.
   OxA-1893   1780 ± 60
   One Σ: cal A.D. c. 140–335
   Two Σ: cal A.D. c. 90–400

APPENDIX 8:
MEASUREMENTS OF MAMMAL BONES
SEBASTIAN PAYNE

A. Domestic mammals:
    1. Cattle — *Bos* dom.
    2. Sheep and goat — *Ovis* dom. and *Capra* dom.
    3. Pig — *Sus* dom. (probably also includes wild boar, *S. scrofa*)
    4. Horse — *Equus* dom.
    5. Dog — *Canis* dom.
    6. Cat — *Felis* dom.

B. Wild mammals:
    7. Red deer — *Cervus elaphus*
    8. Fox — *Vulpes vulpes*
    9. Stoat or weasel — *Mustela* sp.
    10. Hare — *Lepus* sp.
    11. Rabbit — *Oryctolagus cuniculus*

1. *Bos* dom.

Scapula

Context number	A121
Phase	XI/XII
GLP	782
BG	.
SLC	.
Fusion	f

Humerus

Context number	A969	A121	A121	A121	A	
Phase	I	XI/XII	XI/XII	XI/XII	mean	(n)
BT	655	.	629	637	640	(3)
HT	412	425	367	374	395	(4)
HTC	(298)	(318)	292	287	299	(4)
Fusion	p? df	p? dfg	p? df	p? dfg		

Radius

Context number	A969	A964	A149	A121	A121	A	
Phase	I	II	XI	XI/XII	XI/XII	mean	(n)
GL	.	.	2979	.	.		
BpP	737+	907	882+	780+	800	821+	(5)
BFpP	672+	835	807+	721+	712	749+	(5)

SD	.	.	446	.	.
Fusion	pf d?	pf d?	pf df	pf d?	pf d?

Metacarpal

Context number	A957	A69
Phase	VIII	XI
BFd	618	578+
Td	.	293+
Fusion	df	df

Femur

Context number	A104
Phase	XI
DCP	417
Fusion	pu d?

Tibia

Context number	A965	A629	A872	A94	A121	A	
Phase	I	II	IX	X/XI	XI/XII	mean	(n)
GL	.	.	.	.	3168		
BdP	543	612	623+	642+	567	597+	(5)
Fusion	p? df	p? df	p? df	p? df	pf df		

Astragalus

Context number	A541	A543	A6	A69	A121	A	
Phase	II	VII	XI	XI	XI/XII	mean	(n)
GL1	.	598+	614	.	.		
GLm	532+	.	557	591+	534	554+	(4)
Bd	.	.	377	398+	.		

Calcaneum

Context number	A69	A149
Phase	XI	XI
GL	1257	1307
Fusion	f	f

Metatarsal

Context number	A964	A397
Phase	II	VII
GL	2230	(2360)
SD	280	304
BFd	580	613
Td	304	321+
Fusion	df	df

2. *Ovis* dom. and *Capra* dom.

Scapula

Context number	A69	A69	A133	A121	A	
Phase	XI	XI	XI	XI/XII	mean (n)	
GLP	311	.	279+	284+	291+ (3)	
BGP	204	.	.	.		
BG	199	.	.	.		
SLC	180	170	.	160	170 (3)	
Fusion	f	f	f	f		
Identification	?*Ovis*	?	?	?		

Humerus

Context number	A942	A953	A953	A287	A69	A69	A104
Phase	I	I	I	IX	XI	XI	XI
BT	304	(238)	.	.	274	.	.
HT	200	154	152	.	172	163+	169
HTC	147	116	118	138	133	124	136
Fusion	p? df	p? df	pfg df	p? df	p? df	pu df	p? dfg
Identification	.	*Ovis*	*Ovis*	.	*Ovis*	.	*Ovis*
Comment	GRP	GRP	GRP				

Context number	A202	A377	A	
Phase	XI	XI	mean	(n)
BT	.	273	272	(4)
HT	.	182	170+	(7)
HTC	(126)	130+	130+	(9)
Fusion	p? du	p? df		
Identification	.	*Ovis*		
Comment				

Radius

Context number	A942	A942	A953	A954	A69	A212	A	
Phase	I	I	I	VIII	XI	XI	mean	(n)
GL	(1650)	.	.	.	.	.		
BpP	.	.	.	273	299	303	292	(3)
BFpP	.	306+	.	253	275	274	277+	(4)
SD	(163)	162	.	.	.	142	156	(3)
Bd	.	.	242	.	.	.		
Fusion	pf dfg	pf d?	p? df	pf d?	pf d?	pf d?		
Identification	.	.	.	.	?*Ovis*	*Ovis*		
Comment	GRP	GRP	GRP burnt					

Metacarpal

Context number	A942	A942	A927	A462	A69	A323
Phase	I	I	II	VI	XI	XI
GL	1376	1372	1253	.	1256	1325
SD	132	132	.	124	134	122
BFd	253	255	.	243+	235+	234
Dd	167	.	.	158+	.	154
Fusion	df	df	df	df	df	df
Identification	*Ovis*	*Ovis*	*Ovis*	*Ovis*	*Ovis*	*Ovis*
Comment	GRP	GRP				

Context number	A377	A	
Phase	XI	mean	(n)
GL	1245	1305	(6)
SD	133	130	(6)
BFd	241	244+	(6)
Dd	153+	158+	(4)
Fusion	df		
Identification	*Ovis*		

Tibia

Context number	A942	A954	A760	A121	A	
Phase	I	VIII	IX	XI/XIl	mean	(n)
BdP	272	246	243	217+	245+	(4)
Fusion	p? df	p? df	p? df	p? df		
Identification	*Ovis*	*Capra*	.	.		
Comment	GRP					

Astragalus

Context number	A932	A942	A191	A377
Phase	I	I	XI	XI
GLl	268	288	253+	245
GLm	257	278	235	231
Bd	173	187	168+	162+
Identification	*Ovis*	*Ovis*	.	.
Comment		GRP	juv	juv

Calcaneum

Context number	A932	A932	A69	A69	A	
Phase	I	I	XI	XI	mean	(n)
GL	473	595	528+	527	531+	(4)
Fusion	f	f	f	f		
Identification	*Ovis*	*Ovis*	*Ovis*	*Ovis*		

Metatarsal

Context number	A942	A942	A729	A69	A217	A217	A mean	(n)
Phase	I	I	IX	XI	XI	XI	mean	(n)
GL	.	1478	.	1338	.	1335	1384	(3)
SD	119	120	.	110	.	111	115	(4)
BFd	252	252	251	227	234	231	241	(6)
Dd	169	170	173	151	166	.	166	(5)
Fusion	df	df	df	df	df	dfg		
Identification	*Ovis*	*Ovis*	*Ovis*	*Ovis*	*Ovis*	*Ovis*		
Comment	GRP	GRP						

3. *Sus*

Maxilla

Context number	A601	A287	A129	A133	A191	A310	A377
Phase	VIII	IX	XI	XI	XI	XI	XI
dP4 L	.	.	.	147	.	136	131
dP4 WP	.	.	.	112	.	.	106
M1 L	.	.	.	.	*148w	.	174
M1 WA	.	.	.	.	*134w	.	134
M1 WP	.	.	.	.	*134w	.	137
M2 L	232	235	*215−	.	.	.	.
M2 WA	158	183(!)	*161	.	.	.	.
M2 WP	153	163	*158	.	.	.	.
M3 L	.	367	.	.	.	.	.
M3 WA	.	206	.	.	.	.	.

Context number	A377	A377	A377	A377	A377	377	A377
Phase	XI	XI	XI	XI	XI	Xl	XI
dP4 L	.	135	140	146	141	143	.
dP4 WP	.	98	.	.	101	95	.
M1 L	170	.	.	.	.	.	190
M1 WA	135	.	.	.	.	.	140
M1 WP	132	.	.	.	.	.	141
M2 L	219	.	.	.	.	.	.
M2 WA	164	.	.	.	.	.	.
M2 WP	157	.	.	.	.	.	.
M3 L	.	.	.	.	.	.	.
M3 WA	.	.	.	.	.	.	.

Context number	A377	A377	A377	A382	A121	A
Phase	XI	XI	XI	XI	XI/XII	mean	(n)
dP4 L	.	.	.	.	.	140	(8)
dP4 WP	.	.	.	.	.	102	(5)
M1 L	145w	.	.	.	150w	163	(6)
M1 WA	.	.	.	.	.	136	(4)

M1 WP	131w	.	.	.	.	135	(5)
M2 L	.	.	.	.	205	221−	(5)
M2 WA	.	.	.	.	155	164	(5)
M2 WP	.	.	.	155	150	156	(6)
M3 L	.	320	303	.	280	318	(4)
M3 WA	.	179	177	178	168	182	(5)

Mandible

Context number	A768	A865	A865	A968	A969	A927	A575
Phase	I	I	I	I	I	II	X
dP4 L	184	.	.	.	.	.	.
dP4 WP	80+	.	.	.	.	.	.
M1 L	.	.	.	.	.	.	.
M1 WA	.	.	.	.	91+	.	.
M1 WP	.	.	.	.	.	.	.
M2 L	.	*211	.	.	.	.	*201
M2 WA	.	*124	.	.	.	.	*122
M2 WP	.	*126	.	.	.	.	*126
M3 L	.	.	303	.	.	311	.
M3 WA	.	.	148+	152	.	149	.

Context number	A133	A195	A202	A202	A207	A212	A217
Phase	XI	Xl	XI	XI	XI	XI	XI
dP4 L	186	199	196	191	197	185	194
dP4 WP	77	82	81	81	.	80	86

Context number	A222	A222	A223	A261	A309	A377	A377
Phase	XI	XI	XI	XI	XI	XI	XI
dP4 L	187	193	191	197	.	189w	.
dP4 WP	83	.	.	87	.	85w	.
M1 L	.	.	.	.	*151	172	166
M1 WA	.	.	.	.	*101	96	98
M1 WP	.	.	.	.	*110	106	104
M2 L	.	.	.	.	.	.	.
M2 WA	.	.	.	.	.	.	.
M2 WP	.	.	.	.	.	.	.
M3 L	.	.	.	.	.	.	.
M3 WA	.	.	.	.	.	.	.

Context number	A377	A377	A377	A377	A377	A377	A377
Phase	XI	XI	XI	XI	XI	XI	XI
dP4 L	.	.	190	200	179	200	195
dP4 WP	.	.	80+	91	79	86	84
M1 L	.	.	.	.	.	.	.
M1 WA	.	.	.	.	.	.	.

M1 WP	.	.	.	.	.	.	.
M2 L	*202	.	.	.	.	.	.
M2 WA	*125	.	.	.	.	.	.
M2 WP	*132	.	.	.	.	.	.
M3 L	.	345	.	.	.	.	.
M3 WA	.	146	.	.	.	.	.

Context number	A377	A377	A377	A377	A377	A377	A.377
Phase	XI	XI	XI	XI	XI	XI	XI
dP4 L	188	200	183	192	187	185	191
dP4 WP	80	.	80+	88	81	85	85

Context number	A377	A377	A377	A377	A377	A377	A382
Phase	XI	XI	XI	XI	XI	XI	XI
dP4 L	198	193	182	199	200	.	.
dP4 WP	83	84+	77	85	84	80	.
M1 L	.	.	.	.	.	.	.
M1 WA	.	.	.	.	.	.	*106w
M1 WP	.	.	.	.	.	.	.
M2 L	.	.	.	.	.	.	.
M2 WA	.	.	.	.	.	.	.
M2 WP	.	.	.	.	.	.	.
M3 L	.	.	.	.	.	.	.
M3 WA	.	.	.	.	.	.	.

Context number	A382	A382	A88	A88	A88	A88	A88
Phase	XI	XI	X/XI	X/XI	X/XI	X/XI	X/XI
dP4 L	190	.	.	.	.	.	.
dP4 WP	81	.	.	.	.	.	.
M1 L	.	.	.	140w	140w	.	164
M1 WA	.	.	.	.	.	.	105
M1 WP	.	.	.	.	.	.	116
M2 L	.	.	.	198	190	.	.
M2 WA	.	.	.	129	125	.	.
M2 WP	.	.	.	135	133	.	.
M3 L	.	391	300	.	.	272	.
M3 WA	.	159	143	.	.	143	.
Comment			growth arrest	?pair	?pair		

Context number	A91	A121	A				
Phase	X/XI	XI/XII	mean	(n)	CV		
dP4 L	.	.	192	(31)	3.1		
dP4 WP	.	.	83+	(28)	3.9		
M1 L	159	.	156	(7)			

M1 WA	102	.	100+	(7)
M1 WP	110	.	109	(5)
M2 L	.	205	201	(6)
M2 WA	.	125	125	(6)
M2 WP	.	134	131	(6)
M3 L	.	310	319	(7)
M3 WA	.	144	148+	(8)

Humerus

Context number	A69
Phase	XI
HTC	191
Fusion	p? dfg

Radius

Context number	A377	A121
Phase	XI	XI/XII
BpP	281	275
Fusion	pf d?	pf du

Metacarpal III

Context number	A202	A202	A222	A223	A223	A377	A377
Phase	XI	XI	XI	XI	XI	XI	XI
GL	724	785	713	724	699	816	898
Fusion	df	df	dfg	df	df	df	df

Context number	A382	A	
Phase	XI	mean	(n)
GL	843	775	(8)
Fusion	df		

Metacarpal IV

Context number	A202	A202	A223	A348	A	
Phase	XI	Xl	XI	XI	mean	(n)
GL	780	735	714	717	737	(4)
Fusion	df	dfg	df	df		

Femur

Context number	A377
Phase	XI
DCP	243
Fusion	pu d?

Tibia

Context number	A69	A69	A377	A377	A382	A

Phase	XI	X	XI	XI	XI	mean	(n)
BdP	291	274	289	297	315	292	(4)
Fusion	p? df	p? df	p? df	p? du	p? dfg	df+fg	only

Astragalus

Context number	A69	A377
Phase	XI	XI
GLl	459	423
GLm	424	383
Bd	268+	242

Metatarsal III

Context number	A223	A377	A377	A		
Phase	XI	XI	XI	mean	(n)
GL	798	1011	831+	880+	(3)
Fusion	df	df	df		

Metatarsal IV

Context number	A207	A355
Phase	XI	XI
GL	832	897
Fusion	df	df

4. *Equus* dom.

Humerus

Context number	A121
Phase	XI/XII
HTC	366
Fusion	p? df

Radius

Context number	A964
Phase	II
BpP	721
BFpP	643
Bd	.
BFd	.
Fusion	pf d?

Metacarpal

Context number	A121
Phase	XI/XII
GL	2151
Ll	2072
SD	319

BFd   467
Dd   338+
Fusion   df

Tibia
Context number   A121
Phase   XI/XII
GL   (3650)
Bd   811
Dd   475
Fusion   pf df

Metapodial
Context number   A121
Phase   XI/XII
BFd   487
Dd   366
Fusion   df

Phalanx 1

	Context number	A69	A121	A121	A121	A	
	Phase	XI	XI/XII	XI/XII	XI/XII	mean	(n)
	GL	890	789	825	(922)	857	(4)
	Bp	545	483	509	562	525	(4)
	BFp	(505)	(470)	(483)	(522)	495	(4)
	SD	338	298	309	351	324	(4)
	Bd	444+	395	417	.	419+	(3)
	BFd	436	389	(406)	.	410	(3)
	Fusion	pf	pfg	pfg	pf		

5. *Canis* dom.
Mandible
Context number   A69
Phase   XI
dP4 L   123
dP4 B   49

6. *Felis* dom.
Mandible
Context number   A69
Phase   XI
P4 L   74
Ml L   (82)
Ml B   (34)

Femur

Context number	A69
Phase	XI
GL	979
DCP	94
Fusion	pf df

Tibia

Context number	A69
Phase	XI
GL	1070
Fusion	pf df

7. *Cervus elaphus*

Scapula

Context number	A462	A287
Phase	VI	IX
GLP	.	643
SLC	362	403
Fusion	f	f

Humerus

Context number	A287	A88
Phase	IX	X/XI
BT	515	(555)
HT	393	432
HTC	279	311
Fusion	p? df	p? df

Phalanx 1

Context number	A462	A69	A195	A195	A202	202	A223
Phase	VI	Xl	XI	XI	XI	Xl	XI
GL	593	524	560	574	584	599	536
Fusion	pf	pf	pf	pf	pf	pf	pf

Context number	A377	A382	A91	A91	A431	A	
Phase	XI	XI	X/XI	X/XI	X/XI	mean	(n)
GL	617	617	547	631	590	581	(12)
Fusion	pf	pf	pf	pf	pf		

8. *Vulpes vulpes*

Humerus

Context number	A261
Phase	XI
GL	1246+

Bd   215
HTC   81
Fusion   pf df
Comment   GRP
                    (int)

Femur
Context number	A261	A261
Phase	XI	XI
GL	1272	.
DCP	121	121
Fusion	pf df	pf d?
Comment	GRP	GRP
	(int)	(int)

Tibia
Context number	A261
Phase	XI
GL	1351
Fusion	pf df
Comment	GRP
	(int)

Metatarsal II
Context number	A261
Phase	XI
GL	538
Fusion	df
Comment	GRP
	(int)

Metatarsal III
Context number	A261
Phase	XI
GL	646
Fusion	df
Comment	GRP
	(int)

Metatarsal IV
Context number	A261	A261	A261	A	
Phase	XI	XI	XI	mean	(n)
GL	600	657	654	637	(3)
Fusion	df	df	df		
Comment	GRP	GRP	GRP		
	(int)	(int)	(int)		

Metatarsal V

Context number	A261	A261
Phase	XI	XI
GL	605	554
Fusion	df	df
Comment	GRP	GRP
	(int)	(int)

9. *Mustela* sp.

Maxilla

Context number	A430
Phase	X/XI
dP4 L	32

10. *Lepus* sp.

Humerus

Context number	A202	A217	A377	A382	A	
Phase	XI	XI	XI	XI	mean	(n)
GL	.	999	.	.		
BdP	135	126	130	122	128	(4)
HTC	71	65	68	68	68	(4)
Fusion	p? df	pfg df	p? df	p? df		

Radius

Context number	A191	A323	A377	A377	A382	A91	A	
Phase	XI	XI	XI	XI	XI	X/XI	mean	(n)
BpP	95	97	96	97	91+	91	95+	(6)
Fusion	pf d?	pf d?	pf d?	pf d?	pf d?	pf d?		

Metacarpal II

Context number	A195
Phase	XI
GL	290
Fusion	df

Metacarpal III

Context number	A195
Phase	XI
GL	319
Fusion	df

Metacarpal IV

Context number	A195	A282
Phase	XI	XI

GL	257	241
Fusion	df	df

Femur

Context number	A223
Phase	XI
DCP	100
Fusion	pf d?

11. *Oryctolagus cuniculus*

Humerus

Context number	A202	A204	A229	A103	A	
Phase	XI	XI	XI	X/XI	mean	(n)
GL	.	.	.	614		
BdP	90	87	91	94	91	(4)
HTC	44	44	43	41	43	(4)
Fusion	p? df	p? df	p? df	pf df		
Comment	(int)	(int)	GRP	GRP		
			(int)	(int)		

Radius

Context number	A202	A103
Phase	XI	X/XI
GL	.	563
BpP	59	61
Fusion	pf d?	pf df
Comment	(int)	GRP
		(int)

Femur

Context number	A69	A88	A103	A103	A	
Phase	XI	X/XI	X/XI	X/XI	mean	(n)
GL	837	.	807	.		
DCP	68	63	63	64	65	(4)
Fusion	pf df	pfg du	pf df	pf df		
Comment	(int)	(int)	GRP	GRP		
			(int)	(int)		

Tibia

Context number	A229	A229	A103	A103	A	
Phase	XI	XI	X/XI	X/XI	mean	(n)
GL	882	880	885	888	884	(4)
BdP	118	115	121	120	119	(4)
Fusion	pf df	pf df	pf df	pf df		

Comment	GRP	GRP	GRP	GRP
	(int)	(int)	(int)	(int)

Calcaneum

Context number	A229	A103
Phase	XI	X/XI
GL	226	218+
Fusion	f	f
Comment	GRP	GRP
	(int)	(int)

NOTES

All measurements are expressed in tenths of a millimeter. Unless otherwise specified, measurements and their abbreviations follow von den Driesch (1976). For pigs, measurements follow Payne and Bull (1989).

Scapula: BGP is the breadth of the glenoid taken at right angles to GLP; BG is taken as the minimum breadth of the glenoid.

Humerus: HT is the height of the medial part of the trochlea. HTC is the minimum diameter of the distal trochlea at its central constriction (Payne and Bull 1989: Figs 1.8 and 8a, = Duerst, 1926: Measurement 21).

Radius: BpP is the breadth of the proximal end taken at right angles to the sagittal ridge and groove (Payne and Bull 1989: Fig 1.9); BFpP is the breadth of the proximal articular surface taken in the same orientation.

Femur: DCP is the smallest breadth of the caput femoris (Payne and Bull 1989: Fig 1.13).

Tibia: BdP is the breadth of the distal end taken at right angles to the articular grooves (Payne and Bull 1989: Fig. 1.14).

Metapodia: BFd is the distal articular breadth, i.e., taken across the condyles, not across the fusion plane (=Duerst 1926: Measurement 15).

Phalanx 1: BFd is the distal articular breadth (*Equus*); GL is the greatest length taken as on a measuring board (*Equus* and *Cervus* only).

d = distal; f = fused; fg = fusing (see Table 20, notes); GRP = one of group of associated bones; (int) = probably intrusive; p = proximal; u = unfused; w = tooth heavily worn (at or beyond stage j of Grant 1982).

( ) = measurement approximate but within ±2%; + = the specimen is slightly chipped or abraded, but the loss is less than 2%; − = the measurement is slightly too large, but again within 2% (e.g., when the bone has split and warped); * = loose M1/2, identification as M1 or M2 based on size.

APPENDIX 9:
MEASUREMENTS OF BIRD BONES
ENID ALLISON

All measurements given below follow the system of von den Driesch (1976) and are recorded in millimeters.

Measurements of domestic fowl from Castle Copse.

SCAPULA

Phase	GL	DiC
11	—	11.0
	—	11.8
	—	11.3
	—	10.8
	—	12.0
	—	12.4
	—	11.2
	—	12.7
	—	13.4
	—	10.9
	—	11.0
	—	11.2
	—	10.5
	—	11.9
	—	11.5
	—	12.1
	—	12.1
	—	11.3
	—	12.9
	67.2	11.5
	—	11.5
	—	11.0
	—	12.7
	—	12.5
	—	11.6
	—	11.7
	—	12.6
	—	13.0
11/12	—	12.0

CORACOID

Phase	GL	Lm	Bb	BF
9	46.5	45.1	—	11.4
11	49.0	46.7	12.9	10.9
	53.2	51.2	13.8	10.5
	—	—	12.9	11.2
	45.3	43.1	12.3	9.9
	56.8	54.6	14.0	11.5
	55.6	52.5	14.2	11.9
	52.7	50.3	13.4	11.8
	54.2	52.4	14.8	12.6
	52.7	50.7	—	—
	54.2	50.9	14.8	13.0
	48.4	45.8	—	—
	53.1	50.8	14.7	12.8
	57.1	54.5	—	12.4
	—	—	15.0	11.7
	55.0	53.1	—	11.4
	49.1	47.2	—	—
	49.0	46.7	12.0	9.9
	—	—	13.7	11.4
	57.8	55.0	14.9	11.7
	56.1	54.6	14.4	12.5
	55.2	53.5	15.0	12.5
	55.0	52.7	15.4	12.0
	—	—	—	11.2
	56.8	53.7	14.7	12.8
	54.9	52.8	14.1	12.5
	46.2	43.6	—	—
	54.0	—	—	—
	—	—	14.0	11.6
11/12	55.3	53.2	—	11.9

HUMERUS

Phase	GL	Bp	Sc	Bd
9	—	17.7	—	—
10/11	65.6	17.9	6.4	14.1
11	—	—	—	15.4
	—	—	7.1	16.1
	—	—	6.8	15.7
	67.0	17.8	6.8	14.6

GL	Bp	Sc	Bd
70.6	18.8	7.4	15.5
64.8	16.8	6.2	13.4
—	—	—	14.9
70.1	19.6	7.5	15.1
—	—	6.5	—
63.9	16.6	5.9	13.5
—	18.7	6.9	—
—	19.0	—	—
—	17.8	—	—
—	—	6.8	15.3
—	19.0	6.8	—
—	—	—	15.6
—	18.8	—	—
79.6	21.7	7.3	17.3
53.2	16.5	6.4	13.8
—	20.1	—	—
—	19.8	—	—
—	16.8	—	—
—	—	—	15.3
—	18.7	—	—
65.7	18.2	6.3	14.2
72.4	19.2	6.9	15.2
—	—	—	14.9
—	—	—	15.0
—	—	—	16.2
70.0	19.1	6.9	15.2
—	—	6.6	—
—	17.2	—	—
—	19.4	—	—
73.6	19.5	6.7	15.5
—	19.4	7.0	—

RADIUS

Phase	GL	Sc	Bd
10/11	—	—	7.3
	—	3.1	—
11	—	—	7.1
	—	—	6.0
	—	—	7.4
	—	—	6.6
	—	2.8	6.5
	—	—	6.1
	57.5	2.3	5.8

GL	Sc	Bd
66.5	3.6	7.5
63.2	3.1	7.0
—	—	6.8
—	—	7.2
64.7	3.2	7.1
—	2.8	6.3
64.3	2.8	7.1
—	—	6.9
—	—	6.9
—	—	6.3
58.2	2.5	6.3
—	3.0	—
65.1	2.9	7.0
—	—	6.8
—	—	6.3
—	—	6.8
61.3	2.9	6.6
—	—	7.2
—	—	6.3
64.2	2.9	6.8
52.3	2.3	5.8
—	—	6.7
—	—	6.9
—	3.2	7.6
—	—	7.0
—	—	6.7
—	2.8	—
—	—	6.3
—	—	7.5
53.5	2.6	6.0
—	3.1	—
—	2.8	6.9
—	2.8	—
—	3.0	—
—	3.6	—
65.5	3.2	7.2
60.7	2.6	6.5
—	—	6.4

ULNA

Phase	GL	Dip	Bp	Sc	Did
11	—	—	—	—	8.8
	—	—	—	—	8.9
	—	—	—	—	8.9

GL	Dip	Bp	Sc	Did
—	—	—	4.1	9.9
—	—	8.4	—	—
—	—	—	4.6	10.1
64.0	12.2	7.7	4.2	8.9
71.8	—	8.5	4.6	10.3
—	—	—	—	9.8
—	—	—	—	9.9
—	—	—	—	10.0
—	—	—	—	9.0
—	—	—	—	10.0
59.0	10.4	—	3.4	7.9
—	—	—	—	9.9
—	—	—	—	10.7
—	12.9	8.6	4.0	—
—	—	—	3.9	9.0
—	13.8	9.0	—	—
—	—	—	—	8.7
—	—	—	4.1	8.4
—	—	—	—	9.8
—	—	—	4.4	10.2
—	—	—	4.4	10.4
—	—	—	—	9.9
70.7	12.8	—	4.2	9.9
—	—	—	3.8	8.8
75.2	—	—	4.5	10.5
—	11.3	7.6	—	—
—	11.4	7.3	—	—
—	13.3	9.3	—	—
—	—	7.3	—	—
—	—	—	—	8.2
—	—	—	—	10.0
—	—	—	—	10.1
—	—	—	—	9.9
—	—	—	—	8.3
—	—	—	4.6	10.9
—	—	—	4.8	10.4
72.7	13.5	9.1	4.2	10.0
—	—	9.1	4.2	10.0
—	—	9.1	4.7	10.0
62.9	13.0	8.3	4.0	9.7
—	12.3	8.3	—	—
71.2	—	—	4.1	9.8
—	—	4.5	—	—
—	—	4.5	—	—

GL	Dip	Bp	Sc	Did
71.4	13.8	9.0	4.6	10.7
—	14.2	9.3	—	—
—	—	—	—	12.3
—	—	—	—	9.9
—	—	—	—	9.9
—	—	—	—	9.8
—	—	—	—	9.9

CARPOMETACARPUS

Phase	GL	Bp
11	39.8	12.5
	38.6	12.4
	37.2	11.8
	39.4	12.5
	39.4	12.8
	36.3	11.1
	29.2	9.0
	39.0	11.6
	39.4	12.4
	38.2	11.5
	38.8	12.1
	38.0	11.7
	31.8	10.5
	35.9	11.7
	38.6	12.1
	37.6	12.0
	33.6	10.7
	38.7	11.8
	39.9	12.2
	39.3	11.9
	36.9	11.0
	37.8	12.0
	38.5	12.0
	38.6	10.7
	37.3	11.8
	39.6	12.9
	38.8	11.1
	39.9	12.4
	34.4	11.0
	38.1	12.3
	—	11.3
	—	10.3
	—	11.9
	38.7	12.4

	GL	Bp		
	40.0	11.7		
	41.0	12.4		

FEMUR

Phase	Bp	Sc	Bd	Dd	
8	15.5	7.1	—	—	
10/11	15.6	6.6	—	—	
11	—	5.5	—	—	medullary bone present
	—	—	14.6	—	
	—	—	16.1	—	
	—	5.9	—	—	
	—	6.4	—	—	
	17.0	—	—	—	
	16.8	—	—	—	
	16.8	—	—	—	
	—	—	13.5	—	
	15.3	—	—	—	
	14.8	—	—	—	
	13.3	—	—	—	
	13.5	—	—	—	
	16.8	—	—	—	
	13.4	—	—	—	
	13.4	—	—	—	
	15.7	—	—	—	
	15.8	—	—	—	
	—	—	16.5	—	
	—	—	15.6	—	
	—	—	13.3	—	
	13.3	—	—	—	
	17.3	—	—	—	
	13.2	—	—	—	
	16.6	—	—	—	
	—	—	12.7	—	
	—	—	15.6	—	
	—	—	14.9	—	
	—	—	15.4	—	
	16.3	—	—	—	
	—	—	14.4	—	
	13.8	—	—	—	
	16.6	—	—	—	
	16.7	—	—	—	
	16.1	—	—	—	
	13.9	—	—	—	

Bp	Sc	Bd	Dd	
—	—	12.7	—	
15.9	—	—	—	
—	—	14.5	—	
15.1	—	—	—	
—	—	16.1	—	
—	—	11.9	11.0	
15.6	—	—	—	
12.4	—	—	—	
16.1	—	—	—	
—	—	13.4	—	medullary bone present

TIBIOTARSUS

Phase	GL	La	Dip	Sc	Bd	Dd	
11	—	—	—	—	11.2	11.6	
	—	—	21.2	—	—	—	
	—	—	—	5.9	10.3	—	
	—	—	20.4	—	—	—	
	—	—	—	5.8	10.5	10.5	
	—	—	—	6.1	—	—	
	—	—	—	—	10.8	10.8	
	—	—	—	—	11.3	12.2	
	—	—	—	5.8	10.5	—	
	—	—	20.0	—	—	—	
	—	—	—	—	11.4	—	
	—	—	—	—	10.2	—	
	—	—	—	—	11.6	—	
	—	—	21.3	—	—	—	
	—	—	20.6	—	—	—	
	—	—	17.6	—	—	—	
	—	—	20.1	—	—	—	
	—	—	—	—	12.0	—	
	115.5	112.5	20.6	6.3	11.2	—	
	113.0	109.0	20.1	6.0	11.0	11.9	
	—	—	—	—	9.8	9.5	
	—	—	—	5.7	—	—	medullary bone
	—	—	—	—	10.9	11.9	
	—	—	—	5.8	11.4	12.5	
	—	—	—	5.5	—	—	medullary bone
	—	—	19.8	—	—	—	
	—	—	—	—	11.4	12.3	
	—	—	—	—	10.8	11.9	
	—	—	—	—	11.6	—	
	—	—	—	—	9.3	—	
	—	—	—	6.1	—	—	

	GL	La	Dip	Sc	Bd	Dd
	—	—	—	6.1	11.5	—
	—	—	—	—	12.3	12.2
11/12	—	—	20.4	—	—	—

TARSOMETATARSUS

Phase	GL	Bp	Sc	Bd	
10/11	—	12.6	6.2	—	spur forming
	—	—	6.3	—	spur
11	—	—	6.7	12.6	spur forming
	—	—	7.5	—	spur short abraded
	79.5	12.7	6.4	—	spur short abraded
	—	—	5.0	10.6	
	—	11.1	4.7	—	
	66.9	11.4	5.4	11.5	unspurred
	—	12.5	5.8	—	unspurred
	—	—	5.2	11.6	unspurred
	—	—	5.9	—	spur forming
	—	—	—	12.3	
	63.5	11.6	5.4	—	
	—	11.4	—	—	
	63.1	11.6	5.5	10.9	spur 12.9 (well ossified)
	—	—	6.5	—	spur 11.3++ (well ossified)
	—	—	6.4	—	spur 14.8++ (well ossified)
	—	—	6.6	13.0	spur
	—	—	—	13.8	
	—	12.0	—	—	
	—	—	—	—	spur 16.3 (well ossified)
	87.0	—	6.4	13.9	spur forming
	83.4	13.8	6.4	—	spur forming
11/12	—	13.7	—	—	epiphysis still unfused

Mallard measurements from Castle Copse.

CORACOID

Phase	GL	Lm	Bb	BF
10	—	—	23.1	20.0
11	61.0	55.0	—	22.9
	—	—	—	22.0
	—	48.8	—	—
	—	—	—	20.1

GL	Lm	Bb	BF
—	—	22.6	19.8
59.0	53.4	23.5	21.3
56.5	51.8	23.5	20.9
—	—	23.6	22.2
57.6	—	—	—

HUMERUS

Phase	GL	Bp	Sc	Bd
11	—	—	6.7	14.5
	—	—	—	15.7
	—	—	—	15.4
	—	—	—	15.1
	—	21.6	—	—
	—	21.8	—	—
	—	21.1	—	—

RADIUS

Phase	GL	Sc	Bd
11	73.6	3.1	6.6
	—	—	6.7

ULNA

Phase	Did
9	11.2
11	10.0

CARPOMETACARPUS

Phase	GL	Bp	Did
11	57.2	13.1	7.3
	—	—	7.2
	58.9	13.8	7.9
	—	—	7.7

FEMUR

Phase	GL	Bp	Sc	Bd
11	—	—	4.8	—
	—	—	—	10.8
	49.7	—	4.3	—
	—	11.2	—	—
	—	11.0	4.2	—

TIBIOTARSUS

Phase	Sc	Bd
11	3.9	—
	4.2	8.7

Sc	Bd
4.1	—
4.0	8.7

TARSOMETATARSUS

Phase	GL	Bp	Sc	Bd
11	—	—	4.2	—
	44.3	9.6	4.5	9.5
	—	—	4.9	—
	46.3	9.5	4.5	9.7

Measurements of goose bones from Castle Copse.

RADIUS

Phase	Bd
11	10.4
	10.5

CORACOID

Phase	BF
11	29.7

SCAPULA

Phase	DiC
11	21.4

Dove measurements from Castle Copse.

HUMERUS   GL 45.1   Sc 5.1   Bd 11.2
ULNA GL 51.5   Dip 9.5   Bp 6.6   Sc 3.4   Did 7.3
FEMUR   GL 39.9   Lm 37.5   Sc 3.4   Bd 7.6
TARSOMETATARSUS   GL 29.5   Bp 7.3   Sc 3.3   Bd 8.3

APPENDIX 10:
SUMMARY CATALOGUE OF FISH REMAINS
ANDREW K. G. JONES

Identification	Bone	Number	Measurement (mm)
Phase VI			
Anguilla anguilla	vertebral centrum (caudal)	1	2.3
Phase IX			
Salmo salar	basipterygium	1	
Salmo trutta	vertebral centrum (caudal)	1	3.8
Cyprinidae	vertebral centrum (abdominal)	1	2.7
Anguilla anguilla	vertebral centrum (caudal)	1	1.8
Pleuronectidae	anal pterygiophore	1	
Unidentified fish	indeterminate fragment	11	
	vertebral centrum	1	
Phase X			
Anguilla anguilla	vertebral centrum (abdominal)	1	2.0
Pleuronectidae	vertebral centrum (caudal)	1	3.7
Unidentified fish	interneural spine	1	
Phase XI			
Clupea harengus	vertebral centrum (caudal)	1	2.4
	vertebral centrum (abdominal)	10	2.7, 2.7, 2.8, 2.8, 2.9
?Salmonidae	fin ray	1	
Salmonidae	vertebral centrum (caudal)	1	
Salmo salar	hyomandibular	1	
?*Salmo trutta*	vertebral centrum (caudal)	2	3.5, 7.8
	tooth	6	
	vertebral centrum	2	4.6
Salmo trutta	vertebral centrum (caudal)	1	
	dentary	1	37.5
	vertebral centrum (abdominal)	10	3.4, 3.4, 4.4, 5.7
	vertebral centrum	6	2.2
?Cyprinidae	vertebral centrum	1	6.6
Cyprinidae	fin ray	1	
	urohyal	1	
Anguilla anguilla	basioccipital	1	2.2
	vertebral centrum (caudal)	4	3.0

	vertebral centrum (abdominal)	8	2.3, 2.5, 3.3
	vertebral centrum	7	1.8
?Dicentrarchus labrax	spine	2	
Dicentrarchus labrax	maxilla	1	
Trachurus trachurus	vertebral centrum (caudal)	1	3.5
?Sparidae	vertebral centrum (caudal)	2	5.2, 8.8
	scale	1	
	ultimate vertebra	1	3.2
Sparus aurata	premaxilla	1	
Pleuronectidae	anal pterygiophore	3	
	basipterygium	2	
	vertebral centrum (caudal)	25	4.6, 4.9, 5.0, 5.0, 5.2, 5.3, 5.7, 5.9, 5.9, 6.2, 6.7
	vertebral centrum (abdominal)	19	3.5, 4.5, 4.6, 4.7, 5.0, 5.0, 5.3, 5.3, 6.2, 6.2, 6.2, 6.4, 6.5, 6.6, 6.6, 7.2, 7.4
	spine	3	
	vertebral centrum	7	
?Platichthys flesus	anal pterygiophore	1	
Platichthys flesus	epihyal	1	
Unidentified fish	vertebral centrum (caudal)	2	1.7, 7.2
	fin ray	1	
	indeterminate fragment	124	
	vertebral centrum	4	5.3
	vertebral spine	1	

Phase X/XI

Salmo trutta	vertebral centrum (caudal)	1	2.9
?Pleuronectidae	hypural	1	
Pleuronectidae	anal pterygiophore	1	
	vertebral centrum (abdominal)	1	5.2
Unidentified fish	branchiostegal ray	1	
	indeterminate fragment	1	

Explanation of measurements: vertebra   greatest medio-lateral breadth of the centrum (Morales and Rosenlund 1979).

dentary   length of the tooth row from the symphysis to the last tooth-socket.

basioccipital   greatest medio-lateral breadth of the articulating surface (Morales and Rosenlund 1979).

APPENDIX 11:
ENVIRONMENTAL PROCESSING AND RECORDING

KATHRYN L. GLEASON AND FERN FRYER

A combined wet-sieving/flotation process was conducted on an estimated 75% of the contexts defined as layers; these were sampled by taking at least a ten-liter representative sample. In the case of small contexts, the entire deposit was processed. The sample size increased to 10% of contexts in which ten liters was insufficiently representative, with the exception of certain very large contexts, particularly in Sector A, in which increasing the sample size to over forty liters still produced statistically insignificant samples. As a check, however, a few large contexts were processed in their entirety and checked against a ten-liter sample set aside for the purpose.

Weights, Munsell color numbers, and brief descriptions of the soil type were noted before processing. As inclement weather often prevented the drying of samples before processing, each was described as found during excavation. Samples with high clay content were deflocculated in a solution of 10% hydrogen peroxide or Calgon, with limited success.

The combined wet-sieving/flotation process was conducted in a Modified Siraf Tank, a tower sieve with the weir of the Siraf Tank, designed by D. Williams (1973). A spill-trough set in the rim of the plastic-sealed oil drum allowed water to overflow into a detachable 250-micron sieve, while valves in the bottom of the tank allowed for the discharge of silt. Two sieves of 0.07 and 0.001 m were suspended from the tank edge by hooks, with water entering the tub at the rim from a hose.

Samples were poured into the tank and gently agitated to free trapped material. Flot collected in the 250-micron sieve was dried in a fine-mesh wine-making bag. Material, including artifacts, contained in the coarse sieve was removed and sorted. Fine sievings were set to dry; frequently it was necessary to refloat this fine portion to recover more carbonized plant remains. The nonfloating remains were removed later, as were small bones, molluscs, eggshells, and small artifacts. Particularly important deposits, if not too large, were processed by bucket flotation, with 0.005-meter and 250-micron sieves.

Carbonized plant remains were not, in general, well preserved. Difficult to retrieve in the heavy clay soils and damp climate, a large number of small, badly worn assemblages were recovered.

APPENDIX 12:
EXCAVATION PARTICIPANTS 1983–1986

A. Abraham, H. Abraham, C. Alexander, P. Amos, B. A. Ault, D. Barnhill, A. Beckett, D. Berek, S. Brisman, E. Bruns, A. Bullock, M. Burch, H. Butzer, C. Copdici, J. Crawford, S. Cummins, M. G. Davenport, E. Dell'Isola, D. Denson, E. Duffy, R. Dunning, R. Ehrenreich, W. Eyres, S. Falatko, J. Forg, D. Foster, M. Foster, E. Fry, F. Fryer, A. Gallottini, K. Gleason, L. Goldberg, S. Goodarzi, P. Gordon, E. Greenstein, J. Grybowski, D. Gustafson, D. Guzzone, J. Hamblin, S. Hart, H. Hegener, C. Horeisch, E. Hostetter, T. N. Howe, F. Huber, J. Howell, V. Hutchinson, J. E. James, J. Jones, D. K. Keefer, J. Kenfield, J. Klein, M. Lane, C. D. Lathom, S. Liebig, M. Lindsell, M. A. Lynch, E. Maas, C. Mattingly, R. Mayfield, R. McGah, M. Milhous, S. Miller, D. Mok, S. Morgan, N. Murphy, P. Nebergall, A. Oster, V. Paladini, M. Parca, R. Payne, S. Payne, T. Rodriguez, T. Scott, S. Sechrest, B. Stanton, A. St. Clair, J. Sterrenburg, J. Strehle, J. Sutter, S. L. Tuck, E. Weiss, A. Wilmott, S. Wills, D. Yarçan.

TABLES 1–13:
QUANTIFICATION TABLES OF POTTERY FROM CASTLE COPSE

In the following thirteen tables, the vertical axis records fabrics, in the same order as the fabric series in the text chapter 4.11. The numbers of fabrics are added to as new types appear, and the top of the axis is removed by phase as wares cease to appear, even residually. The horizontal axis represents context numbers belonging to the phase, listed in numerical order. The amount of pottery is thus recorded by context and fabric. It is expressed as a ratio, the first figure being the number of sherds, the second being the minimum number of vessels represented by those sherds. The percentage figure that follows is the percentage of vessels in one fabric of all the vessels represented in the context. All percentages are simplified by rounding up or down to the nearest whole number.

TABLE 1. Pottery Quantification Table for Sectors A and C, Phase I: Early Ditch Fills.

Fab. No.	Common Name	A 965-71		C 57		C 59		C 58	
1	Oare Fabric 1	110:65	30%	6:1	3%	29:23	64%	5:5	38%
2	Oare Fabric 2	149:145	67%	32:17	51%	65:8	22%	6:5	38%
3	Silchester Flint-tempered Ware	2:2	1%			6:2	6%		
4	Local Butt Beaker					5:1	3%		
5	Terra Rubra (TR3)					1:1	3%		
6	Terra Rubra (TR2)					50:1	3%		
7	Terra Nigra (TN1)	1:1	1%						
8	Gloucester-type Sandy Ware	4:2	1%	33:15	45%			3:3	24%
9	Highgate C Ware	1:1	1%						
	TOTALS	267:216		71:33		156:36		14:13	

TABLE 2: Pottery Quantification Table for Sector A, Phase II: Terrace Gravel Levelling.

Fab. No.	Common Name	A 152		A 509	A 534	A 541		A 582	
1	Oare Fabric 1							1:1	50%
2	Oare Fabric 2	5:5	83%			1:1	5%		
3	Silchester Flint-tempered Ware	1:1	17%						
4	Local Butt Beaker								
5	Terra Rubra (TR3)								
6	Terra Rubra (TR2)								
7	Terra Nigra (TN1)								
8	Gloucester-type Sandy Ware								

No.	Common Name					
9	Highgate C Ware					
10	Savernake Grog-tempered Ware		1:1 50%	3:3 75%	10:10 50%	1:1 50%
11	Samian Wares			1:1 25%	1.1 5%	
12	Savernake-type Grey Wares				7.7 35%	
13	Hard Sandy Flint Tempered Ware		1:1 50%			
14	Black Burnished Ware 1					
15	White-slipped Redware					
16	New Forest White Ware					
17	New Forest Color-coated Ware					
18	Hard Grey Sandy Ware					
19	Severn Valley Ware					
20	Lower Rhineland Fabric 1					
21	Alice Holt/Farnham Ware				1:1 5%	
	Misc. Sandy Grey Wares					
	TOTALS	6:6	2:2	4:4	20:20	2:2

Fab. No.	Common Name	A 629	A 878	A 927	A 964
1	Oare Fabric 1				
2	Oare Fabric 2				
3	Silchester Flint-tempered Ware	1:1 9%			1.1 0.8%
4	Local Butt Beaker				
5	Terra Rubra (TR3)				
6	Terra Rubra (TR2)				
7	Terra Nigra (TN1)				
8	Gloucester-type Sandy Ware		2:1 25%		
9	Highgate C Ware				
10	Savernake Grog-tempered Ware	6:6 55%	3.3 75%	3:3 21%	74:74 61%
11	Samian Wares				2:2 1%
12	Savernake-type Grey Wares	2:2 19%			30:30 24%
13	Hard Sandy Flint-tempered Ware			1:1 7%	
14	Black Burnished Ware 1	1:1 9%		4:4 36%	5:5 4%
15	White-slipped Redware				3:3 2%
16	New Forest White Ware			2:2 14%	2:2 1%
17	New Forest Color-coated Ware				2:2 1%
18	Hard Grey Sandy Ware				1:1 0.8%
19	Severn Valley Ware	1:1 9%			
20	Lower Rhineland Fabric 1				
21	Alice Holt/Farnham Ware				
	Misc. Sandy Grey Wares			4:4 28%	1:1 0.8%
	TOTALS	11:11	5:4	14:14	121:121

TABLE 3. Pottery Quantification Table for Sector A, Phases V (A433) and VI, Post Structures 1 and 2.

Fab. No.	Common Name	A 433		A 418		A 462	
1	Oare Fabric 1						
2	Oare Fabric 2						
3	Silchester Flint-tempered Ware						
4	Local Butt Beaker						
5	Terra Rubra (TR3)						
6	Terra Rubra (TR2)						
7	Terra Nigra (TN1)						
8	Gloucester-type Sandy Ware					2:2	5%
9	Highgate C Ware						
10	Savernake Grog-tempered Ware	1:1	50%			14:14	33%
11	Samian Wares						
12	Savernake-type Grey Wares			3:3	50%	6:6	14%
13	Hard Sandy Flint-tempered Ware						
14	Black Burnished Ware 1	12:1	50%	2:2	33%	8:8	19%
15	White-slipped Redware						
16	New Forest White Ware					1:1	2%
17	New Forest Color-coated Ware						
18	Hard Grey Sandy Ware					8:8	19%
19	Severn Valley Ware			1:1	17%		
20	Lower Rhineland Fabric 1					2:1	2%
21	Alice Holt/Farnham Ware					2:2	5%
	TOTALS	13:2		6:6		43:42	

TABLE 4. Pottery Quantification Table for Sector A, Phase VII, Construction of First Aisled Building.

Fab. No.	Common Name	A 397		A 543		A 960	
1	Oare Fabric 1						
2	Oare Fabric 2			2:2	9%		
3	Silchester Flint-tempered Ware						
4	Local Butt Beaker						
5	Terra Rubra (TR3)						
6	Terra Rubra (TR2)						
7	Terra Nigra (TN1)						
8	Gloucester-type Sandy Ware						
9	Highgate C Ware						
10	Savernake Grog-tempered Ware	1:1	20%	5:5	23%	2:2	28%
11	Samian Wares			1:1	4%		
12	Savernake-type Grey Wares	1:1	20%			2:2	28%
13	Hard Sandy Flint-tempered Ware					1:1	14%
14	Black Burnished Ware 1			4:4	19%	1:1	14%

15	White-slipped Redware			
16	New Forest White Ware			
17	New Forest Color-coated Ware			
18	Hard Grey Sandy Ware		1:1 4%	
19	Severn Valley Ware	1:1 20%		
20	Lower Rhineland Fabric 1			
21	Alice Holt/Farnham Ware	1:1 20%	4:4 19%	
22	Ironstone-tempered Grey Ware	1:1 20%		
23	Whitehill Farm Wares			1:1 14%
	Misc. Sandy Grey Wares		4:4 19%	
	TOTALS	5:5	21:21	7:7

TABLE 5. Pottery Quantification Table for Sector A, Phase VIII, Occupation of First Aisled Building.

Fab. No.	Common Name	A 395	A 522	A 555	A 574	A 874
1	Oare Fabric 1					
2	Oare Fabric 2				4:4 17%	
3	Silchester Flint-tempered Ware					
4	Local Butt Beaker					
5	Terra Rubra (TR3)					
6	Terra Rubra (TR2)					
7	Terra Nigra (TN1)					
8	Gloucester-type Sandy Ware		6:6 7%		2:2 9%	
9	Highgate C Ware					1:1 1%
10	Savernake Grog-tempered Ware		36:34 39%	16:12 41%	12:12 50%	24:24 46%
11	Samian Wares		1:1 1%	1:1 3%	1:1 4%	1:1 1%
12	Savernake-type Grey Wares			4:4 13%		14:14 27%
13	Hard Sandy Flint-tempered Ware					
14	Black Burnished Ware 1	12:8 89%	10:10 12%	2:2 6%	3:3 12%	2:2 2%
15	White-slipped Redware					
16	New Forest White Ware		3:3 3%		1:1 4%	3:3 5%
17	New Forest Color-coated Ware					
18	Hard Grey Sandy Ware					
19	Severn Valley Ware			2:2 6%	1:1 4%	
20	Lower Rhineland Fabric 1					
21	Alice Holt/Farnham Ware		6:6 7%	3:3 10%		
22	Ironstone-tempered Grey Ware					
23	Whitehill Farm Ware		2:2 2%			
24	Dressel 20 Amphora					
25	Oxfordshire Red Ware		1:1 1%			
26	Wessex Grog-Tempered Ware	1:1 11%				
27	White-slipped Sandy Grey Ware		6:6 7%			
28	Hadham Ware					
29	Nene Valley Color-coated Ware					
	Misc. Sandy Grey Wares		17:17 20%	5:5 17%		7:7 13%
	TOTALS	13:9	88:86	33:29	24:24	52:52

Fab. No.	Common Name	A 877		A 916		A 919		A 920		A 926	
1	Oare Fabric 1										
2	Oare Fabric 2										
3	Silchester Flint-tempered Ware										
4	Local Butt Beaker										
5	Terra Rubra (TR3)										
6	Terra Rubra (TR2)										
7	Terra Nigra (TN1)										
8	Gloucester-type Sandy Ware										
9	Highgate C Ware										
10	Savernake Grog-tempered Ware	2:2	50%	15:15	37%	1:1	25%	9:8	30%	2:2	22%
11	Samian Wares			1:1	2%						
12	Savernake-type Grey Wares			6:6	15%	2:2	50%	6:6	22%	5:5	55%
13	Hard Sandy Flint-tempered Ware										
14	Black Burnished Ware 1			18:18	45%			5:5	18%	2:2	22%
15	White-slipped Redware										
16	New Forest White Ware			4:4	10%			1:1	4%		
17	New Forest Color-coated Ware	1:1	25%								
18	Hard Grey Sandy Ware										
19	Severn Valley Ware										
20	Lower Rhineland Fabric 1										
21	Alice Holt/Farnham Ware			6:6	15%						
22	Ironstone-tempered Grey Ware										
23	Whitehill Farm Ware							4:4	15%		
24	Dressel 20 Amphora										
25	Oxfordshire Red Ware										
26	Wessex Grog-tempered Ware	1:1	25%								
27	White-slipped Sandy Grey Ware										
28	Hadham Ware					5:1	25%				
29	Nene Valley Color-coated Ware										
	Misc. Sandy Grey Wares							3:3	11%		
	TOTALS	4:4		40:40		8:4		28:27		9:9	

Fab. No.	Common Name	A 952		A 954		A 957	
1	Oare Fabric 1						
2	Oare Fabric 2	2:2	40%				
3	Silchester Flint-tempered Ware			1:1	1%		
4	Local Butt Beaker						
5	Terra Rubra (TR3)						
6	Terra Rubra (TR2)						
7	Terra Nigra (TN1)						
8	Gloucester-type Sandy Ware						
9	Highgate C Ware						
10	Savernake Grog-tempered Ware	1:1	20%	88:85	58%	15:15	30%
11	Samian Wares			5:5	3%	4:4	8%
12	Savernake-type Grey Wares	2:2	40%	24:24	16%	31:31	62%
13	Hard Sandy Flint-tempered Ware						
14	Black Burnished Ware 1			14:14	9%		
15	White-slipped Redware						
16	New Forest White Ware						
17	New Forest Color-coated Ware						
18	Hard Grey Sandy Ware						
19	Severn Valley Ware			1:1	1%		
20	Lower Rhineland Fabric 1						
21	Alice Holt/Farnham Ware			7:7	5%		
22	Ironstone-tempered Grey Ware						
23	Whitehill Farm Ware						
24	Dressel 20 Amphora						
25	Oxfordshire Red Ware						
26	Wessex Grog-Tempered Ware			2:2	1%		
27	White-slipped Sandy Grey Ware						
28	Hadham Ware						
29	Nene Valley Color-coated Ware			1:1	1%		
	Misc. Sandy Grey Wares			8:85	5%		
	TOTALS	5:5		150:147		50:50	

TABLE 6. Pottery Quantification Table for Sector A, Phase IX, Construction of Second Aisled Building.

Fab. No.	Common Name	A 287		A 292		A 367	A 374		A 405
1	Oare Fabric 1						1:1	10%	
2	Oare Fabric 2	1:1	4%						
3	Silchester Flint-tempered Ware	1:1	4%	1:1	25%				
4	Local Butt Beaker								
5	Terra Rubra (TR3)								
6	Terra Rubra (TR2)								
7	Terra Nigra (TN1)								

Fab. No.	Common Name									
8	Gloucester-type Sandy Ware									
9	Highgate C Ware									
10	Savernake Grog-tempered Ware	4:4	16%	1:1	25%	7:7	70%	1:1	10%	7:5	55%
11	Samian Wares	3:3	12%	2:2	50%			2:2	20%	1:1	11%
12	Savernake-type Grey Wares					2:2	20%	1:1	10%		
13	Hard Sandy Flint-tempered Ware										
14	Black Burnished Ware 1	4:4	16%			1:1	10%	2:2	20%	3:3	33%
15	White-slipped Redware										
16	New Forest White Ware	2:2	8%								
17	New Forest Color-coated Ware										
18	Hard Grey Sandy Ware										
19	Severn Valley Ware							2:2	20%		
20	Lower Rhineland Fabric 1										
21	Alice Holt/Farnham Ware									1:1	11%
22	Ironstone-tempered Grey Ware							1:1	10%		
23	Whitehill Farm Ware										
24	Dressel 20 Amphora										
25	Oxfordshire Red Ware										
26	Wessex Grog-tempered Ware										
27	White Slipped Sandy Grey Ware										
28	Hadham Ware										
29	Nene Valley Color-coated Ware										
30	Rhenish Ware	2:2	8%								
31	Oxfordshire White Ware	1:1	4%								
	Misc. Grey Sandy Wares	4:4	16%								
	TOTALS	21:21		4:4		10:10		10:10		11:9	

Fab. No.	Common Name	A502	A872
1	Oare Fabric 1		
2	Oare Fabric 2		

3	Silchester Flint-tempered Ware					
4	Local Butt Beaker					
5	Terra Rubra (TR3)					
6	Terra Rubra (TR2)					
7	Terra Nigra (TN1)					
8	Gloucester-type Sandy Ware					
9	Highgate C Ware					
10	Savernake Grog-tempered Ware			9:9	47%	
11	Samian Wares					
12	Savernake-type Grey Wares			1:1	5%	
13	Hard Sandy Flint-tempered Ware					
14	Black Burnished Ware 1	1:1	17%	2:2	10%	
15	White-slipped Redware					
16	New Forest White Ware					
17	New Forest Color-coated Ware					
18	Hard Grey Sandy Ware					
19	Severn Valley Ware	2:2	34%			
20	Lower Rhineland Fabric 1					
21	Alice Holt/Farnham Ware	1:1	17%	1:1	5%	
22	Ironstone-tempered Grey Ware					
23	Whitehill Farm Ware					
24	Dressel 20 Amphora					
25	Oxfordshire Red Ware					
26	Wessex Grog-tempered Ware	2:2	34%			
27	White-slipped Sandy Grey Ware					
28	Hadham Ware					
29	Nene Valley Color-coated Ware					
30	Rhenish Ware					
31	Oxfordshire White Ware					
	Misc. Grey Sandy Wares			6:6	32%	
	TOTALS	6:6		19:19		

TABLE 7. Pottery Quantification Table for Sector A, Phase X, Second Aisled Building before Subdivision.

Fab. No.	Common Name	A10	A646	A760	A897	A939
1	Oare Fabric 1		4:4 28%			
2	Oare Fabric 2					
3	Silchester Flint-tempered Ware				1:1 8%	
4	Local Butt Beaker					
5	Terra Rubra (TR3)					
6	Terra Rubra (TR2)					
7	Terra Nigra (TN1)					
8	Gloucester-type Sandy Ware					

Fab. No.	Common Name								
9	Highgate C Ware								
10	Savernake Grog-tempered Ware			4:4	28%	8:8	47%	7:7	58%	12:12	71%
11	Samian Wares			1:1	7%						
12	Savernake-type Grey Wares	4:4	100%	2:2	14%	2:2	12%			2:2	12%
13	Hard Sandy Flint-tempered Ware										
14	Black Burnished Ware 1					3:3	18%	2:2	16%		
15	White-slipped Redware										
16	New Forest White Ware										
17	New Forest Color-coated Ware										
18	Hard Grey Sandy Ware			4:4	28%						
19	Severn Valley Ware										
20	Lower Rhineland Fabric 1										
21	Alice Holt/Farnham Ware			1:1	7%	3:3	18%	4:1	8%		
22	Ironstone-tempered Grey Ware										
23	Whitehill Farm Ware									2:2	12%
24	Dressel 20 Amphora							1:1	8%		
25	Oxfordshire Red Ware										
26	Wessex Grog-tempered Ware			1:1	7%						
27	White-slipped Sandy Grey Ware										
28	Hadham Ware					1:1	6%				
29	Nene Valley Color-coated Ware										
30	Rhenish Ware										
31	Oxfordshire White Ware									1:1	6%
32	Soapy Sandy Ware									1:1	6%
	TOTALS	4:4		14:14		17:17		15:12		17:17	

TABLE 8. Pottery Quantification Table for Sector A, Phase X-XI, Structures Contemporary with the Second Aisled Building.

Fab. No.	Common Name	A 88		A91		A154		A317	A371	
8	Gloucester-type Sandy Ware	1:1	4%	1:1	3%				1:1	4%
9	Highgate C Ware									
10	Savernake Grog-tempered Ware			3:3	8%	1:1	17%		3:3	12%
11	Samian Wares	4:4	17%	1:1	3%				2:2	8%
12	Savernake-type Grey Wares	20:11	52%						5:5	28%
13	Hard Sandy Flint-tempered Ware									
14	Black Burnished Ware 1	2:2	9%	21:16	41%	3:3	50%		8:8	35%
15	White-slipped Redware									

No.	Common Name					
16	New Forest White Ware					
17	New Forest Color-coated Ware		2:2 5%			
18	Hard Grey Sandy Ware			3:1 17%		
19	Severn Valley Ware	2:2 9%				
20	Lower Rhineland Fabric 1					
21	Alice Holt/Farnham Ware		10:10 26%			4:4 18%
22	Ironstone-tempered Grey Ware				9:7 100%	
23	Whitehill Farm Ware					
24	Dressel 20 Amphora					
25	Oxfordshire Red Ware		1:1 3%			
26	Wessex Grog-tempered Ware		1:1 3%			
27	White-slipped Sandy Grey Ware					
28	Hadham Ware					
29	Nene Valley Color-coated Ware					
30	Rhenish Ware		1:1 3%			
31	Oxfordshire White Ware		1:1 3%			
32	Soapy Sandy Ware					
33	South Midland Shell-gritted Ware	1:1 4%		1:1 17%		
	TOTALS	30:21	44:39	8:6	9:7	23:23

Fab. No.	Common Name	A427	A431
8	Gloucester-type Sandy Ware	1:1 4%	
9	Highgate C Ware		
10	Savernake Grog-tempered Ware	3:3 11%	3:3 27%
11	Samian Wares	2:2 7%	
12	Savernake-type Grey Wares	4:4 14%	6:6 54%
13	Hard Sandy Flint-tempered Ware		
14	Black Burnished Ware 1	6:6 21%	2:2 18%
15	White-slipped Redware		
16	New Forest White Ware	1:1 4%	
17	New Forest Color-coated Ware		
18	Hard Grey Sandy Ware		
19	Severn Valley Ware		
20	Lower Rhineland Fabric 1		
21	Alice Holt/Farnham Ware		
22	Ironstone-tempered Grey Ware		
23	Whitehill Farm Ware		
24	Dressel 20 Amphora		
25	Oxfordshire Red Ware		
26	Wessex Grog-tempered Ware	4:4 14%	
27	White-slipped Sandy Grey Ware		

28	Hadham Ware		
29	Nene Valley Color-coated Ware		
30	Rhenish Ware		
31	Oxfordshire White Ware		
32	Soapy Sandy Ware	1:1 4%	
33	South Midland Shell-gritted Ware		
	TOTALS	28:28	11:11

TABLE 9. Pottery Quantification Table for Sector A, Phase XI, Subdivision and Occupation of Second Aisled Building.

Fab. No.	Common Name	A104	A133	A158	A191	A195
10	Savernake Grog-tempered Ware	4:4 27%	2:2 18%	8:6 85%		4:4 27%
11	Samian Wares					
12	Savernake-type Grey Wares					
13	Hard Sandy Flint-tempered Ware	2:2 13%			1:1 6%	
14	Black Burnished Ware 1	6:6 40%	4:4 36%	3:1 15%	3:3 18%	7:7 60%
15	White-slipped Redware				9:9 54%	
16	New Forest White Ware					
17	New Forest Color-coated Ware		1:1 9%			
18	Hard Grey Sandy Ware				1:1 6%	
19	Severn Valley Ware					
20	Lower Rhineland Fabric 1					
21	Alice Holt/Farnham Ware	2:2 13%	3:3 27%			
22	Ironstone-tempered Grey Ware				2:2 12%	
23	Whitehill Farm Ware				2:2 13%	
24	Dressel 20 Amphora					
25	Oxfordshire Red Ware					
26	Wessex Grog-tempered Ware	1:1 6%				2:2 13%
27	White-slipped Sandy Grey Ware					
28	Hadham Ware		1:1 9%			
29	Nene Valley Color-coated Ware					
30	Rhenish Ware					
31	Oxfordshire White Ware					
32	Soapy Sandy Ware					
33	South Midland Shell-gritted Ware					
34	North Wiltshire Color-coated Ware					
35	Overwey Ware					
	TOTALS	15:15	11:11	11:7	16:16	15:15

Fab. No.	Common Name	A198	A204	A209	A217	A223
10	Savernake Grog-tempered Ware					1:1 4%
11	Samian Wares			1:1 4%		
12	Savernake-type Grey Wares					
13	Hard Sandy Flint-tempered Ware					
14	Black Burnished Ware 1			17:17 71%	3:1 14%	25:23 88%
15	White-slipped Redware					
16	New Forest White Ware					
17	New Forest Color-coated Ware	8:2 100%	2:2 66%		2:2 9%	
18	Hard Grey Sandy Ware					
19	Severn Valley Ware					
20	Lower Rhineland Fabric 1				2:2 9%	
21	Alice Holt/Farnham Ware			1:1 4%	1:1 4%	
22	Ironstone-tempered Grey Ware					
23	Whitehill Farm Ware					
24	Dressel 20 Amphora					
25	Oxfordshire Red Ware				8:8 36%	
26	Wessex Grog-tempered Ware					
27	Rhenish Ware					
28	Hadham Ware					
29	Nene Valley Color-coated Ware					1:1 4%
30	Rhenish Ware					
31	Oxfordshire White Ware					
35	South Midland Shell-gritted Ware					
34	North Wiltshire Color-coated Ware				8:8 36%	
35	Overwey Ware		1:1 33%	4:4 16%		1:1 4%
	TOTALS	8:2	3:3	24:24	24:22	28:26

Fab. No.	Common Name	A229	A232	A310	A323	A355
10	Savernake Grog-tempered Ware					
11	Samian Wares			3:3 12%		1:1 4%
12	Savernake-type Grey Wares					
13	Hard Sandy Flint-tempered Ware					
14	Black Burnished Ware 1			15:15 62%	10:10 100%	18:18 78%
15	White-slipped Redware					
16	New Forest White Ware					

Fab. No.	Common Name					
17	New Forest Color-coated Ware		1:1 20%			7:2 9%
18	Hard Grey Sandy Ware					
19	Severn Valley Ware					
20	Lower Rhineland Fabric 1					
21	Alice Holt/Farnham Ware		1:1 20%	5:5 21%		
22	Ironstone-tempered Grey Ware					
23	Whitehill Farm Ware		3:3 60%	1:1 4%		
24	Dressel 20 Amphora					
25	Oxfordshire Red Ware					
26	Wessex Grog-tempered Ware					
27	White-slipped Sandy Grey Ware					
28	Hadham Ware					
29	Nene Valley Color-coated Ware					
30	Rhenish Ware					
31	Oxfordshire White Ware					
32	Soapy Sandy Ware					
33	South Midland Shell-gritted Ware					
34	North Wiltshire Color-coated Ware					
35	Overwey Ware	6:2 100%				
	TOTALS	6:2	5:5	24:24	10:10	28:23

Fab. No.	Common Name	A377	A121
10	Savernake Grog-tempered Ware	2:2 5%	24:9 11%
11	Samian Wares		10:10 12%
12	Savernake-type Grey Wares		1:1 1%
13	Hard Sandy Flint-tempered Ware		
14	Black Burnished Ware 1	43:35 92%	1:1 1%
15	White-slipped Redware		
16	New Forest White Ware		1:1 1%
17	New Forest Color-coated Ware	3:1 3%	
18	Hard Grey Sandy Ware		
19	Severn Valley Ware		
20	Lower Rhineland Fabric 1		
21	Alice Holt/Farnham Ware		48:21 25%
22	Ironstone-tempered Grey Ware		

23	Whitehill Farm Ware		3:1	1%
24	Dressel 20 Amphora		
25	Oxfordshire Red Ware		4:2	2%
26	Wessex Grog-tempered Ware		8:8	10%
27	White-slipped Sandy Grey Ware		
28	Hadham Ware		
29	Nene Valley Color-coated Ware		2:2	2%
30	Rhenish Ware		
31	Oxfordshire White Ware		1:1	1%
32	Soapy Sandy Ware		
33	South Midland Shell-gritted Ware		
34	North Wiltshire Color-coated Ware		
35	Overwey Ware		22:12	14%
	Misc. Grey Sandy Wares		14:14	17%
	TOTALS	48:38	139:83	

TABLE 10. Pottery Quantification Table for Sector B, Phases III, Early Villa West Wing (B23), IV, Later Villa West Wing, and V, Late Roman Occupation Villa West Wing.

Fab. No.	Common Name	B123	B83	B98	B113
1	Oare Fabric 1			2:2 3%	
2	Oare Fabric 2				
3	Silchester Flint-tempered Ware				
4	Local Butt Beaker				
5	Terra Rubra (TR3)				
6	Terra Rubra (TR2)				
7	Terra Nigra (TN1)				
8	Gloucester-type Sandy Ware			8:1 2%	
9	Highgate C Ware			1:1 2%	
10	Savernake Grog-tempered Ware	14:3 37%		20:20 38%	5:5 24%
11	Samian Wares				
12	Savernake-type Grey Wares	1:1 12%		5:5 9%	1:1 5%
13	Hard Sandy Flint-tempered Ware			5:5 9%	
14	Black Burnished Ware 1	6:4 50%	4:2 66%	17:13 25%	10:2 9%
15	White-slipped Redware				
16	New Forest White Ware				

Fab. No.	Common Name				
17	New Forest Color-coated Ware		1:1 33%	1:1 2%	1:1 5%
18	Hard Grey Sandy Ware				
19	Severn Valley Ware			2:2 4%	1:1 5%
20	Lower Rhineland Fabric 1				1:1 5%
21	Alice Holt/Farnham Ware				
22	Ironstone-tempered Grey Ware				
23	Whitehill Farm Ware				
24	Dressel 20 Amphora				
25	Oxfordshire Red Ware				
26	Wessex Grog-tempered Ware				
27	White-slipped Sandy Grey Ware				
28	Hadham Ware				
29	Nene Valley Color-coated Ware				
30	Rhenish Ware				
31	Oxfordshire White Ware				
32	Soapy Sandy Ware				
33	South Midland Shell-gritted Ware				
34	North Wiltshire Color-coated Ware				
35	Overwey Ware				
36	North Gaulish Fabric 2 Misc. Sandy Grey Wares			7:7 13%	8:8 38%
	TOTALS	21:8	5:3	68:53	29:21

TABLE 11. Pottery Quantification Table for Sector B, Phase VI, Courtyard Surfaces Associated with Main Building.

Fab. No.	Common Name	B116	B124	B125	B126	B131
1	Oare Fabric 1					
2	Oare Fabric 2					
3	Silchester Flint-tempered Ware					
4	Local Butt Beaker					
5	Terra Rubra (TR3)					
6	Terra Rubra (TR2)					
7	Terra Nigra (TN1)					
8	Gloucester-type Sandy Ware	2:2 2%				1:1 4%
9	Highgate C Ware					
10	Savernake Grog-tempered Ware	10:10 11%	2:2 14%	1:1 12%	14:14 63%	3:3 12%

Fab No	Common Name	B132		B140		B141		B142		B143	
11	Samian Wares	3:3	3%	1:1	7%	1:1	12%	5:5	18%	3:3	12%
12	Savernake-type Grey Wares	18:18	20%	3:3	21%	3:3	36%	2:2	9%	9:9	36%
13	Hard Sandy Flint-tempered Ware	10:10	11%	1:1	7%	1:1	12%				
14	Black Burnished Ware 1	15:14	15%	2:2	14%			1:1	4%	5:5	20%
15	White-slipped Redware										
16	New Forest White Ware										
17	New Forest Color-coated Ware			1:1	7%						
18	Hard Grey Sandy Ware										
19	Severn Valley Ware	5:5	6%								
20	Lower Rhineland Fabric 1										
21	Alice Holt/Farnham Ware									2:2	8%
22	Ironstone-tempered Grey Ware			1:1	7%						
23	Whitehill Farm Ware										
24	Dressel 20 Amphora										
25	Oxfordshire Red Ware										
26	Wessex Grog-tempered Ware	2:2	2%								
27	White-slipped Sandy Grey Ware										
28	Hadham Ware					1:1	12%				
29	Nene Valley Color-coated Ware										
30	Rhenish Ware										
31	Oxfordshire White Ware										
32	Soapy Sandy Ware										
33	South Midland Shell-gritted Ware										
34	North Wiltshire Color-coated Ware										
35	Overwey Ware									1:1	4%
36	North Gaulish Fabric 2										
	Misc. Sandy Grey Wares	26:26	29%	2:2	14%						
	TOTALS	91:90		14:14		8:8		22:22		24:24	

Fab No	Common Name	B132		B140		B141		B142		B143	
1	Oare Fabric 1										
2	Oare Fabric 2										
3	Silchester Flint-tempered Ware			1:1	1%						
4	Local Butt Beaker										
5	Terra Rubra (TR3)										
6	Terra Rubra (TR2)										

No.	Common Name					
7	Terra Nigra (TN1)					
8	Gloucester-type Sandy Ware	1:1 1%	2:2 3%	2:2 2%	1:1 11%	
9	Highgate C Ware					
10	Savernake Grog-tempered Ware		3:3 4%	14:14 14%	8:1 11%	6:6 36%
11	Samian Wares		3:3 4%	1:1 1%		
12	Savernake-type Grey Wares	46:46 55%	38:38 51%	11:11 11%	4:4 44%	3:3 18%
13	Hard Sandy Flint-tempered Ware					
14	Black Burnished Ware 1	31:31 37%	17:15 20%	24:24 24%	2:2 22%	3:3 18%
15	White-slipped Redware					
16	New Forest White Ware					
17	New Forest Color-coated Ware					
18	Hard Grey Sandy Ware					
19	Severn Valley Ware			2:2 2%		
20	Lower Rhineland Fabric 1					
21	Alice Holt/Farnham Ware	3:3 4%		3:3 3%		
22	Ironstone-tempered Grey Ware			1:1 1%		
23	Whitehill Farm Ware					
24	Dressel 20 Amphora					
25	Oxfordshire Red Ware					
26	Wessex Grog-tempered Ware	3:3 4%	2:2 3%	33:33 33%	1:1 11%	3:3 18%
27	White-slipped Sandy Grey Ware					
28	Hadham Ware					
29	Nene Valley Color-coated Ware					
30	Rhenish Ware					
31	Oxfordshire White Ware					
32	Soapy Sandy Ware					
33	South Midland Shell-gritted Ware					
34	North Wiltshire Color-coated Ware					
35	Overwey Ware					
36	North Gaulish Fabric 2 Misc. Sandy Grey Wares		9:9 12%	8:8 8%		4:4 21%
	TOTALS	84:84	73:75	99:99	9:9	19:19

Fab. No.	Common Name	B144	B145
1	Oare Fabric 1		
2	Oare Fabric 2		

No.	Common Name				
3	Silchester Flint-tempered Ware	2:2	1%		
4	Local Butt Beaker				
5	Terra Rubra (TR3)				
6	Terra Rubra (TR2)				
7	Terra Nigra (TN1)				
8	Gloucester-type Sandy Ware	12:12	5%		
9	Highgate C Ware				
10	Savernake Grog-tempered Ware	43:43	17%	6:6	42%
11	Samian Wares	6:6	3%	2:2	10%
12	Savernake-type Grey Wares	52:52	20%	1:1	5%
13	Hard Sandy Flint-tempered Ware	10:10	5%		
14	Black Burnished Ware 1	26:26	10%	3:3	21%
15	White-slipped Redware				
16	New Forest White Ware				
17	New Forest Color-coated Ware	5:5	2%		
18	Hard Grey Sandy Ware				
19	Severn Valley Ware	16:16	6%		
20	Lower Rhineland Fabric 1				
21	Alice Holt/Farnham Ware	21:21	8%		
22	Ironstone-tempered Grey Ware	7:7	3%	1:1	5%
23	Whitehill Farm Ware				
24	Dressel 20 Amphora				
25	Oxfordshire Red Ware	8:8	4%		
26	Wessex Grog-tempered Ware	27:27	11%		
27	White-slipped Sandy Grey Ware				
28	Hadham Ware				
29	Nene Valley Color-coated Ware	8:8	4%		
30	Rhenish Ware			1:1	5%
31	Oxfordshire White Ware				
32	Soapy Sandy Ware				
33	South Midland Shell-gritted Ware	6:6	3%		
34	North Wiltshire Color-coated Ware				
35	Overwey Ware	5:5	2%		
36	North Gaulish Fabric 2				
	Misc. Sandy Grey Wares				
	TOTALS	254:254		14:14	

TABLE 12. Pottery Quantification Table for Sector C, Phase III, Roman Building.

Fab. No.	Common Name	C17	C33		C36	C37		C52
1	Oare Fabric 1		3:3	43%		1:1	1%	
2	Oare Fabric 2							
3	Silchester Flint-tempered Ware							
4	Local Butt Beaker							
5	Terra Rubra (TR3)							
6	Terra Rubra (TR2)							

7 Terra Nigra (TN1)					
8 Gloucester-type Sandy Ware				3:3 4%	3:3 12%
9 Highgate C Ware					3:1 4%
10 Savernake Grog-tempered Ware	3:3 33%	3:3 43%	12:12 60%	38:34 49%	19:19 73%
11 Samian Wares			1:1 5%	3:2 3%	
12 Savernake-type Grey Wares			2:2 10%		
13 Hard Sandy Flint-tempered Ware			3:3 15%		
14 Black Burnished Ware 1	4:4 44%	1:1 14%	1:1 5%	5:5 7%	
15 White-slipped Redware					
16 New Forest White Ware					
17 New Forest Color-coated Ware					
18 Hard Grey Sandy Ware					
19 Severn Valley Ware					
20 Lower Rhineland Fabric 1					
21 Alice Holt/Farnham Ware	2:2 22%			6:6 9%	
22 Ironstone-tempered Grey Ware					
23 Whitehill Farm Ware					
24 Dressel 20 Amphora					
25 Oxfordshire Red Ware					
26 Wessex Grog-tempered Ware					
27 White-slipped Sandy Grey Ware					
28 Hadham Ware					
29 Nene Valley Color-coated Ware					
30 Rhenish Ware					
31 Oxfordshire White Ware				2:2 3%	
32 Soapy Sandy Ware					
33 South Midland Shell-gritted Ware				2:2 3%	2:2 8%
34 North Wiltshire Color-coated Ware					
35 Overwey Ware					1:1 4%
36 North Gaulish Fabric 2					
37 Oxfordshire Color-coated Ware			1:1 5%		
Misc. Sandy Grey Wares				14:14 20%	
TOTALS	11:11	7:7	20:20	74:69	28:26

TABLE 13. Pottery Quantification Table for Sector C, Phase IV, Late Activity in Building.

Fab. No.	Common Name	C34		C43		C47		C64	
10	Savernake Grog-tempered Ware	2;2	18%	5:5	21%			1:1	11%
11	Samian Wares	1:1	9%					1:1	11%
12	Savernake-type Grey Wares	1:1	9%						
13	Hard Sandy Flint-tempered Ware								
14	Black Burnished Ware 1	2:2	18%	13:13	54%			3:3	33%
15	White-slipped Redware								
16	New Forest White Ware								
17	New Forest Color-coated Ware								
18	Hard Grey Sandy Ware								
19	Severn Valley Ware								
20	Lower Rhineland Fabric 1								
21	Alice Holt/Farnham Ware					3:3	30%	1:1	11%
22	Ironstone-tempered Grey Ware	4:4	36%	1:1	4%	3:3	30%	2:2	22%
23	Whitehill Farm Ware								
24	Dressel 20 Amphora								
25	Oxfordshire Red Ware								
26	Wessex Grog-tempered Ware								
27	White-slipped Sandy Grey Ware								
28	Hadham Ware								
29	Nene Valley Color-coated Ware								
30	Rhenish Ware								
31	Oxfordshire White Ware								
32	Soapy Sandy Ware								
33	South Midland Shell-gritted Ware	1:1	9%	96:2	8%	1:1	10%		
34	North Wiltshire Color-coated Ware								
35	Overwey Ware			52:2	8%	3:3	30%	2:1	11%
36	North Gaulish Fabric 2								
	TOTALS	11:11		168:24		10:10		10:9	

TABLE 14: Sector A, weights of bone, bird bone, and fish bone, by phase.

Phase	All bone	Bird		Fish			Reptile and	
				0 5%			Amphibian	
	(g)	(g)		|___|			(g)	(g)
A:I	3511.7	7.6	0.2%	|	.	.	0.1	<0.1%
A:II	2974.3	3.0	0.1%	|	.	.	.	.
A:III	92.9	0.7	0.8%	|*	.	.	.	.
A:IV	149.5	.	.	|	.	.	0.1	<0.1%
A:V	317.3	0.1	<0.1%	|	.	.	0.1	<0.1%
A:VI	1316.2	.	.	|	0.1	<0.1%	0.1	<0.1%
A:VII	334.1	0.1	<0.1%	|	.	.	.	.
A:VIII	1438.8	6.0	0.4%	|	.	.	0.3	<0.1%
A:IX	2680.3	15.0	0.5%	|*	1.2	<0.1%	0.1	<0.1%
A:X	170.5	3.4	2.0%	|**	0.2	<0.1%	.	.
A:XI	17136.0	930.7	5.4%	|*****	23.7	0.1%	2.0	<0.1%
A:X/XI	2650.8	24.5	0.9%	|*	1.6	0.1%	0.2	<0.1%
A:XI/XII	6154.2	6.5	0.1%	|	.	.	.	.

Notes to Table 15.

The following bones were counted:

loose teeth: when more than half the tooth is present;

mandibles and maxillae: when they retain one or more teeth of which more than half is present;

scapula: when part of the glenoid or tuber is present;

pelvis: when part of the acetabulum or an acetabular fusion surface is present;

long-bones and metapodia: when part of a proximal or distal articular or fusion surface is present;

patella, carpals, tarsals and phalanges: when part of an articular or fusion surface is present.

Counts are of separate specimens: thus a synostosed radius and ulna are counted as a single specimen, as is a mandible that retains a number of teeth, or even synostosed right and left mandibles. New breaks were mended and teeth were replaced in jaws before recording and counting.

Other skull, mandible, and tooth fragments, vertebra, rib, and other fragments of the axial skeleton, long-bone shaft fragments, and other miscellaneous fragments were checked through rapidly, in case any other species were represented, but are not included in the counts.

"Unidentified": specimens which met the definition of a "countable" specimen, but which could not be closely identified, are grouped in three categories: "large" (effectively a large ungulate category, including specimens identified as ?cattle, ?red deer, cattle/red deer, cattle/horse etc.), "medium" (effectively a medium artio-dactyl category, including specimens identified as ?pig, ?sheep/goat, sheep/goat/pig, etc.), and "small" (i.e., smaller than sheep/goat/pig, e.g., dog, cat, etc.). These counts are included to show that such specimens are relatively scarce (this is a major advantage of using a restricted and defined count list). They have been excluded from the percentage calculations, to which they would make little difference, and have been omitted from the remaining tables.

B = badger, C = cat, D = dog, F = fox, (Gt) = goat (also included in the total count for sheep/goat), H/R = hare/rabbit, La = large, M = *Mustela* sp., Me = medium, (Sh) = sheep (also included in the total count for sheep/goat), Sm = small, * = skeleton(s)/large associated group(s) also present, but not included in count: see text for details.

TABLE 15: Sector A summary of "countable" larger mammal bones by phase.

Phase	Horse	Cattle	Sheep/Goat (Sh) (Gt)	Pig	Red Deer	Roe	Hare	Rabbit	H/R	Carnivores	Total identified	La	Me	Sm	Total
A:I	.	38	28* (3*)	14	.	.	.	.	.	D1	81*	4	3	.	88*
A:II	2	20	9 (1)	4	1	1	.	.	.	D1	38	.	.	.	38
A:III	.	1	3	2	.	.	.	.	.		6	.	1	.	7
A:IV	.	1	1	.	.	.	.	.	1		3	.	.	.	3
A:V	.	1	3	.	.	.	.	.	.		4	.	.	.	4
A:VI	2	10	6 (1)	.	2	.	1	.	.		21	.	.	.	21
A:VII	.	3	.	1	1	1	.	.	.		5	.	.	.	5
A:VIII	.	6	13	5	1	.	.	.	.		25	1	1	.	27
A:IX	3	15	14 (1)	9	5	.	.	1	.		47	.	1	.	48
A:X	.	2	.	8	.	.	.	.	.		10	.	.	.	10
Total I–X	7	97	77* (6*) (1)	43	10	1	1	1	1	D2	240*	5	6	.	251*
	3%	40%	32%	18%	4%	-	-	-	-	1%					
A:XI	4	110	296 (16) (8)	1099	21	1	32	19*	13	D1 F* D/F2 D/F/B6 C6	1605*	4	30	1	1640*
	-	7%	18%	68%	1%	-	2%	1%	1%	1%					
A:XXI	2	13	14	32	10	.	2	3*	2	B1 M1	80	3	1	.	84
A:XI/XII	29	41	8 (1)	8	4	.	.	.	.		90	.	.	.	90
TOTAL	42	261	395* (22*) (10)	1182	45	2	35	23*	16	14*	2015*	12	37	1	2065*

TABLE 16: Sector A, Phases I–X summary of identified larger mammal bones by part of skeleton.

	Horse	Cattle	Sheep/Goat (excl. Grps) (Sh)	(Gt)	Sheep Grp A942 adult	Sheep Grp A953 v.juv.	Pig	Deer Red	Deer Roe	Dog	Hare, Rabbit
Maxilla					1		3				1R
Mx. teeth: Incisor											
Canine											
Deciduous premolar			2								
Premolar		1			3	4					
Molar		3	15		1+[2]	4	[3]				
P/M											[3]R
Mandible		8	10		1		4		1		
Md teeth: Incisor		1	1+[1]		2		2				
Canine							4				
Deciduous premolar		3+[1]	[5]				3				
Premolar		5+[10]	2+[6]		1+[2]	3	2				
Molar		23+[16]	17+[16]		[3]	5	1+[4]		[2]		
P/M	1										
Mx./Md. Incisor	2										
Scapula		1					nc2	3	4		
Humerus proximal			1			1	nc2				
Humerus distal		3	1		1	2		1			
Radius proximal	1	5	1		2		nc2				
Radius distal		3	1		1	1		2			
Ulna proximal	2	3	1				nc1	2		1	1H
Ulna distal		1			1	1					
Carpals					3	5	1				
Metacarpal proximal		3	1		2						
Metacarpal distal		1	2	(2)	2						
Pelvis (acetabulum)	1	4	1		2		nc1	1			
Femur proximal		1				1	nc2				
Femur distal					1	1					
Patella											
Tibia proximal		1			1	2	nc2				
Tibia distal		4	4	(1)	1					1	
Fibula proximal											
Fibula distal					1						
Astragalus		2	1	(1)	1						
Calcaneum		1	3	(2)			nc1				
Other tarsals		2	1		3						
Metatarsal proximal		7	4		1		4	1			

Metatarsal distal	.	2	2	(1)	2	.		1	.	.	. .
Metapodial proximal	.	.	.		.	.	nc7	1	.	.	. .
Metapodial distal	.	.	.		.	4		2	.	.	. 1H/R
Lateral metapodial proximal	.							7			
Lateral metapodial distal								5	.	.	
Phalanx 1	.	10	3		7	.	nc	3	2	.	. .
Lateral phalanx 1								.	.	.	
Phalanx 2	.	2	2		4	.		.	.	.	. .
Lateral phalanx 2								.	.	.	
Phalanx 3	.	1	1		1	.		.	.	.	. .
Lateral phalanx 3								.	.	.	

Notes: For counting method, see notes to Table 15. The total of all entries in any column is often higher than the number of identified specimens given in Table 15 because a single bone may contribute to more than one count: a complete metacarpal, for instance, would be included in the counts for metacarpal proximal and metacarpal distal, and a complete synostosed radio-ulna would be included in the counts for proximal and distal radius and proximal and distal ulna.

For cattle, sheep/goat and deer, counts for lower incisors include canines.

[] = Counts for teeth in jaws are given in square brackets: thus there are 23 loose cattle lower molars and 16 cattle lower molars in mandibles.

Grp = group, (Gt) = goat (also included in counts for sheep/goat), H = hare, R = rabbit, (Sh) = sheep (also included in counts for sheep/goat).
nc = Counts are also given for very juvenile shafts without either end, which are not included in the counts given in Table 15 since they do not have any articular or fusion surface.
P/M = premolar/molar.

TABLE 17: Summary of identified larger mammal bones by part of skeleton, Sector A, Phase XI.

	Horse	Cattle	Sheep/Goat juv (Sh)(Gt)	Sheep/Goat older (Sh)(Gt)	Pig v.juv	Pig older	Deer Red	Deer Roe	Fox Grp A261 adult	Fox Grp A261 juv.	Other Carnivore	Hare	Rabbit Grp A229	Rabbit Other	H/R
Maxilla Mx. teeth:															
Deciduous incisor	.	.	.	3	8	6	.	.	2	1	.	.	.	.	.
Incisor	.	.	.	.	4+[1]	16	.	.	.	.	.	.	.	1	.
Canine	.	.	.	.	.	6	.	.	1	.	.	3	.	.	.
Deciduous premolar	.	.	21	1	17+[10]	.	.	.	.	[2]	.	.	.	.	.
Premolar	.	.	.	30+[3]	.	8+[2]	.	.	[3]	.	.	.	.	[2]	.
Molar	.	1	.	44+[2]	.	5+[7]	.	.	.	.	.	1	.	[2]	.
P/M	.	.	.	.	.	.	.	.	.	.	.	.	.	.
Mandible Md. teeth:															
Deciduous incisor	.	.	4 (1) (1)	7 (1)	7	6	.	1	2	.	1C 1D	.	.	4	.
Incisor	.	.	15	26	28+[1]	2+[1] 29+[1]	.	.	.	.	.	.	.	.	.
Canine	.	1	.	.	.	6	.	.	.	.	[1C]	.	.	[2]	.
Deciduous premolar	.	.	15+[10] (2) (7) [3]	.	34+[9]	1+[5]	.	[1]	[3]	.	[1D]	.	.	.	.
Premolar	1	.	.	7+[9]	.	15+[7]	.	.	.	.	[2C]	1	.	1+[6]	.
Molar	1	5	[1]	9+[13]	.	8+[2]	.	[2]	.	.	[1C]	.	.	1+[6]	.
P/M	1	.	.	.	.	.	.	.	.	.	.	3	.	.	.
Mx./Md.															
Incisor	.	.	.	.	.	.	.	.	.	.	.	.	.	.	.
Deciduous incisor/ canine	.	.	.	.	22	.	.	.	.	.	.	.	.	.	.
Molar	.	.	.	.	.	1	.	.	.	.	.	.	.	.	.

	Horse	Cattle	Sheep/Goat juv (Sh)(Gt)	Sheep/Goat older (Sh)(Gt)	Pig vjuv	Pig older	Deer Red	Deer Roe	Fox Grp A261 adult	Fox Grp A261 juv.	Other Carnivore	Hare	Rabbit Grp A229	Other	H/R
Scapula	.	.	nc1	6	11+nc4	1	.	.	.	1	.	.	1	.	.
Humerus proximal	.	1	.	2	6+nc11	.	.	.	1	.	.	1	1	.	.
Humerus distal	.	1	2	(2) 9	5	2	.	.	1	1	.	4	1	2	.
Radius proximal	.	2	1	(1) 10	9+nc12	1	.	.	1	1	.	6	.	1	.
Radius distal	.	2	4	4	6	1	1	.	.	.	.	.	.	.	.
Ulna proximal	.	2	2+nc1	7	18	5	.	.	1	.	1C	1	1	.	.
Ulna distal	.	1	.	.	.	2	.	.	.	.	.	.	.	.	.
Carpals	.	2	.	1	.	25	.	.	.	.	.	.	1	1	.
Metacarpal proximal	.	1	2+nc1	9	1	67	.	.	.	.	1D/F	5	2	2	1
Metacarpal distal	.	1	3	(3) 4	1	28	.	.	.	.	.	4	1	1	1
Pelvis (acetabulum)	1	3	4	3	7+nc4	.	.	.	.	.	.	5	1	1	1
Femur proximal	.	2	.	3	4+nc6	3	.	.	2	1	1C	2	2	1	1
Femur distal	.	2	.	2	1	.	.	.	1	1	2C	.	1	1	1
Patella	.	1	.	.	.	.	.	.	.	.	.	.	.	.	.
Tibia proximal	.	.	.+nc2	1	5+nc9	5	.	.	2	1	1C	1	2	1	1
Tibia distal	.	.	2	2	6	5	.	.	2	1	1C 1D/F/B.	2	2	.	.
Fibula proximal	.	.	.	.	.	1	.	.	2	.	1C	.	.	.	.
Fibula distal	.	.	.	.	.	.	.	.	.	.	.	.	.	.	.
Astragalus	.	2	2	.	.	2	.	.	.	.	.	.	.	.	1
Calcaneum	.	5	1	(2) 3	7	6	1	.	.	.	.	1	.	1	.
Other tarsals	.	.	.	.	.	17	.	.	.	.	.	.	.	.	.
Metatarsal proximal	.	1	1	(1) 5	.	66	.	.	8	.	.	2	2	2	1
Metatarsal distal	.	.	1	(3) 3	.	14	.	.	7	.	.	3	3	.	.
Metapodial proximal	.	.	.	.	40+nc4	3	.	.	.	.	.	.	.	.	.
Metapodial distal	.	1	1+nc3	.	41	19	.	.	.	.	.	.	.	2	1
Lateral metapodial proximal	.	.	.	.	.	2	178	.	.	.	.	.	.	.	.
Lateral metapodial distal	.	.	.	.	3	138	.	.	.	.	.	.	.	.	1

	Horse	Cattle	Sheep/Goat juv (Sh)(Gt)	Sheep/Goat older (Sh)(Gt)	Pig vjuv	Pig older	Deer Red	Deer Roe	Fox Grp A261 adult	Fox Grp A261 juv	Other Carnivore	Hare	Rabbit Grp A229	Other	H/R
Phalanx 1	1	24	.	12	6	83	8	.	.	.	.	.	.	.	5
Lateral phalanx 1	.	.	.	.	1	73	1	.	.	.	.	.	.	.	.
Phalanx 2	.	27	1	8	4	60	5	.	.	.	1D/F	.	.	.	.
Lateral phalanx 2	.	.	.	.	1	13	.	.	.	.	.	.	.	.	.
Phalanx 3	.	27	1	6	2	56	5	.	.	.	.	.	.	.	3
Lateral phalanx 3	.	.	.	.	1	9	.	.	.	.	.	.	.	.	.

Notes: For counting method, see notes to Table 15. The total of all entries in any column is often higher than the number of identified specimens given in Table 15 because a single bone may contribute to more than one count—a complete metacarpal, for instance, would be included in the counts for metacarpal proximal and metacarpal distal, and a complete synostosed radio-ulna would be included in the counts for proximal and distal radius and proximal and distal ulna.

For cattle, sheep/goat, and deer, counts for lower incisors include canines.

[] = Counts for teeth in jaws are given in square brackets: thus, there are 9 loose sheep/goat lower molars and 14 sheep/goat lower molars in mandibles.

C = cat, D = dog, F = fox, Grp = group, (Gt) = goat (also included in counts for sheep/goat), H/R = hare/rabbit, (Sh) = sheep (also included in counts for sheep/goat), vjuv = very juvenile.

nc = Counts are also given for very juvenile shafts without either end, which are not included in the counts given in Table 15 since they do not have any articular or fusion surface.

P/M = premolar/molar.

TABLE 18: Cut-marks, burning, and gnawing.

	Horse	Cattle	Sheep/Goat excluding Grps	Sheep Grp A942	Sheep Grp A953	Pig	Red Deer
number of "countable" bones, excluding loose teeth	16	198	179	35	17	956	45
number with cut-marks	1 6%	20 10%	4 2%	4 11%	1 6%	23 2%	2 4%
number burnt	. -	3 2%	. -	. -	11 65%	2 -	. -
number gnawed, probably by dogs	. -	. -	3 2%	. -	. -	16 2%	. -
number gnawed by rodents	. -	1 1%	1 1%	. -	. -	2 -	. -

Note: These counts are of bones with definite cut-marks, gnawing, etc.; bones with probable or possible, but not definite, modification are not included.

TABLE 19: Cattle mandibular tooth ageing data (following Grant 1982).

a) mandibles:

		M_1	M_2	M_3	MWS
A927	Phase II	g/h	g/h	b	31-33
A965	Phase I	j	f	-	
A965	Phase I	k/m	f	(e)	36-38
A965	Phase I	-	k/m	g/h	
A878	Phase II	k/m	k/m	j	44-48
A462	Phase VI	k/m	k/m	k/m	45-51

b) individual teeth (including both loose teeth and those in mandibles):

dP_4 Tooth wear stage	a	b/c	d/e	f/h	j/k	l	m	n	Unstaged
A Phases I–X	.	1	.	.	1	.	1	.	.
A Phase XI	.	.	.	.	.	.	.	.	.
A Phases X/XI, XI/XII	.	.	.	.	.	.	.	.	.
total	.	1	.	.	1	.	1	.	.

$M_{1/2}$ Tooth wear stage	a/b	c/e	f	g/h	j	k/m	n	o	p	Unstaged
A Phases I–X	2	.	6	3	3	12	.	.	.	1
A Phase XI	.	.	.	.	1	.	.	.	.	.

A Phases X/XI, XI/XII .   .   1   1   1   .   .   .   .   .

total   2   .   7   4   5   12   .   .   .   1
cumulative
   percentage   7%   30%   43%   60%   100%

M_3 Tooth wear stage	a	b/c	d	e	f	g/h	j	km	Unstaged
A Phases I-X	1	4	.	(1)	.	2	3	1	.
A Phase XI	.	1	1	.	2	.	.	.	.
A Phases X/XI, XI/XII	1	.	.	(1)	.	.	.	.	.
total	2	5	1	(2)	2	2	3	1	.
cumulative percentage	11%	39%	44%	56%	67%	78%	94%	100%	

TABLE 20: Cattle epiphysial fusion data.

	Fused	Fusing	Unfused shaft	Unfused shaft+ epiphysis	Unfused epiphysis	% unfused
Early fusing group: (fusion at <18 mths.)						
Scapula (tuber)	1	.	.	.	.	
Humerus di.	4	3	1	.	.	
Radius pr.	10	.	.	.	.	
Pelvis (acetabulum)	3	.	.	.	.	
Phalanx 1 pr.	31	1	.	.	.	
Phalanx 2 pr.	29	.	.	.	.	
Total	78	4	1	.	.	1%
A Phases I–X	18	1	1	.	.	5%
A Phase XI	52	.	.	.	.	0%
A Phases X/XI, XI/XII	8	3	.	.	.	(0%)
Middle fusing group: (fusion at 24–36 mths.)						
Metacarpal di.	3	.	1	.	.	
Tibia di.	7	.	1	.	.	
Metatarsal di.	3	.	1	.	.	
Metapodial di.	1	.	.	.	1	
Total	14	.	3	.	1	18%
A Phases I–X	7	.	.	.	.	
A Phase XI	1	.	.	.	.	

A Phases X/XI, XI/XII	6	.	3	.	1	

Late fusing group:
(fusion at 36–48 mths.)

Humerus pr.	.	.	.	.	.	
Radius di.	3	1	1	1	.	
Ulna pr.	.	.	2	.	.	
Femur pr.	1	1	.	1	.	
Femur di.	1	.	1	.	.	
Tibia pr.	2	.	.	.	.	
Calcaneum (tuber)	3	.	2	.	.	
Total	10	2	6	2	.	(40%)
A Phases I-X	4	1	.	.	.	
A Phase XI	5	1	4	1	.	(45%)
A Phases X/XI, XI/XII	1	.	2	1	.	

Note: Fusion ages follow Silver (1969: Table A).

An epiphysis is regarded as *unfused* when it separates from the shaft without breakage; as *fusing* when it is joined to the shaft or can be separated from it only by breaking bone, but there are still open areas along the fusion line; and as *fused* when there are no open areas along the fusion line (which may still be visible).

TABLE 21: Comparison of some Roman cattle bone measurements.

Area	Site	Period	Metacarpal Bd (BFd)		Metatarsal Bd (BFd)		Tibia Bd (BdP)	
			n	mean	n	mean	n	mean
SW	Dorchester	75–120	20	52.6	15	46.4	14	55.4
	Dorchester	150–300	12	52.3	14	48.7	4	57.8
	Dorchester	350–450	33	51.9	34	47.1	17	55.3
	Exeter	C1–3	30	48.6	-	-	9	55.4
	Exeter	C4	19	50.0	-	-	11	55.7
SE	Sheepen	C1	40	51.1	52	47.6	-	-
	Colchester BKC E1-3	C1	14	52.9	20	47.9	-	-
	Colchester BKC E6	C3–4	28	56.8	35	53.1	-	-
	Chichester	C1–5	58	55.4	100	50.9	14	56.2
Mid	Dodder Hill	C1	9	51.7	14	47.7		
	Barton Court	C3–5	30	62.1	-	-	-	-
	Castle Copse	C4–early 5	2	59.8	2	59.7	5	59.7
N	Corstopitum	C4-early 5	155	54.4	127	50.3	-	-
	Vindolanda	C4-early 5	33	54	30	50	-	-

Note: The measurements for Chichester are taken from Levitan (1989), for Dodder Hill from S. J. M. Davis (1988), for Dorchester from Maltby (1990), for Exeter from Maltby (1979), and for the other sites from Luff (1982).

TABLE 22: Sheep/goat mandibular tooth ageing data (following Payne 1973 and 1987).

a) mandibles:

	dP_4	P_4	M_1	M_2	M_3	Stage	(estimated age)	sheep/goat
A 729 Phase IX	2Z	-	0	-	-	B	(2–6 months)	?goat
A 555 Phase VIII	14L	-	6A	-	-	C	(6–12 months)	?sheep
A 965 Phase I	16L	-	9A	5B	-	D	(1–2 years)	
A 433 Phase V	-	-	9A	9A	8G	F	(3–4 years)	
A 812 Phase I	-	-	9A	9A	10G	F	(3–4 years)	
A 942 Phase I	-	9A	9A	9A	10G	F	(3–4 years)	[Grp.]
A 927 Phase II	-	9A	9A	9A	-	F/G		
A 927 Phase II	-	-	9A	-	-			
A 462 Phase VI	-	-	10A	9A	11G	G	(4–6 years)	
A 377 Phase XI	7L	-	-	-	-	B	(2–6 months)	?goat
A 69 Phase XI	8Z	-	-	-	-	B	(2–6 months)	?sheep
A 195 Phase XI	13L	-	0	-	-	B	(2–6 months)	goat
A 377 Phase XI	13L	-	-	-	-	B/C		sheep
A 133 Phase XI	14L	-	-	-	-	B/C		sheep
A 377 Phase XI	-	7Z	9A	7A	5A	E	(2–3 years)	
A 377 Phase XI	-	9A	9A	9A	9G	F	(3–4 years)	
A 377 Phase XI	-	-	9A	9A	9G	F	(3–4 years)	
A 377 Phase XI	-	-	-	-	9G	F	(3–4 years)	
A 377 Phase XI	-	9A	9A	9A	11G	G	(4–6 years)	
A 156 Phase X/XI	3–12	-	-	-	-	B/C		goat

b) individual teeth (including both loose teeth and those in mandibles):

dP_4	Tooth wear stage	0	1–6	7–12	13	14	16	>16	Unstaged
	total	.	3	6	5	2	1	.	2
	of which sheep	.	?1	?1	2+?1	1+?1	.	.	.
	goat	.	?1	2+?1	2	.	.	.	1
	A Phases I–X	.	1	.	.	1	1	.	.
	A Phase XI	.	2	6	5	1	.	.	1
	A Phases X/XI, XI/XII	.	.	.	.	.	.	.	1

P_4	Tooth wear stage	0	1–4	5–7	8	9	11	12	>12	Unstaged
	total	1	.	4	1	8	.	.	.	.
	A Phases I–X	1	.	.	1	3	.	.	.	.
	A Phase XI	.	.	4	.	5	.	.	.	.
	A Phases X/XI, XI/XII	.	.	.	.	.	.	.	.	.

$M_{1/2}$	Tooth wear stage	0	1–4	5	6	7	8	9	10	12	15	>15	Unstaged
	total	2	1	1	5	5	.	36	1	.	.	.	.
	cumulative percentage	4%	6%	8%	18%	27%		98%	100%				
	A Phases I–X	1	.	1	4	4	.	22	1	.	.	.	.
	A Phase XI	1	.	.	1	1	.	14	.	.	.	.	.
	A Phases X/XI, XI/XII	.	1	.	.	.	.	.	.	.	.	.	.

M_3	Tooth wear stage	0	1–2	3–4	5	6	7	8	9	10	11	>11	Unstaged
	total	.	.	.	2	1	.	5	5	2	2	.	.
	cumulative percentage				12%	18%		47%	76%	88%	100%		
	A Phases I–X	.	.	.	.	.	.	3	2	2	1	.	.
	A Phase XI	.	.	.	1	.	.	1	3	.	1	.	.
	A Phases X/XI, XI/XII	.	.	.	1	1	.	1	.	.	.	.	.

Note: These counts include the two groups of sheep bones in Phase I.

TABLE 23: Sheep/goat epiphysial fusion data.

	Fused	Fusing	Unfused shaft	Unfused shaft+ epiphysis	Unfused epiphysis	% unfused
Early fusing group (fusion at <16 mths.)						
Scapula (tuber)	4	.	2+1j	.	.	
Humerus di.	9	1	2+2j	.	1	
Radius pr.	7	1	5+1j	.	.	
Pelvis (acetabulum)	5	.	.	.	.	
Phalanx 1 pr.	13	1	6	.	.	
Phalanx 2 pr.	14	.	.	.	1j	
Total	52	3	15+4j	.	1+1j	26%
A Phases I–X	21	.	1	.	.	5%
(without Grps.)	7	.	1	.	.	(13%)
A Phase XI	29	3	14+3j	.	1+1j	35%
A Phases X/XI, XI/XII	2	.	1j	.	.	
Middle fusing group (fusion at 18–28 mths.)						
Metacarpal di.	7	.	1+2j	.	1j	
Tibia di.	6	.	3	.	2j	
Metatarsal di.	6	2	1j	.	.	
Metapodial di.	.	.	.	.	1j	
Total	19	2	4+3j	.	4j	25%
A Phases I–X	12	.	1	.	.	8%
(without Grps.)	7	.	1	.	.	(13%)
A Phase XI	6	1	2+3j	.	4j	42%
A Phases X/XI, XI/XII	1	1	1	.	.	
Late fusing group (fusion at 30–42 mths.)						
Humerus pr.	.	2	1	.	1	
Radius di.	2	1	4+2j	.	2j	
Ulna pr.	1.	.	1	.	.	
Femur pr.	.	.	3	.	.	
Femur di.	.	2	2	.	1	
Tibia pr.	1	2	.	.	1	
Calcaneum (tuber)	5	.	1j	.	.	
Total	9	7	11+3j	.	3+2j	47%
A Phases I–X	4	7	1	.	.	(8%)
(without Grps.)	2	1	1	.	.	-
A Phase XI	5	.	8+3j	.	3+2j	(69%)
A Phases X/XI, XI/XII	.	.	2	.	.	

Notes: Fusion ages follow Silver (1969: Table A).

An epiphysis is regarded as *unfused* when it separates from the shaft without breakage; as *fusing* when it is joined to the shaft or can be separated from it only by breaking bone, but there are still open areas along the fusion line, and as *fused* when there are no open areas along the fusion line (which may still be visible). These counts include the two groups of sheep bones in Phase I (Grp); figures for Phases I–X are calculated both with and without the groups.

j = bone noted as from very young animal.

TABLE 24: Comparison of some sheep/(goat) bone measurements.

Area	Site	Period	Metacarpal Bd (BFd)		Metatarsal Bd (BFd)		Tibia Bd (BdP)	
			n	mean	n	mean	n	mean
SW	Dorchester	75–120 AD	—	—	—	—	62	23.1
	Dorchester	150–300 AD	—	—	—	—	44	24.2
	Dorchester	350–450 AD	—	—	—	—	32	24.4
	Exeter	C1	—	—	—	—	21	23.1
	Exeter	C2–3	—	—	—	—	30	23.3
	Exeter	C4	—	—	—	—	15	23.9
SE	Sheepen	C1	18	21.8	8	20.1	33	22.8
	Colchester BKC E1–3	C1	10	23.3	5	21.3	4	22.9
	Colchester BKC E6	C3–4	3	26.8	2	23.4	12	26.6
	Chichester	C1–5	28	23.5	24	22.4	—	—
Mid	Barton Court	C3–5	13	24.0	9	22.9	38	24.5
	Castle Copse	C4–early 5	6	24.4	6	24.1	4	24.5
N	Rudston	C4	14	21.8	18	20.4	—	—
	Vindolanda		—	—	—	—	4	26.8
	Corstopitum		—	—	10	19.6	—	—

Note: The measurements for Chichester are taken from Levitan (1989), for Dorchester from Maltby (1990), for Exeter from Maltby (1979), and for the other sites from Luff (1982).

TABLE 25: Pig mandibular tooth ageing data (following Grant 1982).

a) Mandibles

		dP_4	P_4	M_1	M_2	M_3
A 865	Phase I	—	—	—	c/d	—
A 968	Phase I	—	—	—	—	a
A 927	Phase II	—	—	—	—	a
A 575	Phase X	—	—	—	e/f	—
A 195	Phase XI	a	—	—	—	—	v.juv.
A 212	Phase XI	a	—	—	—	—	v.juv.
A 217	Phase XI	a	—	—	—	—	v.juv.
A 222	Phase XI	a	—	—	—	—	v.juv.
A 133	Phase XI	a/b	—	—	—	—	v.juv.
A 382	Phase XI	c	—	—	—	—	v.juv.
A 377	Phase XI	j/m	—	c/d	—	—
A 377	Phase XI	—	b/h	g/h	—	—
A 377	Phase XI	—	b/h	—	—	—
A 88	Phase X/XI	—	b/h	—	—	—
A 88	Phase X/XI	—	—	g/h	—	—
A 91	Phase X/XI	—	b/h	g/h	—	—
A 91	Phase X/XI	—	—	—	c/d	a
A 88	Phase X/XI	—	b/h	j/n	g/h	—
A 88	Phase X/XI	—	b/h	j/n	j/n	—
A 88	Phase X/XI	—	—	—	—	(c)
A 88	Phase X/XI	—	—	—	—	(c)

b) Individual teeth (including both loose teeth and those in mandibles)

dP_4	Tooth wear stage	a	a/b	b	c	c/d	d	e	f/h	j/m	Unstaged
	A Phases I–X	1	.	.	.	.	.	.	.	.	.
	A Phase XI	22	2	3	6	1	.	.	.	1	.
	cumulative percentage	63%	69%	77%	94%	97%	.	.	.	100%	
	A Phases X/XI, XI/XII	.	.	.	.	.	.	.	.	.	.
	total	23	2	3	6	1	.	.	.	1	.

P_4	Tooth wear stage	a	b/h	Unstaged
	A Phases I–X	.	1	.
	A Phase XI	2	2	.
	A Phases X/XI, XI/XII	.	4	1
	total	2	7	1

M_1	Tooth wear stage	a	b	c/d	e/f	g/h	j/n	Unstaged
	A Phases I–X	.	.	1	.	.	.	.
	A Phase XI	.	.	1	.	2	.	1
	A Phases X/XI, XI/XII	.	.	.	.	2	2	.
	total	.	.	2	.	4	2	1

M_2	Tooth wear stage	a	b	c/d	e/f	g/h	j/n	Unstaged
	A Phases I–X	.	.	1	1	.	.	.
	A Phase XI	.	.	1	.	.	.	.
	A Phases X/XI, XI/XII	.	.	1	.	1	1	.
	total	.	.	3	1	1	1	.

M_3	Tooth wear stage	a	a/b	b	c/d	e/f	g/h	j/k	Unstaged
	A Phases I–X	3	.	.	.	.	.	.	.
	A Phase XI	1	1	.	2	.	.	.	.
	A Phases X/XI, XI/XII	1	.	.	2	.	.	.	.
	total	5	1	.	4	.	.	.	.

Note: Loose M_1s and M_2s have been distinguished on the basis of their size.

TABLE 26: Pig epiphysial fusion data.

	Fused	Fusing	Unfused shaft	Unfused shaft+ epiphysis	Unfused epiphysis	% unfused (excl. vj)
Early fusing group (fusion at 12 mths.)						
A Phase XI						
Scapula (tuber)	.	.	6vj	.	.	
Humerus di.	.	2	5vj	.	.	
Radius pr.	1	.	9vj	.	.	
Pelvis (acetabulum)	.	.	3vj	.	.	
Phalanx 2 pr.	39	14	5+4vj	.	2	9%
Lat. phal. 2 pr.	11	.	1+1vj	1	.	(15%)
A Phase XI total	51	16	6+28vj	1	2	9%
A Phase I–X	.	.	1vj	.	.	-
A Phases X/XI, XI/XII	3	.	1vj	.	.	-
Middle fusing group (fusion at 24–30 mths.)						
A Phase XI						
Tibia di.	3	1	1+6vj	.	.	
Calcaneum (tuber)	.	.	1+6vj	.	.	
Metapodial di.	17	2	23+42vj	4	15	59%
Lat. mp. di.	19	3	98+3vj	.	18	82%
Phalanx 1 pr.	25	8	33+6vj	10	7	57%
Lat. phal. 1 pr.	12	16	37+1vj	.	6	57%
A Phase XI total	76	30	193+64vj	14	46	66%
A Phase I–X	1	2	6+2vj	.	.	-
A Phases X/XI, XI/XII	5	1	4+1vj	.	1	-
Late fusing group (fusion at 30–42 mths.)						
A Phase XI						
Humerus pr.	.	.	6vj	.	.	
Radius di.	.	.	1+6vj	.	.	
Ulna pr.	.	.	6vj	.	.	
Ulna di.	.	.	2	.	.	
Femur pr.	1	.	1+4vj	.	1	
Femur di.	.	.	1vj	.	.	
Tibia pr.	.	.	5vj	.	.	
A Phase XI total	1	.	4+28vj	.	.	-
A Phase I–X	.	.	.	.	.	-
A Phases X/XI, XI/XII	.	.	3+4vj	.	.	-

Notes: Fusion ages follow Silver (1969: Table A).

An epiphysis is regarded as *unfused* when it separates from the shaft without breakage; as *fusing* when it is joined to the shaft or can be separated from it only by breaking bone, but there are still open areas along the fusion line; and as *fused* when there are no open areas along the fusion line (which may still be visible).

TABLE 27: Sector A small mammals.

Phase	Sorex araneus	Sorex minutus	Clethrionomys glareolus	Microtus cf. agrestis	Apodemus	Mus
A I	.	.	.	.	.	1
A II	.	.	.	.	.	.
A III	+	.	.	.	.	.
A IV	.	.	.	.	.	.
A V	.	.	.	.	.	.
A VI	.	.	.	1	.	.
A VII	.	.	.	.	.	.
A VIII	.	.	.	2	.	1
A IX	1	.	1	1	1	+
A X	.	.	.	.	.	.
A XI	2	1	3	2	1	3
A X/XI	1	1	.	3	.	1
A XI/XII	.	.	.	.	.	.
Total	4	2	4	9	2	6

Note: Counts are of the number of contexts in which jaws or cheek-teeth of each species were found, not of the number of specimens; + indicates that the genus or species was identified as present on the basis of some other part of the skeleton.

TABLE 28: Sector A bird bones by taxon and phase.

Phase Species	I	II	III	V	VII	VIII	IX	X	XI	X/XI	XI/XII
Goose, cf. domestic, Anser anser L.	.	.	.	.	.	.	.	.	29	.	.
Mallard, Anas platyrhynchos L.	.	.	.	.	.	.	1	1	125	3	.
Teal, Anas crecca L.	.	.	.	.	.	.	.	.	6	.	.
Duck sp(p).	.	1	.	.	.	.	1	.	27	2	.
Goshawk, Accipiter gentilis (L.)	.	.	.	.	.	.	?3	.	.	.	.
Domestic fowl, Gallus gallus L.	4	3	.	.	.	4 (2)	8 (3)	5 (4)	842 (154)	17 (7)	5 (1)
Golden plover, Pluvialis apricaria (L.)	.	.	.	.	.	1	.	.	26	1	.
Plover sp., Pluvialis sp.	.	.	.	.	.	.	1	.	31	.	.
Charadriidae sp.	.	.	.	.	.	.	.	.	3	.	.
Woodcock, Scolopax rusticola L.	.	.	.	1	.	.	5	.	34	.	.
Snipe, Gallinago gallinago (L.)	.	.	.	.	.	.	.	.	1	.	.
Scolopacidae sp.	.	.	.	.	.	.	.	.	1	.	.
medium wader(s)	.	.	.	.	.	.	.	.	6	.	.
small wader	.	.	.	.	.	.	1	.	2	.	.
Charadriiformes sp.	.	.	.	.	.	.	.	.	1	.	.
Domestic or rock dove, Columba livia Gmelin or stock dove C. oenas L.	.	.	.	.	.	.	1 (1)	.	16 (7)	.	.
Blackbird, Turdus merula L.	.	.	.	.	.	.	2	.	13	.	.
Blackbird or Fieldfare, Turdus pilaris L.	.	.	.	.	.	.	.	.	3	.	.
Song thrush, Turdus philomelos Brehm	.	.	.	.	.	.	.	.	1+?2	.	.
Song thrush or Redwing, Turdus iliacus L.	.	.	.	.	.	.	.	.	2	.	.
Turdidae sp.	.	.	.	.	.	.	.	.	11	.	.
House sparrow, Passer domesticus (L.)	.	.	.	.	.	.	.	.	2	.	.
Starling, Sturnus vulgaris L.	.	.	.	.	.	.	.	.	?1	.	.
small Passeriformes sp(p).	.	.	.	.	.	.	4	.	44	.	.
Jay, Garrulus glandarius (L)	.	.	.	.	.	.	.	.	1	.	.
Jackdaw, Corvus monedula L.	.	.	.	.	.	.	.	.	4	.	.
Rook, Corvus frugilegus L. or Crow, C. corone L.	.	.	.	.	.	.	.	.	1	1	.
unidentified	.	.	.	.	.	.	.	.	2	.	.
indeterminate fragments	5	.	1	.	2	.	14	1	296	8	1
Total fragments	9	4	1	1	2	5	41	7	1533	32	6

Note: Numbers in brackets give numbers of incompletely ossified bones of young birds included in the total for that species.

TABLE 29: Sector A, Phase XI frequencies of each skeletal part of the major bird species represented in the assemblage.

	Domestic fowl	Goose	Duck	Woodcock	Golden/?Grey Plover	Dove	Small Passerines
Skull/mandible	11	.	4	1	5	.	1
Sternum	18	1	9	1	.	.	1
Furcula	21	1	15	1	.	.	1
Coracoid	76	1	20	5	4	.	5
Scapula	45	1	9	1	.	2	2
Humerus	89	2	20	6	15	2	4
Radius	87	3	4	.	5	1	7
Ulna	113	1	7	3	6	2	10
Carpometacarpus	45	1	6	3	5	1	5
Wing phalanges/carpals	12	3	4	1	2	.	1
Pelvis	21	.	.	1	.	.	.
Femur	101	3	11	2	.	3	3
Tibiotarsus	93	.	25	4	7	1	15
Fibula	7	.	.	.	.	.	.
Tarsometatarsus	27	.	10	4	4	3	8
Posterior phalanges	24	6	9	.	4	.	16
Free vertebrae	37	4	4	.	.	.	.
Notarium	7	.	.	.	.	.	.
Synsacrum	2	.	.	1	.	1	.
Ribs	6	2	1	.	.	.	.
Total fragments	842	29	158	34	57	16	79

TABLE 30: Flotation Samples

Area	Context	Soil vol. (liters)	Flot vol. (ml)	Items/liter	Flot/liter	Items/flot	Context type
AI	615	9.5	1	0.0	0.1	0.0	stakehole
	617	3.5	1	0.0	0.3	0.0	stakehole
	621	2.5	1	0.0	0.4	0.0	stakehole
	814	6	15	0.3	2.5	0.1	posthole
	849	6.5	2	0.2	0.3	0.5	posthole
	942	14	15	11.3	1.1	10.6	burn pit
	944	14	5	2.1	0.4	5.8	posthole
	953	4	110	42.2	27.5	1.7	posthole
AI (beamslot)	816	8	7	12.5	0.9	14.4	beamslot
	*932	14	500	247.0	35.7	6.9	beamslot
	946	14	40	17.5	2.9	6.1	beamslot
AII	689	1.75	10	0.0	5.7	0.0	stakehole
AVII	397	10.0	1.0	—	—	—	floor
	555	10	7	2.3	0.7	3.3	surface
AVIII	*601	11.5	450	0.9	39.1	+	dump (burnt)
	*911	26	1600	4.0	61.5	0.1	fill (industrial)
	*955	35		0.0	55.7	0.0	layer
AX/XI	88	11	60	0.3	5.5	0.1	dump (construction)
	122	10	11	0.8	11.0	0.1	courtyard
	126	10	15	1.8	15.0	0.1	pit in courtyard
	156	10	30	3.2	3.0	1.1	robber cut
	190	15	7.5	1.8	0.5	3.5	robber cut
AXI	133	10	40	6.4	4.0	1.6	hypocaust (burnt deposit)
	202	10	20	0.0	2.0	0.0	floor patch (burnt)
	222	10	7	0.2	0.7	0.3	floor patch (burnt)
	223	9	30	0.6	3.3	0.2	floor patch (burnt)
	310	10	90	2.9	9.0	0.3	floor layer
	355	12	36	3.0	3.0	1.0	floor surface (burnt)
	377	10	20	2.8	2.0	1.4	rubbish dump
AXI	65	10	5	0.1	0.5	+	subfloor
	80	4	12	0.8	3.0	0.3	pit (burn layer)
	*138	12	650	3.6	54.2	+	hypocaust (burn deposit)
	149	9	22	1.5	2.4	0.6	crucible pits
	191	22	26	0.1	1.2	0.1	floor deposit (burned)
	203	10	18	0.3	1.8	1.7	mortar patch
	205	12	22	10.8	1.8	5.9	floor patch (burnt)
	209	10	16	5.8	1.6	3.6	floor debris (burnt)
	218	10	11	0.1	1.1	0.1	dump (with mortar)
	252	10	10	0.5	1.0	0.5	between floors
	259	6	30	1.0	5.0	0.2	burnt layer
	270	1	20	0.0	20.0	0.0	stakehole
	275	2	13	5.0	6.5	0.8	floor deposit (burnt)
	288	9	22	0.8	2.4	0.3	backfill (hypocaust trench)
	295	6	5	2.8	0.8	3.4	fill
	299	10	7	1.0	0.7	1.4	burnt layer
	307	6	19	0.7	3.2	0.2	mortar floor patch

Area	Context	Soil vol. (liters)	Flot vol. (ml)	Items/liter	Flot/liter	Items/flot	Context type
	360	6	30	3.0	5.0	0.6	floor patch (burnt)
	637	12	40	0.6	3.3	0.2	burnt patch
	644	1	1	0.0	1.0	0.0	stakehole
AXI/XII	121	10	110	0.1	11.0	+	ditch
BI	118	10	4	0.3	0.4	0.8	Room 5 posthole
BII	110	9	40	26.1	4.4	5.9	Room 5
	113	10	26	16.4	2.6	6.3	Room 5 subfloor
BIII	116	11	21.5	1.3	2.0	0.7	courtyard
	140	9	45	1.2	5.0	0.3	courtyard
	141	9	170	3.0	18.9	0.2	courtyard
	142	8	3	0.4	0.4	1.0	courtyard
	143	8	34	3.1	4.3	0.7	courtyard
	144	18	40	1.2	2.2	0.5	courtyard
BIV	57	22	40	0.2	1.8	0.1	Room 4
	64	6	10	0.8	1.7	0.5	Room 4
	67	10	20	2.4	2.0	1.2	Room 4
	72	10	9	0.7	0.9	0.8	Room 4
BV	95	10	12	0.3	1.2	0.3	Room 3
	117	20	50	0.7	2.5	0.3	robber trench
BVI	107	18	15	2.9	0.8	3.5	courtyard
BVII	46	9	3.5	0.3	0.4	0.8	courtyard
BVIII	15	6	3	0.2	0.5	0.3	occupation dump
	69	9	8	1.8	0.9	2.0	destruction layer/rubble
	87	10	10	0.7	1.0	0.7	destruction layer/rubble
BX	120	10	10	1.5	1.0	1.5	layer/rubble
CIII	23	10	7	4.8	0.7	6.9	surface (exterior)
	35	9	17.5	2.3	1.9	1.2	surface (interior?)
	37	20	24	13.7	1.2	11.4	surface (exterior)
	52	10	20	14.2	2.0	7.1	ditch
CIV	*34	22	230	10.6	10.5	1.0	debris over burn
	*43	10	280	62.6	28.0	2.2	pit
	47	10	40	3.6	4.0	0.9	burn layer (industrial)
	*64i	20	210	4.2	10.5	0.4	pit
	*64ii	28	176	25.9	6.3	4.1	pit

Percentage examined
A138	25
A601	50
A911	12.5
A932	25
A955	10
C34	22
C43	28
C64i	23
C64ii	22

*less than 100% examined

TABLE 31: Plant remains

Sector:	A	A	A	A	A	B	B	B	B	B	C	C	C
Phase:	I	Beamslot	II–VIII	IX–XII	XI Room 4	I	II–III	IV–VI	VII	VIII	III	IV	IV 64i&ii
CULTIGENS													
Hordeum sativum, hulled grain	3	9	3	5	.	.	.	.	.	.	2	4	2
H. sativum, 2-row rachis frags	.	.	.	.	.	.	1	.	.	.	.	.	.
Hordeum sp., grain	18	25	1	6	3	.	1	.	.	.	4	6[k]	.
Hordeum sp., rachis frags	4	3	.	.	.	.	.	.	.	.	5	.	.
Hordeum/secale, rachis frags	.	2	.	.	.	.	.	.	.	.	.	.	.
Secale cereale, grain	1	2	.	.	.	.	.	.	.	.	.	.	.
Triticum aestivum, grain	.	4	.	.	.	.	.	.	.	.	15	1	20
Triticum cf. *dicoccum,* grain	1	23[b]	.	.	.	.	.	.	.	.	.	.	.
T. cf. *dicoccum,* rachis frags	1	.	.	.	.	.	22	.	.	.	17	1	1
Triticum spelta, grain	.	20[c]	.	1	3[g]	.	5	.	.	3	11	.	1
T. spelta, rachis frags	42	106	4	2	.	.	68	11	.	.	47	2	1
Triticum sp., grain	1	120	3	11	10	1	19	13	.	4	23	37	57
Triticum sp., rachis frags	120	130	1	13	.	.	139	13	1	.	77	3	0
Cerealia, indet., frags	114[a]	414[d]	2[e]	68[f]	15[h]	1[i]	156[j]	23	.	10	150	132	77
Cerealia, indet., rachis frags	.	.	.	.	.	.	.	.	.	.	3	.	.
Linum usitatissimum	.	1	.	12	2	1	.	1	.	.	.	.	1[m]

WOODY PLANTS

Taxon	1	2	3	4	5	6	7	8	9	10	11	12	13
Sambucus nigra	.	.	.	.	.	.	.	.	.	.	.	.	1
Corylus avellana, frags	.	.	1	59	15[h]	.	5	5[e]	.	1	8	.	1
Ficus carica	.	.	1	.	.	.	.	.	.	.	.	.	.
Olea europaea, frags	.	.	.	96	11	.	.	.	.	.	.	2	.
Prunus spinosa, frags	.	.	.	5	.	.	.	.	.	.	.	2[h]	.
Prunus sp., frags	.	.	.	.	.	.	1	.	.	.	.	.	.
Rosa sp.	.	.	.	.	.	.	.	.	.	.	.	.	.
Rubus fructicosus agg.	.	.	.	1	.	.	.	.	.	.	.	.	.

WILD & WEEDY

Taxon	1	2	3	4	5	6	7	8	9	10	11	12	13
Spergula arvensis	.	.	.	.	.	.	1	.	.	.	1	.	1
Stellaria cf. *media*	.	.	.	.	.	.	1	.	.	.	1	.	.
Chenopodium album	.	2	.	1	.	.	.	.	.	.	2	.	1
Chenopodium sp.	.	.	.	.	.	.	1	.	.	.	.	.	.
Centaurea cf. *nigra*	.	.	.	.	.	.	1	.	.	.	.	.	.
Chrysanthemum leucanthemum	.	1	.	.	.	.	.	.	.	.	.	.	.
Lapsana communis	.	1	.	.	.	.	.	1	.	.	.	.	.
Tripleurospermum maritimum	.	3	.	.	.	.	1	.	.	.	.	.	.
Cuscuta europaea	.	.	.	.	.	.	.	1	.	.	.	.	.
Sinapis arvensis	.	.	.	54	3	.	.	.	.	.	15	3	.
Cruciferae, indet.	.	.	.	1	.	.	.	.	.	1	.	.	.
Carex sp.	2	4	.	2	.	.	.	.	.	.	.	2	.
Eleocharis sp.	.	3	.	.	.	.	2	.	.	.	.	.	.
Scirpus sp.	.	.	.	.	.	.	.	.	.	.	1	2	.
Geranium sp.	.	.	.	.	.	.	.	1	.	.	.	.	.
Agrostis sp.	.	.	.	.	.	.	1	.	.	.	.	.	.
Avena sp.	.	3	.	.	.	.	1	.	.	.	6	9	4
Bromus sp.	.	2	.	.	.	.	5	.	.	.	.	.	.
Lolium sp.	6	39	.	2	.	.	.	.	.	.	21	.	.
Poa sp.	.	41	.	1	.	.	1	.	.	.	2	.	.

	1	2	3	4	5	6	7	8	9	10	11	12	13
Gramineae, indet. (small)	13	78	2	6	.	.	12	4	.	3	6	.	4
Gramineae, indet. (large)	18	18	11	4	.	.	3	.	.	.	32	.	.
Labiatae, indet.	.	.	.	.	.	.	.	.	.	.	1	.	.
Melilotus sp.	.	.	.	.	.	.	.	1	.	.	.	.	.
Pisum sativum (small)	.	.	.	.	1	.	.	.	.	.	.	.	.
Trifolium sp.	1	15	.	1	.	.	6	.	.	.	3	4	.
Vicia tetrasperma	.	.	.	1	.	.	.	.	.	.	.	.	.
Vicia/Lathyrus	.	1	1	.	.	.	.	2	.	.	1	4	.
Leguminosae, indet.	5	1	.	1	.	.	.	.	.	.	.	.	.
Linum catharticum	.	.	.	1	.	.	1	.	.	.	.	.	.
Plantago lanceolata	1	.	.	1	.	.	.	.	.	.	.	1	1
Polygonum aviculare	.	13	1	.	.	.	.	.	.	.	1	.	.
Polygonum persicaria	.	7	1	.	.	.	.	.	.	.	.	1	.
Polygonum sp.	.	2	.	.	.	.	1	.	.	.	.	.	.
Rumex acetosella agg.	1	.	.	1	.	.	1	.	.	.	.	5	1
Rumex sp.	5	31	3	3	.	.	3	.	.	.	8	3	1
Ranunculus acris/repens/bulbosa	.	5	.	1	.	.	.	1	.	.	.	.	.
cf. *Geum urbanum*	.	.	.	3	.	.	.	.	.	.	.	.	.
Galium aparine	.	.	.	1	.	.	.	.	.	.	.	2	1
Umbelliferae, indet.	.	.	.	.	.	.	.	.	.	.	.	.	1
Urtica dioica	.	.	.	.	.	.	2	.	.	.	.	.	.
Valerianella dentata	.	2	1	.	.	.	.	.	.	.	.	.	.
Valerianella sp.	.	1	1	.	.	.	.	1	.	.	.	.	.
Unidentified	4	66	5	97	4	0	32	31	3	2	22	37	9

a–includes 52 whole and 1 sprouted
b–includes 3 sprouted
c–includes 4 sprouted
d–includes 413 whole, and 1 sprouted
e–includes 2 whole
f–includes 34 whole
g–includes 1 sprouted
h–includes 1 whole
i–includes 1 sprouted, 2 fragments
j–includes 3 whole sprouted
k–includes 2 fragments
l–"rachis frags" includes mainly glume bases, but also spikelet forks & rachis fragment categories
m–mineralized

LIST OF CONTEXTS OF SECTORS A–C
CONTEXT/PHASE INTERPRETATION

Sector A: The Villa North Wing

A1:XV   Overburden.
A2:XIV   Backfill of eighteenth-century ditch.
A3:XV   Residual topsoil.
A4:XIV   Cut of eighteenth-century ditch.
A5:XV   Residual topsoil.
A6:XIII   Debris on building rubble.
A7:XIII   (=A15, 51) Disturbed silt and rubble.
A8:XI/XII   (=A178) Corridor mosaic.
A9:XIII   Disturbed rubble.
A10:XI   Nave, east room, chalk floor.
A11   Unused number.
A12:XI   Greensand and flint wall.
A13:XV   (=A19, 40, 35, 95) Backfill of Lukis's trench.
A14:XIV   Upcast from eighteenth-century ditch.
A15:XIII   (=A7, 51) Disturbed collapse and robber debris.
A16:XV   Naturally accumulated terrace gravel above rubble.
A17:XIV   (=A43, 44, 73) Lukis's trench, cut.
A18:XIII   Fill/layer, truncated by Lukis's trench.
A19:XV   (=A13, 35, 40, 45) Backfill of Lukis's trench.
A20:XIII   (=A50) Isolated island in Lukis's trench, possibly.
A21:XIV or XV Possibly original upcast from A17, Lukis's original trench cut.
A22:XIII   (=A23?) Burned destruction debris overlying chalk.
A23:XIII   (=A22?) Burned destruction debris, associated with A22.
A24:XIII   (=A49) Fill/layer.
A25:XI or XIII Part of fill of A85, pit in N aisle.
A26:XI or XIII Fill of A28, wall robbing.
A27:XIII   Apparent upcast from robbing.
A28:XIII   Robbing trench for east-west wall of pier support of north column
               no. 4.
A29:XIII   Makeup dump mortar patch.
A30:XIII   Surface of burn-stained Pennant tiles.
A31:XI or XIII Occupational debris over mortar floor.
A32:XIII   Lens of gravel.
A33:XI or XIII Small repair patch, mortar floor.
A34:XI or XIII Charcoal silt on floor.
A35:XV   (=A13, 19, 40, 95) backfill of Lukis's trench.

A36:XIII	Burnt (?) occupational debris or destruction layer.
A37:XIII	Roof collapse.
A38:XIII	Fill of shallow cut A87.
A39:XV	Fill of modern robbing cut.
A40:XV	(=A13, 19, 35, 95) Backfill of Lukis's trench.
A41:XIII	Debris.
A42:XV	Robbing cut?
A43:XV	(=A17, 44, 73) Lukis's trench, cut.
A44:XV	(=A17, 43, 73) Lukis's trench, cut.
A45:XV	(=A101) Fill of robber trench A46.
A46:XV	Robber trench, cut.
A47:XV	Robber trench fill, southwest corner, west wall.
A48:XI or XIII	(=A63): fragment of checkerboard mosaic, not in situ?
A49:XIII	(=A24?) Fill layer cut by ditch A4.
A50:XIII	(=A18) Layer, truncated by Lukis's trench.
A51:XIII	(=A7, 15?) disturbed collapse or robbing debris.
A52:XIII	Collapse rubble.
A53:XI or XIII	Upper fill, greensand lined channel.
A54:XIII and/or XV	(=A97) Fill of cut A60=100, north wall, mosaic corridor.
A55:XIV or XV	Antiquarian cut, filled with A47.
A56:XIII	(=A105) Robber trench fill, mosaic corridor, N wall.
A57:XIII	Rubble/mortar from east-west wall.
A58:XIII	Building collapse layer.
A59:XIII	Robber upcast.
A60:XV	(=A100) Robbing cut, corner N wall mosaic corridor (filled with A54).
A61:XIII	(=A116) Robbing cut, N wall of mosaic corridor.
A62:XIII	Robbing debris, mortary silt.
A63:XI	(=A48) Checkerboard mosaic, N aisle.
A64:XV?	Cut of antiquarian trench.
A65:XI	(=A66, 67, 71, 72, 109) Mortar bedding for checkerboard mosaic A48=63.
A66:XI	Mortar bedding for mosaic.
A67:XI	(=A65, 66, 71, 72, 109) Mortar bedding for checkerboard mosaic A48=63.
A68:XIII	Fill of robbing pit A98.
A69:XI	Hypocaust backfill.
A70:XI	(=A48, 63?) Mosaic fragment.
A71:XI	(=A65, 66, 67, 72, 109) Mortar bedding for checkerboard mosaic A48=63.
A72:XI	Mortar floor or bedding.
A73:XV	(=A17, 43, 44) Lukis's trench cut.
A74:XIII	Fill of east-west robber trench.
A75:XI	Mortar floor/makeup surface.
A76:XIII	(=A124) Robber trench of second south wall.

A77:XI	Burn layer in pit A85.
A78:XI	Mortar makeup patch, upper floor, mortar and greensand.
A79:XI	Mortar fill in pit A85, possibly makeup of redeposited wall plaster.
A80:XI	Burn layer in pit A85.
A81:XI	Mortar makeup in pit A85.
A82:XIII	Dump of mortary soil.
A83:XI	Burning layer in pit A85.
A84:XI	Redeposited clayey gravels, lowest fill of pit A85.
A85:XI	Pit cut.
A86:XI/XII or XIII	Small mortary dump or makeup.
A87:XIII	Shallow cut filled with A38.
A88:XI/XII	Dump of loosely bound building material fill of A89.
A89:XI/XII	Foundation trench cut filled with 88.
A90:X/XI	Chalky soil, pebbles, silt, cut by W wall A130.
A91:X/XI	Silt, fill of E-W trench A92.
A92:X/XI	E-W ditch on N side of Aisled Building II.
A93:X/XI	Redeposited natural exterior clay/gravel.
A94:X/XI	Rubble exterior dump/surface.
A95:XV	(=A13, 19, 35, 40): Lukis's backfill, tree disturbance.
A96:XIII	Rubble dump.
A97:XIII	Fill of robbing feature A100.
A98:XIII	Robbing pit filled with A68, S column no. 4.
A99:XI	Tile floor surface in N aisle, Room 6.
A100:XIII or XV	(=A60) Robbing cut N wall Mosaic Corridor filled with A97.
A101:XIII	Chalky soil.
A102:XIII	Linear dump of flints.
A103:X/XI	Mortar spread.
A104:XI	(=A166) Robbing trench fill, W wall, S end, and S wall.
A105:XIII	(=A56) robber trench fill, N wall, N corridor.
A106:XI	Floor bedding.
A107:XI	Painted wall plaster redeposited in hypocaust backfill.
A108:XIII	Fill of rabbit burrow.
A109:XI	Mortar makeup.
A110:XIII	Fill of robbing pit A112, S column no. 3.
A111:XIII	Fill of robbing trench A124=76.
A112:XIII	Robbing pit for S column base no. 3.
A113:XIII	Robbing trench fill, cut A117, second N wall.
A114:XIII	Fill of robbing trench A130.
A115:IX	Foundation, S column no. 3.
A116:XIII	(=A61) Robbing cut, N wall of mosaic corridor.
A117:XIII	Robbing trench cut, fill 113, second N wall, Aisled Building II.
A118:XI/XII or XIII	Flint and mortar concentration in bottom of A117, possibly remains of wall on footing A88.
A119:XIII/XV	Rabbit burrow.
A120:X/XI	Fill, hypocaust channel, Greensand Quoin Building.

A121:XI/XII	Fill of ditch cut A144.
A122:X/XI	Chalk and mortar lump in courtyard, cut A127.
A123:IX	Foundation cut S column no. 3.
A124:XIII	(=A76) Robber trench of second south wall, Aisled Building II.
A125:XIII	Fill of pit A128.
A126:X/XI	Charcoal-earth fill of A127.
A127:X/XI	Pit in courtyard with mortar-chalk lump.
A128:XIII	Pit.
A129:XI	Mortar floor surface or makeup layer, second from top, Room 4.
A130:XIII	Robbing trench cut, fill A114.
A131:XI	Patch of burning on floor of hypocaust, Rooms 1, 2.
A132:XI	Patch of burning on floor of hypocaust, Rooms 1, 2.
A133:XI	Patch of burning on floor of hypocaust, Rooms 1–2.
A134:XI	Patch of burning on floor of hypocaust, Rooms 1–2.
A135	Unused number.
A136:X/XI	Rubble patch in courtyard.
A137:X/XI	Rubble patch in courtyard.
A138:X/XI	Hypocaust burn deposit.
A139:XIII	Fill of robbing trench A146.
A140 no phase	Material removed in general cleaning.
A141:XI	Layer with *opus vermiculatum*.
A142:XI	Dirty rubble makeup.
A143:IX	Fill of cut A155.
A144:XI/XII	South perimeter ditch, fill A121.
A145:X/XI	Fill of hypocaust channel.
A146:XIII	Robbing trench, S and E walls, mosaic corridor.
A147:X/XI	Mortar spread.
A148:XI	Hypocaust channel fill, Room 3.
A149:XI	Industrial waste in crucible pit A151.
A150:X/XI	Fill of pit A154.
A151:XI	Double bowl crucible pits.
A152:XI/XII	Pebbly courtyard surface.
A153:IX	Packing of foundation pit, N column no. 1
A154:X/XI	Cut filled with A150.
A155:XI	Robbing cut for foundation, S column no. 1.
A156:X/XI	Fill, robbing cut A162.
A157	Unused number
A158:XI	Rubbly soil over hypocaust backfill.
A159:X/XI	Fill, robbing trench for first N wall.
A160:IX	Foundation cut, N column no. 1, fill A153.
A161:XI	Robbing cut, hypocaust channel, fill A148.
A162:X/XI	N wall robbing trench, fill A156.
A163:XI	Rubble fill, robbing trench A165.
A164:XI	Fill of tile-lined hypocaust channel A168=172.
A165:XI	Robbing cut through chalk floor of hypocaust.

A166:XI   Robbing trench fill spur wall S aisle (equivalent A104, cut A180).
A167:XI   Silting within tile-lined channel A168.
A168:XI   (=A172) Tile-lined hypocaust channel.
A169:X/XI   Stones placed in bottom of ditch A92.
A170:IX   Foundation, S column no. 2.
A171:XI   Silting in hypocaust channel, sealed by A148.
A172:XI   (=A168) Tile-lined hypocaust channel.
A173:XI   Robber trench S wall no. 1, filled with A104.
A174:X/XI   Hypocaust channel cut.
A175:X/XI   Hypocaust channel cut.
A176:XI   Wall stub, S colonnade.
A177:IX   Foundation cut, S column no. 2.
A178:XI/XII   (=A8) Corridor mosaic.
A179:X/XI   Cut, robbing trench for first N wall, Aisled Building II.
A180:XI   (=A173) Robbing trench, S wall no. 1, Aisled Building II
A181:XI   Cut, channel hypocaust.
A182:XI   Hypocaust pilae.
A183:XI   Hypocaust pilae.
A184:XI   Chalk floor, S aisle hypocaust.
A185:IX   Greensand footing, W wall, Aisled Building II.
A186:IX   Foundation cut, W wall.
A187:XI/XII   Mortar bedding for corridor mosaic A8=178.
A188:IX   Footings, N wall no. 1, Aisled Building II.
A189:XI   Mortar floor patch.
A190:X/XI   Mortary fill of robbing cut.
A191:XI   Burnt floor or occupation deposit.
A192:XI   Chalk hypocaust subfloor.
A193:XI   Wall/floor material over terrace gravel.
A194:XI   Floor patch.
A195:XI   Occupation floor.
A196:XI/XII   Mortar bedding for mosaic.
A197:XI/XII   Robbing pit.
A198:XI   Mortar floor patch.
A199:XI   Chalk floor patch.
A200:XI   Mortar floor patch.
A201:XI   Mortar floor patch.
A202:XI   Burnt floor patch.
A203:XI   Mortar patch.
A204:XI   Burnt floor patch.
A205:XI   Mortar floor patch.
A206:XI   Mortar floor patch.
A207:XI   Mortar floor surface.
A208:XI   Rubbish deposit against wall.
A209:XI   Burned floor surface and burned debris.
A210:X/XI   Mortar floor.

A211:XI	Mortar bedding for tile floor, over burned floor.
A212:XI	Interior wall bottom course.
A213:XI/XII	Occupation surface.
A214:XI	Robbing cut for partial removal of mortar floor.
A215:XI	Mortar floor, cut by wall A212.
A216:XI	Fill of foundation cut, wall A212.
A217:XI	Floor/occupation surface.
A218:XI/XII	Mortary dump.
A219:XI	Channel hypocaust, fragment.
A220:XI	Floor patch.
A221:XI	Decayed floor surface.
A222:XI	Patch of debris on floor.
A223:XI	Burnt floor surface.
A224:XI	Mortar floor patch.
A225:XI	Burnt floor patch.
A226:XI/XII	Brown soil patch under mosaic.
A227:XI	Mortar floor patch.
A228:XI	Mortar floor patch.
A229:XI	Floor surface overlapping threshold.
A230:XI	Foundation cut, wall A212.
A231:XI	Levelling layer of ash and debris, subfloor from mortar floor.
A232:XI	Burnt floor deposit.
A233:X/XI	Hypocaust channel side wall.
A234:X/XI	Hypocaust channel side wall.
A235:X/XI	Side wall of channel in hypocaust.
A235A:X/XI	Notional foundation cut for wall A235 of channel hypocaust.
A236:X/XI	Wall of channel hypocaust.
A236A:X/XI	Notional foundation cut for wall A236 of channel hypocaust.
A237:X/XI	Fill of hypocaust channel.
A238:X/XI	Wall of channel hypocaust.
A239:X/XI	Wall of channel hypocaust.
A240:XI/XII	Foundation trench for wall A241.
A241:XI/XII	Flint and mortar wall footings, surviving in base of robber trench.
A242:XI	Mortar floor patch.
A243:XI	Chalk floor surface.
A244:XI	Brown silt floor patch.
A245:XI	Burnt floor surface.
A246:XI	Mortar floor patch/remains of floor surface.
A247:XI	Patch on mortar floor of burnt material (possibly used to level surface.
A248:XI	Mortar floor layer.
A249:XI	Burn patch on hard mortar floor.
A250:XI	Hard packed mortar patch.
A251:XI	Mortar floor patch.
A252:XI	Dump of organic material between floors.

A253:XI	Mortar floor patch.
A254:XI	Burned floor patch.
A255:XI	Mortar floor patch, fill of depression.
A256:XI	Mortar surface patch over fine mortar floor surface.
A257:XI	Burnt floor patch, filling hole in mortar floor.
A258:XI	Mortar and silt floor patch.
A259:XI	Burnt layer amid mortar floor patches.
A260:XI	Stakeholes cut in mortar floor.
A261:XI	Hypocaust channel backfill.
A262:XI	Ridge of mortar, hypocaust channel.
A263:XI	Decayed tile threshold?
A264:XI	Channel hypocaust side wall.
A265:XI/XII	Wall pre-dating mosaic A8=178.
A266:XI	Foundation cut for hypocaust wall A233.
A267:XI/XII	Construction cut for hypocaust wall A234.
A268	Unused number.
A269:XI	Single course of mortared flints with greensand: secondary wall in Aisled Building II.
A270:XI	Fill of stakeholes in mortar floor.
A271:XI	Dark brown mortar patch.
A272:XI	Sandy mortar patch.
A273:XI	Mortar floor patch.
A274:XI	Mortar floor patch.
A275:XI	Burnt floor layer.
A276:XI	Hypocaust channel backfill.
A277:X/XI	Wall foundation, S wall, Greensand Quoin Bldg.
A278:X/XI	Wall foundation, S wall, Greensand Quoin Bldg.
A279:X/XI	Foundation cut for wall A277, 278.
A280:XI	Mortar/*opus signinum* patch.
A281:XI	Mortar/*opus signinum* patch.
A282:XI	Mortar, greensand and pebbles floor patch.
A283:XI	Burnt patch on mortar floor.
A284:XI	Mortar floor patch.
A285:XI	Hard fine mortar patch.
A286:XI	Mortar floor patch.
A287:XI	Fill of ditch A339 to S of Aisled Building II.
A288:XI	Backfill of hypocaust trench.
A289:X/XI	Wall of hypocaust
A289A:X/XI	Notional foundation cut for wall A289 of channel hypocaust.
A290:X/XI	Wall of hypocaust channel.
A290A:X/XI	Notional foundation cut for wall A290 of channel hypocaust.
A291:XI	Mortar floor with painted plaster.
A292:IX	Flint pebble and chalk fleck surface.
A293:XI/XII	Six tesserae white and red, remains of mosaic.
A294:XI	E-W cut from foundation of nave wall, Aisled Building II.

A295:XI   Patch of fill on edge of hole or mortar floor patch.
A296:XI   Mortar floor patch.
A297:XI   Shallow oval cut into mortar surface.
A298:XI?   Root disturbance?
A299:XI   Burnt layer.
A300:XI   Sandy mortar layer.
A301:XI   Dark surfaced mortar patch on floor; ancient trample layer on mortar patch.
A302:XI   Chalk base with flint footing for hypocaust pilae.
A303:X/XI   Large flint scatter; fallen wall or robbing rubble.
A304:XI   Mortar floor patch.
A305:XI   Mortar floor patch.
A306:XI   Mortar floor patch.
A307:XI   Mortar floor patch.
A308:XI   Mortar floor patch; fine hard surface.
A309:XI   Fine hard floor patch.
A310:XI   Burnt floor layer.
A311:XI   Flint bedding for chalk platform.
A312:X/XI   Foundation wall for hypocaust channel.
A313:X/XI   Bottom of hypocaust channel.
A314:XI   Ancient trample on mortar surface.
A315:XI   Hypocaust mortar flooring.
A316:X/XI   Cut in flint pebble and chalk surface containing large flint scatter.
A317:X/XI   Hypocaust channel island.
A318:X/XI   Mortar patch overlying fill between foundation walls of hypocaust channel.
A319:XI   Hypocaust mortar island.
A320:XI   Clay and debris pad under flints.
A321:X/XI   Hypocaust island.
A322   Unused number.
A323:XI   Mortar floor patch.
A324:XI   Decayed mortar floor patch.
A325:XI   Hypocaust channel fill with collapsed tiles.
A326:X/XI   Chalk surface.
A327:IX   (=A287) Fill of trench A328 (=A339).
A328:IX   (=A339) Cut of trench filled with A327 (=A287), S wall, Aisled Building II.
A329:XI   Mortar floor patch.
A330:XI   Mortar floor patch.
A331:XI   Mortar floor patch.
A332:X/XI   Surface of crushed chalk.
A333:X/XI   Mortar patch.
A334:X/XI   Mortar patch below with chalk surface.
A335:XI   Wall or threshold mortar.
A336:XI   Hypocaust channel fill.

A337:XI	"Ramp" deposit of silt against wall.
A338:XI	Mortar surface beneath ramp of silt.
A339:IX	Ditch filled with A287 against S wall, Aisled Building II.
A340:XI/XII	Wall A265 foundation cut.
A341:XI	Hard fine mortar floor patch.
A342:XI	Mortar floor patch.
A343:XI	Hard packed sandy layer.
A344:XI	Mortar floor patch.
A345:XI	Mortar floor patch.
A346:XI	Greensand/mortar floor level.
A347:XI	Small mortar patch; floor level.
A348:XI	Layer of ash and burnt material.
A349:XI	White chalk patch.
A350:XI	Mortar floor patch.
A351:XI	Mortar floor patch.
A352:XI	Mortar floor patch.
A353:XI	Wall between Rooms 5 and 6, N aisle.
A354	Unused number.
A355:XI	Destroyed mortar floor; burnt floor surface.
A356:XI	Mortar floor patch.
A357:XI	Mortar floor patch.
A358:XI	Light brown mortar floor patch.
A359:XI	Pure chalk remains of floor patch.
A360:XI	Burnt floor patch.
A361:XI/XII	Wall footing/flint foundation.
A362:XI/XII	Shallow cut for foundation of A361.
A363:III/IV	(=A536) Shallow linear cut with broad flat bottom early ditch, (spur cut).
A364:XI	Mosaic fragments.
A365:XI	Pure white chalk floor patch.
A366:XI	Disturbed mortar and burned patch.
A367:XI	Burnt patch of debris under floor surface.
A368:XI	Heat-affected sandy mortar.
A369:XI	Mortar floor patch with terracotta tiles.
A370:XI	Heat-affected sandy mortar layer.
A371:X/XI	Dump of mixed debris under hypocaust.
A372:X/XI	Dumped or spilled deposit of mortar and flints.
A373:IX	Upper two courses of foundation wall, comprising nondressed flint rubble and greensand.
A374:IX or X/XI	Mixed debris dumped as bedding under channel hypocaust.
A375:XI	Burnt patch on floor.
A376:XI	Medium brown mortar floor patch.
A377:XI	Dark brown debris, fills cut A380.
A378:XI	Burnt floor layer.
A379:XI	Mortar floor surface.

A380:XI	Shallow rectangular cut of pit in floor.
A381:XI	Footing of Aisled Building II, N wall buttress.
A382:XI	Mortar floor surface overlying chalk surface.
A383:XI	Medium brown to yellow sandy mortar patch, burnt floor level.
A384:VII	Dump of mixed debris.
A385:XI	Stakeholes in mortar floor.
A386:XI	Stakehole in mortar floor surface.
A387:XI	Mortar floor patch.
A388:X/XI	Patch of building collapse, dumped debris.
A389	Unused number.
A390:X/XI	Late wall, Aisled Building II, remains in robbing cut A411.
A391:XI	Shallow foundation cut for wall A381.
A392:X/XI	Wall footings, Greensand Quoin Building.
A393A,B:IX	Chalk and flint wall foundation.
A394:XI	Floor patch.
A395:VIII	(=A396) *Opus signinum* floor.
A396:VIII	(=A395) *Opus signinum* floor.
A397:VII	Wall.
A398:VII	Chalk floor patch.
A399:XI	Mixed debris.
A400:XI	Stakehole fill.
A401:XI	Thirty-five stakeholes, Room 4.
A402:XI	Chalk floor.
A403:IX	Corner foundation.
A404:XI	Rubble pack.
A405:IX	Debris layer.
A406:XI	Part of truncated hypocaust retaining wall.
A407:XI	Greensand and mortar plinth, probably part of hypocaust, Room 2.
A408:XI	Part of truncated hypocaust retaining wall.
A409:VIII	(=410) Truncated linear cut.
A410:VIII	(=409) Truncated linear cut.
A411:X/XI	Robbing cut for wall, fill A390.
A412	Unused number.
A413:IX	Wall foundation trench.
A414:XI	Tile threshold.
A415:XI	Burnt floor patch.
A416:XI	Mortar floor and base of threshold.
A417:XI	Building, S aisle, level prior to hypocaust.
A418:VI	Cut.
A419:XI	Stakehole fill.
A420:XI	Compacted chalk and mortar surface.
A421:XI	Robbing cut for stylobate foundation A436.
A422:II	Terrace gravel.
A423:XI	Wall between Rooms 4 and 7
A424:XI	Wall between Rooms 4 and 8.

A425:XI	Wall between Rooms 2 and 4.
A426:X/XI	Hole containing cut A418.
A427:X/XI	*Praefurnium* fill.
A428:XI	Hearth.
A429	Unused number.
A430:X/XI	Chalk floor patch.
A431:X/XI	Mortar patch on corner wall.
A432:XI	Hearth surface.
A433:V	Posthole fill of A471, tile-lined?
A434:XI	Foundation trench for wall 425.
A435:XI	Fill of subsidence hole.
A436:IX	Fill of stylobate pit A438.
A437:XI	Trampled mortar surface.
A438:XI	Cut for stylobate foundation, Aisled Building II.
A439:VIII	Surface cut by chalk foundation.
A440:IX	Chalk and flint wall footing.
A441:IV	Fill of posthole.
A442:IV	Cut of posthole.
A443:IV	Fill of posthole, post withdrawn.
A444:IV	Posthole cut.
A445:IV	Fill of posthole.
A446:IV	Posthole cut.
A447:IV	Fill of post.
A448:IV	Posthole cut.
A449:III	Fill of posthole cut.
A450:III	Posthole cut.
A451:III	Fill of posthole.
A452:III	Posthole cut.
A453:III	Fill of posthole.
A454:III	Posthole cut.
A455:XI	Burn patch in subsidence.
A456:XI	Mortary patch.
A457:VI	Fill of posthole A472.
A458:IX	Cut filled with A431.
A459:XI	Mortar, fill of subsidence hole.
A460:VII	Aisled Building I, W wall.
A461:XI	Foundation trench for wall A353.
A462:VI	Fill of trench A463.
A463:VI	Ditch cut along front of postholes.
A464:IX	Cut of foundation trench for A403.
A465:VII	Stylobate hole, Aisled Building I.
A466:VII	Cut of foundation trench for wall A393B.
A467:X/XI	Cut of foundation trench for wall A392.
A468:IX	Foundation trench, Mosaic Corridor, N side, W end.
A469:VI	Posthole fill, cut A470.

A470:VI	Posthole cut, fill A469.
A471:V	Posthole cut, fill A433.
A472:VI	Posthole cut, fill A457.
A473:V	Posthole fill, cut A474.
A474:V	Posthole cut, fill A473.
A475:V	Posthole fill.
A476:V	Posthole cut.
A477:IV	Posthole fill.
A478:IV	Posthole cut.
A479:V	Posthole fill.
A480:V	Posthole cut.
A481:XI	Compacted chalk floor.
A482:III	Posthole fill.
A483:III	Posthole cut.
A484:V	Posthole fill.
A485:V	Posthole cut.
A486:X/XI	*Praefurnium* cut, fill A427.
A487:VIII	Fill of truncated V-shaped ditch.
A488	Unused number.
A489:IV	Posthole fill.
A490:IV	Posthole cut.
A491:III	Posthole fill.
A492:III	Posthole cut.
A493:I	Posthole fill.
A494:I	Posthole cut.
A495:I	Posthole fill.
A496:I	Posthole cut.
A497:VII	Stylobate packing, Aisled Building II.
A498:VII	Stylobate cut, fill A497.
A499:X/XI	Shallow cut.
A500:VII	Chalk/flint fill.
A501	Unused number.
A502:VIII	Furnace cut.
A503:VIII	Burn patch.
A504:X/XI	Burn patch.
A505:IV	Burn patch.
A506:I	Posthole fill.
A507:I	Posthole cut.
A508:XI	Hypocaust subfloor mortar.
A509:II	Terrace gravel.
A510:IV	Posthole fill.
A511:IV	Posthole cut.
A512:I	Posthole fill.
A513:I	Posthole cut.
A514:III	Posthole fill.

A515:III	Posthole cut.
A516:IV	Posthole fill.
A517:IV	Posthole cut.
A518:III	Posthole fill.
A519:III	Posthole cut.
A520:VII	Stylobate packing, Aisled Building I.
A521:X/XI	Burn patch.
A522:VIII	Gravel floor surface.
A523:II	Terrace gravel.
A524:III	Posthole fill.
A525:III	Posthole cut.
A526:IV	Posthole fill.
A527:IV	Posthole cut.
A528:VIII?	Cut, stakeholes in bottom, fill A521.
A529:II	Terrace gravel.
A530:IV	Posthole fill.
A531:IV	Posthole cut.
A532:I	Fill of beamslot.
A533:I	Fill of beamslot.
A534:II	Terrace gravel.
A535:II	Terrace gravel.
A536:III or IV	(=A363) Cut of ditch.
A537:VII	Foundation cut, Aisled Building I.
A538:II	Terrace gravel.
A539A, B:III or IV	Posthole fill, cut by A474.
A540A, B:III or IV	Posthole cut, fill A539A, B.
A541:II	Terrace gravel.
A542:VIII	Clay floor, Aisled Building I.
A543:VII	Pit cutting beamslot fill A520.
A544:I	Posthole fill.
A545:I	Posthole cut.
A546:X/XI	Ash layer.
A547:III or IV	Thirteen stakeholes, cuts.
A547A-K:III or IV	Thirteen stakeholes, fills.
A548	Unused number.
A549:XI	Floor surface or levelling, Aisled Building II.
A550:XI	Ring slot cut in floor surface.
A551:X	Mortar floor surface set on pebble makeup.
A552:XI	Interior dividing wall between Rooms 3 and 4, Aisled Building II.
A553:I	Posthole fill.
A554:I	Posthole cut.
A555:VIII	Makeup layer.
A556:XI	Greensand and mortar wall hypocaust channel, Room 3.
A557:XI	See A556.
A558:XI	See A556.

A559:XI	See A556.
A560:XI	See A556.
A561:XI	See A556.
A562:XI	See A556.
A563:XI	See A556.
A564:XI	See A556.
A565:XI	See A556.
A566:XI	See A556.
A567:XI	See A556.
A568:XI	See A556.
A569:XI	Cut of hypocaust wall.
A570:XI	Cut of hypocaust wall.
A571:XI	Cut of hypocaust wall.
A572:XI	Cut of hypocaust wall.
573:XI	Cut of hypocaust wall.
A574:VIII	Compacted pebble surface.
A575:X	Surface of creamy-yellow mortar with lime, tile, charcoal flecks; mortar floor.
A576:I	Posthole fill.
A577:I	Posthole cut.
A578:I	Posthole fill.
A579:I	Posthole cut.
A580:I	Posthole fill.
A581:I	Posthole cut.
A582:II	Terrace gravel.
A583:I	Fill of double posthole A584.
A584:I	Cut of double posthole.
A585:X	Slot in floor of Aisled Building I, fill.
A586:X	Slot in floor of Aisled Building I, cut.
A587:XI	Patch on floor: beam impression.
A588:I	Stakehole fill.
A589:I	Stakehole cut.
A590:I	Stakehole fill.
A591:I	Stakehole cut.
A592:XI	Foundation trench for wall A552 between Rooms 3 and 4.
A593–599:I (odd nos.)	Stakehole fills.
A594–600:I (even nos.)	Stakehole cuts.
A601:VIII	Burn dump.
A602–612:I (even nos.)	Stakehole fills.
A603–613:I (odd nos.)	Stakehole cuts.
A614:VIII	Floor surface.

A615–627:I (odd nos.)	Stakehole fills.
A616–628:I (even nos.)	Stakehole cuts.
A629:II	Terrace gravel.
A630–634:I (even nos.)	Stakehole fills.
A631–635:I (odd nos.)	Stakehole cuts.
A636:XI	Mortar floor patch.
A637:XI	Burnt patch.
A638–644:I (even nos.)	Stakehole fills.
A639–645:I (odd nos.)	Stakehole cuts.
A646:X	Floor surface of undivided Aisled Building II.
A647–651:I (odd nos.)	Stakehole fills.
A648–652:I (even nos.)	Stakehole cuts.
A653:I	Fill of post slot.
A654–664:I (even nos.)	Stakehole fills.
A655–665:I (odd nos.)	Stakehole cuts.
A666:I	Beamslot fill.
A667:I	Beamslot cut.
A668–678:I (even nos.)	Stakehole cuts.
A669–679:I (odd nos.)	Stakehole fills.
A680:II	(=A541) posthole fill.
A681–721:I (odd nos.)	Stakehole fills.
A682–722:I (even nos.)	Stakehole cuts.
A723:IX	Stylobate foundation, Aisled Building II.
A724:IX	Cut for stylobate foundation.
A725:IX	Stylobate foundation, Aisled Building II.
A726:IX	Cut for stylobate foundation.
A727:IX	Stylobate foundation, Aisled Building II.
A728:IX	Cut for stylobate foundation.
A729:IX	N wall of Aisled Building II.
A730–758:I (even nos.)	Stakehole fills.

A731–759:I (odd nos.)	Stakehole cuts.
A760:IX	First chalk floor, Aisled Building II.
A761–771:I (odd nos.)	Stakehole fills.
A762–772:I (even nos.)	Stakehole cuts.
A773:X	Fill over Aisled Building I stylobates.
A774–800:I (even nos.)	Stakehole cuts.
A775–801:I (odd nos.)	Stakehole fills.
A802:I	Fill of beamslot.
A803:I	(=A817, 933) Beamslot.
A804:I	Post slot with nine subcircular postholes.
A805:III or IV	Thirteen stakeholes, cuts.
A806–810:I (even nos.)	Stakehole fills.
A807–811:I (odd nos.)	Stakehole cuts.
A812:I	Posthole fill.
A813:I	Posthole cut.
A814:I	Posthole fill.
A815:I	Posthole cut.
A816:I	Beamslot fill.
A817:I	Beamslot cut.
A818	Unused number.
A819–845:I (odd nos.)	Stakehole fills.
A820–846:I (even nos.)	Stakehole cuts.
A847:I	Beamslot fill.
A848:I	Beamslot cut.
A849:I	Posthole fill.
A850:I	Posthole cut with removal spade cut.
A851–863:I (odd nos.)	Stakehole fills.
A852–864:I (even nos.)	Stakehole cuts.
A865:I	Posthole fill.
A866:I	Posthole cut with spade cut.
A867:IX	*Opus signinum* dump.
A868:X	Subsidence fill.
A869:X	Subsidence cut.
A870:VIII	Subsidence fill.

A871:VIII	Subsidence cut.
A872:IX	Burn pit, hearth?
A873:IX	Cut of burn pit.
A874:VIII	Upper dark terrace gravel (Aisled Building I floor).
A875:VIII	Upper dark terrace gravel (Aisled Building I floor).
A876:VIII	Middle terrace gravel (Aisled Building I floor).
A877:VIII	Middle terrace gravel (Aisled Building I floor).
A878:II	Sandy silt layer, terrace gravel.
A879:I	Stakehole fill.
A880:I	Stakehole fill.
A881:I	Beamslot fill.
A882:I	Beamslot cut.
A883:II	Terrace gravel.
A884:VII	Fill.
A885:VIII	Fill of posthole A925.
A886:VIII	Stylobate foundation, Aisled Building I.
A887:VIII	Posthole fill.
A888–894:I (even nos.)	Stakehole fills.
A889–895:I (odd nos.)	Stakehole cuts.
A896:IX	Chalk floor.
A897:IX	(=A760) Chalk floor, Aisled Building II.
A898:IX	Irregular cut.
A899:VII	Stylobate packing, Aisled Building I.
A900:VIII	Position of rotted timber.
A901:VII or VIII	Cut of rotten timber?
A902	Unused number.
A903	Unused number.
A904:I	Stakehole fill.
A905:I	Stakehole cut.
A906:X	Chalk floor patch.
A907:VIII	Posthole filled with A887.
A908:VIII	Greensand patch, chalk.
A909:VII	Orange-beige clay-silt with flint pebbles.
A910:VIII	Silt with patches of black ash and oyster shell.
A911:VIII	Fill of cut (913).
A912:X	Chalk floor.
A913:VIII	Cut of A911.
A914	Unused number.
A915:VIII	Layer.
A916:VIII or IX	Fill of subsidence, patch.
A917:VIII	Layer.
A918	Layer.
A919:VIII	Floor of irregularly laid tiles.

A920:VIII	As A877.
A921:VII	Stylobate cut, Aisled Building I.
A922:IX	Layer.
A923:X	Cut, subsidence void.
A924:VIII	Subcircular cut flat bottom; timber impression.
A925:VIII	Posthole.
A926:VIII or IX	Fill of subsidence void to Aisled Building I.
A927:II	Terrace gravel.
A928:VIII	As A877; middle terrace gravel; floor, Aisled Building I.
A929:VII	Cut for Aisled Building I stylobate.
A930:VII	Stylobate packing Aisled Building I.
A931:VII	Cut for stylobate Aisled Building I.
A932:I	Beamslot fill.
A933:I	Beamslot with occasional subcircular flat-bottomed postholes within the slot.
A934:X	Layer.
A935:X	Layer.
A936:X	Layer.
A937:X	Layer.
A938:VIII or IX	Cut/void over Aisled Building I stylobate subsidence.
A939:IX	(=A760) Chalk floor.
A940:IX	(=A760) Chalk floor.
A941:IX	Cut for wall.
A942:I	Fill of burn pit.
A943:I	Bowl-shaped, concave cut.
A944:I	Fill of posthole.
A945:I	Posthole cut.
A946:I	Beamslot fill.
A947:I	Beamslot cut.
A948:I	Posthole fill.
A949:VII	Stylobate packing, Aisled Building I.
A950:VII	Stylobate cut, Aisled Building I.
A951:IX	Layer.
A952:VIII	Layer.
A953:I	Posthole cut, fill A948.
A954:VIII	Dump of terrace gravel, Aisled Building I floor.
A955:VIII	Layer.
A956:VIII	Layer.
A957:VIII	As A877, middle terrace gravel, Aisled Building I floor.
A958:VII	Stylobate packing, Aisled Building I.
A959:VII	Stylobate cut, Aisled Building I.
A960:VII	Stylobate packing, Aisled Building I.
A961:VII	Stylobate cut, Aisled Building I.
A962:VII	Stylobate packing, Aisled Building I.
A963:VII	Stylobate cut, Aisled Building I.

A964:II	Terrace gravel.
A965:I	Ditch.
A966:I	Ditch.
A967:I	Ditch.
A968:I	Ditch.
A969:I	Ditch.
A970:I	Layer.
A971:I	Layer.
A972:I	Layer.
A973:VIII	Layer.
A974:VII	Layer.

Sector B: The Villa West Wing

B1:XI	Overburden.
B2:XI	Natural soil and building rubble.
B3:X	Destruction debris.
B4:XI	Clayey silt with mixed rubble inclusions.
B5:XI	Rubble spread.
B6:XI	Modern (tree root) disturbance.
B7:X	Silt with mixed rubble and pebble.
B8:X	Mixed rubble from wall robbing; overlies wall fragment adjoining threshold.
B9:X	Rubble spread.
B10:X	Fill of robbing cut B14.
B11:X	Sandy clayey silt with mixed rubble inclusions.
B12:X	Sandy clayey silt with mixed rubble inclusions.
B13:X	Disturbed mortar/rubble dump.
B14:X	Robbing cut filled with A10 for front E wall.
B15:X	Occupation dump.
B16:X	Rubble pack.
B17:X	Sandy silty clay with pebble inclusions.
B18:IV	Interlocking box mosaic (cat. no. **7**)
B19:IV	White mosaic (**8**).
B20:IV	Fragment of mosaic **9**: meander border.
B21:X	Mortary silt with mixed rubble.
B22:X	Mixed rubble in sandy mortary silt.
B23:IV	Cantharus Mosaic (**9**).
B24:X	Silt and mixed rubble, compacted mortar fragments.
B25:X	Chalky clayey silt.
B26:X	Mixed rubble with fragments of painted plaster.
B27:X	Sandy clayey silt with mixed rubble inclusions.
B28:X	Clayey silt with mixed rubble.
B29:IV	Checkerboard mosaic (**10**).
B30:IV	*Opus signinum* wall base molding, Room 4.

B31:VII	Burn patch overlying checkerboard mosaic, Room 4.
B32:IV	Meander border, Cantharus Mosaic (**9**).
833:IV	Fragments of interlocking box mosaic, Room 1.
B34:IV	(=B35) *Opus signinum* wall molding, Room 3.
B35:IV	(=B34) *Opus signinum* wall molding, Room 3.
B36:IV	Mosaic **9**, Room 3.
B37:IV	Terracotta mosaic border (**10**), Room 4.
B38:IV	Sandstone threshold block, Rooms 1 and 3.
B39:IX	Chalk/limestone chippings in sandy silt matrix: threshold across flint wall B55 in courtyard.
B40:X	Tree root disturbance.
B41:X	Rubble spread.
B42:IX	Courtyard/threshold.
B43:X	Loose mixed rubble.
B44:X	Possible mortar bedding for mosaic.
B45:IX	Mixed rubble beneath threshold B42 in courtyard.
B46:IX	Compacted chalk surface, courtyard.
B47:IX	Linear flint, sandstone, and chalk spread in courtyard.
B48:X	Terrace slump.
B49:IX	Clayey silt over wall B55 in courtyard.
B50:IX	Silty clay with rubble over wall B55 in courtyard.
B51:VII	(=B136a) Cut in checkerboard mosaic, Room 4.
B52:X	Clayey mortary silt with rubble and pebble inclusions.
B53:IX	*Opus signinum*, mortar and chalk with mixed rubble: courtyard surfacing?
B54:VIII	Fill of B59, Room 5, with painted plaster.
B55:IX	Mud-mortared flint wall in courtyard.
B56:IX	Clayey silt with rubble and pebble inclusions.
B57:VII	Fill of E-W cut B77, Room 4.
B58:X	Sandy clayey silt with sand, chalk, mortar, and rubble.
B59:VIII	Shallow robbing cut, Room 5, against rear wall.
B60:VII	Upper fill of circular cut B74, Room 4.
B61:VIII	(=B95) Fill of cut B80, Room 3.
B62:X	Sandy mortary silt with mixed rubble inclusions.
B63:IX	Linear spread of sandstone/grey Pennant stone, running from SW to NE in courtyard.
B64:VII	Fill of linear cut B78, Room 4.
B65:VII	Middle fill of circular cut B74, Room 4.
B66:X	Sandy mortary silt with rubble.
B67:VII	Lower fill of cut B74, Room 4.
B68:IX	Sandy clayey silt with rubble, courtyard.
B69:X	Mortary silty sand with rubble inclusions.
B70:IV	Checkerboard mosaic **10**, border, Room 4.
B71:IX	Terracotta tile spread in courtyard.
B72:VII	Fill of E-W linear cut B82, Room 4.

B73:VII	Fill of cut B76 with stakeholes, Room 4.
B74:VII	Irregular cut through E-W linear cut (76=77), Room 4.
B75:X	Sandy mortar with pebble, flint, and chalk.
B76:VII	(=B77) W end of linear slot through checkerboard mosaic **10**, Room 4.
B77:VII	(=B76) E end of linear slot, Room 4.
B78:VII	Linear slot, Room 4.
B79:VIII	Fill of robbing trench B84, Room 4.
B80:VIII	Rectangular robbing cut, Room 3.
B81:VIII	Sandy silt with rubble, painted plaster, Room 3.
B82:VII	(=B86) semicircular cut through linear slot, Room 4.
B83:V	Silty clayey mortar with rubble, Room 5.
B84:VIII	N-S robbing cut filled with B79, Room 4.
B85:VII	Fill of B86, Room 4.
B86:VII	(=B82) Semicircular cut through linear slot B78, truncated by B84, Room 4.
B87:X	Silty clay with mixed rubble W of Room 5.
B88:VII	Sandy silty clay with mixed rubble and pebble.
B89:VIII	Fill of robbing cut B84, Room 4.
B90:VIII	Robbing cut, cut by B84, Room 3.
B91:VIII	Fill of B96 over W wall, Room 5.
B92:VII	Twenty stakeholes, Room 4, E half.
B93:VIII.	Fill of robbing cut B97 over W wall, Room 5.
B94:IX	Flint and chalk rubble in sandy silt, courtyard.
B95:VIII	(=B61) Fill of B80, Room 3.
B96:VIII	Cut over flint wall, Rooms 4 and 5.
B97:VIII	Robbing cut of S section, W wall, Room 5.
B98:V	Slope dump W of villa W wing.
B99:IX	Worn layer of flint and pebbles set in sandy silt.
B100:IX	Sandy mortary silt.
B101:VIII	Silty sand with rubble.
B102:IX	Chalk levelling spread with rubble, courtyard.
B103:IX	Fill of robbing cut B106 for E wall, W wing.
B104:IX	N-S linear spread of tile, fill of B108 in courtyard.
B105:IX	Silt with rubble, courtyard.
B106:IX	Robbing cut for E wall, W wing, fill B103.
B107:IX	Fill of (108) in courtyard.
B108:IX	Narrow N-S linear cut for tile and silt fills B104, B107, courtyard.
B109:IX	Chalk levelling spread, courtyard.
B110:V	Charcoal silt patch, occupation Room 5.
B111:IX	Terracotta and sandstone tile patch, courtyard.
B112:IX	Courtyard dump.
B113:IV	Subfloor of Room 5.
B114:VIII	Fill of robbing cut for central section of front wall of villa W wing.
B115:IV	Rear W wall, villa W wing.

B116:VI	Clayey silt, courtyard: disuse?
B117:VIII	Fill of robber cut B129, square pit, Room 3.
B118:III	Fill of posthole (?) B119, Room 5.
B119:III	Posthole (?) cut, Room 5.
B120:X	Sandy silt layer with mixed rubble.
B121:VIII	Lower fill of robbing cut B129, Room 3.
B122:VI	Compacted mixed rubble in courtyard.
B123:IV/III/II	Clayey layer beneath rear W wall B115, W wing; not fully excavated, visible in evaluation trench.
B124:VI	Mixed rubble in courtyard.
B125:VI	Mixed rubble in courtyard.
B126:VI	Mixed rubble in courtyard.
B127:VIII	Fill of cut B134 in N edge pit cut, Room 3.
B128:VI	Packed flint and mixed rubble in courtyard.
B129:VIII	Robbing cut running W from pit B80, Room 3.
B130:VI	Sandy clayey silt with charcoal, mixed rubble.
B131:VI	Compacted pebbles in sandy silt, courtyard.
B132:VI	Sandy clayey silt with chalk.
B133:VI	Flint layer in sandy silt, courtyard.
B134:VIII	Robbing cut truncated by B80, Room 3.
B135a:VIII	Robbing cut for central section of E wall, W wing.
B135b:VI	Silty mortar, mixed rubble, courtyard.
B136a:VII	(=B51) Cut through border, checkerboard mosaic **10**, Room 4.
B136b:VI	Flint scatter courtyard.
B137:VI	(=B138?) SW-NE linear spread of flints in courtyard.
B138:VI	(=B137?) Irregular layer of flints in courtyard.
B139:VI?	Greensand packing (unexcavated), courtyard.
B140:VI	Silty clay with mixed rubble, courtyard.
B141:VI	Silty clay with chalk, small mixed rubble, courtyard.
B142:VI	Silty clay with small mixed rubble, courtyard.
B143:VI	Silty clay with small mixed rubble, courtyard.
B144:VI	Silty clay with mixed rubble, courtyard.
B145:VI	Clayey silt with mixed rubble, courtyard.
B146:VI	Chalky mortary patch (unexcavated), courtyard.
B147:VI	Chalky mortary patch (unexcavated), courtyard.
B148:VI?	Silt with pebble, (unexcavated), abutting W edge of E wall of villa W wing.
B149:VIII	Fill of robbing cut B151 for wall between Rooms 2, 3.
B150:VI?	Layer beneath A144, visible in evaluation cut against E wall of villa W wing.
B151:VIII	Robbing cut for wall between Rooms 2, 3

Sector C: The Villa South Wing

C1:VI	Topsoil.

C2:VI	Disturbed building material.
C3:VI	Exterior courtyard deposit.
C4:VI	Building rubble.
C5:VI	Possible collapse of exterior S wall.
C6:VI	Fill of cut C7.
C7:VI	Recut of robbing trench C12 of N wall.
C8:VI	Fill of robber trench.
C9:VI	Probable debris levelling.
C10:VI	Rubble deposit.
C11:VI	Robber trench disturbance.
C12:VI	Irregular robber trench cut, fills 8, 11.
C13:VI	Collapse of N wall.
C14:VI	Collapse of S wall.
C15:V	Layer of flints in clay matrix: later "porticus."
C16:V	Layer of flints in clay matrix: later "porticus."
C17:III	Laid pebble surface.
C18:V	Layer of flints in clay matrix: later "porticus."
C19:V	Interior surface of N "porticus."
C20:VI	Dump sealing N wall.
C21:III or IV	Courtyard clay.
C22:VI	Silt with heavy rubble.
C23:III	Chalk/mortar exterior surfacing, earlier N "porticus."
C24:III	Compact layer of flint and pebbles in courtyard.
C25:VI	Mortar patch with flint, chalk; mortar dump.
C26:VI	Dump.
C27:VI	Clay dump.
C28:VI	Building rubble dump.
C29:VI	Dump of sandstone roof tiles.
C30:VI	Collapse of south wall: mudbrick, Pennant slates.
C31:III	Dump of building rubble into earlier N "porticus."
C32:IV	Burnt wood scatter.
C33:II or III	Terrace gravel exposed as possible interior surface.
C34:IV	Mixed debris over burn.
C35:II or III	Compacted pebble layer: terrace gravel exposed as possible interior surface.
C36:II or III	Terrace gravel exposed as courtyard surface.
C37:II or III	Terrace gravel exposed as courtyard surface.
C38:III	Two courses of N wall.
C39:III	Footing of southern wall.
C40:III	Surface laid in earlier N "porticus."
C41:I	Debris in depression.
C42:III	Upper fill of ditch C63 depression.
C43:IV	Fill of pit C55.
C44:II	Natural clay: apparent terrace gravel.
C45:II	Natural clay: apparent terrace gravel.

C46:I	Fill of ditch C63.
C47:III or IV	Burning over pebbles.
C48:III	Foundations for N wall.
C49:III	Footing of N wall.
C50:II	Natural clay: apparent terrace gravel.
C51:III	Sarsens, S wall foundation.
C52:III	Upper fill in ditch C63.
C53:III	Flints and pebbles pressed into surface, earlier N "porticus."
C54:III	Foundation cut, S wall.
C55:IV	Cut of circular pit.
C56:III	Upper fill of ditch C63.
C57:I	Fill of ditch C63.
C58:I	Fill of ditch C63.
C59:I	Fill of ditch C63 with pottery dump.
C60:III	Foundation cut, N wall.
C61:III	N wall foundation.
C62:III	Footings of N wall.
C63:I	Ditch cut.
C64:IV	Fill of pit 55.
C65:IV	Fill of pit 55.
C66:I	Shallow square-bottomed cut, S of S wall.

BIBLIOGRAPHY

Abbreviations for journal titles in text and bibliography are from L'Année Philologique; references not listed therein are:

BAJ Berkshire Archaeological Journal
CBA Research Report = Council for British Archaeology Research Report
OUCA Oxford University Committee for Archaeology.
SAL Research Report = Research Report of the Society of Antiquaries of London
WAM = Wiltshire Archaeological and Natural History Magazine
WANHS = Wiltshire Archaeological and Natural History Society

In keeping with convention, the date cited for articles published in the Wiltshire Archaeological and Natural History Magazine between 1969 and 1984, when publication lagged, refers to the year of actual publication.

Addyman, P. V.
  1972 The Anglo-Saxon House: A New Review. In P. Clemoes (ed.), Anglo-Saxon England I: 273–307. Cambridge: Cambridge University Press.
Ailesbury, C.S.C.B.-B., Marquess of
  1962 A History of Savernake Forest. Devizes.
Alcock, L.
  1972 By South Cadbury is that Camelot. London: Thames and Hudson.
  1980 The Cadbury Castle Sequence in the First Millennium B.C. Bulletin of the Board of Celtic Studies 28: 656–718.
Allason-Jones, L., and R. Miket
  1984 The Catalogue of Small Finds from South Shields Roman Fort. Society of Antiquaries of Newcastle upon Tyne, Monograph 2. Newcastle upon Tyne: The Society.
Allen. D. F.
  1944 The Belgic Dynasties of Britain and Their Coins. Archaeologia 90: 1–46.
  1961 A Study of the Dobunnic Coinage in E. M. Clifford, Bagendon: A Belgic Oppidum. A Record of the Excavations 1954–56: 75–146. Cambridge: W. Heffer.
Allen, J. R. L.
  1986 Interpretation of Some Romano-British Smithing Slag from Awre in Gloucestershire. Journal of the History of Metallurgy Society 20:2: 97–104.
Allison, E. P.
  1985 An Archaeological Study of Bird Bones from Seven Sites in York. Ph.D. diss., University of York.
Anderson, A. C.
  1980 A Guide to Roman Fine Wares. Vorda Research Series 1. Wiltshire: Vorda.
Anderson, A. S.
  1978a Wiltshire Moulded Imitation Samian. In P. Arthur and G. Marsh (eds.), Early Fine Wares in Roman Britain. BAR series 57. Oxford: B.A.R.
  1978b Wiltshire Fine Wares. In P. Arthur and G. Marsh (eds.), Early Fine Wares in Roman Britain. BAR series 57. Oxford: B.A.R.
  1980a The Roman Pottery Industry in North Wiltshire. Swindon Archaeological Society Report 2. Swindon: Thamesdown Borough Council.
  1980b Romano-British Pottery Kilns at Purton. WAM (for 1977–1978) 72–73: 51–58.

Anderson, A. S., and J. S. Wacher
    1980 Excavations at Wanborough, Wiltshire: An Interim Report. *Britannia* 2: 115–26.
Andrews, P., and D. Metcalf
    1984 A Coinage for King Cynewulf? In D. Hill and D. M. Metcalf (eds.), *Sceattas in England and on the Continent: The Seventh Oxford Symposium on Coinage and Monetary History.* BAR British Series 128: 175–79. Oxford: B.A.R.
Annable, F. K.
    1965 Further Finds at Folly Farm, nr. Mildenhall. *WAM* 56: 191–92.
    1962a A Romano-British Pottery in Savernake Forest, Kilns 1–2. *WAM* 58: 142–55.
    1962b Romano-British Burials at Devizes. *WAM* 58: 222–23.
    1965 A (?) Medieval Interment at Marlborough. *WAM* 60: 130.
    1966 A Late First-Century Well at Cvnetio. *WAM* 61: 9–24.
    1976 A Bronze Military Apron Mount from *CVNETIO. WAM* 69 (for 1974): 176–79.
    1978a A Late Bronze Buckle Fragment from *Cunetio. WAM* 70–71 (for 1975–76): 127–28.
    1978b A Bronze Military Mount from Folly Farm. *WAM* 70–71 for 1975–76: 126–27.
Annable, F. K., M. C. C. Corfield, E. Crowfoot, and C. R. Oyler
    1980 A Coffined Burial of Roman Date from Cvnetio. *WAM* 72–73 (for 1977–78): 187–91.
Anonymous
    1860 Account of the Sixth General Meeting Held at Marlborough, 27th, 28th, and 29th September, 1859. *WAM* 6: 245–55.
    1922 Wiltshire Books, Pamphlets and Articles. *WAM* 41: 308–23.
    1932 Roman Sculptural Stone Figure of Atys found at Rudge, in Froxfield, now in the British Museum. *WAM* 46: 108–109.
    1969 Excavation and Fieldwork in Wiltshire, 1968. *WAM* 64: 123–29.
    1988 Excavation and Fieldwork in Wiltshire, 1987. *WAM* 82: 176–82.
Applebaum, S.
    1966 Peasant Economy and Types of Agriculture. In C. Thomas (ed.), *Rural Settlement in Roman Britain,* 99–107. CBA Research Report 7.
    1967 Roman Britain. In H. P. R. Finberg (ed.), *The Agrarian History of England and Wales.* Vol. 1, pt. 2, Cambridge: Cambridge University Press.
Arnold, C. J.
    1982 The End of Roman Britain: Some Discussion. In D. Miles, (ed.), *The Romano-British Countryside.* BAR British Series 103, 2: 451–59. Oxford: B.A.R.
    1984 *Roman Britain to Saxon England.* Bloomington: Indiana University Press.
Atkinson, D.
    1942 *Report on Excavations at Wroxeter: (The Roman City of Virconium) in the County of Salop, 1923–1927.* Birmingham Archaeological Society. Oxford: Oxford University Press.
Audouze, F., and O. Büchsenschütz
    1992 *Towns, Villages and Countryside of Celtic Europe.* Trans. H. Cleere. London: Batsford.
Avent, R., and V. I. Evison
    1982 Anglo-Saxon Button Brooches. *Archaeologia* 107: 77–124.
Avi-Yonah, M.
    1965 La mosaïque juive dans ses relations avec la mosaïque classique. In H. Stern (ed.), *La Mosaïque Greco-Romaine* 325–32. Paris: CNRS.
Barkoczi, L.
    1986 Szazadi Vesett Diszu Üvegek Pannoniabol. *Archeologiai Êrtesítö.* Budapest.
    1988 Pannonische Glasfunde in Ungarn. Studia Archaeologica 9. Budapest: Akadémia: Kiadö.
Barron, R. S.
    1976 *The Geology of Wiltshire.* Bradford-on-Avon: Moonraker.
Bateson, J. D.
    1981 *Enamel-Working in Iron Age, Roman, and Sub-Roman Britain.* BAR British Series 93. Oxford: B.A.R.
Bathurst, W. H., and C. W. King
    1879 *Roman Antiquities at Lydney Park, Gloucestershire.* London: Longmans, Green.

Beal, J. C.

1983 *Catalogue des objets de tablettérie du Musée de la Civilisation Gallo-Romaine de Lyon.* Centre d'Études Romaines et Gallo-Romaines de l'Université Jean Moulin Lyon III. Nouvelle série no. 1 Lyon.

Beresford, M. W.

1959 Poll-Tax Payers of 1377; Poor Parishes of 1429. In R. B. Pugh and E. Crittall (eds.), *A History of Wiltshire.*VCH 4: 304–14. London: Oxford University Press.

Berger, L.

1960 *Römische Gläser aus Vindonissa.* Basel: Birkhauser.

Bersu, G.

1940 Excavations at Little Woodbury, Wiltshire. Part 1: The Settlement as Revealed by Excavation. *Proceedings of the Prehistoric Society* 6: 30–111.

Besly, E.

1983 The Third-Century Hoard from Aldbourne. *WAM* 77 (for 1982): 61–66.

1984 The Aldbourne, Wilts., Hoard. *Coin Hoards from Roman Britain,*Vol. 4. British Museum Occasional Paper 43: 63–102. London: British Museum.

Besly, E., and R. Bland

1983 *The Cunetio Treasure.* London: British Museum Publications.

Biddle, M., H. T. Lambrick, and J. N. L. Myres

1968 The Early History of Abingdon, Berkshire, and Its Abbey. *Medieval Archaeology* 12: 26–69.

Black, E. W.

1987 *The Roman Villas of South-East England.* BAR British Series 171. Oxford: B.A.R.

Blackford, J. H.

1941 *The Manor and Village of Cherhill.* London: Butler and Tanner.

Blagg, T. F. C.

1991 Buildings. In R. F. J. Jones, *Britain in the Roman Period: Recent Trends:* 3–14. Chippenham.

Blair, J.

1985 Secular Minster Churches in *Domesday Book.* In P. Sawyer (ed.), Domesday Book: *A Reassessment,* 104–42. London: Arnold.

Bland, R.

1982 *The Blackmoor Hoard. Vol. 3 of Coin Hoards from Roman Britain.* British Museum Occasional Paper 33. London: British Museum.

Böhme, H. W.

1986 Das Ende der Römerherrschaft in Britannien und die angelsächsische Besiedlung Englands im 5 Jahrhundert. *JRGZ* 33: 469–574.

Bonney, D. J.

1966 Pagan Saxon Burials and Boundaries in Wiltshire. *WAM* 61: 25–30.

1968 Iron Age and Romano-British Settlement Sites in Wiltshire: Some Geographical Considerations. *WAM* 63: 27–38.

1972 Early Boundaries in Wessex. In P. J. Fowler (ed.), *Archaeology and the Landscape; Essays for L. V. Grinsell:* 168–86. London: J. Baker.

1973 The Pagan Saxon Period, c. 500–700. In R. B. Pugh and E. Crittall (ed.), *A History of Wiltshire.* VCH 1:2: 468–84. Oxford: Oxford University Press.

1977 Early Boundaries and Estates in Southern Britain. In P. H. Sawyer, *English Medieval Settlement,* 41–51. London: Arnold.

1978 Early Fields and Land Allotments in Wessex. In H. C. Bowen and P. J. Fowler (eds.), *Early Land Allotment in the British Isles: A Survey of Recent Work,* 49–51. BAR British Series 48. Oxford: B.A.R.

Boon, G.

1950 Excavations at Kings Weston. *Transactions of the Bristol and Gloucester Archaeological Society* 69: 5–58.

1966 Roman Window Glass from Wales. *JGS* 8: 41–45.

Bowen, H. C.

1978 "Ancient Fields" since 1961. In H. C. Bowen and P. J. Fowler (eds.), *Early Land Allotment in the British Isles: A Survey of Recent Work* 1–2, BAR British Series 48. Oxford: B.A.R.

1990 *The Archaeology of the Bokerly Dyke.* (London)

Bowen, H. C., J. G. Evans, and E. Race.

1978 An Investigation of the Wessex Linear Ditch System. In H. C. Bowen and P. J. Fowler (eds.), *Early Land Allotment in the British Isles: A Survey of Recent Work,* 149–53. BAR British Series 48. Oxford: B.A.R.

Bowen, H. C., and P. J. Fowler

1962 The Archaeology of Fyfield and Overton Downs, Wilts (Interim Report). *WAM* 58: 98–115.

1966 Romano-British Rural Settlements in Dorset and Wiltshire. In C. Thomas (ed.), *Rural Settlement in Roman Britain,* 43-67. CBA Research Report 7. London: CBA.

1978 Bowen, H. C., and P. J. Fowler (eds.) *Early Land Allotment in the British Isles: A Survey of Recent Work,* BAR British Series 48. Oxford: B.A.R.

Bradley, R. J., and A. Ellison

1975 *Rams Hill: A Bronze Age Defended Enclosure and Its Landscape.* BAR British Series 19. Oxford: B.A.R.

Brailsford, J. W.

1948 Excavations at Little Woodbury. Part II. *Proceedings of the Prehistoric Society* 14: 1–23.

Brakspear, H.

1904 The Roman Villa at Box. *WAM* 33: 236–69.

Bramwell, D.

1977 Bird Bone. In H. Clarke and A. Carter, *Excavations in King's Lynn, 1963–1970,* 399–402. Society for Medieval Archaeology Monograph Series 7. London: The Society.

Branigan, K.

1971 *Latimer: A Belgic, Roman, Dark Age and Early Modern Farm.* Chess Valley Archaeological and Historical Society.

1973 Gauls in Gloucestershire? *Transactions of the Bristol and Gloucester Archaeological Society* 92: 82–95.

1976 Villa Settlement in the West Country. In K. Branigan and P. J. Fowler (eds.), *The Roman West Country: Classical Culture and Celtic Society:* 120–41. Newton Abbot, North Pomfret (Vt.): David and Charles.

1977a *The Roman Villa in South-West England.* Bradford-on-Avon: Moonraker.

1977b *Gatcombe.* BAR British Series 44. Oxford: B.A.R.

1982 Celtic Farm to Roman Villa. In D. Miles (ed.), *The Romano-British Countryside: Studies in Rural Settlement and Economy,* Vol. 1, 81–96. BAR British Series 103. Oxford: B.A.R.

1985 *The Catuvellauni.* Gloucester: Sutton.

1989 Specialization in Villa Economies. In K. Branigan and D. Miles, *Villas Economies. Economic Aspects of Romano-British Villas:* 42–50. Sheffield: University of Sheffield.

Brentnall, H. C.

1941 The Metes and Bounds of Savernake Forest. *WAM* 49: 391–434.

1948 Bedwyn in the Tenth Century. *WAM* 52: 360–368.

Brodribb, A. C. C., A. R. Hands, and D. R. Walker.

1968 *Excavations at Shakenoak Farm, near Wilcote, Oxfordshire,* vol. 1. Oxford: A. R. Hands, Exeter College.

1971 *Excavations at Shakenoak Farm, near Wilcote, Oxfordshire,* vol. 2. Oxford: A. R. Hands, Exeter College.

1972 *Excavations at Shakenoak Farm, near Wilcote, Oxfordshire,* vol. 3. Oxford: A. R. Hands, Exeter College.

1973 *Excavations at Shakenoak Farm, near Wilcote, Oxfordshire,* vol. 4. Oxford: A. R. Hands, Exeter College.

1978 *Excavations at Shakenoak Farm, near Wilcote, Oxfordshire,* vol. 5. Oxford: A. R. Hands, Exeter College.

Brodribb, Gerald
1987 *Roman Brick and Tile.* Gloucester: A. Sutton.
Brooke, J. W., and B. H. Cunnington
1896–97 Excavation of a Roman Well near Silbury Hill. July and October, 1896. *WAM* 29: 166–71.
Brooks, N.
1964 The Unidentified Forts of the Burghal Hidage. *Medieval Archaeology* 8: 74–90.
Brown, D.
1975 A Fifth-Century Burial at Kingsholm. In H. Hurst et al., Excavations at Gloucester: Third Interim Report: Kingsholm 1966–75. *AntJ* 55: 267–94.
Brown, S.
1989 Report on the Bone from Maddle Farm. In V. Gaffney and M. Tingle, *The Maddle Farm Project. An Integrated Survey of Prehistoric and Roman Landscapes on the Berkshire Downs,* 183–92. BAR British Series 200. Oxford: B.A.R.
Bruce, E.
1854 *In* Donations to the Museum and Library. *WAM* 1: 352.
1854 *In* A List of Articles Exhibited in the Temporary Museum at the Council Chambers, Salisbury. *WAM* 2: 26–39.
Burchard, A.
1971 An Anglo-Saxon Brooch from Grafton, *WAM* 66: 178–79.
Burne, A. H.
1953 Wansdyke West and South. *WAM* 55: 126–34.
Burnett, A. M.
1983 A Late Roman Coin Hoard from near Chisbury Camp. *WAM* 77 (for 1982): 144–45.
Burnett, A. M., and P. H. Robinson
1984 The Upavon, Wilts., Hoard. In *Coin Hoards from Roman Britain* V. British Museum Occasional Paper 54: 89–99. London.
Burnham, B, C., and J. Wacher
1990 *The "Small Towns" of Roman Britain.* London: Batsford.
Burrow, I.
1979 Roman Material from Hill-forts. In P. J. Casey (ed.), *The End of Roman Britain.* BAR British Series 71. Oxford: B.A.R.
1981 *Hillfort and Hill-top Settlement in Somerset in the First to Eighth Centuries A.D.* BAR British Series 91. Oxford: B.A.R.
Bushe-Fox, J. P.
1914 Small Objects in Metal, Glass, Bone, Etc. In J. P. Bushe-Fox, *Second Report on the Excavations on the Site of the Roman Town at Wroxeter, Shropshire, 1913,* 11–23. Oxford: F. Hall.
1916 Small Objects in Metal, Glass, Bone, Etc. In J. P. Bushe-Fox, *Third Report on the Excavations on the Site of the Roman Town at Wroxeter, Shropshire, 1914.* Reports of the Research Committee of the Society of Antiquaries 4: 22–34. Oxford.
1928 *Second Report on the Excavations of the Roman Fort at Richborough, Kent.* SAL Research Report 7.
Butcher, S. A.
1977 Enamels from Roman Britain. In M. R. Apted, R. Gilyard-Beer, and A. D. Saunders (eds.), *Ancient Monuments and Their Interpretation:* 41–70. London: Phillimore.
Cam, H. M.
1944 *Liberties and Communities in Medieval England: Collected Studies in Local Administration and Topographyy.* Cambridge: Cambridge University Press.
Canham, R.
1982 Aerial Photography in Wiltshire 1975–81. *WAM* 76 (for 1981): 3–19.
Carruthers, W. J.
1989 The Carbonised Plant Remains from the Maddle Farm Excavations. In C. Gaffney and M. Tingle (eds.), *The Maddle Farm Project: An Integrated Survey of Prehistoric and Roman Landscapes on the Berkshire Downs,* 179–82. BAR British Series 200. Oxford: B.A.R.

Carson, R. A. G., P. V. Hill, and J. P. C. Kent
1965 *Late Roman Bronze Coinage, A.D. 324–498.* London: Spink.
Carver, M. O. H.
1987 *Underneath English Towns: Interpreting Urban Archaeology.* London: Batsford.
Casey, P. J.
1981 Excavations at Lydney Park, Gloucestershire. *Archaeological Reports of the Universities of Durham and Newcastle* 1980: 30–32.
Chadwick, S. E., and M. W. Thompson
1956 Note on an Iron Age Habitation Site near Battlesbury Camp, Warminster. *WAM* 56: 262–64.
Chambers, C. D.
1920 Romano-British Dovecots. *JRS* 10: 189–93.
Chandler, C. J.
1989 Roman Thamesdown. In C. J. Chandler, H. S. N. Digby, and L. A. Marshman, *"Off the Map of History"?: The Development of North-East Wiltshire to 1600:* 16-32. Swindon: Museums Division, Arts and Recreation, Borough of Thamesdown.
Chapman, D., and N. Chapman
1975 *Fallow Deer. Their History, Distribution and Biology.* Lavenham: Dalton.
Charlesworth, D.
1966 Roman Square Bottles. *JGS* 8: 26–40.
1972 The Glass. In S. Frere, *Verulamium Excavations,* vol. 1, 196–215. SAL Reports 28. Oxford.
Charlesworth, D., and J. Price
1987 The Roman and Saxon Glass. In S. Frere, P. Bennett, and S. Stow, *Canterbury Excavations: Intra- and Extra-Mural Sites, 1949–55 and 1980–84.* Vol. 8 of *The Archaeology of Canterbury,* 220–31. Maidstone: Kent Archaeological Society.
Church, L. E., and L. C. Johnson
1964 Growth of Long Bones in the Chicken. *American Journal of Anatomy* 114: 521–38.
Clairmont, C.
1963 *The Glass Vessels.* Vol. 4, Part 5, of *The Excavations at Dura-Europos.* New Haven: Dura-Europos.
Clapham, A. J.
1986 The Origin, Domestication, Dispersal and Cultivation of Flax *(Linum usitatissimum).* Unpublished paper, University of London.
Clarke, D. L.
1972 A Provisional Model of an Iron Age Society and Its Settlement System. In D. Clarke (ed.), *Models in Archaeology,* 801–69. London: Methuen.
Clarke, G.
1979 Belts and Belt-fittings. In *The Roman Cemetery at Lankhills,*Part 2 of Winchester Studies 3, *Pre-Roman and Roman Winchester,* 264–91. Oxford: Clarendon Press.
Cleere, H. C.
1958 Roman Domestic Ironwork as Illustrated by the Brading, Isle of Wight, Villa. *BIAL* 1: 55–74.
1976 Ironmaking. In D. Strong and D. Brown (eds.), *Roman Crafts.* 127–41. London: Duckworth.
1981 The Iron Industry of Roman Britain. Ph.D. diss., University of London.
Cleere, H., and D. Crossley
1985 *The Iron Industry of the Weald.* Leicester: Leicester University Press.
Colgrave, B., and R. A. B. Mynors (eds.)
1969 *Bede's Ecclesiastical History of the English People.* Translation of the Venerable Bede's *Historia Ecclesiastica.* Oxford: Clarendon.
Collingwood, R. G., and I. Richmond
1969 *The Archaeology of Roman Britain.* London: Methuen.
Collis, J.
1984 *Oppida: Earliest Towns North of the Alps.* Sheffield: University of Sheffield.

Colt Hoare, R.
1819–1821 *The Ancient History of Wiltshire,* vols. 1 and 2. London: Lackington, Hughes, Harding, Maver, and Lepard.

Cookson, N. A.
1984 *Romano-British Mosaics.* BAR British Series 135. Oxford: B.A.R.

Corder, P., and J. L. Kirk
1932 *A Roman Villa at Langton, Near Malton, East Yorkshire.* Roman Malton and District Report 4. Leeds: The Yorkshire Archaeological Society.

Corney, M.
1989 Multiple Ditch Systems and Late Iron Age Settlement in Central Wessex. In M. Bowden, O. Mackay, and P. Topping (eds.), *From Cornwall to Caithness: Some Aspects of British Field Archaeology,* 111–28. BAR British Series 209. Oxford: B.A.R.

Cornwall, I. W., and L. Haglund-Calley
1963 Report on the Dinas Powys Animal Bones. In L. Alcock *Dinas Powys; An Iron Age, Dark Age, and Early Medieval Settlement in Glamorgan,* 192–94. Cardiff: University of Wales Press.

Cotton, M. A.
1947 Excavations at Silchester 1938–39. *Archaeologia* 92: 121–67.

Cox, B. H.
1972–73 The Significance of the Distribution of English Names in -ham in the Midlands and East Anglia. *Journal of the English Place-Name Society* 5: 1972–1983, 15–73.

Crawford, O. G. S.
1921 The Anglo-Saxon Bounds of Bedwyn and Burbage. *WAM* 41: 281–301.
1953a *Archaeology in the Field.* London: Phoenix House.
1953b The East End of Wansdyke. *WAM* 55: 119–25.

Crawford, O. G. S., and A. Keiller
1928 *Wessex from the Air.* Oxford: Clarendon Press.

Crickmore, J.
1984 *Romano-British Urban Defences.* BAR British Series 126. Oxford: B.A.R.

Crummy, N.
1979 A Chronology of Romano-British Bone Pins. *Britannia* 10: 157–63.
1983 Objects of Personal Adornment or Dress. In *The Roman Small Finds from Excavations in Colchester 1971-9,* Colchester Archaeological Reports 2, 7–53. Colchester: Colchester Archaeological Trust.

Cummings, K.
1980 *The Technique of Glass Forming.* London: Batsford.

Cunliffe, B. W.
1971a *Fishbourne; A Roman Palace and Its Garden.* London: Thames and Hudson.
1971b Small Objects of Lead. In B. Cunliffe (ed.), *Excavations at Fishbourne.* Vol. 2, *The Finds.* SAL Research Report 27: 144. London: Society of Antiquaries.
1973 The Period of Romanization, 43–c. 250; The Later Roman Period, c. 250–367; The End of the Roman Era, 367–500. In R. Pugh and E. Crittall (eds.), *A History of Wiltshire.* VCH 1:2: 439–67. Oxford.
1974 *Iron Age Communities in Britain.* London: Routledge and K. Paul.
———, (ed.)
1975 *Excavations at Portchester Castle.* Vol. 1, *Roman.* SAL Research Report 32. London: Society of Antiquaries.
1977 A Romano-British Village at Chalton, Hampshire. *Proceedings of the Hampshire Field Club and Archaeological Society* 33: 45–68.
1978 *Hengistbury Head.* London: Elek.
1984a *Danebury: An Iron Age Hillfort in Hampshire.* CBA Research Report 52. London: CBA.
1984b Iron Age Wessex: Continuity and Change. In B. W. Cunliffe and D. Miles (eds.), *Aspects of the Iron Age in Central Southern Britain,* 12–45 OUCA Monograph 2. Oxford: Institute of Archaeology.

1991 *Iron Age Communities in Britain: An Account of England, Scotland, and Wales from the Seventh Century BC until the Roman Conquest* 3d ed. London and New York: Routledge.
Cunnington, M. E.
1908 Oliver's Camp, Devizes. *WAM* 35: 408–44.
1917 Lidbury Camp. *WAM* 40: 12–36.
1922 4 Pits in Battlesbury Camp. *WAM* 42: 368–73.
1923 *The Early Iron Age Inhabited Site at All Cannings Cross Farm, Wiltshire.* Devizes.
1930 Romano-British Wiltshire. *WAM* 45: 166–216.
1932 Chisbury Camp. *WAM* 46: 4–7.
1933 Excavations at Yarnbury Castle Camp 1932. *WAM* 46: 198–213.
1940 Roman Brick Stamped with Maker's Name from Burderope Race Course Field. *WAM* 49: 117.
Cunnington, M. E., and B. H. Cunnington
1913 Casterly Camp. *WAM* 38: 53–105.
Cunnington, M. E., and E. H. Goddard
1911 *Catalogue of the Antiquities in the Museum of the Wiltshire Archaeological and Natural History Society at Devizes,* vol. 2. Devizes.
1934 *Catalogue of the Antiquities in the Museum of the Wiltshire Archaeological and Natural History Society at Devizes,* vol. 2. Devizes.
Cunnington, W.
1875 Relics of Ancient Population on Oldbury Hill, Wilts. *WAM* 23: 213–28.
Curle, J.
1911 *A Roman Frontier Post and Its People: The Fort of Newstead in the Parish of Melrose.* Glasgow: Maclehose.
Czurda-Ruth, B.
1979 *Die römischen Gläser vom Magdalensberg.* Klagenfurt: Landesmuseums.
Darlington, R. R.
1955 Anglo Saxon Wiltshire; Introduction to the Wiltshire Domesday. In R. B. Pugh and E. Crittall (eds.), *A History of Wiltshire.* VCH 2: 1–34, 42–112. London: Oxford University Press.
Davey, N.
1972 The Conservation of Romano-British Painted Plaster. *Britannia* 3: 251–68.
Davey, N., and R. J. Ling
1982 *Wall-Painting in Roman Britain.* Britannia Monograph Series 3. London: Society for the Promotion of Roman Studies.
Davis, S. J. M.
1987 *Cattle Foot Bones Excavated in 1982 from a 17th/18th Century Pit in Church Street, Dorchester, Dorset.* Ancient Monuments Laboratory Report 222/87.
1988 *Animal Bones from Dodder Hill. A Roman Fort Near Droitwich (Hereford and Worcester), Excavated in 1977.* Ancient Monuments Laboratory Report 140/88.
Davis, S. N., and R. J. DeWeist
1966 *Hydrology.* New York: Wiley.
de la Béydoyere, G.
1991 The Buildings of Roman Britain. London: Batsford.
Deniz, E., and S. Payne
1982 Eruption and Wear in the Mandibular Dentition as a Guide to Ageing Turkish Angora Goats. In B. Wilson, C. Grigson, and S. Payne (eds.), *Ageing and Sexing Animal Bones from Archaeological Sites,* 155–206. BAR British Series 109. Oxford: B.A.R.
Dickinson, T. M.
1974 *Cuddlesdon and Dorchester-on-Thames.* BAR British Series 1. Oxford: B.A.R.
1991 Material Culture as Social Expression: The Case of Saxon Saucer Brooches with Running Spiral Decoration. *Studien zur Sachsenforschung* 7: 39–70.
Dimbleby, G. W.
1971 Pollen Analysis. In H. S. Green, Wansdyke, Excavations 1966 to 1970. *WAM* 66: 129–46.

1978 *Plants and Archaeology* 2d ed. London: Baker.

Donovan, H.

1934 Excavation of a Romano-British Building at Bourton-on-the-Water, Gloucestershire. *Transactions of the Bristol and Gloucester Archaeological Society* 56: 99–128

Down, A.

1978 Roman Small Finds. In A. Down and M. Rule, *Chichester Excavations,* vol. 3, 302–19. Chichester: Chichester Excavations Committee.

1979 The Finds. Iron. In A. Down and M. Rule, *Chichester Excavations,* vol. 4, 151–62. Chichester: Chichester Excavations Committee.

1981 The Finds from the North-West Quadrant (Areas 8 & 9). Objects of Bronze. In A. Down and M. Rule, *Chichester Excavations,* vol. 5, 157–72. Chichester: Chichester Excavations Committee.

Driesch, A. von den

1976 *A Guide to the Measurement of Animal Bones from Archaeological Sites.* Peabody Museum Bulletin 1. Cambridge, Mass.: Peabody Museum, Harvard University.

Droop, J. P., and R. Newstead

1931 Excavations in Deanery Field, Chester, 1928. Part II: The Finds. *Annals of Archaeology and Anthropology* 18: 113–54.

Duerst, J. U.

1926 Vergleichende Untersuchungsmethoden am Skellet bei Säugern. In *Handbuch der biologischen Arbeitsmethoden* 7 (2): 125–530. Berlin.

Dumville, D. N.

1992 *Wessex and England from Alfred to Edgar.* Woodbridge: Boydell.

Dunning, G. C.

1959 The Distribution of Socketed Axes of Breton Type. *Ulster Journal of Archaeology* 22: 53–55.

Eagles, B. N.

1986 Pagan Anglo-Saxon Burials at West Overton. *WAM* 80: 103–19.

Edwards, H.

1988 *The Charters of the Early West Saxon Kingdom.* BAR British Series 198. Oxford: B.A.R.

Ehrenreich, R. M.

1985 *Trade, Technology, and the Ironworking Community in the Iron Age of Southern Britain.* BAR British Series 144. Oxford: B.A.R.

1986 Blacksmithing Technology in Iron Age Britain. *Oxford Journal of Archaeology* 5:2, 165–84.

Ekblom, E.

1917 *The Place-Names of Wiltshire, Their Origin and History.* Uppsala: Appelbergs.

Ellison, A.

1981 *A Policy for Archaeological Investigation of Wessex, 1981 to 1985.* W.A.C. Salisbury.

Ellison, A., and P. Rahtz

1987 Excavations at Whitbury Castle Ditches, Hampshire, 1960. *Proceedings of the Hampshire Field Club and Archaeological Society* 43: 63–81.

Elsdon, S. M.

1989 *Later Prehistoric Pottery in England and Wales.* Shire Archaeology 58. Aylesbury: Shire.

Esmonde Cleary, S. E.

1987 *Extra-Mural Areas of Romano-British Towns.* BAR British Series 169. Oxford: B.A.R.

1989a Constantine I to Constantine II. In M. Todd (ed.), *Research in Roman Britain: 1960-89,* 235–44. Britannia Monograph Series 11. London: Society for the Promotion of Roman Studies.

1989b *The Ending of Roman Britain.* London: Batsford.

Evans, J. G.

1966 A Romano-British Interment in the Bank of the Winterbourne, near Avebury. *WAM* 61: 97–98.

1968 Periglacial Deposits on the Chalk of Wiltshire. *WAM* 63: 12–26.

Evison, V. I.

1963 Sugar-Loaf Shield Bosses. *AntJ* 43: 38–96.

1965 *The Fifth-Century Invasions South of the Thames*. London: University of London Athlone Press.

1977 Supporting-arm Brooches and Equal-arm Brooches in England. *Studien zur Sachsenforschung* I: 127–47.

1978 Early Anglo-Saxon Applied Disc Brooches. Part I: On the Continent; Part II: In England. *AntJ* 58: 88–102, 260–78.

1981 Distribution Maps and England in the First Two Phases. In V. I. Evison (ed.), *Angles, Saxons and Jutes: Essays Presented to J. N. L. Myres:* 126–67. Oxford: Clarendon Press.

Exner, K.

1939 Die provinzialrömischen Emailfibeln der Rheinlande. *Bericht der Römisch-Germanischen Kommission* 29: 31–121.

Farrar, R. A. H.

1973 The Techniques and Sources of Romano-British Black-Burnished Ware. In A. P. Detsicas (ed.), *Current Research in Romano-British Coarse Pottery,* 67–103. CBA Research Report 10. London: CBA.

Faull, M. L.

1975 The Semantic Development of Old English *wealh*. *Leeds Studies in English* 8: 20–44.

Fick, O. K. W.

1974 Vergleichend morphologische Untersuchungen am Einzelknochen europaïscher Taubenarten. Diss. University of Munich.

Fieller, N. J. R., and A. Turner

1982 Number Estimation in Vertebrate Samples. *JArchSc* 9: 49–62.

Finberg, H. P. R.

1964 *The Early Charters of Wessex*. Leicester: Leicester University Press.

Fischer, U.

1973 Grabungen im römischen Steinkastell von Heddernheim 1957–1959. Schriften des Frankfurter Museums für vor- und frühgeschichte. Frankfurt am Main: Kramer.

Flight, C., and A. C. Harrison

1978 Rochester Castle. *Archaeologia Cantinana* 94: 27–60.

Flower, B., and E. Rosenbaum (trans.)

1958 *The Roman Cookery Book: A Critical Translation of* The Art of Cooking *by Apicius; for Use in the Study and the Kitchen*. London: Harrap.

Forbes, R. J.

1955 *Studies in Ancient Technology,* vol. 3. Leiden: Brill.

Ford, S., M. Bowden, V. Gaffney, and G. Mees

1988 The Date of the "Celtic" Field-Systems on the Berkshire Downs. *Britannia* 19: 401–404.

Ford, S., V. Gaffney, M. Tingle, and G. Mees

1994 Field Systems on the Berkshire Downs. In N. Miller and K. Gleason (eds.), *The Archaeology of Garden and Field*. Philadelphia: University of Pennsylvania Press.

Forster, E. S., and E. H. Heffner, (eds. and trans.)

1954 On Agriculture, vol. 2. Translation of Columella, *De Re Rustica*. London: W. Heinemann.

Fowler, E.

1968 Hanging Bowls. In J. M. Coles and D. D. A. Simpson (eds.), *Studies in Ancient Europe,* 287–310. Leicester: Leicester University Press.

1970 Non-Ferrous Metalwork. In H. S. Gracie, Frocester Court Roman Villa, Gloucestershire: First Report, 1961–67. Building A. *Transactions of the Bristol and Gloucester Archaeological Society* 89: 53–66.

Fowler, P. J.

1966 Two Finds of Saxon Domestic Pottery in Wiltshire. *WAM* 61: 31–37.

1967 The Archaeology of Fyfield and Overton Downs, Wiltshire. Third Interim Report. *WAM* 62: 16–33.

1971 Hillforts, A.D. 400–700. In M. Jesson and D. Hill (eds.), *The Iron Age and Its Hill Forts.* Southhampton.

1975a Continuity in the Landscape? A Summary of Some Local Archaeology in Wiltshire, Somerset, and Gloucestershire. In P. J. Fowler (ed.), *Recent Work in Rural Archaeology,* 121–36. Totowa, New Jersey: Rowman and Littlefield.

1975b Review of E. R. B. Pugh and E. Critall (eds.), *A History of Wiltshire. Britannia* 6: 301–303.

Fowler, P. J., and H. C. Bowen
1966 Romano-British Settlements in Dorset and Wiltshire. In C. Thomas (ed.), *Rural Settlement in Roman Britain,* 43–67. CBA Research Report 7. London: CBA.

Fowler, P. J. and J. G. Evans
1965 Plough-marks, Lynchets and Early Fields. *Antiquity* 41: 289–301.

Fowler, P. J., and B. Walters
1981 Archaeology and the M4 Motorway, 1969–71, Tormarton, County of Avon, to Ermin Street, Berkshire. *WAM* 74–75 (for 1979–1980): 69–131.

Fox, A., and C. Fox
1958 Wansdyke Reconsidered. *AJ* 115: 1–48.

Fox, C.
1946 *A Find of the Early Iron Age from Llyn Cerrig Bach, Anglesey.* Cardiff: National Museum of Wales.

1958 *Pattern and Purpose: A Survey of Early Celtic Art in Britain.* Cardiff: National Museum of Wales.

Fremersdorf, F.
1967 *Die römischen Gläser mit Schliff, Bemalung und Goldauflagen aus Koln.* Cologne: Reykers.

Frere, S. S.
1967 *Britannia: A History of Roman Britain.* London: Routledge and K. Paul.

1972 *Verulamium Excavations,* vol. 1. SAL Research Report 28. London: Society of Antiquaries.

1983a *Verulamium Excavations,* vol. 2. SAL Research Report 41. London: Society of Antiquaries.

1983b Roman Britain in 1982. Sites Explored. *Britannia* 14: 279–335.

1984a *Verulamium Excavations,* vol. 3. OUCA Monograph 1. Oxford: Oxford Committee for Archaeology.

1984b Roman Britain in 1983. Sites Explored. *Britannia* 15: 266–332.

1985 Roman Britain in 1985. Sites Explored. *Britannia* 16: 251–316.

1988 Roman Britain in 1987. Sites Explored. *Britannia* 19: 415–26.

1989 Roman Britain in 1988. Sites Explored. *Britannia* 20: 257–319.

1990 Roman Britain in 1990. Sites Explored. *Britannia* 21: 303–64.

1992 Roman Britain in 1991. Sites Explored. *Britannia* 23: 255–308.

Frere, S. S., and J. K. S. St. Joseph
1983 *Roman Britain from the Air.* Cambridge Air Surveys Series. Cambridge: Cambridge University Press.

Frey, O.-H., with J. V. S. Megaw
1976 Palmette and Circle: Early Celtic Art in Britain and Its Continental Background. *Proceedings of the Prehistoric Society* 42: 47–65.

Fulford, M.
1975a The Roman Pottery. In B. W. Cunliffe, *Excavations at Portchester Castle: 1. Roman,* 270–365. SAL Research Report 32. London: Society of Antiquaries.

1975b *New Forest Roman Pottery.* BAR British Series 17. Oxford: B.A.R.

1982 Town and Country in Roman Britain—A Parasitical Relationship. In D. Miles (ed.), *The Romano-British Countryside: Studies in Rural Settlement and Economy,* 403–19. BAR British Series 103 (ii). Oxford: B.A.R.

1984 The Roman Pottery. In M. Fulford, *Silchester: Excavations on the Defences 1974–80.* Britannia Monograph Series 5. 122–187. London: Society for the Promotion of Roman Studies.

1989 The Economy of Roman Britain. In M. Todd, *Research on Roman Britain: 1960–89*, 175–201. Britannia Monograph Series 11. London: Society for the Promotion of Roman Studies.

Gaffney, V., and M. Tingle

1985 The Maddle Farm (Berks.) Project and Micro-Regional Analysis. In S. Macready and F. H. Thompson (eds.), *Archaeological Field Survey in Britain and Abroad.* OPSAL, ns. 6, 67–73. London: Society of Antiquaries.

1989 *The Maddle Farm Project. An Integrated Survey of Prehistoric and Roman Landscapes on the Berkshire Downs.* BAR British Series 200. Oxford: B.A.R.

Galloway, P.

1976 Note on Descriptions of Bone and Antler Combs. *Medieval Archaeology* 20: 154–56.

Galloway, P., and M. Newcomer

1981 The Craft of Comb-Making: An Experimental Enquiry. *BIAL* 18: 73–90.

Gelling, M.

1976 *The Place-Names of Berkshire.* Part 3, *The Old English Charter Boundaries of Berkshire.* English Place-Name Society, vol. 51. Cambridge: Cambridge University Press.

1988 *Signposts to the Past: Place-Names and the History of England* 2d ed. Chichester: Phillimore.

Gentry, A. P.

1976 *Roman Military Stone-Built Granaries in Britain.* BAR British Series 32. Oxford: B.A.R.

Gilchrist, R.

1988 A Reappraisal of Dinas Powys: Local Exchange and Specialised Livestock Production in Fifth-to-Seventh-Century Wales. *Medieval Archaeology* 32: 50–62.

Gillam, J. P.

1976 Coarse Fumed Ware in North Britain and Beyond. *Glasgow Archaeological Journal* 4: 57–80.

Gingell, C. J.

1978 The Excavation of an Early Anglo-Saxon Cemetery at Collingbourne Ducis. *WAM* 70–71 (for 1975–1976): 61–98.

Gingell, C. J., and A. J. Lawson

1985 Excavations at Potterne, 1984. *WAM* 79 (for 1984): 101–108.

Gleason, K. L.

1991 Toward an Archaeology of Landscape Architecture in the Ancient Roman World. Ph.D. diss., Oxford University.

Goddard, E. H.

1897 Notes on Roman Remains at Box. *WAM* 26: 405–409.

1902 Thursday, 18 December 1902. In *Proceedings of the Society of Antiquaries,* 2d ser., 19: 175–89.

1908 Notes on Objects of "Late Celtic" Character Found in Wiltshire. *WAM* 35: 389–407.

1913 List of Prehistoric, Roman, and Pagan Saxon Antiquities in the County of Wilts. Arranged under Parishes. *WAM* 38: 153–378.

1928 Roman Building on Draycott Farm near Huish. *WAM* 44: 270.

Goodburn, R.

1976 Roman Britain in 1975. Sites Explored. *Britannia* 7: 290–377.

1978 Winterton: Some Villa Problems. In M. Todd (ed.), Villas and Romano-British Society. *Studies in the Romano-British Villa,* 93–102. Leicester: Leicester University Press.

1984 The Non-Ferrous Metal Objects. In S. S. Frere (ed.), *Verulamium Excavations,* vol 3., 19–67. OUCA Monograph 1. Oxford: Oxford University Committee for Archaeology.

Goodchild, R., and J. Kirk

1954 The Romano-Celtic Temple at Woodeaton. *Oxoniensia* 19: 15–37.

Gover, J. E. B., A. Mawer, and F. M. Stenton

1939 (1970) *The Place-Names of Wiltshire.* English Place-Name Society, vol. 16. Cambridge: The University Press.

Grant, A.

1982 The Use of Tooth Wear as a Guide to the Age of Domestic Ungulates. In B. Wilson, C. Grigson, and S. Payne (eds.), *Ageing and Sexing Animal Bones from Archaeological Sites*. BAR British Series 109: 91–108. Oxford: B.A.R.

1989 Animal Bones in Roman Britain. In M. Todd (ed.), Research on Roman Britain: 1960–1989. Britannia Monograph Series 11: 135–46. London: Society for the Promotion of British Studies.

Green, C. M.

1980 The Roman Pottery. In D. M. Jones, *Excavations at Billingsgate Buildings "Triangle," Lower Thames Street, 1974*. LMASSP 4: 39–81. London: London and Middlesex Archaeological Society.

Green, F. J.

1981 Iron Age, Roman and Saxon Crops: The Archaeological Evidence from Wessex. In M. K. Jones and G. W. Dimbleby (eds.), *The Environment of Man: The Iron Age to the Anglo-Saxon Period,* 129–53. BAR British Series 87. Oxford: B.A.R.

Green, H. S.

1971 Wansdyke, Excavations 1966 to 1970. *WAM* 66: 129–46.

Green, M. J.

1976 *A Corpus of Religious Material from the Civilian Areas of Roman Britain*. BAR 24. Oxford: B.A.R.

1983 *The Gods of Roman Britain*. Shire Archaeology 34. Aylesbury: Shire.

1986 *The Gods of the Celts*. Gloucester: Sutton.

Greenfield, E.

1963 The Romano-British Shrines at Brigstock, Northhants. *AntJ* 43: 228–63.

Greenough, A. P.

1987 An Examination of Roman Iron Working Residues from Loughour, West Glamorgan, Wales. *Journal of the History of Metallurgy Society* 21:1: 25–27.

Greep, S. J.

1982 Two Early Roman Handles from the Walbrook, London. *AJ* 139: 91–100.

1983 *Objects of Animal Bone, Antler, Ivory and Teeth from Roman Britain*. Ph.D. thesis, University College, Cardiff.

Gregson, M.

1988 The Villa as Private Property. In K. Branigan and D. Miles (eds.), *Villas Economies. Economic Aspects of Romano-British Villas,* 211–33. Sheffield: University of Sheffield.

Greig, J. R. A.

1983 Plant Foods in the Past: A Review of the Evidence from Northern Europe. *Journal of Plant Foods* 5: 197–214.

Grew, F.

1982 Metal Objects. In S. S. Frere (ed.), The Bignor Villa. *Britannia* 13: 135–95.

Griffiths, N.

1983 Early Roman Military Metalwork from Wiltshire. *WAM* 77 (for 1982), 49–60.

Grimal, P.

1963 *The Civilization of Rome*. Trans. W. S. Maguiness. New York: Simon and Schuster.

Grimes, W. F.

1961 Some Smaller Settlements: A Symposium. In S. S. Frere (ed.), *Problems of the Iron Age in Southern Britain*. Institute of Archaeology Occasional Paper 11: 17–28. London: University of London.

Grinsell, L. V.

1957 Gazetteer. In R. B. Pugh and E. Crittall (eds.), *A History of Wiltshire*. VCH 1:1. London: Oxford University Press.

Grose, D. F.

1974 Roman Glass of the First Century A.D., A Dated Deposit of Glassware from Cosa, Italy. *Annales du 6e Congrés de l'Association Internationale l'Histoire du Verre*. Liége.

1977 Early Blown Glass, The Western Evidence. *JGS* 19: 9–29.

1984 Glass Forming Methods in Classical Antiquity: Some Considerations. *JGS* 26: 25–34.

1989 *Early Ancient Glass: The Core-Formed, Rod-Formed, and Cast Vessels and Objects From the Late Bronze Age to the Early Roman Empire, 1600 B.C. to A.D. 50.* New York: Hudson Hills.

Groube, L. M., and M. C. B. Bowden

1982 *The Archaeology of Rural Dorset. Past, Present and Future,* edited by Richard Bradley. Dorset Natural History and Archaeological Society Monograph Series 4. Dorchester.

Grundy, G. B.

1918 The Ancient Highways and Tracks of Wiltshire, Berkshire, and Hampshire and the Saxon Battlefields of Wiltshire. *AJ* 75: 69–194.

1919 The Saxon Land Charters of Wiltshire (First Series). *AJ* 76: 143–301.

1920 Saxon Land Charters of Wiltshire (Second Series). *AJ* 77: 8–126.

Guido, M.

1978 *The Glass Beads of the Prehistoric and Roman Periods in Britain and Ireland.* SAL Research Report 35. London: Society of Antiquaries.

Hallam, S. J.

1964 Villages in Roman Britain: Some Evidence. *AntJ* 44: 19–32.

Hamson, A. C.

1978 Rochester Castle. *Archaeologia Cantiana* 94: 27–60.

Hanley, R.

1987 *Villages in Roman Britain.* Shire Archaeology, 49. Aylesbury, Shire Publications.

Hanworth, R.

1968 The Roman Villa at Rapsley, Ewhurst. *SAC* 65: 1–70.

Harden, D. B.

1947 The Glass. In C. F. C. Hawkes and M. R. Hull, *Camulodunum:* 287–307. Oxford: University Press.

1958 Domestic Window Glass, Roman, Saxon, and Medieval. *Studies in Building History, Essays in Recognition of the Work of B. H. St. J. O'Neil,* 39–63. London: Oldhams.

1963 The Glass. In L. Alcock, *Dinas Powys,* 178–88. Cardiff: University of Wales Press.

Harden, D., and C. M. Green

1978 A Late Roman Grave-group from the Minories, Aldgate. In J. Bird, H. Chapman, and J. Clark, (eds.) *Collectanea Londiniensia: Studies in London Archaeology and History Presented to Ralph Merrifield.* LMASSP 2: 163–76. London: London and Middlesex Archaeological Society.

Härke, H.

1990 Warrior Graves? The Background of the Anglo-Saxon Weapon Burial Rite. *Past and Present* 126: 22–43.

Haselgrove, C.

1984 Celtic Coins found in Britain, 1977–82. *BIAL* 20: 107–54.

1989 The Later Iron Age in Southern Britain and Beyond. In M. Todd (ed.), *Research on Roman Britain, 1960–89,* 1–18. Britannia Monograph Series 11. London: Society for the Promotion of Roman Studies.

Haslam, J.

1976 *Wiltshire Towns: The Archaeological Potential.* Devizes: Wiltshire Archaeological and Natural History Society.

1980 A Middle Saxon Iron Smelting Site at Ramsbury, Wiltshire. *Medieval Archaeology* 24: 1–68.

1984 The Towns of Wiltshire. In J. Haslam (ed.) *Anglo-Saxon Towns in Southern England,* 87–147. Chichester: Phillimore.

Hassall, M., and J. Rhodes

1974 Excavations at the New Market Hall, Gloucester, 1966–7. *Transactions of the Bristol and Gloucester Archaeological Society* 93: 15–100.

Hattatt, R.

1982 *Ancient and Romano-British Brooches.* Sherborne, Dorset: Dorset.

1985 *Iron Age and Roman Brooches: A Second Selection of Brooches from the Author's Collection.* Oxford: Oxbow.

1987 *Brooches of Antiquity: A Third Selection of Brooches from the Author's Collection.* Oxford: Oxbow.

Hattatt, R., and G. Webster

1985 New Light on "Adlocutio" Repoussé Disc Brooches. *AntJ* 65: 434–37.

Haupt, D.

1970 Jahresbericht 1968. Jakobwüllesheim. *BJ* 170: 385–87.

Haverfield, F.

1900 Romano-British Remains. In H. A. Doubleday (ed.), *A History of Hampshire and the Isle of Wight, VCH:* 1: 265–349. London.

Hawkes, S. C.

1968 The Late Roman Military Belt-Fittings. In A. C. C. Brodribb, A. R. Hands, and D. R. Walker, *Excavations at Shakenoak Farm, near Wilcote, Oxfordshire,* Part I, *Sites A and D:* 96–101. Oxford.

Hawkes, S. C., and G. C. Dunning

1961 Soldiers and Settlers in Britain, Fourth to Fifth Century. With a Catalogue of Animal-Ornamented Buckles and Related Belt-Fittings. *Medieval Archaeology* 5: 1–70.

Hedges, R. E. M., R. A. Housley, I. A. Law, and C. R. Bronk

1989 Radiocarbon Dates from the Oxford AMS System: *Archaeometry* Datelist 9. *Archaeometry* 31:2: 207–34.

Hedges, R. E. M., R. A. Housley, I. A. Law, and C. Penny

1988 Radiocarbon Dates from the Oxford AMS System: *Archaeometry* Datelist 8. *Archaeometry* 30:2: 291–305.

Helbaek, H.

1952 Early Crops in Southern England. *Proceedings of the Prehistoric Society* 18: 194–233.

Henig, M.

1978 *Corpus of Roman Engraved Gemstones from British Sites.* 2d ed. BAR British Series 8. Oxford: B.A.R.

1985 Bronzes and Other Non-Ferrous Metalwork. In J. Draper (ed.), *Excavations by Mr. H. P. Cooper on the Roman Site at Hill Farm, Gestingthorpe, Essex,* 29–44. East Anglian Archaeology Report 25. Essex: Essex County Council.

Henkel, F.

1913 Die römischen Fingerringe der Rheinlande und der benachbarten Gebiete. 2 vols. Berlin: Reimer.

Hewitt, A. R. M.

1969 *The Roman Villa, West Park, Rockbourne.* Fordingbridge, Hants.: A. R. M. Hewitt.

Higham, N.

1992 *Rome, Britain and the Anglo-Saxons.* London: Seaby.

Hill, D.

1969 The Burghal Hidage: The Establishment of a Text. *Medieval Archaeology* 13: 84–92.

Hill, D., and D. M. Metcalf

1984 (eds.), *Sceattas in England and on the Continent: The Seventh Oxford Symposium on Coinage and Monetary History.* BAR British Series 128. Oxford: B.A.R.

Hillman, G. C.

1980 Grain Processing at 3rd Century Wilderspool. In J. Hinchcliffe and J. H. Williams (eds.), *Excavations at Wilderspool.* London.

1981 Reconstructing Crop Husbandry Practices from Charred Remains of Crops. In R. Mercer (ed.), *Farming Practice in British Prehistory:* 123–66. Edinburgh: University Press.

1982 Evidence for Malting Spelt. In R. Leech (ed.), *Excavations at Catsgore 1970–1973,* 137–41. Western Archaeological Trust Monograph 2. Bristol: Western Archaeological Trust.

1984 Interpretation of Archaeological Plant Remains: The Application of Ethnographic Models from Turkey. In W. van Zeist and W. A. Casparie (eds.), *Plants and Ancient Man: Studies in Palaeoethnobotany:* 1–42. Rotterdam: Balkema.

Hingley, R.
1982 Roman Britain: The Structure of Roman Imperialism and the Consequences of Imperialism on the Development of a Peripheral Province. In D. Miles (ed.), *The Romano-British Countryside. Studies in Rural Settlement and Economy,* vol. 1, 17–52 BAR British Series 103. Oxford: B.A.R.
1989 *Rural Settlement in Roman Britain.* London: Seaby.
1991 The Romano-British Countryside: The Significance of Rural Settlement Forms. In R. F. J. Jones, *Roman Britain: Recent Trends,* 75–80. Chippenham: Collis.

Hinks, R. P.
1933 *Catalogue of Greek, Etruscan and Roman Paintings and Mosaics in the British Museum.* London: British Museum.

Hirst, S., and P. Rahtz
1976 *Interim Note on Liddington Castle, Wiltshire, England, 1976.* Typescript duplicated.

Hodder, I.
1974a The Distribution of Savernake Ware. *WAM* 69: 67–84.
1974b The Distribution of Two Types of Romano-British Coarse Pottery. *SAC* 112: 86–96.
1974c Some Marketing Models for Romano-British Coarse Pottery. *Britannia* 5: 340–59.
1979 Pre-Roman and Romano-British Tribal Economies. In B. C. Burnham and H. B. Johnson (eds.), *Invasion and Response: The Case of Roman Britain,* 189–96. BAR British Series 73. Oxford: B.A.R.

Hodder, I., and M. Millet
1980 Romano-British Villas and Towns: A Systematic Analysis. *World Archaeology* 12:1: 69–76.

Hooke, D.
1988 Regional Variation in Southern and Central England in the Anglo-Saxon Period and Its Relationship to Land Units and Settlement. In D. Hooke (ed.), *Anglo-Saxon Settlements:* 123–51. Oxford: Blackwell.

Hooper, W. D., and H. B. Ash (trans.)
1935 *Cato and Varro: On Agriculture.* London: Heinemann.

Hostetter, E.
1985 Preliminary Report on Excavations at Castle Copse, Great Bedwyn, 1983–84. *WAM* 79 (for 1984): 233–35.

Hostetter, E., and T. N. Howe
1986a Preliminary Report on Excavations of the Late Roman Villa at Castle Copse, Great Bedwyn, 1985. *WAM* 80: 97–102.
1986b The Romano-British Villa of Castle Copse. *Archaeology* 39:5: 36–43.

Hostetter, E., T. N. Howe, and J. F. Kenfield
1987 Preliminary Report of the Late Roman Villa at Castle Copse, Great Bedwyn, 1986. *WAM* 81: 52–56.

Howe, M. D., J. R. Perrin and D. M. Mackreth
1980 *Roman Pottery from the Nene Valley: A Guide.* Peterborough.

Hull, M. R., and S. C. Hawkes
1987 *Corpus of Ancient Brooches in Britain: Pre-Roman Bow Brooches.* BAR British Series 168. Oxford: B.A.R.

Hurst, H. R.
1985 *Kingsholm.* Gloucester Archaeological Reports 1. Cambridge: Gloucester Archaeological Publications.

Hurst, H. R., D. L. Dartnall, and C. Fisher
1987 Excavations at Box Roman Villa, 1967–68. *WAM* 81: 19–51.

Hutt, F. B.
1949 *Genetics of the Fowl.* New York: McGraw-Hill.

Hutchinson, V. J.
1986 *Bacchus in Roman Britain: The Evidence for His Cult,* 2. BAR British Series 151. Oxford: B.A.R.

IGS

1947 Institute of Geological Sciences (Great Britain), Geological Map of Hungerford (Drift edition). Geological Maps of England and Wales: Sheet 267.

1959 Institute of Geological Sciences (Great Britain), Geological Map of Devizes (Drift edition). Geological Maps of England and Wales: Sheet 282.

1974 Institute of Geological Sciences (Great Britain), Geological Map of Marlborough (Drift edition). Geological Maps of England and Wales: Sheet 266.

1975 Institute of Geological Sciences (Great Britain), Geological Map of Andover (Drift edition). Geological Maps of England and Wales: Sheet 283.

IGS and TWA

1978 Institute of Geological Sciences (Great Britain) and Thames Water Authority, Hydrogeological Map of the South West Chilterns and the Berkshire and Marlborough Downs.

Iliffe, J. H.

1932 Excavations at Alchester, 1928. *AntJ* 12: 35–116.

Isings, C.

1957 *Roman Glass From Dated Finds.* Archaeologica Traiectina, 2. Groningen: Wolters.

Issac, P. J.

1976 Coin Hoards and History in the West. In K. Branigan and P. J. Fowler (eds.), *The Roman West Country. Classical Culture and Celtic Society,* 52–62. Newton Abbot, North Pomfret, Vt.: David and Charles.

Jackson, K.

1953 *Language and History in Early Britain; A Chronological Survey of the Brittonic Languages, First to Twelfth Century A.D.* Edinburgh: University Press.

1970 Appendix II. Romano-British Names in the Antonine Itinerary. In A. L. F. Rivet, The British Section of the Antonine Itinerary. *Britannia* 1: 34–82.

Jackson, R. E.

1854 Leland's Journey through Wiltshire, A.D. 1540–42. With a Memoir and Notes. *WAM* 1: 132–95.

Jarvis, K., and V. Maxfield

1975 The Excavation of a First-Century Roman Farmstead and a Late Neolithic Settlement, Topsham, Devon. *Proceedings of the Devonshire Archaeological Society.* 33: 209–65.

Jessup, R.

1953 *Anglo-Saxon Jewellery.* New York: Praeger.

Johnson, P.

1982 *Romano-British Mosaics.* Shire Archaeology 25. Aylesbury: Shire.

Johnson, P., and B. Walters

1988 Exploratory Excavations of Roman Buildings at Cherhill and Manningford Bruce. *WAM* 82: 77–91.

Jones, A. K. G.

1984 Some Effects of the Mammalian Digestive System on Fish Bones. In N. Desse-Berset (ed.), *2nd Fish Osteoarchaeology Meeting.* Centre de Recherches Archéologiques. Notes et Monographies Techniques 16: 61–65. Paris: C.N.R.S.

1986 Fish Bone Survival in the Digestive System of Pig, Dog and Man: Some Experiments. In D.C. Brinkhuizen and A.T. Clason (eds.), *Fish and Archaeology,* 53–61. BAR International Series 294. Oxford: B.A.R.

1988 Provisional Remarks on Fish Bones from Archaeological Deposits at York. In P. Murphy and C. French (eds.), *The Exploitation of Wetlands.* BAR British Series 186: 117–27. Oxford: B.A.R.

Jones, G. E. M.

1984 Interpretation of Archaeological Plant Remains: Ethnographic Models from Greece. In W. van Zeist and W. A. Casparie (eds.), *Plants and Ancient Man: Studies in Palaeoethnobotany,* 43–62. Rotterdam: Balkema.

Jones, M.
  1981 The Development of Crop Husbandry. In M. Jones and G. Dimbleby (eds.), *The Environment of Man: The Iron Age to the Anglo-Saxon Period,* 95–127. BAR British Series 87. Oxford: B.A.R.
  1982 Crop Production in Roman Britain. In D. Miles, (ed.), *The Romano-British Countryside,* 97–107. BAR British Series 103. Oxford: B.A.R.
  1986 Towards a Model of the Villa Estate. In D. Miles (ed.), *Archaeology at Barton Court Farm, Abingdon, Oxon,* 38–42. Oxford Archaeological Unit Report 3; CBA Research Report 50. Oxford and London: Oxford Archaeological Unit and Council for British Archaeology.
  1989 Agriculture in Roman Britain: The Dynamics of Change. In M. Todd (ed.), *Research on Roman Britain: 1960–89,* 127–34. Britannia Monograph Series 11. London: Society for the Promotion of Roman Studies.
  1991 Food Production and Consumption—Plants. In R. F. J. Jones, *Roman Britain: Recent Trends:* 21–27. Chippenham: Collis.
Jones, M. E.
  1979 Climate, Nutrition and Disease: A Hypothesis of Romano-British Population. In P. J. Casey, *The End of Roman Britain,* 231–51. BAR British Series 71. Oxford: B.A.R.
Jones, M. L.
  1984 *Society and Settlement in Wales and the Marches 500 B.C. to A.D. 1100.* 2 vols. BAR British Series 121. Oxford: B.A.R.
Juhn, M.
  1952 Spur Growth and Differentiation in the Adult Thiouracil-Treated Fowl. *Physiological Zoology* 25: 150–62.
Jukes-Browne, A. J.
  1905 *The Geology of the Country South and East of Devizes.* (explanation of Sheet 282) Memoirs of the Geological Survey, England and Wales. London: H. M. Stationery Office.
  1908 *The Geology of the Country around Andover.* (explanation of Sheet 283) Memoirs of the Geological Survey, England and Wales. London: H. M. Stationery Office.
Keely, J.
  1986 The Pottery. In A. McWhirr, *Houses in Roman Cirencester.* Cirencester Excavations 3: 153–89. Cirencester: Cirencester Excavation Committee, Corinium Museum.
Keller, E.
  1971 *Die Spätrömischen Grabfunde in Südbayern.* Vol. 8 of *Veröffentlichung der Kommission zur archäologischen Erforschung des spätrömischen Raetien der bayerischen Akademie der Wissenschaften.* Munich: Beck.
Kent, J. P. C.
  1981 The Family of Constantine I, A.D. 337–364. Vol. 8 of *The Roman Imperial Coinage,* ed. H. Mattingly et al. 78–89. London: Spink and Son.
Kenyon, K. M.
  1948 *Excavations at the Jewry Wall Site, Leicester.* SAL Research Report 15. London: Society of Antiquaries.
Keynes, S., and M. Lapidge (trans.)
  1983 *Alfred the Great. Asser's Life of King Alfred and Other Contemporary Sources.* Translation of John Asser, *De Rebus Gestis Aelfredi.* Harmondsworth: Penguin.
Kilbride-Jones, H. E.
  1980 *Celtic Craftmanship in Bronze.* London: Croom Helm.
  1987 Repoussé Disc Brooches: Date and Manufacture. *AntJ* 67: 129–30.
King, A. C.
  1978 A Comparative Survey of Bone Assemblages from Roman Sites in Britain. *BIAL* 15: 207–32.
  1984 Animal Bones and the Dietary Identity of Military and Civilian Groups in Roman Britain, Germany and Gaul. In T. F. C. Blagg and A. C. King (eds.), *Military and Civilian in Roman Britain: Cultural Relationships in a Frontier Province,* 187–217. BAR British Series 136. Oxford: B.A.R.

1991 Food Production and Consumption—Meat. In R. F. J. Jones, *Roman Britain: Recent Trends:* 15–20. Chippenham: Collis.

King, C. E.
1981 The Circulation of Coin in the Western Provinces, A.D. 260–295. In A. King and M. Henig (eds.), *The Roman West in the Third Century.* 2 vols. 89–126. BAR International Series 109. Oxford: B.A.R.

King, N. E.
1968 The Kennet Valley Sarsen Industry. *WAM* 63: 83–93.

Kirk, J.
1949 Bronzes from Woodeaton, Oxon. *Oxoniensia* 14: 1–45.

Kirk. J. R., and E. T. Leeds.
1952–53 Three Early Saxon Graves from Dorchester, Oxon. *Oxoniensia* 17–18: 63–76.

Kozelka, A. W.
1933 Spurlessness of the White Leghorn. *Journal of Heredity* 24: 71–78.

Krantz, G. S.
1968 A New Method of Counting Mammal Bones. *AJA* 72: 286–88.

Lamb, H. H.
1972–77 *Climate: Present, Past and Future.* 2 vols. London: Methuen.
1982 *Climate, History, and the Modern World.* London: Methuen.

Landauer, W.
1934 Studies on the Creeper Fowl. VI. Skeletal Growth of Creeper Chickens. *Storrs (Connecticut) Agr. Expt. Sta. Bull.* 193.

Landauer, W., and L. C. Dunn
1930 Studies on the Creeper Fowl. I. Genetics. *Journal of Genetics* 23: 397–413.

Latimer, H. B.
1927 Postnatal Growth of the Chick Skeleton. *American Journal of Anatomy* 40: 1–54.

Leach, P. E.
1982 The Ironwork. In P. E. Leach, *Ilchester,* vol. 1, 255–59. Excavation Monograph 3. Bristol: Western Archaeological Trust.

Leech, R. H.
1976 Larger Agricultural Settlements in the West Country. In K. Branigan and P. J. Fowler (eds.), *The Roman West Country: Classical Culture and Celtic Society,* 142–61. Newton Abbot, North Pomfret, Vt.: David and Charles.

Leeds, E. T.
1933 *Celtic Ornament in the British Isles Down to. A.D. 700.* Oxford: Clarendon Press.

Leopold, L. B.
1974 *Water; A Primer.* San Francisco: Freeman.

Levine, P. J. A.
1986 *The Amateur and the Professional: Antiquarians, Historians, and Archaeologists in Victorian England, 1838–1886.* Cambridge: Cambridge University Press.

Levitan, B.
1989 The Vertebrate Remains from Chichester Cattlemarket. In A. Down, *Chichester Excavations,* vol. 6: 242–76. Chichester: Chichester Excavations Committee.

Limbrey, S.
1975 *Soil Science and Archaeology.* London: Academic Press.

Ling, R.
1985 *Romano-British Wall Painting.* Aylesbury: Shire.

Liversidge, J.
1968 *Britain in the Roman Empire.* London: Routledge and K. Paul.
1969 Furniture and Interior Decoration. In A. L. F. Rivet (ed.), *The Roman Villa, in Britain,* 127–72. New York: Praeger.
1977 Recent Developments in Romano-British Wall Painting. In J. Munby and M. Henig (eds.), *Roman Life and Art in Britain,* Pt. 1, 75–103. British Archaeologic Reports 41: 75–103. Oxford: B.A.R.

————, (ed.) 1982 *Roman Provincial Wall Painting of the Western Empire.* BAR International Series 140. Oxford: B.A.R.

Luff, R.-M.
1982 *A Zooarchaeological Study of the Roman North-Western Provinces.* BAR International Series 137. Oxford: B.A.R.

Lukis, W. C.
1854 Contribution to the Museum and Library. *WAM* 1: 216.
1857 A List of Articles Exhibited in the Temporary Museum at the New Town Hall, Chippenham, Collingbourne Ducis. *WAM* 3: 13–18.

Lukis, W. C., and J. Ward
1860 Great Bedwyn. *WAM* 6: 261–316.

Lyne, M. A. B., and R. S. Jefferies
1979 *The Alice Holt/Farnham Roman Pottery Industry.* CBA Research Report 30. London: CBA.

Lysons, S.
1797 *An Account of Roman Antiquities Discovered at Woodchester in the County of Gloucester.* London: Cadell & Davies.
1813–17 *Reliquiae Britannico-Romanae,* vols. 1–3. London: T. Bensley, Cadell and Davies.

MacDonald, G., and A. O. Curle
1929 The Roman Fort at Mumrills, Near Falkirk. *PSAS* 63: 396–575.

MacGregor, A.
1976 *Finds from a Roman Sewer System and an Adjacent Building in Church Street. The Archaeology of York* 17:1.

MacGregor, M.
1976 *Early Celtic Art in North Britain.* 2 vols. Leicester: Leicester University Press.

MacGregor, M., and D. D. A. Simpson
1963 A Group of Iron Objects from Barbury Castle, Wilts. *WAM* 59: 394–402.

Mack, R. P.
1975 *The Coinage of Ancient Britain.* 3d ed. London: Spink and Son.

Mackreth, D. F.
1973 *Roman Brooches.* Salisbury: Salisbury and South Wiltshire Museum.
1976 The Brooches. In R. A. Chambers and G. Williams, A Late Iron Age and Romano-British Settlement at Hardwick. *Oxoniensia* 41: 25–26.
1983 Small Finds (Part One): The Roman Brooches. In D. Bramwell et al., Excavations at Poole's Cavern, Buxton: An Interim Report. *Derbyshire Archaeological Journal* 103: 62–74.
1986 Brooches. In D. Gurney, *Settlement, Religion and Industry on the Fen-edge: Three Romano-British Sites in Norfolk,* 61–67. East Anglian Archaeology Report 31. Dereham: Norfolk Archaeological Unit.

Mackreth, D. F., and S. A. Butcher.
1981 The Roman Brooches. In A. Down and M. Rule, *Chichester Excavations,* vol. 5, 254–61. Chichester: Chichester Excavations Committee.

Macready, S.
1976 *The Gallus Finds from Wicken Bonhunt.* Unpublished B.A. thesis, University of London; cited by King 1978.

MacWhirr, A.
1982 *Roman Crafts and Industries* Aylesbury: Shire.
1988 Cirencester (Corinium Dobunnorum). In G. Webster (ed.), *Fortress Into City,* 74–90. London: Batsford.

Major, A., and E. J. B. Burrow
1926 *The Mystery of Wansdyke.* Cheltenham: Burrow.

Maltby, M.
1979 *Faunal Studies on Urban Sites: The Animal Bones from Exeter 1971–1975.* Exeter Archaeological Reports 2. Sheffield: Dept. of Prehistory and Archaeology, University of Sheffield.
1990 *The Animal Bones from the Romano-British Deposits at the Greyhound Yard and Methodist Chapel Sites in Dorchester, Dorset.* Ancient Monuments Laboratory Report 9/90.

Manning, W. H.

1966a Caistor-by-Norwich and *Notitia Dignitatum. Antiquity* 40: 60–62.

1966b A Hoard of Romano-British Ironwork from Brampton, Cumberland. *TCWA* 66: 1–36.

1972 The Iron Objects. In S. S. Frere (ed.), *Verulamium Excavations I.* 163–95. SAL Research Report 28. London: Society of Antiquaries.

1974 Objects of Iron. In D. S. Neal, *The Excavation of the Roman Villa in Gadebridge Park, Hemel Hempstead, 1963–8,* 157–87. SAL Research Report 31. London: Society of Antiquaries.

1975 Roman Military Timber Granaries in Britain. *Saalburg* 32: 105–29.

1976a Blacksmithing. In D. Strong and D. Brown (eds.), *Roman Crafts,* 143–53. London: Duckworth.

1976b *Catalogue of Romano-British Ironwork in the Museum of Antiquities, Newcastle upon Tyne.* Newcastle upon Tyne: University of Newcastle upon Tyne.

1984a The Iron Objects. In S. S. Frere (ed.), *Verulamium Excavations,* vol. 3, 83–106. OUCA Monograph 1. Oxford: OUCA.

1984b Objects of Iron. In. S. S. Frere, Excavations at Dorchester on Thames, 1963. *AJ* 141: 91–174.

1985a Ironwork. In J. Draper (ed.), *Excavations by Mr. H. P. Cooper on the Roman Site at Hill Farm, Gestingthorpe, Essex.* EAAR 25: 46–57. Chelmsford, Essex.

1985b *Catalogue of the Romano-British Iron Tools, Fittings and Weapons in the British Museum.* London: British Museum Publications.

Manning, W. H., and C. Saunders

1972 A Socketed Iron Axe from Maids Moreton, Buckinghamshire, with a Note on the Type. *AntJ* 52: 276–92.

Margary, I. D.

1955 (1973) *Roman Roads in Britain.* 2 vols. London: Phoenix House. 3d ed. rev. 1973, London: Baker.

Marsden, B.

1974 *The Early Barrow-Diggers.* Park Ridge, N.J.: Noyes Press.

Mattingly, Harold, et al. (eds.)

1923 *The Roman Imperial Coinage.* 9 vols. London: Spink.

Maxfield, V. A.

1989 Conquest and Aftermath. In M. Todd (ed.), *Research on Roman Britain: 1960–89,* 19–29. Britannia Monograph Series 11. London: Society for the Promotion of Roman Studies.

Meaney, A. L. S.

1964 *A Gazetteer of Early Anglo-Saxon Burial Sites.* London: G. Allen and Unwin.

Mees, G.

1982 Phosphate Analysis at Claydon Pike. Unpublished paper.

Megaw, J. V. S.

1970 *Art of the European Iron Age: A Study of the Elusive Image.* Bath: Adams and Dart.

Megaw, J. V. S., and R. Merrifield

1970 The Dowgate Plaque: A Bronze Mount from the Belgic Iron Age from the City of London. *AntJ* 126: 154–59.

Megaw, M. R., and J. V. S. Megaw

1986 *Early Celtic Art in Britain and Ireland.* Shire Archaeology 38. Princes Risborough: Shire.

1989 *Celtic Art: From Its Beginnings to the* Book of Kells. London: Thames and Hudson.

1991 *The Basse-Yutz, Moselle, Find: Masterpieces of Celtic Art.* SAL Research Report 46. London: Society of Antiquaries.

Melville, R. V., and E. C. Freshney

1982 *British Regional Geology: the Hampshire Basin and Adjoining Areas. Institute of Geological Sciences.* 4th rev. ed. London: H. M. Stationery Off.

Metcalf, D. M.

1984 Monetary Circulation in Southern England in the First Half of the Eighth Century. In D. Hill and D. M. Metcalf (eds.), *Sceattas in England and on the Continent: The Seventh Oxford Symposium on Coinage and Monetary History,* 27–70. BAR British Series 128. Oxford: B.A.R.

Meyrick, O.

1946 Notes on Some Early Iron Age Sites in the Marlborough District. *WAM* 51: 256–63.

1949–50 A Saxon Skeleton in a Roman Well. *WAM* 53: 220–22.

Miles, D.

1977 The Honeyditches Roman Villa, Seaton, Devon. *Britannia* 8: 107–48.

1982 Confusion in the Countryside: Some Comments from the Upper Thames Valley. In D. Miles (ed.), *The Romano-British Countryside. Studies in Rural Settlement and Economy,* vol. 1, 53–79. BAR British Series 103. Oxford: B.A.R.

1984 Romano-British Settlement in the Gloucestershire Thames Valley. In A. Saville (ed.), *Archaeology in Gloucestershire,* 197–203. Cheltenham: Cheltenham Art Gallery and Museums, and Bristol and Gloucestershire Archaeological Society.

1986 *Archaeology at Barton Court Farm, Abingdon, Oxon.* CBA Research Report 50; Unit Report 3. Oxford: Oxford Archaeological Unit, and Council for British Archaeology.

1988 Villas and Variety: Aspects of Economy and Society in the Upper Thames Valley Landscape. In K. Branigan and D. Miles (eds.), *Villas Economies. Economic Aspects of Romano-British Villas,* 60–72. Sheffield: University of Sheffield.

1989 The Romano-British Countryside. In M. Todd (ed.), *Research on Roman Britain: 1960–1989,* 115–34. Britannia Monograph Series 11. London: Society for the Promotion of Roman Studies.

Millett, M. J.

1982 Distinguishing between the *Pes Monetalis* and the *Pes Drusianus:* Some Problems. *Britannia* 13: 315–20.

1990 *The Romanization of Britain.* New York, Cambridge: Cambridge University Press.

Milne, J. S.

1907 *Surgical Instruments in Greek and Roman Times.* Oxford: Clarendon.

Moffett, L.

1987 The Macrobotanical Evidence from Late Saxon and Early Medieval Stafford. Unpublished paper. Ancient Monument Laboratory.

Moore, R. E.

1978 A Newly Observed Stratum in Roman Floor Mosaics. *AJA* 72: 57–68.

Moorhead, T. S. N.

1984 The Easterton Hoard of Mid-Fourth Century Roman Coins. *WAM* 78 (for 1983): 41–49.

1990 Additional Coins to the Aldbourne Hoard. *WAM* 83: 201–205.

Morris, P.

1979 *Agricultural Buildings in Roman Britain.* BAR British Series 70. Oxford: B.A.R.

Mortimer, J. R.

1905 *Forty Years' Researches in British and Saxon Burial Mounds of East Yorkshire.* London: A. Brown and Sons.

Munro, R.

1882 *Ancient Scottish Lake Dwellings or Crannógs.* Edinburgh: Douglas.

Morales, A., and K. Rosenlund

1979 *Fish Bone Measurements: An Attempt to Standardize the Measuring of Fish Bones from Archaeological Sites.* Copenhagen: Steenstrupia.

Myres, J. N. L., and B. Green

1973 *The Anglo-Saxon Cemeteries of Caistor-by-Norwich and Markshall, Norfolk.* SAL Research Report 30. London: Society of Antiquaries.

Neal, D. S.

1981 *Roman Mosaics in Britain.* Gloucester: Alan Sutton.

—— (ed.)

1974 *Excavation of the Roman Villa in Gadebridge Park, Hemel Hempstead, 1963–68.* SAL Research Report 31. London: Society of Antiquaries.

Neal, D. S., and S. A. Butcher

1974 Miscellaneous Objects of Bronze. In D. S. Neal (ed.), *Excavation of the Roman Villa in Gadebridge Park, Hemel Hempstead, 1963–8,* 128–49. SAL Research Report 31. London: Society of Antiquaries.

Northover, P.

   1988 Copper, Tin, Silver and Gold in the Iron Age. In E. A. Slater and J. O. Tate (eds.), *Science and Archaeology, Glasgow 1987*. 2 vols., 223–33. BAR British Series 196. Oxford: B.A.R.

O'Connor, T. P.

   1984 Selected Groups of Bones from Skeldergate and Walmgate. *The Archaeology of York* 15:1. London: CBA.

   1986 The Animal Bones. In J. D. Zienkiewicz, *The Legionary Fortress Baths at Caerleon*. Vol. 2, *The Finds,* 225–48. Cardiff: National Museum of Wales, Welsh Historical Monuments.

   1988 Bones from the General Accident Site, Tanner Row. *The Archaeology of York* 15:2. London: CBA.

O'Neil, H.

   1953 Whittington Court Roman Villa. *TBGAS* 71: 13–87.

Parnell, G.

   1985 The Roman and Medieval Defences and the Later Development of the Inmost Ward, Tower of London: Excavations 1955–77. *Transactions of the London and Middlesex Archaeological Society* 36: 11–80.

Passmore, A. D.

   1914 Liddington Castle (Camp). *WAM* 38: 576–84.

   1920 Roman Wanborough. *WAM* 41: 272–80.

   1921 Notes on Roman Finds in North Wilts. *WAM* 41: 389–95.

   1928 Fieldwork in N. Wilts., 1926–28. *WAM* 44: 240–45.

   1934 A Saxon Saucer Brooch from Mildenhall. *WAM* 46: 393.

   1950 The Rudge Attis. *WAM* 53: 332.

Payne, R.

   1989 Bone Comb. In A. St. Clair and E. P. McLachlan (eds.), *The Carver's Art: Medieval Sculpture in Ivory, Bone, and Horn,* 101–102, no. 62. New Brunswick, N.J.: Jane Voorhees Zimmerli Art Museum, Rutgers.

Payne, S.

   1973 Kill-off Patterns in Sheep and Goats: The Mandibles from Aşvan Kale. *Anatolian Studies* 23: 281–303.

   1985 Morphological Distinctions Between the Mandibular Teeth of Young Sheep, *Ovis* and Goats, *Capra. Journal of Archaeological Science* 12: 139–47.

   1987 Reference Codes for Wear States in the Mandibular Cheek-teeth of Sheep and Goats. *Journal of Archaeological Science* 14: 609–614.

Payne, S., and G. Bull

   1989 Components of Variation in Measurements of Pig Bones and Teeth, and the Use of Measurements to Distinguish Wild from Domestic Pig Remains. *Archaeozoologia* 2: 27–65.

Payne, S., and P. Munson

   1985 Ruby and How Many Squirrels? The Destruction of Bones by Dogs. In N. R. J. Fieller, D. D. Gilbertson, and N. G. A. Ralph (eds.), *Palaeobiological Investigations: Research Design, Methods, and Data Analysis,* 31–39. BAR International Series 266. Oxford: B.A.R.

Peake, H. J. E., and F. H. Cheetham

   1924 Hundred of Kintbury Eagle. In W. Page and P. H. Ditchfield (eds.), *A History of Berkshire.* VCH 4: 156–245. London: Constable.

Peck, R. B., W. E. Hanson, and T. H. Thornburn

   1974 *Foundation Engineering*. 2d ed. New York: Wiley.

Percival, J.

   1976 *The Roman Villa*. London: Batsford.

   1988 The Villa Economy: Problems and Perspectives. In K. Branigan and D. Miles (eds.), *Villas Economies. Economic Aspects of Romano-British Villas,* 5–13. Sheffield: University of Sheffield.

Phillips, B.

   1981 Starveall Farm, Romano-British Villa. *WAM* 74 (for 1979–1980): 40–55.

Phillips, B., and B. Walters

   1977 A Mansio at Wanborough, Wiltshire. *Britannia* 8: 223–27.

1979 Archaeological Excavations in Littlecote Park, Wiltshire, 1978: First Interim Report. Privately published by *Littlecote Estate/Littlecote Roman Research Trust.*

1981 Archaeological Excavations in Littlecote Park, Wiltshire, 1979–80: Second Interim Report. Privately published by *Littlecote Estate/Littlecote Roman Research Trust.*

1983 Archaeological Excavations in Littlecote Park, Wiltshire, 1981–82: Third Interim Report. Privately published by *Littlecote Estate/Littlecote Roman Research Trust.*

1985 Archaeological Excavations in Littlecote Park, Wiltshire, 1983–84: Fourth Interim Report. Privately published by *Littlecote Estate/Littlecote Roman Research Trust.*

Piggott, S.

1953 Three Metal-Work Hoards of the Roman Period from Southern Scotland. *PSAS* 87: 1–50.

Pilloy, J.

1879 Études sur d'anciens lieux de sépulture dans l'Aisne I. St. Quentin.

Pitt-Rivers, A. H.

1892 *Excavations in Cranborne Chase,* Vol. 3, *Excavations in Bokerly and Wansdyke.* London.

Plesters, J.

1963 Examination of Roman Painted Wall Plaster. *WAM* 58: 337–41.

Pole, E. R.

1960 Story of Great Bedwyn. Further Information Collected since 1942. Typescript.

Poulett Scrope, G.

1862 On a Roman Villa Discovered at North Wraxall. *WAM* 7: 59–75.

Pratt, G. D.

1976 Excavations at 51–57 Rayne Road (Site E). In P. J. Drury (compiler), Braintree: Excavations and Research, 1971–76. *Essex Archaeology and History. Transactions of the Essex Archaeological Society* 8: 3–65.

Price, J.

1979 In H. S. Gracie and E. G. Price, Frocester Court Roman Villa, Second Report 1968–1977: The Courtyard. *Transactions of the Bristol and Gloucestershire Archaeological Society* 97: 43–44.

1981 The Glass. In M. Jarrett and S. Wrathmell, *Whitton, An Iron Age and Roman Farmstead in South Glamorgan,* 149–162. Cardiff: University of Wales Press.

1983 Roman Glass Vessels. In C. Heighway, *The East and North Gates of Gloucester,* Bristol: Western Archaeological Trust.

Price, J., and H. E. M. Cool

1985 Glass. *Kingsholm.* Gloucester Archaeological Reports 1: 41–54.

Pugh, R. B.

1981 Malmesbury and 1980. *WAM* 74–75 (for 1979–1980): 133–36.

Rackham, O.

1990 *Trees and Woodland in the British Landscape.* rev. ed. London: Dent.

Radford, C. A. R.

1928 The Roman Site at Westland, Yeovil. *Proceedings of the Somerset Archaeological and Natural History Society* 74: 122–43.

Raftery, B.

1983 *A Catalogue of Irish Iron Age Antiquities.* 2 vols. Veröffentlichung des Vorgeschichtliches Seminars Marburg. Sonderband 1. Marburg: Vorgeschichtliche Seminar.

1984 *La Tène in Ireland: Problems of Origin and Chronology.* Veröffentlichung des Vorgeschichtlichen Seminars Marburg. Sonderband 2. Marburg: Vorgeschichtliches Seminar.

Rahtz, P. A.

1961 Excavation on Bokerly Dyke. 118: 65–99. *ArchJour.*

1976 Buildings and Rural Settlement. In D. M. Wilson, *The Archaeology of Anglo-Saxon England:* 49–98. Cambridge, New York: Cambridge University Press.

Rainey, A.

1973 *Mosaics in Roman Britain.* Newton Abbot: David and Charles.

Rankov, N. B.

1982 Roman Britain in 1981. Sites Explored. *Britannia* 13: 328–95.

Ravetz, A.
1958 A Romano-British Site near Badbury, Wilts. *WAM* 57: 24–29.

Reece, R.
1972 A Short Survey of the Roman Coins Found in Fourteen Sites in Britain. *Britannia* 3: 269–76.
1976 From Corinium to Cirencester—Models and Misconceptions. In A. McWhirr (ed.), *Studies in the Archaeology and History of Cirencester,* 61–80. BAR 30. Oxford: B.A.R.
1978 Bronze Coinage from Roman Britain and the Western Provinces. In R. A. G. Carson and C. M. Kraay (eds.), *Scripta Nummaria Romana: Essays Presented to Humphrey Sutherland,* 124–42. London: Spink and Son.
1980 Town and Country: The End of Roman Britain. *World Antiquity* 12: 77–92.
1981 Coinage and Currency in the Third Century. In A. King and M. Henig (eds.), *The Roman West in the Third Century: Contributions from Archaeology and History.* 2 vols., 79–88. BAR International Series 109. Oxford: B.A.R.
1982 The Roman Coins. In W. J. Wedlake, *The Excavation of the Shrine of Apollo at Nettleton, Wiltshire, 1956–1971,* 112–17. SAL Research Report 40. London: Society of Antiquaries.
1991a *Roman Coins from 140 Sites in Britain.* Cirencester: Cotswold Studies.
1991b Portchester Revisited. *Oxford Journal of Archaeology* 10: 253–60.

Rees, S. E.
1979 *Agricultural Implements in Prehistoric and Roman Britain.* 2 vols. BAR British Series 69. Oxford: B.A.R.

Renfrew, J. M.
1973 *Palaeoethnobotany: The Prehistoric Food Plants of the Near East and Europe.* London: Methuen.

Rennie, D. M.
1971 Bronze Objects. In Excavations in the Parsonage Field, Cirencester, 1958. *Transactions of the Bristol and Gloucestershire Archaeological Society* 90: 79–81.

Rhodes, P.
1950 The Celtic Field Systems of the Berkshire Downs. *Oxoniensia* 15: 1–28.

Richards, J. C.
1976 Three Romano-British Inhumations at Upper Lambourne. *Berkshire Archaeological Journal* 67: 21–28.
1978 *The Archaeology of the Berkshire Downs: An Introductory Survey.* Berkshire Archaeological Committee Publication 3. Reading: Berkshire Archaeological Committee.

Richardson, K. M.
1951 The Excavation of Iron Age Villages on Boscombe Down West, *WAM* 54: 123–68.

Richmond, I.
1969 The Plans of Roman Villas in Britain. In A. L. F. Rivet (ed.), *The Roman Villa in Britain,* 49–70. New York: Praeger.

Rickman, G. E.
1971 *Roman Granaries and Store Buildings.* Cambridge: University Press.

Rigby, V.
1981 The Gallo-Belgic Wares. In C. Partridge, *Skeleton Green: A Late Iron Age and Romano-British Site,* 159–95. Britannia Monograph Series 2. London: Society for the Promotion of Roman Studies.
1982 The Coarse Pottery. In J. Wacher and A. McWhirr, *Cirencester Excavations I: Early Roman Occupation at Cirencester,* 153–209. Cirencester: Cirencester Excavation Committee.

Rigold, S. E., and D. M. Metcalf
1984 A Revised Check-list of English Finds of Sceattas. In D. Hill and D. M. Metcalf (eds.), *Sceattas in England and on the Continent: The Seventh Oxford Symposium on Coinage and Monetary History,* 245–68. BAR British Series 128. Oxford: B.A.R.

Rivet, A. L. F.
1969 Social and Economic Aspects. In A. L. F. Rivet (ed.), *The Roman Villa in Britain,* 173–272. London: Routledge and K. Paul.

1970 The British Section of the Antonine Itinerary. *Britannia* 1: 34–82.

Rivet, A. L. F., and C. Smith

1979 *The Place-Names of Roman Britain*. Princeton: Princeton University Press.

Robertson, A.

1970 Roman Coin Hoards from Non-Roman Sites. *WAM* 65: 199–200.

Robinson, P.

1975 The Savernake Forest Find of Ancient British and Roman Coins (1857). *BNJ* 45: 1–11.

1977a A Local Iron Age Coinage in Silver and Perhaps Gold in Wiltshire. *BNJ* 47: 5–21.

1977b Roman Gold Coins from Wiltshire. *WANHS Bi-annual Bulletin* 23: 10–12.

1981 A Pin of the Later Saxon Period from Marlborough and Some Related Pins. *WAM* 74–75 (for 1979–1980): 56–60.

1982 Recent Acquisitions by Devizes Museum of Ancient British, Saxon and Norman Coins. *WAM* 76 (for 1981): 83–91.

1984 Review of E. Besley and R. Bland, *The Cunetio Treasure: Roman Coinage of the Third Century A.D.* London: British Museum Publications, 1983. In *WAM* 78 (for 1983): 137–38.

Robinson, M., D. Bramwell, J. Pernetta, and J. J. West

1973 Excavations at Copt Hay, Tetsworth, Oxon. *Oxoniensia* 38: 41–115.

Rodwell, K. A.

1988 *The Prehistoric and Roman Settlement at Kelvedon, Essex*. Chelmsford Archaeological Trust Report 6. CBA Research Report 63. London: Chelmsford Archaeological Trust; CBA.

Rose, F.

1981 *The Wild Flower Key*. London: Warne.

Rowley, T.

1978 *Villages in the Landscape*. London: Dent.

———— (ed.) 1974 *Anglo-Saxon Settlement and Landscape: Papers Presented to a Symposium, Oxford 1973*. BAR 6. Oxford: B.A.R.

Ryan, N. S.

1988 *Fourth-Century Coin Finds from Roman Britain: A Computer Analysis*. BAR British Series 183. Oxford: B.A.R.

Salter, C., and R. M. Ehrenreich

1984 Iron Age Iron Metallurgy in Central Southern Britain. In B. Cunliffe and D. Miles (eds.), *Aspects of the Iron Age in Central Southern Britain*, 146–61. Oxford Archaeology Monograph 2. Oxford: OUCA.

Salway, P.

1981 *Roman Britain*. Oxford: Clarendon Press.

Savory, H. N.

1964 A New Hoard of La Tène Metalwork from Merionethshire. *Bulletin of the Board of Celtic Studies* 20: 449–75.

1966 Further Notes on the Tal-y-llyn (Mer.) Hoard of La Tène Metalwork. *Bulletin of the Board of Celtic Studies* 22: 88–103.

1971 *Excavations at Dinorben 1965–9*. Cardiff: National Museum of Wales.

1973 La Tène Wales. *EC* 13: 685–709.

1976a *Guide Catalogue of the Early Iron Age Collections*. Cardiff: National Museum of Wales.

1976b The La Tène Shield in Wales. In P.-M. Duval and C. F. C. Hawkes (eds.), *Celtic Art in Ancient Europe: Five Protohistoric Centuries. Proceedings of the Colloquy Held in 1972 at the Oxford Maison Française*, 185–99. London, New York: Seminar Press.

Sawyer, P. H.

1968 *Anglo-Saxon Charters. An Annotated List and Bibliography*. Royal Historical Society Guides and Handbooks 8. London: Royal HIstorical Society.

Sellwood, L.

1984 Tribal Boundaries Viewed from the Perspective of Numismatic Evidence. In B. Cunliffe and D. Miles (eds.), *Aspects of the Iron Age in Central Southern Britain*, 191–204. OUCA Monograph 2. Oxford: OUCA.

Sharrock, J. T. R.

1976 *The Atlas of Breeding Birds in Britain and Ireland.* Berkhamsted: Poyser.

Sheail, J.

1971 *Rabbits and Their History.* Newton Abbot: David and Charles.

Sherlock, R. L.

1960 *British Regional Geology, London and Thames Valley.* 3d ed. London: H. M. Stationery Off.

Simpson, C. J.

1976 Belt-Buckles and Strap Ends of the Later Roman Empire: A Preliminary Survey of Several New Groups. *Britannia* 7: 192–223.

Skempton, A. W., and J. N. Hutchinson

1969 Stability of Natural Slopes and Embankment Foundations. In *Proceedings from the 7th International Conference on Soil Mechanics and Foundation Engineering, Mexico City,* 291–340. Mexico City: Sociedad Mexicana de Mecanica de Suelos.

Smith, C. A.

1977 Late Prehistoric and Romano-British Enclosed Homesteads in Northwest Wales. *Archeologia Cambrensis* 126: 38–52.

Smith, D. J.

1965 Three Fourth-Century Schools of Mosaic in Roman Britain. In H. Stern (ed.), *La Mosaïque Greco-Romaine* I: 95–116. Paris: CNRS.

1969a The Mosaic Pavements. In A. L. F. Rivet (ed.), *The Roman Villa in Britain,* 71–125. New York: Praeger.

1969b New Light on the Corinian School. *AntJ* 49: 235–45.

1975 Roman Mosaics in Britain before the Fourteenth Century. In Henri Stern, *La Mosaïque Greco-Romaine,* vol. 2. Paris: Picard.

1978 Regional Aspects of the Winged Corridor Villa in Britain. In M. Todd (ed.), *Studies in the Romano-British Villa:* 117–47. Leicester: Leicester University Press.

Smith, H. E.

1852 *Reliquiae Isurianae.* London: Hilton.

Smith, I. F.

1969 Neolithic Pottery from Rybury Camp. *WAM* 60: 127.

Smith, M. J.

1982 A Survey of Worked Bone from Iron Age Sites in Wiltshire. Undergraduate diss. Department of Archaeology, University of Southampton.

Smith, J. T.

1963 Romano-British Aisled Houses. *Archaeological Journal* 120: 1–30.

1978a Villas as a Key to Social Structure. In M. Todd (ed.), *Studies in the Romano-British Villa,* 149–85. Leicester: Leicester University Press.

1978b Halls or Yards. A Problem of Villa Interpretation. *Britannia* 9: 349–56.

1982 Villa Plans and Social Structure in Britain and Gaul. *Caesardodunum* 17. Bulletin de l'Institut d'Études et du Centre de recherches. A. Piganiol. Actes du colloque: "La Villa Romaine dans les provinces du nord-ouest": 321–36.

Smith, R. A.

1908–09 A Hoard of Metal Found at Santon Downham, Suffolk. *PCAS* 13: 146–63.

Smith, R. J.

1987 *Roadside Settlements in Lowland Roman Britain. A Gazetteer and Study of Their Origins, Growth and Decline, Property Boundaries, and Cemeteries.* BAR British Series 157. Oxford: B.A.R.

Smith, I. F., and D. D. A. Simpson

1964 Excavation of Three Roman Tombs and a Prehistoric Pit on Overton Down. *WAM* 59: 68–85.

Soames, C.

1890 A Find of Roman Coins near Marlborough. *Numismatic Chronicle* ser. 3, 10: 282–84.

1892 A Find of Roman Coins near Marlborough. *WAM* 26: 39–41.

Speake, G.
1989 *A Saxon Bed Burial on Swallowcliffe Down.* Archaeological Report 10. London: Historic Buildings and Monuments Commission for England.

Spratling, M. G.
1966 The Date of the Tal-y-llyn Hoard. *Antiquity* 40: 229–30.
1972 Southern British Decorated Bronzes of the Late Pre-Roman Iron Age. 3 vols. Ph.D. thesis, University of London, Institute of Archaeology.
1979 The Debris of Metal Working. In G. J. Wainwright, *Gussage All Saints: An Iron Age Settlement in Dorset.* Department of the Environment Archaeological Reports 10. London: H. M. Stationery Office.

Stead, I. M.
1971 Beadlam Roman Villa: An Interim Report. *YAJ* 43: 178–86.

Stenton, F. M.
1913 *The Early History of The Abbey of Abingdon.* Reading: University College.
1971 *Anglo-Saxon England.* 3d ed. Oxford: Clarendon Press.

Stern, H. (ed.)
1965 *La Mosaique Greco-Romaine,* vol. 1. Paris.
1975 *La Mosaique Greco-Romaine,* vol. 2. Paris.

Stevens, C. E.
1966 The Social and Economic Aspects of Rural Settlement. In C. Thomas (ed.), *Rural Settlement in Roman Britain,* 108–28. CBA Research Report 7. London: CBA.

Stevens, P.
Forthcoming. *Wicken Bonhunt, Essex. The Animal Bone from the Romano-British to Saxo-Norman Periods.*

Stevenson, J. H.
1983 Selkley Hundred. Preshute. C. R. Elrington (ed.), *A History of Wiltshire.* VCH XII (Oxford), 160–84.

St. Joseph, J. K. S.
1953 Air Reconnaissance of Southern Britain. *JRS* 43: 81–97.

Strong, D., and D. Brown
1976 *Roman Crafts.* London.

Stuiver, M., and R. Kra
1986 Proceedings of the 12th International Radiocarbon Conference, Trondheim, Norway. *Radiocarbon* 28 (2A and 2B).

Swan, V. G.
1975 Oare Reconsidered and the Origins of Savernake Ware in Wiltshire. *Britannia* 6: 37–61.
1977 Relief Decorated Imitation Samian Cups from Wanborough, Wiltshire. In J. Dore and K. Greene (eds.), *Roman Pottery Studies in Britain and Beyond.* BAR Supplementary Series 30. Oxford: B.A.R.
1984 *The Pottery Kilns of Roman Britain.* Royal Commission on Historical Monuments Supplementary Series 5. London: H.M.S.O.

Swanton, G. R.
1987 The Owen Meyrick Collection. *WAM* 81: 7–18.

Swanton, M. J.
1973 *The Spearheads of the Anglo-Saxon Settlements.* London: The Royal Archaeological Institute.
1974 *A Corpus of Pagan Anglo-Saxon Spear-Types.* BAR British Series 7. Oxford: B.A.R.

Taylor, C.
1982 The Nature of Romano-British Settlement Studies—What Are the Boundaries? In D. Miles (ed.), *The Romano-British Countryside. Studies in Rural Settlement and Economy,* vol. 1, 1–15. BAR British Series 103. Oxford: B.A.R.

Taylor, C. C.
1967 Late Roman Pastoral Farming in Wessex. *Antiquity* 41: 304–306.

Thomas, C. (ed.)
1966 *Rural Settlement in Roman Britain*. CBA Research Report 7. London: CBA.

Thomas, N.
1956 Excavation and Field-work in Wiltshire: 1956. *WAM* 56: 231–52.
1960 *Guide to Prehistoric England*. London: Batsford.

Thompson, N. P.
1971 Archaeological Research in the Pewsey Vale. *WAM* 66: 58–75.

Thorn, C., and F. Thorn (eds.)
1979 *Doomsday Book*. Vol. 6, *Wiltshire*, gen. ed., John Morris. Chicester: Phillimore.

Thun, E.
1967 Mediaeval Tommarp, Archaeological Investigations 1959–1960. *Acta Archaeologica Lundensia* 8 (ser. 5).

Todd, M.
1978 Villas and Romano-British Society. In M. Todd (ed.), *Studies in the Romano-British Villa*, 197–208. London: Leicester University Press.
1985 Oppida and the Roman Army. A Review of Recent Evidence. *OJA* 4: 187–99.
1989 Villas and Fundus. In K. Branigan and D. Miles (eds.), *Villas Economies: Economic Aspects of Romano-British Villas*, 14–20. Sheffield: Dept. of Archaeology and Prehistory, University of Sheffield.

Tomber, R. S.
1985 The Pottery. In T. Wilmott and S. P. Q. Rahtz, An Iron Age and Roman Settlement Outside Kenchester (*Magnis*) Hertfordshire: Excavations 1977–79. *TWNFC* 45: 101–45.

Tomkins, R.
1983 *Wiltshire Place Names*. Swindon: Redbrick.

Toynbee, J. M. C.
1964 *Art in Britain under the Romans*. Oxford: Clarendon Press.
1981 Apollo, Beasts and the Seasons: Some Thoughts on the Littlecote Mosaic. *Britannia* 12: 1–5.
1982 Bronze, Ivory and Iron Objects Recovered from the Floor of the Later Improvised Shrine. In W. J. Wedlake, *The Excavation of the Shrine of Apollo at Nettleton, Wiltshire, 1956–1971*, 143–49. SAL Research Report 40. London: Society of Antiquaries.

Trow, S., and S. James
1989 Ditches Villa, North Cerney: An Example of Local Conservatism in the Early Roman Cotswolds. In K. Branigan and D. Miles (eds.), *Villas Economies: Economic Aspects of Romano-British Villas*, 83–87. Sheffield: Dept. of Archaeology and Prehistory, Univ. of Sheffield.

van Lith, S. M. E.
1979 *Römisches Glas aus Valkenburg, Oudheidhundige Mededelingen uit het Rijksmuseum van Oudheden te Leiden* 59–60 (1978–1979).

Wacher, J.
1989 Cities from the Second to the Fourth Centuries. In M. Todd (ed.), *Research on Roman Britain: 1960–89*, 91–114. Britannia Monograph Series 11. London: Society for the Promotion of British Studies.

Wainwright, G. P.
1970 An Iron Age Promontory Fort at Budbury, Bradford on Avon, Wiltshire. *WAM* 65: 108–66.

Walters, B.
1983 The Orpheus Mosaic in Littlecote Park, England. In R. Farioli (ed.), *Colloquio Internazionale sul Mosaico Antico Ravenna, 6–10 Settembre, 1980,* vol. 2. 433–42. Ravenna: Girasole.
1976 The Roman Villa on the North Wiltshire Chalk. Undergraduate thesis, Cardiff University.

Walters, B., B. Phillips, and K. T. Greene
1973 Some Romano-British Material Salvaged from Wanborough, Wilts. *WAM* 68: 64–70.

Walthew, C. V.
1975 The Town House and Villa House in Roman Britain. *Britannia* 6: 189–205.
1982 Possible Standard Units of Measurement in Roman Military Planning. *Britannia* 12: 15–35.

WAR 1978 Wiltshire Archaeological Register for 1974–75. *WAM* 70–71 (for 1975–76): 132–38.
1980 Wiltshire Archaeological Register for 1976–7. *WAM* 72–73 (for 1977–78): 201–208.
1981 Wiltshire Archaeological Register for 1978–79. *WAM* 74–75 (for 1979–80): 201–208.
1983 Wiltshire Archaeological Register for 1981. *WAM* 77 (for 1982): 157–62.
1986 Wiltshire Archaeological Register for 1984. *WAM* 80 (for 1984): 240–44.
1987 Wiltshire Archaeological Register for 1985. *WAM* 81: 140–43.
1988 Wiltshire Archaeological Register for 1986. *WAM* 82: 183–86.
1990 Wiltshire Archaeological Registers for 1987 and 1988. *WAM* 83: 224–35.
1991 Wiltshire Archaeological Register for 1989. *WAM* 84: 146–51.

Ward, J. W.
1860 Great Bedwyn. *WAM* 6: 261–316.
1911 *The Roman Era in Britain*. London: Methuen.

Warren, F. C.
1938 Excavations on a Roman Site in Brail Wood, Great Bedwyn, in 1936 and 1937. *WAM* 48: 318–20.

Waterman, D.
1959 Late Saxon, Viking and Early Mediaeval Finds from York. *Archaeologia* 97: 59–105.

Waugh, H., and R. Goodburn
1972 The Non-Ferrous Objects. In S. S. Frere (ed.), *Verulamium Excavations I*, 114–45. SAL Research Report 28. London: Society of Antiquaries.

Webster, G.
1969 The Future of Villa Studies. In A. L. F. Rivet (ed.), *The Roman Villa in Britain*, 217–49. London.
1970 The Military Situation in Britain between A.D. 43 and 71. *Britannia* 1: 179–97.
1982 The Small Finds. In G. Webster and L. Smith, The Excavation of a Romano-British Rural Establishment at Barnsley Park, Gloucestershire, 1961–1979: II: c. AD 360–400. *Transactions of the Bristol and Gloucester Archaeological Society* 100: 107–39.
1985 *The Roman Imperial Army of the First and Second Centuries A.D.* 3d ed. London: A. & C. Black.

Webster, J.
1975 Objects of Bronze and Silver; Objects of Iron. In B. W. Cunliffe (ed.), *Excavations at Portchester Castle*. Vol. 1, *Roman*, 198–215, 233–47. SAL Research Report 32. London: Society of Antiquaries.

Webster, L. E. and J. Cherry
1974 Medieval Britain in 1973. *Medieval Archaeology* 18: 174–223.
1977 Medieval Britain in 1976. *Medieval Archaeology* 21: 204–62.

Wedlake, W. J.
1982 Bronze Objects; Iron Objects. In W. J. Wedlake, *The Excavation of the Shrine of Apollo at Nettleton, Wiltshire, 1956–1971*, 204–19, 223–34. SAL Research Report 40. London: Society of Antiquaries.

Welch, F. B. A., and R. Crookall
1935 *British Regional Geology: Bristol and Gloucester District*. London: H. M. Stationery Office.

Welch, M. G.
1976 45. Disc, Gilt Bronze, from an Applied Brooch. In B. W. Cunliffe, *Excavations at Portchester Castle*. Vol. 2, *Saxon*. SAL Research Report 33: 206–11. London: Society of Antiquaries.

West, S. E., with J. Plouviez
1976 The Romano-British Site at Icklingham. *East Anglian Archaeology Report* 3: 63–102.

Wheeler, R. E. M.
1943 *Maiden Castle, Dorset*. SAL Research Report 12. Oxford: University Press.

Wheeler, R. E. M., and T. V. Wheeler

1928 V. The Roman Amphitheatre at Caerleon, Monmouthshire. *Archaeologia* 78: 111–218.

1932 *Report on the Excavation of the Prehistoric, Roman, and Post-Roman Site in Lydney Park, Gloucestershire.* SAL Research Report 9. London: Society of Antiquaries.

Whitaker, W., and F. H. Edmunds

1925 *The Water Supply of Wiltshire from Underground Sources.* Memoirs of the Geological Survey, England and Wales. London: H.M.S.O.

White, H. J. O.

1907 *The Geology of the Country around Hungerford and Newbury.* Memoirs of the Geological Survey, England and Wales. London: H.M.S.O.

1925 *The Geology of the Country around Marlborough.* Memoirs of the Geological Survey, England and Wales. London: H.M.S.O.

White, R. H.

1988 *Roman and Celtic Objects from Anglo-Saxon Graves: A Catalogue and an Interpretation of Their Use.* BAR British Series 191. Oxford: B.A.R.

Whitelock, D. (ed.)

1955 *English Historical Documents c. 500–1042.* D. C. Douglas, general editor. London: Eyre and Spottiswoode.

Whitelock, D., D. C. Douglas, and S. I. Tucker (eds.)

1961 *The Anglo-Saxon Chronicle. A Revised Translation.* London: Eyre and Spottiswoode.

Wild, J. P.

1970 *Textile Manufacture in the Northern Roman Provinces.* London: Cambridge University Press.

1982 Wool Production in Roman Britain. In D. Miles (ed.), *The Romano-British Countryside. Studies in Rural Settlement,* vol. 1, 109–22. BAR British Series 103. Oxford: B.A.R.

Willcox, G. H.

1977 Exotic Plants from Waterlogged Sites in London. *Journal of Archaeological Science* 4: 269–82.

Williams, D. F.

1977 The Romano-British Black Burnished Industry: An Essay on Characterization by Heavy Mineral Analysis. In D. P. S. Peacock (ed.), *Pottery and Early Commerce: Characterization and Trade in Roman and Later Ceramics,* 163–200. London: Academic Press.

Williams, J. H.

1971a Roman Building-Materials in South-East England. *Britannia* 2: 166–95.

1971b Roman Building Materials in the South-West. *TBGAS* 90: 95–119.

Wilson, D. G.

1979 Horse Dung from Roman Lancaster: A Botanical Report. *Archaeo-Physika* 8: 331–50.

Wilson, D. R.

1968 Roman Britain in 1967. *JRS* 58: 176–214.

Wilson, D. R., and D. A. Sherlock

1980 *North Leigh Roman Villa.* London: H. M. Stationery Office.

Winbolt, S. E., and G. Herbert

1967 *The Roman Villa at Bignor, Sussex.* Chichester: Moore and Tillyer.

Winterbottom, M. (ed. and trans.)

1978 *The Ruin of Britain, and Other Works, by Gildas.* General ed., J. Morris. London: Phillimore.

Woodfield, C.

1983 The Pottery. In A. E. Brown and C. Woodfield, Excavations at Towcester: The Alchester Road Suburb. *Northhants. Archaeol.* 18: 43–110.

Woods, P. J.

1977 *Brixworth Excavations.* Vol. 1, *The Romano-British Villa, 1965–70.* Northampton: Northampton Museums and Art Gallery.

Wormald, P.

1982 The Burhs. In J. Campbell (ed.), *The Anglo-Saxons,* 152–53. Oxford: Phaidon.

Wright, R. P.

1952 A Parallel from Amiens for the Rudge Cup. *WAM* 54: 361–62.

1970 Bronze Rings. In J. R. Collis, Excavations at Owslebury, Hants: A Second Interim Report. *AntJ* 50: 246–61.

Young, C. J.

1977 *The Roman Pottery Industry of the Oxford Region.* BAR 43. Oxford: B.A.R.

1986 The Upper Thames Valley in the Roman Period. In G. Briggs, J. Cook, and T. Rowley, *The Archaeology of the Oxford Region,* 58–63. Oxford: Oxford University, Dept. for External Studies.

———, (ed.) 1980 *Guidelines for the Processing and Publication of Roman Pottery from Excavations.* London: Department of the Environment.

Youngs, S.

1992 A Late Seventh-Century Anglo-Saxon Gold Pendant from Pewsey. *WAM* 85: 149–50.

Zippelius, A.

1953 Das vormittelalterliche dreischiffige Hallenhaus in Mitteleuropa. *Bonner Jahrbücher* 153: 13–45.

CONTRIBUTORS

ENID ALLISON, University of York

BRADLEY AULT, Assistant Professor, State University of New York at Buffalo

THEODORE V. BUTTREY is Professor Emeritus of Greek and Latin, University of Michigan, and former Keeper of Coins and Medals, Fitzwilliam Museum, Cambridge University. From 1989 to 1994 he was President of the Royal Numismatic Society. His publications lie primarily in the fields of ancient and modern numismatics, and he has published finds of ancient coins from the American excavations of Cosa in Italy, Morgantina in Sicily, Sardis in Turkey, and Cyrene in Libya.

ALAN CLAPHAM, Institute of Archaeology, London

BRUCE N. EAGLES is Head of the Archaeological Monuments Section of the National Monuments Record, a part of the Royal Commission on Historical Monuments. He is author of *The Anglo-Saxon Settlement of Humberside* and other articles and papers in British journals and publications.

ROBERT M. EHRENREICH is Staff Scientist/Archaeologist with the National Research Council and is the editor of *Archeomaterials,* the international journal of artifact studies. His research concerns the analysis of complex societies, early industrial organization, and cultural context.

LAURA FLUSCHE, Program in Art History, School of Art and Design, University of Illinois, Urbana-Champaign

FERN FRYER, Department of Landscape Architecture, University of Pennsylvania

KATHRYN L. GLEASON is Assistant Professor in the Department of Landscape Architecture, Cornell University.

DAVID FREDERICK GROSE is a Full Professor in the Classics Department, University of Massachusetts, Amherst.

MARGARET GUIDO, independent scholar, Devizes, England.

ERIC HOSTETTER is Associate Professor in the Program in Art History, School of Art and Design, at the University of Illinois at Urbana-Champaign. He has directed a replication project of Lydian architectural terracottas at Sardis on behalf of the Harvard-Cornell Sardis Expedition and the excavation of the Roman villa at Great Bedwyn on behalf of Indiana University. Hostetter is currently directing excavations on the eastern slope of the Palatine Hill on behalf of the Soprintendenza Archeologica di Roma and the American Academy in Rome. His publications include *Bronzes from Spina I: The Figural Classes,*

Lydian Architectural Terracottas: A Study in Tile Replication, Display, and Technique. Illinois Classical Studies, Supplement 5, and various articles on Etruscan, Roman, and Lydian art and archaeology.

THOMAS NOBLE HOWE is Associate Professor of Art History, Architectural History, and Architecture at Southwestern University. He has served as Senior Architect at the Harvard-Cornell Sardis Expedition as Assistant Director, Architect/Surveyor at the Indiana University excavation at Castle Copse, and as Associate Director, Architect at the American Academy Palatine East Slope Excavation.

ANDREW K. G. JONES, University of York

DAVID K. KEEFER is a geologist with the United States Geological Survey and is the author or coauthor of more than 100 monographs, articles, reports, and abstracts. In addition to his work in archaeological geography, his specialties include engineering geology, surficial geologic processes, and geologic hazards, especially landslides.

JOHN F. KENFIELD is Associate Professor of Art History, Rutgers University.

RUTH MEGAW, Department of Visual Arts, Flinders University

VINCENT MEGAW, Department of Visual Arts, Flinders University

MARYLINE PARCA, Department of Classics, University of Illinois, Urbana-Champaign

ROSEMARY PAYNE, Cambridge, United Kingdom

SEBASTIAN PAYNE, English Heritage Commission

VALERIE HUTCHINSON PENNANEN is an independent scholar. She has taught classics and art history at Tulane University, The University of Michigan, and Arkansas State University. Her publications include *Bacchus in Roman Britain: The Evidence of His Cult* and articles on "Ecstasy" and "Communion" for *The Encyclopedia of Comparative Iconography.*

PAUL ROBINSON is an archaeologist and the curator of Devizes Museum. He is the author of several papers on Iron Age coinage in Britain and is part-author of the forthcoming *Catalogue of the Iron Age Collections at Devizes Museum.*

ARCHER ST. CLAIR is Associate Professor of Art History, Rutgers University, and Associate Director at the American Academy in Rome Palatine East Excavation.

ANTHONY R. WILMOTT, English Heritage Commission, Historic Buildings and Monuments Commission for England

INDEX